Heterodoxy
in Late
Imperial China

Heterodoxy
in Late
Imperial China

Edited by
Kwang-Ching Liu
and
Richard Shek

UNIVERSITY OF HAWAI'I PRESS
HONOLULU

Library of Congress Cataloging-in-Publication Data

Heterodoxy in late Imperial China / Edited by Kwang-Ching Liu
and Richard Shek.
    p. cm.
Includes bibliographical references and index.
ISBN 0-8248-2538-1 (alk. paper)
1. China—Religion—History. 2. Heresy. I. Liu, Kwang-Ching.
II. Shek, Richard Hon-Chun.
BL1800.H47 2004
200'.951—dc22

                    2003018418

Designed by the University of Hawai'i Press production staff

Printed by The Maple-Vail Book Manufacturing Group

Contents

PART IV. LATE QING PERSPECTIVES

Preface

Kwang-Ching Liu and Richard Shek

ectarianism and Religious Persecution in China, by the Dutch
scholar J. J. M. de Groot, appeared nearly a century ago.* Published in the aftermath of the Boxer Uprising (1900), the two-volume
work was written largely as a polemical defense of Christian missionary presence in China and as a condemnation of China's long tradition of religious intolerance as he saw it. But de Groot unwittingly
identified a major issue in Chinese cultural and religious history,
namely, orthodoxy versus heterodoxy. De Groot equated orthodoxy
in China with "the Religion of the State, practised by the emperor
and his ministers for their own good and the welfare of the people."
All other religious traditions "are therefore absolutely unclassical
(puh king [*bujing*]) and anti-Confucian; they are incorrect and heterodox (puh ching [*buzheng*], puh twan [*buduan*], i twan [*yiduan*],
sie [*xie*], or yin [*licentious*]) . . . and in the eyes of the State they have
no right to exist."

In the hands of Max Weber (1864–1920), de Groot's formulation of orthodoxy and heterodoxy received the test of social theory,
with documentation from a wide range of European-language
sources up to the First World War. Weber's essays on China were
conveniently brought together in English translation by The Free
Press in 1951, in a volume entitled *The Religion of China: Confucianism and Taoism*. Confucianism he identified as orthodoxy, not as a
school of thought only, but also as a pattern of institutions, the kin
group, and the imperial state. Daoism, both philosophical and reli-

* Original version published in Verhandelingen der Koninklijke Nederlandse Akade-
mie van Wetenschappen, Afdeling Letterkunde, Nieuwe Reeks. First edition Amsterdam, 1903–1904. Reprinted by Irish University Press, Shannon, Ireland, 1973. Quotation is from volume 1, page 15.

gious, he identified with heterodoxy. Weber did not go deeply into the question of popular religious sects and secret societies, referring to the former as distinguished chiefly by "ecstasy and orgy" at their cult meetings.

Like its companion volume, *Orthodoxy in Late Imperial China* (Berkeley: University of California Press, 1990), this volume, now considerably transformed, originated in a conference on "Orthodoxy and Heterodoxy in Late Imperial China," held in August 1981 in Montecito, California, and sponsored by the Joint Committee on Chinese Studies of the American Council of Learned Societies and the National Foundation for the Humanities. We wish to thank all participants of that conference for their contributions. We also wish to thank Robert N. Bellah and Myron L. Cohen for enlightening conversations, which they probably no longer remember. For valuable comments we are grateful to anonymous readers of this long manuscript. We are most thankful to Yu-Yin Cheng of Marymount Manhattan College, who drew the two maps for chapter 8 and expertly compiled the glossary for this volume. For indispensable work on the preparation of the final manuscript, we wish to thank Debbie Lyon and Eteica Spencer of the History Department of the University of California, Davis. For her thorough and skillful copyediting of the manuscript, we are greatly indebted to Karen Weller-Watson. We are, as always, grateful for the help of Edith Liu and Kitty Shek.

Introduction

Kwang-Ching Liu and Richard Shek

D issent and rebelliousness are the concern of many historical works, on China and other lands; yet the nature and goals of the protests are not always systematically explored. Dissent and rebelliousness could, of course, represent opposition merely to a political regime or to a certain policy, but could also be the reaction to an entire system of central values. The study of heterodoxy, which means views that vary or depart from orthodoxy, therefore entails the quest for doctrines that offer an alternative—in the Chinese context an alternative worldview and social ethics. Heterodoxy is not identical with religious practices proscribed by law, although government in late imperial China sometimes identified *xiejiao* (heterodox or heretical teaching) with such practices. In the historian's view, heterodoxy is dissent that challenges certain premises of culture—the beliefs and meanings of the established norm.

Such cultural, indeed, socioreligious, protests frequently incurred government suppression. The usage of such terms as *"xie,"* *"zuodao"* (deviance), and *"yiduan"* (alien principles) was established in imperial pronouncements and in law codes in the Ming-Qing period.[1] The animus of the government toward heterodoxy was important because it affected the views of at least some of the literati and gentry who dominated cultural expression. Yet to adopt the concept of *xie* held by the state or the ruling class is to leave out of consideration the value content of the ideas and practices inherent in certain strains of Daoism and Buddhism, in Manichaeism, and in the Eternal Mother Religion of later imperial China. It seems obvious to a student of modern China that one simply cannot interpret the Taiping Rebellion in terms of the Qing government's denunciations.

Studies of dissent and rebellion must be grounded in material life. Belief and interest are closely associated, and a vast literature has been produced, especially in the People's Republic of China (PRC), identifying the class background of the rebellions.[2] This literature is extremely valuable in pointing to protests that stemmed immediately from the reaction to injustice and exploitation. Yet after every effort has been made to relate class consciousness to the history of culture, historians in the PRC have found themselves returning to such categories as religion and kinship.[3] One needs to confront the fact that among people of similar class background, different and dissenting ideas may arise. While it is important to have more refined studies of the social contexts of various heterodox rebellions, it is also essential to place them in the perspective of beliefs and values.

Orthodoxy and heterodoxy are often represented as the beliefs, respectively, of the elite and of the common people. Max Weber was perhaps the originator of this rigid division, suggesting in the early twentieth century that orthodoxy in China was embodied in the sober and agnostic literati, while the opposing Daoist heterodoxy was upheld by the masses, oriented to magic and ecstasy.[4] C. K. Yang, who defined Confucian ethics as the "moral orthodoxy" of imperial China, offered a more realistic analysis of the religious beliefs that coexisted with Confucian ethics:

> The Confucians did not constitute a group separate from the general current of religious life of traditional Chinese society. They shared with the rest of the population a basic system of religious belief in Heaven, fate, and other supernatural concepts. More important was the steady interflow of religious ideas between the Confucians and the general population.... The Confucians, therefore, cannot be regarded as a distinctively different group on religious grounds, but must be regarded as part of the general pattern of Chinese religious life with only relative differences due to their social and economic position.[5]

In his article of 1974, Maurice Freedman has stated that "the elite as a group was bound to the masses indissolubly by its religious beliefs and practices." For "elite and peasant religion rest on a common base, representing two versions of one religion."[6] Freedman undoubtedly had in mind such matters as ancestor worship and geomancy, belief which was indeed shared by the Chinese elite and the populace.

Analyzing Chinese rebel ideology in the eighteenth and nineteenth centuries, Muramatsu Yuji wrote that "Some Chinese rebels were strongly influenced by Taoism [Daoism] and Taoicized [Daoicized] Buddhism. At the same time, they seem to have shared with the emperor and literati a reliance upon the benevolence of Heaven, and in this way they were drawn into the historical constellation of Confucian ideas." Muramatsu thus warned that "one cannot associate Confucian orthodoxy solely with Confucian rulers, and rebel ideologies solely with non-Confucian heterodoxy."[7] This observation is apt and will serve as a point of departure for our ensuing discussion.

Religious Pluralism and Moral Orthodoxy

If one defines the heterodox, as the dictionary does, as "not in accordance with established doctrines or opinions, or those generally recognized as right or 'orthodox,'"[8] then one could say that by the Eastern Han dynasty (A.D. 25–220), with Confucian classics being especially honored and with official histories becoming Confucian in tone, orthodoxy had been officially defined and Daoism and Buddhism had thereafter to take heed of its core values. Confucian polemics against Buddhism and Daoism were not lacking, especially in the middle period of Chinese history, from the breakup of the Han empire through the fall of the Tang dynasty—roughly from the third to the early tenth centuries. But once Buddhism and Daoism came under the bureaucratic control of the state, they were no longer condemned seriously as heterodoxy.[9] A major characteristic of late imperial China of the Ming-Qing period was that different religions could be tolerated—by the state and by the society at large—if they did not conflict with the interests of the state and with what had been regarded as essential, namely, social ethics and certain accompanying rituals. In *Orthodoxy in Late Imperial China*, edited by Kwang-Ching Liu, it has been argued that the core of orthodoxy in imperial China was *lijiao*, literally "ritual and teaching." More interpretively, *lijiao* may be translated either as "institutionally- and ritually-based ethics," or as "socioreligious ethics." The concept has been discussed at length, and here it suffices to provide a brief summary of the argument as counterpoint to the theme of heterodoxy in the Chinese tradition.

Originating in the Han dynasty (206 B.C.–A.D. 220), *lijiao* was reaffirmed by the neo-Confucians of the Song dynasty and thereafter. It actually constituted a belief system accepted by the major religions of China, the famous Three Teachings—Confucianism, Daoism, and

Buddhism. The focus of *lijiao* was ethics and ritual, yet it had firm roots in a worldview more or less accepted by all the Three Teachings. Specifically this worldview included such assumptions as yin-yang dualism and the *Yijing* (Book of changes) principles regarding life and fate. *Lijiao* was not only ortho*praxis*, but ortho*doxy*, because of its cosmological and indeed religious underpinnings.

The ethics of *lijiao* centered on the doctrine of Three Bonds— the obligations of child to parents, wife to husband, and official to monarch—which was expressed ritualistically in ancestor worship, marriage ceremonies, and the complex rites at the imperial court, including the sacerdotal exercises of the emperor himself. Not only did the imperial court find it necessary (and advantageous) to endorse the socioethical orthodoxy, the leading Confucian scholars provided philosophic and scholastic justification for its prevalence. Leaders of the Buddhist and Daoist establishment, too, found it desirable to render their unreserved support to this moral orthodoxy, even arguing that subscription to filial piety and other cardinal virtues was a precondition for salvation and immortality. For many, the Three Bonds, alternatively known as *gangchang lunli* (ethical principles of the [Three] Bonds and [Five] Constant Virtues) and *zhongxiao zhi dao* (way of filiality and loyalty to the monarch), had become the ultimate concern from which the meaning in life was derived and for which lives would be sacrificed.[10] To be sure, these ethical obligations were not always binding, and individual or communal practices often failed to measure up to the rigorous standards. Nevertheless, it remains true that these values were consistently and unequivocally upheld as self-evident and immutable. Here was a norm that guided the behavior of men and women, emperors and officials, wealthy landowners and impoverished peasants, even Buddhist monks and Daoist priests, cutting across socioeconomic and religious lines.

Controversy and Unity

Different schools within the Confucian tradition continued to emerge. Scholars disagreed on the authenticity of texts, the centrality of certain metaphysical concepts, or the effectiveness and legitimacy of certain policies, making claims of orthodoxy for themselves and hurling charges of heterodoxy against their rivals along the way. Nonetheless, all but the rarest exceptions agreed on the sanctity of *gangchang lunli.* Thus Zhu Xi (1130–1200) and Wang Yangming (1472–1529) might differ fundamentally over philosophic issues, yet their common adherence to the principles of *zhong* and *xiao* made them both advocates of this moral orthodoxy. Similarly, despite their personal idiosyncrasies and eccentric tendencies, mavericks such as Wang Gen (ca. 1483–1540) and Lin Zhao'en (1517–1598) did not seem to have stepped beyond the bounds of *zhongxiao zhi dao.* As Hao Chang has so ably pointed out, neo-Confucianism may have contained numerous critical impulses that at times created tremendous tensions with this orthodoxy; yet in the end it failed to offer an alternative worldview and system of values.[11] Notwithstanding the glorification by He Xinyin (1517–1579) of friendship as the essential human relationship, and the oblique denial by Huang Zongxi (1610–1695) of any ultimate sanctity in the emperor's status, there was no real breaking away from the *lijiao* orthodoxy among the Confucian literati of the late imperial period.

The hold of *lijiao* orthodoxy on the non-Confucian traditions of Buddhism and Daoism was surprisingly strong. Although Chinese Buddhism long held to the teaching that "leaving the home" *(chujia)* was a solution to life's endless suffering, this ideal very early had to come to terms with the requirements of filial piety, and Buddhist rituals were adapted to the needs of Confucian funerary and graveside memorial services. The sangha eventually accepted the control of the state. From the Northern and Southern dynasties through the Tang, the principle of the monk not paying homage to the temporal ruler was actually circumvented by some monarchs assuming the mantle of chakravartin king and being accorded obeisance on that basis. Whalen W. Lai, in an important essay here, analyzes afresh the fact that the Buddhist establishment had by and large accommodated itself to the ethical orthodoxy of *lijiao* by the Ming-Qing period, if not long before.[12] The late-Ming Buddhist divine Zhuhong (1535–1615), in his popular morality book, the *Zizhi lu* (Record of self-knowledge), assigned *zhong* and *xiao* to the very first category of meritorious deeds that ultimately would lead to rebirth in the Pure Land. Zhuhong singled out filial piety as the foremost virtue that would enable one not only to attain personal salvation but also to bring about deliverance of other sentient beings.[13] Deqing (1546–1623), another eminent Buddhist of the late Ming, continued to fulfill his obligation as a filial son even after he had entered the sangha and achieved some fame as a prominent monk; and he showed his ardent support for the Ming imperial house by organizing a grandiose assembly to pray for the birth of an heir to the reigning Wanli emperor.[14]

Although no prominent spokesman like Zhuhong or Deqing existed for the Daoist establishment in the Ming-Qing period, the Celestial Master recognized by the throne continued to play the role of obedient minister and submissive subject. He served as a chief administrator and helped the state to control, supervise, and regulate all the activities of the certified members of the Daoist "church"—indeed the church was only a branch of the state.[15] Among Daoist texts there was, for example, the *Taishang ganying pian* (Treatise of the Exalted One on retribution and punishment), which was conceived under Confucian and Buddhist influences during the Song dynasty and published in an ever greater number of copies and circulated widely throughout the empire in the Ming-Qing period, exhorting people to adhere to their obligations to the family and the state as well as to exhibit good faith and compassion in order to reap rewards and to avoid disasters.[16]

In late Ming there was also the growing influence of a Daoist sect named Jingming zhongxiao dao (The Loyal and Filial Way of the Pure and Perspicacious), studied here by Richard Shek.[17] Its origins going back to the Eastern Jin dynasty (317–419) during the lifetime of the adept Xu Sun, this sect developed under local auspices in the Tang period and enjoyed the patronage of emperors in the Song and Yuan periods. It produced the first *Ledger of Merits and Demerits (Gongguo ge)*, in 1171, that served later as the prototype for many others, including the aforementioned *Zizhi lu*, by the Buddhist Zhuhong. According to the sect's teachings, the virtues of filial piety and loyalty to the monarch were not only ethically desirable but also religiously valuable, enabling one to attain the Daoist goal of life everlasting.

Their own religious characteristics notwithstanding, Buddhism and Daoism seem to have generally accommodated themselves to the orthodox ethics of Confucianism. The result was a blurring of distinctions and an increasing tendency toward harmonious coexistence among the Three Teachings of China. Some Confucian purists would continue to rail against Buddhist and Daoist unorthodoxy. Indeed, there were enough Confucian purists to create an entire movement in classical scholarship to purge Buddhist influences on Confucianism itself and to renew the proper focus on unquestioned obligations in the daily conduct of life.[18] The purists continued to regard Buddhism as heterodoxy—witness the essay entitled *On Refuting Heresies (Poxie lun)* written by the famed enlightened scholar Huang Zongxi late in his life.[19]

Nonetheless, there were many Confucians who would not denounce either Buddhism or Daoism as outright heterodoxy. Quite apart from the Unity-of-Three-Teachings movement of Lin Zhao'en,[20] who was considered heterodox on account of his pro-Daoist orientation and his appeal to the masses, there was actually a broad syncretic trend built on the basis of moral orthodoxy. That is, religious pluralism was allowed to exist on the basis of a unifying socioethics. The primacy of either Mind or Principle could be endlessly debated, the Buddha's Pure Land could be longed for, Daoist immortality could be sought, even ghosts and fox-spirits could be believed in, as long as the basic precepts of *zhong* and *xiao* were abided by and remained unchallenged. For women, there was the precept of *jie* (firm integrity, in this case devotion to one husband, dead or alive), which most Buddhists and Daoists, like most Confucian scholars, complacently approved.

It is important to realize that this moral orthodoxy was not merely decreed by the state but was based on a cultural norm, as reflected in primers and axioms and in the literature of exhortation often distributed by religious societies and philanthropists. So pervasive was this socioethics in society at large that Ming and Qing monarchs could declare, "Under Heaven there is no alternative way; among the sages there is no divergent mind."[21] Among officials there were many men of rectitude who protested against the abuses of imperial or bureaucratic power. A rich literature of social commentary was, moreover, available in the Ming-Qing period in the form of essays or in the tales of popular storytellers. The behavior of local officials and yamen underlings, the arbitrariness of the family patriarch, the discriminatory treatment received by women—all were the subjects of criticism and satire.[22] Chinese life was never so monolithic as to preclude unconventional or critical expression in word or deed. Yet criticism or protest does not always amount to the advocacy of alternate beliefs or values—views not in accordance with and, moreover, maintained in competition with the established ones. It is the beliefs and values that challenged or seemed to challenge those prevalent in late imperial China that we look for when the focus shifts to popular culture.

Popular Religion and Shamanism

Religious pluralism is especially evident in the vast domain of popular religion, honoring a variety of protective deities. To the ubiquitous Lord Guan (Guan Gong), Guanyin (Avalokitesvara), and Tudi (local earth god) are added noble and heroic deities such as Marshal Wen, the god of epidemics, here studied by Paul R. Katz.[23] In his lifetime under the Tang dynasty, Wen was a rebellious youth who died young as a result of his reckless exploits. In some hagiographic treatments, he is described as a demon god fed on bloody raw meat, but he then reforms and accepts only incense and tea. He is ordered by the Jade Emperor to poison the wells of a village as punishment for the misdeeds of its inhabitants. But he decides to take the thousand plague pills himself and, of course, instantly dies. The altruistic deed is recognized by the Jade Emperor, and Wen is appointed to be the Loyal and Pacifying King (Zhongjing wang) in charge of prevention of epidemics. As Katz explains, "Unregulated cults featuring spirit mediums and bloody sacrifices represented disorder and chaos, and due to the fact that they resisted Daoist norms, came to be labeled heterodox and licentious." To conform to Daoist norms is to be orthodox.

What these norms were can be seen in Donald S. Sutton's essay on the late imperial Chinese elite's attitude toward shamanism.[24] Shamanism is defined as the capacity to become possessed by gods who can speak of past, present, and future. A shaman (he or she) is employed for purposes of exorcism, witchcraft, or clairvoyance. The practice has been common among villagers and some city-dwellers and reflects the religious life of many Chinese living in comparatively obscure areas.

In the late imperial period of the Ming-Qing dynasties, the neo-Confucian elites were hostile to the shamans and their practice. One of Sutton's themes is that magico-religion as such was not only prevalent among the common people but was shared by the elite as well. For filial sons among the elite who believed they could cure a sick parent by dissolving in the medicinal soup a piece of the son's own flesh, the notion was based on filial impulse, to be sure, yet also on supernatural assumptions. The elite reformers—at any rate, the ideologically prim neo-Confucians—were hostile to shamanism, not simply because the shamans claimed to invoke heterogeneous deities but because the shamans' manner and demeanor offended the Confucian sense of propriety. Sutton cites Cooper and Sivin's remark about "an element of snobbery or social prejudice in Chinese judgements about heterodoxy." [25] Sutton believes this is true of the elite attitude toward the shamans, with their uncouth manners and violations of Confucian *li* (propriety and ritual)—heteropraxis indeed.

Both Katz and Sutton employ the term *heteropraxis* (as opposed to *orthopraxis*). The sacrifice of raw meat to "heterodox deities" not named in imperial registers and the employment of shamans in appealing to even less known deities are described by Katz as well as Sutton as heteropraxis—wrong practice, or action without the backing of a system of correct belief. Yet as Sutton puts it: "Actually the dualistic separation of action from belief is a Western notion that would have been incomprehensible to the writers I have quoted. *Li* as a practice was supposed to reflect a universal moral order. Appropriate behavior, therefore, was not a matter of pure decorum, but an effort to approximate that ideal state of affairs. . . . Just as to be orthoprax was to be orthodox, so heteroprax violators of the principles of *li* were subsumed to the heterodox and tarred with the same brush."

Historical Roots of Heterodoxy

Just as *lijiao* orthodoxy was predicated on certain cosmological assumptions, heterodoxy, too, was based on principles—principles that either rejected those assumptions or offered entirely different ones. In a jointly written article by Kwang-Ching Liu and Richard Shek, the inherent radical nature of Daoism is explored through the historical background. [26] Daoist values of equality may be found in *Laozi* itself. Although the text is subject to different interpretations, it can be read to signify a moral ambiguity that challenges what was to become conventional ethics:

> There is a thing undifferentiatedly formed,
> Born before heaven and earth,
> Silent and void
> It stands alone and does not change.
> Goes around and does not weary. [27]

How else are we to read this definition of *dao* except as affirmation of a nonhierarchical, primitivist ideal of no high and low, no debased and superior, in short, no differentiations? In what appear to be ante-cedents of heterodoxy in late imperial China, Liu and Shek argue, even as Daoism developed into a religious tradition, some of its adherents adopted antiestablishment postures and espoused egalitar-ian and even eschatological hopes that challenged views then deemed orthodox.

Similarly, Buddhism was not to abandon entirely its salva-tional ideals and their cosmological basis, despite the compromise its spokesmen had been making with the Chinese society. In a remark-able essay, Whalen Lai discusses such compromises between Bud-dhism and the Confucian concept of filial piety.[28] Going beyond earlier views of this topic held by Michihata Ryōshū and Kenneth Ch'en, Lai analyzes the problem in an original contribution. Lai accepts that the historic Buddhist of the Sui and Tang periods had high praise for the virtue of filiality, as witness the remarks of Zhiyi (538–597), Shandao (d. 681), Zongmi (786–841), and others. Yet despite their endorsement of *xiao,* they were good Buddhists–and would still follow the nibbanic, not the kammatic path. They put filiality in the Buddhistic perspective; however, this was no longer true with Zhuhong. The most prominent Buddhist monk of the Ming dynasty, Zhuhong believed that without being filial, no one, no matter how pious and how virtuous otherwise, could enter the West-ern paradise. Lai shows how Zhuhong actually tampered with Bud-dhist texts to reconcile them with Confucian ethics; Zhuhong gen-uinely believed that *xiao* was a Buddhist virtue, and that his editing was faithful to Buddhism and Confucianism as well.

Looking at the other side of the coin, Lai finds that the much-maligned White Lotus sect actually preserved elements of authentic Buddhism. Harking back to early Buddhist experience, Lai invokes the sixth-century *Xiangfa jueyi jing* (Sutra to resolve doubts in the age of the Semblance Dharma), which describes a sangha-organized peasant community:

> Sons of Good Families, in the future age, when myriad ills rise, monks and laymen alike should cultivate great friendliness and compassion, bear all kinds of derision and think only of how all human beings are from before the beginning of time one's father, mother, brother, sis-ter, wife and relative. Because of that, one should show all human beings compassion, helping all according to one's ability, risking one's life if necessary in exercising such means to aid the needy.[29]

With such Buddhist groups as the Maitreyans and the later, metamorphosed White Lotus, the Buddhist goal of salvation was maintained through an ardent eschatology. Richard Shek here traces the
historical unfolding of the Buddhist chiliasm, which posed a great
threat to the existing order. Shek also identifies Manichaeism as an
important element in sectarian heterodoxy.[30]

As late as the sixteenth century, the sectarian movement still
retained the social as well as the spiritual values inherent in early
Buddhism and Daoism and had, moreover, combined them with a
consciousness that emphasized the in-group community of the elect.
The Eternal Mother was equated with heaven yet was more intimate
than heaven. The assemblies and networks of men and women as
individuals honored charismatic leaders as religious masters. Furthermore, the inherent millenarian faith periodically called for action
"in response to the kalpa." From the standpoint of Confucian-Bud-
dhist-Daoist orthodoxy, this constituted a contrary and outrageous
belief system, quite apart from its potential threat to the state.
Thanks to the works of Daniel Overmyer and Susan Naquin, in
North America, and to scholars in Japan under the leadership of the
late Suzuki Chūsei, the doctrines, practices, and organizational techniques of the Eternal Mother tradition have been meticulously documented.[31] The contribution of this volume is to offer a major case
study and to put this sectarian tradition in a historical context in reference to certain themes that seem to require special emphasis.

The Eternal Mother Religion

In the sectarian scriptures (*baojuan*, lit. "precious volumes") studied
by Overmyer for the period up through the mid-nineteenth century,
he has found teachings representing "explicit values" that were predominantly Confucian or lay Buddhist, sometimes combined with
elements of Daoism.[32] While the earliest *baojuan* texts focused
mainly on religious deliverance, "beside which conventional ethical
injunctions are of secondary importance or even without validity," in
such texts from late Ming to the mid-nineteenth century he has
found a curious duality: "the split is between the explicit values and
implicit dissenting ones."[33] According to Richard Shek and Noguchi
Tetsurō's study on sectarian values and ethics, the "implicit" values
of the *baojuan* actually predominated. What was especially significant
in this mature form of sectarian belief was the appearance in the

early sixteenth century of a female supreme deity, the Venerable Mother of Unborn Eternality (Wusheng laomu), or Eternal Mother. Allegiance to the Eternal Mother actually challenged Buddhism with a heretical Daoist deity. Moreover, such worship recognized men and women of different generational status to be all children of the progenitor that transcended time—children whose return to her womb, or salvation, she tearfully awaited.[34] Sectarian scriptures or mantras could teach filial devotion as well as respect for the socially superior; they could also subscribe to elements of Pure Land Buddhism. But such admixture of values and beliefs was just that—not syncretism that involved conscious reconciliation. Sectarian practitioners are known to have performed mortuary rites on behalf of other families for pay. But as Naquin has written of the "meditation sects" in what she called the "White Lotus religion," the members generally did not focus their attention on the transition of the soul at death: "We seldom find funeral rituals performed by these sects. Believers relied instead upon announcements to the Eternal Mother of their membership to establish their place among the elect."[35] Compare this mode of soteriology with the Confucian, Buddhist, and Daoist rituals regarding the dead, and one can understand how under certain circumstances the "explicit values" in the *baojuan* could be relegated to the background.

Shek and Noguchi probe into the psychology as well as the politics of Eternal Mother millenarianism. Relying on their charismatic authority, many sect masters of the Ming and Qing periods would predict the date for the "turning" of the kalpa believed to be the final one, typically during severe natural or man-made disasters. Despite the sectarians' comparatively universalistic soteriology, once the consciousness of cosmic crisis was brought to the fore, in-group self-righteousness would take over—the saved would set themselves apart from the damned by successful violence.[36]

Rebellious eschatology was not free of political considerations. The sect master's course of action could reflect his impatience with a wicked society in disarray, or merely his dilemma as to how to maintain an organization's cohesiveness and solvency while forestalling government arrest. Naquin has emphasized that for networks of spatially scattered members, the desire for an "encompassing" community justified the risk of daring action. Rebellion was one of the outcomes of the impulse to compete with the elite, born of resentment of the powerful who monopolized the symbols of legitimacy.[37] But did the sectarians really believe that they would succeed?

According to Shek and Noguchi, millenarian rebellion that honored the Eternal Mother was not so much a matter of desperation as a return to one's "true original home." The degenerate world, which human endeavor could no longer redeem, was to be thoroughly cleaned by the Maitreya Buddha, and the brothers and sisters were to return to the Eternal Mother's embrace. Success was not a question, for although the elect's total commitment must be shown by violent action, what was assured was Maitreya's supernatural intervention. This was a matter of faith. "Return to the origins" was the Daoist inspiration behind sectarian piety in the first place. One can understand such a psychology in the context of a hierarchical, ritual-ridden society, which left many human aspirations unfulfilled. But the stress that was being relieved was further ameliorated by the sectarians' own rituals and practices—the daily prayer to heaven where the Eternal Mother dwells, magical curing, martial arts, and shamanistic ecstasy.

A historic case of religion-inspired rebellion in late imperial China is the White Lotus uprising of the mid-Qing period (1796–1804), the subject of Kwang-Ching Liu's chapter 8.[38] Relying on published archival materials that contain depositions of the rebels, Liu explores the socioreligious dimensions of this movement that centered in Hubei, one which came close to shaking the foundations of the Manchu dynasty. Liu contends that in addition to economic deprivation and official malfeasance, sectarian eschatology was the principal factor among the causes of the rebellion. He argues that the chiliastic hopes of the rebels must be taken seriously in order to understand the zeal and fanaticism with which they fought the government forces. The belief in the Eternal Mother and her promise of salvation was a powerful motivating force that drove many sect leaders, including a major woman leader, into taking armed action against the state and all the injustices it represented. Liu's essay also highlights the intricate network of relationships that existed among separate but doctrinally similar sects, which facilitated massive mobilization of sectarian forces in times of crisis. Ironically, by the same token, sectarian division and the teacher-disciple relationship also set the limits of greater coordination in war as in peace among the friendly sects.[39]

The Triads

Do we find a parallel between the sectarians' in-group consciousness and the in-group comradeship extolled and practiced by the late Qing Triads? Sworn brotherhoods that developed into secret societies, the Triads were characterized by complex initiation and other rituals believed to be transformative processes.[40] Their "unquestioning comradeship" (*yi*) could transcend the concerns of kinship on which the organization was modeled. The chapters by Wen-hsiung Hsu and by David Faure in this volume present a critical overview of the early history of the Triads.[41] Both papers suggest that the worship of Lord Guan, the bodhisattva Guanyin, and other popular deities was merely instrumental with the Triads. These sworn brotherhoods were not possessed by any millenarian consciousness, while their ties with the conventional kinship morality appeared to remain rather strong. Hsu points out, for example, that members pledged aid to the society brothers' families, including womenfolk. On the other hand, Faure observes that the anti-Manchu Ming loyalism of the Triads did not become a prominent part of their ideology until the early nineteenth century. He finds that sedition, in the sense of wanting to overthrow the government, was not really the Triads' goal.

These two chapters on the Triads hold a view rather different from that advanced by Barend ter Haar, who in a recent work suggests that the Triads, at least at one time, possessed a "demonological and messianic paradigm."[42] He argues that the Triads, somewhat akin to the sectarians, had their roots in a paradigm that included: "the restoration of the Ming dynasty and its young ruler, the most important Triad ancestors, the City of Willows as a safe haven, the use of special dates, and some other, minor elements."[43] We do not feel, however, that this list qualifies the Triads to belong to a fully developed heterodox tradition. Their reference to the Ming regime, summarized in the slogan "Oppose the Qing and restore the Ming," was intended to gain legitimacy for their existence. They did not, according to presently available evidence, visualize any change in organization for the restored dynasty. Insofar as they defied the law and, moreover, placed the pseudo-family above their natural kin and shared the classic novel *Water Margin*'s value of *yi* (unquestioning comradeship, not Confucian "righteousness" or "appropriate duty"), they must be viewed as unorthodox, as well as illegal. In view of their many unusual rituals with political implications, they should perhaps be described as "politically subversive," but not heterodox in the sense of espousing socioethical values contrary to the orthodox.

Pseudo-Christian Heterodoxy

There was, however, a major religiously iconoclastic movement in nineteenth-century China, more than half a century before imperial rule came to an end. The Taiping Rebellion (1851–1864), which again threatened the foundations of the Manchu dynasty, may be viewed as the world's greatest millenarian movement, unless one counts Mao Zedong's Cultural Revolution of 1966–1969 as also chiliastic. P. Richard Bohr's essay for this volume not only delineates in chronological order the development of Hong Xiuquan's theology, but includes a wide-ranging comparison between Taiping and traditional sectarian theory and practice.[44] The vengeful Old Testament God inspired among the early Taipings an even more fervent egalitarian ethic than did the Eternal Mother of the Ming-Qing sects. Despite the elite personal background of a few of the Taiping leaders, the pauperized Hakka peasants in the Guangxi hill country harbored not only a degree of class consciousness but also utter resentment of the old settlers who treated them as outcasts and feuded with them.

Hong never seems to have preached an apocalypse in cosmic terms: soteriology to him was at first on a personal level only.[45] But the "doomsday omens of man-made and natural calamity," together with Yang Xiuqing's shamanistic performance, uttering the inspired words of the Heavenly Father himself in addition to his magic healing and exorcism, precipitated collective hopes and fears. Desperation among the growing membership of the Society of God Worshipers generated visions of an earthly order of divinely sanctioned happiness and paved the way for the creation of the Heavenly Kingdom of Great Peace in 1851. Hong Xiuquan subsequently made the claim that he was Melchizedek, the messianic hero of Genesis, thus retrospectively putting the movement in the Old Testament framework.

When compared with other millenarian movements of the Ming-Qing period, the Taipings were the most successful. Their claim to a new and alternative orthodoxy is demonstrated by their declaration that all women were literally "sisters" and all men "brothers," and by their denunciation of the ancestral cult and iconoclastic destruction of the Buddha, Laozi, and other idols of popular

Chinese religion. Their well-organized forces occupied Nanjing for eleven years, even as their shamanistic theocracy thoroughly denied the very principle behind Confucian monarchy. The Taiping Land System of 1853 not only envisaged equal division of farmland among the tillers, male and female alike, but also aimed at strict control over them by grassroot officials supervising all aspects of life.

It is not surprising that the Taipings would soon revert to Confucian positions on filial piety and gender relations, as well as loyalty to the Heavenly King and to a bureaucratic hierarchy. The orthodoxy of the Chinese tradition was simply too deeply rooted to disappear in the course of a decade. What is not usually stressed by historians is that the Taipings, at least in the post-1853 phase, came to rely on the *Water Margin,* or Triad-type of unquestioning comradeship *(yi),* as well as old-style loyalty to the monarch and his commanders as their operating ethics.[46] In the Taipings, we may perhaps see a form of Maitreyan faith in combination with strong shamanism as well as vestiges of Confucianism. Despite the "moral universalism" of the Christian influence on the Taipings, in the last analysis it was their particularly strong in-group solidarity, Hakka self-identity combined with the self-consciousness of a chosen people, that forged the powerful army that fought so effectively—even after the internecine struggle of 1856 the Hakka identity was still a factor for solidarity.

Elite Heterodoxy

It should not be expected that the beliefs of the plebeian Eternal Mother sectarians and the Taipings had exerted an important influence on the young literati elite who challenged the orthodoxy of their own heritage during the last two decades of the imperial era. However, one can nonetheless draw a rough analogy between elite and popular heterodoxy. The radical intellectuals who precipitated the Reform of 1898 and the revolutionaries whose ideas helped create the Republic in 1912 were, perhaps even more than the folk sectarians, egalitarian in their ethics. Although as individuals they continued to cherish familistic sentiments and were to enjoy the patronage of Emperor Guangxu, both Kang Youwei (1858–1927) and Tan Sitong (1865–1898) bitterly inveighed against the hierarchical interpersonal obligations in favor of a newly defined human-heartedness *(ren)* that would recognize the individual's "right of autonomy" *(zizhu zhi quan).*

In Tan's philosophical treatise written in 1896, the constraining Three Bonds as well as the "doctrine of name" *(mingjiao)* were vigorously attacked—the bond between monarch and subject being to him particularly dark, stultifying, and oppressive of humanity. Behind this iconoclasm lay a profound change of worldview. Kang and Tan both had intense interest in Buddhist ideas of equality, so long submerged under the orthodox ethics. But the latent values took on new force when they were merged with the implications of Western science. The stars visible through a telescope changed the heaven of ancient Chinese cosmology. Knowledge of elementary physics made "ether" *(yitai)* more real than yin and yang. The concept of evolution introduced through social Darwinism came close to becoming a faith for the new heterodox elite, to whom the Western peoples, by virtue of their emphasis on citizenship qualities and on progressive change, seemed the fittest to survive. As they worked for China's survival as a nation, the reformers and revolutionaries looked to a Golden Age in the future, not the past, and they sought inspiration from abroad, not just from the Chinese classics or from their own intuition.[47] The obscure classical theory of three-stage development toward the "great peace" was given a new interpretation, and the classical utopian ideal of the "grand unity" *(datong)* was reconciled to parliamentarianism and women's rights.

The Twentieth-Century Perspectives

The complex history of elite iconoclasm in post-imperial China is beyond the scope of our inquiry. It is hoped, however, that the last paper in this volume will provide some early twentieth-century perspective on the volume's main theme. How did the Chinese elite, awakened to science and democracy, view popular heterodoxy and the rural peasants at large?

Harking back, in a sense, to Donald Sutton's perspective on popular shamanism, Don C. Price has documented how the reformers and revolutionaries toward the end of the Qing dynasty saw the Taipings, the Boxers, the sects, and the Triads.[48] By the early twentieth century, science and the evolutionary cosmology had won the minds of the elite activists. The rational outlook of the literati was strengthened. The reformers and revolutionaries alike considered the sectarian groups and Triad-type societies "atavistic," even though they needed the latter's help, especially in attempted uprisings. The

Triads and the Taipings were commended for their anti-Manchu stand. But they, as well as the folk religious sects, to say nothing of the Boxers, were criticized for ignorance and irrationality. The heroic "knight-errantry" of the Triads was especially appreciated. Song Jiaoren (1882–1913), who in his youth had admired "the heroes of the forest" (i.e., hero bandits), had quite subjectively read into the *Water Margin* Robin Hood–style chivalry and sense of justice. But he gave up this fancy after he had acquired some knowledge of Western science and institutions. By 1907, Song's nationalism and anti-Manchu sentiments were accompanied by his new faith in the Western democratic process. Like so many other patriots of that decade, Song (on a trip from Japan to Manchuria) sought out popular dissidents to join in the common cause of overthrowing the Manchus. However, as the revolutionaries found more effective comrades among the patriots within the Qing dynasty's new provincial armies, their need for alliance with popular associations declined.

Yet Price also finds in the writings of the revolutionaries continued appreciation of the "people's spirit" *(minqi)* as reflected in popular heterodoxy. This image accorded with the elite radicals' self-image of the stalwart young hero capable even of martial exploits—itself not necessarily incompatible with Confucian orthodoxy. However, some among the radicals, including the small group of early Chinese intellectual anarchists, soon combined the heroic ideal with a strong voluntarism emphasizing the efficacy of human will and with a populist faith in the virtue and power of the people going beyond merely appreciation of *minqi*.[49] It is a central question of twentieth-century Chinese history whether voluntarism and populism could be reconciled with the equally new Marxist-Leninist historical determinism.

In the extraordinary career of Mao Zedong, Marxism was combined with voluntarism and peasant populism. Mao did not believe in the turning of the kalpa except one willed by himself, his unique version of historical dialectics allowing the exercise of his will, generalized as the aspiration of the masses. Although Mao, too, censured the Triads and the Red Spears as backward, his mystique of the "grand union of popular masses" may well have been inspired by the heterodoxy of the past, *Water Margin* being his favorite reading and Tan Sitong an author he admired.[50] In launching the Cultural Revolution in the mid-1960s, he saw himself as the incarnation of the masses who, as in his version of the "Foolish Old Man" story, could literally and miraculously move mountains. Equally remarkable, however, was the complete faith reposed in him by the idealistic and youthful Red Guards. Distressed and disoriented by economic hard times and resentful of the power of Party bureaucrats, radicals of the Cultural Revolution bombarded the headquarters of the power structure with only a dim vision of the blissful permanent revolution that Mao promised. Theirs was the millenarian frame of mind: a new heaven and a new earth were at hand, and rebelliousness was for the moment an end in itself.

From the standpoint of the ritual and social morality of late imperial China's culture and society, the Maoist Cultural Revolution must be viewed as supreme heterodoxy—this is simply a historical perspective, not a value judgment. The Buddho-Daoist egalitarianism of the Eternal Mother tradition has persisted only among a tiny minority, but the Maoist message of "Serve the people" has at one time inspired millions. On the other hand, the active millenarian movement induced by Mao, with its emphasis on militant anti-bureaucratic and even antiparty "class struggle," appears to have failed decisively, as many such millenarian movements had failed in the past.

Notes

1. For the meanings of the terms *xie, zuodao, yiduan,* etc., as used by the state and the elite, see the appendix in this volume. See also the excellent discussion in Paul A. Cohen's *China and Christianity: The Missionary Movement and the Growth of Chinese Antiforeignism, 1860–1870* (Cambridge, Mass.: Harvard University Press, 1964), esp. pp. 4–20, and in Barend J. ter Haar, *The White Lotus Teachings in Chinese Religious History* (Leiden: E. J. Brill, 1992).

2. Frederic Wakeman Jr., "Rebellion and Revolution: The Study of Popular Movements in Chinese History," *Journal of Asian Studies* 36.2 (Feb. 1977): 201–237; James P. Harrison, *The Communists and Chinese Peasant Rebellions: A Study in the Rewriting of History* (New York: Atheneum, 1969), 16–37; Kwang-Ching Liu, "World View and Peasant Rebellions: Reflections on Post-Mao Historiography," *Journal of Asian Studies* 40.2 (Feb. 1981): 295–326.

3. For trends in PRC historiography in the early 1990s see, for example, the following works on family and kinship: Chen Zhiping, *Jin wubainian Fujian de jiazu shehui* [Lineage society in Fujian province during the last five hundred years] (Shanghai: Sanlian, 1991); Zheng Zhenman, *Ming Qing*

Fujian qinzu zuzhi yu shehui bianqian [Lineage organization and social change in Ming-Qing Fujian] (Hunan jiaoyu chubanshe, 1992); Feng Erkang and Zhang Jianhua, *Qingren shehui shenghuo* [Social life of the Qing people] (Tianjin: Renmin, 1990); Ye Xian'en, *Ming-Qing Huizhou nongcun shehui* [Rural society in Ming-Qing Huizhou] (Anhui: Renmin, 1983).

4. Max Weber, *The Religion of China: Confucianism and Taoism*, trans. Hans H. Gerth (New York: Free Press, 1968), chaps. 5, 6, 7, esp. pp. 173, 181. See also C. K. Yang's introduction in the same volume, p. xxxiv.

5. C. K. Yang, *Religion in Chinese Society* (Berkeley: University of California Press, 1961), 276–277.

6. Maurice Freedman, "On the Sociological Study of Chinese Religion," in Arthur P. Wolf, ed., *Religion and Ritual in Chinese Society* (Stanford: Stanford University Press, 1974), 37, 40.

7. Muramatsu Yuji, "Some Themes in Chinese Rebel Ideologies," in Arthur F. Wright, ed., *The Confucian Persuasion* (Stanford: Stanford University Press, 1960), 242.

8. *The Oxford English Dictionary*, 1961 reprint; see also *Webster's International Dictionary of the English Language*, 1955 ed. For a discussion of concepts of orthodoxy, orthopraxy, heterodoxy, and heresy, see Sheila McDonough, "Orthodoxy and Heterodoxy"; Judith Berling, "Orthopraxy"; Kurt Rudolph (Matthew J. O'Connell, trans.), "Heresy"; and Burton Russell, "Christian Concepts," in Mircea Eliade, ed., *The Encyclopedia of Religion* (New York: Macmillan, 1987), 9:269–279; 11:124–132.

9. Suppression of Buddhism was carried out in 446–454 under Northern Wei, in 574–577 under Northern Zhou, in 840–846 under Tang, and 955–959 under the Later Zhou. Under the Song, there was a brief period of persecution in 1110–1119 under Huizong (r. 1101–1125). But by the Ming dynasty, Buddhism had become an integral part of elite life. See Timothy Brook, *Praying for Power: Buddhism and the Formation of Gentry Society in Late Ming China* (Cambridge, Mass.: Harvard University Press, 1993).

10. See Kwang-Ching Liu, "Socioethics as Orthodoxy: A Perspective," in *Orthodoxy in Late Imperial China* (Berkeley: University of California Press, 1990), 53–100. See also Chen Yinko, *Hanliutangji* [Collected writings of the Cold Willows Hall] (Shanghai: Guji, 1980) 58; *Chen Yinko shiji* [Collected poems of Chen Yinko] (Beijing: Tsinghua University Press, 1993), 10–11. Commenting on Song ideas regarding the family, Denis Twitchett has written: "I do not think that there is anything fundamentally new in Song ideology regarding the family; a new emphasis on descent perhaps, just as there is a renewed focus on hierarchical submission in the growing emphasis on *xiao* and *zhong*, but these are hardly new ideas." There was a new emphasis on ritual forms and unity, but the major development was "the gradual change of China into an ideological society with a strong sense

of orthodoxy. Perhaps what we see is not so much any change in ideology as a change in attitudes toward existing ideology. People in the late Song began to take it all very seriously and literally." See Twitchett, "Comments on J. L. Watson's Article," *China Quarterly* 92 (1982): 625–626.

11. Hao Chang, "Confucian Cosmological Myth and Neo-Confucian Transcendence," in Richard J. Smith and D. W. Y. Kwok, eds., *Cosmology, Ontology, and Human Efficacy: Essays in Chinese Thought* (Honolulu: University of Hawai'i Press, 1993), 11–34.

12. Chapter 3, this volume. See also Michihata Ryōshū, *Bukkyō to Jukyō rinri* [Buddhism and Confucian ethics] (Kyoto: Heirakuji, 1968); Kenneth Ch'en, *Chinese Transformation of Buddhism* (Princeton: Princeton University Press, 1973).

13. Chün-fang Yü, *Renewal of Buddhism in China: Chu-hung and the Late Ming Synthesis* (New York: Columbia University Press, 1981), 18, 90.

14. Sung-peng Hsu, *A Buddhist Leader in Ming China: The Life and Thought of Han-shan Te-ch'ing 1546–1623* (University Park: Pennsylvania State University Press, 1978), 74, 78.

15. For a general discussion of the patriarchs of the Celestial Master tradition in the Ming, see Huang Zhaohan, "Mingdai de Zhang Tianshi" [Celestial Master Zhang of the Ming dynasty], in *Daojiao yanjiu lunwenji* [Essays on Daoist studies] (Hong Kong: Chinese University of Hong Kong Press, 1988), 9–38. For a more detailed study on the subject, see Zhuang Hongyi, *Mingdai daojiao Zhengyi pai* [The Orthodox Unity School in Ming Daoism] (Taibei: Xuesheng shuju, 1986).

16. See Sakai Tadao, "Confucianism and Popular Educational Works," in Wm. Theodore de Bary, ed., *Self and Society in Ming Thought* (New York: Columbia University Press, 1970), 341–342.

17. Shek's article in this volume, chapter 4. See also Akizuki Kan'ei, *Chūgoku kinsei dōkyō no keisei—jōmyodō no kisoteki kenkyū* [The formation of modern Daoism in the history of China—a fundamental study of the Jingming dao] (Tokyo: Sobunsha, 1978); Cynthia J. Brokaw, *The Ledgers of Merit and Demerit: Social Change and Moral Order in Late Imperial China* (Princeton: Princeton University Press, 1991), 45 n. 56, 50–51, 62.

18. Kai-Wing Chow, *The Rise of Confucian Ritualism in Late Imperial China: Ethics, Classics, and Lineage Discourse* (Stanford: Stanford University Press, 1994).

19. *Huang Zongxi quanji* [Complete works of Huang Zongxi] (Hangzhou: Zhejiang Guji, 1985), 192–207.

20. See Judith Berling, *The Syncretic Religion of Lin Chao-en* (New York: Columbia University Press, 1980).

21. For examples of such imperial pronouncements, see the essays of the Ming founder in *Ming Taizu yuzhi wenji* [Essays by His Majesty himself Ming Taizu], 20 *juan* Ming edition, 11:9b, 18b. Cf. Romeyn Taylor, "An

Imperial Endorsement of Syncretism: Ming T'ai-tsu's Essay on the Three Teachings, Translation and Commentary," *Ming Studies* 16:31–38 (1983).

22. See Robert E. Hegel, *The Novel in Seventeenth Century China* (New York: Columbia University Press, 1981); Paul S. Ropp, *Dissent in Early Modern China: Ju-lin wai-shih and Ch'ing Social Criticism* (Ann Arbor: University of Michigan Press, 1981).

23. Chapter 5, by Paul R. Katz, this volume.

24. Chapter 6, by Donald S. Sutton, this volume.

25. See William C. Cooper and Nathan Sivin, "Man as a Medicine," in Shigera Nakayama and Nathan Sivin, eds., *Chinese Science* (Cambridge, Mass.: MIT Press, 1973), 271.

26. Chapter 1, by Liu and Shek, this volume.

27. D. C. Lau, trans., *Lao Tzu, Tao Te Ching* (Harmondsworth, England: Penguin, 1963), 82. Slightly adjusted.

28. Chapter 3, by Whalen W. Lai, this volume.

29. See Taishō Shinshū Daizōkyō (Tokyo: Kaho Kai, 1924–1934), 85:1338a.

30. Chapter 2, Richard Shek, this volume. See also the two seminal articles by Erik Zürcher, "Eschatology and Messianism in Early Chinese Buddhism," in W. L. Idema, ed., *Leyden Studies in Sinology* (Leiden: E. J. Brill, 1981), 34–56; and " 'Prince Moonlight': Messianism and Eschatology in Early Medieval Chinese Buddhism," *T'oung Pao* 68 (1982): 1–75. Wu Han's thesis regarding Manichaeism and the Ming dynasty remains basic; see his *Dushi daji* [Notes from reading history] (Beijing: Sanlian, 1956), 235.

31. The major book that brought the historical dimension of this dissenting movement to the attention of the Western scholarly world is Daniel L. Overmyer, *Folk Buddhist Religion: Dissenting Sects in Late Traditional China* (Cambridge, Mass: Harvard University Press, 1976). Unsurpassed social history of two sectarian uprisings may be found in Susan Naquin, *Millenarian Rebellion in China: The Eight Trigrams Uprising of 1813* (New Haven: Yale University Press, 1976) and *Shantung Rebellion: The Wang Lun Uprising of 1774* (New Haven: Yale University Press, 1981). Suzuki Chūsei's pioneering and invaluable works are represented by *Shinchō chūkishi kenkyū* [A study of mid-Qing history] (Toyohashi: Aichi University Research Institute on International Issues, 1952); and *Chūgoku ni okeru kakumei to shūkyō* [Revolution and religion in China] (Tokyo: Tokyo University Press, 1974). Suzuki was also general editor of a special volume dedicated to the study of millenarianism in Asia. See *Sennen ōkoku teki minshu undō no kenkyū* [A study of millenarian mass movements] (Tokyo: Tokyo University Press, 1982). His younger colleagues on this project have since published monographs on their own. See Noguchi Tetsurō, *Mindai byakurenkyōshi no kenkyū* [Study of the history of the White Lotus in the Ming dynasty] (Tokyo:

Yuzankaku, 1986); and Asai Motoi, *Min-Shin jidai minkan shūkyō kessha no kenkyū* [Study of folk religious associations in the Ming-Qing period] (Tokyo: Kenbun shuppan, 1990).

32. Overmyer, *Folk Buddhist Religion,* and his more recent *Precious Volumes: An Introduction to Chinese Sectarian Scriptures from the Sixteenth and Seventeenth Centuries* (Cambridge, Mass.: Harvard University Press, 1999).

33. Overmyer, "Values in Chinese Sectarian Literature: Ming and Ch'ing *pao-chuan,*" in David Johnson, Andrew Nathan, and Evelyn Rawski, eds., *Popular Culture in Late Imperial China* (Berkeley: University of California Press, 1985), 219–254, esp. 253. Overmyer writes that "with the exception of the egalitarianism and utopian hope of the late Ming *pao-chuan,* values in Chinese sectarian literature are quite conservative." Ibid., 221. This "exception" is extensive! The egalitarianism and utopianism of the late Ming *baojuan* persisted as elements in later sectarian texts, including the nineteenth-century materials that the Qing official Huang Yubian saw.

34. Chapter 7, by Shek and Noguchi, this volume.

35. Susan Naquin, "The Transmission of White Lotus Sectarianism in Late Imperial China," in Johnson, Nathan, and Rawski, eds., *Popular Culture in Late Imperial China,* 225–291, esp. 280. Cf. Naquin, "Funerals in North China: Uniformity and Variation," in James L. Watson and Evelyn S. Rawski, eds., *Death Ritual in Late Imperial and Modern China* (Berkeley: University of California Press, 1988), 37–70, esp. 51.

36. See chapters 7 and 8 in this volume. For the millenarian consciousness among sectarians who did not immediately stage a violent revolt, see Richard Shek, "Millenarianism without Rebellion: The Huangtian Dao in North China," *Modern China* 8.3 (1982): 337–360.

37. Naquin, *Millenarian Rebellion in China* and *Shantung Rebellion.* See also idem, "Connections Between Rebellions: Sect Family Networks in Qing China," *Modern China* 8.3 (1982): 337–360. For a workmanlike Chinese study of the Eight Trigrams sect, see Ma Xisha, *Qingdai bagua jiao* [The Eight Trigrams sect of the Qing dynasty] (Beijing: Chinese People's University Press, 1989).

38. Chapter 8, this volume. Despite the complaint made by ter Haar in his *White Lotus Teachings,* (see note 1 above), we do not apologize for using the term "White Lotus rebellion," since this is how the 1796–1804 uprising is referred to in current textbooks without a pejorative implication. Cf. John K. Fairbank and Edwin O. Reischauer, *China: Tradition and Transformation,* rev. ed. (Boston: Houghton Mifflin, 1989), 179, 240–241.

39. Cf. Blaine Gaustad, "Prophets and Pretenders: Inter-sect Competition in Qianlong China," *Late Imperial China* 21.1 (June 2000): 1–40.

40. See Barend J. ter Haar, *Ritual and Mythology of the Chinese Triads: Creating an Identity* (Leiden: E. J. Brill, 1997). "Its ritual and narrative lore provided a Triad group with a long term identity and a supra-local frame of

reference, thereby masking its essentially contingent nature. . . . Ultimately, the Triad groups remain local groups enmeshed in local webs of interests and conflicts" (p. 443).

41. Chapters 9 and 10, by Hsu and Faure respectively, in this volume. See also Frederic Wakeman Jr., "The Secret Societies of Kwangtung, 1800–1856," in Jean Chesneaux, ed., *Popular Movements and Secret Societies in China, 1840–1950* (Stanford: Stanford University Press, 1972), 29–47. A recent and important survey of secret societies *(huidang)* in the Qing period is Liu Zhengyun, "Qingdai huidang shikong fenbu chutan" [A preliminary chronological and spatial survey of secret societies in the Qing period], in *Zhongguo jinshi shehui wenhua shi lunwenji* [Papers on the society and culture of early modern China] (Taibei: Institute of History and Philology, Academia Sinica, 1992), 429–479. Based on extensive archival sources, Liu's article includes data on 92 secret societies with different names (except for two with the same name known to be different groups). Of the 916 cases of incidents involving secret societies, 209 cases concerned the Heaven and Earth Society (Tiandihui), 184 the Three Dots Society (Sandian hui or Sanhe hui), and 222 the Elder Brother Society (Gelao hui). The former two societies shared similar organization and ritual practices, and were active mainly in the southern provinces; for the sake of convenience, they are described as Triads in the present volume. On the Gelao hui, see, *inter alia,* Liu Zhengyun, "The Ko-lau hui in Late Imperial China" (Ph.D. dissertation, University of Pittsburgh, 1983). See also his articles on this secret society in Chinese, including "Gelao hui de renji wangluo—Guangxu shiqi'nian Li Hong anli de ge'an yanjiu" [Personal networks of the Gelao hui—a study of the Li Hong case in 1891], *Bulletin of the Institute of History and Philology, Academia Sinica,* 62 (1993): 39–64. On the Tiandi hui, see Lu Baoqian's classic study, *Lun wan-Qing liang-Guang de Tiandi hui zhengquan* [On the Tiandi hui regime in Guangdong and Guangxi provinces in late Qing] (Taibei: Institute of Modern History, Academia Sinica, 1975).

42. Ter Haar, *Ritual and Mythology,* chapters 6–7, 224–305.

43. Ibid., 263.

44. Chapter 11 in this volume; see also Bohr's "Liang Fa's Quest for Moral Power," in Suzanne Wilson Barnett and John K. Fairbank, eds., *Christianity in China: Early Protestant Missionary Writings* (Cambridge, Mass: Harvard University Press, 1985), 35–46. The historiography on Taiping religion is simply too huge to be listed comprehensively here. But Jonathan Spence's *God's Chinese Son: The Taiping Heavenly Kingdom of Hong Xiuquan* (New York: Norton, 1996) is highly recommended. For another interpretation, see Robert Weller, *Resistance and Control in China: Taiping Rebels, Taiwanese Ghosts, and Tiananmen* (Seattle: University of Washington Press, 1994).

45. See Philip A. Kuhn, "Origins of the Taiping Vision: Cross-Cultural Dimensions of a Chinese Rebellion," *Comparative Studies in Society and History* 19.3 (July 1977), 350–366.

46. This is evident in Li Xiucheng's famous deposition of 1864. For an English translation, see C. A. Curwen, *Taiping Rebel: The Deposition of Li Hsiu-ch'eng* (Cambridge: Cambridge University Press, 1977).

47. Hao Chang, *Chinese Intellectuals in Crisis: The Problems of Order and Meaning, 1880–1911* (Berkeley: University of California Press, 1987); San-pao Li, "A Preliminary Analysis of K'ang Yu-wei's Earliest Extant Essay, *K'ang-tzu nei-wai-pien* [Inner and outer chapters of Master Kang's writings]," *Tsing Hua Journal of Chinese Studies,* new series, 11.1–11.2 combined issue (1975): 213–247; and his "K'ang Yu-wei's *Shih-li kung-fa ch'uan-shu* [A comprehensive book of substantial truths and universal principles]," *Bulletin of the Institute of Modern History,* Academia Sinica, 7 (1978): 683–725.

48. Chapter 12, by Don C. Price, this volume.

49. See Charlotte Furth, "Intellectual Change: From the Reform Movement to the May Fourth Movement, 1895–1920," in John K. Fairbank, ed., *The Cambridge History of China,* vol. 12 (Cambridge: Cambridge University Press, 1983), 322–405; Maurice Meisner, *Li Ta-chao and the Origins of Chinese Marxism* (Cambridge, Mass.: Harvard University Press, 1967), esp. 22–28, 80–88, 166–170, 248–256.

50. See Frederic Wakeman Jr., *History and Will: Philosophical Perspectives of Mao Tse-tung's Thought* (Berkeley: University of California Press, 1973), esp. chap. 20.

PART 1

The Early Sources

CHAPTER I

Early Daoism in Retrospect
Cosmology, Ethics, and Eschatology

Kwang-Ching Liu and Richard Shek

There is a thing undifferentiatedly formed.
Born before heaven and earth.
Silent and void.
It stands alone and does not change.
Goes round and does not weary.
It is capable of being the mother of the world.
I know not its name.
So I style it "the Way." [1]

This famous passage from *Laozi* is one of the most important among Chinese religious and philosophical texts but was, in the formative period of imperial China, either directly contravened or given interpretations that deprived it of meaning. The doctrine that opposed or disfigured it gained ascendancy during the Eastern Han dynasty (A.D. 25–220). The imperial council honored the doctrine based largely on the *Yijing* (Book of changes), the *Liji* (Book of rites), and other Confucian classics, and in general following the religious and cosmological tradition of Dong Zhongshu (ca. 195–ca. 105 B.C.). This led to the dogma of the Three Bonds *(sangang)* becoming the core of a secular religion that constituted orthodoxy in the Chinese tradition. [2]

The original message of *Laozi* was never lost, however. The challenge of a doctrine that honored the Grand Unity (Taiyi), the deity of unwrought simplicity that had existed before the creation of "heaven and earth" (two words that will be referred to here in low-ercase in the Daoist context and capitalized for the Confucian usage), helped to explain the hardening of Han orthodoxy during the century and a half before the council of A.D. 79. Earlier, in many pas-

sages of the eclectic work *Huainanzi,* a collection of essays written
for (or by) Prince Liu An (ca. 180–122 B.C.), the *Laozi* vision of the
cosmos had been reaffirmed and elaborated. The doctrinal challenge
of *Huainanzi* to Confucian writings that had been gaining esteem at
the Han court, as well as the imperial favor enjoyed by quasi-Daoist
magicians *(fangshi)*—with their amoral disdain for the Confucian
canons and their esoteric formulas for attaining physical immortality—produced a situation not unlike the challenge of Arianism to the
ascendant Christian church in the late Roman Empire.[3] Orthodoxy
was forced to define itself by what was considered heterodoxy.
Although Daoist-oriented works continued to be read by the scholar-
official elite, their message came to be submerged in the growing general acceptance of the ethical and behavioral norms dictated by the
Confucian secular religion. It was not until the original Daoist message, in a cruder form, to be sure, was taken up by groups among the
populace and was combined with collective action inspired by a new
soteriology—indeed a hint of eschatology—that Daoism was branded
"supernaturally evil" *(yaowang),* a standard phrase by which heterodoxy was denoted in the Chinese tradition.[4]

Exploring this theme through some six centuries of complex
history, this essay can do little more than highlight certain basic facts
and propose new inquiries. The influence of Buddhism in stimulating new challenge to the imperial authority cannot be ignored, perhaps even under the Eastern Han dynasty. Yet it may be suggested
that some aspects of Daoism had provided the principal indigenous
challenge to the Han orthodoxy.[5] This essay begins with an exposition of certain concepts inherent in Daoist and Confucian writings
through the period of so-called mystic learning *(xuanxue),* then exam-
ines certain developments within the Daoist movement itself through
the fifth century A.D. It will be stressed that even as certain Daoists
of the early imperial era were making accommodations to an "external orthodoxy"[6]—that is, the essentially Confucian secular religion
—a heterodox Daoism persisted, as indicated by a remarkable work
of the late Eastern Han period, a bit uncouth but unmistakable in its
depiction of a Daoist peaceful utopia, *Taiping jing* (Canon of the
great equity). Well-established views of Han Daoism, including the
Huang-Lao school (Daoism that honors the Yellow Emperor as well
as Laozi), are acknowledged here; such issues as Holmes Welch's
"parting of the Way," and the mysteries of alchemy and internal
hygiene will be referred to only briefly.[7] The focus will be on certain

Daoist motifs—beliefs regarding cosmology and ethics and regarding change in the environment and in institutional life.

Cosmos and Change in Confucian and Daoist Thought

Scholars of the past have often spoken of a common denominator in Chinese thought—to wit, an ideal of harmony that underlay both Confucian and Daoist philosophies: dualisms that were "complementary and mutually necessary rather than hostile and incompatible . . . [dualisms that were] the expression of the concept of harmony based upon hierarchical differences."[8] Such a concept of harmony is indeed of great importance in the Chinese tradition. Yet the question may be asked whether this was always the case, especially with Daoism. It is possible that there were at least two views of the cosmos in the Chinese tradition—and accordingly at least two views of what is natural. The first inquiry of this essay is therefore whether, at least in early imperial China, there were indeed two such contradictory worldviews.

In contrast to Laozi's cosmogony as indicated in the opening quotation of this essay, one can point at once to the world view presented in the *Yijing Appendices* (commonly known as *Shiyi* or *Ten Wings*). These were in existence by the beginning of the Western Han dynasty (206 B.C.–A.D. 8), if not earlier.[9] Their influence on Han thought was profound and merits further study.

Although some passages in the *Yijing Appendices* appear to have been derived from *Laozi,* they differ fundamentally from *Laozi* in affirming that Heaven or the hexagram *qian* is "great and originating" *(yuan).*[10] The *Appendices* state it more explicitly: "Great indeed is the sublimity of *qian* to which all beings owe their beginning and which permeates all Heaven."[11] The Heaven here is moral, and it prescribes, moreover, a mode of social ethics patterned after its relationship with Earth. "Heaven is high, the Earth is low: thus the positions *(wei)* of *qian* and *kun* are determined. In correspondence with this difference between low and high, inferior and superior positions are established."[12] The *Yijing Appendices'* ethics was therefore unavoidably hierarchical, based on the natural order of the trigrams and hexagrams.

In the *Yijing Appendices,* the state of things prior to Heaven's coming into being is only briefly alluded to, yet it is suggested clearly enough that nothing preceding Heaven's existence was contrary to the will of Heaven. Thus, in a famous passage, "The great man *(daren)* accords in his character with Heaven and Earth; in his light, with the sun and moon. . . . When he acts in advance of Heaven, Heaven will not contradict him *(Xian Tian er Tian bu wei),*" which may be read as "he will not contradict the heaven which is to come into existence." "When he succeeds Heaven, he adapts himself to the time-scheme of Heaven. If Heaven itself does not contradict him, how much less can persons, or can the spirits and gods!"[13]

One finds many passages in the *Yijing Appendices* that prefigure what was to become the orthodoxy in the Eastern Han period. On the monarch-subject relationship that constitutes one of the Three Bonds, for example, it is stated in reference to those trigrams in which either yang or yin predominates, "The *yang* trigrams have one ruler and two subjects. This shows the way of the superior person. The *yin* trigrams have two rulers and one subject. This is the way of the inferior person."[14] All of the Three Bonds are indeed spelled out, and the need to regulate them through "ritual propriety and dutifulness" *(liyi)* firmly stipulated:

> After there are Heaven and Earth, there are the individual things,
> After individual things have come into being, there are the
>   two sexes,
> After there are male and female, there is the relationship between
>   husband and wife,
> After the relationship between husband and wife exists, there is
>   the relationship between father and son,
> After the relationship between father and son exists, there is the
>   relationship between monarch and subject,
> After the relationship between monarch and subject exists, there is
>   the difference between superior and inferior,
> After the relationship between superior and inferior exists, the rules
>   of ritual propriety and dutifulness can operate.[15]

Dong Zhongshu, who served Emperor Wu (r. 141–87 B.C.), was an "erudite" (official scholar) specializing in the *Chunqiu* (Spring and autumn annals), and wrote little directly on the *Yijing*. However, the *Yijing Appendices* undoubtedly had an influence on his cosmology that synthesized the four seasons, yin and yang forces, the predetermined positions of Heaven and Earth, and the interactions between Heaven and humanity. Dong was not concerned with the problem of cosmogony raised by Laozi. He took the word *"yuan,"* or *"yiyuan,"* (single origin) from the *Spring and Autumn Annals* and from the *Yijing* and he wrote: "What is called the single origin is the great beginning."[16] Yet he quickly relegated this vague "origin" to the background. Unlike Laozi, he did not equate the "undifferentiatedly formed" dao with the beginning of the cosmos. Instead, he identified dao with Heaven. He wrote: "The great source of dao is Heaven. Heaven will not change and dao will not change." Dong thus in fact reversed the *Laozi* premises, which, as we have seen, regarded Dao as anterior to Heaven's coming into being. Dong also said that "Heaven was the progenitor of the multitude of things."[17] Heaven, which he saw as the supreme deity, possesses consciousness and a moral purpose. It is Heaven's will that the monarch—the Son of Heaven—should see that the people all have means of livelihood and that they be taught proper rituals and social morality. In his famous memorials in reply to Han Wudi's request for advice on policy, Dong warned that it was Heaven that invested the monarch with the mandate to rule. Heaven, according to Dong's cosmology, would respond to misgovernment with calamitous and extraordinary occurrences, such as long and severe drought and earthquakes. Dong wrote in one of the memorials:

> Your servitor respectfully notes that in the *Spring and Autumn Annals* deeds of an earlier time are examined in order to perceive those occasions when the affairs of Heaven and of humanity interacted. It is most awesome! Whenever the state was on the verge of failure from a loss of the Way *(dao)*, Heaven first would send forth calamities and prodigies as warning. When [the rulers] were incapable of examining themselves, Heaven again would send forth strange and extraordinary phenomena in order to make them worry and to frighten them. When they still did not change their ways, injury and downfall then came upon them.[18]

Dong Zhongshu thus spoke of the yin-yang cosmology and the belief in interactions between Heaven and human society through the reigning monarch. From the *Spring and Autumn Annals,* he derived a view of authority and of social morality that is profoundly hierarchical. He wrote of the parallel nature of *zhong* (loyalty to the monarch) and *xiao* (filial piety). He defined the Heaven-conferred responsibility of the ruler *(jun)* to "bring about the people's filiality toward their parents and obedience to the elders."[19] The *Spring and Autumn Annals* provides cases of "the Way of the servitor and the son *(chenzi zhi dao)* serving [the ruler or the father] unto death." Events recorded in the *Spring and Autumn Annals* are believed to have demonstrated "the faithfulness of women of firm integrity *(zhenfu zhi xin).*" The general political lesson to be learned is "that there is no way to control power when the ruler is deprived of authority, and that the ruler's position cannot be intact when there is no differentiation between the noble and the mean *(guijian).*[20]

Throughout the chapters of the *Chunqiu fanlu* (Luxuriant gems from *Spring and Autumn*) that are believed to include authentic writings of Dong, the distinctions between high and low, the noble and the mean; between close and distant relationships, and the legitimate and illegitimate statuses, are emphasized and juxtaposed with the distinction between yang and yin. In other parts of the text of *Chunqiu fanlu* believed to have been written in the Eastern Han period mainly by the followers of Dong and his disciples, the cosmological basis of polity and society are further elaborated.[21] Dong, in his lifetime, had prefigured the Eastern Han doctrine of name or status *(mingjiao)*, which overlapped with what has been known as the doctrine of ritual propriety *(lijiao)*. As is stated in chapter 9 of *Chunqiu fanlu:*

> Ritual propriety forms a continuum with Heaven and Earth, embodies the *yin* and *yang* forces, and makes careful distinction between the primary and the secondary. It observes correct order regarding the position *(wei)* of the high and low, the honored and the mean, the great and the small.[22]

And to give another example, it is stated in chapter 12 that the Three Bonds *(sangang)* are part of the kingly way of government *(wangdao)* based indeed on Heaven's will:

> The regulations for benevolence, dutifulness, and institutions are wholly derived from Heaven. Heaven acts as the ruler, who confers benefits. Earth acts as the subject, who assists and supports [the ruler]. The *yang* acts as the husband, who procreates. The *yin* acts as the wife, who gives assistance. Spring acts as the father, who procreates. Summer as the son, who supports [the parents]. . . . The Three

Bonds, comprising the Way of the King *(wangdao)*, may be sought for in Heaven.[23]

The cosmological concepts and ethics of Dong Zhongshu's school were clearly reflected in the text produced by the imperial council of A.D. 79, transcending the old-text and new-text controversy in classical scholarship. Such norms and values were also generally upheld by the elites of the Eastern Han and successor regimes. The increased dissemination of the *Xiaojing* (Book of filial piety) put the father and, by extension, the monarch in the position of associates of Heaven. At least according to the *Liji,* the husband was himself Heaven to the wife, whose position corresponded to that of Earth. Of the principle that governs the relationship between husband and wife, the *Liji* says: "It is in accordance with this same idea that Heaven takes precedence over Earth, and the ruler over the subject."[24]

It must not be supposed, however, that as Han Confucianism gained ascendancy as the imperially sanctioned doctrine, the Daoist cosmology was lost to the Chinese consciousness—elite or popular. The book of *Huainanzi* continued to be read after Prince Liu An's suicide by imperial order—or his ascending to heaven as immortal, according to Daoist legend—in 122 B.C. Several editions with commentaries were prepared by such great scholars as Xu Shen. An unorthodox worldview was apparently tolerated, at least until A.D. 184, when the outbreak of large-scale rebellions made a Daoist work, the *Taiping jing,* anathema to the imperial authorities.[25]

As is well known, the anthology of Prince Liu An is a less than homogeneous work. Nonetheless, the work has a distinct vision and it highlights and expands the Daoist tradition.[26] Its ethics, based on Laozi's teaching of "turning back" to the beginning of existence, implies a strong dissent from Confucian social morality.

Employing mythological imagery, the passages of *Huainanzi* that could be identified as Daoist represent a repossession and an elaboration of Laozi's cosmogony. In the opening passage of chapter 3, *Huainanzi* visualizes that "when heaven and earth did not yet have form, there was a state of amorphous formlessness. Therefore this is termed the Great Beginning (Taishi). Dao began with an empty extensiveness, and this empty extensiveness produced the cosmos. The cosmos produced primal breath (*qi,* often translated as ether), which moved within boundaries. The breath that was clear and light collected to form heaven. That which was heavy and turbid congealed to form earth."[27] What is especially noteworthy is that although heaven is believed to have formed before earth (since "the congealing of the heavy and turbid was particularly difficult"), there was no fixed position of heaven or earth in the process of creation. At one stage, as related in chapter 2, "the breath of heaven first descended, and the breath of earth first ascended. The *yin* and *yang* mixed and got together. They moved at ease and competed for expansiveness within the cosmos. Possessing energy and intending harmony, they interpenetrated and united. They wished to have contact with things, yet there was no appearance of any created form."[28]

The essays in *Huainanzi* were written in a period when many Han Chinese aspired to personal physical immortality, which they believed could be achieved by visiting islands off the east coast or the Kunlun mountains in the northwest where forces of nature or magic could remove the cause of death. These forces could even be encapsulated in immortality pills produced by alchemy. The extant chapters of *Huainanzi* advised, however, the more intellectual salvationist formula of "turning back" to the beginning, or "returning to being the uncarved block," repossessing knowledge of primitivity and making oneself a true person *(zhenren)*—"who is not separated from the Great Oneness (Taiyi)."[29] While contemplative self-realization was the principal preoccupation, this Daoist ideal nonetheless carried a challenge to the conventional ethics of the Confucians—and to the orthodoxy of the Eastern Han period.

As in *Laozi* and *Zhuangzi*, the artificial norms of dutifulness *(yi)* and ritual propriety *(li)* were criticized in *Huainanzi*. "Great harmony" *(taihe)* and primitive response to "nature" *(ziran)* were believed to have been corrupted by the externally imposed socioethics. "People of antiquity shared the breath of heaven and earth. . . . Ritual propriety, dutifulness, integrity, and sense of shame were not established [as norms]; nor were blame and praise, humaneness or contempt. Yet none of the multitude transgressed, deceived, or tyrannized each other, being in a state of undifferentiated unawareness *(hunmin)*."[30] A scathing attack on Confucianism is particularly reminiscent of the world of *Laozi:*

> Acting on one's heavenly nature is called Dao: obtaining one's heavenly nature is called De [i.e., that which one obtains from Dao]. Only

after the nature is lost is humaneness *(ren)* esteemed; only when Dao is lost is ritual propriety esteemed.[31]

Despite Liu An's aristocratic status, the *Huainanzi* essays were sometimes influenced by the mystical *Zhuangzi* to affirm equality from a relativist perspective:

> Each thing is equal to and cannot exceed the other. A bright mirror is appropriate for reflecting forms; in steaming food it is not as good as a bamboo colander. The red hair of a victim ox is fitting in temple sacrifice; for bringing rain it is not as good as a black snake. Viewed in this light, there is neither nobility *(gui)* nor baseness *(jian)* in things. If one is to acknowledge nobility, then there is nothing which does not possess nobility. If one is to acknowledge baseness, there is nothing which is not base.[32]

Zhuangzi's philosophical relativism does not, however, actually call for a sense of equity or justice between the high and the low classes in society, the mystical insight as depicted in *Zhuangzi* seeming to have the effect of blurring the reality of life. On the other hand, a number of sayings in *Laozi,* also inspired by transcendence, could be construed to be affirmations of social or even political equality (although these passages in *Laozi* were not directly referred to in *Huainanzi*).[33] Laozi stresses the value of equitableness *(jun)*, at the same time teaching the virtues of simplicity and the lowering of desire. Thus it is written in chapter 32:

> Though the uncarved block is small,
> No one in the world dares claim its allegiance,
> Should lords and princes be able to hold fast to it,
> The myriad creatures will submit of their own accord,
> Heaven and earth will unite and sweet dew will fall,
> And the people will be equitable *(jun)*, though no
>   one so decrees.[34]

Laozi's vision called for action inherent in nonaction. For example, in chapter 37:

> The Way never acts yet nothing is left undone,
> Should lords and princes be able to hold fast to it.
> The myriad creatures will be transformed of their own accord.

After they are transformed, should desire raise its head,
I shall press it down with the weight of the nameless uncarved
    block.[35]

Or chapter 77:

Is not the way of heaven like the stretching of a bow?
The high it presses down,
The low it lifts up:
The excessive it takes from
The deficient it gives to.[36]

That *Laozi*'s vision of cosmos and ethics had been applied by
some lowly literati—perhaps those of the *fangshi* magician type—to
the problems of the deprived lower classes is indicated by an early
scripture of the Daoist religion, the *Taiping jing,* the main part of
which is believed to have been written in the Eastern Han period.[37]
At least one group among the rebels that staged uprisings in A.D. 184
was known to have access to one version of *Laozi,* identified as
Wuqian wen (Book of five thousand words), but it seems that the
Taiping jing was also known to some of the rebels.[38] The *Taiping jing,*
even more eclectic than *Huainanzi,* incorporated many Confucian
notions stemming from the *Classic of Filial Piety,* and even from the
Book of Mencius. In its universalistic concern for humanity and belief
in the supramundane forces, the *Taiping jing* has been compared
especially with the altruistic *Mozi.*[39] Yet it was a predominantly
Daoist work. Written sometimes in barely coherent language, it
developed some of *Laozi*'s ideas to bring out a populist theme, con-
strained as it was by the yin-yang concepts of the Han cosmology.

The *Taiping jing* states that heaven and earth originated with a
primordial force—a force that was "confused yet natural *(huanghu
ziran),*" indeed sharing the qualities of Dao itself. "The 'primordial breath' *(yuanqi)* adheres to Dao and operates itself to produce
heaven and earth." Therefore, "Dao is the root of all transformation
(dahua) and the mentor of all transformation."[40] The primordial
breath also associates itself with the "breaths" of nature *(ziran)* and
of perfect harmony *(taihe)*—both being attributes of Dao.

The *Taiping jing* recognizes at the same time a middle-level
harmony *(zhonghe),* this middle level being in the interval between
heaven and earth, yin and yang. "The primordial breath and the

breaths of Nature and of Perfect Harmony merged . . . they congealed and begot heaven and earth. Heaven and earth, on their part, were infused with the Middle-level Harmony, working together with a common mind, and produced all things."[41] It was at the level of the middle-level harmony that humanity, acting as link between heaven and earth, played a crucial part. Humanity—not just the imperial ruler but all the people—could, together with heaven and earth (referred to also as the "great yang" and the "great yin"), generate the "Breath of Great Equity (Taiping qi)" that was to purge the world and the cosmos of accumulated sins *(chengfu)*.[42]

As is emphasized by Max Kaltenmark, Barbara Hendrischke, and others, the *Taiping jing* is a religious work not only because it offers methods of attaining longevity and immortality (although none of them particularly esoteric), but because it focuses on inherited sinfulness that stemmed from humanity's neglect of the Dao and De (virtue derived from Dao), of goodness, and of the responsibility that came with material riches.[43] The *Taiping jing* was itself a work of revelation—comprising teachings revealed by the Celestial Master ('Tianshi), a divine being sent by heaven for a very brief appearance on earth to impart the way toward salvation. This divine being was not himself a messiah, nor did he entrust his task to a messiah.[44] His role was to transmit through six accomplished Daoists *(zhenren)* a message to a "ruler of virtue" *(youde zhi jun)*—not necessarily the ruling sovereign—ultimately to be disseminated among people of all stations. Remarkably enough, the *Taiping jing* saw each individual among the people (male, female, and of whatever social status) as being as sagelike as any other, and the salvation of all eventually as lying in their own hands. All people were responsible for the *chengfu* sinfulness that had not only affected the ruler (who had, to be sure, his own share of blame) but also polluted the earth and its vegetation and heaven itself. The burden of sinfulness was believed to have accumulated through the generations; unlike the Buddhist karma, it did not involve reincarnation and was broadly cosmic in its repercussions. Except in the case of physical immortality being achieved, human life simply ends with death. Yet there was a continuous interaction between human deeds, on the one hand, and natural disasters, on the other. "Heaven and earth produced all things, yet they were impaired by the lack of [human] virtue. . . . Earth may have the fault of harming things, yet it is human beings that bear the sinful responsibility [for the degeneration of earth]."[45]

The individual's moral responsibility and his prospects for intellectual—and therefore social—attainment were recognized. Society was to be hierarchical, but mobility through the ranks was possible. The *Taiping jing* sets forth a nine-level spiritual and occupational hierarchy: (1) the divine person "without shape and endowed with the [primordial] breath" *(wuxing weiqi zhi ren);* (2) the great divine person *(da shenren);* (3) the perfected person *(zhenren);* (4) immortals *(xian¹ren)* (the numeral indicates the tone of pronunciation); (5) persons possessing great Dao *(dadaoren);* (6) sages *(sheng-ren);* (7) worthies *(xian²ren)* (again, the numeral indicates the tone of pronunciation); (8) the common people *(fanmin);* and (9) male or female slaves *(nubi).* The slaves could be bought and sold like merchandise, yet it was possible for them to ascend the spiritual-social ladder to become common people, worthies, and sages, and eventually divine persons. Repentance as well as intelligence were necessary for ascending to a higher spiritual-social level. For all people, expiation was to be found not just in repentance of a few persons with divine help, but in the reform of the conduct of the many.[46]

For all aspiring persons, meager diet and living alone in a thatch-roofed hut were advised "to attain union with the primordial breath." It was necessary for all nine human categories, from divine person to slave—and indeed all who held political and economic power as well—to conduct themselves so that the breath that stems from the middle-level harmony would rise and join the primordial breath of the Dao, out of which would come the "breath of Great Equity (Taiping qi)."[47] This term is explained as follows:

> *Tai* means great, referring to the accumulation of such great deeds as heaven has done. . . . *Ping* refers to the perfect rule of equity. All matters are well managed, never with treachery and selfishness. *Ping* is like earth which, being below, stands for holding fast to equity *(zhi-ping)*. . . . *Tai* means great; *ping* means justice *(zheng); qi* means giving life and support in interacting harmony.[48]

The arrival of the "breath of Great Equity," which signaled universal salvation, was more concretely the result of extensive communication between the ruler and the populace. The *Taiping jing*'s concept of rulership is surprisingly enlightened. It is stated that "human beings are the offspring of heaven" and that the emperor *(diwang)* is only heaven's "first noble son" *(diyi guizi)*—he is not different in kind from the rest of mankind as Han Confucianism would have it.[49] The ruler should govern by doing little *(wuwei)*, yet he must first be fully aware of the wishes of the governed. He should send emissaries to the people in various localities to gather information, but in addition, he should establish "lodges of goodness" *(shanhao zhai)* along the main thoroughfares where the populace can deposit signed texts expressing their views on what is to be done by government. As Kaltenmark has summarized it:

> The prince shall then examine the texts that were collected in this way and have the best of them extracted [by a council of sages and immortals]. . . . This text, which represents the quintessence of universal wisdom, shall in turn be redistributed, among the people so that they shall become converted to the good and be ignorant of the evil; "that is called completely obtaining the heart of Heaven, of Earth, of Man and of the Barbarians, so that great joy appears day by day, so that the world becomes one family and together constitutes a total order."[50]

Kaltenmark describes the *Taiping jing*'s political process as one in which "The ideas [comprising information and wisdom] should circulate from the people to the capital and *after decantation,* from the capital to the people" (italics added). The ruler and his elite advisors undoubtedly played a part in this decantation. Still, it is perhaps not wrong to say that the *Taiping jing*'s Daoism includes a populist element, for the prevalence of the "breath of Great Equity" presupposes unimpeded communication between different levels of the polity. As Kaltenmark explains, it is necessary that the three estates of heaven, earth, and humanity "love one another and mutually communicate *(xiangtong)* in order that there may be no evil."[51]

As is the *Taiping jing*'s view of the political process, its advocacy of social justice is remarkable. At a time of hardship in the countryside that witnessed widespread female infanticide, the *Taiping jing* lashes out against this practice as harmful to the "system of earth" *(ditong)* and thus to the balance between heaven and earth, indeed threatening to "exterminate the human species" itself. The *Taiping jing* concedes that a man could have two wives—as suggested by the symbol of the two short lines for "yin" and a single long line for "yang," according to the *Yijing*. But it is repeatedly emphasized that "man and woman must find each other suitable *(xiangde).*" "Only when there is sensual compatibility *(se xianghao)* can there be birth of offspring." That the *Taiping jing* takes a view contrary to the Han orthodoxy, in cosmology as in gender relationship, is indicated by the statement: "Heaven is the father and earth is the mother. Both father and mother are persons; what is the difference [between them]?"[52]

At a time when rampant local power was in the hands of self-aggrandizing officials, themselves often the largest landowners, it is perhaps not surprising that the *Taiping jing* should be concerned with the abuses by the powerful and wealthy. It suggests, for example, that the powerful and the rich are the rats in the granary, alone enjoying the produce levied from thousands of families.[53] When popular unrest had caused many among the poor to be imprisoned and to suffer cruel penalties, equity in the treatment of such pauperized rebels was an urgent issue. Echoing *Laozi*'s injunction that "the superior must have the inferior as root; the high must have the low as base,"[54] the *Taiping jing* goes further and asserts that the low can indeed sometimes "change and admonish" *(gejian)* the high:

> According to the nature of heaven and earth, the low can change or admonish the high, just as the high can change or admonish the low. Each has strength and weakness and therefore complements the other. Only thus will heaven's way and all affairs find their appropriate places. Therefore, sacred as the august heaven is, it has shortcomings and cannot match earth's strength. This is why all things receive their decree *(ming)* from heaven, yet their bodies are nourished by earth.[55]

Undoubtedly with many unjust adjudications in mind, the *Taiping jing* frequently dwells on the unequal status accorded to different members of society and comments from the standpoint of the *Laozi* cosmology and ethics. Justice is regarded as the principal quality of a virtuous ruler or parent:

> When heaven gives and earth transforms on an equal basis *(tiandi shihua de jun)*, and when the high and the low, the great and the small, are all treated identically *(zunbei daxiao jie ruyi)*, there will then be no disputes or lawsuits. Thus one is fit to be ruler, father, and mother.[56]

Whether the breath of Great Equity arises to bring cosmic and individual salvation indeed hinges on the ruler's administration of justice. "Being equitable so there will be no grievances—this is *ping*. Therefore once the virtuous ruler governs in this way, the breath of Great Equity will arrive immediately." On the other hand, if the ruler does not make "his government a just one" *(ping qi zhi)*, upon his death his soul will be condemned to dwell below the earth, amidst pernicious miasmas.[57]

Was the Celestial Master of the *Taiping jing,* divine messenger that he was, prophesying doom or deliverance? As compared with the Confucian beliefs regarding historical change as determined by the cyclical Five Phases and the *Yijing* hexagrams, the *Taiping jing* seems at least to have suggested an eschatological warning and to some extent an assurance. The *Laozi* states that "turning back is how the Dao moves,"[58] presumably back to the primordial beginning. But should the society fail to make such a return, without the oneness that informs the cosmos, heaven and earth may yet be destroyed; thus chapter 39 of *Laozi* begins with a statement on the universal, egalitarian oneness *(yi)*—in Lau's translation:

> Of old, these came to be in possession of the One:
> Heaven in virtue of the One is limpid;
> Earth in virtue of the One is settled;
> Gods in virtue of the One have their potencies;
> The valley in virtue of the One is full;
> The myriad creatures in virtue of the One are alive;
> Lords and princes in virtue of the One become leaders in
>   the empire.

Without the oneness or leveling equity that underlay the political system, disaster was indeed, according to this reading of *Laozi,* in store for the cosmic as well as the social order:

> It is the One that makes these what they are.
> Without what makes it limpid heaven might split;
> Without what makes it settled earth might sink;
> Without what gives them their potencies gods might spend
>   themselves;
> Without what makes it full the valley might run dry;
> Without what keeps them alive the myriad creatures might perish;
> Without what makes them leaders lords and princes might fall.[59]

In the *Taiping jing,* there is warning of cosmic and societal catastrophe—essentially a Daoist message, though mixed with some of Dong Zhongshu's theory of interaction between Heaven and humanity. Disaster was certain if the inherited sins were not expiated and heaven's warning conveyed by omens and prodigies not heeded.

> If severe illness is not cured in time, one will die. If astronomical happenings are not rectified, disaster will ensue. The four seasons will lose their atmosphere, and the Five Operating Phases will be tangled up. The Three Lights [sun, moon, and stars] will lose their proper brightness and paths and then be destroyed. The people will be in turmoil, losing their abodes. The old and weak will be carried away from home and half of the people will die young. The state will suffer misgovernment, in chaotic delusion; the great Dao and the good De will be separated. . . . Is this not severe illness? Therefore one must do one's utmost to cure it.[60]

During the third century, even after widespread rebellions inspired partly by the Daoists had been suppressed (see below), the malaise of the times was by no means cured. The so-called mystic learning (*xuanxue,* sometimes translated as neo-Daoism) reflected an existential crisis among a small elite of literati of high birth and political connections who were involved in—or were attempting to be disengaged from—the frenzied power struggle at court in the period of Wei-Jin transition. The pressure of *mingjiao* (doctrine of status) that involved not simply official duties but family obligation and endless ritual observances added to the burden on the psyches of the few gifted libertines and libertarians.[61] They turned to *Laozi* and *Zhuangzi* for intellectual solace, as some of them resorted to heavy drinking. They took pride in being unconventional. Yet the Han orthodoxy persisted not only in the surviving imperial structure and kinship system, but also in the teaching of the *Yijing Appendices* regarding fixed positions for individuals in society. With the *Yijing* still preeminent as a guide, it was extremely difficult to arrive at the vision of a complete upheaval.

How hard it was to transcend the Han socioethics may be seen in the writing of Wang Bi (226–249), the youthful genius who, before his death, at the age of twenty-three, had written profound commentaries on both *Laozi* and the *Yijing.* Wang Bi arrived at a philosophical position that acknowledges nonbeing *(wu)* as the Dao itself,

which therefore must be upheld as substance *(ti)*. Yet nonbeing had
to express itself in the useful functions of society, and for this category of application *(yong)*—the *tiyong* dichotomy being Wang's
invention—it was still necessary to honor the authority of the monarch, hoping only that he could practice nonintervention *(wuwei)*,
thus letting things take their own course and spontaneously arrive at
good government.[62] Wang Bi was in fact attempting to reconcile
Laozi and the *Yijing:* in other words, he was for less state interference, but he was for the preservation of the imperial ruler and of
bureaucracy. Wang's annotation on a line in *Laozi* 32, for example,
reads:

> TEXT: When first there were instructions and regulations, there
> were names.[63]
>
> WANG'S COMMENTARY: "When first there were institutions and
> regulations" describes the time when the uncarved block *(pu,*
> pristine simplicity) was dispersed and there first were officials
> and rulers. When institutions and regulations, officials and
> rulers are initiated, it is impossible not to establish names
> and statuses *(mingfen)* by which to determine superior and
> inferior; therefore when first there are institutions and
> regulations, there will be names.[64]

The issue here was whether such inherited institutions as monarchy and bureaucracy could be regarded as "natural" and meet the
Daoist ideal of spontaneity. Guo Xiang (d. 312), who wrote lengthy
annotations of *Zhuangzi,* commented on chapter 2, "Discussion on
making all things equal":

> Whether one is a ruler or servitor, a superior or an inferior, and
> whether it is the hand or the foot, the inside or the outside, follows
> from the spontaneity of Natural Principle *(tianli zhi ziran)*. How could
> it be thus directly from man's actions? . . . The one whom the age
> takes to be worthy becomes the ruler, while those whose talents do
> not correspond to the demands of the age become servitors. It is
> analogous to heaven's being naturally high and earth naturally low,
> the head being on top and the feet occupying naturally the inferior
> position.[65]

While Wang Bi and Guo Xiang, who were outstanding figures
among neo-Daoists, were willing in fact to recognize *mingjiao* or

lijiao as "natural," there were others who derived from *Laozi* and *Zhuangzi* views that could not be reconciled with orthodoxy—and one part found to be incompatible was none other than the relative positions of heaven and earth in *Laozi*'s "undifferentiatedly formed" early cosmos. Ruan Ji (210–263), who adhered more closely to original Daoism perhaps out of temperament, went even beyond *Zhuangzi* in questioning the "naturalness" of monarchy and bureaucracy. His *Biography of Master Great Man (Daren xiansheng zhuan)*, written in poetic prose, declares that in the distant past there were indeed no monarchs or officials to oppress the people:

> In the ancient past when heaven and earth were just assuming form, all the myriad things together came into existence. The great were delighted in their nature, the lesser placidly accepted their forms. . . . The weak were not in fear of oppression, and the powerful did not exploit their strength. For there were no monarchs and everything was in order; there were no officials and every matter went well.[66]

Ruan went further. In a moment of drunkenness or desperate inspiration, he envisioned the disintegration of the cosmos itself, resulting in the collapse of heaven and earth and *"yin* and *yang* having gone awry *(shiwei)."*[67] In *Biography*, he warned the hypocrites who were the gentleman-officials of his times:

> Let me tell you. In the past, heaven was below and earth was above. They flipped over and were upside down and were not secure. How could we put them in place in the exact and constant position? Heaven is shaken by earth. The mountain falls and the river rises. . . . Where can you gentlemen find a place to walk in and keep step with music?[68]

Further on in the prose-poem, Ruan portrays an apocalypse seen at the very moment of writing:

> Heaven and earth disintegrate and the cosmos opens up,
> Stars are falling, the sun and moon decaying,
> I lift myself up there but what do I feel?

Ruan found the sun and the moon fallen and the sea frozen; the earth crumbled, and the cold hit him. He was leaving what had been heaven and earth but was not certain what would happen next.[69]

Orthodoxy and Heterodoxy Within the
Daoist Movement

Ruan Ji's eschatological vision was rare among the elite neo-Daoists of the third century. But even as the first Chinese empire decayed, to be followed by nomadic invasions and the surging influence of Buddhism, the Daoist movement broadened, although there was now a real "parting of the ways." This was not between philosophical-mystical inspiration on the one hand and the cult of immortality on the other. Nor was it between the various modes of achieving immortality—whether it was elixir of life produced through the alchemical process, involving pills made of gold and cinnabar; or less expensive "internal alchemy," involving meditation, breathing exercise, and sexual regimen; or, alternatively, especially with the Tianshi dao (the Way of the Celestial Master), through belief in the blessings of talismans dispensed by Daoist masters who could communicate with the deities. Actually, the line was increasingly drawn between Daoists who accommodated, indeed championed, the "external orthodoxy" of the Three Bonds and the *mingjiao* and *lijiao,* and those who had mass appeal in time of stress, representing an egalitarian revolt in an aristocratic age and destructive impatience with the established institutions. This demarcation within the Daoist movement *was* a matter of doctrine and was over the issue of whether such virtues as loyalty to the monarch and complete devotion to the family were indeed part of Daoist nature—a question which even Ruan Ji's friend Xi Kang (223–262) had answered in the affirmative. Despite his heroic and turbulent life, Xi Kang's political ideal was: "The ruler above is quiescent, while his servitors below are agreeably compliant. . . . They harbor loyalty and cling to dutifulness without being aware of their reasons for doing so."[70] Over this issue of the social content of "nature" there were to be deep differences within the Daoist movement, even as its activity increased and esoteric scriptures multiplied throughout the vicissitudes of the second to fifth centuries.

   The principal facts regarding the two strands of Daoism, many of which are already known, need to be briefly recapitulated. While there were throughout the Han period numerous popular "Huang-Lao groups"—groups honoring the legendary Yellow Emperor and Laozi—that combined shamanistic worship with techniques for achieving immortality, it was the two major Daoist popular movements in the second century that transformed Daoism into a fully

institutionalized religion, complete with clerical, scriptural, and ritu-
alistic traditions.[71] The movement in eastern China was led by Zhang
Jue and his brothers and was known as the Taiping dao. Zhang Jue
allegedly was acquainted with the *Taiping jing.* It was his group that
staged the Yellow Turban Rebellion in present-day Henan in A.D.
184. The group in the west, in Sichuan, was said to be headed by
Zhang Ling (Zhang Daoling), who was succeeded by his son Zhang
Heng and later by his grandson Zhang Lu. Together known as the
Three Zhangs, they were eventually to maintain a theocratic organization called the Way of Five Pecks of Rice (Wudoumi dao). Since
Zhang Ling was believed to have been invested in seance by Laozi
with the title of Celestial Master (Tianshi), this movement was also
referred to as the Tianshi dao. Its principal text was the *Laozi,* to
which was added annotations known as the *Xiang'er Commentary*
(now available in English translation).[72]

  This account of the Three Zhangs in Sichuan must, however,
be modified by a more critical historiography highlighting a fourth
Zhang—Zhang Xiu, who was not related to the other three. *The History of the Three Kingdoms,* the principal source regarding the Three
Zhangs, states in other contexts that the rebellion of the Five Pecks
of Rice in Sichuan that broke out in 184 (the first year of the Zhong-
ping era) was led by Zhang Xiu, who was a successful leader of the
cult until he was attacked and replaced by Zhang Lu (an event probably no earlier than 188).[73] Both Zhang Xiu and Zhang Lu introduced innovations in religious and community practices, but the latter was less of a rebel and more of a sub-warlord. Tradition has it
that Zhang Lu's mother, a beautiful woman, was a priestess and had
influence on Liu Yan, governor of the region, and it was she who
secured for Zhang Lu an official status that enabled him to govern
the Hanzhong area for more than twenty years. Even after Zhang
Lu's surrender to the warlord Cao Cao in 215, the organization and
ideology of the Five Pecks of Rice continued to grow.

  As compared with the movement in Sichuan, the one in east
China—that is, the Taiping dao, which inspired the Yellow Turban
Rebellion—was more radical.[74] Both movements in east and west
saw physical ailments as punishment for the accumulation of sins
and insisted on reflection and repentance as the way to healing. The
rallying cry of the Taiping dao included "The Blue Heaven is dead
and the Yellow Heaven is to establish [its rule]"—implying perhaps
not only the goal of establishing a new dynasty, but also an impend-

ing cosmic change. Perhaps it was an eschatological vision that explains why it was under the banner of the Taiping dao that large-scale revolts broke out in east China, bestriding the territory of eight commanderies *(zhou)*.

Although the activities of the Tianshi dao were continued by Zhang Lu in Sichuan and Shaanxi, the overall response among the populace was not enthusiastic. However, with the decimation of the Taiping dao after the failure of the Yellow Turban Rebellion, the field was left wide open for the more complacent Tianshi dao to expand and to make inroads into traditionally Taiping dao territory. The Tianshi dao under Zhang Lu introduced innovations including hostels offering food and lodging free of charge and religious officers (known as *jijiu,* or libationers) performing civil as well as military functions. Laozi was honored as the highest god—the Most Exalted Venerable Lord (Taishang laojun). Instead of the morally neutral and antiritual teaching of Laozi, however, it was taught that "When Dao prevails, subjects are loyal and sons filial and the state is easy to govern."[75] Zhang Lu's surrender to Cao Cao in 215 gained further respectability for his sect and allowed it to become the only well-organized Daoist movement in the Three Kingdoms (220–280), the Western Jin (265–317), and the Eastern Jin (317–419) periods. Thus the Tianshi dao became the only organized Daoist movement and its accommodation with orthodoxy was notable. In a later Tianshi dao text (circa A.D. 255) titled *Instructions and Admonitions for the Families of the Great Dao (Dadao jia ling jie)* and attributed to Zhang Lu himself, the movement's espousal of orthodox values was unequivocally expressed:

> All of our households should transform one another through loyalty and filiality, so that fathers are magnanimous and sons filial, husbands faithful and wives chaste, elder brothers respectful and the younger obedient.[76]

The ceaseless intrigues and power struggle within the Eastern Jin court and the onslaught of the "barbarians" from the north, together with the increasing presence of Buddhist teachers from Inner Asia, afforded a stimulating environment for the Tianshi dao to refine its doctrine and to attract recruits from the upper classes. By the fourth and fifth centuries, with the migration of many magnate families to southeast China, many prominent lineage groups in both north and south had become Tianshi dao believers. The Wangs of Langye, the Ges, the Xus, and the Taos of Danyang, in the south, as well as the Cuis and the Lus from the north were outstanding examples.[77] Members of these families played very important roles in the further unfolding of Daoism in this period. Moreover, men and women at court, including such monarchs as the emperors Ai (r. 362–363) and Jianwen (r. 371) of Eastern Jin and Emperor Taiwu (r. 424–452) of the Northern Wei had also become ardent Daoist converts.

At the same time, however, the rapid expansion of the Tianshi dao resulted in decentralization and the dilution of doctrinal purity. Because of war and migration, many Tianshi dao followers formed splinter groups, worshiped new gods, and practiced "heretical" rituals, much to the chagrin of the purists of the tradition. They chastised the "excessive cults" (yinsi) for everything from making blood sacrifices of raw meat, worshiping on wrong days, and incurring ruinous expenditures in carrying out ceremonies, to using mediums and propitiating uncanonical gods.[78] Even more alarming were the numerous rebellions staged by such cults in pursuit of the utopian world. It was under these circumstances that the necessity was felt for the definition of orthodoxy within the Daoist movement. The line between orthodoxy and heterodoxy was gradually drawn.

One direct result of this awareness of orthodoxy versus heterodoxy was the outburst of reforming zeal among the self-styled orthodox Daoists. Between the middle of the fourth century and the latter part of the fifth, large numbers of Daoist texts were "revealed" to individual reformers, who dutifully transcribed them and created new scriptural traditions, which in turn led to the formation of new schools of Daoism.

An early scripture of the Tianshi dao was the Sanhuang jing (The three sovereigns canon), compiled by Bao Jing (also known as Bao Xuan), teacher of Xu Mai (300–348). Bao Jing was the father-in-law of Ge Hong (283–363), of whom more will be said in the following pages. Another scripture of the fourth century may be traced to a woman Daoist, Wei Huacun (251–334), daughter of a prominent official in the Western Jin court and herself a "libationer" (jijiu) of the Tianshi dao. Wei had been instrumental in the compilation of the Huangting neijing jing (Inner effulgence canon of the Yellow Court), a most important early Daoist text. But it was her revelations after her death, together with those of several other immortals, to a certain young man named Yang Xi (b. 330) during the years 364 to 370 that really commenced the process of textual compilation for the Shangqing (Higher Clarity) school.[79] During that seven-year period, she and others visited Yang repeatedly and instructed him in the canons of the Shangqing Heaven, one that was even higher than the Taiqing Heaven of the original Tianshi dao. After Yang had transcribed his visionary instructions into thirty-one texts, he had them recopied by his pupil Xu Mi (303–373) and the latter's youngest son Xu Hui (341–ca. 370).[80] It is noteworthy that both the Ge and the Xu families were old aristocratic lineages from Jurong in Jiangsu and were related by marriage for several generations. Since Bao Jing was also related to the Xus and the Ges, it is apparent that the prominent southern aristocratic families were at the center of the Daoist reformation within the old celestial masters tradition.

Almost thirty years after the transcription of Shangqing texts by Yang Xi and the two Xus, another set of new Daoist texts, the *Lingbao jing* (Divine Treasure canon) appeared on the scene.[81] From 397 to 401, a series of scriptures were revealed to Ge Chaofu, grand-nephew of the famous Ge Hong. These became the core of the Lingbao scriptural corpus later catalogued and codified by Lu Xiujing (406–477), one of the most important Daoist figures in the southern dynasties.[82]

Coinciding with this fervent reform activity in the south was a similar movement in the north.[83] Spearheaded by Cui Hao (381–450), chancellor to the Tuoba Wei court and senior member of the most prestigious lineage in the north, and Kou Qianzhi (365–448), Daoist visionary and younger brother of another prominent official in Northern Wei, the campaign against the "spurious teaching of the Three Zhangs" was launched. The purpose of this movement was to purge the abuses of the Tianshi dao, of which both the Cui and the Kou families were members for generations, specifically including the exorbitant rice levies *(zumi)* and cash taxes *(qianshou)* exacted from the members, as well as the techniques for the "union of vital forces between male and female" *(nannü heqi zhi shu)*.[84]

Receiving direct revelations from the deified Laozi and from his "great-great grandson" Li Puwen, on two separate occasions in 415 and 423 respectively, Kou Qianzhi compiled the *Yunzhong yinsong xinke zhi jie* (Articles of a new code to be chanted to musical notation amidst the clouds) and the *Lutu zhenjing* (Perfect book of talismans and designs; no longer extant) and submitted them to

Emperor Taiwu of Northern Wei. With the patronage of Cui Hao at
court, Kou was able to convince Emperor Taiwu that Taiwu was the
Perfect Ruler of Great Peace of the North (Beifang taiping zhenjun)
who was destined to bring peace and prosperity to all under heaven.
A theocratic rule was thus initiated.[85]

Against this background, the doctrine of this reformed yet
orthodox Daoism may now be described as the elite reformers themselves defined it. The orthodox religious leaders were ever aware of
the existence of the "excessive cults" and of the Daoist rebels. Interestingly enough, their idea of orthodoxy paralleled much of the *mingjiao* or *lijiao* ethical norm championed by the state since Han times.
In other words, they perceived the attainment of the ultimate Daoist
goal—immortality and perfection—as contingent upon adherence to
the principles of the Three Bonds. Their labeling of rival Daoist
groups as heterodox was based on what they saw as the latter's flouting of such principles.

Ge Hong, who died several decades before this reform period
actually began, had already set the tone for the argument. Ge Hong
was the principal spokesman for the *danding* (alchemical) school of
Daoism, which was perhaps consciously reacting against the *fulu* (talismans) orientation of earlier popular Daoist groups that included
the rebels. Ge Hong's *Baopuzi* (its "Inner Chapters" in particular) is
significant not only as a compendium of elite Daoist thought up to
the middle of the fourth century, but also because it provides detailed
description of the techniques for attaining immortality the Chinese
had experimented with by that time. Yet it was Ge's view that all such
techniques would be rendered ineffective if they were not accompanied by the observance of *mingjiao* or *lijiao* morality, especially filial
piety, loyalty to the monarch, and respect for hierarchy. He puts it
this way:

> Those who are in pursuit of immortality should regard filial piety,
> loyalty, harmonious deference *(heshun)*, benevolence, and trustwor-
> thiness as fundamental. If they are negligent in cultivating their moral
> behavior, but concentrate only on the techniques, immortality will be
> beyond their reach.[86]

Ge's book makes very clear that such moral values not only do
not impede the pursuit of immortality but are, on the contrary, cru-

cial to its success. The same chapter provides a specific "schedule" for attaining immortality:

> Those wishing to become terrestrial immortals *(dixian)* should accumulate 300 meritorious deeds; those wishing to become celestial immortals *(tianxian)* should acquire 1200. If, after accumulating 1199 good deeds, one commits one single transgression, all the previously accumulated merit will be lost, and one has to start anew. . . .
>
> If one has not performed all the necessary meritorious deeds, even the ingestion of immortal medicine will not help in attaining perfection. On the other hand, if one does not consume any immortal medicine but performs good deeds anyway, then one can at least avoid the tragedy of sudden death, though immortality may be out of the question.[87]

Filial piety, loyalty to the monarch, and "harmonious deference" Ge deemed essential in the Daoist pursuit of perfection. This line of thinking later exerted considerable influence on popular Daoism. The well-known morality books *(shanshu)* of the Song dynasty (960–1279) and, later, *Taishang ganying pian* (Treatise of the Most Exalted One on moral retribution), *Gongguo ge* (Ledger of merits and demerits), and *Yinzhi wen* (Essay on karmic retribution) all contain the same theme outlined in the *Baopuzi.*

Ge Hong's embracing of the Confucian socioethics is also to be seen in his attack on Bao Jingyan, a contemporaneous writer who espoused a clear-cut antimonarchical theory, believing that the Mandate of Heaven was a false notion and that in the ideal society of antiquity there were neither royalty or officials. Bao went further than Ruan Ji in attacking the hierarchical society and its inherently arbitrary and unjust nature. Ge Hong criticized Bao for taking Daoist cosmogony too seriously when the latter affirmed the undifferentiated primitivity prior to division of yin and yang and of the hexagrams. Ge wrote in reference to Bao, quite unconscious of his own forgetfulness of Laozi's adulation of primitive nature:

> If you think that undifferentiated darkness is beautiful, then perhaps *qian* and *kun* [symbolizing heaven and earth] should never have been divided. If you think that the nameless *(wuming)* is the loftiest, then the Eight Trigrams *(bagua)* should never have been drawn. . . . Your

elegant discourse simply adulates nature *(ziran)*. Now it is in the nature *(xing)* of many animals to know only the mother, forgetting the father. Prostration in homage [of sovereign and parents] seems to be a minor matter of appearances. However, human nature should not be unconstrained: it is necessary to honor one's father. Appearances cannot be dispensed with; prostration in homage must be performed. To be unconstrained and abandon [all appearances]—will that make you feel at ease?[88]

This concern with social ethics and proper ritual was common to all the reformers of Daoism in the fourth and fifth centuries, although particularly evident with Cui Hao and Kou Qianzhi.[89] It may be recalled that both Cui and Kou came from prominent families which had for generations been associated with the Tianshi dao. Disturbed by the total degeneracy of some of their onetime fellow Celestial Master believers, whose disregard for proper ritual they absolutely deplored, and alarmed by the rebelliousness of others, such as maverick Tianshi dao members Sun En and Lu Xun (see below), both Cui and Kou sought to purify the Daoist tradition and to reestablish an ideal society based on the orthodox morality of monarchy and kinship. For Cui, the goal was to implement the policy of "regulating and rectifying human relationships and separating and clarifying surnames and lineages" *(qizheng renlun, fenming xingzu)*.[90] He envisioned a society very similar to that described in the *Zhouli* (Rites of Zhou), with five orders of nobility at the top and the subject people knowing their place below. For Kou, the reformed Daoist tradition must be guided exclusively by rules of ritual behavior *(zhuan yi lidu wei shou)*[91] that the elect or chosen people *(zhongmin)* should effortlessly observe. A confluence of practical interest and a particularistic interpretation of Daoist spontaneity—one which undoubtedly had accommodated the ideology of the *Yijing Appendices*—brought the two men together.

Kou's preoccupation with the "external orthodoxy" may be seen in the following passage from *Laojun yinsong jiejing,* the extant version of the *Yunzhong yinsong xinke zhi jie:*

Taishang laojun . . . proclaims: Large numbers of people nowadays commit iniquitous acts. Fathers are not loving, children are not filial, and ministers are not loyal. Their fate is such that pestilence and poison will be visited upon them and all the evil people will perish.[92]

Kou regarded laxity in social morality as the greatest cause for disaster. He was especially incensed by the other Daoist groups that, using the name of Li Hong (popularly believed to be the incarnation of the deified Laozi), repeatedly rebelled against existing regimes.[93] Speaking through Laojun, Kou expressed his indignation:

> The false prophets and charlatans attack the orthodox Dao *(zhengdao)* and delude the ignorant people. They proclaim that "Laojun should reign and Li Hong should appear." Throughout the realm there are crowds of rebels. Year after year they use the name of Li Hong and rebel. Some of them stir up demons and gods, so that people can see them in broad daylight. They lure and confuse the people with what they call the language of the gods and demons. . . . They assume official functions and titles, attract followers as numerous as ants, and devastate the land. . . .
>
> Those fools are deceitful without end and have all taken to disloyalty, this band of criminals and fugitives, serfs and slaves, falsely calling themselves Li Hong! To think that I would stoop so low as to mingle with this vulgar, stinking group, these slaves, dogs, and demons, to engage in evil subversion! These villainous imposters spout heresies and destroy the orthodox teaching *(zhengjiao)!*[94]

This passage clearly indicates how the awareness of orthodoxy had been strengthened. The awareness deepened with the rise of heterodoxy—what was perceived as misinterpretation or degeneration of the original teaching. The "excessive cults" and the rebels had forced the elite, orthodox-minded Daoists to define, or redefine, themselves and what they believed in, again in a manner comparable to that in which the Arians forced the early Christian church to stake out its own position. The outcome was the formulation of an orthodoxy based on the morality of the Three Bonds and the related rituals, which enabled the elite Daoists to have common ground with Confucian scholars and politically preeminent Buddhist monks. From the religious and ritualist standpoint, Daoist groups such as the adepts of the Li family (Lijia dao), famous for longevity and charisma since the third century, were denounced because they did not practice the proper rituals and because they made false claims regarding the age they attained.[95] From the political standpoint, Daoist groups such as those led by Sun En and Lu Xun were condemned because they harbored antidynastic intentions. They were, moreover, labeled heterodox—not just because they were politically disloyal, but because they embraced an eschatological vision that involved a challenge to existing institutions and moral values.[96]

The Sun En–Lu Xun rebellion raged for a decade in the early fifth century, wreaking havoc in the coastal areas of Zhejiang-Jiangsu, and decisively damaged the Eastern Jin regime.[97] Sun's family had for generations been followers of the Tianshi dao. His brother-in-law Lu Xun came from a prominent Daoist family and was himself the cousin of Cui Hao (Cui's mother was Lu's aunt on his father's side). Both Sun and Lu took the belief in *shijie* (release from the corpse) seriously and, when their movement failed, drowned themselves, in 402 and 411 respectively, in an attempt to gain immortality. Many of their supporters followed suit, some throwing their children into the water first. The movement was definitely both zealous and millenarian in nature.

Although Sun and Lu's rebellion ended in failure by 411, the cult of Li Hong proved much more resilient and therefore more threatening to the authorities.[98] Actually, Li Hong, the incarnation of the deified Laozi now known as the Sage Lord of the Latter Age (Housheng daojun), was a deity worshiped by the Shangqing Daoists. Originally a mortal, Li attained perfection through rigorous Daoist practices outlined in some Shangqing texts.[99] He was, however, also closely associated with an apocalyptic vision of the imminent end of the present world. His appearance signaled the onset of a cataclysmic disaster in the aftermath of which only a chosen few would survive.[100] In this capacity Li Hong was on occasion used by religious rebels as the clarion call for action. Beginning in 324 and extending over the next two centuries, there were at least seven recorded uprisings or conspiracies involving Li Hong as the reputed leader.[101] It is for this reason that the orthodox reformer Kou Qianzhi was so vituperative in his condemnation of the Li Hong cult. What made the cult so awesome was precisely its eschatology, which consists of a full range of well-integrated ideas, from the prediction of an imminent crisis, the identification of the messiah/savior who will solve it, and the designation of the elect who will help in this task, to the apocalypse that will separate the saved from the doomed and the "New Jerusalem" that the survivors will enjoy.[102] The scripture that fully illustrates this eschatology is the *Taishang dongyuan shenzhou jing* (Sacred chants from the deep vault of the Most Exalted One, Daozang, 335).[103] This text is worthy of examination in some detail.

Scholars who have studied this scripture almost unanimously agree that at least the first few *juan* of it were completed by the beginning of the fifth century.[104] This places it squarely in the same time period as Kou Qianzhi's moral writings. The contrast in tone cannot be more clear.

The Crisis. Like most of the religious Daoist texts compiled around this time, the *Shenzhou jing* conveys a strong sense of crisis. The phrase *"dajie chuizhi"* (the great calamity is imminent) occurs regularly throughout the text. The following passage is typical:

> The Dao says: The great calamity is fast approaching. The monarch's rule is in total disarray, and the people are full of grief. The weather loses its regularity and the five grains fail to ripen. The people develop evil intentions, becoming rebellious and subversive. Parents and children, younger and elder brothers, they all scheme against one another until they perish.[105]

The crisis is man-made and not divinely intended. It is the direct result of the moral degeneracy of mankind. Thus the *Shenzhou jing* declares: "The people of this world have accumulated much evil. They do not subscribe to the teaching of the Dao. Consequently, only the sound of mourning for the dead can be heard, but not the melody of the immortals' songs."[106] As a punishment for this accumulation of human depravity, a catastrophe of cosmic proportions is about to take place.

It should be noted, however, that evil is here defined as not believing in the teaching of the Dao and not, as in the case of the elite Daoists, transgression against a certain ethical norm. In other words, good and evil are not determined by external orthodoxy, but by the demonstration of true faith. This is made clear in other parts of the text: "While the evil ones in the world are numerous, the good ones are few and far between. This is because the people are ignorant of the perfected teaching of the Three Vaults."[107] Elsewhere it is stated that "after the years *xinsi* [441] and *jiawu* [454], 80 million demons of pestilence will come to slaughter the people. The evil people are those who do not subscribe to the Dao."[108] In yet another section the text declares: "Evil ones exist in multitudes. They are ignorant of the Dao. Even when they see it, they refuse to follow. This is the reason for the large number of deaths."[109]

The Messiah. Once the seriousness of the crisis has been

demonstrated and its cause explained, the stage is set for the introduction of the messiah, or savior, who will help solve it. The description of this messiah appears almost entirely in the first *juan* of the
Shenzhou jing, the oldest portion of the text. He is the "Perfect Lord
Who Is To Come" (Danglai zhenjun), and is none other than Li
Hong himself, the villain in Kou Qianzhi's *Laojun yinsong jiejing!* The
passage in question runs as follows: "The Dao says: Listen to me
attentively! I will speak to you now about the era to come and the
period of the end. . . . In the *jiawu* year [454] . . . the doctrine of the
Dao prospers and Muzi Gongkou [Li Hong's name written in four
characters] is destined to rise again."[110] Elsewhere the identification
of Li Hong with the Perfect Lord is made even more explicit: "If you
receive the 20 *juan* of this text you will see The Perfect Lord Who is
to Come. . . . The Perfect Lord is Muzi Gongkou."[111]

Further description of the Perfect Lord is found later in the
same chapter: "The Perfect Lord is sixteen feet tall. His face and eyes
are radiant—there is no comparably handsome appearance among
men. One does not get tired of looking at him."[112] Thus, from being
a rather obscure sage of the first century B.C., Li Hong has evolved
first into the object of a local cult in Sichuan, then into the semidivine inspirer of fourth-century rebel leaders who operated under his
name, finally being canonized as the Perfect Lord.[113] As the messiah
figure, he will come to cleanse the world of all inequities through a
catastrophic upheaval and a rearrangement of the cosmic order:
"The Perfect Lord is not far away. Calamities will arise in the year
jiashen [444–445], and the world will be thrown into total chaos. The
empire will be completely destroyed, while heaven and earth will be
reconstituted. Then the Perfect Lord will manifest himself!"[114]

The Elect. Li Hong is not to accomplish the task of world-
cleansing by himself. He will be assisted by saints, sages, and immortals, and more importantly by his followers, who are the elect. This is
where the notion of the chosen people *(zhongmin)* becomes important.[115] A clear message of the *Shenzhou jing* is the guarantee of the
survival of the faithful. The faithful are all those who embrace the
doctrine of the Perfect Lord and worship the *Shenzhou jing,* regardless of sex, social status, wealth, even educational level. The following passage is typical:

> Young men and women, whether you are emperors, kings, noblemen
> with 2000 piculs of rice stipend, or ignorant masses, servants, and
> slaves, if you will receive this text and this talismanic contract, your

names will be entered in the list of immortals and you will not die a tragic death.[116]

Indeed, the chosen people need not demonstrate any religious zeal, as is evidenced by the following passage: "Even if you are illiterate, you can receive this text and hire people to re-copy it and install it in a clean and quiet room to worship it. Then all the vicious demons will be kept at bay and may not get near you."[117]

The *Shenzhou jing* repeatedly assures the faithful that they are predestined to be the elect, that they have been sent from heaven to assist the Perfect Lord to usher in the millennium.[118] At the same time, it admonishes them not be complacent about their own guaranteed salvation, but to exert themselves to popularize the text and to convert others.[119] Then they will be ready for the apocalypse and will survive it.

The Apocalypse. The bulk of the *Shenzhou jing* is concerned with the great upheaval and how to survive it. References are made to devastating floods and war,[120] but the greatest emphasis is on disease and pestilence. A dazzling array of demons, goblins, and evil spirits are mentioned throughout the text. They are described as the executioners who will slaughter all the iniquitous elements and purge the world in preparation for the coming of the Perfect Lord. The different kinds of epidemics and ailments with which they can afflict people are as hair-raising as they are bizarre. This incidentally makes the *Shenzhou jing* the single most important source for the study of demonology and infectious diseases in fifth-century China.

The "New Jerusalem." Once the demons have finished their work, the millennium under the rule of the Perfect Lord arrives:

> The Dao says: The Perfect Lord is Li Hong who will reign over the empire as king. The world will be in great joy. One sowing will yield nine crops. Human lifespan will increase to three thousand years, after which mankind will be rejuvenated and transformed afresh. Heaven and earth will be in perfect order without any turmoil. The sun and moon will shine brighter than they do now. . . .
>
> When the Perfect Lord manifests himself, he will reign by non-intervention *(wuwei)*. There will be no more suffering by war, torture, and imprisonment. Under the reign of the Sage, people will have abundance and joy. They will be free from greed and avarice. There will be no more ordinary domestic animals. Instead the phoenix and the white crane are now the domestic fowls, and the unicorn and lion

the domestic animals. . . . Men and women will be chaste and free from lust.[121]

This portrayal of utopia completes the eschatology of the *Shenzhou jing,* in which each concept is logically linked to another, forming a sequence. A crisis is identified. The savior who will solve it will manifest himself. He will be assisted by his chosen people. The apocalypse will occur, and the predestined elect will survive it to live as immortals and to enjoy a reconstructed world of affluence and peace. The text maps out no concrete plan for the faithful to hasten the arrival of the new age, but it is quite obvious that its eschatology is subversive in a sweeping way. It anticipates the destruction of the existing institutions and the demise of the current political authority.[122] It preaches an egalitarianism quite contrary to the hierarchy envisioned by orthodox reformers like Cui Hao and Kou Qianzhi.

Thus the battle line between orthodoxy and heterodoxy in early Daoism is complete. It is clear from the vantage point of the fifth century that there were two kinds of Daoism: one which made accommodation with external orthodoxy and believed the "fixed positions" in the natural and social cosmos to be spontaneous and natural; and one which never forgot *Laozi*'s vision of the "undifferentiatedly formed" beginning—a beginning that would also be the end, except for the elect endowed with the individual mystic knowledge and capacity to return to the origins, transcending heaven and earth and the social cosmos.

Notes

1. D. C. Lau, trans., *Lao Tzu, Tao Te Ching* (Harmondsworth, England: Penguin, 1963), 82, slightly adjusted. See also Ariane Rump, Commentary on the *Lao Tzu by Wang Pi* (Honolulu: University of Hawai'i Press, 1979), 75. Robert G. Henricks's translation of this passage based on the Mawangdui texts (discovered in 1973) is as follows:

> There is something formed out of chaos.
> That was born before Heaven and Earth.
> Quiet and still! Pure and deep!
> It stands on its own and does not change.
> It can be regarded as mother of Heaven and Earth.
> I do not know its name:
> I "style" it "the Way."

Robert G. Henricks, *Lao-Tzu, Te-Tao Ching: A New Translation Based on the Recently Discovered Ma-wang-tui Texts* (New York: Ballantine Books, 1989), 77:236–237. For the convenience of the reader, we have referred to the widely available Penguin edition of Lau's translation in the text and Henricks' version in the footnotes, throughout this chapter. The Mawangdui text in Chinese characters is given in Henricks and in D. C. Lau, trans., *Chinese Classics: Tao Te Ching* (Hong Kong: The Chinese University Press, 1982). The latter also includes the Chinese characters for the traditional Wang Bi text.

2. Kwang-Ching Liu, "Socioethics as Orthodoxy: A Perspective," in *Orthodoxy in Late Imperial China* (Berkeley: University of California Press, 1990), 53–100.

3. Ibid., 59 ff.

4. See note 37. It may be noted, here, that although the *Taiping jing* is a nonviolent treatise and does not contain a clear eschatology, it had been criticized by at least one official of the Eastern Han court in the reign of Shundi (126–144) as "demonic, deluding, and unorthodox" *(yaowang bujing)*. *Hou-Han shu* [History of the Later Han dynasty] (Beijing: Zhonghua, 1959), 30b:1084.

5. The term "Daoism" is here used in a broad sense, including both philosophical and religious Daoism—both "Daojia" and "Daojiao" in the modern meaning of those terms. We have found still useful Arthur Wright's typology of Daoism, especially subtradition 3b: "dissenting political Taoism." *History of Religions* 9.2 and 3 (1969–1970), 248–255, esp. 250. For a survey of Western-language studies of Daoism, see Anna Seidel, "Chronicle of Taoist Studies in the West, 1950–1990," *Cahiers d'Extreme Asie* 5 (1989–1990): 223–347, esp. 254–258. Cf. Seidel, "Taoism: The Unofficial High Religion of China," *Taoist Resources* 7.2 (1997): 39–72. See also Franciscus Verellen, "Taoism," Chinese Religions: The State of the Field, part 2, *Journal of Asian Studies* 54.2 (1995): 322–346.

6. For this concept, see chapter 3, by Whalen Lai, this volume.

7. See Holmes Welch, *The Parting of the Way: Lao Tzu and the Taoist Movement* (Boston: Beacon Press, 1957). See also the discussion in the English translation of Kristofer Schipper's *Le corps taoist, The Taoist Body*, trans. Karen C. Duval (Berkeley: University of California Press, 1993); Max Kaltenmark, *Lao Tzu and Taoism*, trans. Roger Greaves (Stanford: Stanford University Press, 1969); Rolf A. Stein, "Remarques sur les movements du taoisme politico-religieux au deuxième siècle après J.C.," *T'oung Pao* 50.1–3 (1973): 1–78.

8. See Derk Bodde, "Harmony and Conflict in Chinese Philosophy," in Arthur F. Wright, ed., *Studies in Chinese Thought* (Chicago: Chicago University Press, 1953), 10–80.

9. On a major appendix, see Willard J. Peterson, "Making Connec-

tions: 'Commentary on the Attached Verbalizations' of the *Book of Change* [*sic*]," *Harvard Journal of Asiatic Studies* 42.1 (1982): 67–116.

10. James Legge, trans., *The Sacred Books of China: The I Ching,* 2d ed. (Oxford: Clarendon, 1899; reprint, New York: Dover, 1963), 57.

11. Richard Wilhelm and Cary F. Baynes, trans., *The I Ching or Book of Changes,* 3d ed. (Princeton: Princeton University Press, 1967), 370. *Qian,* translated by Wilhelm and Baynes as "The Creative," is here untranslated. The rendering of *tongtian* as "permeates all Heaven" is compatible with Legge's version: "contains all the meaning belonging to [the name] Heaven." *The I Ching,* 213.

12. Wilhelm and Baynes. *The I Ching,* 280, slightly adjusted.

13. Ibid., 382–383, slightly adjusted.

14. Ibid., 337, slightly adjusted.

15. Ibid., 540, slightly adjusted.

16. Su Yu, *Chunqiu fanlu yizheng* [Evidence on the meaning of the *Luxuriant dews from the spring and autumn annals*] (1910), 3:1.

17. *Han shu* [History of the Former Han dynasty], Zhonghua ed., (1962), 26:2515, 2518–2519.

18. *Han shu,* 26:2498.

19. Su Yu, *Chunqiu fanlu,* 11:2b. Also 1:23b, 9:5b, 11:4.

20. Ibid., 4:20b–22.

21. See Sarah A. Queen, *From Chronicle to Canon: The Hermeneutics of the Spring and Autumn, According to Tung Chung-shu* (Cambridge: Cambridge University Press, 1969), 77–101.

22. Su Yu, *Chunqiu fanlu,* 9:9b–10.

23. Ibid., 12:4; translation from Fung Yu-lan, *A History of Chinese Philosophy,* 2 vols., trans. Derk Bodde (Princeton: Princeton University Press, 1953), 2:43.

24. See Liu, "Socioethics as Orthodoxy," 56–64, 86–87. For the imperial council of A.D. 79, see especially *Po Hu T'ung: The Comprehensive Discussions in the White Tiger Hall,* trans. Tjan Tjoe-som, 2 vols. (Leiden: E. J. Brill, 1949 and 1952).

25. See note 4, this chapter, and the appendix, this volume, on the usage of the Chinese term for heterodoxy.

26. Cf. Charles Le Blanc, *Huai-nan Tzu: Philosophical Synthesis in Early Han Thought* (Hong Kong: Hong Kong University Press, 1985), 21–30.

27. *Huainanzi* (Sibu beiyao ed.), 3:1; translation from Fung, *A History,* 1:396, slightly adjusted.

28. *Huainanzi,* 2:1 (cf. translation in Fung, 1:195), 3:1 ff.

29. Ibid., 14:1. The passage referred to here is translated by Girardot as follows: "Having form, one is ruled by things. But one who is able to return to that from which he was born and become formless again is called

a True Man. The True Man is one who has not been separated from the Great One." Norman Girardot, *Myth and Meaning in Early Taoism: The Theme of Chaos (hun-tun)* (Berkeley: University of California Press, 1983), 134. On "True Man," or the "Perfected Human Being," see also *Huainanzi*, 2:7b–12; 7:5–7.

30. Ibid., 6:4; 8:3b.

31. Ibid., 11:1. For a translation and analysis of the chapter cited here, see Benjamin E. Wallacker, *The Huai-nan Tzu, Book Eleven: Behavior, Culture, and the Cosmos* (New Haven: American Oriental Society, 1962).

32. *Huainanzi*, 11:3, translation by Wallacker.

33. Donald Munro has written: "In Taoist thought, egalitarianism is carried to its ultimate extreme: men are equal in the descriptive sense of the term, since the Tao is equally found in all; and being also of equal worth (equality in the evaluative sense), they should be treated impartially." Donald J. Munro, *The Concept of Man in Early China* (Stanford: Stanford University Press, 1969), 141. But it is difficult to say that the mystic wisdom in Zhuangzi led to real insistence that persons of different social station should be treated equally.

34. Lau, *Lao Tzu, Tao Te Ching*, 91. Henricks' translation from the Mawangdui texts is as follows (*Lao-Tzu, Te-Tao Ching*, 84:250–251):

> Though in its natural state it [the uncarved block or Tao]
>   seems small,
> No one in the world dares to treat it as a subject.
> Were marquises and kings able to maintain it,
> The ten thousand things would submit to them on their own,
> And Heaven and Earth would unite to send forth sweet dew,
> By nature, it would fall equally on all things, with no one among
>   the people ordering that it be so.

35. Lau, *Lao Tzu, Tao Te Ching*, 96. The first line of this chapter in the Mawangdui texts is especially variant (Henricks, *Lao-Tzu, Te-Tao Ching*, 89):

> The Tao is constantly nameless,
> Were marquises and kings able to maintain it,
> The ten thousand things would transform on their own,
> Having transformed, were their desires to become active,
> I would subdue them with the nameless simplicity.

36. Lau, *Lao Tzu, Tao Te Ching*, 139. Henricks' translation of this chapter from the Mawangdui texts reads (Henricks, *Lao-Tzu, Te-Tao Ching*, 48:180–181):

> The Way of Heaven is like the flexing of a bow,
> The high it presses down: the low it raises up,

From those with a surplus it takes away: to those without enough
it adds on.

37. Tang Yongtong, *Wangri zagao* [Miscellaneous past writings] (Beijing: Zhonghua, 1962), 56 ff.; Max Kaltenmark, "The Ideology of the T'ai-
p'ing ching," in Holmes Welch and Anna Seidel, eds., *Facets of Taoism* (New
Haven: Yale University Press, 1979), 19–21. The history of the *Taiping jing*
and scholarship on it are reviewed by J. Mansvelt Beck, "The Date of the
T'ai-p'ing ching," *T'oung Pao* 66, 4–5 (1980): 149–181. Beck concludes
that the Wang Ming edition of this work (see below, note 40) "remains, in
my view, a genuine Later Han text." Barbara Kandel [Hendrischke], *Taiping Jing, the Origin and Transmission of the "Scripture on General Welfare": The
History of an Unofficial Text* (Hamburg: Gesellschaft für Natur- und Volker-
kunde, 1979), concludes that the present version of the *Taiping jing* "was
composed in the second century A.D. and that on the basis of this old text
it was re-edited in the 6th century" (p. 2). Articles by Chinese scholars have
confirmed the view of Ofuchi Ninji (see his *Dōkyō to sono kyōten* [Daoism
and its canonical works] (Tokyo: Sōbunsha, 1997), and of other Japanese
scholars in favor of assigning the text to Eastern Han. A recent synoptic
work is by Kamitsuka Yoshiko, "Taiheikyō no sekai" [The world of the Taiping jing], in Noguchi Tetsurō, et al. eds., *Kōza Dōkyō* [Symposium on
Daoism] vol. 1 (Tokyo: Yūzankaku, 1999), 76–92. Wang Ming believes that
part A *(Jiabu)* is a later interpolation, but finds the present text to be otherwise a work of the early second century, jointly composed by a number of
writers. See Wang Ming, *Daojia he Daojiao sixiang yanjiu* [Studies in Daoist
philosophical and religious ideas] (Chongqing: Xinhua, 1984), 183–214,
esp. 200. Yü Ying-shih has maintained that *Taiping jing* is essentially an Eastern Han work representing the confluence of elite and popular culture. See
his "Life and Immortality in the Mind of Han China," *Harvard Journal of
Asiatic Studies* 25 (1964–1965), esp. 84–96, 112–119; "'O Soul, Come
Back!' A Study in the Changing Conceptions of the Soul and Afterlife in
Pre-Buddhist China," ibid., 47:2 (1987), 363–392.

38. The suggested evidence is summarized in Qing Xitai, *Zhongguo
Daojiao sixiang shigang* [Outline history of Daoist thought in China]
(Chengdu: Sichuan renmin, 1981), 64–70, 134, 142, 148–149, 153–154.

39. See Wang Ming, *Daojia he Daojiao*, 99–107.

40. Wang Ming, ed., *Taiping jing hejiao* [Consolidated texts of the
Taiping jing, critically compared] (1960; reprint, Beijing: Zhonghua, 1979),
12–13, 16–18, 21, 78, 96, 166, 544, 647, 662.

41. Ibid., 24, 148–149, 524.

42. Ibid., 18, 22–24, 57–59, 70, 75, 124, 146, 461, 640.

43. Kaltenmark, "The Ideology"; Barbara Hendrischke, "The Concept of Inherited Evil *(chengfu)* in the *Taiping jing*," *East Asian History* 2
(1991): 1–30.

44. See Lin Fushi, "Shilun Taiping jing de zhuzhi yu xingzhi" [On the themes and nature of *Taiping jing*], *Bulletin of the Institute of History and Philology*, Academia Sinica, 69.2 (1998): 205–244; Jens Ostergard Petersen, "The Anti-Messianism of *Taiping jing*," *Studies in Central and East Asian Religions* 3 (1990): 1–41.

45. Wang Ming, *Taiping jing*, 50.

46. Kaltenmark, "The Ideology," 26–27, 31–32 n. 20.

47. Ibid., 31; Wang Ming, *Taiping jing*, 88–91.

48. Ibid., 148–149, 398–399, 451.

49. Ibid., 164, 303, 342–343. The human being *(ren)* is also described as "the child of heaven and earth and the superior among the myriad things," p. 124.

50. Kaltenmark, "The Ideology," 23, 26, 27–29.

51. Ibid., 28–29. For an excellent discussion of communication in the context of *Taiping jing*'s ethics and eschatology, see Barbara Hendrischke, "The Daoist Utopia of Great Peace," *Oriens Extremus* 35 (1992): 61–89, esp. 72–74.

52. Wang Ming, *Taiping jing*, 33–34, 44, 114, 220–221, 518–519.

53. Ibid., 242–249, esp. 247.

54. Lau, *Lao Tzu, Tao Te Ching*, 100; Henricks' translation from the Mawangdui texts is as follows (*Lao-Tzu, Te-Tao Ching*, 8:100–101):

> Therefore it must be the case that the noble has the base as its root;
> And it must be the case that the high has the low as its foundation.

55. Wang Ming, *Taiping jing*, 102. Also 33–38, 44, 114.

56. Ibid., 683. Cf. 362, 398, 451, 491, 594–595, 614, 643.

57. Ibid., 450–451; Kaltenmark, "The Ideology," 36.

58. Lau, *Lao Tzu, Tao Te Ching*, 101. In Henricks' translation of the Mawangdui texts, the verse reads (Henricks, *Lao-Tzu, Te-Tao Ching*, 10:104–105):

> "Reversal" is the movement of the Tao.

59. Henricks' translation of the Mawangdui text of chapter 39 reads in part (*Lao-Tzu, Te-Tao Ching*, 8:100–101):

> Of those in the past that attained the One—
> Heaven, by attaining the One became clear;
> Earth, by attaining the One became stable;
> Gods, by attaining the One became divine;
> Valleys, by attaining the One became full;
> Marquises and kings, by attaining the One made the whole land
>   ordered and secure.
> Taking this to its logical conclusion we should say—
> If Heaven were not by means of it clear, it would, I'm afraid,
>   shatter;

If the Earth were not by means of it stable, it would, I'm afraid,
    let go.
If the gods were not by means of it divine, they would, I'm afraid,
    be powerless,
If valleys were not by means of it full, they would, I'm afraid,
    dry up,
And if marquises and kings were not by means of it noble and
    high, they would, I'm afraid, topple and fall.
Therefore it must be the case that the high has the low for
    its foundation.

60. Wang Ming, *Taiping jing*, 188. Cf. 122, 318, 324–326.

61. See Yü Ying-shih, *Zhongguo zhishi jieceng shilun: Gudai bian* [Historical essays on Chinese intellectuals as a social stratum: the ancient period] (Taibei: Lianjing, 1980), 329–358. Also Etienne Balazs, "Political Philosophy and Social Crisis at the End of the Han Dynasty," in Balazs, *Chinese Civilization and Bureaucracy: Variations on a Theme,* ed. Arthur F. Wright (New Haven: Yale University Press, 1964), 187–225.

62. On Wang Bi's outlook, see Fung, *A History,* 2:179–189; Kung-chuan Hsiao, *A History of Chinese Political Thought,* trans. F. W. Mote, (Princeton: Princeton University Press, 1979), 607–608, 611–612.

63. This verse, *"Shizhi youming,"* is translated in Lau, *Lao Tzu, Tao Te Ching,* as: "Only when it [the uncarved block] is cut are there names" (p. 9); and by Henricks as: "As soon as we start to establish a system, we have names" (*Lao-Tzu, Te-Tao Ching,* 84:250–251).

64. Hsiao, *A History,* 1:612; Lou Yulie, ed., *Wang Bi ji jiaoshi* [Textual comparison and annotations of Wang Bi's works] (Beijing: Zhonghua, 1980), 1:82.

65. Hsiao, *A History,* 1:612, 613; cf. Burton Watson, trans., *The Complete Works of Chuang Tsu* (New York: Columbia University Press, 1968), 36 ff. On Guo Xiang's philosophy, see Fung, *A History,* vol. 2, chap. 6. Although he was for "taking no action" or little action on the part of the ruler, Guo Xiang nonetheless affirmed the need for a ruler: "When a thousand people are collected together, if one is not made their master [*zhu,* or ruler] they must either be disorderly or become scattered. Thus it is that though many may be worthy, there cannot be many masters, and even though none is worthy, yet neither can there be no master. This is the way of heaven and humanity [or: the natural way of humanity], and the appropriate condition to be arrived at." Hsiao, *A History,* 2:613, slightly adjusted.

66. *Ruan Ji ji* [Collected works of Ruan Ji] (Shanghai: Guji, 1978), 66, our translation. On Ruan Ji, see Donald Holzman, *Poetry and Politics: The Life and Work of Juan Chi, A.D. 210–263* (Cambridge: Cambridge University Press, 1976). Holzman's translation of the same passage reads: "In the past, when heaven and earth divided and the ten thousand things were

all born together, the great among them kept their nature tranquil, and the small kept their forms clean. . . . The weak were not cowed by oppression, nor did the strong prevail by their force. For them there was no ruler, and all beings were peaceful; no officials, and all affairs were well ordered" (ibid., 195).

67. *Ruan Ji ji*, 73, in Holzman, *Poetry and Politics*, 203. See also Fukunaga Mitsuji, "Chūgoku ni okeru tenchi hōkai no shisō—Gen Seki no 'Daijin sensei ka' to To Ho no 'To Jionjito shi ni tsuite'" [The idea of cosmic collapse in China—with respect to Ruan Ji's "Biography of Master Great Man" and Du Fu's "Poem on climbing the pagoda of the Ci'en Temple"] in *Yoshikawa hakase taikyū kinen Chūgoku bungaku ronshū* [Festschrift on Chinese literature commemorating Dr. Yoshikawa's retirement] (Tokyo: Chikuma shobō, 1968).

68. *Ruan Ji ji*, 65, in Holzman, *Poetry and Politics*, 194: "I am going to explain it to you. In the past, at one time the heavens were below and the earth was above; they turned over time and again, and had not yet reached a stable condition. How [if you had been living then] could you not have lost your 'rules' and 'models'? How then could you have counted them as 'prescribed'? When the heavens moved with the earth, the mountains crashed down and the rivers rose up . . . how then could you have been able to 'choose the very ground you walk on' or 'make your pace in walking conform to a musical beat'?" (p. 194).

69. *Ruan Ji ji*, 70–73, in Holzman, *Poetry and Politics*, 199–200:

The heaven and earth become undone;
The six directions spread apart;
The stars and their constellations drop;
The sun and the moon tumble down.
I will leap up into the heights;
What would I take to heart?

See also Holzman's translation, 203–204: "The sun and moon have fallen! The earth cracks open; rocks split; the yang freezes; how the cold stings the breast! . . . The ocean freezes over and no longer flows; cotton threads break; one cannot breathe; how the cold stings and splits!"

70. Xi Kang, *Xi Zhong shan ji* [Collected writings of Xi Kang] (*Sibu beiyao* ed.), 5:11; Hsiao, *A History*, 1:618. See Donald Holzman, *La vie et la pensée de Hsi Kang, 223–262 après J.C.* (Leiden: E. J. Brill, 1957).

71. On aspects of the original Han religion, which Daoism incorporated, see Anna Seidel's magistral essay, "Traces of Han Religion in Funeral Texts Found in Tombs," in Akizuki Kan'ei, ed., *Dōkyō to shukyō bunka* [Daoism and religious culture] (Tokyo: Hirakawa, 1987), 21–57. For a recent summary of the two Daoist groups in later Han, see Sawada Akitoshi, "Dōkyō kyōdan no keisei—Gotobei dō to Taihei dō [The formation

of Daoist groups—the Five Pecks of Rice group and the Great Peace group]," in Noguchi Tetsurō, ed., *Kōza Dōkyō* [Symposium on Daoism] vol. 2 (Tokyo: Yūzankaku, 2000), 12–33. For a similar survey in English, see Barbara Hendrischke, "Early Daoist Movements," in Livia Kohn, ed., *Daoism Handbook* (Leiden: E. J. Brill, 2000), 134–164.

72. For a full translation as well as discussion, see Stephen R. Boken-kamp, *Early Daoist Scriptures* (Berkeley: University of California Press, 1997), esp. 29–148.

73. *Sanguo zhi* [History of the Three Kingdoms] (Beijing: Zhonghua, 1959): *Wei shu* [History of the Wei kingdom], 1:263, cf. 264, and *Shu shu* [History of the Shu kingdom], 865–866. For a discussion regarding Zhang Xiu and Zhang Lu, see Ren Jiyu, ed., *Zhongguo Daojiao shi* [History of Daoism in China] (Shanghai: Shanghai renmin chubanshe, 1990), 34–37.

74. Zhang Jue claimed to be a *da xian liang shi* (great worthy and good teacher), and he predicted that the year of his rebellion, the first of the sixty-four-year cycle *(jiazi)*, was to be the most auspicious for the event. *Hou-Han shu*, 71:2299–2300. Cf. Fang Shiming, "Huangjin qiyi xianqu yu wu ji yuanshi Daojiao de guanxi" (Precursors of the Yellow Turban Rebellion and its relationship to shamanism and primitive Daoism), *Lishi yanjiu* (1993) 3:3–13.

75. *Sanguo zhi*, 1:264; Rao Zongyi, ed., *Laozi Xiang'er zhu* [The Xiang'er commentary on *Laozi*] (Hong Kong: privately published, 1956). This commentary has been ascribed to either Zhang Daoling or Zhang Lu; see pp. 1–5.

76. Bokenkamp, *Early Daoist Scriptures*, 181.

77. Chen Yinke, "Tianshi Dao yu binhai diyu de guanxi" [The relation between coastal regions and the Celestial Master sect], *Bulletin of the Institute of History and Philology*, Academia Sinica, vol. 3, no. 4 (1934), later collected in *Chen Yinke xiansheng lunji* [Collected studies of Mr. Chen Yinke] (Taibei: Academia Sinica, 1972), 217–298.

78. See Rolf A. Stein, "Religious Taoism and Popular Religion from the Second to Seventh Centuries," in Welch and Seidel, eds., *Facets of Taoism*, esp. 127–192.

79. For a survey of the Shangqing movement, see Isabelle Robinet, "Shangqing—Highest Clarity," in Livia Kohn, ed., *Daoism Handbook*, 196–224.

80. See Michel Strickmann, "The Mao Shan Revelations: Taoism and the Aristocracy," *T'oung Pao* 63 (1977): 3, 40; also Strickmann, "On the Alchemy of T'ao Hung-ching," in Welch and Seidel, eds., *Facets of Taoism*, esp. 127–192.

81. For a summary of the Lingbao tradition, see Yamada Toshiaki, "The Lingbao School," in Livia Kohn, *Daoism Handbook*, 225–255.

82. Ofuchi Ninji, "The Formation of the Taoist Canon," in Welch

and Seidel, eds., *Facets of Taoism*, 254. On Lu Xiujing and the Lingbao scriptures, see Stephen R. Bokenkamp, "Sources of the Ling-pao Scriptures," in Michel Strickmann, ed., *Taoist and Tantric Studies in Honor of R. A. Stein* (Brussels: Institut Belge des Hautes Etudes Chinoises, 1983), 2:434–486; and Catherine Bell, "Ritualization of Texts and Textualization of Ritual in the Codification of Ling-pao Liturgy," *History of Religions* 27.4 (1988), 366–392. Bell writes: "Both the Shang-ch'ing and the Ling-pao revelations alluded to cosmic realms that transcended the traditional three-tiered cosmos populated by gods, people, and demons. These new realms were referred to as the three 'prior' or 'highest,' while the traditional cosmos was referred to as the 'posterior' or 'later' heavens. . . . The role of the Ling-pao-empowered liturgical master was to mediate relations between these two sets of heavens, the traditional cosmos and this newly revealed dimension of the Tao. Thus, this form of mediation could distinguish itself from any accusations of *lèse majesté*. The roots of this formulation, which is nothing less than a differentiation of religious and political spheres, probably goes back to the reformulations and compromises of the Way of the Heavenly [Celestial] Master that accompanied its subordination to the state in the third century" (ibid., 380–381).

83. For a summary treatment of the Celestial Masters in the north, see Livia Kohn, "The Northern Celestial Masters," *Daoism Handbook*, 283–308.

84. The section on Daoism in the treatise on Buddhism and Daoism in *Wei shu* [History of the Northern Wei dynasty], 8:3025–3065, is almost entirely devoted to this development in the north. For analysis of this and other sources, see Chen Yinke, "Cui Hao yu Kou Qianzhi" [Cui Hao and Kou Qianzhi], *Lingnan xuebao* 11.1 (1950), 111–134; Yang Liansheng, "Laojun yinsong jiejing jiaoshi" [Collation and annotation of the text *Laojun yinsong jiejing*], *Bulletin of the Institute of History and Philology*, Academia Sinica, 28.1 (1956), 17–54; and Richard B. Mather, "K'ou Ch'ien-chih and the Taoist Theocracy at the Northern Wei Court, 425–451," in Welch and Seidel, eds., *Facets of Taoism*, 102–22.

85. See articles by Chen Yinke, Yang Liansheng, and Richard Mather cited in note 84.

86. Wang Ming, *Baopuzi neipian jiaoshi* [The "Inner Chapters" of Master Who Holds Fast the Uncarved Block, critically collated and annotated] (Beijing: Zhonghua, 1980), 47; cf. the different translation in James R. Ware, trans., *Alchemy, Medicine, and Religion in the China of A.D. 320: The Nei P'ien of Ko Hung* (Cambridge, Mass.: MIT Press, 1966), 66.

87. Wang Ming, *Baopuzi* 47–48; cf. Ware, *Alchemy*, 66–67.

88. Ge Hong, *Baopuzi waipian* [The "Outer Chapters" of Master Who Holds Fast the Uncarved Block], *juan* 48, cited in Qing Xitai, *Zhongguo daojiao*, 1:226–227. On Bao Jingyan, see Hsiao, *A History*, 623–630.

89. For some examples of the Confucianization of Daoist texts, see Liu Lin, "Lun Dong-Jin Nanbeichao daojiao di biange yu fazhan" [On Daoist reform and development in Eastern Jin and during the Northern and Southern dynasties], *Lishi yanjiu* 5 (Oct. 1981), 125. See also Yoshioka Yoshitoyo, "Rikuchō dōkyō no shumin shisō" [The notion of the chosen people in Six Dynasties Daoism], in his *Dō kyō to Bukkyō* [Daoism and Buddhism], vol. 3 (Tokyo, 1976), 248.

90. *Wei shu*, 3:1045; see also 3:807–828; and Mather, "K'ou Ch'ienchih," 112.

91. "Shi-Lao zhi" [Treatise on Buddhism and Daoism] in *Wei shu*, 8:3025–3065.

92. *Laojun yinsong jiejing*, 4a–b, quoted in Yang Liansheng, "Laojun," 40.

93. For a summary discussion of the transformation of Laozi into the messianic figure of Li Hong, see Kikuchi Noritaka, "Rikō shinko no seisei to henyō" [The formation and transformation of the Li Hong belief], in *Kōza Dōkyō* [Symposium on Daoism], vol. 1 (Tokyo: Yūzankaku, 1999), 202–221.

94. Quoted in ibid., 41. See also Anna Seidel, "The Image of the Perfect Ruler in Early Taoist Messianism: Lao Tzu and Li Hung," *History of Religions* 9.2–3 (Nov. 1969–Feb. 1970): 241.

95. Wang Ming, *Baopuzi*, 158–159; cf. Ware, *Alchemy*, 158–160. See also Yamada Toshiaki, "Rikadō to sono shūhen" [The adepts of the Li family and their environs], *Tōhō shūkyō* 52 (1978), 15–27. On the famous adepts of the Bo family, see Stein, "Religious Taoism and Popular Religion," 54–55.

96. The issue of eschatology in the Daoist tradition is worth exploring. See the discussions by Kristofer Schipper, "Millenarisme et messianisme dans la Chine ancienne," in *Understanding Modern China, Proceedings of the Twenty-sixth Conference of Chinese Studies* (Rome: Instituto Italiano per il Medio ed Estremo Oriente, 1979); Christine Mollier, *Une apocalypse taoiste du Ve siècle: le Livre des incantations divines des grottes abyssales* (Paris: Institut des Hautes Études Chinoises, 1990); Kikuchi Noritaka, "Dōkyō no shūmatsu shisō" [Eschatological ideas in Daoism], in *Kōza Dōkyō* [Symposium on Daoism] 4:84–109; Kobayashi Masayoshi, "Tōjinki no Dōkyō no shūmatsu ron" [Daoist eschatology in the Eastern Jin period], in *Kamata Shigeo hakase kanreki kinen ronshū: Chūgoku no Bukkyō to bunka* [Festschrift celebrating the sixtieth birthday of Dr. Kamata Shigeo: Buddhism and culture in China] (Tokyo: Okura shuppan, 1988); Jiang Sheng, "Kandai Dōkyō kyōten no shūmatsuron ni tsuite" [On the eschatology of Han dynasty Daoist scriptures], trans. Yamada Shun, *Tōhō shūkyō* 92 (1998); and Li Fengmao, "Liuchao daojiao de zhongmolun" [Eschatological thought in Six Dynasties Daoism], in Chen Guying, ed., *Daojia wenhua yanjiu* [Study of Daoist culture], vol. 9 (Shanghai: Guji chubanshe, 1996).

97. W. Eichhorn, "Description of the Rebellion of Sun En," *Mitteilungen des Instituts für Orientforschung* 2.1 (1954); Miyakawa Hisayuki, "Son On–Ro Jun no ran ni tsuite" [On the Sun En–Lu Xun Rebellion], *Tō yō shi kenkyū* 30.2–3:1–30 (1970).

98. For a study that attempts to trace the lineage of Daoist rebelliousness from the Taiping dao, through the Lijia dao, and up through the Li Hong movement, see Fang Shiming, "Shi 'Zhang Jue Li Hong duliu Hanji'—Lijia dao yu Han-Jin Nanbeichao de Li Hong qiyi" [An explanation of the phrase "Zhang Jue and Li Hong ravaged the country during the end of Han"—the Way of the Li family and the Li Hong uprisings of the Han, Jin, Northern and Southern dynasties period], *Lishi yanjiu* 2 (1995), 40–51.

99. See the introduction to and translation of "The Upper Scripture of Purple Texts inscribed by the spirits" ["Lingshu ziwen shangjing"], in Bokenkamp, *Early Daoist Scriptures*, 275–372.

100. Ibid., 295–297, 339–362.

101. See Sunayama Minoru, "Ri Kō kara Kō Kenshi e: seireki shi-go seiki ni okeru shūkyō teki hanran to kokka shū kyō" [From Li Hong to Kou Qianzhi: Religious uprisings and state religion in the fourth and fifth centuries], *Shūkan Tōyōgaku* 26 (1971): 2–4.

102. There is an interesting parallel between the Li Hong cult and the Buddhist Maitreyan cult later. See Kikuchi Noritaka, "Ri Kō to Miroku —Tenshidō no kaikaku to Chūgoku bukkyō ni okeru kyūseishu shinkō no seiritsu" [Li Hong and Maitreya—the reform movement of the Tianshi dao and the formation of soteriology in Chinese Buddhism], in Yamada Toshiaki and Tanaka Fumio, eds., *Dōkyō no rekishi to bunka* [History and culture in Daoism] (Tokyo: Yuzankaku, 1998).

103. The edition used here is reproduced in Yamada Toshiaki and Yusa Noboru, eds., *Taijō dōen shinjukyō* (Tokyo: Sōundō, 1984). We are grateful to Professor Yamada for the gift to Richard Shek of a signed copy. The most detailed monographic study of this text is Christine Mollier's *Une apocalypse taoiste du Ve siècle*, mentioned in note 96.

104. Ofuchi Ninji, *Dōkyō shi no kenkyū* [Study of the history of Daoism] (Okayama, 1964), 435–482. See also Yoshioka Yoshitoyo, *Dōkyō kyō ten shiron* [Historical essay on Daoist scriptures] (Tokyo: Taisho daigaku shuppansha, 1955), 193–304; Miyakawa Hisayuki, "Jindai dōkyō no ichi kōsatsu: Taijō dōen shinjukyō o megurite" [An investigation of Daoism in the Jin dynasty; with special reference to the *Taishang dongyuan shenzhou jing*], *Chūgoku gakushi* 5 (1968): 79–102.

105. *Shenzhou jing* (hereafter *SZJ*), 1:4.

106. *SZJ*, 1:1.

107. *SZJ*, 2:2.

108. *SZJ*, 3:2–3.

109. *SZJ*, 4:11.

110. *SZJ*, 1:3–4. See also Seidel, "Image of the Perfect Ruler," 238.

111. *SZJ*, 1:10.

112. *SZJ*, 1:11.

113. Seidel, "Image of the Perfect Ruler," 236–244. Other Daoist texts lend support to the claim that Li Hong is the apotheosis of Laozi. Cf. *Santian neijie jing*. Both the Shangqing text *Housheng daojūn lieji* [Biography of the Daoist Lord Who Is to Come] and the Lingbao text *Yuanshi wuliang duren shangpin miaojing* [Superior wondrous text on the boundless deliverance of mankind by the primordial beginning] identify Li Hong as the august lord of the golden portico *(jinjue dijun)*.

114. *SZJ*, 1:10.

115. *SZJ*, 1–2. See Yoshioka Yoshitoyo, "Rikuchō dōkyō no shūmin shisō," cited in note 89.

116. *SZJ*, 1:3. See 1:5 for similar message.

117. *SZJ*, 1:8–9.

118. *SZJ*, 1:5, 1:10, 4:8, 5:1, 5:8, 6:9, 8:1, 9:2–3, 9:6–8, 16:3.

119. *SZJ*, 1:7, 5:6, 8:4.

120. *SZJ*, 1:4, 1:7, 1:8.

121. *SZJ*, 1:10–11.

122. It is true that the text pays lip service to the Liu Song dynasty apparently during whose rule it was compiled. Yet the overall apocalyptic version of the text makes such perfunctory declaration of support for the ruling regime insincere.

CHAPTER 2

Ethics and Polity

The Heterodoxy of Buddhism, Maitreyanism, and the Early White Lotus

Richard Shek

As an alien faith that transplanted itself in China by the beginning of the common era, Buddhism immediately posed a threat to the Chinese orthodoxy discussed in chapter 1. Its "conquest"[1] of China was by no means a smooth, unresisted process but was instead a long and arduous journey that required concession, adaptation, and "transformation."[2] Reasons for objection to Buddhism by the guardians of Chinese orthodoxy are varied.[3] They include the unabashedly chauvinistic argument that disparages Buddhism as a "barbarian" creed unsuited for the high culture of China, and the utilitarian view that accuses the Buddhist community as being parasitical and unproductive. The more serious charges, at least from the perspective of this volume, however, pertain to the putative heterodoxy of Buddhism, specifically its rejection of the authority of the ruler, and its violation of the principle of filial piety.

Concerning the first point, namely the intransigence of the Buddhist sangha to submit to the authority of the imperial court, the charge seems to be valid, when the Buddha's teaching is properly understood and when the early history of Buddhism in China is examined. According to the Buddhist tradition, the Buddha, at his birth, was given two career options. He could follow the career of a householder, a lord of the Dharma Wheel, a righteous ruler, and a universal monarch (chakravartin). He could, alternatively, choose to go forth into the homeless state to become a redeemer of all life-forms. Between these two choices, that of being a "world conqueror" and that of being a "world renouncer,"[4] the Buddha unhesitatingly chose the latter, thus unequivocally revealing his preference and his assessment of the relative value of the two careers.

Moreover, in one of the longest, and decidedly one of the most authoritative, Buddhist texts, the *Chang Ahan jing* (*T* 1, no. 1), the Buddha discourses at length on the genesis of the world and the evolution of society, which also sheds light on the original Buddhist view of kingship and secular power. In this discussion, the world begins as an ethereal mind and evolves progressively toward materialization and differentiation. Disorder sets in, which necessitates the institution of a king, one who is most handsome in physical form and most perfect in conduct, to impose order and regulation in society. Hierarchy develops, followed by all kinds of fetters and bondage. Then, a new personality appears—the *bhikkhu* (*biqiu* in Chinese, i.e., Buddhist monk)—who is homeless and is therefore free from all fetters and bondage. The upward course of the *bhikkhu* liberates him, and subsequently all others as well, from the confinement of materiality and social entanglement, ending with the ultimate freedom of nirvana.[5]

In this breathtaking description of the evolution of the natural world and human society, the king and the Buddhist monk represent two central ideals. The former is indeed a crucial figure who maintains order in the world, but the latter is paramount in importance, as he breaks through all the confining elements of the natural and social order and arrives at a state of total liberation and transcendence. The superiority of the monk is thus made apparent, and the tradition of the king paying homage to the *bhikkhu* is established. This tradition had existed for a long time in Buddhist-dominated regions in India, Ceylon, Thailand, Burma, and Cambodia.

When Buddhism arrived in China, it was confronted by an equally long tradition of imperial authority buttressed by cosmological and religious claims. The Chinese ruler was no mere political head of state but was at the same time a religious figure who embodied the creative and transformative powers of the cosmos and who was given a mandate by Heaven to care for the welfare of the people. As such he was the supreme priest and king of all under Heaven, unequalled by any other individual. It was certainly impossible, even unthinkable, for the Buddhist community to insist upon the superiority of the monk over the monarch in this case. Still, it did try to assert a special and independent status for itself vis-à-vis the Chinese ruler, one enjoyed by the sangha elsewhere in the Buddhist world up to that time. It insisted that it should be governed by its own monastic laws, unfettered by the ritual requirements of the imperial government

Nowhere is this insistence more clearly and resolutely articulated than by the eminent monk Huiyuan (334–416). At issue was whether Buddhist monks should pay homage to the emperor, just as all other Chinese subjects did.[6] The controversy actually began in 340 when Yü Bing, regent to Emperor Qing of the Eastern Jin dynasty, decreed that monks should perform the ritual of respect to the emperor. He was opposed by He Chong, a powerful official and an ardent patron of Buddhism. The matter was unresolved and set aside, for a while at least. In 402 the would-be usurper Huan Xuan reopened the debate by declaring that monks, who owe their existence to the benevolence of the emperor, should not be allowed to "receive the fruits of the emperor but neglect the Rites, to be blessed by his favor but abstain from reverence."[7]

When the ministers failed to come to a consensus, and to convince him with a powerful counterargument, Huan Xuan turned to Huiyuan, the most respected member of the clergy in the south and a great defender of the faith, for advice. That Huan should have chosen to consult Huiyuan on this matter is interesting enough. Surely, he should have expected Huiyuan to object to his declaration. What he had really intended, then, was to be convinced by the most articulate and authoritative representative of the Buddhist community as to why the sangha should be exempted from the ritual obligation of giving obeisance to the ruler. Huiyuan did not disappoint him.

In his reply, and later in a more developed treatise entitled *Shamen bujing wangzhe lun* (On the sramana not paying homage to the ruler),[8] Huiyuan outlined a cogent and forceful argument concerning the autonomy of the sangha. It is a firm, uncompromising position that argues, albeit in respectful language, that the sangha is a brotherhood outside the mundane world. It therefore abides by its own rules without regard to the obligations of secular society. Part of the discussion runs as follows:[9]

> According to the Buddhist texts, there are two categories of Buddhists: [lay people] who espouse the teaching while dwelling in the world, and [monks] who cultivate the Way, having left the household *(chujia)*. Those who remain in the world observe the rites of service to the superiors and respect for the elders. . . .
>
> But the monk who has abandoned the household is a stranger living outside the world of human relations. His behavior is different from others. . . . His principles run counter to those of the world, and

his Way is contrary to the common way. Therefore all who have left the household retire from the world so as to satisfy his yearning, and to depart from the normative behavior so as to make perfect his Way. Having departed from the normative behavior, they cannot submit to the Rites imposed by the civil codes. . . . Only through this can they save the drowning world. . . . Hence the sramana is the one who greets the emperor as if they stood on the same level. . . .

What Huiyuan has in mind is clear. Delineating the Buddhist community into two camps, he concedes that Buddhist laymen can and should be subjected to the ritual requirements of society, but he adamantly maintains that the clergy, by abandoning the household in search of salvation, is free from such obligations. The monk abides by a different set of principles, having voluntarily become a stranger to, and living apart from, secular society. He is, in a sense, the equal of the ruler. His independence from imperial authority is therefore total and nonnegotiable. The monk must remain autonomous, as submission to imperial prerogatives will bind him to the mundane world and prevent him from attaining his own salvation as well as that of others.

In another letter to Huan Xuan in 402, Huiyuan even went so far as to assert, "If the monastic rules of those who shave their heads and mutilate their bodies are entangled with the rites of China, it is a sign of the mutual interference of different species, something which makes me feel uneasy."[10] This indicates that for Huiyuan, the Buddhist clergy and the rites of Chinese orthodoxy are two entirely separate and equal entities, not meant to be mixed, and definitely not requiring the former to submit to the latter. As Kenneth Ch'en has so shrewdly observed, what Huiyuan claims "amounted to extraterritorial status."[11]

Huiyuan's bold and unyielding assertion apparently was persuasive enough. When Huan Xuan did finally usurp the throne, in 404, he issued an edict that exempted the monks from paying homage to the ruler. However, the issue was far from being permanently settled. Numerous clashes between the court and the Buddhist establishment on the matter recurred, each time ending with the rather shaky victory of the latter, which managed to keep its independence and dignity, however precariously.

The last noteworthy address on the subject occurred in 662, when Emperor Gaozong of the Tang dynasty once again revived the issue by proposing that Buddhist monks and nuns should honor the imperial family as well as their own parents. As expected, the Buddhist community responded negatively. Led by the famous monk Daoxuan, it objected to the imperial proposal vehemently. Daoxuan's argument echoed much of what Huiyuan had stated more than two centuries earlier:

> In the manner of living, the monk has no regard for wealth and sensuous beauty, and is not shackled by honors and emoluments. He considers mundane matters as floating clouds, and his form and life as a bright flame. Therefore he is proclaimed as one who has left the household life. One who has done so no longer embraces the rites of one who remains in the family; one who has forsaken the world is no longer immersed in the practices of the world. Such a principle is self evident, and is the unchanging model for a hundred generations.[12]

To further bolster his position, Daoxuan cited from the *Fanwang jing* (Sutra of the Dharma Net) (*T* 24.1008c): "Those who leave the household life do not reverence the ruler, the parents, and the six relationships"; and also from the *Nirvanasutra* (*T* 12.399c): "Those who have left the household life should not reverence the householder."[13]

This argument, as in the case of Huiyuan's, succeeded in keeping the autonomy of the sangha, at least for the time being and as far as the issue of paying homage to the ruler was concerned.[14] But this time the victory was only partial, as erosion of such independence had already begun. Gaozong's final decision, while exempting the sangha from paying obeisance to the ruler, nevertheless required that it honor the parents. More significantly, other forms of government control were instituted, definitely by the middle of the Tang dynasty, to deprive the Buddhist clergy of its special status. The ordination and registration of monks increasingly came under the control of the state, which also empowered itself with the authority to defrock undesirable elements in the sangha. The behavior and conduct of the monks too became regulated by secular codes, while the construction of temples and monasteries also gradually came under government supervision. As Kenneth Ch'en has put it, "All in all, therefore, what we see here is a gradual de-emphasis of the sangha as a special religious group devoted mainly to religious matters, and an increasing tendency for the clerics to become just like any other Chinese subject in the empire."[15] Instead of being separate from and transcending the secular state, as was the case in the original Buddhist world, the sangha had become, since the middle of Tang, compromised with the moral orthodoxy of China, succumbing to its demand of loyalty and submission.

An even more serious charge leveled against Buddhism as it sought to gain acceptance in China was its violation of the most cardinal principle of Chinese orthodoxy—filiality. The Buddha's renunciation of the mundane world in order to attain nirvana not only brought him into direct confrontation with the prerogatives of the ruler, it also made him an unfilial son, an unloving husband, and an uncaring father. In other words, his was the worst case of a selfish, malevolent individual who had done the greatest injustice to his family. By Chinese ethical standards, his leaving the household, shaving his head, mutilating his body, and practicing celibacy and mendicancy had turned him into the most glaring example of unfiliality. For the Chinese, the family was the most sacrosanct institution and the basis of morality. Filial piety involves the subjugation of the individual to the interests of the family—in the caring of aging parents, in the continuation of the patrilineal succession through the procreation of male offsprings, and in the preservation of the body intact as a living monument of the blessing received from the parents. The Buddha had violated every single maxim of filial devotion with his teaching and personal behavior. The sangha, who followed the Buddha's teaching of nonattachment, adopted the same lifestyle and behavioral pattern, thus making itself equally an example of unfiliality. It was a problem that Buddhism had to deal with almost from the beginning of its history in China.[16]

The *Mouzi lihuo lun* (On the settling of doubts by Master Mou), an early Buddhist apologetic treatise, with portions dating back to the third century, acknowledges the problem head-on and attempts to defend the Buddhist mode of life by citing ancient Chinese paragons of virtue who had either performed mortifications on themselves or who had starved themselves to death.[17] Yet there is no denial that fundamentally, the Buddhist view of secular life, in particular family life, is far from sanguine. The family is seen as the fountainhead of all evil and impurities. Kang Senghui's preface to the *Fajing jing* (mid third century) is indicative of this perception:

> The desires of the family are insatiable. They are like the ocean swallowing up the streams, or fire getting hold of wood. The cruelty of the Six Evils [for the individual] is greater than the harm done to fish by

prickly nets. The obsequiousness of women parallels that of the Three Demons. Their goodness is artificial, and they yearn to reach widow-hood. This is the calamity of [having] a family. When the evil and the impure are honored, when the pure and the perfect are belittled, when the trivial and the petty are congregated, when the sagely and the worthy are slandered, when litigation is initiated, and when the nine relationships are severed, they are all caused by the family![18]

Kang Senghui continues by pointing out that the monastic life of detachment and seclusion is the best antidote to this evil. Only by withdrawing from and rupturing with the family can one attain the Buddhist goal of salvation.

Other Buddhist apologists were, however, not so outspoken or unequivocal in their criticism of secular and family life. Huiyuan, whose *Shamen bujing wangzhe lun* has been referred to earlier, adopts a rather interesting view. While insisting upon the separateness and sanctity of the monastic life, Huiyuan nevertheless makes a special point to observe: "within [the family] the monks deviate from the veneration due to natural relationships, yet they are not opposed to filial piety; outside [the family] they are negligent in honoring the ruler, yet they do not lose their respect for him."[19] This of course represents a concession and a departure from Kang Senghui's earlier position. In Huiyuan's opinion, Buddhist monks do not observe filial piety, yet they do not find it objectionable either. On the contrary, filial devotion and Buddhism are by no means incompatible.[20]

Once this compromise was acknowledged, others went further.[21] They pointed out that filial piety was stressed in numerous Buddhist texts; they also forged a group of apocryphal texts that emphasized filial devotion; and finally, they even argued that Buddhists espoused a superior form of filiality.[22] It was in this connection that the Ghost Festival, which was itself based upon one of the most well-known Buddhist texts, the *Yulanpen sutra* (*T* 16, no. 685), became a most interesting case of Buddhist accommodation to Chinese orthodoxy.[23]

Central to the *Yulanpen sutra* is the myth of Mulian saving his mother.[24] According to this story, Mulian (Maudgalyayana, or Moggallana) is a disciple of the Buddha and upon attaining arhatship wants to repay his parents' kindness. To his chagrin and alarm, Mulian finds his mother being reborn among the hungry ghosts, having to endure torture and starvation in the lowest level of hell.

Even after he performs the usual mortuary rites by offering his mother a bowl of rice, she cannot take it because the food changes into flaming coals as soon as she tries to put it in her mouth. Much aggrieved, Mulian seeks advice from the Buddha and is told that since his mother's sins are heavy, his efforts alone are not enough to alleviate her sufferings. Instead, Mulian is instructed "to make offerings to the assembly of monks, those of great virtue of the ten directions," and "to place food and drink of one hundred flavors in the yulanpen and offer it to the monks," who emerge from their retreat on the fifteenth day of the seventh month.[25] By partaking of such offerings, the monks can collectively through their accumulated virtues cause the release from purgatory of seven generations of Mulian's ancestors. Mulian follows the Buddha's instruction, and indeed, his mother is rescued from her miserable existence. The sutra closes with the Buddha's assurance that the same practice can be carried out by all pious Buddhists who wish to save their living parents and deceased ancestors from the horrors of hell.

This sutra, with its unmistakable theme of filial devotion, was exceedingly popular in China and other parts of East Asia, and it spawned an entire genre of Mulian literature, as well as sealed the popularity of the Ghost Festival. What is particularly noteworthy here is the centrality of the Buddhist monk in the ritual performance of filiality. The *Yulanpen sutra* places "the renouncer at the very center of secular life."[26] The Ghost Festival reveals the belief that the very act of leaving the household allows the monk to acquire the power that can be redirected to enhance the ideal of filial piety. It is small wonder that the eminent monk Zongmi (780–841), in his celebrated *Commentary on the Yulanpen Sutra* (*T* 39, no. 1792), writes with pride and approval that Buddhism is not only not inimical to the orthodox doctrine of filial piety, but is in fact most supportive of it:

> Beginning in primordial chaos, filling all of heaven and earth, uniting humans and spirits, connecting the noble and the lowly, and revered by Confucians and Buddhists alike—it is the Way of Filial Devotion! Responding to the sincerity of filial sons, saving parents from suffering, repaying heaven's kindness—it is the teaching of yulanpen.[27]

Indeed, Zongmi even went so far as to claim that the Buddha's withdrawal from the household was motivated by no other reason than to become enlightened so as to repay his parents![28]

With that, Buddhism's accommodation with Chinese orthodoxy appears to be complete. From its original world-renouncing
stance, it had become increasingly entangled with Chinese polity and
family. Despite the gallant attempts of monks such as Huiyuan in
defending the faith and in preserving its independence, the Buddhist
community had inevitably come under imperial supervision, thereby
requiring it to be loyal; at the same time, it felt compelled to out-
Confucian the Confucians, thereby making it uphold the principle of
filial piety. Nevertheless, there continued to exist a subterranean tradition within Buddhism that remained "undomesticated." At times
it came to the surface to challenge both imperial and patriarchal
authority, by which the Buddhist establishment had been co-opted.
Subscribers to this tradition were generally lay believers who had
assumed monastic roles and prerogatives that allowed them to retain
some of the original ethical teachings of Indian Buddhism. This tradition may be labeled militant Maitreyanism, characterized by its
intense eschatology and fervent messianism. In time it was joined by
another tradition—Manichaeism—to form a very potent soteriolog-
ical movement commonly referred to as the White Lotus of the late
Yuan period. The remainder of this essay is devoted to the examination of the process by which these movements came about.

Maitreyanism

Belief in the periodic dissolution of the universe is part of classical
Buddhism, though by no means the most salient part of it. According to traditional Buddhist cosmology, as related in the *Lokadhatu-
sutra* (*Daloutan jing, T* 1, no. 23),[29] world systems evolve and disin-
tegrate through a series of cosmic periods known as aeons. At the
end of each great aeon *(dajie)*, the physical universe is destroyed by
the three "kalpa-disasters" of water, fire, and wind. After an intervening period of emptiness and darkness, a new "receptacle-world"
comes into being and a new cycle begins.[30]

Paralleling this idea of kalpa-disasters marking the end of a
world is the equally potent notion of the gradual (but inexorable)
decay and final disappearance of the Buddha's teaching.[31] This pes-
simistic view, expressed in Buddhist canonical writings and reem-
phasized by numerous "apocryphal texts" compiled in China in the
late Six Dynasties, envisions three stages *(sanjie)* for the unfolding of
the Buddha's doctrine, each to last several centuries.[32] Starting with

the Buddha's *parinirvana*, the first period is that of the "true doctrine" *(zhengfa)*, during which the Buddha's precepts are faithfully followed. In the second period, known as the time of "counterfeit doctrine" *(xiangfa)*, the Buddha's teaching is adulterated and undermined by distortion and immorality of both the *sangha* and the laity. In the third period, that of the "end of the doctrine" *(mofa)*, even the semblance of religious devotion is abandoned and the world is plunged into darkness and ignorance, lost in sin and injustice. In time, the next Buddha will appear and the dharma will be restored.[33]

The twin ideas of periodic destruction and *mofa* degeneration are disparate and unconnected in original Buddhism. As Erik Zürcher has pointedly observed, "In the Buddhist complex . . . the general situation of decay and sin has no connection with the destruction of the world at the end of a Great Aeon." Obviously a certain linkage has to exist before any Buddhist eschatology is possible, and Maitreya, the next Buddha after Sakyamuni, provides that linkage.[34]

As the Buddha "who has yet to come," Maitreya is a perfectly respectable figure in classical Buddhism. His abode is the Tusita heaven, where he will dwell to await the time of his descent, some five hundred and seventy-six million years after Sakyamuni's nirvana. When his descent takes place, the world will be under the reign of a perfect chakravartin, "Sacred King, Turner of the Dharma Wheel" *(zhuanlun shengwang)*, which is characterized by universal peace, longevity, and material well-being. Meanwhile, pious devotees can take the vow to be reborn in his Tusita heaven, there to enjoy his elucidation on the dharma and the pleasures of his paradise until the time of his descent. Or they can visualize *(guan)* his august being, even in this life, through mental concentration, and receive his blessings.[35] Indeed, this kind of Maitreyan devotionalism was popular among some elite circles of the Eastern Jin period, notably the group headed by the eminent monk Dao'an (312–385).[36] Its further popularization among the devout Buddhists in the early sixth century is evidenced by the large number of stone statues and other images of the Maitreya Buddha in the cave temples of Longmen.[37] They attest the respectability Maitreyan worship enjoyed at that time. In fact, statues of Maitreya far outnumbered that of Amitabha during this period, indicating that the wish to be reborn in his Tusita heaven was widespread. It was, in a way, a form of Pure Land devotionalism that antedated Amitabha's.[38]

In his capacity as the future Buddha, Maitreya is, in essence, a revealer of the doctrine. His incarnation will take place in the distant future, amidst peace and prosperity. He is therefore in no way associated with the *mofa* situation, which, if related to this Maitreyan belief at all, is supposed to have taken place and been finished with *prior* to his descent. In any event, this classical view of Maitreya puts him in the same category as other great bodhisattva, whose principal function is to facilitate the spiritual advancement of individual beings. His arrival has no social or political implications, and he is certainly no messiah who answers the plea for help from his chosen but suffering people, comes to their rescue, eliminates all evil, and establishes a millennium on earth afterwards. As a matter of fact, the world as such cannot be saved by him or anybody else, as it runs its own inexorable course of cyclical decay and prosperity. Besides, in classical Buddhism, all existences are considered ultimately unreal and mired in illusory suffering anyway.

This canonical view of Maitreya notwithstanding, an alternative and potentially more subversive brand of Maitreyan devotionalism made its appearance in the late Six Dynasties period. The arrival of Maitreya came to be understood in the here/now mode described by Jan Nattier.[39] The earliest expression of this belief appeared during the Northern Wei (386–534), when the Tuoba rulers exploited the monk Faguo's declaration that "the emperor is the Buddha" and proclaimed themselves incarnation of Maitreya.[40] Later, during the Tang dynasty, Empress Wu also made use of this belief to suggest her identification with Maitreya.[41] But such appropriations of the myth by those in power were rare. The vast majority of the subscribers to this faith were antiestablishment groups who needed a powerful religious justification to overthrow the status quo. Moreover, as no canonical text supporting this active apocalyptic tradition existed, "apocryphal texts" had to be compiled to provide the doctrinal foundation. As expressed in some apocryphal texts compiled during this period, Maitreya was, for the first time, the focal point of an intense eschatological-messianic devotionalism. Zürcher has pointed out this shift succinctly:

> The decisive deviation from the common Maitreya devotion consisted in a chronological shift of the person of the savior himself: Maitreya has been moved forward from an era of prosperity and happiness in the very distant future to an imminent period of decay and

misery, which in turn is not only associated with the *mofa,* but also with the kalpa-disasters at the end of an aeon.[42]

This transposition in the timing of Maitreya's descent, together with his association with the *mofa* and kalpa-disaster expectations, finally transformed him into a fully messianic figure. The former benign teacher of the dharma is now a wrathful messiah and a world redeemer, ready to save the faithful and damn the evil. He will rid the world of all misery and injustice and create a millennium of unspeakable happiness, peace, and prosperity. This radically different image of Maitreya, again according to Zürcher, is the result of "hybridization" between Buddhism and Daoism during the Six Dynasties.[43] Furthermore, the main features of this Buddhist "eschatological-messianic" complex are modeled after its Daoist counterpart, presumably from the Yellow Turbans down to the Li Hong followers.[44] Thus Zürcher asserts:

> It was the Taoist vision that provided a coherent complex of eschatological expectations into which all these disconnected Buddhist themes became incorporated and welded into an integral whole, and it was also Taoism that filled some essential gaps by providing the materials for which there was no Buddhist counterpart: the apocalyptic battle, the judgment, and the creation of an ideal world.[45]

How Maitreya came to embody his full messianic attributes is an interesting story to pursue. Before that, however, a little digression is in order: for, before Maitreya's descent as a savior, some Chinese Buddhists envisioned another messianic figure who would serve as his herald and precursor. This was the Yueguang tongzi (Candraprabha-kumara), which Zürcher has poetically translated as "Prince Moonlight."[46] It is to this forerunner of Maitreya that my discussion shall briefly turn.

Prince Moonlight Messianism

Candraprabha-kumara in original Indian Buddhist hagiography is a minor figure. He is the young son of Srigupta, a local chieftain in northern India who, incited by slanderers of the Buddha, plans to murder the Buddha by letting him fall into a fire pit. Upon learning of this plot, Candraprabha-kumara remonstrates with his misguided father, but to no avail. Anyway, the plot fails, for the Buddha escapes injury by turning the fire pit into a lotus pond. Deeply ashamed, Srigupta begs for forgiveness and is converted.[47] While the original story focuses on Srigupta's conspiracy and his conversion, the Chinese translations (at least two of them) contain interpolations that highlight the son, Prince Moonlight. He is praised by the Buddha for his moral rectitude and for his courage to stand up to his errant father. But more significantly, he is prophesied by the Buddha to be a saintly ruler in China at the time of *mofa*, and he will revive the Buddha's doctrine, at least for a while.[48] This supposed prophecy has been fully exploited by Emperor Wen of the Sui dynasty, and by Empress Wu in early Tang, both claiming to be incarnations of Prince Moonlight.[49] In this capacity as the ideal ruler of China who restores the Buddha's teaching at a time of approaching decay, Prince Moonlight is understood primarily as a chakravartin (universal monarch) and a great revivalist, with no messianic attributes. His role is one that affirms and maintains the existing order, not one that puts an end to it or replaces it.

In several of the sutras compiled in China (the so-called apocryphal texts), however, Prince Moonlight assumes an entirely different persona. In the *Famiejin jing* (Sutra on the total annihilation of the doctrine; *T* 396, probably fifth century), he is depicted as a saintly ruler who, for fifty-two years, arrests the decline of the Buddha's teaching in the age of darkness. Though not yet fully messianic, he is nevertheless closely associated with a very critical nodal point in human history, marked by widespread degeneration within the Buddhist clergy, a devastating deluge, the destruction of the wicked, and the preservation of the chosen people. He is, moreover, described in this text as the savior who comes before the eventual arrival of Maitreya.

In two other texts compiled in China in the sixth century— which had been expunged from the Buddhist canon because of their radical sectarianism but had been rediscovered among the Dunhuang remains—Prince Moonlight comes across as the true and full-fledged messiah. The two texts in question are the *Shouluo biqiu jing* (Sutra of the monk Shouluo; *T* 2873) and the *Puxian pusa shuo zhengming jing* (Sutra of the realization of understanding related by the bodhisattva Samantabhadra; *T* 2879). Together they create an eschatology centering on the messianic figure of Prince Moonlight that is at once breathtaking and astounding. The main themes of this eschatology include:

The Cosmic Crisis: As the world approaches its own end, it is ravaged by three kalpa disasters *(sanzai)*—floods, epidemics, and murderous demons. Water, for instance, will stand forty *li* high upon flat land, and inundate the world with raging waves and thundering noise. Epidemics will afflict the survivors from the flood with innumerable forms of disease, causing widespread disability and death. And demon kings, riding on dragon horses and brandishing clubs and axes, will descend on earth and shout, "Kill!" The world will be plunged into darkness for seven days, during which the demons will devour more people. Finally the whole world is burned down in a cosmic conflagration.[50]

The Apocalyptic Battle: The military engagement between the forces of destruction and salvation is described as titanic in scale. The demon armies led by Mara kings are defeated and slaughtered by divine troops whose leader also rides a dragon-horse.

The Judgment: There will be a complete separation of the saved and the doomed, with the line sometimes running right through even the closest of relatives, who may find themselves in opposite camps. Small in number (only eighty-four or eighty-seven thousand), the chosen people are the lay Buddhists who in stark contrast to the clerical establishment, which is steeped in sin, have faithfully observed the Buddhist vows and are now physically transported to a magic city of great splendor.

The Reconstructed World: The surviving electi will enjoy a restored world of unspeakable opulence. The surfaces of the earth and mountains will be covered with gold, and the trees made of silver, the innumerable palaces adorned with luminous jewels of all kinds. Human lifespan will be extended to eighty-seven-thousand years, after which one is reborn into an even more spectacular heaven.

At the center of these cosmic happenings is the savior Prince Moonlight, who is also called "Prince of Light" (Mingwang)[51] or "Prince of Peace and Equality" (Pingjun). He predicts and describes all the events just mentioned, and instructs his faithful believers on the methods that can be followed to survive the end of the world. When he appears in the world, they recognize him in all his glory and are saved. He has a coterie of assistants who will help him in his task of salvation.

This amazingly detailed eschatology centering on Prince Moonlight, who is the forerunner of Maitreya himself, is highly suggestive. It enables us to get a glimpse not only of the Buddhist sectarian mentality as it developed in the late Six Dynasties but also of the form of Maitreyan messianism that might have evolved contemporaneously. As such it has been worth our while to examine this minor savior figure, who was the object of worship by a small group of devout followers. The only threat to the government posed by this group took the form of a cult around a nine-year-old boy, in 516–517, who was touted as Prince Moonlight's incarnation.[52] With Maitreyan messianism, on the other hand, the threat would be much greater, and the effect more serious.

Apocalyptic Maitreyanism

In contrast to the *shangsheng* (rebirth in heaven) belief characteristic of classical Maitreyan devotionalism, apocalyptic Maitreyanism is noted for its preoccupation with the future Buddha's imminent descent in the age of moral degeneration and widespread suffering. Its focus is on Maitreya's *xiasheng* (incarnation). While taking the vow to be reborn in his Tusita heaven necessitates no confrontation with the existing political order, yearning for his descent in the age of *mofa* to rid the world of immorality and injustice implies a condemnation of the establishment, both clerical and political. By its very nature, therefore, this *xiasheng* devotionalism is "subversive" and almost automatically invites the suspicion and hostility of the authorities, be it the state or the ecclesiastic hierarchy. Zürcher has correctly noted that "no political regime could accept the idea that the *mofa* era was at hand, because that period is characterized, inter alia, by a cruel, corrupt, and tyrannical government; and the established church could not approve it either, because in *mofa* texts the traditional sangha is described invariably as degenerate, ignorant, and indulging in all kinds of forbidden practices."[53]

That Maitreya has come to be associated with the main themes of eschatological expectations is evidenced in the titles of sutras related to his cult, many of which have been expunged from the Buddhist canon and are preserved only in bibliographies since the sixth century. They show how Maitreya is "incarnated to separate the sinful ones from the blessed," to "save the faithful from suffering and danger," and to "deliver [them] from the three disasters of the great kalpic transition."[54] More than anything else, however, it was the deep concern about the onset of the *mofa* age in late–Six Dynasties

China that was responsible for the maturation of Maitreya into a
messianic figure.[55] The fear of *mofa* became all the more real when
Emperor Wu of Northern Zhou launched his devastating anti-Buddhist campaigns between 574 and 577. Witnessing both oppression
from the state and corruption within the sangha, many pious Buddhists were driven to the conclusion that the end of the doctrine was
at hand. Maitreya, as the next Buddha, was the logical choice to be
called upon to redeem this world and to punish all external oppres-
sors and internal renegades of Buddhism. In some extreme cases,
believers of Maitreyan messianism took matters into their own hands
and staged antidynastic, anticlerical uprisings to usher in the reign of
their savior, thinking that, with him on their side, they would be
invincible and victory would be guaranteed.

Some notable Maitreyan rebellions in the Northern Wei, Sui,
Tang, and Song periods include the following:

1. A.D. 515: The monk Faqing rebelled and used the slogan "The
   New Buddha has appeared; the Old Devil will be eliminated."
   The "New Buddha" was a clear reference to Maitreya, while
   the "Old Devil" might mean the clergy. This movement was
   vehemently anticlerical, slaughtering monks and nuns, and
   burning down temples as it moved along. It promised its followers that mass slaughter would earn them higher status as a
   buddha. The movement was at times so fanatical that "fathers,
   sons, and brothers did not recognize one another."

2. A.D. 610: On the day of the lunar New Year, a band of white-
   robed Maitreyan believers, with incense and flowers in hand,
   entered the Sui palace through the Jianguo Gate. They "prepared for rebellion" by seizing the weapons of the palace
   guards.

3. A.D. 613: Two incidents occurred involving Maitreyan followers. The first was headed by Song Zixian, who called himself
   the incarnation of Maitreya and planned a grand assembly for
   his followers during which he had plotted to attack the carriage
   in which the Sui emperor Yangdi was riding. The second was
   under the leadership of a monk named Xiang Haiming, who
   also claimed to be the Maitreya Buddha. Adopting princely
   titles, he began the reign of Baiwu (White Crow).

4. Mid 710s: A certain Wang Huaigu declared that "the Sakyamuni Buddha has declined; a New Buddha is about to appear.

The house of Li (Tang Dynasty) is ending, and the house of
Liu is about to rise."
5.   A.D. 1047: Wang Ze, an army officer, used an almost identical
slogan as that adopted by Wang Huaigu three centuries earlier.
He proclaimed that "the Sakyamuni Buddha has declined: the
Maitreya Buddha should rule the world."[56]

All of these Maitreyan uprisings ended in failure soon after they
erupted. Yet they demonstrated the persistence and resilience of the
belief in Maitreya's messiahship. They also signaled the inability of
the establishment to stamp out this heterodox faith. When it was
merged with other powerful eschatological traditions, as it apparently
was during the early fourteenth century, the appeal was even more
overwhelming and the menace was even more threatening.

Manichaeism: Its History in China and Its Eschatology

Another tradition that severely tested orthodoxy in China was Manichaeism, which was introduced from Persia. Its founder was Mani
(216–276), who put together a syncretic mixture of Christianity
(primarily Gnosticism), Buddhism, and traditional Persian beliefs,
and turned them into an intensely eschatological religion.[57] Reaching
China perhaps as early as the fifth century,[58] it was not officially presented to the court until 694, when Empress Wu was on the throne.
From the time of its formal introduction to its 843 proscription by
Emperor Wuzong of Tang, it enjoyed uninhibited growth, particularly among the Uighurs, with the exception of one brief episode of
state intervention in 732. But even then the prohibition was applied
only to the Chinese converts, not the "barbarian" practitioners of the
faith, who were far greater in number. Manichaean temples, known
as Great Cloud Temples of Light (Dayun guangming si), were built
in considerable numbers in the lower Yangzi basin as well as in
Henan and around the capital.

The proscription against Manichaeism in 843, coming right
upon the heels of the decline in Uighur influence in Tang politics,
was much more damaging and lasting.[59] Occurring two years before
the 845 general persecution of all alien faiths (Buddhism being the
main target), this event signaled the "sectarianization" of Manichaeism in China, for after 843 this religion was driven underground,
never to be tolerated by the state again. Nevertheless, the Mani-

chaean tradition did not die out; instead it spread to the provinces of Fujian and Zhejiang, where it remained popular even among educated elites throughout the Song, and possibly Yuan, period.[60] In fact, most of the informative sources on Manichaeism in China date from the Song dynasty.[61]

This religion was referred to as Moni jiao in Tang, a simple transliteration of the word "Mani." After the ninth century, it was also known as Ming jiao (Religion of Light).[62] By the Song period, it was pejoratively called *chicai shimo* (practicing vegetarianism and serving Mani, or demon, as the two words for "Mani" and "demon" are homophones in Chinese), although the same appellation was also occasionally used against the White Lotus and the White Cloud sects.[63] Its doctrines, as understood by the Chinese, could be summarized by the term *erzong sanjie* (two principles and three stages).[64] The "two principles" refer to Light and Darkness, while the three stages are past, present, and future.

According to Mani's original teaching, which was heavily influenced by ancient Iranian dualism, two elements existed before creation: God and Matter, or Light and Darkness, or Truth and Light.[65] Being eternal substances, they never went through the process of creation themselves but were responsible for the creation of all other things. During the first stage, or the first epoch, Light and Darkness were clearly separated. The realm of Light was characterized by peacefulness, goodness, and wisdom; while the realm of Darkness was filled with swirling agitation, jostling, and pushing. The realm of Light was unbounded on three sides—east, west, and north—but to the south it came up against Darkness, thereby setting the stage for the second epoch when, upon seeing the calm and harmony of his neighbor, Darkness (now personified as "Prince") broke from below into the realm of Light in an attempt to disrupt this peaceful setting and partake of the illumination.

With this intrusion of Darkness into Light, the second epoch was begun. His realm having been thrown into convulsion by this disruption, Light (now personified as "King" and "Father") was forced to respond. Since he was all pure and pacific, the Father was unsuited to struggle and strife. He thus "called" (Mani never used the word "create," but always the verb "to call") into being the "Mother of Life," who in turn "called" the "Primaeval Man" (*"yuanren"* or *"churen"* in Chinese).[66] Clad in his armor of five light elements, which represented not only his protection but actually his own being and his proper self, Primaeval Man set out to do battle with Matter, Darkness, and Evil, which was now assisted by a large army of cohorts. In this first encounter, however, Primaeval Man was defeated by the prince of Darkness and his host, and his five light elements were devoured by the demons, while he himself lay in a stupor, overwhelmed by Evil.

Whereupon Father of Light "called" another deity, the "Living Spirit," who proceeded to the boundary of Darkness and summoned Primaeval Man. In turn, the latter answered. In Manichaeism, "the Call" symbolizes the message of redemption while "the Answer" represents humankind's willingness to be saved. Stretching out his hand, which was seized by Living Spirit, and soaring like a victorious light out of Darkness, Primaeval Man was returned to the paradise of Light, where he was reunited with his mother. The joy of return and the emotional reunion with the mother marked a high point in the Manichaean myth. The stirring scene of the mother embracing and kissing her son, whom she thought had been lost to her forever, is vividly described.[67]

Though Primaeval Man was rescued, his light elements were still left behind in captivity in the world of Darkness. This set in motion an even more complicated plot. Living Spirit first began to undertake the task of liberation by purifying those light particles that had not been defiled. He turned them into sun and moon, the two vessels of light, according to the Manichaeans. Those particles that had been partially befouled he transformed into stars. Those that remained in Darkness had to be retrieved through a very circuitous procedure.

A third messenger was "called," who sailed across the vault of heaven and showed himself to the demons below. To the male demons, he displayed the radiant, naked beauty of his femininity in the shape of the virgin of Light, while to the female demons he assumed the form of a naked, shining youth. As a result, the male demons, in their violent sexual excitement, discharged the particles of light, which they had previously taken from Primaeval Man, in the form of sperm that thereafter sprouted as plants and vegetables on earth. The female demons bore offspring, who also fell to earth as animals and, having eaten the plant buds, also assimilated the particles of light. Consequently, Manichaeans held the belief that plants and vegetables contain the remaining particles of light still hidden in Matter, with animals harboring some even smaller portions of them,

The rest of the second epoch is preoccupied with the struggle between Light and Darkness that unfolds in the human realm. Human beings were created by Darkness, yet they also retained portions of the light particles. If they could practice vegetarianism and thereby enhance their light "count," they could participate in the struggle on the side of Light and come to enjoy the fruits of destined victory. These will be the elect of the Manichaean faith, who were endowed with divine intelligence to know what needed to be done. They included such perfect individuals as Noah, Abraham, and Enoch, as well as founders of religions: the Buddha, Zoroaster, and Jesus. The final and most complete manifestation of the Great Nous (intelligence) was, of course, Mani himself.

The third epoch is ushered in when, following a fierce apocalyptical battle, Light finally triumphs over Darkness after retrieving all the light particles. Then the physical world is destroyed in a general conflagration, the last Judgment will follow, and the Good will be separated from the Evil. Darkness is driven back to its original realm, and peace and harmony will be restored, with Light and Darkness forever separated thereafter.

The preceding discussion of Mani's teaching helps us understand Manichaeism as it was practiced in China. One particular feature of Manichaeism in China was its close association with Buddhism. Mani taught that the Buddha conveyed the same revelatory message that he was given. During its march toward China, Mani's teaching began to display certain signs of assimilation with Buddhism, which, after all, was then the most dominant religion there. More interestingly, among his followers in China, Mani himself also took on certain attributes of the Buddha. To some, he was the Maitreya, the Buddha to be; to others, he was Mani the Buddha of Light (Moni guangfo).[68] It was thus no surprise that Manichaeism was persecuted alongside Buddhism in the middle of the ninth century. However, it survived and even prospered by the Song dynasty, having spread to Fujian and Zhejiang, and having taken on a Daoist guise as well. One of the most detailed and informative sources on the Manichaean groups in Song China is provided by Zhuang Jiyu in his *Jile pian,* which I quote at length here:

> The Chicai shimo sects spread from Fujian to Wenzhou, and then Zhejiang. When Fang La rebelled, the sects also got involved. Their teaching prohibits meat and wine, and the worship of gods, deities,

and even ancestors. They do not entertain guests. At death they are buried naked. Before the body of the deceased is put in the coffin, it is at first fully dressed and capped. Then two of their members sit next to the body. One asks the other, "When he was born, did he have a cap?" When the answer is no, the cap is removed. In like manner all the other clothing is removed one by one until the body is stark naked. Then one asks again, "What did he have when he was born?" The answer is that he had his placenta. Thus the body is put in a cloth sack. Ignorant people say that one gets rich after joining this sect. They do not realize that if you refrain from wine and meat, stop all entertainment of guests, and dispense with elaborate funerals, getting rich will be easy. Moreover, one may be poor when one joins the sect, but then all others in the sect contribute money to help him out. In time he can accumulate some wealth and become affluent. When they travel, even members previously unknown to them will provide food and lodging. Everything is used and shared communally; they call themselves one family. . . . Their leader is called the Manichaean (demon) King, his assistants are known as Manichaean Fathers and Manichaean Mothers. . . . They do not worship deities and buddhas, only sun and moon do they worship as true buddhas. Their texts declare that their "doctrine is egalitarian, with no distinction between high and low". . . . They also regard life as painful. Thus killing someone is to end his pain. This they call deliverance. He who "delivers" large number of people may become a buddha himself. Congregating into large groups, they create opportunities to foment trouble. Taking delight in killing, they are the greatest source of worry. They harbor special hostility toward the Buddhist clergy, because the latter's prohibition against killing runs counter to their practice.[69]

This long account reveals several major features of the Manichaean groups in Song China. First, they practiced strict vegetarianism and abstinence from alcohol. Second, they worshiped no deities and observed no ancestor worship. Third, they observed extreme frugality. Fourth, they conducted naked burials. Fifth, they emphasized mutual aid. Sixth, they worshiped sun and moon. Seventh, they promoted egalitarianism. Eighth, they regarded death as liberation. Among these, the practice of vegetarianism is understandable because Manichaeans believe that plants have the largest concentration of light particles among Matter. The worship of sun and moon is also logical, as they are regarded by Manichaean believers as the vessels of light. Only the description of wanton killing is disturbing and uncharacteristic of Manichaean beliefs and practices. Even some of the Manichaeans' Buddhist detractors attested to their strict adherence to nonviolence, as it shall be shown later.

Zhuang Jiyu's description of the Manichaeans is corroborated by at least two other sources, also from the Song period. One is Liao Kang's memorial to urge the court to proscribe Manichaeans:

> The Manichaean sects are popular throughout the lower Yangzi region. . . . When one member gets into trouble with the law, all others will contribute five hundred or a thousand cash each to collect enough money to bribe officials for his release. When a member dies, his body is cremated on a bier, with no need for coffin or funeral dress. There is no more funeral rite or ancestor worship. All they try is to abolish human relationships. They are totally neglectful of the distinction between monarch and subject, and high and low.[70]

This conforms to the earlier sources in several respects. The Manichaeans were reported to have a strong sense of group solidarity. They also practiced mutual aid, simple or no funerals, and dispensed with ancestor worship. The last feature, in particular, invited the wrath of the reporters who accused them of abolishing all human relationships.

The other corroboratory source is also a memorial, submitted by one Wang Juzheng in the 1130s:

> Your minister has learned that among those who worship Mani (demons), there are one or two crafty types in each village who are called Manichaean chiefs *(motou)*. These men record the names of all the villagers, then swear an oath of association with them to make them Manichaean followers. All Manichaeans abstain from meat-eating. When one family has trouble, all the other members join together to help out. Vegetarianism saves money, therefore self-sufficiency can be attained. Through association with other members they become close, and mutual aid becomes natural. All matters can be more easily accomplished.[71]

Once again, this source confirms the vegetarianism of the Manichaeans, the relative affluence of the membership, and the emphasis on mutual aid. Thus from these three accounts, all provided by Song scholars and officials (who were by no means unbiased reporters), one gets a rather consistent picture of the Manichaean groups active in the Fujian-Zhejiang area. With the exceptions of the alleged refusal to honor ancestors and their love of killing, which might have been government slander to make them appear more heterodox than they really were, all the other features were "neutral" descriptions, in that the government would benefit little in fabricating them. Thus it is fairly safe to conclude that the Manichaeans in the Song period insisted on strict abstinence from meat and wine, practiced naked burial, worshiped sun and moon but not other deities, maintained a frugal lifestyle that resulted in the accumulation of wealth, and emphasized group solidarity through the practice of mutual aid.

Added to this is the Buddhist perception of some Manichaeans, which introduces a different perspective. The *Fozu tongji* (Record of the traditions of buddhas and patriarchs) (published 1260–1270), by Zhipan relates the following information about a rebellious group inspired by Manichaeism:

> In the sixth year of Zhenming of the Liang Dynasty (920), the Manichaeans in Chenzhou assembled to stage a rebellion. They put forth Muyi as their emperor. The court dispatched troops to capture him and had him executed. Members of this group did not eat meat or drink wine. They assembled at night to engage in licentious and dirty acts. Their picture depicted a seated Mowang (Manichaean King), with the Buddhas washing his feet. They claimed that while Buddhism was the Great Vehicle *(dacheng)*, their doctrine was the Most Supreme Vehicle *(shang shangcheng)*. Such was their lawless irreverence! [72]

From this complaint it is evident that Manichaeism during the Five Dynasties period came into direct competition with Buddhism, and on at least one occasion instigated a rebellion. The charge of licentiousness is interesting, as it is not supported by any other source. In fact, this accusation is undermined by another Buddhist source, the *Shimen zhengtong* (Orthodox tradition of Buddhism) (published 1256), by Zongjian:

> The teaching of Two Principles (Manichaeism) requires that men and women remain celibate and not marry. They should stay aloof from one another and not even converse with one another. When they are

sick, they take no medicine: and when they die, they are buried naked.
. . . Its doctrines prohibit meat-eating and wine-drinking. Its members sleep in the daytime and become active at night. Using incense
as signals, they secretly maintain contacts and address one another as
friends of virtue *(shanyou)*. . . . Ignorant people are most willing to join
such Manichaean groups. Their members maintain a strict observance of vegetarianism, teetotalism, avoidance of killing, and inges-
tion of spices. Members of the Buddhist community who are careless
in their conduct are ridiculed and held in contempt by them. For
those of us who have entered monkhood and have dedicated ourselves
to the observance of the Buddha's laws, should we not take heed of
such criticisms?[73]

Zongjian not only undercut the accusation of licentiousness against
the Manichaeans, he painted a picture of highly puritanical behavior
practiced by them. The point about Manichaean celibacy may be
authentic, as Mani's original teaching did discourage sex and, in particular, procreation, as it would further delay the complete retrieval
of light particles by having more human beings born.[74] Moreover,
the insistence on nonviolence and non-killing is equally an integral
part of Mani's ethics.[75] Thus in Zongjian's portrayal, Manichaeism
comes across as a puritanical tradition with a strict ethical standard,
one that can put a morally degenerate Buddhist sangha to shame.

There is some debate on whether the most devastating rebellion in Northern Song, the one led by Fang La in 1120–1121, was
principally inspired by Manichaeism.[76] That Manichaeism was very
popular among sectarians in Zhejiang, Jiangxi, and Fujian during the
twelfth century is beyond doubt. It was precisely in Zhejiang that
Fang La's rebellion began and gained momentum. Moreover, Qiu
Daoren (Qiu the follower of the Way), one of Fang La's cohorts, was
himself leader of an active Manichaean group. So was Lü Shinang,
another Fang La supporter. It appears that some Manichaeans *did*
take part in this large rebellion, which, along with the capture of the
emperors Huizong and Qinzong by the Jin, effectively put an end to
the Northern Song dynasty.

With the failure of the Fang La rebellion, Manichaeism suffered even more disrepute and persecution. It apparently underwent
a gradual loss of identity and simply merged with other proscribed
sectarian traditions. In the fourteenth century, however, its influence

was once again impressively demonstrated. Under the innovative syncretism effected by Han Shantong (d. 1351), Manichaean eschatology was merged with Maitreyan messianism and White Lotus sectarianism, producing a powerful and explosive movement that in the end brought down the Mongol regime.[77]

The White Lotus Movement of Han Shantong

The Maitreyan cult, though severely persecuted, survived all the dynastic transitions from Sui to Yuan. In the early fourteenth century, echoes of the same messianic call for the descent of Maitreya could be heard in the incidents involving Guo Pusa (Guo the bodhisattva) (1325) and Bang Hu (Hu the Cudgel) (1337). In the meantime, Maitreyan eschatology also interacted with other sectarian traditions, such as Manichaeism and White Lotus, and gradually merged with them. The most spectacular example of this syncretic mutation was that undertaken by Han Shantong, the innovative leader of a White Lotus group.[78]

Before Han Shantong's appearance on the scene, there were already two distinct White Lotus traditions in Yuan China. The first, known as the White Lotus school (Bailian zong), traced its origin back to Huiyuan's Amidist devotionalism. Though by this time it was chiefly a lay-oriented devotional organization, the White Lotus school was considered orthodox and perfectly respectable. Its principal spokesman was Pudu, author of the *Lianzong baojian* (Precious mirror of the lotus school) (published 1312), who discreetly dropped the word "white" in order to distinguish it from another White Lotus tradition, which he vehemently denounced. Referred to as the White Lotus assembly (Bailian hui), it was portrayed by Pudu as a degenerate and distorted form of White Lotus teaching. He complained that this imposter and corrupt tradition was "neglectful of productive undertakings," "transmitted heterodox doctrines," "mingled the sexes to disrupt proper human relationship," "used reckless words to delude the multitudes," and "irresponsibly discoursed on fortunes and misfortunes."[79] As it turned out, government officials had discovered in 1281 just such a White Lotus group. They reported that it used all sorts of prognostication devices, exorcising charms, and astrological charts to deceive people and foment trouble.[80] It should be noted that no mention of Maitreya worship or Manichaean rituals was made. Han Shantong's grandfather seems to have belonged to one of these White Lotus assemblies, and passed down his belief to Shantong.

Han Shantong proved to be an innovator. Under him the incorporation of the most potent eschatology to date, which was derived from Maitreyan and Manichaean sources, was accomplished. His religion was the White Lotus sect (Bailian jiao). Evidence of this merger of Maitreyan and Manichaean elements can be found in the slogan used by Han at the start of his rebellion in 1351: "The empire is in utter chaos *(tianxia daluan)*. Maitreya Buddha has incarnated, and the King of Light has appeared in this world *(Mile xiasheng, mingwang chushi)*."[81] This was the ultimate eschatological and messianic declaration. Maitreya and the King of Light merged into one personality and promised to appear at the time of utter chaos to deliver the suffering masses and install the millennium on earth. But the coming of this super messiah would be attended by cataclysmic destructions throughout the empire.[82] One poem composed during the tumultuous late Yuan period illustrates vividly the destructiveness of the savior:

> What kind of god is this Maitreya, who has sown so many seeds
>   of misfortune?
> The flying squirrels shake the earth, and stir up huge dust storms.
> Smoldering smoke blankets the land, and people's livelihood has
>   been made unbearable.
> Blood stains all the rivers, while the ghosts and spirits wail bitterly.
> Only once in a hundred years will people encounter such disasters.
> As of when have the punishing weapons of Heaven, which stretch
>   for thousands of miles, announced their arrival?
> Even in a barren field (wicked world) there may be hidden
>   precious jade (good people).
> But alas! They all perish into a heap of ashes![83]

Han Shantong never lived to realize his messianic dream. He was captured and executed soon after the rebellion began. His son Lin'er was later located by one of his lieutenants, was enthroned as the Lesser King of Light (Xiao mingwang), and adopted the dynastic name of Song. But it was Zhu Yuanzhang, one of the numerous ambitious soldiers of fortune in Han's service, who finally emerged triumphant as the next emperor. To eliminate all threats to his empire-building efforts, Zhu had Han Lin'er drowned, in 1366, but adopted Ming as his dynastic name two years later in an attempt to placate his former religious associates. He was trying to convince them that their true King of Light had indeed ascended the throne!

Conclusion

In this short essay, I have examined the process of development from Buddhism, through Maitreyanism and Manichaeism, to the culmination in late-Yuan White Lotus sectarianism. Collectively this development represents another heterodox tradition that challenged Chinese orthodoxy during the medieval period. The main purpose of this chapter is to provide linkage to the essay on Daoist heterodoxy that appears earlier in this volume, and to the one on Eternal Mother religion, which comes later. Together, these three chapters should show the existence of a resilient countercurrent that ran against the socioethical orthodoxy discussed in the introductory essay in this volume, paralleling it from the time of its inception in Han. It is apparent that this heterodox tradition was derived from numerous sources and underwent various mutations. Daoism was one such source; Buddhism was another. For the period under consideration in this essay, it was principally represented by Maitreyan messianism and Manichaean chiliasm.

The Maitreyan and Manichaean vision of salvation has three major components: (1) the expectation of an imminent cosmic disaster, which precedes the arrival of a messianic figure who will bring a violent end to the existing world, (2) the deliverance of the faithful (the electi) from oppression and misery, and (3) the apocalyptic battle from which the savior and his chosen people will emerge triumphant. From the standpoint of orthodoxy, this eschatological vision, with its corollary expectations of strife and struggle by the community of the elect, posed the most threatening challenge to the existing order.

For one thing, the very anticipation of the advent of a new age implies a negation of the present one, thereby undermining the authority, and even legitimacy, of the current establishment, be it political or ecclesiastical. The imminent arrival of the millennium, envisioned by both the Maitreyans and the Manichaeans, denies the existing order's claim to immutability and permanence. It allows the sectarians to realize that this world is not the best of all possible worlds and that a new beginning will arrive in time to replace the current age and to sit in judgment over the entire past. In effect, the present world is relativized and doomed for oblivion.

More ominously, the present world is not expected to pass in a peaceful, quiet way. Instead, it is anticipated to be plunged in the throes of unspeakable violence, afflicted by all kinds of terrifying catastrophes so devastating that the majority of humanity will perish, the entire universe will be torn asunder, and the physical face of the earth as well as the structure of the heavens will be rearranged.

Equally unsettling is the notion of predestined election held jealously by the Maitreyans and the Manichaeans. It defies the orthodox assumption of universal salvation or at least communal betterment. It creates a "sectarian" mentality that is exclusionist and focuses only on in-group solidarity and well-being. As a result, it becomes less dependent on the services provided by the state and the religious establishment, thereby lessening their holds on sect members. In turn, the sect offers a "competing hierarchy of authority" to orthodoxy. In addition, this new identity with the community of the elect may engender alternative ethical standards, such as social egalitarianism and non-distinction of the sexes. If the charges of sectarian refusal to worship ancestors, honor imperial authority, and separate the sexes are valid, this will clearly show how far afield the sectarians have departed from the socioethical orthodoxy. Even if they are mere fabrications designed to tarnish the reputation of the sectarians, they are equally indicative of what the guardians of orthodoxy perceived to be heterodox and absolutely unacceptable. When they leveled this charge of heterodoxy against the Maitreyans and Manichaeans, they betrayed the threat they must have felt coming from these sectarians.

Finally, the horrors of the apocalyptic battle, complete with divine armies lined up against demon troops, may engender a psychological frame of mind among the sectarians that violence and conflict, especially with their participation in them, may be unavoidable. Buttressed by the promise of certain victory, some of them may be tempted into creating situations in which armed struggles with the existing political and clerical authorities are staged, with the hope that the arrival of the millennium may thus be triggered. After all, the vision of apocalyptic warfare may help to dull the sensitivity toward violence and the aversion toward killing. When, as the authorities charge, killing is seen as deliverance, and death as liberation, there is little deterrence to their occurrence.

To be sure, only a few of the Maitreyans and Manichaeans rebelled, and for those that did, factors other than their chiliasm might have been at play as well. It is not my intention to suggest that these sects were invariably seditious or violence prone. Nevertheless, it remains true that, precisely because of their eschatological vision and messianic hope, Maitreyan and Manichaean groups were always potentially subversive. That the majority of them did not rebel does not reduce their subversiveness; that at times they were allowed to exist unharassed does not lessen their heterodoxy. As Daniel Overmyer has so shrewdly observed, though the explicit values of the Chinese sectarians may be conventional and proper, it is their implicit values that are, at the very least, nonconformist and dissenting in nature, if not even heretical.[84] Their eschatological and millenarian yearnings create a sense of urgency and immediacy not present in orthodox religion. Their salvationism accepts and even welcomes the violent demise of the present world. It is in this sense that they may be considered subversive. Their chiliasm offers an alternative ethic that runs counter to the one governing the existing society. It is in this sense that they may be considered heterodox.

Notes

1. Taken from the title of Erik Zürcher's classic, *The Buddhist Conquest of China*, 2 vols. (Leiden: E. J. Brill, 1959).

2. Taken from the title of Kenneth Ch'en's revisionist approach to the history of Chinese Buddhism, *The Chinese Transformation of Buddhism* (Princeton: Princeton University Press, 1973).

3. The anti-Buddhist polemics as well as the Buddhist apologetics during the first half-millennium of Buddhism's introduction are contained in the collections *Hongming ji* (*T* 52, no. 2102, compiled by Sengyou between 515 and 518, hereafter abbreviated as *HMJ*) and *Guang hongming ji* (*T* 52, no. 2103, compiled by Daoxuan in 664, hereafter abbreviated as *GHMJ*). *T* stands for *Taishō shinshū daizōkō* [The Buddhist canon newly compiled during the Taishō reign] (Tokyo: Taishō shinshū daizōkyō kankōkai, 1924–1929).

4. Taken from S. J. Tambiah's highly suggestive monograph, *World Conqueror and World Renouncer: A Study of Buddhism and Polity in Thailand*

against a Historical Background (Cambridge: Cambridge University Press, 1976).

5. This Buddhist scheme of genesis and evolution is described in ibid., 13–14.

6. Details of the debate are recorded in the *HMJ*. See Zürcher, *Buddhist Conquest,* 1:106–110, 156–157, 160–163, 231–253, 256–259. See also Ch'en, *Chinese Transformation,* 69–78.

7. Quoted in Zürcher, *Buddhist Conquest,* 1:232.

8. The letter can be found in *HMJ,* 12 (*T* 52.83c–84b). The treatise is collected in *HMJ,* 5 (*T* 52.29c–32b). For a complete translation of this treatise, see Leon Hurvitz, "'Render Unto Caesar' in Early Chinese Buddhism," in the Liebenthal Festschrift, *Sino-Indian Studies* 5.3–4 (1957): 96–114.

9. Quoted in the biography of Huiyuan, translated as Appendix to chap. 4 in Zürcher, *Buddhist Conquest,* 1:251–252. I have made some modifications in the translation here.

10. *HMJ,* 12 (*T* 52.84b)

11. Ch'en, *Chinese Transformation,* 77.

12. Quoted in ibid., 79.

13. Ibid.

14. As a matter of fact, the special independent status of the clergy had already been compromised in North China earlier. One glaring example of this loss of autonomy was when the monk Faguo, under Emperor Taizu (r. 386–409) of the Northern Wei, was given an official appointment, which immediately obligated him to pay homage to the ruler. Even though he cleverly rationalized his submission to imperial authority by explaining that Emperor Taizu was a present-day Buddha, thus his bowing to him was actually a gesture of respect to the Buddha, the defense had been breached. Control of the sangha by the secular government in the Northern dynasties was therefore far more pervasive and effective.

15. Ch'en, *Chinese Transformation,* 114.

16. The most detailed discussion of this issue has been done by Michihata Ryōshū. See his *Bukkyō to Jukyō rinri* [Buddhism and Confucian Ethics] (Kyoto: Heirakuji, 1968).

17. This text is collected in *HMJ*. See also Fukui Kōjun, "Han minzoku no rinri to Bukkyō" [Ethics of the Han people and Buddhism] in his *Fukui Kōjun chosakushū* [Collected works of Fukui Kōjun] (Kyoto: Hōzō-kan, 1988), 3:162–184. See also Ch'en, *Chinese Transformation,* 16–18.

18. This preface is collected in the *Chu sanzang jiji, juan* 6, no. 10 (*T* 55.46b).

19. *HMJ,* 12 (*T* 52.84b). Quoted in Zürcher, *Buddhist Conquest,* 1:251, 258.

20. In a recent article, Gregory Schopen points out that even before

the common era, filial piety was an integral and pervasive part of Indian Buddhism, as evidenced by the large number of inscriptions at Indian and Central Asian temple complexes that recorded dedications to parents by monks and nuns. See his "Filial piety and the Monk in the practice of Indian Buddhism: A Question of 'Sinicization' viewed from the outside," *T'oung-pao* 70, nos. 1–3 (1984): 110–126.

21. The ensuing discussion of this surrender to "external orthodoxy" dovetails with what Whalen Lai addresses in chapter 3 of this volume.

22. These efforts are discussed in detail in Ch'en, *Chinese Transformation,* 18–50.

23. An in-depth study of the Ghost Festival is Stephen F. Teiser's *The Ghost Festival of Medieval China* (Princeton: Princeton University Press, 1988).

24. See Kenneth Ch'en's brief discussion of the story of Mulian in *Chinese Transformation,* 24–27. See also David Johnson "Ritual Opera, Operatic Ritual: 'Mu-lien Rescues His Mother,'" *Chinese Popular Culture* (Berkeley: University of California Press, 1989).

25. *Yulanpen jing* (*T* 16.779b–c).

26. Teiser, *Ghost Festival,* 14.

27. *Yulanpen jingshu* (*T* 39.505a).

28. Ibid.

29. Translated by Bo Fali and Bo Faji around A.D. 300. The relevant part on the destruction of the world is found on pp. 302c–305a.

30. See Erik Zürcher, "Eschatology and Messianism in Early Chinese Buddhism," in W. L. Idema ed., *Leiden Studies in Sinology* (Leiden: E. J. Brill, 1981), 38.

31. For a full discussion of this subject, see Jan Nattier, *Once Upon a Future Time: Studies in a Buddhist Prophecy of Decline* (Berkeley: Asian Humanities Press, 1991).

32. It is interesting to note that a Buddhist sect by the name of Sanjie jiao (Three Stages Teaching) founded by Xinxing (540–594) was active in the Sui-Tang period. Though it espoused no millenarian belief in the saving power of the Maitreya, it was nevertheless populist and anticlerical in character. It was decimated in the persecution of 713. Cf. Yabuki Keiki, *Sangaikyo no kenkyū* [A study of the Sanjie jiao] (Tokyo: Iwanami, 1927).

33. Zürcher, "Eschatology and Messianism," 39. Nattier identifies the first explicit reference to this three-period system to a work completed in A.D. 558 by the monk Huisi (515–577); see her *Once Upon a Future Time,* 110–111.

34. Cf. Alan Sponberg and Helen Hardacre, eds., *Maitreya, the Future Buddha* (Cambridge: Cambridge University Press, 1988).

35. This form of Maitreyan devotionalism, i.e., rebirth in his Tusita heaven and visualization of encounter with him, is called *shangsheng xinyang.*

The text most representative of this belief is the *Guan Mile pusa shangsheng doushuaitian jing* [Sutra on visualizing bodhisattva Maitreya and rebirth in the Tusita heaven] (*T* 452).

36. See Erik Zürcher, *Buddhist Conquest*, 1:194–195.

37. Kenneth Ch'en, *Buddhism in China* (Princeton: Princeton University Press, 1964), 172. See also Tsukamoto Zenryū, *Tsukamoto Zenryū chosakushū* [Collected works of Tsukamoto Zenryū], vol. 2, *Hokuchō bukkyōshi kenkyū* [Study of Buddhism in the Northern Dynasties] (Tokyo: Daitō, 1974), 241–261.

38. Jan Nattier has devised a neat typology to describe the various modes of Maitreyan belief. It focuses on *where* and *when* the encounter between Maitreya and his believers will take place. The combinations are: there/now (mystical visualization); there/later (Maitreyist Pure Land); here/later (standard and oldest devotionalism); and here/now (Maitreyan messianism, discussed later). See her "The Meanings of the Maitreya Myth: A Typological Analysis," in Sponberg and Hardacre eds., *Maitreya*.

39. See ibid.

40. Ibid., p. 31.

41. Cf. Antonio Forte, *Political Propaganda and Ideology in China at the End of the Seventh Century* (Naples: Instituto Universitario Orientale, 1976).

42. Erik Zürcher, "'Prince Moonlight' Messianism and Eschatology in Early Medieval Chinese Buddhism," *T'oung Pao* 68 (1982): 13.

43. Erik Zürcher, "Eschatology and Messianism," 35.

44. See notes 96, 98, and 102 in chapter 1 of this volume for works dealing with the eschatological aspects of Daoism.

45. Zürcher, "Prince Moonlight," 10.

46. See the two articles by Zürcher cited previously. Of the two, "Prince Moonlight" contains a much fuller treatment. In addition, see Sunayama Minoru, "Gekko doshi Ryukeihi no hanran to Shura-bikukyō" [The uprising of Prince Moonlight Liu Jinghui and the scripture of the monk Shouluo] *Tōhōgaku* 51 (1976): 1–17.

47. Several Chinese translations of this story exist in different degrees of elaboration. See *Yueguang tongzi jing* [Sutra of Prince Moonlight] (*T* 534); *Shenri jing* [Sutra of Srigupta] (*T* 535); *Shenri er benjing* [Original sutra on the son of Srigupta] (*T* 536), and *Dehu zhangzhe jing* [Sutra on the elder Srigupta] (*T* 545).

48. My discussion of Prince Moonlight is largely based on Zürcher's articles. In fact, it is a summary of his main findings.

49. For Sui Wendi's association with Prince Moonlight, see *Dehu zhangzhe jing*, *juan* 2. For Empress Wu's self-identification with Prince Moonlight, see *Baoyu jing* [Sutra of precious rain] (*T* 660), *juan* 1.

50. See the appended text in Zürcher, "Prince Moonlight," p. 65, lines 105–112, and p. 69, lines 187–190, 197–198.

51. As indicated below (see note 79), the title "Prince Moonlight," used identically by the late Yuan rebel Han Shantong, has been used to support the argument that Han was influenced by this Maitreyist tradition rather than the Manichaean one. See Barend J. ter Haar, *The White Lotus Teachings in Chinese Religious History* (Leiden: B. J. Brill, 1992), 121–123.

52. Sunayama Minoru, "Gekko doshi," and the "Xingfa zhi" [Section on punishments] in the *Wei Shu* [History of Wei], *juan* 111.

53. Zürcher, "Prince Moonlight," 14.

54. *Dazhou jianding zhongjing mulu* [Published bibliography of the various texts under the Great Zhou Dynasty] (*T* 55.2153), *juan* 15.

55. For the emergence of *mofa* thought in China, see Yuki Reimon, "Shina bukkyō ni okeru mappō shisō no kōki" [The rise of *mofa* thought in Chinese Buddhism] *Tōhō gakuho* 6 (1936): 205–216; for *mofa* ideas in the Sui-Tang period, see Takao Giken, "Mappō shisō to Zui-Tō shoka no taido" [The attitudes of the Sui-Tang Buddhist schools towards *mofa*], in his *Chūgoku bukkyō shiron* [History of Chinese Buddhism] (Kyoto: Heirakuji 1952), 54–96.

56. Shigematsu Shunshō, "To-So jidai no miroku kyōhi" [Maitreyan sectarians in the T'ang-Sung period] *Shien* 3 (1931): 68–103. Also the more recent article by Kegasawa Yasunori, "Zuimatsu mirokukyō no ran o meguru ichi kosatsu" [An investigation into the Maitreyan uprisings in the late Sui period], *Bukkyō shigaku kenkyū*, vol. 23, no. 1 (1980): 15–32. See also the authoritative treatment by Tsukamoto Zenryū, *Tsukamoto Zenryū chosakushū*, vol. 2, chap. 5, "Hoku-Gi no bukkyōhi" [Buddhist sectarians in Northern Wei], 141–185.

57. See Geo Widengren, *Mani and Manichaeism* (London: Weidenfeld and Nicolson, 1965), for a good synoptic discussion of this religion. See also Samuel N. C. Lieu, *Manichaeism in the Later Roman Empire and Medieval China: A Historical Survey* (Manchester: Manchester University Press, 1985). There are two more-recent and significant works in Chinese that study the teaching of Mani and trace its history in China: Lin Wushu, *Monijiao ji qi dongjian* [Manichaeism and its eastward expansion] (Beijing: Zhonghua shujū, 1987), and Wang Jianchuan, *Cong Monijiao dao Mingjiao* [From Manichaeism to the Religion of Light] (Taibei: Xinwenfeng chuban gongsi, 1992).

58. For speculation on its introduction before the seventh century, see Liu Ts'un-yan, "Traces of Zoroastrian and Manichaen Activities in pre-T'ang China," *Selected Papers from the Hall of Harmonious Wind* (Leiden: E. J. Brill 1976), 30–55; also Shigematsu Shunsho, "To-So jidai no manikyō to makyō mondai" [On the question of Manichaeism and demon worship in Tang and Song], *Shien* 12 (1936): 85–143, esp. 97–98. For a history of Manichaeism in China, see Chen Yuan, "Moni jiao ru Zhongguo kao" [A study of the introduction of Manichaeism to China], collected in his *Chen*

Yuan shixue lunzhu xuan [Selected historical studies by Chen Yuan] (Shanghai: Renmin chubanshe, 1981), 133–174. See also E. Chavannes and P. Pelliot, "Un traite manichéen retrouvé en Chine," *Journal Asiatique* (1913): 99–302. A Chinese translation of this monograph was published by Feng Chengjun in 1927 under the title *Moni jiao liuxing Zhongguo kao* [A Study of the popularization of Manichaeism in China] (Shanghai: Shangwu yinshuguan, 1927). Needless to say, the two works by Lin Wushu and Wang Jianchuan mentioned in note 57 contain more updated information. See also Wu Han, "Mingjiao yu DaMing diguo" [Manichaeism and the Ming Empire], *Dushi daji* [Miscellaneous notes from reading history] (Beijing: Sanlian 1956), 235–270. Peter Bryder's *The Chinese Transformation of Manichaeism—A Study of Chinese Manichaen Terminology* (Leberod: Bokforlaget Plus Ultra, 1985) is also worth noting.

59. Many of the Manichaean priests were ordered killed, according to the Japanese Buddhist pilgrim Ennin. See Lieu, *Manichaeism*, 197.

60. For Manichaeism's popularity among Song scholars and lower officials, see Lu You's *Weinan wenji, juan* 5, and *Laoxue'an biji, juan* 10; both have been cited by Chen Yuan, "Moni jiao," 164–165, and Wu Han, "Ming jiao," 246, 251–253. See also Lieu, *Manichaeism*, 225–255. Lin Wushu's "Song-Yuan shidai Zhongguo dongnan yuanhai di siyuanshi Moni jiao" [Ecclesiastical Manichaeism along China's southeastern coast during the Song and Yuan era], included in his *Moni jiao ji qi dongjian*, 145–158, is also instructive.

61. For more details, see Wu Han, "Ming jiao," 235–270.

62. Evidenced by a stone inscription carved in 814. See ibid., 241.

63. A number of scholars have argued that the term *"chicai shimo"* was rather indiscriminately used against all kinds of heterodox groups, by the scholar-officials, and was by no means reserved for the Manichaeans. See Chikusa Masaaki, "Kissai jima ni tsuite" [Eating vegetables and serving demons], *Chūgoku bukkyō shakaishi kenkyū* [Study of Chinese Buddhist social history] (Kyoto: Dōhōsha, 1982), 199–227; Chikusa's argument is supported by Lin Wushu, Wang Jianchuan, and Barend J. ter Haar. See Lin Wushu, *Monijiao ji qi dongjian*, 135–144; Wang Jianchuan, *Cong Monijiao dao Mingjiao*, 233–269; Barend J. ter Haar, *White Lotus Teachings*, 48–55.

64. See Hong Mai's characterization in his *Yijian zhi*, cited in Zhipan's *Fozu tongji* [Records of the traditions of buddhas and patriarchs], *juan* 48, (*T* 49, 431). Also Wu Han, "Ming jiao," 237–238; Lin Wushu has a detailed discussion on this term in *Moni jiao ji qi dongjian*, 12–34.

65. For a summary of Mani's teaching, see Widengren's *Mani and Manichaeism*, 43–73; and Lieu's *Manichaeism*, 5–24.

66. It is in this connection that Manichaeism might have influenced the myth centering on the Eternal Mother in later sectarianism. See Richard

Shek and Tetsurō Noguchi, "Eternal Mother Religion: Its History and Ethics," chap. 7 in this volume.

67. This is the most poignant part of the Manichaean myth and is most reminiscent of the Chinese Eternal Mother myth that developed in the sixteenth century. Though the background events are different in nature, the moving portrayal of the reunion between the mother and child in the Manichaean version may have directly influenced the strikingly similar story in the Eternal Mother myth later.

68. See Lieu, *Manichaeism*, 208–211.

69. Chen Yuan, "Moni jiao," 170–171, and Wu Han, "Ming jiao," 247–248. The relevant passages are also translated in Jacques Gernet, *Daily Life in China on the Eve of the Mongol Invasion, 1250–1276* (New York: Macmillan, 1962), 208–210. See also the translation by Lieu, *Manichaeism*, 236–238, and a more detailed translation in Kao Yu-kung, "Source Materials on the Fang La Rebellion," *Harvard Journal of Asiatic Studies* 26 (1966): 223–225.

70. Chen Yuan, "Moni jiao," 171, and Wu Han, "Ming jiao," 247.

71. Cited in Li Xinchuan, *Jianyan yilai xi'nian yaolu* (Chronicles by the year since the Jianyan era), *juan* 76, quoted in Chen Yuan, "Moni jiao," 163.

72. *Fozu tongji*, juan 42, 54, cited in Chen Yuan, "Moni jiao," 152; also Wu Han, "Ming jiao," 243.

73. "Chiwei zhi" [Chastising falsehood], in *Shimen zhengtong*, quoted in *Fozu tongji*, juan 39, and cited in turn in Chen Yuan, "Moni jiao," 172.

74. Widengren, *Mani and Manichaeism*, 97.

75. Ibid., 96.

76. Both Chen Yuan, "Moni jiao," 164, and Vincent Shih, "Some Rebel Ideologies," *T'oung-pao* 44 (1956): 177, seem to doubt the direct connection between Fang La and Manichaeism. Their view is echoed recently by Zhu Ruixi, "Lun Fang La qiyi yu Moni jiao di guanxi" [On the relationship between the Fang La uprising and Manichaeism], *Lishi yanjiu* (1979): 67–84, and by Wang Jianchuan, *Cong Moni jiao dao Ming jiao*, 233–234. In Japan, Chikusa Masaaki also discounts the direct connection between Fang La and Manichaeism. See "Hōra no ran to kissai jima" [The Fang La rebellion and eating vegetables and serving demons], in *Chūgoku bukkyō shakaishi kenkyū*, 229–259. On the other hand, Kao Yu-kung insists on the connection; see "A Study of the Fang La Rebellion," *Harvard Journal of Asiatic Studies* 24 (1962–1963): 57–60.

77. Barend J. ter Haar, in *White Lotus Teachings*, suggests that the commonly assumed Manichaean influence on Han Shantong may be unfounded (121–122). He cites Zürcher and Forte to argue that Han Shantong's reference to the advent of a Mingwang (King of Light) might have been the

result of Maitreyan messianic belief rather than Manichaean influence. The term appears in the texts associated with the Prince Moonlight cult. Wu Han and the Japanese scholars, however, think otherwise. I also find ter Haar's revisionist discussion not necessarily convincing; see argument in note 82.

78. Studies on Han Shantong and his White Lotus group are too numerous to be listed comprehensively here. A good synopsis is provided by Tetsurō Noguchi, *Mindai byakurenkyōshi no kenkyū* [A study of white-lotus history during the Ming] (Tokyo: Yuzankaku, 1986), 107–127. Another good account is provided by Soda Hiroshi, "Byakurenkyō no seiritsu to sono tenkai" [The origin and development of the white lotus sect], in *Chūgoku minshū hanran no seikai* [The world of rebellions of the Chinese masses] (Tokyo: Suiko shobo, 1974), 147–191. Daniel L. Overmyer also has an adequate discussion in his *Folk Buddhist Religion: Dissenting Sects in late Traditional China* (Cambridge, Mass.: Harvard University Press, 1976), 98–100. See also Wu Han, "Ming jiao," 235–270.

79. Noguchi Tetsurō, *Mindai byakurenkyōshi*, 131 n. 43.

80. This was the case of Du Wanyi, recorded in the *Da Yuan tongzhi tiaoge* [Rules and regulations of the comprehensive institutions of the Great Yuan], *juan* 28, as quoted in Noguchi Tetsurō, *Mindai byakurenkyōshi*, 90, 129.

81. Gao Dai, *Hongyou lu, juan* 7, quoted in Wu Han, "Ming jiao," 260.

82. Ter Haar maintains that "Han Shantong's religious message fits into old indigenous Maitreyist tradition, by no means linked to Manichaen religion or to the White Lotus tradition"; see his *White Lotus Teachings*, 123. See also note 77 above. His argument is that the term "Mingwang" was already in use by Maitreyist cults such as the Prince Moonlight cult. Thus there is no need to borrow from Manichaeism. Yet the Prince Moonlight cult was active only in the sixth century. There is no indication that the Maitreyan tradition in the fourteenth century was still knowledgeable about Mingwang. Moreover, we know that Mani was also associated with Maitreya and his teaching was known as *mingjiao* by the Song dynasty and beyond. So the merger between Manichaeism and Maitreyism is not as far-fetched as ter Haar contends.

83. A poem by Li Fu, collected in the *Caomu zi, juan* 4, and quoted in Suzuki Chūsei, *Chūgokushi ni okeru kakumei to shūkyō* [Revolution and religion in Chinese history] (Tokyo: Todai shuppankai, 1974), 73–74.

84. Daniel Overmyer, "Values in Chinese Sectarian Literature: Ming and Ch'ing Pao-chuan," in David Johnson, et al. eds., *Popular Culture in Late Imperial China* (Berkeley: University of California Press, 1985), 219–254).

CHAPTER 3

The Origins of
Ming Buddhist Schism

Whalen W. Lai

B uddhism is not a religion particularly known for being dogmatic. There may be a basic creed, such as the Three Refuges, and even the idea of a "right view" and a series of "noble practices," but the Buddha would be the first to disown the idea of a "right belief" as the sole means to enlightenment. The goal of nirvana, being ineffable, is hardly any logos that can be formulated with logocentric exactitude. The liberal attitude was such that while the Pudgalavadins, a sect in early Indian Buddhism that believed in there being a provisional self *(pudgala)*, were considered by all other sectarian Buddhists to be misguided in so reintroducing the Hindu idea of a self *(atman)*, no critic ever said the Pudgalavadins could not attain enlightenment! And although it is true that the *vinaya* (monastic precepts) allows the sangha to expel monks who sowed schism in the fellowship, there never was a single papal authority to enforce universal compliance. Thus the controversial Daosheng (ca. 360–463) was expelled from the fellowship for teaching universal Buddha-nature when he did not have the scripture to back him up. Huiguan (ca. 424–453) requested the expulsion from the reigning emperor in the north. Daosheng left only to be made welcome by the circle at Lushan, in the south, who regarded him differently. All in all, it would seem that heretics and heresies are not characteristics of the rather liberal and tolerant Buddhist religion.

External vs. Internal Standard of Orthodoxy

Late imperial China did witness an open schism in the Buddhist ranks. A general consensus emerged among the self-proclaimed "orthodox" Buddhists that there was an obvious "heresy" to denounce, namely, the White Lotus sectarians infamous for stirring up many an uprising.[1] To be sure, political expediency has meant that "mainline" Buddhists generally bowed to the existing political order, but not every Buddhist would yield to such external pressure. In any century since circa 400 C.E., some monks had stood up to the state, and some "deviant" elements had staged rebellions. Nevertheless it was not until the Ming dynasty that we see anything like an absolute divide between an orthodox and a heterodox camp. That schism cannot be attributed to an unfortunate misunderstanding, because no prior schism ever perpetuated itself with such persistence. The phenomenon has to be considered as being unique to Ming-Qing times and needs to be dealt with in historical specificity.

The Christian experience that underwrites the use of the terms "orthodoxy" and "heterodoxy" might be tied to a logocentrism of its own. Still, the circumstance leading to their rise may be instructive here. It has been noted that there was, in those early days, not a singular Church but a number of churches and that "orthodoxy" rose not so much out of a natural self-consciousness but more as a reaction to a perceived threat coming from certain groups holding a "wrong belief," or heterodoxy. The so-labeled heretics, of course, did not consider themselves to be adhering to a wrong article of faith. They knew themselves to be true Christians and their faith to be the genuine article.[2] But once the majority had so decided on its orthodoxy, that Church was obliged to specify what is the "right faith." The official creed might subsequently be phrased in positive terms, but that formulation was crafted originally as a denial. It tells one more about what *not* to believe—how not to follow the heterodox formula for understanding the mystery at the heart of the Christian faith. We also know that in settling these early disputes, the final rulings on who was right and who was wrong leaned on—the decision was enforced by—the power of the state. God or the Holy Spirit that guided the Church might be the final judge, but on earth it was Emperor Constantine who set his imperial seal on the document issued from the council at Nicaea. It was his sword that empowered the Church to outlaw those heretics that the council ruled against. In the history of Indian Buddhism, Maurya King Asoka performed a similar function. He supposedly called a council, at which time he also took steps to "purify the sangha" by removing those elements deemed undesirable. Pali Buddhism reported and traced itself back to a Theravada orthodoxy that way. This set a historical precedent.

Henceforth it was possible for other kings to assume that righteous duty to purge corruption from within the clerical fellowship. Chinese rulers from the time of the Northern (Tuoba) Wei exerted that right to oversee the sangha.[3]

After a long and complex history of negotiation between "state power and sangha authority," the Ming dynasty initiated a new pattern of purging heresies that was not sudden and haphazard, that is to say not like the four major Buddhist persecutions that went before. It was rational and patient and drew a hard-and-fast line that created a permanent schism within the sangha—between a deliberate orthodoxy and a persistent heterodoxy with the blanket label of the White Lotus. That ideological divide came about as follows. Considered potentially dangerous, the White Lotus sectarians were banned by the Yuan government in the early fourteenth century. By the middle of the sixteenth century, the term "White Lotus" under the Ming had become a catch all for a hodgepodge of folk syncretic movements charged, sometimes rightly but sometimes wrongly, with political sedition. Now, the original White Lotus rebels of the mid-fourteenth century seem to have their roots in a Pure Land devotional society under the Song. At the time, the distinction between the so-called Lianshe, the orthodox "Lotus lineage," and the Bailian, the heretical White Lotus, was yet unknown. That ideological distinction was initiated by the Yuan monk Pudu (fl. 1300–1312). In his *Lushan lianzong baojian* (The precious mirror to the lotus school of Lushan), he defended the legitimate school as *shimen zhengtong* (the orthodox line of the house of Sakyamuni). Since Pudu dedicated this work to the throne in the tenth lunar month of 1308, after the state had issued a ban on the heretical White Lotus in the fifth month, the work was meant to dissociate the orthodox line from the banned heretics. The rebels were charged with contaminating the purity of the Pure Land faith with their expectation of the imminent coming of Maitreya, the future Buddha; those last days would involve a cosmic battle between Light and Darkness. However, what anticipated that systematic proscription against the White Lotus has to be the ironic career of the future Ming emperor. He was an ex-monk and one of the rebels who fought on the side of the Light and would later give his dynasty that unusual appellation, Ming for Light.

Ming Emperor Taizu ended up acting the reverse of Emperor Constantine. A pagan, Constantine was so converted to Christ that he ended the Roman persecution of the early Church, proclaimed

Christianity the state religion, and empowered the Church to perse-
cute heretics within its fold. An ex-monk, Taizu led a band of rebels
belonging to the White Lotus movement started by Han Shantong
and continued after 1354 by Shantong's son Han Lin'er. The rebellion removed the Mongol rulers, but instead of proclaiming the
White Lotus faith the state religion, Ming Taizu turned against the
very forces that put him on the throne. Had he acted like Constantine, the history of Chinese Buddhism would be very different
indeed.[4] As he had not, he would help to split the orthodox (pious
and harmless) Lianshe from the heterodox (millenarian and anomic)
Bailian. The Ming founder chose instead to make neo-Confucianism the state orthodoxy. With the imposition of such an "external
orthodoxy," Buddhists soon found themselves having to choose
whether to serve two masters; some would and some would not.
Among Buddhist leaders who sided with the orthodox Pure Land
faith were the more populist Luo Qing (Luozu, fl. 1509–1522) and
the more eminent and erudite Zhuhong (1535–1615). Luozu
"reformed" the popular, lay-oriented White Lotus tradition, purged
it of any elements that the state might regard as seditious, but was
independent enough from "canonical" Buddhism that he founded a
new lineage of teachings (with his writings forming a new canon).
The schools that rose therefrom, such as the Wuwei sect, were syn-
cretist and for incorporating non-Buddhist teachings, and often
could not avoid being charged by more orthodox Buddhists with
being heretical. Some suffered state persecution despite their harmless pietism. The greater public acclaim went to Zhuhong, heir to
the proper Pure Land lineage (he was counted as being in its patriarchal line). A monastic reformer, he ensured that his code of Pure
Land practice would be acceptable to the established monastic community. But as we shall see, he too might have tampered with earlier
Pure Land teaching by being overly accommodating to the "external
orthodoxy" that was the neo-Confucian socioethics. If so, a legitimate question may be raised about whether the "orthodox" Buddhism of Zhuhong is really Buddhist orthodoxy.[5] And if so, may it
not also be asked if the "heretical" White Lotus might not, in some
measures, be deemed legitimately Buddhist?

This essay looks into this issue of the Buddhist accommodation
or nonaccommodation to an "external orthodoxy" of the Chinese
society. In what ways did Zhuhong, who rebuilt Buddhist monasti-
cism and guided highly respectable gentry Buddhists, bend to the

external demand for "loyalty to throne, devotion to family"? In what ways might the heretical White Lotus sectarians refuse to bend and, for that, be unkindly labeled "heterodox"? If we apply standards inherent to Buddhism—acknowledging that there is more than one standard there—might not Zhuhong, who regarded it as a monk's duty to bow to parents, be violating the precepts? And if we apply a liberal Mahayana standard that allows Buddhism to be "world-conquering" and householder bodhisattvas to answer the call to arms in "defense of the Dharma," then might not the notorious White Lotus have just cause to repudiate the authority of an unrighteous rule?[6] It is in this context that the doctrine of the Three Bonds is important to the present discussion. Rooted in ancient China and already formalized by the Later Han, the priority of the Three Bonds was reaffirmed during the Song and made into a virtual "sacred edict" from the Ming on. The neo-Confucians campaigned for it, fully aware of the Buddhist threat to this article in Chinese socioethics.[7] Of these Three Bonds, our focus will be on those between son and father, and minister (or subject) and ruler, as applied to the "orthodoxy" of Zhuhong and the "treachery" of the White Lotus.

Orthodox Accommodation to Family Values

The history of the Buddhist attitude toward China's family ethics has been documented by Michihata Ryōshū and Kenneth Ch'en.[8] A bolder characterization of certain epochal shifts may, however, be appropriate here. As a general rule, the later in time it was, the more accommodating Buddhism would be to traditional Chinese values. That, in one sense, is to be expected. When Buddhism first took root in China during the Age of Disunity, its call to men to leave home and world behind was timely. With the world in chaos, the monastery proved a true refuge spiritually as well as politically and economically.[9] When China was reunited under Sui and Tang, the same offer of a haven from the woes of this world became increasingly less attractive. Meanwhile, the state often reasserted its authority and sought to curtail the privileges granted the sangha. But more than loyalty to the throne, it was filial piety that was being remade more and more into a Buddhist virtue. The Five Dynasties, however, provided renewed instability for new social experiments at community building by Buddhists, Daoists, and Confucians alike. But it was the success of the Song neo-Confucians in revitalizing the family system

and the clan organizations and their conscious campaign against
Buddhism and the foreign (non-Chinese) customs it fostered that
would put the Buddhist monk leaders on the defensive. Times had
changed, and so did the challenge that was once the Buddhist vocation. Before the Tang, the monastic order was a threat to the family
system. After the Tang, the monasteries had turned generally conservative.[10] They served the interest of the family so well that the new
threat to the family now came from some independent Buddhist lay
organizations that sprang up outside the monastic order proper. That
initiative came not from Chan monastics as much as from the Pure
Land devotional associations. How the "heretical" White Lotus grew
out of those is examined later in greater detail. First, a terse review
of the Buddhist attitude toward the family.

Since Gautama left home and attained enlightenment as a
renunciant, there was a distinction made between the higher calling
of the monk and the mundane duties of the lay householder as a
world-bound "family man." If the Chinese Buddhists liked to count
a set of works loosely referred to as "filial sutras," these were based
on the Buddha's teaching intended for laymen. Since renunciation
is not possible for everyone in this lifetime, the Buddha generally
endorsed, for his lay followers, a set of duties tied to the kammatic
world. Though critical of the caste system, he was not about to over-
haul Hindu society. Indian society had its own version of the Three
Bonds, and the Buddha only ameliorated its hierarchic structure with
a fraternal ideal with more stress on the reciprocal duties. So the ruler
should be obligated to the subject, the father to the son, the husband
to the wife, and not just always the other way around. This teaching
of reciprocity, comparable to the golden mean taught by Confucius,
is found in Buddha's instructions to the layman Singala.[11] The one
difference is that the Buddha valued greater achievement ("a brah-
min is what he does—not what he is born into") while Confucius
stayed more with the ascribed roles. The Buddha also made special
allowance for the renunciant as Confucius would not. We see that in
the *Singala Sutta*. The son observes the duty to be filial and obedient to his father; and the father in turn has the duty of providing him
with a wife—unless, of course, the son decides to "leave home." In
that case, no Buddhist parent should stand in the way of the son's
decision but should support it. In Buddhist countries, parents are
more than willing because they would acquire merits for so releasing
a son to the sangha.

Other Buddhist "filial sutras" in China were drawn from the *jatakas* and *avadanas,* stories about the careers of the Buddha or other Buddhas and bodhisattvas. So as a dutiful son, the Buddha went up to the Heaven of the Thirty-Three to preach to his mother, Maya, so that she, who died soon after giving birth to him, would not be denied the opportunity to hear the dharma and attain liberation thereby. So too, in a previous life, the Buddha was the youth Syama, who risked his own life to get deer milk for his parents.[12] Though given filial sutra status by the Chinese Buddhists, these two exemplars do not abrogate the higher status of the nibbanic path. So Maya still bowed to her son and not vice versa. If Syama did not receive homage from his parents, that is because he had not renounced the world yet. In the Six Dynasties, Buddhists cited these stories to appease their Confucian critics and show how Buddhist lay ethics was not against family values. It was not easy but the Buddhist monks in this period held on to their higher calling fairly well. The status distinction between the nibbanic monks and the kammatic laymen, parents included, stayed fairly intact.

The situation changed somewhat in Sui and early Tang. By the sixth century, Buddhist services for the dead had won over many Chinese hearts, somewhat to the chagrin of Confucian ritual purists. The Yulanpen festival, a kind of Buddhist All Souls' Day, had become routine. Based on the *Ullambana Sutra,* it tells of how Mulian aided his mother, suffering in hell, by offering maigre feasts to monks—and any hungry ghost that might be out begging for food that night—and transferring the merits gained thereby to her deliverance. The popularity of this festival was acknowledged by a filial sutra compiled in China. Titled *Fumu Enzhongjing,* it tells of the "heavy debt owed by sons to parents" and how to repay it by feeding hungry ghosts on that autumnal Ghost Festival.[13] Though this was claimed as a Buddhist filial sutra, it has few distinctively Buddhist teachings, so that with a few changes, it became a Daoist text, the *Fumu Enzhongjing* as taught by the Taishang laojun (i.e., Laozi). The tone of the text is too operatic to induce any nirvanic impassivity. Confucian "human feeling" overwhelms Buddhist detachment. At one point, the aged parents complain tearfully to the Buddha about how their son, more attentive now to his new bride, is growing forgetful of them.[14] The *Ullambana Sutra* did not deserve a serious clerical commentary; a tiny episode, it aroused none in Theravada. That Zongmi (780–841) provided such a commentary only showed how the tenor of Buddhism had changed by his time; that he should win kudos for so doing—he still does—says more about the unwitting diluting of the nirvanic dharma by his time and among Zongmi's admirers.

If Zongmi so sinicized Buddhism, Zhuhong in the Ming dynasty would further accommodate his brand of "orthodox" Buddhism to the requirement of filial piety. This we can see by comparing the reading by Zhuhong and that by Zhiyi (538–597) of the Tiantai school of a line from another Chinese-compiled sutra. The *Fanwang jing* (Brahma net sutra) is suspected of being compiled in the Qi dynasty (479–502) in the south. Considered a major "Mahayana Precepts" text, it contains a bold endorsement of filial piety:

> When Sakyamuni attained supreme enlightenment under the bodhi tree, he first formulated the bodhisattvic precepts which call for filial obedience *(xiaoshun)* to parents, to one's Buddhist master, and to the Three Jewels. When *xiao* is perfected, it is none other than *sila* (precept) or self-discipline.[15]

The sentiment resonates with the *Classic of Filial Piety,* a Han text that elevated *xiao* into being the all-encompassing virtue. Coming before its list of major and minor Mahayana precepts, the passage above seems to regard filial piety as the summum bonum of all virtues. Yet if we read the passage in its setting and do not let the single term *"xiao"* leap off the page, then the passage probably says no more than how one should be grateful to one's parents; and how when one joins the order, one should be obedient to one's precept master; and that everyone, lay or monk, should also take refuge in the Buddha, the dharma, and the sangha. That was precisely how the passage was read by Zhiyi, its first major commentator.

Before coming to Zhuhong, we should note some other markers in the history in between. A century after Zhiyi, Shandao (d. 681) of the Pure Land school commented on another sutra, the *Guanjing* (Amitayus-dhyana sutra) and used it to legitimize simple, lay devotion to Amitabha as a means for ordinary people to enter his Western Happy Paradise. The sutra made "filial upkeep of parents" one of the prerequisites for gaining birth in Pure Land, but listed the other requirements, such as "reverent service to [one's Buddhist] master" and general "compassion, nonviolence and the performance of Ten Good Deeds."[16] Shandao's commentary stressed filial duty as a "heavy debt owed the parents."[17] Without them, we would not be here. But Shandao had enough good Buddhist sense not to play up, as the *Fumu enzhongjing* would, the biological tie between parent and child—at least, not any further than necessary. That is because in Confucianism, we are beholden to parents for our being. But in Buddhism, we are ultimately the authors of our own rebirth, our parents (semen and womb) supplying only the secondary condition, *pratyaya*, necessary for karmic transmigration.[18] That fine distinction known to Shandao[19] would later be blurred by Zhuhong who ruled, as the sutra did not, that unfilial sons are not eligible for Pure Land.[20]

A century after Shandao, Zongmi, who advocated a unity of the Three Teachings, sang the praises of *xiao* sky high in his commentary on the *Yulanpenjing*. There, enlarging upon the passage in the *Fanwang jing* cited earlier, he said: "Filial piety fills Heaven and Earth from the beginning of time; it is what unites men and gods, the superiors and the subordinates; it is revered by Buddhists and Confucians alike." And "the prince Siddhārtha left the throne and home because he hoped that by attaining the Dao he might so repay his parents.... Mulian hoped to save his parents and repay their kindness, received as a baby, so he left home to cultivate the Way until he secured the first supernatural power that allowed him to see his mother suffering as a hungry ghost."[21] This is putting the cart before the horse and reversing the nibbanic/kammatic values. The Buddha left home in a quest for nirvana; he did not look for the Truth to repay his parents. Mulian left home before his mother passed away; he did not cultivate yogic powers just to acquire the ability to see where she ended up. Zongmi had turned the monk's vocation into a means to fulfilling filial piety.[22]

Zhuhong and the Confucianization of Buddhism

Zongmi was writing in the Tang dynasty. By the Ming, with neo-Confucianism being made a state ideology, Zhuhong would yield even more to the demand for filial compliance. He knew personally that when a son left home and assumed a new Buddhist name, he had left his natal self and family behind. For that reason, he should no more bow to his parents. In Theravada society, the Buddhist parents would know well enough to bow to him instead. In Ming society, though, where such a gesture was frowned upon by the neo-Confucian mainstream, Zhuhong knew better than to offend that external orthodoxy. He echoed its view: parents should not have to bow to a son who had joined the order; the latter should bow to the parents instead. Why? Because "parents are like Buddhas to him."[23] Of course, if the parents as pious laymen should choose to return the favor and bow to their son-turned-monk, Zhuhong would understand. But he would rather have those knowing parents hasten forward to prevent their dutiful son from completing the bow.[24] A *vinaya* purist might charge Zhuhong with being "less than Buddhist," but for Zhuhong, who truly believed in a possible unity of the Three Teachings (and did so with less of a hierarchic structure, compared with Zongmi), filial piety could well be seen as a Buddhist virtue to be observed by lay and monk alike. In the ledger of merits and demerits *Zizhi lu* (Record of self-knowledge), he rated filial piety highest under the category of good deeds.[25] He even bothered to compile a record of the lives of twelve filial monks, showing how their nibbanic calling was not incompatible with this kammatic duty.[26]

There is always a place in Buddhist literature for such apologetic treatises. A proposal supportive of a Unity of the Three Teachings need not be contrary to the Buddha dharma. The question remains always: at what point might such compromises distort the original intent of a Buddhist teaching? A good test case would be Zhuhong's 1594 compilation, *Wangshengji* (Record of [pious faithfuls gaining] yonder birth [in Pure Land]). It is based largely on previous collections. The preface notes:

> Herein have I selected 166 cases [of reported birth in Pure Land], adding here and there critical comments in order to bring out the hidden message. Titled *Wangshengji*, it is offered in hope that a person would, upon reading it, recognize [the truth] that so-and-so achieved liberation . . . ; so-and-so was single-minded . . . ; so-and-so was most sincere . . . ; so-and-so was compassionate . . . ; so-and-so was repentant at the last minute thereby changing his fate—and how these all thereby were born in Pure Land.[27]

When Zhuhong's retelling of these legends is checked against the earlier versions, we find telling redactions of the originals and, in his appended remarks, new agendas. For example, Zhuhong edited out a famous episode in Huiyuan's life. At his conversion to the dharma, Huiyuan declared, "Confucianism, Daoism and the Nine Branches [of teachings] were chaff" when compared with the truth of the Buddha's insight. Finding that judgment offensive to his commitment to a unity of the Three Teachings, Zhuhong left it out.[28] Prizing filial piety, he also added an aside to the life of Liu Yimin, noting how Liu was a filial son. Liu was a famous lay follower in the Lotus Society headed by Huiyuan of Lushan, but no prior *wangsheng* collection thought his filial piety was pertinent to his birth in Pure Land.[29] Zhuhong went further than that. Noting how the *Guanjing* had ranked filial piety as first among the pure deeds and a prime qualification for entering Pure Land, he concluded that a person who is not filial would never attain Pure Land, however diligent he might be in chanting (calling upon) Amitabha.[30] That is overstating the case. The sutra did not make filial piety a prerequisite for admission. To do so would be putting "good works" ahead of or above "sincere and deep faith." This moral conservatism on Zhuhong's part is most evident when he consciously redacted the case of Hongjun, a monk who "broke precepts, misused collected donations, left the order to become a soldier [to kill, thus taking life] and then rejoined the order to avoid persecution." In the original version, when Yama was about to drag Hongjun off to Hell, Hongjun shouted, "If I should enter hell, it would prove the Buddha a liar." The reason? Because anyone who sincerely chanted Amitabha's name was promised salvation. Yama yielded and Hongjun was ferried off to the Western Paradise.[31] An annoying tale—it ruffles our sense of justice—it was also sacred lore. No compiler ever tried to tamper with this case of "an evil man gaining yonder birth" until a moralistic Zhuhong found it necessary to tell "what really happened."

> Hongjun of Tang was a native of Chengdu. An audacious man, he would not keep to the monastic precepts. He left the order at one point to become a soldier and then rejoined it. Just because he heard the *sutra* say, "With just one praise of the name of the Buddha, eight million *kalpas* of sins are erased," he rejoiced and said, "I can rely on this." Although he was evil, he recited the name nonstop. In the second lunar month (of what would be 1252), he suddenly passed away but then came back to life. He had been, he said, dragged down to hell but was told that he had been summoned by mistake. "Though you practice *nianfo* [recitation of the name of Amitabha Buddha]," the hell official said, "you lack deep faith. Go back to your lot on earth and persevere the more." People thought he was lucky to have escaped hell thus. What actually happened is that he then retired to the mountains, kept to a vegetarian diet and practiced *nianfo* for four

more years. It was in the third lunar month (of what would be 1256) that he summoned the people and told them of his imminent departure. He had a message sent to his parents in the city, informing them how he gained Pure Land by *nianfo* and not just by a lucky chance. Amidst the chit-chat and the laughter, he passed away while cross-legged.[32]

Zhuhong had rewritten the narrative so that the evil man made good by years of penance between the two deaths. He also turned the man into a filial son, dutifully reporting to his parents before his final leave-taking.[33] So successful was Zhuhong's insistence that only good men or women are eligible for salvation that in the Qing collection of this genre, the *Jingtu shengxianlu* (Record of sages and worthies of the Pure Land), the category of "evil men gaining birth" disappeared altogether.[34] The compiler, the layman Peng Shaosheng (also Jiqing, or Chimu, 1740–1796), was clearly influenced by Zhuhong, whom Peng regarded as his spiritual mentor. The frightening thing about this Qing collection is that all candidates for salvation were proverbially filial sons, loyal officials, or chaste widows. It is as if Pure Land admits only people of neo-Confucian moral rectitude—like, say, a Christian Heaven populated only by WASPs.[35] Such redaction of Buddhist tradition makes one wonder if the mainline Buddhists had not bent too far backward in their accommodation to external orthodoxy. And if so, the reverse question is then whether there might not be just cause for the emergence of the proverbially maligned White Lotus heretics.

A Higher Loyalty: The White Lotus Rebels

At first glance, Buddhism should not condone rebellions. As Buddhists are committed to nonviolence, there are few recorded armed uprisings in Indian or Southeast Asian Buddhist histories, at least not until the modern period as notably in Sri Lanka and Burma. Even Korea and Japan, which knew some Buddhist-inspired rebellions, had nothing as persistent as the one attributed to the White Lotus in late dynastic China. In China, Buddhist-led revolts had a long history. They went as far back as the late Northern Wei period. The Tuoba rulers had tapped into the world-conquering ideology of Buddhist politics. They billed themselves as Tathagata-Kings and regarded the crown prince as a future Tathagata, that is, Maitreya.[36] Little wonder that peasant rebels copied that and used similar sym bols in their cause. One early sixth-century movement called itself Dacheng (Mahayana); and a first explicitly Maitreyan rebellion was recorded under Sui. In that sense, the White Lotus rebellion led by Han Shantong in the fourteenth century was a continuation of that legacy. The major difference is that the White Lotus was originally an Amitabha cult seeking rebirth in the Pure Land. Somehow by late Yuan, Maitreyan millenarianism became a part of its teaching. Leaving that ideological history to others,[37] we will consider below the organizational innovations.

The Protestant Reformation has been called a "revolt of the laity" because the priesthood of all believers made it possible for the layman to usurp what was once the prerogative of the priest. As an "inner worldly ascetic," he could also co-opt the lifestyle of the monk. To appreciate the White Lotus heresy, we have to consider the possibility of a similar development within Chinese Buddhism. It is well known that the Buddha, in organizing his fellow renunciates into a fraternity, turned eremites into monastics. That was a historical first. The monastic sangha then held itself up as an alternative social organization. Because the Buddha set the sangha off from regular society, he also left the Hindu caste society basically unchanged. The monks did not have to, but the laymen should honor their parents and obey their kings. The clear divide between the kammatic and the nibbanic, this world and the other shore, has fostered the impression that this is a tradition of "otherworldly mystics" who could little change the socioeconomic structure of this world. That is not true; we just need to know where to look. Under favorable conditions, the fraternal organization of the sangha could impinge upon or be emulated by the lay world. In theory, Mahayana claimed to bridge the divide between samsara and nirvana, the householder bodhisattva and the monk bodhisattva. As a major text of bodhisattvic precepts, the *Fanwang jing* sang the praise of filial piety (in one passing line, cited earlier). It also laid out this communal ideal that looks far beyond the natal family:

> With a heart of compassion, practice the release of life (freeing captive men or animals). [That is because] all men are my father and all women are my mother. In all my many past rebirths, I have assumed

so many different life forms that (in some way), all living things in the six paths of rebirth are [could well have been once] my parents. Those who take life are taking the life of my parents and my life.[38]

This might appear to be a simple, harmless, common, pious sentiment of no great consequence. A person usually does not think that way; no normal person seriously considers his household cat and dog to be his parents. But the sentiment is not untrue. This idea of a brotherhood of all living things underwrites a universal ethics of mutual obligation known as *bao'en* that does inform Buddhist behavior. *Bao'en* extends the ethics of reciprocity captured in the native word *"bao"* itself.[39] That this call to love even nonhumans seems impractical—Weber called it "acosmic"—does not mean it could not be brought down to a manageable level and be made realizable as a social experiment. The Christian Church was founded on the principle of its being an alternate family to the natal one.[40] In Chinese Buddhist history, the first major organization of laymen into a larger sangha family occurred under the Northern Wei. Tanyao created it on Buddhist preceptory grounds. The sangha-household experiment founded in 470–476 drew in peasant families, even whole villages. Called *yiyi*, the villages *(yi)* were "adopted" *(yi)* as extended members *(huren)* of a household attached to the sangha as a "family of monks" *(sengjia)*.[41] The fraternity of the monk fellowship had been extended to this predominantly lay householder community. It is suspected that the *Fanwang jing* was inspired by the same Mahayana bodhisattvic ethics that were being brought to the South from migrating northern monks.

The sangha-household experiment was so successful that it invited a persecution by the state in 574. So much sangha grain was bound up in this association of confessional peasant families (they gathered every fortnight to chant their simple lay precepts) that the state had to reclaim its lost revenue by force. Administered initially by conscientious monk elders adhering to a Buddhist principle of economic justice (equal division of donation among the Three Jewels with aid going also to the needy), its demise was lamented openly by the *Xiangfa jueyi jing* (Sutra to resolve doubts in the age of the semblance dharma), compiled in North China between 517 and 520. The text recalled the design of the merit fields, one to glorify the Three Jewels and one to aid the orphaned and the widowed—all sentient beings, down to the tiniest of ants.[42] The second one, being based on compassion, is ranked higher.

> Sons of Good Families, in the future age when myriad ills arise, monks and laymen alike should cultivate great friendliness and compassion, bear all kinds of derision and think only of how all human beings are from beginningless time one's father, mother, brother, sister, wife, and relative. Because of that, one should show all human beings compassion, helping all according to one's ability, risking one's life if necessary in exercising such means to aid the needy.[43]

The text was not excessively eschatological. It spoke of the passing of the age of the true dharma and dated itself to the then-current *xiangfa* (semblance dharma) era. The later White Lotus movement would respond to a more anxious *mofa* (end of dharma) crisis. More importantly, the text defended the right of sangha self-rule and protested the abuse by secular officials of both "the servants and the property of the Three Jewels." That change came about after 512 when the clerical bureau lost firm control over the sangha grain; by 574 the sangha was disestablished altogether. Nonetheless, a precedent had been created and the stage would be set for future Buddhist protests against "rendering unto Caesar" what belonged to the Buddha. The right to sangha autonomy, the extralegal exemption from tax, draft and corvee labor as well as the sanctity of its holdings would fuel later Buddhist movements that the state naturally dubbed heretical but which could well just be the pious souls answering to a higher authority. In this essay, we skip the Buddhist organizational developments in the Tang.[44]

The sangha-household experiment was never called heretical because it was set up under the auspices of the ruler in response to a petition from the official head of the sangha. The monk elders were behind this program; the lay peasant householders who took their precepts from the monks never dared to displace or challenge the clerical leadership.[45] Such was not always the case in the new devotion and organization that sprang up in the Song dynasty. A "revolt of the laity" under a consciously Mahayanist banner was a real possibility. Instead of a two-tiered (monk and lay) hierarchy, there was this new vision of cosmic bodhisattvic "interdependence" with universal buddha-nature now granted for all.[46]

The White Lotus movement began as one such pious *nianfo* society.[47] Mahayana in intent, the message was liberation and not, as with the sangha-household, just a better rebirth within the paths of men and gods. The means to attaining it was primarily through faith and not through works. To the extent that monks previously earned their higher standing by their cultivation of pure deeds, this emphasis on *nianfo* and faith (which was accessible to everybody) undermined their special standing somewhat. The perception that mankind was living in the evil *mofa* age only leveled the monk/lay distinction even more. A pious "householder bodhisattva" could now even be presumptuous enough to lecture the monks. And this did happen. Song lay evangelical Wang Rixiu, in his *Longshu jingtuwen* (Writings on the Pure Land by the lay Buddhist Longshu), so lectured monks about the superior path of faith. The Northern Wei Buddhists were known for copying sutras and sponsoring stupas or statues. The Song Pure Land pietists, out to save souls, were more into popular pamphleteering and preaching. So many monk and lay alike were swept up in this religious zeal that if we go by a naive numerical count of lives told in the *wangsheng* records, then more people in Song went to Pure Land than ever before or, for that matter, ever after.

Song society also witnessed a flourishing of "release of life" societies (buying up birds, turtles, fishes and releasing them to water and air)[48] as well as lay observance of a vegetarian diet. Such facts might seem minor or incidental, but considering how *ahimsa* (nonviolence to life) was the prerogative of the monks, this amounted to the laity co-opting the sanctity of monkhood. Since Chinese Buddhist monks were distinguished from the regular laymen primarily in just two areas (food and sex),[49] the lay abstinence from meat in the diet was a symbolic act of consequence. In the balance of merits, it raised the layman's sanctity far more than we moderns might realize. It is in this context of a cultivated "revolt of the laity" that we should appraise the birth of the White Lotus.

The Roots of the White Lotus "Heresy"

The Song period was when the legend of Huiyuan founding a "White Lotus" association at Lushan gained currency and got blown out of proportion. People then emulated his example and started founding *nianfo hui* all over. It started with eminent monks enrolling cultured

gentlemen. Soon after, the cultured lay gentlemen organized themselves in similarly small and rather exclusive groups. Then around
A.D. 1000 the size of such groups exploded, and a shift in leadership
soon became noticeable. The catalyst, the figure responsible for this
change, was the learned Tiantai monk, Master Siming Zhili (960–
1028). He came up with the idea of opening membership to the elite
and the populace alike to form a society ten-thousand-members
strong based on a multiple of the number (48) of vows Amitabha
made:

> The way to form a *she* is to recruit first 210 group leaders, each com-
> missioned to recruit 48 members. Each of the [10,080] members is
> to recite a list of Buddha-names, confess [sins], and make the [bodhi-
> sattvic] vow [of wisdom and compassion]. . . . There will be a record
> kept [on a calendar] which is to be delivered together with 48 strings
> of cash to the [main] temple on an annual basis. At the death of each
> member, all fellow members must attend the passage chanting the
> Buddha's name [a duty only overridden by death in one's own fam-
> ily or that of one's original Buddhist master; a new member is to be
> recruited to fill the slot].[50]

So successful was Zhili with this model of organizing the devotional groups of which so many people wanted to be a part, he had
to farm it out to others, who set up their own satellite groups. This
growth was not just a matter of the more the merrier, because
according to the Buddhist accounting of merits, "sharing in the gift
and the joy of recompense" multiplies the beneficence geometrically.
In Mahayana this *jieyuan* (making connections) further contributes to
an infinite network of enlightenment.[51] A preceptory record of sponsorship and membership would be scrupulously kept at the head-
quarter temple; a list of dues, duties, and obligations followed that;
all the while the ardent hope was held that all the members would
literally meet again in the Pure Land. This method of evangelizing
was duly adopted by Mao Ziyuan (1086–1166), the founder of the
original "orthodox" White Lotus society. Remnants of that practice
can still be detected in the way the later "heretical" White Lotus
organized itself.

No heretic ever considers himself heretical as charged; trusting
he is in the right, he would just as readily reverse the accusation. So
how the "orthodox" White Lotus "devolved" into the "heterodox"

White Lotus was never that simple an affair. If we look at the four standard charges lodged against the heretics, we can find their roots or inspirations to have come no less from the orthodox forerunners.[52]

First, it is said that the White Lotus *zhai,* or vegetarian community, repudiated family and state. The reference to *zhai* here might not be accidental. Vegetarianism was being cultivated as a mark of a holy life, the sanctity of which could challenge both family and state. It also happened to be a mark of the Manicheans. At issue here is how membership in the White Lotus could have set a devotee apart from and above regular society as if he were a monk. The answer would be that Mao Ziyuan made this more possible with certain innovations. He subsumed, or telescoped, the observance of the five lay precepts (not to kill, steal, indulge in sex, lie, or drink alcoholic beverages) into five *nianfo* chants. He condensed the whole of the Mahayana teachings into a four-character mantra: *pu jue miao dao* (universal enlightenment into the wonderful Way), which he then used for making up the dharma-names of his followers. Granting such names to laymen could amount to creating a lay order.[53] We find such usage in orthodox monks' names like Pudu; we find its continual usage by Luo Qing and his sect, even after he severed all ties with the heretical White Lotus.[54] Members sworn to a brotherhood designated with such dharma names were obligated to render assistance to one another. Under special circumstances, that obligation might even supersede the duties to kin and king.

Second, it was said that the White Lotus heretics violated the monk precepts. If by that it is meant they were not strict monastics, this could be due to the further laicization of the faith after the time of Mao Ziyuan. A certain Little Mao succeeded him and led a "neither monk nor lay" *(feiseng feisu)* fellowship that repudiated celibacy and encouraged married priesthood. The charge of "neither monk nor lay" also hounded Shinran in Japan; like Luther, Shinran also married an ex-nun. If Luther granted thereby a calling *(beruf)* to lay professions, Little Mao could also have made it possible for the laymen to claim the same. Unlike with Luther and Shinran, there is no indication that White Lotus leveled the monk/lay distinction on the grounds of man's inherent and universal sinfulness. Rather, Mao Ziyuan made access to Pure Land easy and open to all. He justified this by transcribing the Tiantai theory of the Four Pure Lands into "one single page," and he condensed their essentials into four diagrams, each just "one inch square." Concerning Amitabha's Pure Land, he wrote:

> Few know this way of cutting across the Three Realms.
> But have no doubt about its being the Easy Path.
> Though defilement remains, one may be enlightened as such.
> So just single-mindedly trust his vow and chant his name.
> The proper recollection at death secures a sure birth.
> Within three or five days one's destiny is known.
> Once there, you hear the Dharma preached perpetually.
> Who needs fear not being counted among the enlightened?
>
>> Explanatory note [by Mao Ziyuan]: Here there is no termination of defilement, no abandoning of family and home, no need to cultivate meditation (as the monk's vocation traditionally would require).[55]

Mao eliminated the grades of the three paths (for monk, nun, and layman) and considered Amitabha's Pure Land—deemed lowest and the most expedient of the four in the original Tiantai understanding—the easiest but also the most all-inclusive (containing the lights, sun, moon, stars, of the other three). In endorsing its "mixed residence of sages and commoners" (monk and layman), he could have provided the pretext for Little Mao to initiate a married clergy. That probable conflation of monk status and lay status was in part a by-product of Song and Yuan policy. The Song state could supervise the sangha more effectively than the Tang had been able to do. But to raise needed revenue, it also started selling "monk certificates." The initial sale was priced low, so many laymen bought monkhood-in-name. The second sale was priced so high that many monks ended up nominally as laymen. That created this "neither-monk-nor-lay" phenomenon. Some of these ended up in a class known as "men of the Way," and they seem to have staffed the devotional group known as the White Cloud.[56]

Third, it was said that the White Lotus practiced acts of licentiousness. The first detailed report on this by Pudu seems to substantiate it. The sect compared the act of intercourse to realizing the oneness of dharmata *(heyixiang)*. This could just be using a Mahayana nondual wisdom to sanctify a married life. The reason could also be location: the White Lotus that emerged in north China spread and flourished in areas where the new Daoist sects of the Song-Yuan era also flourished. Sexo-yoga had a long history in Daoist practice. That itself could also have been influenced by the Tantrism patronized by the Yuan court.[57]

Fourth, it was said that the White Lotus sectarians "gathered at night and dispersed in the morning, practicing vegetarianism and serving the devil." The description fits easily the Manicheans who served Mo, for Moni or Mani. Mani had traveled to India and incorporated Buddhist ascetic practices into his church. Centuries later, Chinese Manicheans followed tradition and regarded both the Buddha and Mani as saviors. Though we have yet to know exactly how Manichean beliefs entered into a Maitreyanized Pure Land tradition,[58] it is not too difficult to imagine their mutual attraction. With the Pure Land equated with a pure mind, the paradise beyond could be moved into the here and now. Such a Chan-inspired reading of Pure Land is found in the poems of Mao Ziyuan. And since Song Pure Land pietists vowed to return to this world as bodhisattvas to better their society, that social activism could easily take a millenarian form of helping to hasten a Maitreyan reign. With Mani being called the Buddha of Light and Amitabha being the Buddha of Eternal Light, the two could slide easily into one another. In a cosmic battle between Light and Darkness at the end of time, Light will triumph.[59] Now, the Manichean tradition had had a long history in China, going back to perhaps even the fifth century. After being banned in the 845 persecution, it went underground, apparently blending its dualism with the yin-yang paradigm, and succeeded in having its scriptures included in the Song Daoist canon. Manicheans not only observed vegetarianism as the sectarian Buddhists might, but they also dressed in white—and the expression "the white-clothed" *(baiyi)* applied equally to the Buddhist laity. And it just so happened that Maitreya would be born to a *Cakravartin* (cosmic king) who would unite the world, while in Manicheaism, a similar Mingwang (King of Light) was expected to come at the end of time. Somehow the two myths fused into a historical reality: the White Lotus rebellion that toppled the Mongol rule and put Ming Taizu, as that King of Light, on the throne.

This essay has described, in a general and theoretical fashion, two major trends of development affecting monastic and lay Buddhism. If we think of Buddhism as being divided into two tiers and two paths, namely, the monk's nibbanic quest and the layman's kammatic duties, then it may be said that after the Ming, the mainline monks increasingly accommodated the requirements of filial piety—until a Zhuhong would endorse the external orthodoxy of a neo-Confucian society. Meanwhile, elements within the laity sought independence and some even hoped to bring about a new brotherhood of men on earth—which resulted in the extremism of the White Lotus. Judged seditious by the state and considered heretical by the mainstream monks, the White Lotus could well be the "revolt of the laity" that China knew. It was similar to, but it also fell short of, the Protestant Reformation in the West or the new Buddhism of Kamakura. These sectarians lived fairly peaceful lives most of the time, but some of them could and did turn violent at intervals, not unlike the episodes of the Anabaptists in Germany or the *ikko ikki* in Japan. That the White Lotus did not gain legitimacy is not without reason. One irony, though, is that, in one sense, it succeeded all too well. It put an ex-monk on the throne who just decided to turn his back to it. It is that which created, since the Ming, a new two-tiered structure in the sangha. With respectable clerics like Zhuhong "purifying" monastic practices, the less respectable lay groups, unguided or misguided, drifted further and further from the standards of the old canonical Buddhism. They went their own way and later found their own voice in a new set of scriptures, the *baojuan* (precious scrolls). They worshiped a new deity, the Wusheng Laomu (the Venerable Mother of the Unborn), her name expressing Buddhist ideas and native cults. In this sense, apropos of the topic of orthodoxy and heterodoxy, what we perhaps have is that while neo-Confucianism became the state ideology, the folk Buddhist religions—to use Overmyer's term—held out to the people the hope of a utopia.[60]

Notes

1. On the use and abuse of the phrase "White Lotus," see Barend J. ter Haar, *The White Lotus Teachings in Chinese Religious History* (Leiden: E. J. Brill, 1992).

2. The mainstream Byzantine Church might consider Nestorius to be a heretic; but east of Edessa on the Silk Road, Nestorian and other Gnostic churches were de facto (and de jure, by their own council) the mainline churches.

3. Calling that "State Buddhism," as if there were a unilateral control of the sangha by the state, is like reducing the Orthodox or the Anglican Church to being nothing more than Caesaropapism. That simply oblit-

erates the many complicated and nuanced negotiations that went on between "church and state" in the Northern Dynasties, maneuvers that gave Buddhism there a strength the monks in the Southern Dynasties— where Huiyuan did not bow before the king—never knew.

4. See Edward L. Farmer, "Social Regulations of the First Ming Emperor: Orthodoxy as a Function of Authority," in Kwang-Ching Liu, ed., *Orthodoxy in Late Imperial China* (Berkeley: University of California Press, 1990), 103–125.

5. Contrast this evaluation with a thorough, and more kind, treatment of Zhuhong by Chün-fang Yü, *Renewal of Buddhism in China: Chu-hung and the Late Ming Synthesis* (New York: Columbia University Press, 1981); see chap. 1, 1–8.

6. For these concepts, see S. J. Tambiah, *World Conqueror and World Renouncer: A Study of Buddhism and Polity in Thailand against a Historical Background* (Cambridge: Cambridge University Press, 1976).

7. See Kwang-Ching Liu, "Socioethics as Orthodoxy: A Perspective," in *Orthodoxy in Late Imperial China*, 64–100; also Fung Yu-lan, *A History of Chinese Philosophy*, 2 vols., trans. Derk Bodde (Princeton: Princeton University Press, 1953), 2:566–571, 610–612.

8. Michihata Ryōshū, *Bukkyō to Jukyō rinri* [Buddhism and Confucian ethics] (Kyoto: Heirakuji, 1968); and Kenneth Ch'en, *The Chinese Transformation of Buddhism* (Princeton: Princeton University Press, 1973).

9. In the north, Buddhist holy men turned hierocrats protected the flock by pleading its case before the foreign rulers. Temple manors in both north and south, winning privileges, then took in peasants as tenants or as serfs. In an age of war, these temple manors acted as sanctuaries; they prospered and often survived better than the secular manors.

10. Owing either to a conservative turn within or to pressure from without, the Song Chan monasteries were more ready to compromise with family values than before. So Chan monks regularly delivered sermons at a lay patron's funeral. Buddhist funerals soon became the major source of monastic income, as land was donated to the "merit cloisters" set up for the welfare of the departed. See the chapter on Song "grave cloisters," in Chikusa Masaaki, *Chūgoku bukkyō shakaishi kenkyū* [Study of Chinese Buddhist social history] (Kyoto: Dōhōsha, 1982), 111–143. This monastic function (and income) was undercut by similar offerings from non-Buddhist, clan-based counterparts, especially under the Qing.

11. Pali, *Singavada-sutta;* see *Taishō Shinshu Daizokyō* (Tokyo: Kanko Kai, 1924–1934; henceforth *T*), 1:251b; see also Ch'en, *Chinese Transformation*, 19 n.

12. See Ch'en, *Chinese Transformation*, 20–23, 34–35; Michihata, *Bukkyō to Jukyō rinri*, 64, 77–78. Recast as a Chinese youth, Syama made his way into the Song compilation of the *Twenty-Four Tales of Filial Piety*.

13. See Michihata, *Bukkyō to Jukyō rinri*, 90–100. Michihata infers from the impoverished background of the parents that the text is of lower-class origin. Not so. The language is far too polished; and the depiction of poverty was only a literary device to highlight their suffering.

14. One should not drag God or Buddha into family quarrels. In Sri Lanka, Buddhists observe a division of labor between the Buddha detached from the world and Hindu gods involved in the same. The emotionally charged Hindu gods are there to handle human affairs. Not the impassive Buddha.

15. *T* 24:10004a. The translation is mine; see Ch'en, *Chinese Transformation*, 30, where *shiseng* is read as "teacher and monk" instead of "Buddhist master."

16. See *T* 12:277a.

17. See *T* 39:505a; also excerpted in Ch'en, *Chinese Transformation*, 40.

18. Strictly speaking, it is the *vijnāna* (consciousness) burdened with *samskāra* (karmic impulse) that assumes *namarūpa* (name-and-form, i.e., human existence) in accordance with the law of the twelve chains of causation.

19. See Shandao, *Guanjingshu*, *T* 37:259a–b; Ch'en, *Chinese Transformation*, 41, has a less exact translation of the chain of causation involved.

20. According to the *Guanjing*, only those who committed one of the five grave sins [murder of father, of mother, of *arhat*; making the Buddha bleed; and sowing dissension in the fellowship] would not be admissible to the Pure Land. Otherwise any repentant wayward son could still be saved. See Mochizuki Shinkō, *Bukkyō daijiten* [Buddhist dictionary], (Tokyo: Sekai seiten Kankō Kyōkai, 1933–1936), 1124c–1126b.

21. *T* 39:505a; my translation.

22. To be fair, Zongmi was writing here as an apologist. He knew well the higher goals of Buddhism; see his "Essay on Man" *(Yuanrenlun)*.

23. The argument is the same as Faguo's justification for bowing before Northern Wei Emperor Taizu (r. 386–409). More observers criticized Faguo than Zhuhong.

24. Michihata, *Bukkyō to Jukyō rinri*, 244 and 293–295. This is a privilege granted superiors. The son-turned-monk should also so interrupt his parents' gesture. No such diplomacy is needed in Theravada Sri Lanka.

25. Yü, *Renewal of Buddhism in China*, Appendix 1, item no. 1, p. 233. Loyalty to the ruler comes soon after, in item no. 8.

26. No one before Zhuhong felt the need to do such a compilation, although there is a Korean text (*T* 49:1017b–c) that does include filial piety as a category of Buddhist virtues.

27. *T* 51:126c. Prior collections did not find it necessary to explain the moral lessons of the legends.

28. Compare his account (*T* 51:127a) with any previous *Wangsheng-zhuan* account of Huiyuan; see his biography as translated by E. Zürcher, *The Buddhist Conquest of China*, 2 vols. (Leiden: E. J. Brill, 1959), 1:240.

29. *T* 51:138b. Liu's filiality is reported in his biography found in the dynastic record.

30. *T* 51:138c.

31. From the *Wangsheng xifang Jingtu Ruiyingzhuan* [Record of auspicious responses concerning birth in the Western Pure Land] in *T* 51:106b.

32. *T* 51:146c.

33. Filial sons are required to inform their parents upon going out of or returning to the house.

34. Zhuhong retained this category of "evil men's rebirth" in his *Wangshengji* but, fearful that the idea might be abused, stipulated that the doctrine of "evil men gaining birth" was meant for "evil men of the past" and not "evil men of the present." Men in the past learned a lesson; men of the present are just opportunists. "Those in the past were good men within the evil lot; those in the present are evil men of the evil lot." See *T* 51:147b.

35. Of course, since one does not usually speak ill of the dead, most people who went to Pure Land in the earlier collections were also proverbially "good men and women." They typically "believed in karmic retribution" or "worshiped the Three Jewels." The Ming-Qing collections just dressed them up in Confucian moral gowns instead. The Japanese *Myōkō-ninden* did better in this regard; it preserves the Buddhist intent, or a deep faith, even as it accommodates to the feudal morality.

36. Cakravartins and the Tathagata share the same set of extraordinary bodily marks, allowing their identities to overlap. Under Northern Wei, it is thought that the reigning king was perceived as the Buddha of the present while the crown prince was decked out as the bodhisattva of the future.

37. As an object of devotion, Amitabha overshadowed Maitreya by the Tang period. Xuanzang did give Maitreya renewed respect, and Empress Wu even claimed to be him/her. But after that, Maitreya generally was eclipsed until he was revived in Yuan. In Korea and Japan, Maitreya tended to have national and regal—not populist—associations. Textually and iconographically, Maitreya (the friendly one) was not presented as militant except in China. See chapter 2, by Richard Shek, in this volume.

38. *T* 24:1006b.

39. See Lien-sheng Yang, "The Concept of *Pao* (Reciprocity) as a Basis for Social Relationship in China," in John K. Fairbank ed., *Chinese Thought and Institutions* (Chicago: Chicago University Press, 1957), 291–309.

40. This is captured in a Gospel narrative: Being summoned home by his mother, Jesus declared his fellowship to be his brothers and sisters.

41. These remarks are drawn from my essay "The Earliest Buddhist

Folk Religion: the *Ti-wei Po-li ching* and its Historical Significance," in David W. Chappell ed. *Buddhist and Taoist Practices in Medieval Chinese Society*, in the series *Buddhist and Taoist Studies II* (Honolulu: University of Hawai'i Press, 1987), 11–35; and from "Dating the Hsiang-fa chueh-i ching," in *Annual Memoirs of the Otani University Shin Buddhist Comprehensive Research Institute* 4 (1986): 61–91.

42. *T* 85:1336b.

43. *T* 85:1338a.

44. On the *she* in Tang, see three essays on this topic by Naba Toshisada in his *Tōdai shakai bunkashi kenkyū* [Studies in the social and cultural history of Tang Buddhism] (Tokyo: Sōbunsha, 1974) and the more recent studies of Chikusa Masaaki, *Chūgoku bukkyō shakaishi kenkyū,* part 2, on Dunhuang Buddhist communities, 329–557.

45. I do not want to overly romanticize this early Buddhist communitarianism. The peasants as members of a monastic manor would, by mid-Tang, be turned into tenant farmers. And in the powerful Dunhuang temple estates, records (admittedly late) indicate that the "serf/servants" were indentured slaves, because offspring born to such serfs in marriages contracted with outsiders were deemed to be temple-owned.

46. This ideology was formulated already by Xinxing of the Three Periods Sect that innovated a city-based "Inexhaustible Treasure" (a community chest) during the Tang dynasty. Supervised by monks, this too was eventually outlawed by the state.

47. The analysis in this chapter is drawn from my study of the *wangshengzhuan* genre in "Tales of Birth in Pure Land and the Later Pure Land Tradition," in James Foard, Michael Solomon, Richard Payne eds. *The Pure Land Tradition: History and Development* in the Berkeley Buddhist Studies series (Berkeley: University of California Press, 1996), 173–232. Basic statistics can be found in Ogasawara Senshū, *Chūgoku Jōdōkyōka no kenkyū* [Studies in the teachings of the Chinese Pure Land masters] (Kyoto: Heirakuji, 1951), esp. 81–99, and *Chūgoku kinsei jōdōkyōshi no kenkyū* [Studies in the history of early modern Chinese Pure Land teaching] (Kyoto: Hakke'en, 1962), esp. 46–49.

48. On this cult, see Takao Giken, *Sōdai bukkyōshi no kenkyū* [Study of Song dynasty Buddhist history] (Kyoto: Hakke'en, 1975). Zhuhong is considered an authority on how to conduct this rite to release life.

49. Except in very strict monasteries that Zhuhong would revive, the average monk in China observed basically only the novice's ten precepts, five more than the layman. Wine, judging from Dunhuang manuscripts, had long been a part of the monk's permissible diet. Clothing, shaven head, and residences are, of course, different, but the lay Buddhist retiree could imitate most of that.

50. From *Siming Zhili jiaoxinglu* [Record of the teaching and conduct

of (Master) Siming Zhili]; my translation with interpolated explanations. For a more literal rendition, see Kenneth Ch'en, *Buddhism in China* (Princeton: Princeton University Press, 1964), 402–403 n.

51. For the Tang contribution to this networking technique and mystique, see the classic analysis by Naba Toshisada, *Tōdai shakai bunkashi kenkyū*, esp. 459–574.

52. For details on the charges, see ter Haar, *White Lotus Teachings*, chap. 2, 44–55.

53. Shek and Noguchi find that a wife having joined the society earlier than her later-joining spouse would be acknowledged as his senior. See chapter 7 in this volume. Naquin writes in reference to some White Lotus sectarians: "Pupils regularly paid ritual obeisance to their teachers, even if the latter were younger or female—that is, sect hierarchy took precedence over conventional relationships." Susan Naquin, "The Transmission of White Lotus Sectarianism in Late Imperial China," in David Johnson, Andrew Nathan, and Evelyn Rawski, eds., *Popular Culture in Late Imperial China* (Berkeley: University of California Press, 1985), 281. This went beyond the monastic Buddhist norm, where nuns traditionally defer to monks, are segregated, and always walk behind the male elders. Generally, the secular triad-type of "secret societies" seems to set greater store by the rankings according to age, generation, and sex among the families of members. Cf. articles by Shek and Noguchi, Hsu, and Faure, in this volume.

54. Cf. ter Haar, *White Lotus Teachings*, chaps. 2 and 3; esp. 39, 79. Among Dunhuang documents from the late Tang period, there seem to be few instances of such a common first character in lay Buddhist names (as "Pu" would be in White Lotus circles).

55. *T* 37:131c–141c.

56. See Chikusa Masaaki, *Chūgoku bukkyō shakaishi kenkyū*, 17–82; 262–292. Also Daniel L. Overmyer, "The White Cloud Sect in Song and Yuan China," *Harvard Journal of Asiatic Studies* 42.2 (Dec. 1982): 615–642.

57. See Zhang Shengyan, *Minmatsu chūgoku bukkyō no kenkyū* [Studies on Chinese Buddhism of the late Ming] (Tokyo: Sangibō, 1975), 55–57.

58. This Manichean trait might be there as early as the Fang La revolt. See Chikusa Masaaki, *Chū goku bukkyō shakaishi kenkyū*, 199–227, 229–260.

59. The *Fanwang jing*, for example, prohibits the storing, not to mention the bearing, of arms. It rules out any participation in war (including acting as messenger between kingdoms). It even discourages the pious from approaching men of power for personal gain, and it outlaws avenging the death of one's lord; see *T* 24:1005c–1006b. The traditional, pacifist response to persecution by evil kings is to stand firm and try to salvage the Three Jewels; see *T* 24:1005a, 1007b, 1008b, 1009b.

60. The story is more complicated than this, of course. Susan Naquin discerned two types among these sectarians of the Qing period: those whose activities were characterized by regular meetings for sutra chanting, and those who stressed meditation and the martial arts. Barend J. ter Haar believes that the former type was actually similar to the original Song White Lotus tradition. Naquin, "The Transmission of White Lotus Sectarianism," 255–291; ter Haar, *White Lotus Teachings,* 297 ff.

PART II

Aspects of Popular Religion

CHAPTER 4

Daoism and Orthodoxy
The Loyal and Filial Sect

Richard Shek

The generalization may be offered that Daoism, with its original alternative cosmological views and its subsequent eschatological aspirations, was intrinsically unorthodox.[1] Yet this observation should in no way obscure the fact that ever since Zhang Lu's surrender to Cao Cao in A.D. 216, the Daoist establishment (represented by the Celestial Master tradition and its offshoots) has consistently toned down this original difference from orthodoxy and has made numerous accommodations to orthodox ethics and political authority. Indeed, serious students of Daoism insist that organized Daoism had always been supportive of the state and orthodox morality.

The opinions of Nathan Sivin and Michel Strickmann are, for example, representative of this view. Sivin argues that "far from being politically revolutionary, orthodox Taoist sects after the Han period played no active role in rebellions, messianic or otherwise, and never represented rebellions as desirable. . . . Instead, the Taoist religious organizations consistently sought the favor of the temporal powers, provided support for the government, and modeled relations with the gods on the usages of the imperial bureaucracy."[2] Similarly, Michel Strickmann contends: "(Farewell, I hope, to the lingering myth of the subversive Taoist). Both secular sources and texts in the Canon attest the close relationship of Taoist organizations to the state; under every dynasty priests furnished supportive tokens to the central government and performed rituals for its security."[3] These views of Sivin and Strickmann are borne out by most of the early canonical Daoist texts, which generally express a moral code very much supportive of Confucian, therefore orthodox, values.[4] The *Five Sentiments of Gratitude*, written by the Lingbao (Spiritual Treasure) master Lu Xiujing (406–477), is particularly illustrative. The first such sentiment, as identified by Lu, pertains to one's parents:

> Father and mother engendered me and gave me life, nourished me and nurtured me. Coming and going, they cradled me in their arms, soothed and comforted me, caressed and tended me. They damaged their health with anxiety and wore themselves out with worry. When I was unwell or fell ill, they were distressed and preoccupied on my account, their hearts burning as if on fire. Apprehensive day and night, they forgot their food and gave up their sleep; with growing agitation, they became emaciated. Shedding ceaseless tears they yearn for my growth and development. Enabled to become as I am now, I am mindful of their great, their immeasurable kindness. I sincerely vow to repay the boundless beneficence of my parents! . . . I wish that my father and mother shall ascend to the Hall of Felicity, forever escape the Eight Hardships, and never again suffer distress. May my small sincerity afford them sustenance.[5]

These lines could have been written by any Confucian scholar!

This Daoist accommodation to orthodoxy has, regrettably, seldom been documented in full-length monographic studies, in the manner that the works of Michihata Ryōshū and Kenneth Ch'en have done for Buddhism.[6] The appearance of Akizuki Kan'ei's path-breaking work on the Jingming zhongxiao dao (The Loyal and Filial Way of the Pure and Perspicacious) in 1978 can therefore be seen as a major effort undertaken to fill the gap. The present essay on the history and doctrine of this important Daoist order owes much to Akizuki's pioneering study, as well as to the writings by other scholars that appeared after it. This essay attempts, however, to go beyond previous works in the analysis of the popular socioethical orthodoxy which Jingming zhongxiao dao exemplified.[7]

Hagiography of Xu Sun the Grand Patriarch

The grand patriarch of this tradition was Xu Sun (239–272, or 374)[8] of the Jin period. What we know about Xu is primarily derived from hagiographies, which offer divergent accounts of him, ranging from rather concise and undramatic portrayals to highly elaborate and fanciful descriptions.[9] One of the latest, therefore most complete, hagiographical sources on the life of Xu is the *Jingming daoshi Jingyang Xu zhenjun zhuan* (Biography of the perfect lord Xu of Jingyang, teacher of the way of the pure and perspicacious). It is contained in the compendium dated 1327, *Jingming zhongxiao quanshu* (Complete works of the Jingming zhongxiao dao), the single most important work on this sect.[10]

According to this biography, Xu Sun's father Xu Su moved the family to Yuzhang (also known as Yuchang, Zhongling, and Hong-zhou, present-day Nanchang in Jiangxi province) to escape the ravages of war during the last years of the Han dynasty. In 239 his mother dreamt a golden phoenix deposited a shining pearl from its mouth into her palm. Afterward Xu Sun was conceived. From childhood, Xu was known to have had an impressive appearance and kind disposition. When he was still young, he went hunting one day and shot a deer. The deer turned out to be pregnant; Xu watched in horror as the baby deer emerged from the wound of the mother and fell to the ground. Though the mother deer was dying, she still licked her baby in an instinctive act of maternal love. Deeply moved and distressed by this sight, Xu broke his arrow and returned home empty-handed. Thenceforth he devoted himself to study, with special interest in the way of the immortals.

Later Xu studied with Wu Meng, a renowned Daoist and paragon of filial piety.[11] Xu also reportedly befriended Guo Pu, a famous scholar. Together they practiced Daoist cultivation and performed meritorious acts in the community. In 280 Xu's fame finally reached the court. He was appointed prefect of Jingyang county, in Shujun, purportedly in present-day Sichuan province.[12] In that capacity, he was an able and compassionate administrator. He admonished his yamen underlings to be lenient toward the people, and he paroled all prisoners after lecturing to them on the virtues of love and frugality. In times of famine, he used his magical power to turn bricks and tiles into gold to buy food for the starving people. When plagues afflicted the locality, he prescribed special formulas to heal the sick. In time, however, he was disillusioned with the Jin court and resigned. Many people from Jingyang followed him back to Yuzhang, where they settled down and adopted the surname of Xu just so they could stay close to him.

Afterward Xu and Wu Meng traveled extensively in search of more knowledgeable masters and more subtle teaching. Their encounter with the female adept Mother Zhan (Zhanmu) proved to be fateful. It turned out that Mother Zhan herself had been entrusted with sacred texts, bronze talismans, iron contracts, and golden elixir, as well as the teaching of filiality by the enlightened king *(xiaodao mingwang zhi fa)*, by yet another immortal, Lord Orchid (Langong). It was Lord Orchid who, having himself received these symbols and the sacred teaching of filiality from the King of Filial Piety and Brotherly Deference (Xiaodi wang, a deity from the Great Dipper), had predicted the arrival of Xu and Wu and had instructed Mother Zhan to give the same to them. Mother Zhan was therefore well prepared when the two showed up at her door.

After Xu and Wu examined the symbols and the texts, they discovered that only Xu was designated to be the transmitter of this teaching of filiality. Thus Wu Meng, former teacher of Xu, must now defer to the latter and submit himself as a disciple. Shortly thereafter, Xu received further instruction from the two august lords of Sun and Moon. This additional doctrine was titled *Jingming lingbao zhongxiao zhi dao* (The way of loyalty and filiality, of the pure and perspicacious Lingbao [Spiritual Treasure] tradition).

As Xu Sun increasingly gained insight into the teaching of *jingming zhongxiao*, his magical prowess improved even further. He slew gigantic snakes and sea monsters, subdued fiends, and banished evil spirits. He was besieged by people who wanted to become his disciples. To test their integrity, Xu transformed sticks of charcoal into pretty ladies and sent them at night to seduce these prospective students. Of the several hundred who sought his instruction, only ten passed the test by having no charcoal marks on them in the morning (proof that they did not have intimate contact with these charcoal-turned-beauties, thereby maintaining their purity). He took these ten as his worthy disciples and, together with Wu Meng, formed the group of Twelve Perfect Lords (Shi'er zhenjun).[13] Their principal center of activity was West Mountain (Xishan), not far from present-day Nanchang.

Finally, after performing much beneficial work for the community, Xu was informed by two immortals sent from heaven that he should prepare for his return to the celestial realm. On the designated day, the fifteenth day of the eighth month in 374, the two immortals returned and, amidst much pomp and solemn heavenly proclamations, announced Xu's attainment of immortality and his ancestors' elevation to numerous divine posts. Accompanied by his family and six of his favorite disciples (totaling forty-two altogether), as well as by his domestic animals, Xu "ascended to Heaven in broad daylight."[14]

What the preceding account of Xu Sun's life relates is an elaborate hagiographic representation of the founder of a tradition that later culminated in the establishment of the Jingming zhongxiao dao. It portrays him as a man of compassion, an able and caring official, a "culture hero" who slays monsters and subdues demons, and, finally, as an accomplished immortal who has been divinely ordained to establish the most orthodox of Daoist traditions. It attempts to leave the impression that the teaching of *jingming zhongxiao* is what Xu Sun preached right from the beginning.

Other sources, however, tell a somewhat different story. The *Xu Sun zhenren zhuan* (Biography of the perfect immortal Xu Sun) in the Song Daoist compendium *Yunji qiqian* (Seven slips from the bookbag of the clouds, in *DZ* 37, 95–860), for example, indicated that Xu never studied with, nor even met, Wu Meng. Furthermore, it reveals that Wu was a well-known teacher of "the way of filial piety" *(xiaodao)* in his own right. Xu was, however, very much an ardent admirer of Wu and worshiped him from afar. Before Wu Meng ascended to heaven, this source continues, he predicted that Xu would come to mourn him, and instructed his son to hand over to Xu his talisman of perfection *(zhenfu)*. Xu did eventually show up after Wu's ascent, and having then received the talisman, Xu put it to use in his practices. He surpassed Wu in his Daoist cultivation.[15] Obviously this biography of Xu contradicts the assertion in *Quanshu* that Wu Meng was a disciple of Xu in the teaching of filial piety. More significantly, this source makes no mention of the terms *"jingming"* (pure and perspicacious) and *"zhong"* (loyal), a conspicuous omission that does not make any sense if indeed these qualities are part of the original teaching of Xu. As *Yunji qiqian* appeared at least two centuries before *Quanshu,* the absence of such key terms in it may suggest that they were not part of Xu Sun's teaching, even in the early part of the eleventh century, when this text was compiled.

In fact, this speculation finds support in another text, the *Xiaodao Wu-Xu er zhenjun zhuan* (Biographies of the perfect lords Wu and Xu of the way of filial piety), a ninth-century compilation and one of the earliest sources on the Xu Sun cult.[16] As suggested by the title of the text, the teaching propagated by Wu Meng and Xu Sun is represented here as the way of filial piety, with no mention of loyalty at all. Furthermore, throughout that text the term *"jingming"* is nowhere to be found. It should be recalled that the teaching supposedly transmitted to Xu and Wu by Lord Orchid and Mother Zhan is called "the way of filiality by the enlightened king." The details of this transmission take up considerable space in the text, further suggesting that the Xu Sun tradition was associated much more closely with the theme of filial piety than with loyalty. Thus, we can assume that, as late as the ninth century, Xu's teaching was known simply as *xiaodao.*[17]

In any event, we must now turn our attention to the development of the Xu Sun tradition after the master's departure.

The Xu Sun Tradition in Tang and Song

After Xu Sun's reported ascent to heaven, a shrine was built in his memory by his nephew. Many of his personal belongings, as well as the parting poems he composed on the eve of his ascent, were kept there. The shrine itself came to be known as Shrine of the Wandering Mat (Youwei guan), after the story that subsequent to Xu's ascent, the brocade mat on which he used to sit flew back to West Mountain and hovered in the sky for three days before disappearing again.

In time, a cult centering on Xu developed, with the Youwei guan as the focal point.[18] The *Biographies of the Perfect Lords Wu and Xu* relates that "from the time the Perfect Lord and his family ascended to Heaven, until the fourteenth year of the Yuanhe era in the Tang (819 A.D.), approximately five hundred and sixty-two years have passed."[19] In successive generations, the people from the four neighboring counties congregated at the Youwei guan to hold the Great Retreat of the Yellow Register (Huanglu dazhai). They invited Daoist masters to conduct a service of three days and three nights, during which they ascended the altar and presented memorials to Laozi. They also performed rituals and burned incense, and with utmost sincerity petitioned for blessings for both the living and the dead.[20] These rites were conducted each year on the fifteenth day of the first, fifth, and eighth months, with the last date being the most important, as it traditionally marked the day of Xu's ascent to heaven. It is noteworthy that at such gatherings, the Xu Sun worshipers offered prayers for the safety and fortune of kings and officials, in addition to the common people.[21]

Apart from the solemn rituals, the annual retreats also featured processions, songs, and dances.[22] The following is a vivid description of these occasions:

> On the Xishan at Zhongling is the *Youwei guan*, which is the residence from where the Perfect Lord Xu rose to Heaven. Every year during the mid-Autumn festival [that is, the day of the ascent], the people of Wu, Shu, Chu and Yue come from afar to attend this celebration. Many take along high-grade incense, precious fruits, rolls of silk, and gold money, to hold a Retreat and Offering in order to pray for blessings. At that time of the year, tens of thousands of people gather at Zhongling, chariots and horses with much noise jam the place. Men and women, standing close to each other like the teeth of a comb, link their arms and dance and sing.[23]

Records of such ecstatic devotions date from the ninth century. Two centuries prior to that, however, the Youwei guan had actually gone through some lean years, as some sources indicate. *Quanshu* reveals that the shrine was burned down during the time of Yangdi (604–617) of the Sui and was not repaired until the last years of the seventh century.[24] The *Biographies of the Perfect Lords Wu and Xu* also concedes that "by the first year of the Zhenguan era in the Tang [627], the state no longer patronized the shrine and the people who came were few. The buildings fell into disrepair, shrouded by an air of melancholy and desolation."[25] It was through the appearance of a charismatic leader in the second half of the seventh century that the Xu Sun cult was rejuvenated.

That leader, Hu Huichao, was a mysterious figure who arrived on the scene out of nowhere and, distressed by the dilapidated state of the Xu Sun shrine, almost single-handedly restored it, in 682–683. Hu was not associated with the shrine prior to that time, and his understanding of Xu Sun's teaching was limited to a brief revelatory experience with the "two Lords of Sun and Moon, who instructed him on the teaching of Loyalty and Filiality, of the Pure and Perspicacious Lingbao tradition."[26] Still, he was pivotal in reviving the Xu Sun tradition in early Tang, not only through his restoration work on the Youwei guan but apparently also through his authorship of the earliest known biographical accounts of Xu and his disciples, *Jin Hongzhou Xishan shi'er zhenjun neizhuan* (Intimate biographies of the twelve perfect lords of West Mountain, in Hongzhou, during the Jin dynasty).[27] For this reason, Hu has been given a most exalted position in *Quanshu.*

It was during the Tang dynasty that Xu Sun's way of filial piety came to be closely affiliated with the Daoist Lingbao tradition in both ritual and liturgy. The late Tang Daoist erudite Du Guangting (850–933) asserted that "the ritual of the Way of Filial Piety is little different from that of the Lingbao tradition. The people of Yuzhang have been practicing it for generations."[28] In fact, Du's famous ritual handbook on the Yellow Register Retreat, *Huanglu zhaiyi,* provides detailed descriptions of the rites, which correspond closely to the Lingbao tradition.[29]

One more significant development for the Xiaodao in the Tang was the formulation of one of its earliest doctrinal works, *Yuanshi dongzhen cishan xiaozi bao'en chengdao jing* (Text on the attainment of the way by the compassionate filial son who repays his debt to his parents, from the cavern of perfection in the primordial beginning).[30] In this text the theme of filial devotion is given the highest priority, this virtue being portrayed as the single most indispensable ingredient for the attainment of immortality. It also lends support to the suspicion that the Xu Sun tradition was principally concerned with filial piety in the Tang.

The fortune of *xiaodao* improved even more with the founding of the Song dynasty. During the reigns of Zhenzong (933–1023) and Huizong (1101–1125), two of the most pro-Daoist Song emperors, *xiaodao* enjoyed unprecedented imperial patronage. Zhenzong's commission for the compilation of a new manuscript of the *Daoist Canon (Daozang)* is well documented.[31] Less well known is his bestowal of the name of Yulong (Jade Eminence) on the Youwei guan in 1010. He also elevated the status of the Xu Sun shrine from *guan* to *gong* (palace). Furthermore, he forbade lumbering on the now sacred West Mountain, ordered reduction of all taxes for the area, and established the sinecure post of commissioner *(tiju)* for the support of respected scholars and retired officials there.[32] The Xu Sun shrine underwent several renovations during the following decades. Prominent scholar-officials such as Zeng Gong (1019–1083) and Wang Anshi (1021–1086) are known to have written commemorative verses and essays on one such restoration of the Yulong gong.[33]

By the time of Emperor Huizong, the influence of the Xu Sun cult had reached new heights. The honor of *shengong miaoji* (divine efficacy and wondrous saving power) was conferred on Xu Sun in 1112. A grand service lasting seven days and involving thirty-seven Daoist priests was held for the occasion.[34] Four years later, the additional title of *wanshou* (longevity) was given to the Xu Sun shrine, thus making it the Yulong wanshou gong (Palace of Jade Eminence and Longevity), a name it kept from that time on until the late nineteenth century. Further renovation or reconstruction was carried out at the shrine in the same year (1116).

This generous bestowal of imperial favor has to be viewed in the context of the general ascendancy of Daoism at this time. The Shenxiao (Divine Empyrean) movement headed by the Daoist Lin Lingsu was in its heyday. Through his shrewd and ingenious recompilation of a Lingbao text, the *Duren jing* (Scripture of salvation), Lin persuaded Emperor Huizong that he, the emperor, was actually the incarnation of the Jade Emperor's eldest son, the Grand Lord of Long Life, sovereign of the Divine Empyrean, and destined savior of the world.[35] Thus the Shenxiao sect, with the Song emperor himself as both high priest and supreme deity, became the most favored Daoist order of the time. The years 1116–1117 should also be remembered as an extremely active period in the development of Daoism. The compilation of the first printed *Daoist Canon* was complete and the carving of the printing blocks was ready to begin. So it was a milieu highly favorable to Daoism, and the Xu Sun followers enjoyed the full benefits of it. As a result, *xiaodao* became closely identified with the state and its fortune.

With the disastrous conclusion of Huizong's reign and the ensuing factional intrigues at court, not to mention the intense buildup of pressure on the frontier, *xiaodao* faced a most serious crisis. As its fortune was now linked to that of the court and the state, it was forced to tap deeper into its spiritual reserve to seek solutions for the crisis that threatened both the state and itself.

The situation became even more pressing when the marauding army of the Jurchens captured Kaifeng, in 1126, and effectively ended the rule of the Song dynasty in the north. During the next two decades, the Song and Jin forces engaged in numerous skirmishes, with the Jurchens sometimes breaching the Song defense and crossing the Yangzi River to wreak havoc in the south. Those long years of war caused extensive suffering among the ravaged populace in both north and south. The Yulong wanshou gong itself was once nearly destroyed by Jurchen troops as they tried to set it on fire. But, miraculously, water poured out of the beams and rafters of the shrine and, observing this, the Jin soldiers beat a hasty retreat. Even more alarming and insufferable was the specter of the potential demise of China as a civilization. For this reason, loyalist sentiments erupted spontaneously, prompted by the logic that if the Song royal house could be preserved, then China herself could also be saved. There were impassioned calls to exert one's loyalty to the utmost in order to repay one's indebtedness to the state. Thus Southern Song generals such as Yue Fei, Han Shizong, and Zhang Jun all stressed the fervently patriotic theme of dying for the country *(baoguo)*.

It was during such an intensely emotional and trying period that *xiaodao*—the fate of which had by now become inextricably intertwined with that of the imperial house—adopted the notion of *zhong* (loyalty) as part of its central doctrine. He Zhengong, He the Perfect Master, then heading the *xiaodao* movement, was instrumental in this major doctrinal addition. His earnest prayers to Xu Sun for guidance to cope with the troubled times and the menacing prospect of dynastic demise were reportedly answered. Through a revelatory encounter with the founding patriarch Xu, He was given instruction in a new teaching.

As recorded by his disciple He Shouzheng,[36] this new teaching pertained to the *Lingbao jingming mifa* (Esoteric formula of purity and perspicacity of the Lingbao tradition) and the *zhongxiao lianshen zhi dao* (Way of loyalty, filiality, incorruptibility, and prudence).[37] However, the *Quanshu*, compiled nearly two hundred years later, asserts that the new revelation was actually the *Feixian duren jing* (Scripture of salvation by flying immortals) and the *Jingming zhongxiao dafa* (Grand formula of purity, perspicacity, loyalty, and filiality).[38] Despite the discrepancy, it is clear that for the first time, the terms *"jingming"* and *"zhong"* appeared in the doctrinal teaching of the Xu Sun tradition, making them as central concepts as *xiao*.[39] With this new revelation, He Zhengong transformed the original *xiaodao* into a religious order very much influenced by, and in tune with, the crisis of its time. He built an altar to mark the significance of the occasion, and transmitted the instruction to over five hundred disciples.

It should be noted that during this highly critical time in Song history, a reforming mood prevailed in other Daoist groups as well. Under Jurchen rule in the north, "reformed" sects appeared in rapid succession: the Taiyi (Grand Unity) sect, founded by Xiao Baozhen in 1138–1140; the Zhen dadao jiao (True Great Way), by Liu Deren in 1142; and the Quanzhen (Total Perfection) sect, by Wang Zhe in 1163. With the possible exception of the Taiyi, these new Daoist groups abandoned the alchemical and magical orientation of traditional Daoism. Instead they stressed moral cultivation and ethical practice as more important in the attainment of their religious goals. Kubo Noritada, one of Japan's leading authorities on Daoism, has gone so far as to call this new phenomenon the "Chinese Religious Reformation."[40]

Amidst this Daoist reorientation toward ethical rectitude and moral cultivation, two extremely influential and popular tracts made their appearance. These were the *Taishang ganying pian* (The text on moral retribution revealed by the Most Exalted One), by Li Changling, and the *Taiwei xianjun gongguoge* (Ledger of merits and demerits revealed by the immortal lord of supreme subtlety), by a Daoist named Youxuanzi who resided at West Mountain. Both texts became prototypes for the later morality books *(shanshu)*, which played important roles in the popularization of China's ethical orthodoxy.[41] Of the two, the latter deserves particular attention, as it has been argued, rather convincingly, that Youxuanzi was a member of Xu Sun's reformed group.[42] An analysis of this text follows later in this chapter.

In any event, it is apparent that while the Taiyi, the Zhen dadao jiao, and the Quanzhen represented reformed Daoism in the north, Xu Sun's Zhongxiao dao (it can be so labeled now) symbolized this same reforming trend in the south. There is ample evidence that the Yulong wanshou gong became a very popular religious center in Southern Song, attracting a large following. In *Zhuzi yulei* (Classified conversations of Master Zhu), Zhu Xi (1130–1200) specifically commented on the religious fervor demonstrated by the faithful at the Xu Sun shrine on West Mountain, and expressed much consternation that the ignorant masses should be so deluded by this sect that they would make yearly pilgrimages to the Yulong wanshou gong despite the arduous journey and the huge expense involved.[43] It is truly ironic that Zhu should denigrate the Zhongxiao dao out of sheer elitism and philosophic partisanship, when in fact his own emphasis on *zhong* and *xiao* as the core values of orthodoxy was totally supported by this accommodated Daoist sect. Zhu's hostility toward the sect notwithstanding, other Southern Song officials and scholars were quite accepting of the tradition and were not at all averse to being affiliated with it. Indeed, the last of the great neo-Confucian scholars of the Song dynasty, Zhen Dexiu (1178–1235), even served as commissioner of the Yulong wanshou gong, as did another famous literary figure, author of the celebrated *Yijian zhi* [Record of the listener], Hong Mai (1123–1202).[44]

The Xu Sun Tradition in Yuan, Ming, and Qing

He Zhengong's Zhongxiao dao would have suffered the same fate as the Taiyi and Zhen dadao jiao—which faded into oblivion after the Yuan dynasty—had it not been for the appearance of a number of charismatic leaders from within its own ranks. Toward the end of the thirteenth and the beginning of the fourteenth centuries, these new leaders brought the prestige as well as the doctrinal sophistication of the Xu Sun tradition to new heights, despite the ascendance of Buddhism after 1255.[45] Liu Yu (Yuzhenzi, 1257–1310) was the first such reformer. During the 1280s he reportedly had numerous visions of encounters with Xu Sun and Hu Huichao, the *xiaodao* patriarch in early Tang, and received from them instructions in the most profound aspects of the Xu Sun teaching. These instructions, received over a sixteen-year period, finally reached a climax in 1297 when, having reportedly penetrated the innermost core of the doctrines of the sect, Liu attained total enlightenment and renamed the sect Jingming zhongxiao dao. The avowed focus of his new teaching was to "regard loyalty and filial piety as fundamental to venerate Heaven and exalt the Way, and to provide relief for the living as well as deliverance for the dead."[46] Thus it seems that under the leadership of Liu Yu, Xu Sun's tradition finally reached its mature form, almost a millennium after its inception.[47] At the same time, the stewardship of Liu also gained much prestige and imperial patronage for the sect, culminating in the further canonization of Xu Sun by Emperor Chengzong (1295–1307), when the additional illustrious attribution of *zhidao xuanying* (ultimate way and mysterious correspondence) was conferred upon Xu.[48]

Liu Yu was succeeded by Huang Yuanji (1270–1325), who hailed from a prominent family near West Mountain. During Huang's tenure as patriarch of the Jingming zhongxiao dao, in the early fourteenth century, the sect's influence advanced further. He maintained cordial friendship with the thirty-ninth Celestial Master, the court-appointed "pope" of Daoism in southern China. He was awarded numerous honorific titles; his intellectual acumen earned him many acquaintances among the prominent officials of the time.[49] Some of these scholar-officials showed genuine admiration for the teaching of the sect, as we shall see later.

With Huang's death, in 1325, the patriarchy was passed down to Xu Yi (1291–1352). It was under Xu's supervision that *Jingming zhongxiao quanshu,* the compilation of which was begun by Huang Yuanji, was completed, in 1327. This work represents the culmination of all hagiographical accounts of the major patriarchs. It also contains important doctrinal expositions by the masters, especially those by Liu Yu. The six prefaces written by the leading scholar-officials of the time, most of whom were friends of Huang Yuanji, are highly revealing. Uniformly laudatory and admiring, these prefaces bespeak the degree of acceptance by the guardians of orthodoxy that the sect had gained. The two extracted here are typical and illustrative. The first, composed by Zhang Gui, a Hanlin scholar, reads in part:

> The *jingming* teaching, initiated by the Lord Immortal Xu Sun and elucidated by Master Liu Yu of Xishan, is based on the moral principles of *zhong* and *xiao*. Without *zhong* there is no ruler, without *xiao* there are no parents. To be disloyal [not *zhong*] and unfilial [not *xiao*] is something not even ordinary mortals should do, how much more should it be avoided by practitioners of the immortal Way? Conversely, if *zhong* and *xiao* are moral values espoused even by the practitioners of the immortal Way, how much more should they be embraced and followed by the ordinary mortals? The ancients have suggested that in order to pursue the way of the immortals [*xiandao*], it is best to pursue the way of the mortals [*rendao*] first. The *jingming* teaching is the best way to put this suggestion into practice.[50]

The second, written by Zhao Shiyan, vice-censor-in-chief and co-compiler of the *Huangchao jingshi dadian* (Great compendium on statecraft), is in a similar vein:

> The duty of a minister is to be *zhong,* that of a child is to be *xiao*. Those who abide by the Three Bonds and the Five Constant Virtues walk the path of *zhongxiao*. The way of the sage-kings Yao and Shun teaches filiality and brotherly deference *(xiaodi)*, while that of our sage master Confucius exalts loyalty and reciprocity *(zhongshu)*. Thus the

essentials of the great way and the supreme morality are inherent in the *Jingming* Sect [which teaches *zhongxiao* as fundamental].[51]

Other prefaces contrast the ethical emphasis of the Jingming zhong-xiao dao with the magical, alchemical, and exorcistic nature of traditional Daoism, and state their unqualified preference for the former. They also stress the compatibility between the ethical teaching of this sect and the core values of Confucianism, thereby recognizing the orthodox nature of the Jingming zhongxiao dao.[52]

The influence of the Jingming zhongxiao dao does not seem to have been adversely affected by the collapse of the Yuan dynasty and the founding of the Ming, even though the Yulong wanshou gong did suffer heavy damage at the hands of the Red Turbans in 1352. Liu Yuanran (1351–1432), patriarch of the sect in early Ming, was head of the Daolu si, the highest agency in the central government in charge of Daoist affairs, during the reigns of Taizu (1368–1398) and Chengzu (1403–1424). He also held the title of *zhenren* (perfect master), which effectively put him on equal footing with the Celestial Master, upon whom the same title was also conferred by the Ming court.[53]

An imperial prince, the seventeenth son of Taizu, was an accomplished Daoist and a practitioner of the Jingming zhongxiao dao.[54] But more notable was the Daoist Hu Qingxu in the sixteenth century. A master of the Jingming zhongxiao teaching of considerable renown, Hu gave instruction to such "left-wing" Wang Yangming followers as Wang Ji (1498–1582) and Luo Rufang (1515–1588), influencing their attitude toward Daoism as well as their method of self-cultivation.[55] The acceptance of the Jingming zhongxiao dao by more conservative scholars can also be discerned in the recorded conversations of Gao Panlong (1562–1626), a leader of the Donglin group. Gao professed that "all my friends at the Donglin Academy know nothing about Daoism. But we do understand that among the various Daoist groups, the one founded by Xu Sun is the most orthodox [i.e., correct]. What it teaches are the four concepts *jing, ming, zhong,* and *xiao*. Those engaging in Daoist studies must try to understand these four words thoroughly. When they do, they will become genuine Daoists."[56] For Tu Long (1542–1605), a *jinshi* degree holder in late Ming and a respected literary figure as well, Daoism was best represented by the Jingming zhongxiao dao.[57]

The influence of Xu Sun was also evident in late Ming popular literature. There was a full-scale novel describing some of the magical exploits of Xu written by Deng Zhimo and entitled *Tieshu ji* (The iron tree). This was in turn adapted by Feng Menglong in his *Jingshi tongyan* (General words to warn the world) and renamed *Jingyanggong tieshu zhenyao* (The suppression of demons by the iron tree in the Xu Sun shrine).[58]

The Jingming zhongxiao dao entered a period of irreversible decline after the founding of the Qing dynasty. There were, to be sure, a few outstanding leaders in early Qing, such as Xu Shoucheng (d. 1692) and Zhou Defeng, who maintained some semblance of continuity in the teaching of the sect. Yet the vigor and vitality of the organization were already dissipated. The Yulong wanshou gong underwent several more reconstructions during the eighteenth and nineteenth centuries, the last one taking place in 1867 after the devastation by the Taipings. The *Records of the Yulong wanshou gong* was published twice during the Qing dynasty. The first edition appeared in the Qianlong reign (1740, reprinted in 1846), while the second was printed in the Guangxu era (1878), indicating that interest in the Xu Sun tradition had been sustained at least through the end of the imperial period.[59]

Worship of Xu Sun persisted in popular religion as practiced, for example, by the Jiangxi merchants' guilds. The stone inscription of a Jiangxi merchants' guild in Suzhou dated 1734 reads in part:

> The Perfect Lord [Xu Sun] is a Confucian *(ruzhe)*, who personally cultivates the ultimate virtue. The ether of his Dao ascends above the clouds and the great, long dragons with scales are subdued. . . . All watery lands have shared the wondrous benefits of his transformative and spiritual influences. His merits are not less than those of Yü [sage-king of antiquity who controlled the great flood]. He [Xu Sun] is pure in his filial piety, loyalty, firm integrity *(jie)*, righteousness, and statecraft. . . . His legacy is filiality and loyalty, initiating the heritage of the [Three] Bonds and [Five] Constant Virtues for thousands of years.[60]

The stele of a Jiangxi merchants' guild dated 1796 refers to Perfect Lord Xu Sun as "the filial and loyal immortal of Jiangxi, where he is the astral god of good fortune."[61] The popular belief continued to be cherished in the late Qing period, as evidenced by the stone inscription of a Jiangxi guild hall (Yuzhang huiguan) in Shanghai that was founded in 1849.[62] Moreover, worshipers of Xu Sun can still be found in Taiwan today,[63] while the Wanshou gong of Nanchang (formerly Yuzhang) still exists and continues to attract adherents.[64]

The Evolution of the Central Doctrines

From its beginnings in the fourth century to its maturity in the thirteenth, the Xu Sun tradition had undergone a most interesting metamorphosis. As Schipper and Boltz have observed, it originated as a local cultic worship of folk heroes who slew dragons and snakes and exorcised demons. There was nothing particularly "Daoist" about the exploits of Xu Sun and the other early patriarchs.[65] Such worship of the saints, represented by the annual festivals at West Mountain, was in time justified and legitimized by the presence of Daoist masters who "ascended the altar and presented memorials" on behalf of the worshipers. This, as explained by Schipper, might have signaled the existence of a local leadership that sought and obtained the confirmation of its position through the Daoist rites of investiture.[66] As evidenced by the Retreat of the Yellow Register, the association of the Xu Sun festival with the Daoist Lingbao liturgy was completed by the Tang period, if not earlier. But more pertinent to our interest is that the Xu Sun tradition had, by Tang times, also come to be identified with the ethical principle of filial piety. From this perspective a closer look at the content of the *Yuanshi dongzhen cishan xiaozi bao'en chengdao jing,* a text affirmed by Schipper to be a late Tang work, seems appropriate.

This text is a glowing celebration of the efficacy of filial piety. It declares that the instruction it imparts will enable "the enlightened kings of the world to rule the realm with filial piety, and the filial sons to repay the debt they owe their parents."[67] It assures the reader that when filial piety is practiced, "the myriad spirits of Heaven and Earth will guard the filial son day and night, so that when he engages in Daoist exercises and preserves the One, he will naturally attain the Way."[68] In other words, filial piety is not only ethically desirable but religiously useful. As explained by the text later, "The virtuous man embraces lofty filial sentiments. His Way is in accord with Heaven and earth. Thus Heaven cannot kill him, the Way cannot eliminate him, and the earth cannot bury him."[69] This filial piety, moreover, is the sustaining force in the universe, regulating the seasons, healing diseases, and providing livelihood for the multitudes.[70] This text is thus a veritable psalm that glorifies filiality.

This emphasis on filial piety by the Xu Sun tradition was revised in the twelfth century to include loyalty and other ethical values as a result of the dynasty's crisis mentioned earlier. Under the leadership of He Zhengong, the sect entered a feverishly creative period during which important texts were compiled and new doctrines were formulated. Specifically mentioned by divergent sources were the *Lingbao jingming mifa* and the *Feixian duren jing,* which respectively illuminated the way of loyalty, filiality, incorruptibility, and prudence, and the grand formula of purity, perspicacity, loyalty, and filiality.

In the *Daoist Canon,* two texts that correspond rather closely to the two titles mentioned above do exist. The first is the *Taishang lingbao jingming mifa* (The esoteric formula of the most exalted one in the Lingbao and the purity-and-perspicacity tradition).[71] The other is the *Taishang lingbao jingming feixian duren jingfa* (Textual formula of salvation by flying immortals in the Lingbao and the purity-and-perspicacity tradition).[72] It is difficult to determine if these two are actually the same texts that existed in the twelfth century. However, their contents do indicate some correlation with the problems of the age and stress unequivocally such themes as *zhongxiao* and *lianshen* (incorruptibility and caution). The *Taishang lingbao jingming mifa,* for example, contains talismans meant to help the user to "repay ruler and parent above and deliver the multitudes below."[73] This is a likely response to the critical moment in the 1120s and 1130s when there was widespread turmoil and devastation. Even more indicative of the crisis of the time is one of the incantations listed in the text that supposedly would repel barbarians, who were referred to as "unloving fathers and unfilial sons who invaded China."[74] The text can be seen as a reflection of the yearning to eliminate the threat posed by the Jurchens—if only they could be driven away by the invocation of a mantra!

Lengthier and doctrinally far more cogent is the *Feixian duren jingfa.* Far from being merely a plagiarized and abridged version of Lin Lingsu's *Duren jing,* as Akizuki has characterized it,[75] the text encapsulates many of the concepts allegedly revealed to He Zhengong. It also lends support to the contention that the reformed Xu Sun tradition in Southern Song might have been responsible for the compilation of the first *Ledger of Merits and Demerits.* At the beginning, the Eight Ultimates *(baji)* are discussed: "*Zhong* [loyalty] is the ultimate of respectful submission; *xiao* [filiality] is the ultimate of obedience; *lian* [incorruptibility] is the ultimate of purity; *jin* [prudence] is the ultimate of abstinence; *kuan* [leniency] is the ultimate of broad-mindedness; *yu* [abundance] is the ultimate of delight; *rong* [tolerance] is the ultimate of harmony; and *ren* [forbearance] is the ultimate of intelligence."[76] The first four terms—"*zhong*," "*xiao*," "*lian*," and "*jin*"—definitely bear a strong resemblance to the teaching of *zhongxiao lianshen* supposedly revealed to He Zhengong in 1131. In fact, "*jin*" and "*shen*" are so similar in meaning that they form a compound word. Along with the additional precepts of *kuanyu* and *rongren,* they form the so-called Eight Precious Instructions *(babao chuixun)* of Xu Sun.

Elsewhere in the text the *zhongxiao* theme is given further elucidation:

> As human beings, our parents are those who are dearest to us while our ruler is the person whom we respect the most. When we realize the benefaction of our ruler, ancestors and fathers, and think of repaying our debt to them, we practise *zui, du,* and *anzhen. Zui* is to recite scriptures and use talismans to provide comfort and solace for our deceased ancestors and relatives on their journey through the underworld. *Du* is to recite scriptures and use talismans to secure blessings for our living forebears and other relatives. *Anzhen* is to recite scriptures and use talismans to wish longevity for our ruler so that he can pacify the four corners of the empire, summon the dragons to provide timely rainfall, protect the people and their property, as well as make offerings to the astral gods.[77]

This passage clearly illustrates the degree to which Xu Sun's followers in the Song dynasty had committed Daoist rituals and liturgy to the exaltation of orthodox moral principles. This preoccupation with ethical precepts also led to an interest in moral accounting—that is, the conscious and systematic recording of one's behavior to determine one's moral standing. In this regard the *Duren jingfa* is highly revealing. One of the cardinal moral acts it advises is to keep a daily record *(rilu):* "Daily records are for us to examine and reflect upon our moral action. . . . When we use them to record our daily deeds, we will realize that those which we are too embarrassed or ashamed to write down are indeed the wrongful deeds and we should rectify them. Daily records are therefore teachers who need not instruct, friends who need not counsel, rulers and fathers who need not decree, and rules and regulations that need not discipline."[78] If this text was indeed compiled in the 1130s, then it attests to the prevalent practice of daily recording of personal behavior among the Xu Sun followers at that time.

Indeed, other texts of the Xu Sun tradition not dated also indicate that this practice of moral accounting was quite common among the believers. For example, the *Taishang lingbao jingming rudao pin* (Introductory text of the Most Exalted One for entry into the way of Lingbao purity and perspicacity) advises the keeping of a small notebook by the faithful to record their daily actions for self-reflection.[79] The *Lingbao jingmingyuan xingqian shi* (Ritual forms at the Lingbao purity and perspicacity) similarly mentions a *Jingming ji gongguobu* (Notebook for the recording of merits and demerits) commonly kept by followers of the *jingming* teaching.[80] Seen in this context, the compilation of the first printed *Ledger of Merits and Demerits,* the *Taiwei xianjun gongguoge,* by one of the members of the Xu Sun tradition in 1171 is therefore entirely plausible, as Akizuki has so vigorously argued.[81] The content and significance of this ledger will be discussed later in this chapter.

With the systematization of Xu Sun's teaching in early Yuan, the Jingming zhongxiao doctrine reached a high level of sophistication and coherence. In the words of Liu Yu, the great synthesizer of the sect's doctrine in the late thirteenth century, "*Jingming* is nothing other than the rectification of the mind *(zhengxin)* and the making sincere of the will *(chengyi). Zhongxiao* is nothing other than bolstering and propagating the Three Bonds and the Five Constant Virtues *(fuzhi gangchang).*"[82] In other words, the teaching of the sect is based on the premise of moral transformation while its central purpose is the affirmation of orthodox values and institutions. On the surface, therefore, there is nothing particularly "Daoist" about this doctrine. Liu readily concedes that the way of Jingming zhongxiao is no ordinary Daoist teaching, which is merely concerned with the refinement of essence and breath.[83] However, he insists that the Daoist goal of attaining immortality cannot be attained without, first of all, a purified and moralized mind. Unless this firm foundation is laid, Liu contends, all the traditional Daoist practices of magic, alchemy, and exorcism are nothing more than useless tricks. Therefore the practice of *zhongxiao* is the primary, indispensable step in the pursuit of immortality:

> For those who can establish *zhongxiao* as their basis and maintain purity and perspicacity within their hearts, their mind is linked without any obstruction to the Cosmic Breath of Yellow Centrality *(huangzhong daoqi)* in Heaven. There will be mutual response and penetration. In time, union with the Way to achieve perfection will be made possible, like water returning to the ocean.[84]

This insistence on the primacy of moral cultivation and the dismissal of traditional Daoist exercises as secondary are found in other *Jingming* texts as well. The *Taishang lingbao jingming dongshen shangpin jing* (Supreme text from the cavern of spirituality of the Lingbao purity and perspicacity tradition) is representative:

> The body of the parents is the body of the Celestial Venerable *(tianzun)*. If one can serve one's parents, the Celestial Venerable will send down spirits to save oneself. If one wishes to worship the astral gods, one must practise brotherly respect. The body of one's brother is that of the perfected beings of the various heavens. All who realize this fact are qualified to refine the elixir and to use talismans. The myriad demons will tremble at the very mention of their names. However, those who fail to put it into practice are not qualified to enter the Way and worship the Three Purities. The spirits of hell will devour their flesh and the evil demons will slaughter their souls. Even though one possesses thousands of volumes of texts on immortality, one may not rise to perfection. Even though one has ten thousand chests of talismans, one may not be able to harness the power of the spirits. The evil demons will only sneer and be ready to kill. Only when one knows *zhongxiao* can one learn the Way. . . . The Supreme Lord will dispatch perfected beings to earth and teach one the genuine instructions, which will enable one to cultivate oneself and help others and to accumulate meritorious deeds to become immortal.[85]

Perhaps the most coherent and detailed discussion of the relationship between *zhongxiao* and the Daoist goal of immortality is contained in the *Gaoshang yuegong taiyin yuanjun xiaodao xianwang lingbao jingming huangsushu* (The book of yellow elements, belonging to the Lingbao purity-and-perspicacity tradition and revealed by the immortal king of filiality who is the primordial lord of Taiyin from the lunar palace on high). The following passage is most illuminating:

> The names of *zhong* and *xiao* are established for the sake of the ruler and the parents. They emphasize honest sincerity and gentle courtesy. In the discharge of official duties, honest sincerity is of primary importance; as is gentle courtesy in the serving of the parents. Honest sincerity leads to discernment, therefore gossips cannot move it. Gentle courtesy results in respectful prudence, therefore license and deviancy cannot penetrate it. When *zhongxiao* is extended to financial matters, it is called incorruptibility *(lian)*; when manifested in words and actions, it is called prudence *(shen)*. It dwells upon generous affluence *(kuanyu)* and ends in tolerant forbearance *(rongren)*. When it is further regulated by rituals *(li)* and made sincere by trustworthiness *(xin)*, the Ten Virtues *(shishan)* are then complete. Ruler and subject have their respective duties, their constancy should not be violated. There is affection between father and son, their status should not be violated. Husband and wife are differentiated, their harmonious feelings should not be violated. There is precedence between senior and junior, their order should not be violated. Among friends there is faithfulness, their feelings of exchange should not be violated. Then the Five Violations *(wu'ni)* will be eliminated. The mind will be as clear as still water. How can external matters confuse it? Can there be any failure in one's pursuit of the Way then? . . . One's name will be absent from the records of evil-doers but will appear in the records of the virtuous. It is then entered into the register of the immortals. Should this be doubted at all? When such moral cultivation is practised within and assisted by the pursuit of the Way without, is it not like the refinement of pure gold to extend its utility and the carving of exquisite jade to further manifest its beauty?[86]

This lengthy quote illustrates how the Xu Sun followers rationalized the connection between moral cultivation and the Daoist goal of attaining immortality. The practice of orthodox morality is thus doctrinally justified, and the accommodation of Daoism with orthodoxy is complete. As a fitting conclusion to this discussion of the doctrinal teaching of the Jingming zhongxiao dao, the postscript to *Quanshu,* written by one Shao Yizheng in mid-Ming, will be examined:

In order to cultivate the way of the immortals, the way of the mortals
must first be perfected. Hence the *Jingming* Sect regards *zhong* and
xiao as the root of cultivation. To nurture and sustain an immutable
human relationship is the primary task for immortals bent on accumulating merit. For *zhong* and *xiao* are the major tenets in the way of
the mortals. They are also the source of all moral deeds. In *zhong*,
there is nothing greater than not to deceive, and not deceiving the
monarch is the greatest *zhong*. In *xiao*, there is nothing greater than
love, and loving one's parents is the greatest *xiao*. Hence to practise
the way one must begin with the monarch and the parents. . . . When
one can be both *zhong* and *xiao*, one's nature is not clouded. When
one's nature is not clouded, one is at once pure *(jing)* and perspicacious *(ming)*.[87]

The Taiwei xianjun gongguoge

This study of the Jingming zhongxiao dao would not be complete
without at least a cursory examination of the *Taiwei xianjun gongguoge*, the earliest published *Ledger of Merits and Demerits* still extant.
This text is the prototype for a number of highly popular ledgers
compiled by the scholar-official Yuan Huang (1533–1606) and the
Buddhist monk Zhuhong (1535–1615) in the late sixteenth century.[88] Known as morality books, these ledgers exerted a strong influence on popular thought even among the illiterate members of late
imperial Chinese society. They also played a central role in the popularization and the inculcation of orthodox values. This being the
case, the *Taiwei xianjun gongguoge* deserves serious attention.

The publication of this *Ledger of Merits and Demerits,* in 1171,
represents the culmination of the Daoist concern for moral accounting that dates back to Ge Hong (283–363). In the "Inner Section" of
Ge's *Baopuzi* (The master who embraces simplicity), it is stated that:

> There is a God in Heaven and Earth who metes out punishment to
> moral offenders in accordance with the gravity of their transgressions.
> He makes deductions in the original life allotment of these people.
> When such deductions are made, the offender will suffer poverty and
> ailments. He will repeatedly be subjected to privation and anxiety.
> When retribution is completed, the person will die. Those offences
> that result in retribution number several hundreds—they cannot be

listed exhaustively here. Within every person there are entities called *sanshi* (three decaying agents) which, though lacking form, are spirits in actuality . . . On each *gengshen* day they report to the Heavenly Tribunal on the offences committed by each person. On the night of the last day of the month the Kitchen God also reports to Heaven on each man's transgressions. Grave offences result in the deduction of *ji*, which is three hundred days; while minor ones lead to the deduction of *suan*, which is three days.[89]

Elsewhere in the *Baopuzi* the rewards for good deeds are also enumerated:

When man aspires to become a terrestrial immortal, he should accumulate three hundred good deeds. If he aspires to become a heavenly immortal he should perform twelve hundred good deeds. He who after having accomplished eleven hundred and ninety nine virtuous deeds, does but a single evil one, loses all the previous good deeds and will have to start afresh.[90]

Thus the whole theory of reward and punishment for moral behavior was clearly enunciated in the fourth century. It had also been established that the carrying out of acts of virtue is an integral part of the pursuit of life eternal.

This line of thought runs through the teachings of Lu Xiujing (406–477) and the Shangqing (Upper Clarity) Daoists. Toward the end of the Tang dynasty, the notion of moral retribution was heavily emphasized in the *Sanyuan* (Three primordials) texts of the Maoshan branch of Daoism. By the time of Du Guangting, there was already mention of the existence of a ledger or format *(ge)* that enables one to establish merits and make up for demerits *(ligong buguo)*.[91]

With the appearance of such a ledger during the Tang-Song transition, the practice of moral accounting entered a new age. Instead of having impersonal divine bureaucrats automatically and mechanically recording human actions, as was believed in earlier times, the new way was a conscious and deliberate recording of moral behavior by the individual human beings themselves. This change offered the satisfaction and assurance that human beings are in control of their own destiny, that there is nothing mysterious or inscrutable about their fate. By accumulating merits and avoiding demerits, the practitioners of this kind of moral accounting can feel confident that reward is in store for them. This internalization of morality, resulting in self-discipline and self-regulation according to certain clearly defined moral precepts, contributed much to the triumph and proliferation of orthodoxy.

As indicated earlier, it was common for followers of the Xu Sun tradition to be always vigilant about their behavior and habitually record their daily deeds for reflection and introspection. Thus the publication of the *Taiwei xianjun gongguoge* can be seen as a natural outcome of this customary practice. The compiler of this work was a person who used the pseudonym of Youxuanzi, named after one of the thirty-six buildings within the sprawling complex on West Mountain.[92] In his preface Youxuanzi claimed that the text was revealed to him by the immortal lord of supreme subtlety, Taiwei, who was believed by Daoists to be the chief deity in charge of rewarding and executing retribution for all human moral or immoral deeds.[93] As explained by the compiler: "There are thirty-six items of meritorious acts and thirty-nine items of wrongful acts. Both the merits and demerits are divided into four categories each, so as to make easy the calculation. The text is entrusted to the practitioners of perfection (*xiuzhen zhi shi*) so that they can clearly enter the dates and record their own meritorious or wrongful deeds themselves. At the end of each month they should draw up a minor balance sheet: at the end of each year, a major one. In this way, the exact quantity of their merits and demerits will be known. Their reward should match those kept in the Heavenly Tribunal and no discrepancy should exist. . . . When this practice is followed, evil will be shunned and virtue will be approached. This will be genuine cultivation, and immortality will be within reach."[94]

The four categories for merit are: charity and relief (12 items), religious fidelity (7 items), prayers and rituals (5 items), and public affairs (12 items). The four for demerit include: malevolence (15 items), sacrilege (8 items), unrighteousness (10 items), and uncanonical acts (6 items). The highest merit is to instruct a Daoist priest, worth one hundred points. The severest demerit is the taking of human life, also one hundred points. All other acts fall between one and one hundred points in increments of ten, except for points below ten. All of them are assigned specific points. Later in the *Gongguoge* the exact procedure for entering records is described:

The ideal method of using this ledger is to keep ready at all times brushes, ink boxes, and notebooks at one's bedside. First enter the month, then the day. Below that make two columns, one for merits, the other for demerits. Before going to bed, each day's behavior is entered into the ledger under the appropriate column. A virtuous act is registered under the merits column; a bad deed, the demerits column. There should not be concealment of wrongful deeds and only entry of good deeds. At the end of a month the merits and demerits should be tallied and balanced to see if one outnumbers the other. The result will be apparent at a glance and should be duly recorded. When the months accumulate to a year, a summary accounting should be undertaken. In this manner one knows exactly if reward or punishment is due. There will be no guessing about luck or misfortune.[95]

This description reveals a highly rationalized form of ethical-religious practice. Luck and misfortune are not the result of the whims of gods, but are the direct consequence of one's behavior, over which one has total control. There is nothing left to chance in one's pursuit of fulfillment in life. The course of action one takes can be charted with certainty, and the power of the deities and spirits can be harnessed to achieve one's goals, as long as they are morally acceptable. Thus instead of trying to propitiate the inscrutable spirits and hoping that they will grant one's wishes, one can actually compel them to perform wonders on one's behalf as long as one occupies the moral high ground. The ledger of merits and demerits is a powerful tool for the user to exercise control over his own destiny, enabling him to gain a sense of confidence hitherto unavailable to him.

Conclusion

The Jingming zhongxiao dao is a Daoist tradition with a fifteen-hundred-year history. This study traces its development from a local cult of saints and folk heroes to becoming a mainline Daoist order, complete with its own rituals and liturgy. But more importantly, it highlights the accommodation that an established Daoist order makes with the socioethical orthodoxy. Not only has the Jingming zhongxiao dao accepted the ethical values of the Three Bonds, it has actually integrated them into its central religious doctrine, making them the primary and cardinal precepts in the attainment of immortality. To be sure, this integration is by no means unique to the Jingming zhongxiao dao. As observed in chapter 1 of this volume, many of the early canonical Daoist texts express a moral inclination very much in line with the orthodox values of filiality and loyalty. All three of the major established Daoist traditions—the Celestial Master, the Shang-qing, and the Lingbao—gave prominence to Confucian virtues.[96] Similarly, Ge Hong in the fourth century also supported such syn-thesis between Daoist goals and orthodox ethics. He stated explicitly that "those who do not carry out acts of virtue and are satisfied only to practise magical acts will never obtain Life Eternal. For those seeking immortality, they should regard as fundamental the values of *zhong* (loyalty), *xiao* (fidelity), *he* (harmony), *shun* (obedience), *ren* (benevolence), and *xin* (trustworthiness)."[97] This sect simply car-ried this exhortation the farthest, making *zhong* and *xiao* part of its very name.

As a "reformed" Daoist order, reaching its maturity at a time when the survival of China as a civilization was threatened, the Jing-ming zhongxiao dao shared certain features with other "reformed" groups such as the Quanzhen sect. They departed from the classical Daoist orientation toward magic, alchemy, and exorcism. Instead they emphasized inner discipline, purification of the mind, and eth-ical practice. Theirs was clearly a more "rationalized" form of reli-gion. Moreover, in the face of this cultural crisis of unprecedented proportions, they closed ranks with other religious traditions in an attempt to preserve what they regarded as the essence of Chinese civ-ilization. Thus the Quanzhen sect advocated the combined reading of the *Heart Sutra,* the *Daodejing,* and the *Book of Filial Piety.* Likewise, leaders of the Jingming zhongxiao dao insisted that the three reli-gions were in fact identical. Liu Yu's remark is representative: "There is only One substantial teaching. What is meant by One? The Purity and Perspicacity *(jingming)* of Laozi, the Loyalty and Reciprocity *(zhongshu)* of Confucius, and the Mahayana teaching *(dacheng)* of the Buddha are all identical with this One."[98]

Perhaps the most lasting and influential contribution of the Jingming zhongxiao dao was its publication of the oldest extant ledger of merits and demerits. It provided a mechanism for religious practitioners to take control of their own lives and to internalize moral values for self-discipline. It enabled the orthodox moral values to percolate down to the lower levels of society, thereby further guaranteeing the proliferation of orthodoxy.[99] Seen in this light, the Jing-ming zhongxiao dao was certainly one of the most important Daoist orders in late imperial China, its contribution to the triumph of orthodoxy was enormous.

Notes

1. See chapter 1, by Kwang-Ching Liu and Richard Shek, in this volume.

2. Nathan Sivin, "On the Word 'Taoist' as a Source of Perplexity," *History of Religions* 17.3–4 (1978): 323.

3. Michel Strickmann, "History, Anthropology, and Chinese Religion," *Harvard Journal of Asiatic Studies* 40.1 (1980): 211.

4. The content of several of the texts has been discussed in chapter 1 of this volume. See Stephen R. Bokenkamp, *Early Daoist Scriptures* (Berkeley: University of California Press, 1997).

5. Included in Wm. Theodore de Bary and Irene Bloom, eds., *Sources of Chinese Tradition*, 2d ed. (New York: Columbia University Press, 1999), 404–406.

6. Michihata Ryōshū, *Bukkyō to Jukyō rinri* [Buddhism and Confucian ethics] (Kyoto: Heirakuji, 1968); Kenneth Ch'en, *The Chinese Transformation of Buddhism* (Princeton: Princeton University Press, 1973).

7. Akizuki Kan'ei, *Chūgoku kinsei dōkyō no keisei—jōmyōdō no kisoteki kenkyū* [Formation of modern Daoism in the history of China—a fundamental study of the Jingming dao] (Tokyo: Sōbunsha, 1978). Akizuki has published numerous articles since, refining his thesis and debating with reviewers of his work. Some of his more recent publications include: "Jōmyodō kenkyūjo no ni san no mondai" [Two or three questions in the study of the Pure and Perspicacious Sect], *Tōhō shūkyō* 57 (May 1981); "Jōmyōdō kenkyūjo no ni san no mondai—dōkyō shi no shitsugi ni yosete" [Two or three questions in the study of the Pure and Perspicacious Sect—toward the inquiry about the history of Daoism], *Tōhō shūkyō* 58 (Oct. 1981): 1–15; "Kyo Son no kyozō to jitsuzō" [Illusory and concrete images of Xu Sun], *Tōhō shūkyō* 67 (June 1986): 59–70; "Jōmyōdō keisei ronkō—chūgoku ni okeru saikin no kenkyū seika o yonde" [A discussion of the founding of the Pure and Perspicacious Sect—on reading the fruits of recent research conducted in China], *Tōhō shūkyō* 78.23–44 (Nov. 1991); and his most recent article on Xu Sun, "Kyo Son to Jōmyodō" [Xu Sun and the Jingming dao], in Noguchi Tetsurō, ed., *Kōza dōkyō*, vol. 1 (Tokyo: Yuzankaku, 1999), 222–241. In recent years, Chinese scholars have also shown great interest in this Daoist tradition. The following is a partial list of publications: Li Fengmao, "Wei-Jin nanbeichao wenshi yu Daojiao zhi guanxi" [The rela-

tionship of literati and Daoism in the Wei, Jin, and North-South dynasties period], (Ph.D. diss., National Chengchi University, Taibei, 1978), 253–256; Liu Ts'un-yan, "Xu Sun yu Langong" [Xu Sun and Lord Orchid], *Shijie zongjiao yanjiu* 3.40–59 (1985); a Japanese version of the Liu Ts'un-yan essay appeared as "Tōdai ni itaru made no Kyo Son no imeji" [The image of Xu Sun up to the Tang dynasty], *Tōhō shūkyō* 64.1–27 (1985); Qing Xitai and Zhan Shichuang, "Xu Sun yu Jingming dao zhi gaige" [Xu Sun and the reform of the Jingming dao], in *Zhongguo wenxue yu Zhongguo zhexue* [Chinese literature and Chinese philosophy] (Shenzhen, 1983); Li Yangzheng, "Jingming dao yu zhongxiao shenxian" [The Jingming dao and loyal and filial immortals], in *Daojiao gaishuo* [General study of Daoism] (Beijing: Zhonghua shujü, 1989); Zhan Shichuang, "Jingming dao de xingcheng" [The formation of the Jingming dao], in *Nan-Song Jin-Yuan de daojiao* [Daoism in Southern Song and the Jin and Yuan dynasties] (Shanghai: Guji chubanshe, 1989); Ren Jiyu, "Ru-Dao ronghe de dianxing: Jingming dao" [A quintessential example of the synthesis of Confucianism and Daoism: The Jingming dao], in *Zhongguo daojiao shi* [History of Chinese Daoism] (Shanghai: Renmin chubanshe, 1990); Li Gang, "Jingming dao fasheng yu Tangdai Xu Sun chongbai" [The rise of the Jingming dao and Xu Sun worship in the Tang], *Zhongguo daojiao* 4 (1990); Zeng Shaonan, "Jingming dao de lixue tese" [The neo-Confucian characteristics of the Jingming dao], *Zongjiaoxue yanjiu* 2–3 (1988); Zhang Zehong, "Xu Sun yu Jingming dao" [Xu Sun and the Jingming dao], in *Wei-Jin Nanbeichao Sui-Tang ziliao* [Source materials on the Wei, Jin, North and South dynasties, Sui, and Tang period] (Wuhan: Wuhan daxue chubanshe, 1991). See also Judith M. Boltz, *A Survey of Taoist Literature: Tenth to Seventeenth Centuries* (Berkeley: Institute of East Asian Studies, 1987), 70–78, for a survey of sources pertaining to this sect. A more recent work by Cynthia J. Brokaw, *The Ledgers of Merit and Demerit: Social Change and Moral Order in Late Imperial China* (Princeton: Princeton University Press, 1991), also contains a brief discussion of the sect, particularly from the perspective of the practice of merit-making; see pp. 43–52.

8. The dates for Xu are by no means certain. The year of death, in particular, is problematic. Most sources accept the 374 date. Moreover, the very historicity of Xu is also a matter of dispute, as official historical records, such as the *Jinshu,* contain no account of him. Finally, as shall be made clear later, there is considerable divergence of opinion on the issue of whether Xu should be regarded as the founder of the sect that came to be known as Jingming zhongxiao dao.

9. See Akizuki, *Chūgoku kinsei,* 4–5 for the various sources. See also Boltz, *Survey of Taoist Literature,* 70–78.

10. Hereafter referred to as *Quanshu,* this compendium is collected in the *Daozang,* the *Daoist Canon.* Hereafter, all quotations from the *Daozang*

(conventionally abbreviated as *DZ*) are based on the Taiwan reprint of the original edition published in 1665 with a supplement published in 1606 (Taibei: Xinwenfeng chuban gongsi, 1977) *DZ* 41: 481–531.

11. *Jinshu* [History of the Jin dynasty] relates that, as a child, Wu Meng often left himself naked in the summer so that the mosquitoes would bite him and would leave his parents alone (see *juan* 95). For this he became one of the twenty-four Exemplars of Filiality. Miyakawa Hisayuki offers a brief biographical account of Wu in "Local Cults around Mt. Lu at the time of Sun En's Rebellion" in Holmes Welch and Anna Seidel eds., *Facets of Taoism* (New Haven: Yale University Press, 1979), 92–94; See also K. M. Schipper, *"Taoist Ritual and Local Cults of the T'ang Dynasty,"* Proceedings of the International Conference on Sinology, 1980, Vol. 4, *Popular Customs and Culture* (Taipei: Academica Sinica: 1981) 102–104. As shall be explained later, other sources partial to Xu would change the relationship between the two, making Xu the master and Wu the disciple. Many of Wu's heroic feats would also be credited to Xu.

12. It is commonly assumed that Jingyang is located in Sichuan, but Akizuki argues that it could be the Zhijiang county of Hubei; see Akizuki, *Chūgoku kinsei*, 57. Most Chinese scholars now concur with Akizuki.

13. It is interesting to note that nearly half of the Twelve Perfect Lords were actually Xu Sun's closest relatives. His son-in-law, two nephews, and a father-in-law of his own son, were among his most trusted disciples. This clearly reflects the sect's emphasis on family and blood ties. That the sect should stress filial piety and family ethics is understandable. See Akizuki, *Chūgoku kinsei*, 101–102.

14. This hagiographical account is summarized from the biography of Xu Sun in *Quanshu*.

15. *Yunji qiqian, juan* 106, *DZ* 37:363b.

16. *DZ* 11:693–699.

17. This is precisely the title adopted by Schipper in his discussion of the Xu Sun tradition in the Tang dynasty, in "Taoist Ritual," 108–110.

18. The Youwei guan was, however, by no means the only center of Xu Sun worship. There was a Black Stone Shrine (Wushi guan) in Fengcheng County not far from Yuzhang where another Xu Sun following maintained cultic worship of Xu for several hundred years. At the time of Tang Taizong, it even obtained imperial patronage to renovate the shrine. See Akizuki, *Chūgoku kinsei*, 105–106.

19. The calculation here is problematic. Taken literally, this statement will make A.D. 257 the year of the ascent, a rather improbable happening— as Xu was born in 239 and would have thus made his ascent at age 18, which would not allow for all of his alleged accomplishments in later life.

20. *DZ* 11:697.

21. Ibid., 699. *Juan* 1 to 9 of the *Huanglu zhaiyi*, by Du Guangting,

describes in detail the canonical rites for the three-day service. Cf. Schipper, "Taoist Ritual," 110.

22. A portrayal of such a procession is contained in the *Xishan Xu zhenjun bashiwu hualu* [Records of the perfect lord Xu of Western Mountain in eighty-five segments], published in 1247 by Sun Yuanming, abbot of the Xu Sun Shrine. Cf. *DZ* 11:678–680.

23. Quoted from the *Lishi zhenxian tidao tongjian* [Comprehensive mirror of the embodiment of the way by immortals of all ages], (*DZ* 8:305–788) quoted in Schipper, "Taoist Ritual," 111.

24. *Quanshu*, 1:10; *DZ* 41:490.

25. *DZ* 11:699.

26. See Hu's biography in *Quanshu*, 1:15; *DZ* 41:491.

27. This text, unfortunately, is now lost. *Taiping guangji* contains several entries that are reportedly taken from this work. Hu's authorship is asserted by *Tangshu* and *Tongzhi;* see Schipper, "Taoist Ritual," 103.

28. Quoted in Schipper, "Taoist Ritual," 109, without attribution.

29. Ibid., 110. A recent interpretation of the Lingbao tradition may be found in Catherine Bell, "Ritualization of Texts and Textualization of Ritual in the Codification of Taoist Liturgy," *History of Religions* 27.4 (May 1988): 366–392.

30. As identified by John Lagerway, this text is identical to the *Taishang dongxuan lingbao baxianwang jiaojie jing*. Cf. Schipper, "Taoist Ritual," 109 n. 28.

31. The surviving specimen of this canon, in excerpted form, is in *Yunji qiqian*, which was completed in 1019 by Zhang Junfang and others.

32. Cf. *Quanshu*, 1:10; *DZ* 41:490. Eminent Song scholars such as Hong Mai and Zhen Dexiu had served as *tiju* at the Yulong gong. Cf. Akizuki, *Chūgoku kinsei*, 119, 139.

33. Ibid., 126–130. For a description of the physical layout of the Yulong gong from the Song dynasty to 1871, see *Xiaoyaoshan wanshou gong zhi*, comp. Jin Guixing and Qi Fengyuan, 1878, reprinted in vols. 6–9 of the *Daojiao wenxian*, ed. Du Jiexiang (Taibei: Danqing tushu, 1983).

34. *Quanshu*, 1:10; *DZ* 41:490. See also Akizuki, *Chūgoku kinsei*, 30, 117.

35. For the best account of Lin Lingsu's ascendancy at the court of Emperor Huizong, see Michel Strickmann, "The Longest Taoist Scripture," *History of Religions* 17.3–4 (1978): 331–351.

36. Most Chinese scholars regard He Zhengong and He Shouzheng as the same person.

37. See He's preface to *Lingbao jingming xinxiu jiulao shenyin fumo mifa*, *DZ* 17:649.

38. *Quanshu*, 1:19; *DZ* 41:494.

39. Both texts, or texts with almost identical titles, are extant in the

Daozang. An analysis of the two texts will show that they are quite similar in emphasis. It should be pointed out that some Chinese scholars, notably Qing Xitai and Li Yangzheng, regard He Zhengong as the true founder of the Jingming zhongxiao dao.

40. See his *Chūgoku no shūkyō kaikaku* [Chinese religious reformation] (Kyoto: Hōzōkan, 1968).

41. The two texts receive substantial discussion in Cynthia Brokaw's *Ledgers,* 36–52.

42. See Akizuki, *Chūgoku kinsei,* chaps. 8 and 9, 195–246.

43. *Zhuzi yulei, juan* 106, quoted in ibid., 130–132.

44. As a matter of fact, a total of twenty-six prominent scholar-officials of the Song period had served as commissioner of the Xu Sun shrine. See Akizuki, *Chūgoku kinsei,* 137–139.

45. For an account of Daoism in early Yuan and the Buddho-Daoist debates under Kublai Khan, see Janet Rinaker Ten Broeck and Yiu Tung, "A Taoist Inscription of the Yuan Dynasty: The Tao-chiao-pei," *T'oung-pao* 40 (1950): 60–112.

46. *Quanshu,* 2:23; *DZ* 41:496.

47. Because of Liu's doctrinal contribution to the sect, many scholars, including Akizuki Kan'ei, Zeng Shaonan, Zhang Zehong, and others, argue that he was the true founder of the Jingming zhongxiao dao.

48. *Quanshu,* 1:12; *DZ* 41:496.

49. *Quanshu,* 1:25–27; *DZ* 41:497–498.

50. *Quanshu, juan* 1; *DZ* 41:481.

51. Ibid.

52. See in particular the prefaces of Zeng Sunshen and Peng Ye.

53. Akizuki, *Chūgoku kinsei,* 150–160.

54. Ibid., 161–163.

55. Ibid., 174–175. It should be pointed out that other sources, notably the *Complete Works of [Wang] Longxi* (*Longxi quanji, juan* 19), indicate that it was Hu who was the student of Wang, thereby reversing the roles. Also, Luo Rufang is known to have used a copy of the *Ledger of Merits and Demerits* for his own moral cultivation.

56. *Gaozi yishu* [Surviving works of Master Gao] *juan* 5. Cf. Akizuki, *Chūgoku kinsei,* 176.

57. *Hongbao ji, juan* 22, quoted in Akizuki, *Chūgoku kinsei,* 176.

58. Cf. Feng Menglong, *Jingshi tongyan* [Popular words to admonish the world] (Beijing: Renmin chubanshe, 1956), 593–647.

59. See Timothy Brook, *Geographical Sources of Ming-Qing History* (Center for Chinese Studies: University of Michigan Press, 1988), 144.

60. Cited in Liu Guangjing (Kwang-Ching Liu), *Jingshi sixiang yu xinxing qiye* [Statecraft thought and newly risen enterprises] (Taibei: Lianjing, 1990), 320.

61. Ibid. It is interesting to note that virtually all of the commercial guilds representing Jiangxi sojourner merchants throughout China in the Qing period were called *wanshou gong* (longevity palace). To what extent the Xu Sun tradition served as the glue for Jiangxi merchant identity and solidarity remains to be explored.

62. Shanghai bowuguan tushu ziliao shi [Office of Books and Resources of the Shanghai Museum], comp., *Shanghai beike ziliao xuanpian* [Selected stone inscription materials in Shanghai] (Shanghai, 1980), 336. The main temple was devoted to Xu Sun, the side altar to the god of wealth, and the upstairs altar to the literary god.

63. See Zhou Dezai, *Taiwan miaoshen zhuan* [Biographies of temple gods in Taiwan] (Jiayi: Fulo yinwuguan, 1980), 80–82.

64. See Ren Jiyu, *Zongjiao cidian* [Encyclopedia of religion] (Shanghai: Cishu chubanshe, 1981), 46.

65. Schipper, "Taoist Ritual," 103, 113.

66. Ibid., 114–115.

67. I am using an identical text with a different title, *Taishang dongxuan lingbao baxianwang jiaojie jing.* See note 28; *DZ* 41:545.

68. *DZ* 41:544.

69. *DZ* 41:545.

70. *DZ* 41:544.

71. *DZ* 17:638–648.

72. *DZ* 17:655–729.

73. *DZ* 17:638.

74. *DZ* 17:646–647.

75. Akizuki, *Chūgoku kinsei,* 122.

76. *DZ* 17:668.

77. *DZ* 17:668–669.

78. Ibid.

79. *DZ* 17:613.

80. *DZ* 18:901.

81. Cynthia Brokaw has a section on the *Taiwei xianjun gongguoge* in her *Ledger,* 43–52.

82. *Quanshu,* 3:1; *DZ* 41:503.

83. *Quanshu,* 3:7; *DZ* 41:506.

84. *Quanshu,* 3:8; *DZ* 41:507.

85. *DZ* 41:451.

86. *DZ* 17:577–578.

87. This was found in a Ming edition of *Quanshu,* 77a, in the collection of *Naikaku bunkō* in Japan.

88. For Yuan Huang, see Sakai Tadao, "Confucianism and Popular Educational Works," in Wm. Theodore de Bary ed., *Self and Society in Ming Thought* (New York: Columbia University Press, 1970), esp. 342–345. See

also the more recent work of Cynthia Brokaw, *The Ledgers of Merit and Demerit: Social Change and Moral Order in Late Imperial China* (Princeton: Princeton University Press, 1991), 61–109. For Zhuhong, see Chün-fang Yü, *Renewal of Buddhism in China: Chu-hung and the Late Ming Synthesis* (New York: Columbia University Press, 1981), chap. 5, 101–137.

89. *Baopuzi, juan* 3, 8b–9a.

90. Ibid.

91. For a detailed analysis of the history of *gongguo* (merits and demerits) thought, see Akizuki, *Chūgoku kinsei,* 235–238. See also Sakai Tadao, *Chūgoku zensho no kenkyū* [Studies on the Chinese morality books] (Tokyo: Kōbundō 1960), chap. 5, esp. 356–372; Brokaw, *Ledgers of Merit and Demerit,* passim.

92. Akizuki has actually located the building as described in *Records of the Yulong wanshou gong, juan* 10. See Akizuki, *Chūgoku kinsei,* 211. Cynthia Brokaw inexplicably refers to this individual as Master Yu [You], thereby giving the erroneous impression that You is the family name. See her *Ledgers,* 43.

93. See the detailed description of the celestial bureaucracy, particularly the agency for moral accounting, in *Taishang lingbao jingming dongshen shangpin jing, juan shang,* 1, *DZ* 41:450.

94. *DZ* 5:289.

95. *DZ* 5:290.

96. Stephen Bokenkamp makes a special observation in connection with the Tianshi dao and the Shangqing texts he translated. See his *Early Daoist Scriptures,* 155–157, 299–300.

97. *Baopuzi,* "Inner Section," *juan* 3.

98. *Quanshu,* 5:8; *DZ* 41:518.

99. Cynthia Brokaw observes that some elite scholar-officials regarded the teaching and mentality of the ledgers as "heterodox," because they were originally inspired by Buddhist and Daoist doctrines and they exhorted people to do good in hopes of personal gains, a premise that orthodox Confucian teaching would frown upon; see *Ledgers,* 52–60. Yet at the same time she also concedes that, at least for those scholar-official elites who supported the Xu Sun tradition, they "seem to have been impressed with the potential usefulness of the text and the sect in the transmission of 'Confucian' values supportive of social stability" 52.

CHAPTER 5

Daoism and Local Cults
A Case Study of the Cult of Marshal Wen

Paul R. Katz

Few problems in the study of Chinese religion deserve greater attention than the complex process of interaction between Daoism and local cults. Unfortunately, few problems have also been as thoroughly misunderstood. In considering the scholarly literature on this topic, one can see the emergence of two nearly diametrically opposed viewpoints. On one side are scholars researching Daoism, many of whom tend to view it as a "higher" or "elevated" form of Chinese popular religion, one which structured cult worship through the "Daoist liturgical framework."[1] On the other, there are scholars devoting their efforts to the study of local cults, of whom most downplay or underestimate the important role Daoism could play in the growth thereof. Some have even argued that lay believers could not worship the deities summoned by Daoist priests in their rituals.[2] While each of these views is grounded in an element of truth (Daoism certainly presents itself as superior to local cults, while many esoteric Daoist deities are seldom worshiped by non-Daoists), both fail to appreciate the degree to which Daoism and local cults shaped each other, indeed depended on each other. I explore this problem through a case study of the cult of a popular deity named Wen Qiong, also known as Marshal Wen (Wen yuanshuai) or the Loyal and Pacifying King (Zhongjing wang). Wen's cult enjoyed a high degree of popularity from the Song dynasty onward, as he was worshiped by Daoist priests *(daoshi)*, Daoist and local ritual masters *(fashi* or *faguan)*, and lay believers throughout southern China (particularly the provinces of Jiangsu, Zhejiang, and Fujian). His cult continues to be popular in Taiwan, and is now making a comeback in China following the dark years of the Cultural Revolution (1966–1976). In the course of this study, I address the following questions: How did

Daoist priests attempt to distinguish the deities they worshiped from those of local cults? In what ways did they try to influence such cults? To what extent did their efforts succeed?

In discussing what is generally referred to as "religious Daoism" (Daojiao), I basically concur with Nathan Sivin and the late Michel Strickmann (1942–1994), who define as "Daoist" those religious movements that shared a recognition of the First Heavenly Master Zhang Daoling as one of their patriarchs and promoted the worship of deities representing "pure emanations of the Dao."[3] However, I also concede that the use of such a definition makes it difficult to consider as "Daoist" socio-ethical movements like Quanzhen dao (the Way of Perfect Realization) and Jingming zhongxiao dao (the Loyal and Filial Way of the Pure and Perspicacious), or local ritual movements like the Divine Empyrean (Shenxiao) discussed below. The main reason for this is that, as Judith Boltz points out, for members of these movements "homage to Zhang Daoling may have been little more than an afterthought, reflecting the unquestioned primacy of the [Orthodox Unity] Cheng-i [Zhengyi] lineage."[4] While such groups are invariably included in general histories of Daoism, it is important to realize that the term "Daoism" in Chinese religious history has been used to encompass all manner of religious movements, many of which espoused very different agendas.[5]

This point becomes abundantly clear when considering the various forms of orthodoxy and orthopraxy occurring in different Daoist movements.[6] As Richard Shek points out in chapter 4, in his essay on the Loyal and Filial Way, this type of Daoist movement actively attempted to accommodate the "socioethical orthodoxy" discussed by Kwang-Ching Liu and others in *Orthodoxy in Late Imperial China*,[7] or the "moral orthodoxy" described by C. K. Yang,[8] by stressing ethical values such as loyalty to the state and filial piety.[9] Such groups tended to look down on Daoist exorcistic rituals such as those featuring Marshal Wen, stressing instead that proper ethical behavior was the "indispensable step in the pursuit of immortality."[10] However the Daoist movements discussed in this essay, the Divine Empyrean movement and the Way of the Heavenly Masters (Tianshi dao; also known as the Way of the Orthodox Unity [Zhengyi dao]), shared a very different concern. As evidence in the following shows, members of these movements constantly strove to establish a Daoist spiritual hierarchy in which Daoist and local deities were accorded proper sacrifices based on their position therein. In addition, they attempted to define which ritual traditions should be considered orthodox and which were heterodox. Such efforts reflect a profound concern with what I would tentatively define as "liturgical orthopraxy." This does not mean that Daoism featured a rigid dichotomy between socioethical orthodoxy and liturgical orthopraxy. Heavenly Master Daoists also expressed a concern for the former,[11] while members of the Loyal and Filial Way did not reject all Daoist rituals out of hand, for example, rituals such as Daoist offerings (jiao) and retreats (zhai) were perfectly acceptable. The Heavenly Master Daoists' concern with liturgical orthopraxy also represented a form of accommodation to orthodox Confucian ideology having to do with ritual propriety and the state cult. I should also stress that the distinction between socioethical orthodoxy and liturgical orthopraxy is not meant to suggest a Western dualism between belief and action.[12] Nevertheless, I do believe that this distinction can help us better appreciate the various ways in which different Daoist movements tried to identify or define themselves.

Why were the members of various Daoist movements so deeply concerned with orthodoxy and orthopraxy? I believe that such concerns largely reflect their desire to distinguish themselves from and establish their religious superiority over local cults. As the late Michel Strickmann pointed out, Daoism's chief rival throughout Chinese history was not Buddhism, or even the state; rather, it was the "nameless religion" of the masses.[13] A careful reading of any general history of Daoism reveals that the growth of this religion since its formation in Han-dynasty Sichuan has been marked by an ongoing effort to absorb, co-opt, reform, and even eradicate the numerous cults and ritual traditions it encountered in the regions to which it spread.[14] In many ways, Daoism enjoyed considerable success, with Daoist priests being among the key figures behind the growth of numerous local cults throughout China. These religious specialists compiled hagiographies of local deities written in classical Chinese, helped found and restore temples in which such deities could be worshiped, and invoked them in their rituals. Daoist priests also performed many of the major rituals marking the growth of local cults, particularly the offering rituals and retreats mentioned above. They continue to play such roles throughout parts of China, Taiwan, and Hong Kong, as well as among overseas Chinese communities. At the same time, however, Daoism was never fully able to achieve its goal of reforming or even eradicating those local cults it considered to be heterodox. Frequently labeled by Daoists "licentious shrines" *(yinci)* or "licentious sacrifices" *(yinsi)*,[15] such cults were said to feature worship of "heterodox deities" *(xieshen,* usually the ghosts of the unruly dead or various nature spirits). These deities (or demons) were invariably served by spirit mediums *(wu)*, who led rituals to placate them with "bloody (i.e., meat) offerings" *(xueshi)*. If heterodoxy is to be understood as a form of dissent or resistance,[16] then those local cults that failed to conform to "orthodox" Daoist values would certainly have been seen as heterodox by Daoist priests. However, although Daoist priests made mighty efforts to eliminate such forms of heteropraxy, their success seems to have been rather limited. Far more common are the cases of Daoists absorbing and attempting (again unsuccessfully) to redefine local deities as orthodox Daoist gods, at times even grudgingly accepting the hated representations of those heterodox deities they had once attempted to destroy.[17]

In their opposition to local cults and their rituals, Daoist priests expressed attitudes strikingly similar to those of the Ming-Qing elites described by Donald Sutton in this volume, as well as the late imperial state as studied by Richard J. Smith and Romeyn Taylor in *Orthodoxy in Late Imperial China*.[18] Consequently, they faced a somewhat similar dilemma. On the one hand, Daoism's claim to liturgical authority depended in part on its ability to absorb popular deities (like Marshal Wen) into the Daoist heavenly bureaucracy. On the other hand, its declared allegiance to the state and the Confucian values it represented (a relationship established during the Three Kingdoms period and maintained to the present day) compelled Daoism to defend itself against any form of contamination by "heterodox" practices.[19]

The existence of such a dilemma appears to reflect what might best be termed a "Daoist identity crisis." As I have mentioned, Daoism interacted extensively with numerous local cults and ritual traditions as it spread throughout China. This resulted in Daoism and local cults being both in competition with and yet also "embarrassingly similar" to each other. Even in recent decades, some scholars and most laymen (including government officials) tend to equate the terms "Daoism" and "popular religion."[20] Faced with such an awkward situation, and well aware of the implications of being considered just another local movement and labeled as "illicit" or "heterodox,"[21] Daoist priests made concerted efforts to define themselves as "orthodox" or "correct." In doing so, they attempted to portray themselves as being both morally and ritually superior to those same cults they attempted to absorb, reform, or aid the state in suppressing.

We can see such a process at work in the development of the very first Daoist movement, the religious organization established in Sichuan by Zhang Lu and his followers.[22] While most histories refer to this movement as the Way of the Five Pecks of Rice (Wudoumi dao), such a term is merely a label (or exonym) used by the scholar-officials who recorded the activities of this cult. In fact, members of this movement identified themselves by using autonyms such as "the Way of the Heavenly Masters," or more importantly "the Way of the Orthodox Unity" (Zhengyi dao).[23] Why did they choose to do so, and why in particular did they use the latter appellation?[24] The answer to this question lies in this movement's origins in Sichuan, a region with a highly active body of local cults and spirit mediums (even Zhang Lu's mother was said to have belonged to a "way of demons" or *guidao,* in all likelihood a local cult). Zhang and his successors seem to have attempted to absorb some of these mediums' practices (including healing rites, music, ecstatic possession, etc.)[25] while at the same time identifying themselves as a separate and superior movement, which aimed at reforming many popular practices deemed "excessive" or "heterodox."

This sense of identity appears quite clearly in a number of this movement's earliest scriptures. For example, a fragment of one text entitled *Zhengyi jing* (Scripture of orthodox unity) preserved in the Daoist collectanea *Yunji qiqian* (Seven lots from the bookbag of the clouds), compiled by Zhang Junfang (fl. 1008–1029), describes a divine encounter between Zhang Daoling and Laozi (said to have occurred in 142 C.E.) as follows:

> I [Zhang Daoling] received [this scripture? this covenant?] from the Venerable Lord on High (Taishang laojun), who instructed me in the newly revealed Way of the Orthodox Unity . . . to study the orthodox and uproot the heterodox"[26]

A more detailed account of these events is supplied in the *Santian neijie jing* (Scripture of the internal commentaries of the three heavens), a text ascribed to the fifth century:

The Most High [Laozi] said: "Men of the world do not respect the true and the orthodox, but only honor pernicious demons. That is why I have taken the name of Old Lord Newly Appeared." Then he installed Zhang as Master of the Three Heavens, of the Orthodox One Energy of Peace of the Great Mysterious Capital; he revealed to him the Way of the Covenant with the Powers of the Orthodox One *(Zhengyi mengwei zhi dao)* . . . [The Heavenly Master] made a contract with the Three Officials *(sanguan)* of Heaven, Earth, and Water respectively, as well as with the generals of the star of the Great Year (Taisui), so that they then entered the orthodox system of the Three Heavens and no longer oppressed the faithful [by requiring bloody offerings or lavish temples].[27]

Here we see the first evidence of the "system" presented in Marshal Wen's hagiography, a system in which popular deities joined the Daoist heavenly bureaucracy (or hierarchy; see note 102) and accepted only pure offerings (vegetarian foods and incense). We also see Daoism attempting to distinguish itself from and establish its authority over local cults by declaring that only it represented the "orthodox" way. Given the importance of this claim, it is no surprise that many of the early titles of this movement's leaders also included the term "orthodox unity."[28]

The extent to which Daoism was able to succeed in lording it over local cults is another matter entirely. As scholars such as Rolf A. Stein, Hisayuki Miyakawa, Richard B. Mather, and Peter Nickerson have shown, while the Daoist priests of China's medieval era frequently condemned "licentious shrines" and their "heterodox deities," and even joined with the state in attempting to suppress them, such efforts rarely bore fruit, particularly since many new converts to Daoism (both lay worshipers and those who had originally belonged to local ritual movements) persisted in worshiping local deities with bloody offerings, despite the exhortations of their leaders.[29] Daoism of that era undoubtedly considered itself to be a reform movement, with an agenda clearly set out in numerous scriptures. However, the degree to which these reforms were actually able to take hold among the supporters of local cults appears to have been rather limited.

We see a similar phenomenon in Song China as well, particularly in the southern regions of the empire. As Judith Boltz and others have shown,[30] numerous new ritual movements arose throughout the region during that time, including the Divine Empyrean movement to be discussed in the following pages. Such movements, which were extensively influenced by both local mediumistic traditions and Tantric Buddhism, featured numerous forms of exorcistic and healing rituals centering on powerful martial deities like Marshal Wen. Many of these ritual movements were soon absorbed into the Way of the Heavenly Masters, while others merely chose to acknowledge its supremacy. Members of the Way of the Heavenly Masters also absorbed many of the deities and rites of these ritual movements, while simultaneously attempting to redefine them in terms of the liturgical orthopraxy mentioned. We see just such a process at work in the hagiography and ritual traditions of Marshal Wen.

The Hagiography of Marshal Wen

The hagiography of Marshal Wen contained in the *Daoist Canon* is entitled *Diqi shangjiang Wen taibao zhuan* (A hagiography of Grand Guardian Wen, supreme general of the earth spirits).[31] This text has been extensively studied by a number of scholars,[32] so there is no need to give a detailed presentation of it here. Instead, I will briefly discuss its author, summarize its contents, and then proceed to analyze the concept of orthopraxy as it appears in this text.

Wen's hagiography was composed in 1274 by a Divine Empyrean priest named Huang Gongjin, a disciple of the famous ritual master Liu Yu (fl. 1258) of Fengcheng (Jiangxi).[33] In a colophon preserved in the *Daofa huiyuan,* which probably was meant to accompany Wen's hagiography, Huang portrays himself as having been a young scholar who initially developed an interest in Chan (Zen) Buddhism but converted to Daoism in 1247 after having successfully used Daoist charms to cure illnesses. He later kowtowed to Liu as his master, and spent seven years under him learning how to write charms and perform rituals, as well as an additional seven years practicing meditation and alchemy.[34] As for his motives in composing Wen's hagiography, Huang indicates that this arose out of an urgent sense of a need for liturgical orthopraxy:

> [When I studied under Liu Yu], he transmitted to me the various [ten] ritual techniques of the earth spirits. But now there are many different schools and sects *(zongpai),* whose teachers transmit different forms [of these ritual techniques]. They [willfully] increase and decrease the incantations and formulas *(zhoujue)* used, thereby falsi-

fying [these techniques'] true original form *(zhen yuan ben)*.... Today, those who study these techniques are as numerous as the hairs of an ox, while those who succeed [in their studies] are as few as the horns of a griffin.... Therefore, I decided to print up this hagiography of General Wen, and compose this colophon.[35]

Despite Huang's concern with liturgical orthopraxy, however, in the hagiography itself Wen seems anything but the image of an orthodox deity. He is not a scholar-official but a martial figure over nine feet tall, who serves the Tang commander Guo Ziyi (697–781) in his campaign against the An Lushan rebels. He proves an effective warrior, not simply because of his knowledge of strategy and tactics but because he is able to transform himself into a one-horned snake and spit out a poisonous black fog to rout his enemies. Eventually Guo becomes aware of the unusual nature of this officer, and Wen flees to the foot of Mount Tai (Tai Shan), not to practice self-cultivation but to work as a butcher. Wen then has a spiritual encounter with Lord Bingling (Bingling gong; said to be the third son of the Emperor of the Eastern Peak [Dongyue dadi]), who admonishes Wen to give up being a butcher yet also informs him that he lacks the potential (literally "bones") to become an immortal.[36] Subsequently, Wen joins the Temple of the Eastern Peak as a "master of alms" *(huazhu)*. His devout ways eventually earn him the attention of the Emperor of the Eastern Peak, who reveals through a temple medium *(taibao;* also referred to as a "general" *[jiangjun])*[37] that Wen will become a deity once a statue of himself is metamorphosed, an event that takes place on the ninth day of the fifth lunar month.

The rest of the hagiography describes Wen's transformation into an orthodox Daoist deity, as well as his subsequent exploits in the fight against heteropraxy. After his death, the court awards Wen an official title, while villagers around Mount Tai propose erecting a temple to him. Wen's spirit refuses both honors, however, claiming that he has no interest in official titles or popular temples (and their rituals featuring bloody offerings), desiring instead to "support the orthodox Way" *(fuchi zhengdao)*. This greatly impresses the Emperor of the Eastern Peak, who accepts Wen into the temple's spiritual bureaucracy by placing him in charge of the registers of life and death. Wen also refuses a temple offered by the residents of Wenzhou after he ended a drought there, informing the locals that he would prefer that they hold a Daoist offering *(jiao)* and submit a memorial recounting his good deeds to Dark Emperor (Xuandi, also known as Supreme Emperor of the Dark Heavens [Xuantian shangdi]). News of Wen's merit soon reaches the attention of the thirtieth Heavenly Master Zhang Jixian (ritual name [*faming*], Xujing) (fl. 1092–1126).[38] Zhang visits Mount Tai during the Xuanhe reign (1119–1125) and, impressed by Wen's desire to "convert to the orthodox Way" *(guiyi zhengdao)*, promotes Wen to the rank of earth spirit *(diqi)* and creates an "orthodox ritual technique" *(zhengfa)* in his name.

Wen's first act in the service of orthodox Daoism is to help Zhang Jixian exterminate the remnants of a demon horde at Qingcheng Shan (in Sichuan) originally vanquished by the first Heavenly Master.[39] These demons seem suspiciously similar to the popular deities Daoist priests were always railing against, having been awarded temples and official titles. Wen incinerates their temple and beheads the members of the demon horde,[40] prompting Zhang to award him the Daoist (*not* official) title of "Grand Guardian and Commissioner of Martial Prowess" who aids ritual techniques and assists the spirits *(zhufa yiling zhaowu dashi taibao)*. Zhang also presents Wen with a force of three thousand spirit soldiers and cavalry.

The story then backtracks in time to the reign of the Zhenzong emperor (998–1023), with Wen assisting a Daoist named Wang Zongjing (who had allegedly studied under Zhang Jixian)[41] in performing exorcisms. Wen also helps Wang's disciple Wu Daoxian to destroy the temple of a Buddhist deity in Fujian known as King Qieluo (Qieluo wang). This deity had used a form of sorcery known as "gold cocoon gu poison" *(jinjian gudu)* to control people by capturing their souls *(shou ren hunpo)*.[42] In order to overcome the deity, Wu utilizes the Tantric Buddhist technique of "catoptromancy" (summoning a deity by use of a mirror) to call on Marshal Wen, while also relying on the "incantation of (Marshal) Tianpeng (Tianpeng zhou)" to bolster his efforts.[43] This time, Wen uses a combination of thunder and fire to destroy the temple. As news of Wen's power spreads, the ritual techniques featuring him and his fellow earth spirits become extremely popular. Wu ends up transmitting these techniques to a total of 532 disciples, but only 106 of these prove successful in mastering these techniques, and over 200 disciples disobey the heavenly codes *(tianlü)* and are beaten to death by Wen.

The hagiography continues with an account of Wen's victory over a heterodox Buddhist movement in Jiangsu known as the Three Altars (Santan),[44] with Wen devouring some of its leaders alive. He then goes on to destroy a plague-demon cult in Sichuan, which includes a fellow earth spirit named King Kang (Kang wang). King Kang receives one hundred blows as punishment for his misdeeds.[45] There is also an addendum *(buyi)*, which contains a number of additional stories about Wen that Huang may have considered inappropriate to place in the main hagiography, including the highly popular tale of his disobeying his superiors in the Daoist heavenly bureaucracy and drinking the plague poison he is ordered to use against wicked people. The addendum also contains stories of how Wen aids local officials in the destruction of a temple, in Anhui, to the Five Manifestations (Wuxian, originally a group of mountain goblins known as the Wutong who were later awarded official titles),[46] destroys a monstrous fish *(nian; parasilurus asofus)* afflicting the people of Jiangxi, and vanquishes a group of animal demons in Pucheng county of Jianning prefecture (Fujian) who possess young girls and cause them to have seizures.

Wen's hagiography in the *Daoist Canon* provides invaluable information on the ways in which Southern Song Daoists conceived of liturgical orthopraxy.[47] For example, Wen is frequently praised for his adherence to orthodox Daoism or "the orthodox Way" *(zhengdao)*. In addition to the two examples cited above, a passage describing Wen's fight against the Three Altars movement notes that "the Grand Guardian constantly protected and supported the orthodox Way" *(huchi zhengdao)* (11a). The "orthodox Way" referred to could be religious Daoism in general, but it is also possible that Huang Gongjin intended this term to indicate the Way of Orthodox Unity (Zhengyi dao).[48] Wen's hagiography further reveals Huang's concern (expressed in the colophon) that the "orthodox Way" was in trouble. For example, when Wang Zongjing instructs Wu Daoxian to battle King Qieluo in Fujian, he laments that the people there "do not worship the orthodox Way" *(bufeng zhengdao)*, and that the province is a place of liturgical heteropraxy, full of "evil and heterodox devils and demons" *(yaoxie mogui)*.

In addition to local cults, Buddhism also comes under attack as being heterodox. The clearest example of this occurs when Wu Daoxian, after his victory over King Qieluo, asks Wen: "Buddhism is not

the orthodox Way *(fei zhengdao)*. Why don't you simply destroy it?"
(Wen replies that while Buddhism does contain heterodox elements,
Laozi decided to sanction its existence because it teaches people to
be compassionate). When Wu passes through Quanzhou, he also
notes that the locals' adherence to a heterodox religion like Buddhism has prevented the growth of the orthodox Way *(zhengdao
buzhen)*. It is not clear why Huang possessed such a powerfully negative attitude toward Buddhism, particularly as he had begun his religious career as a Buddhist practitioner. Nevertheless, the statements
cited, as well as the account of the Three Altars movement, leave
little room for doubt as to where his sympathies lay.

Marshal Wen's hagiography also reveals the ways in which deities could support the orthodox Way, the most important of which
involved adherence to Daoist liturgical orthopraxy by rejecting official titles and worship in popular temples (because it would involve
accepting bloody offerings). Wen is allowed to join the spiritual
bureaucracy of the Temple of the Eastern Peak, and is later awarded
a ritual technique by Zhang Jixian, precisely because he refuses such
honors offered by the residents of Mount Tai and Wenzhou. Such
behavior prompts Huang to describe Wen as "proper (orthodox)
and upstanding" *(zhengzhi)*, and classify him as an "orthodox deity"
(zhengshen). Wen also refers to himself in these terms when refusing
the honors offered by the residents of Wenzhou, saying: "I have made
a vow to be proper and upstanding, thereby aiding the people. . . . I
care not for official titles and temples." The heterodox deities Wen
vanquishes are precisely those deities who accept such honors. At the
same time, however, it is important to note that deities like Wen who
adhere to the orthodox Way *are* allowed to accept other titles: those
awarded by a Heavenly Master like Zhang Jixian or an orthodox
Daoist deity like the Emperor of the Eastern Peak. This represents
the ideal relationship between Daoism and local cults portrayed in
early texts such as the previously cited *Santian neijie jing*, according
to which, local deities willingly submit to Daoism. There are numerous examples of Wen being awarded (and accepting) Daoist titles,
the highest of which is "Superintendent of Temples under Heaven"
(Tidian tianxia shenmiao), effectively placing him in charge of all
local cults.[49]

Wen's hagiography also indicates that apart from convincing
local deities to accept a position in the Daoist spiritual bureaucracy,
liturgical orthopraxy could also be achieved through the transmis-

sion of "orthodox ritual techniques" *(zhengfa)*, a concern clearly addressed by Huang in the colophon he composed. Heavenly Master Zhang Jixian himself states that ritual techniques for the earth spirits are orthodox, though Huang later notes such techniques constitute an "inferior grade" *(xiapin)* in the hierarchy of Daoist liturgy. Huang (and his master Liu Yu) were also keenly aware that orthodox ritual techniques could be misused and abused. Huang's compilation of Wen's hagiography, and the ritual techniques to be discussed hereafter, represent Huang's attempt to deal with this liturgical crisis. Things are much simpler in the hagiography, as Wen simply beats to death all of Wu Daoxian's disciples who flout the heavenly codes.

In considering Wen's hagiography as a whole, I tend to agree with John Lagerwey that this text represents an attempt to formulate a "system" for Chinese religion, one in which Daoists supervise all local cults throughout the empire, judging which should be classified as orthodox and which as heterodox, and taking action against the latter.[50] A deity like Wen, initially a heterodox figure who transforms himself into a snake in battle and butchers animals for a living, can be accepted into the Daoist heavenly bureaucracy, but only if he agrees to adhere to the tenets of liturgical orthopraxy by refusing titles, temples, and, most importantly, bloody offerings.[51] As Lagerwey points out, Wen's hagiography is intended to demonstrate:

> All power in heaven and on earth was in the hands of Zhang Daoling and his successors, and all powers [including deities like Wen] had to either enroll in his ranks, that is, support and protect the Orthodox Way, join the System, perform public services, or else "go into the opposition" and so expose themselves to constant persecution, not to mention execution. . . . In a word, henceforth there was an Orthodoxy.[52]

The hagiography of Marshal Wen also confirms Terry Kleeman's theory about the existence of two ritual continuums. The first continuum consisted of the state cult and local cults, and featured bloody sacrifices. The second consisted of the "institutional religions" of Buddhism and Daoism, which distinguished themselves from the first continuum through their rejection of such sacrifices.[53] Huang's hagiography of Wen clearly views Daoism as belonging to the second continuum, yet also allows for the absorption of deities from the first continuum, provided that they first relinquish all claims to bloody offerings.[54] In fact, we know from non-Daoist sources that Wen was worshiped in local temples, received bloody offerings, and was awarded official titles. Nevertheless, Huang's work is important in that it reveals one form of the liturgical orthopraxy that Daoists tried so hard and for so long to establish.

The Rituals of Marshal Wen

Huang Gongjin did more than compose a hagiography about Marshal Wen; he also compiled two sets of ritual techniques featuring this deity entitled *Diqi Wen yuanshuai dafa* (Great ritual techniques of the earth spirit Marshal Wen). In the colophon mentioned, Huang also gives a thorough account of his motives for doing so, revealing once again his concern for maintaining a Daoist liturgical orthopraxy:

> In practicing the ritual techniques of the earth spirits, one must be aware of which sect's version one uses. If the sect is not authentic *(buzhen)*, then the generals *(jiang)* [summoned] will be unorthodox *(buzheng)*. What do I mean by unorthodox? For example, when our ritual colleagues among the wandering priests *(jianghu fayou)* practice these techniques and fall on hard times, even if they have these texts . . . they are unable to summon any generals. As a result, various demons and [popular] deities *(guishen)* will assume the names and usurp the places of the generals, causing them unlimited harm. . . . [In this way], the orthodox transmission of these techniques is lost, and even if one can summon the generals and their subordinates for a while, one will not be able to do so in the future. Those studying [these techniques] should carefully consider this, and heed the warning of my words![55]

Both Huang and and his master Liu Yu insist that the ritual techniques of Marshal Wen and his fellow earth spirits were first transmitted by the thirtieth Heavenly Master Zhang Jixian. Zhang is also listed as the administrator of ritual *(fazhu)* for the two sets of ritual techniques featuring Wen compiled by Huang as previously noted. However, there is no evidence in the biographical sources about Zhang to indicate that he had ever practiced Wen's ritual techniques,[56] and this claim seems little more than an attempt by Liu and Huang to enhance the legitimacy of the ritual techniques they so valued (and make them appear more orthodox).[57] It is significant, however, that these members of the Divine Empyrean movement chose to recognize the authority of the Way of the Heavenly Masters (which was only granted authority over Daoist movements in south China in 1280), as this implies that these men had begun to identify themselves as Daoists in the strict sense of the term, and that in doing so they may have sought to assume this movement's mantle of liturgical orthopraxy.

Huang Gongjin and Liu Yu were united in viewing Marshal Wen as an "orthodox deity" *(zhengshen)* who could aid them and their fellow Daoists in the ongoing struggle against heteropraxy. For example, in a text entitled *Diqi fa* (Ritual techniques of the earth spirits) Liu claims that those utilizing these techniques would be able to "distinguish between the orthodox and the heterodox" *(bian zhengxie)*, and that Wen was a deity who "supported the orthodox and eliminated the heterodox" *(fuzheng quxie)*.[58] The *Diqi Wen yuanshuai dafa* also places great emphasis on Wen's role as a deity who can overcome heterodox forces. For example, one passage describing Wen's iconography portrays him as a deity who "expels the heterodox and supports the orthodox" *(quxie fuzheng)*, while another slightly later in the text lauds his ability to "capture and hold heterodox essences" *(shouzhuo xiejing)*.[59] These ritual texts, which contain numerous charms and incantations to be used in the fight against "heterodox demons" *(xiegui)*,[60] follow Wen's hagiography in portraying him as a deity who "protects and supports the orthodox Way" *(huchi zhengdao)*. In addition, he is credited with helping to preserve the "orthodox energies" *(zhengqi)* and "true essences" *(zhenjing)* of the cosmos.[61] Even ritual texts about Wen in the *Daofa huiyuan* that were not compiled by Huang Gongjin, such as the *Dongyue Wen taibao kaozhao bifa* (The secret ritual technique for investigations and summonses of Grand Guardian Wen of the Eastern Peak), which contain representations of Wen very different from Huang's, listed hereafter, also describe him as a deity in the service of orthodox Daoism who fights against heterodox forces.[62]

Daoist Ritual Unity?

A number of scholars researching Daoism have been profoundly impressed by what they define as the "ritual unity" of this religious movement.[63] However, it is also important to be aware of the significant degree of diversity within Daoism. In the case of Marshal Wen's

hagiography and ritual texts, the extent to which Huang's ideals were
accepted by other Daoist priests, not to mention ritual masters and
lay believers, is a matter of considerable doubt. Much of the evidence
to be presented below indicates that Huang's works appear to have
had relatively little influence on contemporary and later worshipers.

Take for example the text in the *Daofa huiyuan* immediately
following Liu Yu's and Huang Gongjin's writings, the *Dongyue Wen
taibao kaozhao bifa* (*DFHY*, 254). This text, apparently not compiled by Huang, opens with an anonymous preface entitled "A Preface for Numinous Writings" ("Lingwen xu"). The preface presents
a very different representation of Marshal Wen, portraying him not
as a martial figure but as a young scholar who mastered the classics
of various schools of thought, including Daoism. The text also claims
that Wen refused to take a wife, so as not to spoil his "heavenly perfection" *(tianzhen)*. While Wen remains in the service of the Emperor
of the Eastern Peak, the text does not mention any link to Zhang
Jixian, claiming instead that Wen had helped Heavenly Master Ye
Fashan (616–720/722?) overcome a horde of plague demons in
Sichuan and that Ye was the one who had transmitted Wen's ritual
techniques.[64] The text also quotes Wen as making a vow to assist all
the ritual masters *(faguan)* under heaven in catching wicked forces
and curing illnesses; Daoist priests *(daoshi)* receive no explicit mention.[65] Taken as a whole, this text appears somewhat similar to a
hagiography of Wen written by the late Yuan/early Ming scholar-
official Song Lian (1310–1381), particularly in portraying Wen as a
scholar and stating that he had served under Ye Fashan, discussed
hereafter. How and why such different representations of Wen had
arisen within Daoism is unclear. Perhaps this text represents the
view of Divine Empyrean ritual masters who had not yet submitted
to the authority of the Way of the Heavenly Masters. It is also possible that this text was written during the early years of the Southern
Song dynasty, before the Way of the Heavenly Masters had gained
primacy. Whatever the case may be, the presence of such vastly different representations of the same deity in texts compiled by members of the same ritual movement suggests that any claims to "ritual
unity" among Daoists may need to be approached with a considerable degree of caution.

Even in considering the contents of these ritual texts, we find
considerable variation. For example, in the *Dongyue Wen taibao kaozhao bifa*, Wen is said to command a group of four generals (repre-

senting the four cardinal directions).[66] This differs from the hagiography composed by Huang Gongjin, which claims that Wen only commanded two generals (the names of these generals are different as well). The *Diqi Wen yuanshuai dafa* compiled by Huang even places Wen in command of the "four sages" *(sisheng)*, Marshals Tianpeng, Tianyou, Yisheng, and Yousheng.[67] In addition, the *Dongyue Wen taibao kaozhao bifa* contains a different set of instructions on how to write the Bingding Charm (Bingding fu) from that found in the *Diqi Wen yuanshuai dafa*.[68] We know from the passages of Huang's colophon cited above that numerous variations could be found in the ritual techniques featuring Wen and his fellow earth spirits. Huang's attempt at providing a standard form of these rituals apparently met with only limited success.

Other ritual texts featuring Marshal Wen that were written by members of the Divine Empyrean movement provide a very different representation of this deity and his function from those of the texts compiled by Huang Gongjin. Take for example a set of three ritual texts members of this movement used to counter the ravages of epidemics.[69] While these texts occasionally refer to certain Heavenly Masters and the Way of Orthodox Unity,[70] their overall emphasis is not on combating heteropraxy but rather on the problem of ritual efficacy. While they portray calamities, such as epidemics, as resulting from immoral behavior, this appears to have less to do with liturgical orthopraxy than moral orthodoxy. I have argued that such rites, in attempting to address the social problems that provoke the wrath of the deities in the Daoist heavenly bureaucracy, may in some ways resemble what Victor Turner has described as "rites of affliction."[71]

Popular Representations of Marshal Wen

If Huang Gongjin's work on Marshal Wen had a limited impact on his fellow Daoists, it had even less influence on those individuals or groups who had not been initiated into Daoism. This is not to deny the important role that Daoists played in the spread of Wen's cult throughout Zhejiang, as many of his cult's earliest temples there were founded or restored by Daoist priests.[72] However, the sources on the history of his cult there also indicate that the Daoist representations of Wen presented here may not have appealed to a broader audience. Take for example the stele inscription composed in 1355 by Song Lian, entitled "Wen Zhongjing Wang miaotang bei" (A stele for the temple to loyal and pacifying King Wen), written for a temple to Wen that had been founded by a Daoist in 1344.[73] According to this hagiography, Wen was the only son of a Tang dynasty aristocratic family. His mother had been unable to bear a son for many long years but finally conceived him during a miraculous dream following devoted prayers to the Jade Emperor. As a child, Wen soon mastered the main classics of the Three Religions, while also learning to perform rituals such as the Steps of Yu (Yubu).[74] However, he proved unable to pass the examination for the *jinshi* degree, and subsequently made a vow to serve "the deity at Mount Tai" (the Emperor of the Eastern Peak) in ridding the world of all manner of epidemics. He formulated a series of thirty-six charms and transmitted them to others, and then transformed himself into a *yaksa (yecha)* (lowly demon) and passed away. He is credited with assisting Ye Fashan in ridding Sichuan of "noxious vapors," and is also said to assist readily any Daoist priests in performing exorcistic rituals.[75]

Song Lian's hagiography of Marshal Wen, while linking him to rituals and deities that were a part of Daoism (and local ritual traditions as well), differs from Huang's work in failing to present Wen as being in the service of the "orthodox Way." In addition, Wen is said to have created his own charms, and not relied on the services of a Daoist Heavenly Master. His title in the hagiography, "Mighty and Fierce Loyal and Pacifying King of Orthodox Blessings and Manifest Response" (Zhengfu xianying weilie zhongjing wang), appears to be an official title, not a Daoist one; it is certainly the most frequently mentioned title in Zhejiang local gazetteers.[76] All in all, Song does not seem to have viewed Wen as a martial Daoist figure but instead as a broad-minded Confucian scholar well versed in the teachings of Buddhism and Daoism. In some respects, Wen seems remarkably similar to Song Lian himself, who mastered all manner of ancient texts in his childhood.[77]

A somewhat similar hagiography of Marshal Wen may be found in the *Sanjiao yuanliu shengdi fozu soushen daquan* (Complete compendium of the origins of the deities, sage emperors, and buddhas of the three religions), which diverges even further from Huang's account in the *Daoist Canon*.[78] It is not clear whether this version of Wen's hagiography is older than the preceding two, or whether it circulated more widely. It does follow Song's stele inscription in including the following features: miraculous impregnation, birth on the fifth day of the fifth lunar month, failing the examinations, and service to the Emperor of the Eastern Peak. Nevertheless, there are also some important differences, starting with the statement that Wen was born during the Han dynasty (in the same year, 142 C.E., during which Zhang Daoling encountered Laozi). His studies do not include Buddhist and Daoist works, and he fails both civil and military examinations. His vow reads: "As a man, I could not serve my ruler and aid the people; therefore (I vow that) after I die I will aid the Emperor [of the Eastern Peak] in punishing evil and exterminating heterodox forces" *(zhujian miexie)*. He also composes a gatha, the first two lines of which mention the orthodox values of filial piety, loyalty, and righteousness.

When the Emperor of the Eastern Peak hears of Wen's awesome abilities, this source claims, he summons him to become his assistant. After performing many meritorious acts, Wen is awarded a title by the Jade Emperor, who also grants him a jade flower (*qionghua;* said to confer immortality), a jade circlet, and a gold tablet inscribed in seal script with the characters "the carefree man of the empyrean" *(wuju xiaohan)*. He is later appointed commander of all the forces of the Five Peaks (Wuyue), and is the only marshal permitted an audience before the Jade Emperor.

According to the *Complete Compendium,* Wen received bloody offerings *(xueshi)* at Wenzhou, where he was both feared and respected by the city's residents. The thirty-sixth Heavenly Master Zhang Zongyan (1244–1291)[79] subsequently drafted the forces of the Five Peaks to carry out his own set of ritual techniques, establishing a group of ten grand guardians *(taibao)* with Wen as their leader. Zhang also ordered temples enshrining their images to be built; one such temple was founded in Hangzhou during the thirteenth century.[80] This temple's links to the Way of the Heavenly Masters have yet to be determined.[81]

This hagiography seems to give somewhat more primacy to Daoism, in that the Jade Emperor bestows a title on Wen, and the thirty-sixth Heavenly Master creates ritual techniques in Wen's name. However, the overwhelming emphasis of this text is not on Wen's prowess as a defender of orthodox Daoism but on his desire to serve the state and the people. His scholarly background receives even greater attention than in Song Lian's stele inscription, while the ideals of filial piety, loyalty, and righteousness are the focus of his gatha. Finally, the text clearly portrays Wen's function as a popular deity who received bloody offerings, without any hint of disapproval.

While it also mentions Zhang Zongyan's inclusion of Wen as one of ten grand guardians, it does not indicate that such a move made Wen more orthodox, or resulted in a cessation of bloody offerings on the part of his lay worshipers.

Quite a different representation of Marshal Wen may be found in late imperial fiction, as well as modern folktales. Such sources do not portray Wen as either an orthodox Daoist or Confucian figure; rather, he is someone who defies the Daoist heavenly bureaucracy in order to save the people. Huang Gongjin included one such story in the supplement *(buyi)* to Wen's hagiography. It recounts how Wen chose to swallow one thousand pills of plague poison rather than obey the Jade Emperor's orders to use them to spread epidemics among people judged as "evil" by orthodox Daoist deities. This story, which contradicts the principal values espoused by Huang in his hagiography of Wen by portraying Wen as *defying* the system, was probably not invented by Huang but instead represents his recording of a popular folktale.

We find a much more detailed version of this story in chapter 19 of the novel *Journey to the North*, which was edited and published by the Fujian publisher Yu Xiangdou (fl. 1588–1609) during the late Ming.[82] It states that the stove god of a certain village reported to the Jade Emperor that all its inhabitants persistently engaged in evil deeds. Livid with rage, the Jade Emperor summons one of the Five Commissioners of Epidemics (Wuwen shizhe), Zhong Shigui (the deity in charge of epidemics occurring during the winter months),[83] and orders him to use plague poison to exterminate all the village's inhabitants. Zhong takes his poison down to the earth god of the village, and instructs him to scatter some in every well the next morning. On hearing this, the earth god admits that most of the villagers are a sorry lot who deserve to die, but he also petitions Zhong to save one meritorious individual, named Xiao Qiong,[84] who makes a living selling bean curd. Zhong agrees, and the earth god proceeds to warn Xiao of the impending calamity, advising him not to drink any water the next day.

Terrified by this warning Xiao thinks to himself: "If a deity sent by Heaven is to poison the wells tomorrow and kill all the people, can I conceal what I know and preserve my own life? I would rather die myself and save the lives of the villagers; such an act would add to this old man's hidden merit" *(yinde;* believed to bring rewards in this life or the next). The story goes on to recount how Xiao Qiong went to one of the wells the very next day to confirm the earth god's warning. Before long, he spots an old man (the earth god) approaching the well with a packet of poison in his hand. Just as the old man is about to cast its contents into the waters, Xiao charges forward, snatching the packet away and swallowing the lot. Xiao dies on the spot, his body turning black all over.

The earth god, shocked by this unexpected turn of events, promptly takes Xiao's three yang and seven yin souls *(sanhun qipo)* to present to the Jade Emperor. The Jade Emperor, being deeply moved by Xiao's spirit of self-sacrifice, orders him to be enfeoffed as the Mighty Spirit and Marshal of Epidemics (Weiling wen yuanshuai; here the character *"wen"* means "epidemics"), and bestows on him a hat, a jade flower, and a golden tablet inscribed with the characters "the carefree man of the divine empyrean" *(wuju xiaohan)*.[85] Xiao persuades the Jade Emperor to spare the villagers, and warns them in a dream to change their evil ways. He later serves the Supreme Emperor of the Dark Heavens.[86]

Although the surname of the deity featured in this story has changed, there is little doubt that he is in fact Marshal Wen. His given name (Qiong) and iconography are identical to those in the other versions of his hagiography previously mentioned, and he is also portrayed as serving the Supreme Emperor of the Dark Heavens. The fact that his surname has changed may be due to the influence of spirit mediums. Some sources from Wenzhou give his surname as Lin or Ling,[87] while some Shaoxing sources also give Wen's surname as Lin.[88] In Taiwan, spirit mediums appear to have been largely responsible for creating the over one hundred different surnames of the Royal Lords (Wangye), including Wen, who populate that island's temples (see below).[89]

Of all the hagiographical accounts concerning Marshal Wen, those recounting his attempts to prevent epidemics appear to have had the widest circulation. According to one account by the late Qing writer Fan Zushu:

> The Earth Spirit Marshal (Diqi yuanshuai), enfeoffed as the Loyal and Pacifying King of Eastern Wenzhou, has the surname Wen. According to legend, he was a government student of the previous [Ming] dynasty who came to the provincial capital [Hangzhou] for the examinations. One night he overheard demons putting plague poison in a well, and threw himself into the waters in hopes of saving

the people. When they fished his body out the next day, it had turned black all over, and they knew that he had been poisoned [so nobody dared drink the water]. He was enfeoffed as a deity at that time.[90]

In Shaoxing, a serpent was responsible for poisoning the waters, while in both Lishui and Jiaxing plague demons are blamed.[91] The Reverend Hampden C. DuBose recorded a similar story of a deity worshiped in Suzhou, but does not give that deity's surname.[92]

Stories of deities like Marshal Wen drinking plague poison or preventing people from drinking poisoned waters have also spread to Taiwan, although their protagonist is not Wen Qiong but one of Taiwan's most popular Royal Lords, Lord Chi (Chi wangye). Most of these stories portray Lord Chi as an official, usually a district or prefectural magistrate (note the steady rise in Wen's status from commoner to scholar to scholar-official), and state that he swallowed plague poison in order to save the people under his jurisdiction.[93] Despite the differences in name and title, Lord Chi appears remarkably similar to Marshal Wen in terms of hagiography and iconography, and I have argued elsewhere that Lord Chi represents a transformation of Marshal Wen, which occurred in southern Fujian.[94] Of Taiwan's 700-plus Lord temples, at least 131 enshrine Chi as their sole principal deity (zhushen). If one were to include all the temples in which Chi is worshiped along with other Royal Lords in a group of main deities, or as a subsidiary deity (peishen), the number of temples enshrining him would exceed half of all the Lord temples on the island.[95]

These folktales, as well as Huang's hagiography in the Daoist Canon, all portray Marshal Wen as a deity linked to epidemics. Huang's version goes so far as to portray Wen as a deity with the power to inflict others with epidemics, even though he declines to use it. Such stories indicate the strong possibility that Wen may have originally been worshiped as a spirit capable of spreading epidemics, particularly during the initial period of his cult's growth. There are a number of reasons to suspect that this may have been the case. For one thing, Wen's birthday is celebrated on the date of the Dragon Boat Festival, the traditional time for expelling epidemics in south China and also the birthday of the Five Commissioners of Epidemics. There are also numerous records, including a passage in The Story of the Stone, of people in north China worshiping a deity named the Marshal of Epidemics whose iconography resembles Marshal

Wen's.[96] Wen is also referred to as the Marshal of Epidemics in some Zhejiang folktales, as well as the *Journey to the North*. In addition to this, the *Daoist Canon* version of Marshal Wen's hagiography mentions that he could transform himself into a snake and belch black fog to overcome his foes. Snakes with the power to harm others using the vapors they spat out were an integral part of the folklore of south China.[97] While these serpentine features were quickly expunged from later versions of Wen's hagiography and iconography, their presence in the earliest known version of his hagiography indicates that at least some worshipers saw him as a potentially dangerous spirit with the power to infect others. It is even possible that the use of the character *wen* (meaning "warm"; also a Chinese surname) instead of *wen* ("fevers" or "epidemics") in Marshal Wen's titles may have represented an attempt to cover up his cult's sinister origins, as well as link it to its cult center at Wenzhou.

As Wen's cult continued to grow, however, the nature of his links to epidemics appears to have undergone a change.[98] It appears that while Marshal Wen may originally have been represented as a demon who could spread epidemics, he eventually became worshiped as a deity with the power to prevent them. Even though some of his titles retained the character *"wen"* (epidemics), I have not found any evidence to indicate that Song dynasty or later worshipers viewed him as a deity who could spread contagious diseases. How Wen became transformed from a demon into a deity is not clear, but the process involved may have been somewhat similar to what frequently occurs in Taiwan. Field data on a number of cults there, including those of some Royal Lords, indicates that the souls of those who die premature or violent deaths, and prove powerful enough to resist attempts at exorcism, are considered to be "vengeful ghosts" *(ligui)*. Not all vengeful ghosts are alike, however, as those able to acquire an individual identity and also prove efficacious when approached by worshipers may end up being worshiped as gods.[99] The numerous versions of Wen's hagiography presented here all reveal that he died young (before marrying and fulfilling his Confucian obligation of fathering descendants), and in a highly unusual or violent fashion. This implies that he was originally conceived of as a vengeful ghost with the power to harm individuals or communities by infecting them with contagious diseases. Furthermore, the novel *Journey to the North* and other sources indicate that Marshal Wen may originally have been a plague demon lacking any individual features, as seen in his title "Marshal of Epidemics." The fact that his surname frequently changed also hints at the nebulous nature of his identity. Wen appears to have acquired a clear hagiography and iconography only by the Song dynasty, and it is probably no coincidence that his first temples were built at that time.

Apart from his links to epidemics, a significant feature of these popular stories about Wen is their portrayal of him as someone who defies the "system," that is to say the Daoist heavenly bureaucracy. As the *Journey to the North* and folktales make clear, the epidemics to be inflicted on the populace do not represent arbitrary forms of divine wrath; rather, they are a justly deserved retribution for wrongful behavior. Therefore, deities like the Five Commissioners of Epidemics were not conceived of as rampaging demons but as officials in the Daoist heavenly bureaucracy who only acted on orders of the Jade Emperor.[100] The study of Daoist rituals used to combat epidemics also indicates that such calamities were viewed as representing the inevitable consequences of immoral behavior and social decay, and were invariably inflicted by a just and fair spiritual bureaucracy.[101] One of the great contradictions of Chinese popular religion may be the fact that it envisions epidemics as a form of divine punishment, yet also allows for the presence of deities like Marshal Wen, who intercede on behalf of the people to prevent them from receiving their just desserts.[102] One wonders how Daoists like Huang Gongjin would have reacted to such stories, which, while portraying Wen as a compassionate figure, also emphasize his defiance of the Daoist heavenly bureaucracy. Such defiance would normally be enough to cause a deity to be considered heterodox by Daoists, particularly since his actions were meant to save the very people who sacrificed to him using heterodox bloody offerings.

Conclusion

The evidence presented indicates that many different representations of Marshal Wen circulated among his worshipers, indeed that more than one Marshal Wen existed in the minds of the late imperial Chinese. However, I do not mean to imply that each of these representations constituted an isolated and insulated set of beliefs, as constant interaction among different representations occurred through a process I have termed "reverberation."[103] In the case of Wen's hagiography, the data indicate that people who were not Daoist priests still believed that Wen had served the Way of the Heavenly Masters, while Daoists like Huang Gongjin also recorded popular folktales. The belief that Wen had been a scholar appeared in Song Lian's stele inscription, the *Complete Compendium* hagiography, and the *Dongyue Wen taibao kaozhao bifa,* eventually influencing the folktales about him previously described. The fact that the process of reverberation occurred during the circulation of Marshal Wen's hagiography not only means that Daoist representations of Wen could gain some acceptance among lay believers, but also that lay representations of Wen could influence Daoist ones. At the same time, however, we find that each representation generally had only a limited impact on the other. Thus, while Huang recorded the story about Wen's drinking plague poison, his version suggests that Wen can only redeem himself by going through the proper procedures of the Daoist heavenly bureaucracy. Similarly, while Song Lian and the authors of the *Complete Compendium* accepted the idea that Wen had served the Way of the Heavenly Masters, they did not portray Wen as working to support the orthodox Way but, rather, fulfilling a typical Confucian scholar's ambition of serving the state to bring peace and order to the world. The process of reverberation may have encouraged interaction between different representations of a deity, but it certainly did not mean that one representation could achieve hegemony over the others.[104]

This is abundantly clear in the case of Huang Gongjin's hagiography of Marshal Wen, a work that portrays Wen as a deity who gained recognition and status by loyally serving Daoists belonging to the Way of the Heavenly Masters and helping them maintain spiritual and cosmic order. As numerous scholars of Daoism have shown, one of the key facets of Daoism is that it presents itself as able to maintain social, spiritual, and cosmic order through its establishment of a heavenly bureaucracy and the performance of rituals like the *jiao* (or "rite of cosmic renewal").[105] The "bureaucratic metaphor," so important to lay worshipers in their understanding of the spiritual world,[106] also occupied an integral place in Daoist cosmology.[107] For Daoism, therefore, one way to maintain order in the universe was through the attainment of liturgical orthopraxy, something that could be achieved in part with the help of deities like Marshal Wen, who accepted and knew their place in the Daoist heavenly bureaucracy.

Unregulated cults featuring spirit mediums and bloody sacrifices represented disorder or chaos and, due to the fact that they resisted Daoist norms, came to be labeled as heterodox or licentious.[108]

In considering the relationship between Daoism and local cults, it might be useful to compare Daoist attempts to influence the latter to the early Christian practice of converting popular local deities into saints while transforming their hagiographies (as well as iconographies and rituals) to fit the criteria of Christianity.[109] As the Christian church tried to absorb the ancient cults of various nature and tutelary spirits and transform such deities into more acceptable saints, so Daoist movements from the Han dynasty onward strove to mold those local gods whose cults could not be eradicated into deities conforming to Daoist norms. However, the evidence on the cult of Marshal Wen presented above, as well as that concerning other popular deities such as the Wutong/Wuxian, suggests that the Daoists proved far less successful than the Christians in their efforts. The reasons for this have yet to be fully understood, but probably involved the various "institutional" weaknesses discussed by C. K. Yang,[110] as well as the problem of a text's "audience" and "reception."[111] Daoism's influence over local cults has declined even further in modern societies like Taiwan, where certain rituals, such as those for feasting plague deities, once the exclusive "intellectual property" of Daoist priests,[112] are now performed by members of the temple committee.[113]

Another factor that undermined Daoism's influence on local cults involved the tendency on the part of many worshipers to transform the deities they worshiped into more orthodox figures by portraying them as conforming to Confucian socioethical or ritual norms (for example, stressing Guan Gong's loyalty to the state over his martial prowess).[114] In the case of Marshal Wen, I have already mentioned that most folktales describe him as an official, not a young scholar or warrior as in earlier written sources. Furthermore, fieldwork in Wenzhou reveals that the city's residents have bestowed a wife on him, whose statue is worshiped next to Wen's, despite the fact that all the hagiographies about him previously mentioned either claim he refused to marry or ignore the issue of his family life entirely. Such a phenomenon is hardly unusual, as deities like the stove gods, the earth gods, the city gods, and some Royal Lords in Taiwan are also represented as having wives. In Taiwan today, a number of the most famous Mazu temples now feature statues of her parents, showing that she is a filial daughter who takes care of her parents, in spite of the awkward reality that she never married or had children. In addition to this, the leaders of local cults often tried to upgrade the status of the deities they worshiped by using the term "orthodox" as an autonym (take for example Wen's title Mighty and Fierce Loyal and Pacifying King of Orthodox Blessings and Manifest Response), a phenomenon still seen among local cults in Taiwan today (for example, the earth god there is often referred to by the title Orthodox Deity of Blessings and Virtue (Fude zhengshen).

In considering this problem, I concur with Laurence Thompson's argument that official and popular religion represent two levels of orthodoxy, which, while certainly not identical and involving a degree of tension, could frequently coexist without open hostility.[115] Local gazetteers are full of the names of deities like Marshal Wen who were not incorporated into the register of sacrifices *(sidian)*, but whose worship was tolerated and at times even openly supported by government officials. Such officials often found it sound politics to curry favor with the local elite by offering a plaque or composing a poem at the local temples they patronized.[116] Scholar-officials and local elites certainly did not label such cults as heterodox or licentious, and did not find it beneath their dignity to worship at their temples. Such a combination of official tolerance and semi-official support, combined with a strong sense of self-declared orthodoxy among cult worshippers, made the acceptance of Daoist-imposed norms even more problematic.

Notes

Abbreviations

The following abbreviations are used in the text and notes to this chapter:

CT   *Concordance du Tao-tsang, titres des ouvrages,* vol. 102 (Paris: Publications de l'École Française d'Extrême Orient, 1975).

DFHY   *Daofa huiyuan* [A corpus of Daoist ritual], in *DZ* 884–941 (see *CT* 1220).

DZ   *(Zhengtong) Daozang* [Daoist canon of the Zhengtong reign] (1445), including the *Wanli xu daozang* [Supplement to the Daoist canon of the Wanli reign] (1607), 1120 threadbound vols. (Shanghai: Hanfenlou, 1923–1926), reprinted in 60 hardbound vols. (Taibei: Xinwenfeng chubanshe, 1983).

1. See Kristoffer Schipper, *The Daoist Body* (Berkeley: University of California Press, 1993), 2, 7–8, 69, 86, 89; John Lagerwey, *Daoist Ritual in Chinese Society and History* (New York: Macmillan Publishing Company, 1987), 246–247, 249, 250, 270–271; and Kenneth Dean, *Daoist Ritual and Popular Cults in Southeast China* (Princeton: Princeton University Press, 1993), 12–18.

2. Valerie Hansen, *Changing Gods in Medieval China, 1127–1276* (Princeton: Princeton University Press, 1990), 26.

3. Nathan Sivin, "On the Word Daoist as a Source of Perplexity," *History of Religions* 17:3–4 (Feb.–May 1978), 306; and Michel Strickmann, "On the Alchemy of T'ao Hung-ching," in Holmes Welch and Anna Seidel, eds., *Facets of Taoism* (New Haven: Yale University Press, 1979), 165.

4. Judith M. Boltz, *A Survey of Daoist Literature: Tenth to Seventeenth Centuries* (Berkeley: Center for Chinese Studies, 1987), 17.

5. For more on Strickmann's definition, and its problems, see Stephen R. Bokenkamp, *Early Daoist Scriptures* (Berkeley: University of California Press, 1997), 14. For more on the history of Quanzhen daoism, see Vincent Goossaert, *"La création du taoïsme moderne: L'ordre Quanzhen"* (Ph.D. diss., École Pratique des Hautes Études, 1997).

6. While I use the terms "orthodoxy"/"orthopraxy" (both expressed by the Chinese term *"zheng"*) and "heterodoxy"/"heteropraxy" *(xie)*, I also realize that in a Daoist context the Chinese terms *"zheng"* and *"xie"* may just as easily be translated as "correct" and "perverse," "true" and "deviant," or even "good" and "evil." For more on this problem, see Michel Strickmann, "History, Anthropology, and Chinese Religion," *Harvard Journal of Asiatic Studies* 40 (1980): 222–225.

7. See Kwang-Ching Liu, "Preface," in *Orthodoxy in Late Imperial China* (Berkeley: University of California Press, 1990), ix; and "Socioethics as Orthodoxy: A Perspective," in ibid., 53.

8. C. K. Yang, *Religion in Chinese Society* (Berkeley: University of California Press, 1961), 279.

9. See Richard Shek, "Daoism and Orthodoxy: The Loyal and Filial Sect," chap. 4, in this volume.

10. Ibid., 158.

11. Heavenly Master Daoists also adhered to orthodox Confucian norms in that they married, fathered children, took care of their parents, and worshiped their ancestors, just like most self-respecting Chinese.

12. See Donald Sutton's lucid discussion of this problem in chapter 6, this volume.

13. See Michel Strickmann, *Chinese Magical Medicine: Therapeutic Rituals,* ed. Bernard Faure (Stanford: Stanford University Press, 2000); and Lin Fu-shih (Lin Fushi), "Chinese Shamans and Shamanism in the Chiangnan Area during the Six Dynasties Period (3rd–6th Century A.D.)" (Ph.D. diss., Princeton University, 1994), 229–232, 239–242.

14. See for example Kubo Noritada, *Dōkyō-shi* [History of Daoism] (Tokyo: Yamakawa Shuppansha, 1977); Fukui Kōjun, et al., eds., *Dōkyō* [Daoism], 3 volumes (Tokyo: Hirawaka Shuppansha, 1983); Ren Jiyu, ed., *Zhongguo Daojiao shi* [History of Daoism in China] (Shanghai: Shanghai renmin chubanshe, 1990); Qing Xitai, ed., *Zhongguo Daojiao shi* [History of Daoism in China], 4 volumes (Chengdu: Sichuan renmin chubanshe, 1988–1994).

15. The term *"yin"* has been variously translated as "excessive," "licentious," "illicit," "improper," "perverse," "profane," and "profligate." I believe that the way one chooses to translate this term depends on its context. For example, I would argue that the term *"yin"* as found in official documents and elite writings adhering to an official point of view should be translated as "illicit," as the authors thereof mainly objected to the fact that such cults were not included in the register of sacrifices *(sidian).* However, the term *"yin"* as found in the writings of Daoist priests and other members of the elite may be translated as "licentious" or "excessive," as such people were clearly offended by what they considered to be heterodox or improper practices, including the prominence of spirit mediums and offerings of bloody sacrifices.

16. For more on the problem of resistance in Chinese culture, see Robert Weller, *Resistance, Chaos and Control in China: Taiping Rebels, Taiwanese Ghosts and Tiananmen* (Seattle: University of Washington Press, 1994).

17. For a striking example of this phenomenon, see Ursula-Angelika Cedzich, "The Cult of the Wu-t'ung/Wu-hsien in History and Fiction: The Religious Roots of the Journey to the South," in David Johnson, ed., *Ritual and Scripture in Chinese Popular Religion: Five Studies* (Berkeley: Chinese Popular Culture Project, 1995), 137–218, esp. 139, 158, 180–192.

18. See chapter 6, this volume; Richard J. Smith, "Ritual in Ch'ing Culture," in Kwang-Ching Liu, ed., *Orthodoxy*, 288; and Romeyn Taylor, "Official and Popular Religion and the Political Organization of Chinese Society in the Ming," in *Orthodoxy*, 130. See also Daniel L. Overmyer, "Attitudes Toward Popular Religion in the Ritual Texts of the Chinese State: *The Collected Statutes of the Great Ming,*" *Cahiers d'Extrême Asie* 5 (1989–1990), 191–221; and Chiang Chu-shan (Jiang Zhushan), "Cong daji yiduan dao suzao zhengtong: Qingdai guojia yu Jiangnan cishen xinyang" [From suppressing heterodoxy to creating orthodoxy: popular religion and the state in Qing-dynasty Jiangnan] (master's thesis, National Tsing-hua University, 1995).

19. For more on the early relationship between Daoism and the state, see Ren, *Zhongguo Daojiao shi*, 42–48; Anna Seidel, "Der Kaiser und sein Ratgeber—Lao Tzu und der Daoismus der Han-Zeit," *Saeculum* 29 (1978): 18–50; and idem, "Imperial Treasures and Daoist Sacraments," in Michel Strickmann, ed., *Tantric and Daoist Studies in Honor of Rolf Stein* (Bruxelles.

Institut Belge des Hautes Études Chinoises, 1983), 2:291–371. For a slightly
later example, see Franciscus Verellen, "Liturgy and Sovereignty: The Role
of Taoist Ritual in the Founding of the Shu Kingdom (907–925)," *Asia
Major,* 3rd series, vol. 2, no. 1 (1989), 59–78. See also Bokenkamp, *Early
Daoist Scriptures.*

20. Holmes Welch, "Introduction," in Welch and Seidel, eds., *Facets
of Taoism,* 7.

21. Daoist movements were frequently labeled as "heterodox" by
government officials, members of the elite, and members of the Buddhist
sangha, not to mention many early sinologists who accepted those labels.
See for example Max Weber, *The Religion of China,* trans. and ed. Hans H.
Gerth (New York: The Free Press, 1964), 181–190, 205–213.

22. For more on the early history of Daoism, see the following works
by Anna Seidel: *La divinisation de Lao Tsu dans le Daoisme des Han* (Paris:
Publications de l'École Française d'Extrême Orient, 1969); "The Image of
the Perfect Ruler in Early Daoist Messianism: Lao Tzu and Li Hung," *History of Religions* 9.2–3 (1970): 216–247. See also Ursula-Angelika Cedzich,
"Das Ritual der Himmelmeister im Spiegel früher Quellen: Übersetzung
und Untersuchung des liturgischen Materials im dritten *chüan* des *Teng-chen
yin-chüeh*" (Ph.D. diss., Julius-Maxmilians Universität, Würzburg, 1987), as
well as Seidel's review in *Cahiers d'Extrême Asie* 4 (1988): 199–204. Cf. chapter 1, this volume.

23. See Qing, *Zhongguo Daojiao shi,* 1:147–149; Zhang Jiyu, *Tianshi
dao shilue* [A brief history of the Heavenly Master movement] (Beijing: Huawen chubanshe, 1990), 14–16, 216–219; and Sun K'o-k'uan (Sun Kekuan),
Yuandai Daojiao zhi fazhan [The development of Daoism during the Yuan
dynasty] (Taizhong: Tung-hai University, 1968), 17–18.

24. The use of the autonym "Heavenly Master" is somewhat easier
to grasp, as such a figure occupies a prominent position in early scriptures
such as the *Taiping jing* (Scripture of supreme peace). See for example Max
Kaltenmark, "The Ideology of the T'ai-p'ing Ching," in Welch and Seidel,
eds., *Facets of Taoism,* 19–52.

25. See for example Chen Guofu, *Daozang yuanliu kao* [A study of
the *Daoist Canon* and its origins], 2 vols. (Beijing: Zhonghua shuju, 1963),
2:260–261; and Zhang, *Tianshi dao,* 27–31.

26. See *Yunji qiqian* (*DZ* 677–702; *CT* 1032), 6:4, quoted in Chen,
Daozang yuanliu kao, 1:98.

27. *Santian neijie jing* (*DZ* 876; *CT* 1205), 1:1b, translated in Schipper, *The Daoist Body,* 61. The entire text has been translated in Bokenkamp,
Early Daoist Scriptures, 186–229; the relevant passage is on p. 216. For more
on the idea of covenant in Daoism, see Lagerwey, *Daoist Ritual,* 27, 28, 97,
159, 246.

28. See Kaltenmark, "Ideology," 52 (comment by Kristofer Schip-

per); Chen, *Daozang yuanliu kao,* 1:98–99 and 2:275; and Zhang, *Tianshi dao,* 217 218.

29. See Rolf A. Stein, "Religious Taoism and Popular Religion from the Second to Seventh Centuries," in Welch and Seidel, eds., *Facets of Taoism,* 53–81; Hisayuki Miyakawa, "Local Cults around Mount Lu at the Time of Sun En's Rebellion," in ibid., 83–101; Richard B. Mather, "K'ou Ch'ien-chih and the Daoist Theocracy at the Northern Wei Court, 425–451," in ibid., 103–122; Peter Nickerson, ed. and trans., "Abridged Codes of Master Lu for the Daoist Community," in Donald S. Lopez Jr., ed., *Religions of China in Practice* (Princeton: Princeton University Press, 1996), 347–359. See also Lin, "Chinese Shamans and Shamanism," 232–239, 242–248.

30. See Boltz, *Survey,* 23–53; Chen Bing, "Yuandai Jiangnan Daojiao" [Daoism in Jiangnan during the Yuan Dynasty], *Shijie zongjiao yanjiu* 2 (1986): 65–80; Michel Strickmann, "Sōdai no raigi: Shinshō undō to Dōka nanshū ni tsuite no ryakusetsu" [Thunder rites during the Song: a brief study of the Divine Empyrean movement and the southern branch of Daoism], *Tōhō shūkyō* 46 (1975): 15–28; and Lowell Skar, "Ritual Movements, Deity Cults, and the Transformation of Daoism in Song and Yuan Times," in Livia Kohn, ed., *Daoism Handbook* (Leiden: E. J. Brill, 2000), 413–463.

31. *DZ* 557; *CT* 780. While the term *"taibao"* can be used as an official title (meaning "grand guardian"), in the context of Wen's hagiography it is also used to refer to spirit mediums working at the Temple of the Eastern Peak (see note 33).

32. See Boltz, *Survey,* 97–99; Lagerwey, *Daoist Ritual,* 241–252; and Paul R. Katz, *Demon Hordes and Burning Boats: The Cult of Marshal Wen in Late Imperial Chekiang* (Albany: SUNY Press, 1995), chap. 3.

33. Huang's biography of Liu may be found in *DFHY,* 253:10a–12a.

34. Ibid., 3b–4b.

35. Ibid., 4a, 9b–10a.

36. See Schipper, *Daoist Body,* 58.

37. Lagerwey states that the term *"taibao"* refers to "Daoist priests when they perform military rituals"; see Lagerwey, *Daoist Ritual,* 242. However, the term *"taibao"* was commonly used to refer to mediums in south China as early as the Song. See Yu Yan (fl. 1260s), *Shuzhai yehua* [Evening conversations in a scholar's studio], 1:4b, in Yen Yi-ping (Yan Yiping), ed., *Xuju zhenben congshu* [Supplemental collection of rare volumes] (Taibei: Yiwen yinshuguan, 1972), vol. 37. See also *Songjiang fuzhi* [Songjiang prefectural gazetteer] (1884), 5:13a; and Yi Xijia, et al., "Taibao yu zuoshe" [Spirit mediums and tutelary deity rituals], in *Zhongguo minjian wenhua* [Chinese popular culture] (Shanghai: Xuelin chubanshe, 1992), 7:199–214.

38. *DFHY,* 253:3a, 5b, 7b.

39. See the Ming-period *Han Tianshi jiashi* [Family genealogy of the

Chinese Heavenly Master] (*DZ* 1066: *CT* 1463), *juan* 2; and Zhao Daoyi (fl. 1294–1307), *Lishi zhenxian tidao tong jian* [A comprehensive mirror on successive generations of perfected transcendents and those who embody the dao] (*DZ* 139–148; *CT* 296), *juan* 18, for accounts of the first Heavenly Master's battle against these demons.

40. For more on Daoists using thunder and fire rituals against "licentious cults," see Judith M. Boltz, "Not by the Seal of Office Alone: New Weapons in the Battle with the Supernatural," in Peter N. Gregory and Patricia Buckley Ebrey, eds., *Religion and Society in T'ang and Sung China* (Honolulu: University of Hawai'i Press, 1993), 241–305.

41. This is, of course, an impossibility and reveals that Huang composed Wen's hagiography with little regard for historical fact.

42. See Feng Han-yi and John K. Shryock, "The Black Magic in China Known as *Ku,*" *Journal of the American Oriental Society* 55 (1935): 1–30; and J. J. M. de Groot, *The Religious System of China,* 6 volumes (Leiden: E. J. Brill, 1982–1910), 5:826–869.

43. For more on the Tianpeng incantation and its links to the cult of Marshal Tianpeng, see *DFHY, juan* 156–168, esp. 157:18, 159:3–11, 159: 19–23, 164. Like Marshal Wen, Marshal Tianpeng was an exorcistic deity who served under Supreme Emperor of the Dark Heavens.

44. I have not been able to locate any information on such a movement. It may have been purely fictional, concocted by Huang as an allegorical device.

45. It is rather odd that Huang portrays King Kang as a plague demon, as all other sources about him I have seen emphasize his ability to fight epidemics. See *Zhongguo minjian zhushen* [Chinese popular deities] (Hebei: Hebei renmin chubanshe, 1985), 603–606. The *Zhishun Zhenjiang zhi* [Zhenjiang gazetteer compiled during the Zhishun reign] (1332), 8:2b–3a, contains an account of King Kang's exploits in fighting epidemics.

46. For more on the history of this cult, see Cedzich, "The Cult of the Wu-t'ung/Wu-hsien in History and Fiction," esp. p. 182; and Richard von Glahn, "The Enchantment of Wealth: The God Wutong in the Social History of Jiangnan," *Harvard Journal of Asiatic Studies* 51.2 (Dec. 1991): 651–714.

47. For more examples, see essays by Boltz, Cedzich, and Strickmann cited.

48. See also Lagerwey, *Daoist Ritual,* 246–249.

49. For more on Daoists portraying themselves as "caretakers" of local cults, see Terry F. Kleeman, "The Expansion of the Wen-ch'ang Cult," in Ebrey and Gregory, eds., *Religion and Society,* 61.

50. Lagerwey, *Daoist Ritual,* 246.

51. Ibid., 249.

52. Ibid., 246.

53. See Kleeman, "Expansion of the Wen-ch'ang Cult," 62; and *A God's Own Tale: The Book of Transformations of Wenchang, the Divine Lord of Zitong* (Albany: SUNY Press, 1994), 44. See also his "Licentious Cults and Bloody Victuals: Sacrifice, Reciprocity, and Violence in Traditional China," *Asia Major* 7.1 (1994): 185–211.

54. While some scholars have argued that any interaction between these two continuums did not occur until the Song dynasty, we find considerable evidence for such interaction in sources dating back to the Six Dynasties, if not even earlier. See Stein, "Religious Daoism and Popular Religion"; Lin Fu-shih, "The Cult of Chiang Tzu-wen in Medieval China" (paper presented at the conference on The Cult of Saints and the Cult of Sites: Sources of Chinese Local History and Hagiography, sponsored by the École Française d'Extrême Orient, Paris, May 29–June 1, 1995); and Kristofer Schipper, "The Immortal Cult of Tang Gongfang (revisited)" (also presented at the conference on The Cult of Saints and the Cult of Sites).

55. *DFHY*, 253:5b, 6b.

56. For more on Zhang's life and career, see Boltz, *Survey*, 48, 63, 194–195; Sun, *Yuandai Daojiao*, 33–41; Zhang, *Tianshi dao*, 83–84, 196; and Chuang Hung-i (Zhuang Hongyi), *Mingdai Daojiao Zhengyi pai* [The Daoist Orthodox Unity Sect during the Ming dynasty] (Taibei: Xuesheng shuju, 1986), 36–43.

57. Numerous ritual movements of the Southern Song attempted to augment their liturgical authority by claiming that their ritual techniques had been created or transmitted by this famous Heavenly Master; see Boltz, *Survey*, 47–48, 187, and nn. 255, 259.

58. *DFHY*, 253:3a.

59. *DFHY*, 255:1a, 2a.

60. *DFHY*, 256:7b.

61. *DFHY*, 255:7b.

62. *DFHY*, 254:7b, 8a, 10b.

63. Schipper, *Daoist Body*, xx; Dean, *Daoist Ritual and Popular Cults*, 176–178.

64. Ye is often referred to by the title Heavenly Master, but whether he was a member of this movement is a matter of some debate. While Zhang Jiyu refers to Ye as "a member of the Heavenly Master movement" (Zhang, *Tianshi dao,* 76), most other works on the history of this movement, including those compiled by Heavenly Masters themselves, do not make such a claim. See, for example, the Ming-period *Han Tianshi jiashi* (see n. 39); Chuang, *Mingdai Daojiao Zhengyi pai*, 36–43, (see n. 56); Zhang Yuanxian (sixty-fourth Heavenly Master), *Lidai Zhang Tianshi zhuan* [Biographies of Successive Heavenly Masters with the Surname Zhang] (Ying-ko: Sihan Tianshi Fu, 1988); and Zhang Jinyuan (nominal Heavenly Master in the PRC), *Zhongguo Longhu Shan Tianshi dao* [The Heavenly Master movement

at Dragon-Tiger Mountain in China] (Nanchang: Jiangxi renmin chuban-she, 1994), 20. For more on Ye's biography in the *Daoist Canon,* see Boltz, *Survey,* 96–97.

65. *DFHY,* 254:1a–2a.

66. Ibid., 3a–5a.

67. *DFHY,* 256:9b–10b.

68. Compare *DFHY,* 254:11b–12b to *DFHY,* 256:2a–3b.

69. These are the *Shenxiao duanwen dafa* (Great ritual technique of the Divine Empyrean for stopping epidemics; *DFHY,* 219); the *Shenxiao qianwen songchuan yi* (Divine Empyrean ritual for expelling epidemics and sending off the [plague] boat; *DFHY,* 220); and the *Shenxiao qianwen zhibing juefa* (Divine Empyrean formulas and ritual techniques for expelling epidemics and curing diseases; *DFHY,* 221).

70. *DFHY,* 219:1a; *DFHY,* 221:10a.

71. See Paul R. Katz, "The Pacification of Plagues: A Chinese Rite of Affliction," *Journal of Ritual Studies* 9.1 (winter 1995): 55–100.

72. See Katz, *Demon Hordes and Burning Boats,* chap. 4.

73. For more on this and other temples to Marshal Wen in Wenzhou, see *Zhejiang tongzhi* [Zhejiang prefectural gazetteer] (1736): 225:3b–4a; *Wenzhou fuzhi* [Wenzhou county gazetteer] (1605): 4:6a; *Wenzhou fuzhi* (1756): 9:4b–5b; *Yongjia xianzhi* [Yongjia county gazetteer] (1566): 4:5a–b; *Yongjia xianzhi* (1682): 3:51a–b; and *Yongjia xianzhi* (1882): 4:31a–32a. See also Ye Dabing, "Wen Yuanshuai xinyang yu Dongyue miaohui" [The cult of Marshal Wen and the festival of Eastern Peak], *Minsu quyi* 72/73 (1991): 102–128.

74. For more on this and other paces *(bufa, bugang)* performed by Daoist and local specialists, see Paul Andersen, "The Practice of *bugang:* Historical Introduction," *Cahiers d'Extrême Asie* 5 (1989–1990): 15–54.

75. See *Song Xueshi wenji* [The collected writings of academician Song (Lian)] (Congshu jicheng edition), *juan* 16, 560–561; and *Song Wen-xiangong quanji* [The collected writings of Song (Lian), Lord of Magnificent Letter] (Sibu beiyao edition), 41:3b–4a. Song's inscription has also been preserved in numerous Zhejiang gazetteers.

76. The *Songshi* [History of the Song dynasty] and the *Song huiyao jigao* [A draft version of the important documents of the Song dynasty] contain no record of such a title having been awarded, but these sources are far from complete, and the latter only records titles awarded before the 1230s. See Hansen, *Changing Gods,* 80–81 (see n. 2).

77. See L. Carrington Goodrich and Fang Chao-ying, eds., *Dictionary of Ming Biography,* 2 volumes (New York: Columbia University Press, 1976), 2:1225–1231.

78. A number of later hagiographical anthologies also reproduce this version of Wen's hagiography, including *Jishuo quanzhen xubian* [Supple-

mental compilation of collected sayings and explanations of veracity] (1880), *juan* 14a–15a, pp. 35–37; and *Shishen* [Explanations about the gods] (1812), *juan* 5, pp. 41–42. Both these works may be found in Wang Qiugui and Li Fengmao, eds., *Zhongguo minjian xinyang ziliao huibian* [Collected source materials on Chinese popular religion] (Taibei: Xuesheng shuju, 1989).

79. See Boltz, *Survey*, 58 n. 248; Chuang, *Mingdai Daojiao Zhengyi pai*, 43–46, 53, 80; Zhang, *Tianshi dao*, 85–86, 95–96.

80. For more on the cult of the ten grand guardians in Hangzhou, see *Xianchun Lin'an zhi* [Gazetteer of Lin'an (Hangzhou) of the Xianchun Reign] (1274), 73:16b; *Zhejiang tongzhi* (1736), 217:7b; *Hangzhou fuzhi* [Hangzhou prefectural Gazetteer] (1579), 47:28a; *Hangzhou fuzhi* (1764), 8:9a; and *Hangzhou fuzhi* (1922), 9:32a.

81. See *Sanjiao yuanliu shengdi fozu soushen daquan, juan* 5, in Wang and Li, eds., *Zhongguo minjian xinyang ziliao huibian*, 218–220. See also *Sanjiao yuanliu soushen daquan* [Complete compendium of the origins of the deities of the three religions] (1907 reprint of Ming edition by Ye Dehui), *juan* 5 (Taibei: Lianjing, 1980), 150–152.

82. This work has been studied and translated by Gary Seaman. See "The Divine Authorship of the *Pei-yu chi*," *Journal of Asian Studies* 45.3 (May 1985): 483–497; and *The Journey to the North* (Stanford: Stanford University Press, 1988). For more on Yu Xiangdou, see Cedzich, "The Cult of the Wu-t'ung/Wu-hsien in History and Fiction," 142–145.

83. For more on these deities, see Katz, *Demon Hordes and Burning Boats*, chap. 2.

84. This is the surname given in most editions of the novel I have seen. The Shijie shuju edition (Taibei, 1975) gives his name as Lei Qiong, as does Seaman's translation.

85. A painting of Wen from the Museum of Fine Arts in Boston has been reproduced in Stephen Little, with Shawn Eichman, *Daoism and the Arts of China* (Chicago: The Art Institute of Chicago in association with University of California Press, 2000), 264–265.

86. This combined summary/translation is based on the *Beifang Zhenwu zushi xuantian shangdi chushen zhizhuan* [Record of the life of Supreme Emperor of the Dark Heavens, True Warrior and Patriarch of the North], in *Guben xiaoshuo congkan*, ser. 9, vol. 1 (Beijing: Zhonghua shuju, 1990), 191–194. Seaman's translation of this story may be found in *Journey to the North*, 175–177.

87. See *Wenzhou fuzhi* (1765), *juan* 9; and "Wenzhou fengsu zhi" [Record of local customs in Wenzhou] (unpublished twentieth-century manuscript, n.d.), 27.

88. See *Zhejiang fengsu jianzhi* [Brief treatise on the local customs of Zhejiang] (Hangzhou: Zhejiang renmin chubanshe, 1986), 328.

89. See my *Taiwan de wangye xinyang* [The cult of the royal lords in

Taiwan] (Taibei: Shangting, 1997). See also Huang Yuxing, *Penghude min-jian xinyang* [Popular religion in the Pescadores] (Taibei: Taiyuan chuban-she, 1992), 82–122.

90. Fan Zushu, *Hangsu yifeng* [The lost customs of Hangzhou] (1864) (Shanghai: Wenyi chubanshe, 1989), 15–17.

91. See *Zhejiang fengsu jianzhi*, 277, 328, 578.

92. See Rev. Hampden C. DuBose, *The Dragon, Image, and Demon* (New York: A. C. Armstrong and Son, 1887), 220–221.

93. See Cheng Chih-ming (Zheng Zhiming), "Wangye chuanshuo, xia" [Legends of the royal lords, part 2], *Minsu quyi* 53 (June 1988): 104, 110–111.

94. See Katz, *Demon Hordes and Burning Boats*, chap. 4.

95. See Ch'iu Te-tsai (Qiu Decai), *Taiwan miaoshen zhuan* [Hagiographies of temple deities in Taiwan] (Tounan: Jongjing xiaoxintang shuju, 1979) 588–602.

96. See *The Story of the Stone*, trans. David Hawkes (Harmondsworth: Penguin Books, 1973–1986), 2:275. For more on the cult of the Marshal of Epidemics in north China, see Amano Genosuke, *Chūgoku nōgyō keizairon* [Treatise on Chinese agricultural economics] (Tokyo: Ryukai shosha, 1978), 3:290; and Li Jinghan, *Ding xian gaikuang diaocha* [Investigation of the general situation in Ding county] (Beijing: Zhonghua pingmin jiaoyu cujinhui, 1934), 431.

97. See Paul R. Katz, "Demons or Deities—The *Wangye* of Taiwan," *Asian Folklore Studies* 46.2 (spring 1987): 197–215; and *Demon Hordes and Burning Boats*, chap. 2.

98. The spread of Wen's cult is documented in Katz, *Demon Hordes and Burning Boats*, chap. 4.

99. See C. Stevan Harrell, "When a Ghost Becomes a God," in Arthur P. Wolf, ed., *Religion and Ritual in Chinese Society* (Stanford: Stanford University Press, 1974), 193–206; David K. Jordan, *Gods, Ghosts and Ancestors: The Folk Religion of a Taiwanese Village* (Berkeley: University of California Press, 1972), 164–171; and Lin Fu-shih (Lin Fushi), *Guhun yu guixiong de shijie: Bei Taiwan de ligui xinyang* [The world of lonely souls and the violent ghosts: Vengeful ghost beliefs in Northern Taiwan] (Bangqiao: Taibei County Cultural Center, 1995).

100. For more on this problem, see Kleeman, *A God's Own Tale*, 107–109.

101. See Katz, "The Pacification of Plagues."

102. For more on this phenomenon, see Stephan Feuchtwang, *The Imperial Metaphor: Popular Religion in China* (London and New York: Routledge, 1992), 58–59.

103. See Katz, *Demon Hordes and Burning Boats*, chap. 3.

104. For more on the concept of hegemony, and its application to the

study of Chinese religions, see Paul R. Katz, *Images of the Immortal: The Cult of Lü Dongbin at the Palace of Eternal Joy* (Honolulu: University of Hawai'i Press, 1999), 19–23, 195–201.

105. Apart from the works of Schipper and Dean cited, see Norman Girardot, *Myth and Meaning in Early Taoism: The Theme of Chaos* (Berkeley: University of California Press, 1983), esp. 279–281; and Michael Saso, *Daoism and the Rite of Cosmic Renewal* (Pullman, Wash.: University of Washington Press, 1972).

106. See Arthur P. Wolf, "Gods, Ghosts, and Ancestors," in Wolf, ed., *Religion and Ritual in Chinese Society*, 131–182.

107. However, it is also important to note that Daoism featured deities who belonged to spiritual hierarchies without functioning as bureaucrats (such as heavenly worthies and stellar deities), as well as deities who were strongly nonbureaucratic in nature (such as Lü Dongbin and his cohorts among the Eight Immortals). See Anna Seidel, "Chronicle of Daoist Studies in the West, 1950–1990," *Cahiers d'Extrême Asie* 5 (1989–1990); 254–258; and Katz, *Images of the Immortal.*

108. For more on this problem, see P. Steven Sangren, *History and Magical Power in a Chinese Community* (Stanford: Stanford University Press, 1987), 171–178.

109. See for example Peter Brown, *The Cult of the Saints: Its Rise and Function in Latin Christianity* (Chicago: University of Chicago Press, 1981), esp. chap. 6; and Robert Hertz, "St. Besse: a Study of an Alpine cult," trans. by Stephen Wilson, in Wilson, ed., *Saints and their Cults* (Cambridge: Cambridge University Press, 1983), 55–100.

110. See Yang, *Religion in Chinese Society*, 301–340. However, it is important to note that Daoist movements like The Loyal and Filial Way of the Pure and Perspicacious could effectively circulate their views and assert a degree of influence through the use of media, like morality books *(shanshu)*. See chapter 4 of this volume, as well as Cynthia Brokaw, *The Ledgers of Merit and Demerit* (Princeton: Princeton University Press, 1991); and Sakai Tadao, *Chūgoku zenshō no kenkyū* (Research on Chinese morality books) (Tokyo: Kōbundo, 1960).

111. See W. F. Hanks, "Text and Textuality," *American Review of Anthropology* 18 (1989), 95–127; and David Johnson, "Communication, Class, and Consciousness in Late Imperial China," in David Johnson, Andrew Nathan, and Evelyn Rawski, eds., *Popular Culture in Late Imperial China* (Berkeley: University of California Press, 1985), 34–74.

112. For more on this problem, see Simon Harrison, "Ritual as Intellectual Property," *Man*, n.s. (1992), 225–243.

113. See Katz, "The Pacification of Plagues"; and *Taiwan de wangye xinyang.*

114. For more on elite attempts to "standardize" local cults, see

James L. Watson, "Standardizing the Gods: The Promotion of T'ien Hou ('Empress of Heaven') Along the South China Coast," in Johnson, et al., eds., *Popular Culture in Late Imperial China*, 292–324. See also Prasenjit Duara, *Culture, Power, and the State: Rural North China, 1900–1942* (Stanford: Stanford University Press, 1988); and Michael Szonyi, "The Illusion of Standardizing the Gods: The Cult of the Five Emperors in Late Imperial China," *The Journal of Asian Studies* 56.1 (1997): 113–135.

115. See Laurence G. Thompson, "Orthodox Official Religion and Orthodox Popular Religion in Early Ch'ing Taiwan" (paper presented at the Conference on Orthodoxy and Heterodoxy in Late Imperial China, Montecito, California, August 1981). See also Sangren, *History and Magical Power,* 176–177. It is also important to recall Kleeman's argument that official and local religion belonged to the same ritual continuum.

116. See Katz, *Demon Hordes and Burning Boats,* chap. 4. For more on elite patronage, see Timothy Brook, *Praying for Power: Buddhism and the Formation of Gentry Society in Late Ming China* (Cambridge, Mass.: Harvard University Press, 1993).

CHAPTER 6

Shamanism in the Eyes of Ming and Qing Elites

Donald S. Sutton

The animus against shamans or spirit mediums is a striking feature of Ming and Qing Chinese elites. The legal code provided
that a doctor who accidentally killed a patient was simply forbidden
to practice, but a spirit medium *(duan gong)* or Daoist priest who did
so while using heterodox *(yiduan)* healing techniques was strangled.[1]
The gazetteers celebrated local hermits, Daoist priests, Buddhist
monks, and the workers of medical miracles, but individual mediums
became part of the historical record only as the cause or beneficiary
of Confucian good works: there are the cases of Cao E of the later
Han period, who committed suicide when her spirit medium father
died in waterside ritual,[2] and a more obscure fellow-provincial who
gave up his own life in place of his father, sentenced for sorcery;[3]
there are also a few instances where temples erected in memory of
particular mediums were too popular to ignore.[4] At the end of the
Qing period, local spirit mediums were still acknowledged to be the
principal healers in peripheral counties or localities, yet gazetteer
compilers dismissed their healing work as worse than useless, and
singled them out as necessary targets of official repression and reform
by the local elite.

Hostility and indifference were not confined to officials and the
gazetteer compilers, men generally steeped in orthodox neo-Confucianism. For all their eclecticism, Confucian borrowers from Daoism
and Buddhism and even the late-Ming Three Teachings syncretists
stopped short of adopting shamanic elements. Nor did enthusiasm
for the meticulous critical scholarship known as *kaozheng* or fascination with the poetic theme of the cosmic itinerary[5] inspire literati
interest in the social role of contemporary mediums or their trance
experiences.

In order to put into sharper focus the peculiarity of Ming/Qing
attitudes and consider the applicability of the terms "orthodoxy" and
"heterodoxy" in this context, it will be necessary to begin with a cursory examination of the rich literature on spirit mediums by Tang and
Song writers. I shall then argue that the subsequent opposition to
shamanism was not canonical or rationalist or based on a different
theoretical conception but rather was the expression of a particular
literate subculture, that of the neo-Confucian elite. I shall show that
the repellent style of a lower status group, along with its implicit challenge to proper social roles as defined by the elite, lay at the heart of
the antagonism, and suggest that the Ming/Qing effort at establishing tighter control over society necessarily brought the elite closer to
unanimity in opposition to shamanism than before.

A spirit medium may be defined as a person who is recognized
to have the capacity for ecstatic possession by a deity and is employed
for purposes of exorcism, witchcraft, or clairvoyance. Such a definition appears to fit most Chinese historical references to *wu* or *wuxi*,
as well as *wushi, shipo, duan gong, shamen, shenwu*, and *tongji*, among
the variant regional terms. They are possessed exorcists, working
sometimes as mediums, or, very rarely, practicing black magic. A
medium's effectiveness derives from the manipulation of a god, or
spirit familiar *(shen)*, who comes down into his or her body as the
result of rhythmic shaking or dancing. Once possessed, the medium
may be able, if the spirit is cooperative, to see the future or the past,
or to affect present or future conditions by exorcism. Exorcism is
accomplished by removing ghosts or curses responsible for sickness
or other misfortunes, and sometimes by recovering the lost soul of
the sick person. Chinese spirit mediums have been used to cope with
a variety of other dangerous social transitions apart from sickness,
such as the climate (impending flood or drought), and calendrical
events, very rarely at the family "passages of life," from conception
to burial. Local gazetteers suggest that by the nineteenth century the
wu concentrated on magical healing.

Tang and Song Elites' Acceptance of Spirit Mediums

There is abundant material in Tang and Song collections to indicate
that spirit mediums' social position was very different from their successors' in the late imperial period.[6] They were widely consulted by
men of power and education, including most of the Tang emperors

before Dezong (r. 780–805).[7] There were lute-playing mediums in the Tang, showing some assimilation of upper-class culture,[8] and many in both Tang and Song worked from temples,[9] a likely sign of local financial support. Members of the Tang elite appeared to believe in sorcery, judging from the recorded motive for numerous prosecutions,[10] and from the Tang legal code, which specified life exile for the use of sorcery to gain a parent's doting love.[11] When mediums figure in short stories written by the elite, even as tricksters[12] or bumpkins,[13] they give every impression of being accepted, though not necessarily cultivated, members of society, and remarkable powers are attributed to them. Li Fuyan, a late Tang author, takes his reader's credulous interest in shamanism for granted in describing a medium's seance with a disappointed former official who answers questions about existence after death.[14] A Northern Song tale has a magistrate arriving at his post to find his office pervaded by the stench of a next-door temple grove infested with birds and animals. He gets a medium to order the local spirit (tudishen) to clear up the mess within two days, or have his temple razed to the ground. The job is accomplished, before the deadline, by a flock of birds and a great rainstorm.[15] A similar tone of wonder and credulity animates Song tales of wu, whether about sorcerers or exorcists. One example among many in Hong Mai's twelfth-century collection the Yijian zhi (The record of the listener) depicts the cure of a virgin's false pregnancy in a series of vividly theatrical scenes. Two small boys dive into a pond as the rituals are taking place, and apparently drown. Their angry parents threaten to turn the medium over to the county magistrate. She (or he) asks for patience to give her arts time to work. The village people gather round the pond and wait. Suddenly amid a series of explosions like thunder, the two boys emerge unscathed from the water, dragging the culprit, a dead carp. The medium exorcises its curse and terminates the false pregnancy by smashing a jar placed on the girl's distended belly.[16] Yet there is an undercurrent of hostile and skeptical opinion from at least the Six Dynasties period. Spirit mediums were inseparable from the wasteful expense, singing and dancing, healing rites, animal sacrifices, and uncodified gods denounced as "improper cults" (yinsi) by Confucians and Daoists and sporadically repressed by officials.[17] Yan Zhitui (531–595) in his Family Instructions warned against consulting mediums, but they continued to be employed widely by the elite; as late as the eighth century they took part in Tang imperial sacrifices.[18] The poet Yuan Zhen

(779–831) inveighed against the expense and futility of *wu* healing and cult practices, and various late Tang tales refer to shaman "delusions."[19] In the eleventh century a series of local persecutions accompanied an imperial order to destroy "improper temples" *(yinci)* south of the Yangzi;[20] further repressions are reported in the following century and under the Yuan, evidently at the initiative of local officials.[21] While the success of such localized suppressions was probably short-lived, they surely reflect a split within the elite. Spirit mediums could not support cults and temples without the connivance of some local people of substance. On the other hand a serious attack on them presupposed the backing of other influential local leaders. The neo-Confucian revival strengthened the interventionists at the expense of those tolerant of shamanic practices. The opposition of Zhu Xi (1130–1200) to the foreign religion of Buddhism is well known, but his writings contain many denunciations of *wu* and popular cults, as inspired by private greed, destructive of society, and disruptive of good government.[22] The spread of the neo-Confucian orthodoxy in later centuries would leave no room for support of mediums. The educated elite would lose their mingled fear and admiration, cease to consult them (openly at least), and echo Zhu Xi's condemnation.

Toward an Anti-shamanism Consensus

Nineteenth-century gazetteers give an impression of a general reduction of shamanic practice except in peripheral places.[23] One gazetteer published in Republican times put it like this:

> The absurdity *(wang)* of shamanic arts, *wushu*, is recognized by people living near to the capital who have imbibed the teaching of the *li* [proper Confucian conduct], but the ignorant people *(yumin)* of remote areas hold fast to these practices and never cease their reverential worship.[24]

Such a "trend" may be wishful thinking among Confucian authors. There are, however, indications in early modern times of a gradual shift away from open elite patronage. For Xie Yingtang, a native of Wujin (modern Jiangsu province), who lived during the transition from Yuan to Ming, spirit mediums were a familiar sight.[25] "As a boy," he wrote in his *Refutation of Delusions,* "whenever I saw shamans *(wuzhe)* worshipping the spirits for my relatives, spitting out vulgar phrases, chasing some obscure blessing, I felt embarrassed and left. After I had grown up, I cut myself off from these people and did not even pay them the proper courtesies when I encountered them"[26] Xie saw himself as a reformer among his peers, for he goes on: "Alas, the ignoramuses in the women's quarters who believe in them blindly and employ their services do not deserve censure; but cannot the gentlemen *(shidafu)* who are deluded feel some shame? If one wishes to improve mores and customs, put an end to what is weird and disorderly, and shun the shamanizers, it must begin in the houses of the gentlemen." In an epidemic in 1329–1330, most of the inhabitants of neighboring villages had died after vainly offering improper sacrifices *(yinsi)*. Xie's entire family and his maternal relatives survived, because, he believed, they had turned instead to doctors and medicine.[27] Such evidence was not persuasive to many of Xie's peers. One older literatus argued that prayer to the spirits manifested a respectful, trusting heart, "just as the *junzi* of old invariably spoke of *yinyang* and *guishen* in a spirit of respectful trust," and he dismissed Xie's attack on the popular custom of shamanism as "a dog barking at snow."[28]

Two generations later, a shamanic cult flourished for a time near the great center of Ningbo in the lower Yangzi without interference from officialdom or the local elite. A reformist literatus Yang Yifan, having issued written denunciations without effect, went in person to the chief spirit medium and struck him to the ground.[29] Several hundred adherents dispersed meekly after this display of righteous Confucian anger. The account suggests an easy tolerance of popular shamanic cults by the elite even near an advanced center of learning and commerce, but little or no elite involvement; otherwise Yang's success could not have been so easy.

How widespread shaman cults and medium healing were in Yang Yifan's time is unknown, but by the time of the philosopher and military commander Wang Yangming (1472–1529), shamanic healers were a phenomenon one expected to find only in out-of-the-way places. One of his poems records his falling sick on a trip through the mountains where medicines were unobtainable, and considering a spirit medium *(shenwu)* treatment in conformity with local custom. This idea caused such consternation in his entourage as to suggest that neither Xie Yingfang nor Yang Yifan would have had to wage their struggle single-handed had they lived in Confucian circles in the early sixteenth century.[30]

In the interior of China various forms of shamanism persisted undiminished. Lu Can (1494–1551), a younger contemporary of Wang Yangming, recalled a wave of shamanism in western Hunan, during the heyday of a celebrated shamanic swindler named Jiang Cong. Mediums promised good fortune in return for donations of food and wine, and threatened disaster if their demands were refused. They assisted locally in the preservation of corpses, thereby facilitating the practice, abhorrent to Confucians, of delaying burial pending the location of a propitious grave site. This high point of shamanism, which abated with Jiang Cong's exposure and dispatch to the capital for execution, was located far from the more-developed centers of Ming life: Chu (Hunan and Hubei) was, according to Lu Can, a region where there was a particular "fondness for ghosts," and Jiang Cong had been active in the undeveloped far southwest of the region. On the near side of Dongting Lake, wrote Lu, "shamanic arts could not be very efficacious."[31] He thus sustains the impression of declining medium use by Ming elites in the more advanced areas.

The late Ming author Xie Zhaozhe (fl. 1592–1607) commented that while shamanism flourished throughout the area south of the Yangzi, its most vigorous expression was in Fujian and Guangdong. Writing about his native Fujian, he noted that "even in rich and distinguished families the women revere and worship shamanic spirits no differently than the spirit of heaven (tianshen). When they have some small illness, no day is missed and no ghost omitted in their religious parades and prayers."[32] He blamed nine out of ten fatalities in recurring epidemics on the futile or harmful practices current in Fujian, such as continual incense burning and prayer to "heterodox spirits" (xieshen), complete avoidance of doctors and medicine, the shutting of doors and windows, which had the effect of blocking yang vapors (yangqi), and the employment of spirit mediums to launch paper boats at the water's edge and thereby carry away evil influences.

An invidious comparison lies behind Xie's denunciation of rich female patrons in his native Fujian: he is implying that, two centuries after Xie Yingtang, in regions more familiar to his readers, such as the lower Yangzi, mediums were no longer patronized by the elite.

That Ming and Qing literati viewed mediums differently from Tang and Song elites is supported by evidence from fiction. In tales of the supernatural, sorcery is rarely attributed to wu; it occurs in gu witchcraft, practiced more often than not by nonexperts and localized in southern frontier regions heavily populated by minorities.[33] Shamans are not portrayed admiringly or credited with marvelous powers. Of two figuring in the late Qing collection *Chiwen lu* (Record of close listening), one commits murder during the distraction of an exorcism to cover up his adultery, another is himself victimized by a prankster who replaced with a poisonous snake a toad hidden in a mulberry branch for ritual use. This, says the author, is the kind of fate deserved by those who practice shamanism.[34] A Ming work exposes a medium as a fraud when he diagnoses a plum stone hidden in a man's cheek as a "nail abscess" *(dingchuang)* resulting from failure to respect the spirits.[35] For these literati and their audience, mediums are no better than charlatans and fools, and at worst, troublemakers.

Respectable people were not expected to consult spirit mediums. Pu Songling (1640–1715) does give a factual account of women conducting possession rituals within their own clans, but this special Manchu-style clan shamanism is not mentioned by other Chinese writers.[36] The more common view is humorously indicated in another story. The ghost of an eccentric Ming calligrapher, famous for his ill temper, is contacted by a *wu* medium in an effort to discover who robbed and killed him, but the literatus denounces his interlocutors through the mouth of the medium: how dare they use the despised *wu* to address him?[37] Snobbery about shamans had been present even in Tang accounts, but now the elite seems to have withdrawn its patronage altogether.

An unfavorable image of shamans pervades serious Qing writing. While shamanism figures as a significant popular social custom in one gazetteer out of three or four in the last Qing decades, it is almost invariably as the target of criticism.[38] Noncommittal reports are few and far between in the more casual *biji* (random notes) genre, Pu Songling's account being the best known.[39] Administrative, criminal, and customary law is sharply hostile. When Manchus familiarizing themselves with Chinese ways consulted a phrase book for the Six Boards, they received the following explanation of the term *wuxi tiaoshen* (shamanic spirit-dancing): "A shaman *(wuzhe)* pretends to dance on the pretext that a spirit has attached itself to his [or her] person," and the term is included among the phrases that an official in the Board of Punishments would be likely to come across.[40] Both

Ming and Qing codes prohibited "spirit mediums *(shiwu)* who, on the pretense of calling down heretical spirits, write charms, recite spells, do spirit writing and pray to saints," and lumped them together with secret societies as deceptive and inflammatory influences on the people. The leaders were to be sentenced to death by strangling, and their followers to one hundred blows and exile to 3,000 *li*.[41] Popular versions of the Sacred Edict also inveighed against spirit mediums.[42] Some clan rules forbade consulting them. Others ordered that males who became spirit mediums be removed from the clan registers.[43] Thus the old strains of credulity and wonder, fear of sorcery, and matter-of-fact acceptance of magical healing and clairvoyance had been replaced by disbelief in the *wu*'s power for good or ill, and dismay at their social influence.

The Control of Popular Religion

The opposition to spirit mediums must be related to the general disparagement in print of popular religious practices. With his stress on official control and proper order, the late-fourteenth-century writer Xie Yingfang (cited earlier) offers a foretaste of the Ming/Qing elite consensus on the subject.[44] He traced the profusion of *yinci* in his own times to the disruptions of the Tang dynasty in decline, and urged official action against them. He criticized the spontaneous generation of new gods and the popular attempt to rank them hierarchically, and ridiculed the crude linguistic "errors" made in their popular titles. He disapproved of nameless ghosts and "ghosts who were not one's own to worship" *(feiqigui)*. Yet while Xie denied the power of ghosts and gods to bring about sickness, he did not deny their existence. Besides one's ancestors, it was quite appropriate to pay homage to the spirits of local worthies, so long as they were from one's own locality or region. Yue people, for example, should worship historical Yue heroes, but not those of Wu. Nor was there anything wrong with building a Confucian school temple, providing the gods were fittingly represented: Xie waged a successful campaign to have the god's female partner removed from a shrine next to one such temple, dedicated to a *diling,* or local god, on the grounds that her presence ignored the principle, hallowed in the *Confucian Record of Rites (Liji)*, the segregation of sexes. Like other writers, he also criticized the extravagance of *jiao* festivals (great ceremonies of renewal), which were conducted even in times of famine, and deplored the greed of mediums whose fees ruined patients or obliged them to beg for help from collateral relations in other villages.

It was a similar concern with proper order, combined with the belief that official intervention was the best way to assure it, that inspired a series of attempts to systematize and codify popular religion under the Board of Rites, beginning with the Ming founder. (See Romeyn Taylor, "Official and Popular Religion and the Political Organization of Chinese Society in the Ming," in *Orthodoxy in Late Imperial China*, ed. Kwang-Ching Liu, 126–157.) The rationale for such attempts is illustrated by one Li Mingzhong of Jiangyi in a ten-point critique of religious parades *(saihui)*. Li objected particularly to the confusion of social categories, whether literally, through the intermingling of the sexes during these unruly gatherings, or in the affront to the ritual order prescribed by the sacrificial regulations.

> Each prefecture or other district has its altars *(tan)* to the mountains and rivers, its temples *(miao)* to the Gods of Literature and War and the City God, and its shrines *(ci)* in honor of local worthies and famous officials. It is all set out in the sacrificial regulations *(sidian)* what is appropriate for officials and people to sacrifice and worship in spring and autumn. As for this or that local spirit, or such and such a spirit, prince, general, or minister, these are not set forth in the sacrificial regulations. Since names and ranks differ, there is no precedence from humble to noble, ancient and recent are turned upside down and the rites and ritual objects are inconsistent. This is what is called *yinsi*, improper sacrifices.[45]

Like Xie, Li emphasized the ruinous cost of religious practices. He also attacked in detail the socially disruptive effects of the parades themselves, such as gambling and brawling, and the cover they offered to criminals and incendiarists.

The purposes implicit in these two comments—the maintenance of a conventional hierarchical symbolic order and of a tractable and orderly society—would continue to inspire efforts to assert official control. The local officials tried to co-opt popular religion by conducting regular observances, centered at the city god's temple, at specified periods in the lunar calendar and in times of drought and flood. Wu Rongguang (1773–1843), author of the *Wuxuelu* (My own learning), explained: "This is because the city god is in charge of the whole locality, and goodness and happiness, ruin and depravity are

basically administered by him." But the attempt at co-optation was
not a complete success. Wu went on with the usual disdainful recital
of complaints about popular religion.

> The ignorant common folk, not content with righteousness and fate,
> unaware of cultivation and restraint, say that a disaster can be avoided
> and blessings brought nigh. So on top of the annual sacrifices, there
> is also the so-called birthday of the city god on which they invite the
> god out of the temple and parade him round the streets and alleys,
> with booming gongs and drums and earsplitting firecrackers, for the
> purpose of flattering him and seeking blessings. The deception has
> become extreme, but none of the local officials has prohibited it.[46]

It continued to be the custom, in the lower Yangzi, to hang portraits of a consort in the city god's "bed chamber," six centuries after
Xie Yingfang's effort at reform. A similar outcome of elite pressure to
co-opt has been well described by James L. Watson in the case of the
Mazu cult in the south and southeast. Watson demonstrates that the
elite adopted an official interpretation of the cult and a ritual to go
with it, without eliminating the various popular rituals and accompanying interpretations.[47]

In discussing the neo-Confucian attempt at control and reform,
it is difficult to detach shamanism from other aspects of popular religion, most obviously because it lacked a textual canon or an institutional tradition of its own. Its rites necessarily elaborated upon
existing local beliefs, and were frequently interwoven with local ritual practice. Spirit mediums, for example, participated in the cult of
Wutong, originally a malicious female spirit. Within the lower Yangzi
region, some are said to have treated a pretty girl with a fever by
conveying her to the god's local temple and declaring she was chosen
for his bride—an honor that consoled the parents when the illness
proved fatal.[48] In some popular cults mediums actually played a central role, for example, as escorts of the god's image in the southern
Fujian processions that took on a new life in Taiwan.[49]

While in consequence any attack on popular religious practice
necessarily fell on spirit mediums, they presented some special problems for official reformers. The limits of official power would have
made repression infeasible at the village level where most mediums
worked: there was no large-scale equivalent of European witch persecutions. Most forms of co-optation were scarcely easier. Taking

over the medium's god as an object of worship, on the model of the official city god and Mazu cults, was not feasible. Noteworthy gods could be given official rituals, and mediums could probably be excluded from a particular temple, but it was hardly possible to co-opt all the gods that possessed them, or all the temples and village shrines where they practiced. Substituting official control over the targets of shamanic work was attempted in the Ming founder's insti-tution of formal annual sacrifices to wandering ghosts, but if these official rituals were ever widespread below the county level, they lacked "any prominent place in the religious experience of rural inhabitants,"[50] and in any case, could only reinforce the common shamanic diagnosis of collision with unhappy ghosts and the patient's tendency to seek a shaman cure. Absorbing the mediums themselves into official religion was briefly tried, in a modification of another early Ming policy, at Hui'an in east Guangdong: they were made offi-cial *shefu*, "temple managers," and authorized to conduct exorcistic rituals,[51] but the sheer cost of such appointments would have pro-hibited their spread. Appropriating a shamanic weather exorcism in a formalized and supervised official ritual was perhaps the only form of co-optation that went as far as the official city god and Mazu wor-ship. Thus it became respectable, even obligatory, for Ming and Qing officials to post messages and officiate personally at placatory cere-monies to the appropriate god in times of drought, flood, and plague, though without stamping out the corresponding shamanic and Dao-ist rites below the county level. Rather than these various attempts to undercut shamanism via official or gentry co-optation, it was prob-ably by the slow process of education that officials actually limited the spirit mediums' practice. Even so, as I argue elsewhere (see note 23), the elite could not impinge on their popularity in the urban lower class or in rural areas far from prosperous centers.

Intellectual Anti-shamanism?

It is odd that the efforts at co-optation of popular religious practices involved an extension of concepts of ritual propitiation and divine intervention at a time when neo-Confucian writers were developing a relatively secular metaphysical system. As indicated in the preced-ing text, the spread of official cults was seen as a means to control abhorrent popular cults; that is, to adumbrate this essay's main theme, ritual orderliness and political security took priority over any

attempt to impose an orthodoxy of belief. Yet the issue of an intellectual basis for anti-shaman sentiments should not be hastily dismissed, whether it might be canonical, rationalist, pragmatic, or
philosophical. Certainly anti-shaman writers found little support in
the classics. It is true that Confucius had urged respect for ghosts
and spirits but insisted on "keeping them at a distance," which no
medium could do without giving up his or her work, and besides,
Confucian decorum was contravened by shaman ritual. On the other
hand, they had to acknowledge that *wu* took part in Zhou state rituals, that Confucius spoke of them in the same breath as doctors, citing southerners for a saying that "constancy" was required of both,
and that Mencius also recognized *wu* as healers.[52] A case could be
made that *wu* of the Zhou period "sincerely prayed to the spirits" and
so were very different from the "wildly spirit-dancing" *wu* of later
times,[53] but the classical canon did not contribute directly to neo-
Confucian anti-shamanism. When Mencius denounced the heterodox *(xie)*, he referred to the un-Confucian doctrines of fellow think-
ers like Yang Zhu and Mo Di, not the likes of mediums.[54]

　　Some of the opposition to shamanism can be described as
"rationalistic" in the sense of being firmly this-worldly. In the Six
Dynasties, a military advisor to Emperor Xiaoming of Wei (r. 515–
527) named Bian Lan, rejected the "water method" proposed for
his sore throat by a shamaness *(wunü)* trusted by the emperor. His
grounds were that "illnesses should be cured by medical prescriptions, why believe in this?" The belief that medicine was more effective than the gods was the stated motive of sweeping local anti-
shaman campaigns, like that of Xia Song in the Song period, who
destroyed nineteen hundred homes of spirit mediums while serving
as a magistrate in Jiangxi.[55] The same assumption is reflected in
many late Qing gazetteers, which compare the relative popularity of
the two forms of healing. But the term "rationalism" is not readily
applied to Ming and Qing writers in the full post-Renaissance Western sense of the term. The religious nature of Confucianism has been
well established by C. K. Yang,[56] and others, and to argue for a rise
in rationalism coincident with increasing unanimity about the evils
of shamanism, one would have to explain away the increasing elaboration of religious observances conducted by officials (previously
noted), the persistent private religious practices connected with
ancestor worship, and the widespread use of the Confucian *Yijing* and

the (officially disapproved) *fuji* spirit writing among the elite. Only in the twentieth century was the term *"mixin"* (superstition) adopted (probably from Japanese) and used of religious beliefs in general. As I shall show, popular culture diverged from that of the elite not so much in its underlying ideas as in the way these ideas[57] were concretely elaborated in practice.

Did shamanism excite elite opposition as a result of conflicts on the conceptual level? This possibility is vulnerable to several arguments. First of all, there was too much disagreement about whether gods *(shen)* and ghosts *(gui)* existed or not, whether they interfered with human existence, and whether they were morally purposive. Although Zhu Xi favored an abstract metaphysical interpretation, there are many passages of his dialogues with disciples that speak of *gui* and *shen* as tangible entities, and their nature continued to be an area of argument, not consensus, among the educated, for example, in medical literature.[58] On the other hand at the more general level, concepts of disease involving *qi* and the balance between yin and yang elements seem very widely shared if not universal within both the elite and popular traditions,[59] so there is no cause for conceptual opposition on those grounds.

Opposition on grounds of wrong belief, which would best fit the Western concept of heterodoxy, is almost entirely absent. Note, however, a critical account "About the Woman Mediums" ("Ji nüwu"), by Li Dongyang (1447–1516), the early Ming Grand Secretary and poet. These mediums in his native Beijing owed their popularity to people's belief that "everyone who died became a spirit and all spirits leveled curses [on the living]"; thus people would take home images of the medium's god to receive their offerings and prayers. Li considered that in doing this they were "abandoning their ancestral tablet and turning their parents into ghosts."[60] He concluded by comparing these mediums unfavorably to the useless female healers *(nüyi)* who treated many of the city's women and children: "While the healers only kill people's bodies, the mediums can destroy their heart-minds *(xin)*." By spelling out shamanism's implications as something people believed in, Li Dongyang was in effect criticizing it as heterodox; for him, the ancestral cult is the orthodox belief violated, and terrible harm to the self is the result. This attention to belief rather than practice alone is rare among critics of the mediums, as we shall shortly see.

Elite Magic and the Magic of the Mediums

The question of why Ming and Qing Confucians objected to spirit mediums is best approached by contemplating their strange tolerance for quite similar practices and attitudes. How did Confucian magic —or direct manipulation of the supernatural—differ from the popular varieties of which shamanism was one?

Even shamans themselves are sometimes put down with Confucian magic. The locus classicus is the *Fengsu tongyi,* describing an organized contest before the Emperor Wu of the former Han dynasty between Dong Zhongshu and the Yue *wu.* While the *wu* uttered imprecations and cast spells, Dong calmly faced south and read the classics aloud—and one or more *wu* fell dead on the spot.[61] Two such confrontations may be cited from late imperial times. The first, a Ming magistrate who had a shaman severely beaten, without ostensibly inflicting pain, then pressed his official seal on the medium's back; with the resumption of beating, the medium died.[62] In the second, there is more Confucian magic, in an official's biography in which a telling childhood incident prefigures a brilliant career. Overhearing the commotion of a shamanic exorcism in a neighbor's house, the child went to investigate. As the child appeared in the doorway, the medium's god abruptly stopped the proceedings and informed the gathering: "Since his Honor has arrived, I do not venture to stay."[63] Evidently shamanism was no match for secular power in the eyes of literati who reported or invented these confrontations. They wanted to feel that their culture, symbols, and persons represented more than simple coercion, the power of law, or even the moral power *(de)* of the ideal Confucian ruler. No less than that of the medium through her spirit, their literatus-hero's authority is mystical, producing *ling,* the magical efficacy attributed to the most responsive spirits or temples. To imitate the *wu* was to flatter them. In these magical duels, the literati authors betray a certain respect for the *wu*'s sorcery, in spite of themselves.

Far from being restricted to dealings with supernatural experts, this kind of thinking characterizes some of the biographies of filial sons and zealous young brothers in the local histories, which had to supply plausible if somewhat idealistic models of behavior for a literate Confucian audience. A first reading of the three "Xiaoyou" (Filiality and friendliness) chapters in the 1736 edition of the Zhejiang provincial gazetteer turns up magical themes in twenty-six out of several hundred "filial devotion and friendliness" cases. In most of these, an adult male seeks to cure a sick parent by medicine and prayer, offering his own life if all else fails. A god appears in a dream, to grant the wish.[64] Or if prayers are unanswered, the son may secretly cut out his "liver" *(gan)* or a piece of thigh and feed it in a soup to the invalid,[65] a custom linked with filial devotion as early as the Three Kingdoms period and denounced in vain by Han Yü (768–824).[66] Other biographies describe devoted mourners in the same vein. In one, tigers (another conventional motif) steer clear of the grave and its mourning hut;[67] in another, a god in a dream declaims a riddle, locating a burial site in a rocky spot missed by expert geomancers. In order to spare the son an arduous daily climb for water, a spring gushes forth nearby, flowing precisely for the specified three years of mourning.[68] The magico-religious thinking of these solemn exemplary biographies is striking. Their origin in commercially and educationally progressive Shaoxing and Hangzhou is still more so.

The distinctive meaning of this Confucian magic is suggested by the way in which filial deeds are evaluated. The writers display very little interest in the mechanism of cure. They have their heroes trying out medicine, prayer, and self-mutilation almost indiscriminately. They rarely specify particular medicines or name the spirits contacted, except for the officially approved city god *(chenghuang)* or a generalized heaven *(tian)*.[69] What counts is the son's devotion, not his technique. In one filial biography, the despairing son goes off to a temple and, fortunately ignorant of human anatomy, cuts away at his ribs until he falls down unconscious. Regaining his senses, he notices on the knife a purple bloodstain a foot long resembling a liver, takes it home to treat his mother, and finds the substitute no less effective than the real thing.[70] Like the behavior of another hero who "exhausted his sincerity in meditation and prayer *(jiecheng yidao)*,"[71] this selfless act manifests the force of sincerity. Because supernatural agencies operate like humanity within a moral universe, such human sincerity has the potential to influence them to act upon mundane life. Significantly, this influence does not need to be mediated by priests or shamans. The one resort to a spirit medium in this collection is involuntary. It occurs when a man who has saved his mother with his thigh flesh goes into seclusion, apparently to avoid upsetting her with an analysis of the curative soup's ingredients. He faints in his hiding place from loss of blood and is rescued through the vision of a possessed medium in a nearby temple.[72] Here the medium is passive, no more than a channel of communication. Again, filial devotion works its own direct magical effect without the benefit of supernatural expertise.

This elite magic was seen to contrast with popular religion in motive, method, and form. Take for example two excerpts in a late Ming work, the *Xiyuan wenjian lu* (Observations from my western garden). One describes a prefect who deals with a drought by suspending (capital) punishment (a standard practice) and by "omitting no god in his prayers" *(zhu)*. Since the people were saying the Dragon King had the greatest magical effect *(ling)*, he sent a subordinate to pay respects at the latter's temple, but he then learned that a shaman *(wuzhe)* there was "behaving in a disorderly fashion" *(wanwei)*. The official went to the god's officiant *(shenzhu)* and said, "The Dragon King is a substance *(wu)*; clay and wood are not a dragon. If it does not rain in three days it [the image] will be exposed to the sun, and in six days it will be burned." After six more days of drought, he burned it, "the rain fell in torrents, and the grain grew tall."[73] According to this anonymous text, the official is a long way from being a skeptic: he avoids denying the existence of the rain dragon or denouncing rain-inducing rituals in principle; indeed we are supposed to infer that by destroying the rain dragon's image, he actually produces the magical effect its worship had intended. What he disliked was the crudeness of the shaman's disorderly methods and of the clay-and-wood imagery.

The crudely direct relationship with the spirits that was typified in rain dragon ceremonies was seen to sully the worshiper's motives. Another writer, Zhu Yigong, equates god worship with currying favor from officials. "The gods take orders from Heaven, the officials obey the law *(fa)* from the ruler. To induce awe of officials nothing surpasses the ruler's law: to induce awe of gods nothing surpasses Heaven's law (or mandate, *Tianming*). Is it not just as erroneous to ignore Heaven's law and chase after blessings from gods as it is to ignore the ruler's law and chase after blessings from officials?"[74] Like Confucius, this author does not deny the existence of gods but prefers to keep his distance.

Proper form even in supernatural encounters did matter for the many literate people who accepted the popular notion of the celestial bureaucracy, as a story in the Qing collection *Lüyuan conghua* illustrates.[75] A young and impoverished teacher, a *zhusheng*, catches a sudden fever, which a shaman interprets as a curse from the deity Dongpingwang, "the King of Eastern Peace." The teacher seemingly accepts this diagnosis, for he does not seek a second practitioner's opinion, but objects vehemently when he finds out that his quick recovery has been magically assured with a loan of five thousand in cash, thanks to the mediation of an old woman neighbor. He addresses a petition of complaint to the god of the eastern peak (usually understood as the celestial equivalent of the emperor), reminding him that "the King of Eastern Peace" is a *zhengshen,* an orthodox or upright spirit. Why should he demand ritual sacrifices from people and impose burdens on a poor scholar?[76] Later he dreams that he is taken before a court session of the god of the eastern peak. The god ascertains that it is not the King of Eastern Peace but his hostler who is responsible, commands the latter's execution, and promises the teacher that he will recover the money. He does indeed find a five-thousand-cash note by the roadside at the place predicted by the god. The teacher's supernatural quest for justice unquestionably reflects a magico-religious sentiment, but it is one distinctly different from the popular equivalent. While the medium's ability to make contact with the world of gods is not denied here, the literatus hero prefers to manipulate that world by his written request and dream encounter. His magic is orderly and discreet, and follows the proper form.

To judge from the norms of behavior suggested by these various sources, the objection to popular magic focused on form rather than substance. Supernatural contacts were not excluded, but they had to be made in an appropriate way. While moral commitment was essential, without correct style and demeanor the petitioner could not hope for success.

Defending a Style of Life

To be consistent with this argument, ritual not belief should have marked the starkest contrast between elite and shaman religious forms. This was indeed the case. Confucian rites were planned in advance and often in writing, being theoretically based on the prescriptions of the Board of Rites. Physical movements were slow and restrained, sometimes actually choreographed; diction and musical accompaniment were measured and solemn, and the descent, presence, and ascent of a spirit in some rites would be indicated by the officiant and imagined by the audience, not dramatically portrayed or perceived by the senses. Spirit mediums by contrast literally let their hair down, danced and shook, half-dressed, amid the rhythmic clamor of drums and conch or horn, and behaved spontaneously, even unconsciously, having to be supported or restrained by assistants while in trance. What they said was rich in atmosphere but largely metaphorical in meaning. Generation after generation, elite commentators expressed their distaste for the mediums' "wild" (*kuang*) dancing, their vulgar (*bili*), incomprehensible language, and the din of their music.

The contrast, however, was more than purely stylistic. In a Confucian rite the arrangement of the participants took careful account of their rank and status, but the medium and her spirit were unambiguously at the center of a performance and paid no deference to anyone. Moreover, to borrow Mary Douglas's parallel of body and society,[77] just as the restraint of Confucian rites reflected emotional self-control and submission to the social order, so the physical spontaneity of shamanic performance implied the relaxing of social controls over the individual. Thus the performance itself posed a challenge to Confucian values.

That many literati saw the shamans as a type of performer, and at least as confusing to proper social roles and behavior as other performers, is indicated in several late imperial works. The mid-Ming author of the *Danqianlu* pointed out that the *wu* of the *Chuci* and other ancient books "used song and dance to charm his spirit; what difference is there in clothing and deportment from the singing actors of today?"[78] Indeed, he argued that the *wu* serving his spirit was the origin of the actor's vocation. Shen Zinan, Qing author of the *Yilin huikao* adopted this view by giving a chapter over to the "mediums and actors." (The remaining chapters included more readily grasped social entities such as servants and concubines, relatives and dependents, and military men.) Quoting from the *Danqianlu* and a variety of other works, he passed almost imperceptibly from mediums to actors to puppets and to female and boy prostitutes.[79] Arbitrary though it may appear, this categorization is revealing. Most obviously all were dressed in costume, danced in a seductive, rhythmic, or hypnotic fashion, and entertained for money. But a more fundamental similarity seems to link these social categories for the writer and his intended readers: mediums, actors, puppets, and prostitutes all assumed new roles in a wild Dionysiac mode, and thereby deliberately suspended the normal order of things. Some mediums put aside their sexual roles by cross-dressing or adopting in trance the mannerisms of the opposite sex.[80] Such role suspension became increasingly repulsive and threatening in a society seen to be governed by *li*, in which social roles were clearly demarcated, and proper duties were specified for each social position.

Unlike many social elites who have tolerated role-undermining behavior for special occupations or on carnival occasions, the Ming-Qing elites did their best to reduce it to a minimum or drive it to the social and geographic fringes of their influence. I contend that for many Confucian opponents of shamanism, such behavior was a defining feature and a principal reason for their distaste.

Cooper and Sivin have noted "an element of snobbery or social prejudice in Chinese judgements about heterodoxy."[81] This is a point to be underscored. In the elite view of shamans I have outlined, centering on form and style, colored by worry about upholding proper roles and behavior, the element of snobbery seems uppermost.

Snobbery here is not purely the attitude of a self-conscious elite toward its class inferiors; it has also spatial and sexual aspects. Commentators in the gazetteers and the *biji* sources like to distinguish regions, the south from the north, Guangdong and Fujian from the rest of China, in the degree of reverence for ghosts. Particular counties, even parts of counties, are seen as especially credulous; the country people are more superstitious than the townsfolk. Official suppressions are undertaken usually in marginal regions or near the periphery,[82] and inevitably by the men from wealthier places who staffed most of officialdom; their actions are represented as a civilizing mission, bringing the benighted interior into the light of Confucian civilization. Similarly women are repeatedly blamed for their foolish and ignorant patronage of shamans and extravagant pursuit of religious festivities. Insofar as social snobbery justifies the ascendancy of a particular social group in its own eyes, looking down on shamanism, and popular religions as a whole, rationalized the prevailing patterns of geographical and sexual dominance.

Some puzzling problems noted earlier may be resolved if it is noted that for the literati, illiteracy was an index of social rank, a target of social snobbery, and had a key mental association with shamanism.[83] Spirit mediums had the style and manners of illiterates; that is surely why they were less likely than Buddhist or Daoist priests to be present at the family passages of life or to be entered in the historical record, which celebrates the literate elite and its like. It may also be why the literati, though skeptical of the doctors' skills, preferred them to shamans: the better doctors were learned, long-gowned, and properly behaved—virtually social equals who could be admitted to their homes and secrets without anxiety. Similarly, only writing could make divination and supernatural quests acceptable—hence the popularity of the *Chuci* and the literatus vogue of (officially banned) spirit writing, along with the canonically sanctioned *Yijing*. Only texts, or topics that could be traced to texts, warranted careful investigation—hence in part the failure of great Qing scholars, as distinct from eccentrics like Pu Songling, to record the concrete details of shamanic ritual. Of course, illiteracy had a moral connotation in Confucian society; that explains why the (invariably reform-oriented) compilers of gazetteers point most often not to violent extirpation of shamanism as the remedy for illiteracy but rather to the spread of Confucian values by education and example.

It is difficult to ascertain how much spirit mediums were feared as competitors. They did claim to control part of the supernatural; and by perceiving aspects of this world, past, present, and future, that other mortals were unaware of, they did assert their power, at an exorcism or clairvoyant session, over the human participants as well as unseen beings. The Confucian state and its servants also tried to bring the cosmic and social worlds into harmony by manipulating each. The more Confucian leaders worked to strengthen social control in the Ming and Qing period, the more likely they were to regard mediums as arrogant and to deplore their influence over the people.

What made shamanism seem menacing was that mediums were less amenable to state control than the examination elite or organized religion. After the Song period they generally appear in fiction, *biji*, and local gazetteers as villagers, remote from bureaucratic supervision. Unlike Buddhist or Daoist priests, who, however illiterate, owed their authority ultimately to a written tradition, they derived theirs from the spirit they summoned to possess them. Access to such authority was nearly as common as possession illness, not a rare thing in Chinese society. While in a state of possession, the humblest peasant used this borrowed power to influence village society. Though such power did not adhere permanently to the borrower or give any day-to-day prestige in the community, its dangerous possibilities must have been glimpsed by many of the elite.

Nonetheless shamanism per se did not pose a direct threat. On the rare occasions that cults formed around a charismatic like Jiang Cong, these lacked the political potential of the sect, with its initiation rites, organizational routine via sutra readings, messianic vision, and perhaps a martial routine of some sort.[84] Ecstatic possession, it is true, could be adapted for political purposes, as both the Taiping and Boxer movements proved. Hong Xiuquan's conversion followed the classic course of an initiatory shamanic illness—lacking education and exposure to Christian tracts he might have made an excellent village shaman—and as Vincent Shih's study demonstrates, the Taiping leaders' divine communications constituted a political application of shamanism.[85] In the case of the Boxers, a possession cult merged with secret society and martial arts traditions without possession being monopolized by a few leaders—which helps to explain the amorphous nature of Boxer organization.[86] Practicing mediums qua mediums are not known to have been a recruiting base for either movement, and it is hard to see how the elite could fear illiterate village mediums unless it was the fear underlying its sense of social superiority.

European historians, noting the participation of medieval European elites in popular as well as elite culture, have argued that such biculturalism was gradually lost between the Reformation and 1800.[87] This is not unlike the transformation I have suggested during Ming times, at least where spirit mediums were concerned, following the characteristic tolerance and credulity of Tang and Song. The Chinese elites turned away from shamanism and similar forms of religious practice under the influence of a more prim and austere mentality, which had its expression on the intellectual plane in the neo-Confucian orthodoxy and was undoubtedly affected by the ideological controls newly exercised by the Ming and Qing state. Widely influenced by the neo-Confucian mentality, the rich, powerful, and socially ambitious seem to have followed the lead of literati such as the authors I have relied on in this essay. As in post-Reformation Europe, however, the masses remained largely unaffected by reforms in the realm of ideas, hence the elite's alienation from popular culture.

This shift must be understood in wider social terms, that is, as part of the increasing, self-conscious integration of the elite and its detachment from the common people. It resulted from many intersecting factors, notably the transforming effects of the civil service competition, the rise of local lineages, the spread of Mandarin, and rote memorization of the classics.[88] Ideology also mattered. Kai-Wing Chow explains the sharpened demarcation between gentry and commoners in terms of the "ritualist reorientation" of Confucianism in Qing times following a late-Ming effort at dialogue.[89] This new tendency within neo-Confucianism also may help to explain the intensification of anti-shamanism in Qing times.

It does not follow that mediums were outcasts. They did not vanish from local society. Not only did they satisfy the needs of country people, but they probably acted as doctors' surrogates for the wives and daughters of the elite and as principal consultants wherever the supernatural seemed overwhelming, for example in the mountainous periphery, and in cases of ghost possession. Where the latter affected childless wives and reluctant brides,[90] mediums who solved the problem served the vital interests of the patriarchal family order; they produced neither a philosophical rebuttal of Confucianism nor a seditious political ideology. From the point of view of writers in the Confucian tradition, shamanism could not be classified with Buddhism as a heretical doctrine, or simply as superstition, a concept of Western-style rationalism. When, as I have suggested, neo-Confucians criticized shamanism, they did so as a class elite and as moral reformers. Driven by the urge to order the Chinese world after their own fashion, they resisted mass ritual behavior that offended their special brands of morality and liturgy, chaotic services or nocturnal meetings that disturbed the local peace. It was heteropraxy that affronted them, not heterodoxy.

The medium, one can say, was the message; that is to say what mediums did, and who they were, accounted for the animus against them. Disorderly and disruptive behavior was what seemed to matter. Does that mean that in neo-Confucian eyes, beliefs counted for less than behavior (or practice)? A recent difference of opinion on this topic, between the editors of a symposium on Chinese death rituals, may be exaggerated. One can agree both with James L. Watson that Confucian reformers did make the reform of practice their priority, and with Evelyn Rawski that they were far from unconcerned about belief.[91] Actually, the dualistic separation of action from belief is a Western notion that would have been incomprehensible to the writers I have quoted. *Li* as a practice was supposed to reflect a universal moral order.[92] Appropriate behavior, therefore, was not a matter of pure decorum but an effort to approximate that ideal state of affairs. The belief that this order was attainable as well as desirable was implicit in *li* practice, and inconceivable without it. It was as practitioners of *li* in this sense that neo-Confucian writers trying to further and deepen the reform of Chinese society included shamanism so prominently among their targets. Just as to be orthoprax was to be orthodox, so heteroprax violators of the principles of *li* were subsumed to the heterodox and tarred with the same brush.

Notes

A grant from the ACLS Committee on Chinese Civilization, and the hospitality of the Department of Anthropology, Stanford University, and of the Hoover Institution, assisted the preparation of this chapter. I wish also to thank K. C. Liu, Susan Mann, Ramon Myers, G. William Skinner, and Ann Waltner for help of various kinds. For an extended version of the argument, with more evidence especially on earlier periods, see "From Credulity to Scorn: Confucians Confront the Spirit Mediums in Late Imperial China," *Late Imperial China*, vol. 21, no. 2 (December 2000), 145–183. The scope of the topic is very large, and I hope others will take up some of the many issues raised.

The following are abbreviations for series titles cited in the notes for this chapter. Date and place of publication are given whenever possible for individual titles in a series as they appear in the notes.

CSJC	*Congshu jicheng* [A collection of series works]
SBCK	*Sibu congkan* [A collection of publications under Four Categories (classics, history, philosophy, and literature)]
SKQS	*Siku quanshu* [Complete works of the Four Treasuries (classics, history, philosophy, and literature)]
TPGJ	*Taiping guangji* [Comprehensive records of the Taiping (Great Peace) era]
TPYL	*Taiping yulan* [Imperial records on the Taiping (Great Peace) era]
TSJC	*Gujin tushu jicheng* (A collection of ancient and modern books including illustrations)
ZJTZ	*Chixiu Zhejiang tongzhi* (Imperially ordered gazetteer of Zhejiang province)

1. Wu Rongguang, *Wuxuelu chubian* [Record of my own learning, first part] (1832; reprint, Taibei: Zhonghua, 1966); Xue Yunsheng, comp., *Duli cunyi* [Doubts noted down while perusing the substitutes of the Qing code] (1905; reprint, Taibei: Chengwen, 1970), 421.

2. *Chixiu Zhejiang tongzhi* [Imperially ordered gazetteer of Zhejiang] hereafter *ZJTZ*] (1736 ed., 280 *juan; SKQS* reprint), 210:22b.

3. *ZJTZ*, 185:9a–b (in Shaoxing prefecture: Ming, Wanli period).

4. E.g., the Canton *nüwu* (female shaman) for whom the Jinhua temple *(miao)* was founded. Qiu Chishi, ed., *Yangcheng guchao* [Old material on Canton], 8 *juan* (1806; reprint, Taibei: Wenhai, 1969), 3:14b.

5. David Hawkes, "The Quest of the Goddess," *Asia Major* 13 (1967): 71–94; Edward H. Schafer, *The Divine Woman: Dragon Ladies and Rain Maidens in T'ang Literature* (Berkeley: University of California Press, 1973).

6. See the "Spirit medium," chapters of the tenth-century encyclopedic collections: Li Fang et al., comp., *Taiping Yulan* [Imperial records from the Taiping era] (originally dated 983; hereafter *TPYL*), *juan* 734–735 and idem et al., comp., *Taiping guangji* [Comprehensive records of the Taiping era] (originally dated 987; hereafter *TPGJ*), *juan* 283.

7. *TPGJ*, 2255 no. 4, 2256 no. 8, 2257–2258 no. 12; *TPYL*, 735:1b; J. J. M. De Groot, *Sectarianism and Religious Persecution in China* (Amsterdam: Proceedings of the Royal Academy of Science, 1903–1904), 2:1235.

8. *TPGJ*, 2256–2257 nos. 9–10.

9. E.g., *TPGJ*, 2254 no. 3 (from *Youming lu* [Record of the underworld]), no. 10; Bo Xingjian, "Sanmeng ji" [Record of three dreams], in Tao Zongyi, comp., *Shuofu* [Speaking of this realm] (unpaginated 120 *juan* ed. cited here and below using reprint, Taibei: Shangwu, 1983), *juan* 114. Hong Mai, *Yijian wuzhi* [Records of the listener, part *wu*] (Biji xiaoshuo daguan ed.), 3, 8–9. For translation of this title, see Valerie Hansen, *Changing Gods in Medieval China 1127–1276* (Princeton: Princeton University Press, 1990).

10. E.g., *TPGJ*, 2255 no. 6.

11. Wallace Johnson, trans., *The T'ang Code, vol. 1: General Principles* (Princeton: Princeton University Press, 1979), 74, 95. See also 69.

12. Zheng Chang, "Qiawen ji" [Heard-by-chance collection], *Shuofu*, *juan* 32.

13. *TPGJ*, 2256 nos. 9–10.

14. Li Fuyan, "Xu youguai lu" [More records of the strange], *Shuofu*, *juan* 117.

15. Xu Xuan, *Jishenlu* [Records of marvels], (*TSJC* ed.), 6.51. For similar tales incorporating shamans without denunciation, see ibid., 2.15, 3.23–24, 6.50.

16. *Yijian bingzhi* [The record of the listener, part *bing*], section 6.6a–b. See also Shen Gua (1031–1095), *Mengqi bitan* [Jottings from dream

creek] (*CSJC* ed.), 20.22a–b, on his uncle's encounter with a clairvoyant *wu*.

17. Rolf A. Stein, "Religious Taoism and Popular Religion from the Second to Seventh Centuries," *Facets of Taoism: Essays in Chinese History,* ed. Holmes Welch and Anna Seidel (New Haven: Yale University Press, 1979).

18. Yan Zhitui, *Yanshi jiaxun* [Mr. Yan's family instructions] (reprint, Taibei: Zhonghua, 1966); De Groot, *Sectarianism,* 2:1236.

19. See *Peiwen yunfu* on *wu,* and Yuan Zhen, *Yuanshi changqingji* [Mr. Yuan's long blessings collection] (Taibei: Zhonghua, 1966), 1.44–45; 25.5–6. See four of the last five accounts in *TPYL,* 735.1b.

20. De Groot, *Sectarianism,* 2:1238–1239.

21. Hansen, *Changing Gods,* 84–86; Li Cefen, *Yuanshi Xinjiang* [New lectures on Yuan history] (Taibei: Taibei municipality, 1978), 5.514–515.

22. When his disciples spoke one by one of "such ubiquitous phenomena as the heterodox *wu (yinwu)* and the damage done by blind fortune-tellers, the Master just sat with furrowed brow and sighed." *Zhu Wengong zhengxun* [Zhu Xi's instructions on governing] (Taibei: Xinwenfeng, 1985), 13. See also a commentary of his, calling for the extirpation of *wu, zhu* (exorcists), *yin* (nuns), and *ao* (traders in human beings) in the *Xiaoxue jizhu* [Collected annotations on *Elementary Learning*] (n.p.: Santangtang, 1830), 5.12b; also 11b. See also note 58.

23. Discussed in Donald S. Sutton, "Pilot Surveys of Chinese Shamans, 1875–1949: A Spatial Approach to Social History," *Journal of Social History* 15 (1981): 39–50.

24. *Gusong xianzhi chukao* [Preliminary draft of the Gusong county gazetteer] (Gusong: Qingan Benevolent Association, 1931), 8.45a–b.

25. Xie Yingtang (1296–1392), *Bianhuo bian* [Refutation of delusions] (*SKQS* ed.), 1.15.

26. Ibid., 2.1.

27. Ibid., 1.18. This may have been the Black Death, which McNeill believes struck Henan in 1331 on its way to Europe. See William McNeill, *Plagues and Peoples* (New York: Doubleday, 1976), 143–145. Doctors' visits can have done little other than spread the plague bacillus—but no doubt less efficiently than communal rituals of exorcism!

28. Xie, *Bianhuo,* appendix.

29. Cited in Zhang Xuan, *Xiyuan wenjian lu* [Observations from my western garden] (1632; reprint, Taibei: Huawen, 1968), 106.13a–b.

30. Wang Shouren, *Wang Yangming quanji* [Complete works of Wang Yangming] (Taibei: Zhengzhong, 1955), 337. I found no evidence of differences in attitudes toward shamans in the Wang Yangming and Zhu Xi schools of neo-Confucianism.

31. Lu Can, "Chuwu" [The shamans of Hunan and Hupei], *Gengsi bian* [Written in a nonexistent year] (*TSJC* ed.), 8:164. The phrase *gengsi*

refers to a nonexistent year beyond the sixty-year cycle. The work was probably written between 1510 and 1519. See Zhonghua shuju edition of the identical work (Beijing, 1987), 1.

32. Xie Zhaozhe, *Wu zazu* [A collection of oddments] (Beijing: Zhonghua 1959), 178.

33. On *gu,* see Feng Han-yi and J. K. Shryock, "The Black Magic in China Known as Ku," *Journal of the American Oriental Society* 25 (1935): 1–30, and Donald S. Sutton, "Ethnicity in Late Imperial China: *Ku* Witchcraft Reinterpreted" (paper presented at the Conference of the International Society for the Comparative Study of Civilizations, Pittsburgh, May 1982). I take sorcery to be actual rituals performed to bring harm to an individual's enemies, and witchcraft to be the imaginary ones attributed to scapegoats at times of stress in certain societies.

34. *Yongua jushi* [Wen Rugua] (1760–1814), *Chiwen lu* [(Record of close listening], 12 *juan* (Taibei: Xinwenfeng, 1985), 1.5.

35. Lu Rong, *Shuyuan zaji* [Miscellanea written in my vegetable garden], 7.8b, cited by Victoria B. Cass, "Hags, Nursemaids and Doctors of Physique: Women's Work in Beijing" (paper presented at the Conference of the American Oriental Society, Austin, Texas, March 1982).

36. Pu Songling, *Liaozhai zhiyi* [Strange tales from the Make-do Studio] (Beijing: Zhonghua, 1962), 755–756.

37. Qian Yong, *Lüyuan conghua* [Chitchat from my garden walks] (Taibei: Guangwen, 1969), 15.1–2.

38. Sutton, "Chinese Shamans."

39. Besides Pu's account (see note 36), Fan Xingrong wrote a late-nineteenth-century description of spirit dancing after reading the *Liaozhai.* Fan Xingrong, *Danying ji* [Luring the shadows], section reproduced in Wang Xingzhen, ed., *Mixin zai Zhongguo* [Superstition in China] (Taibei: Xingguang, 1981), 135–138.

40. Naitō Kenkichi, *Rokubu seigo chūkai* [Annotated customary expressions used by the Six Boards] (Tokyo: Daian, 1962), 113.

41. Xue Yunsheng, *Duli cunyi,* 421.

42. See the record of an oral version in Leon Wieger, *Moral Tenets and Customs in China* (Ho-kien Fu: Catholic Mission Press, 1913).

43. See Taga Akigoro, *Sōfu no kenkyū* [An analytical study of Chinese genealogical works] (Tokyo: Tōyō Bunko, 1960), especially: *Yimen Chenshi jiabu* (Hefei, Anhui), 782; *Huangshi zongpuji* (Tongcheng), (Anhui), 838; *Fanshijiabu* (Huangpuzhuang, Zhejiang), 843.

44. Xie, *Bianhuo,* appendix, 2–6.

45. *Lüyuan conghua,* 21.14–15.

46. Wu, *Wuxue lu,* 9.9b–11a.

47. James L. Watson, "Standardizing the Gods: The Promotion of T'ien-hou ('Empress of Heaven') Along the South China Coast, 960–1960," in David Johnson, Andrew Nathan, and Evelyn S. Rawski, eds., *Popular Cul-*

ture in Late Imperial China (Berkeley: University of California Press, 1985), 292 324.

48. Wu, *Wuxue lu*, 10b–11a. For a memorial of 1824 confirming the cult's link with shamans and its persistence, see De Groot, *Sectarianism*, 2:21–22.

49. See David K. Jordan, *Gods, Ghosts and Ancestors: The Folk Religion of a Taiwanese Village* (Berkeley: University of California Press, 1972), 45–49, 80–81; Donald S. Sutton, "Ritual Trance and the Social Order: The Persistence of Taiwanese Shamanism," in Andrew Barnes and Peter Stearns, eds., *Social History and Issues in Consciousness* (New York: New York University Press, 1989; paperback, 1990), and "Self-Mortification and the Temple Community: Taiwanese Spirit-Mediums in Comparative Perspective," *Journal of Ritual Studies* 4.1 (winter 1990): 99–125.

50. Kung-chuan Hsiao, *Rural China: Imperial Control in the Nineteenth Century* (Seattle: University of Washington Press, 1960), 223. Cf. Romeyn Taylor, "Official and Popular Religion and the Political Organization of Chinese Society in the Ming," in Kwang-Ching Liu, ed., *Orthodoxy in Late Imperial China* (Berkeley: University of California Press, 1990), esp. 134, 146–147.

51. Li Tiaoyuan (1734–1803), *Nanyue biji* [Jottings on Southern Yueh] (*TSJC* ed.), 4.7.

52. James Legge, trans., *The Chinese Classics* (1893, reprint, Hong Kong: University of Hong Kong Press, 1960), vol. 1, *Confucian Analects*, 191–192, 272–273; 2, *The Works of Mencius*, 204.

53. Wang Sancai, *Yiquan chubian* [The powers of medicine, part one] (*TSJC* ed.), appendixes 3–4.

54. De Groot, *Sectarianism*, 1:11–12.

55. Xie, *Bianhuo*, 2.2–3.

56. C. K. Yang, *Religion in Chinese Society* (Berkeley: University of California Press, 1969).

57. Cf. Maurice Freedman, "On the Sociological Study of Chinese Religion," in Arthur P. Wolf, ed., *Religion and Ritual in Chinese Society* (Stanford: Stanford University Press, 1974), 19–41.

58. Li Guangdi, ed., *Zhuzi quanshu* [Complete works of Master Zhu], 66 *juan* (1714), 51.9–10, 52–53. See the eighteenth-century Xu Dazhong, *Yixue yuanliulun* [On the sources of medical learning] (*SKQS* ed.), 1.28–29, acknowledging the existence of spirits, which are like "malignancies of the winter's cold or the summer humidity," the efficacy of planchette, and the uses of prayer for diseases caused by ghost collision, but denying the spirits can really harm people. Early Qing writers are examined by Paul S. Ropp, *Dissent in Early Modern China: Ju-lin wai-shih and Ch'ing Social Criticism* (Ann Arbor: University of Michigan Press, 1981).

59. Cf. Xie Yingfang, *Bianhuo bian*, appendix 2, 63, or any standard medical treatise, with the analysis of Emily Martin Ahern, "Sacred and Oc-

ular Medicine in a Taiwan Village: A Study of Cosmological Disorders," in Arthur Kleinman et al., eds., *Medicine in Chinese Cultures: Comparative Studies of Health Care in Chinese and Other Societies* (Washington, D.C.: U.S. Department of Health, Education and Welfare, 1975).

60. Li Dongyang, *Huailutang ji* [Collection of the hall cherishing the foot of the mountains] (1518) (*SKQS* ed.), 38.3–4. Li's concern for the "heart-mind" of ordinary people and his implicit incorporation of them in ideas of reform is typical of Ming but not Qing scholars. See note 89. This is one of the aspects of this topic that needs further exploration.

61. Ying Shao, *Fengsu tongyi* [Comprehensive analysis of popular customs] (*SKQS* ed.), 9.11.

62. De Groot, *Sectarianism*, 2:1239–1240.

63. *Jifu tongzhi* [Gazetteer of the capital district] (reprint, Taibei: Huawen, 1968), 299.18.

64. In one case, the god informs the father that his appointed time has come in spite of the display of filiality. *ZJTZ*, 183.25b (Ming, Jiaxing prefecture).

65. E.g., *ZJTZ*, 186.18 (Qing, Wenzhou prefecture), 186.23b (Ming, Quzhon prefecture), etc. Filial self-mutilation was claimed and recorded as late as the 1890s. See two cases in *Baxian zhi* [Ba county gazetteer (Sichuan)] (1939; reprint, Taibei: Xuesheng, 1967), 2.19b; and 12–26 passim.

66. *Peiwen yunfu* on "Kegu."

67. *ZJTZ*, 185.16b (Yuan, Shaoxing prefecture).

68. *ZJTZ*, 183.23b–24a (Ming, Hangzhou prefecture).

69. *ZJTZ*, 183.24b (Ming, Hangzhou prefecture), 185.11b–12a (Ming, Shaoxing prefecture).

70. *ZJTZ*, 186.4 (Ming, Quzhou prefecture).

71. *ZJTZ*, 185.38a (Ming, Jinhua prefecture).

72. *ZJTZ*, 186.4a (Ming, Quzhou prefecture).

73. Zhang Xuan, *Xiyuan wenjian lu*, 106.23b–24a.

74. Ibid., 106.12b.

75. Qian Yong, *Lüyuan conghua*, 22.9b–10a.

76. Ibid., 9a.

77. Mary Douglas, *Natural Symbols: Explorations in Cosmology* (New York: Random House, 1970), chap. 5.

78. Yang Shen (1488–1599), *Danquian zalu* [Miscellaneous revisions] as cited by Shen Zinan, *Yilin huikao* [Compendium of studies on the arts) (Taibei: Shangwu, 1971). The compilers of the *Leshan Xianzhi* [Leshan county gazetteer] (Sichuan, 1934; Taibei: Xuesheng, 1967) were also reminded of actors.

79. Shen Zinan, *Yilin huikao*, passim.

80. For references to transvestism among shamans, see Sun Jintai,

"Shina no miko ni tsuite" [On China's shamans], *Minzokugaku* [Ethnology] 2.4 (April 1936): 1–19; *Hejiang xianzhi* [Hejiang county gazetteer] (Sichuan, 1929; Taibei: Xuesheng, 1967).

81. William C. Cooper and Nathan Sivin, "Man as a Medicine," in Shigeru Nakayama and Sivin, eds., *Chinese Science* (Cambridge, Mass.: MIT Press, 1973), 271.

82. In the sense of G. William Skinner's regional systems analysis. See Skinner, ed., *The City in Late Imperial China* (Stanford: Stanford University Press, 1977).

83. This argument is also consistent with the dichotomy drawn between literate and pre-literate by Jack Goody, *The Domestication of the Savage Mind* (Cambridge: Cambridge University Press, 1977).

84. As described in Daniel L. Overmyer, *Folk Buddhist Religion: Dissenting Sects in Late Traditional China* (Cambridge, Mass.: Harvard University Press, 1976).

85. Vincent Shih, *The Taiping Ideology: Its Sources, Interpretations, and Influences* (Seattle: University of Washington Press, 1967), chap. 10.

86. Cf. Joseph W. Esherick, *The Origins of the Boxer Rising* (Berkeley: University of California Press, 1987).

87. Peter Burke, *Popular Culture in Early Modern Europe* (New York: New York University Press, 1978; also Harper and Row, 1978).

88. Benjamin A. Elman and Alexander Woodside, in the afterword to their edited work *Education and Society in Late Imperial China, 1600–1900* (Berkeley: University of California Press, 1994), 549–551, 532.

89. Kai-Wing Chow, *The Rise of Confucian Ritualism in Late Imperial China: Ethics, Classics, and Lineage Discourse* (Stanford: Stanford University Press, 1994).

90. See *Yijianzhi bu* [The record of the listener supplement], 22.1a for a Song tale of a doctor's daughter with bride possession. A *wu* is employed, but the cure in this case is effected through Daoist exorcism. Equally conservative is the role of spirit mediums serving the Tang lineage at Pingshan, Kowloon, New Territories, in the 1960s: lineage members saw them as controllers of the vengeful ghosts of downtrodden local women. See Jack M. Potter, "Cantonese Shamanism," in Wolf, *Religion and Ritual*, 207–231 (see n. 57).

91. James L. Watson and Evelyn S. Rawski, eds., *Death Ritual in Late Imperial and Modern China* (Berkeley: University of California Press, 1988). It was Watson who introduced the term "orthopraxy" into discussion of late imperial China.

92. On mid-Qing understandings of *li* at court, see Angela Zito's *Of Body and Brush: The Grand Sacrifice as Text/Performance in Eighteenth Century China* (Chicago: University of Chicago Press, 1997).

PART III

Eternal Mother Religion

CHAPTER 7

Eternal Mother Religion:
Its History and Ethics

Richard Shek and Tetsurō Noguchi

B y the sixteenth century, both orthodoxy and heterodoxy in China
had solidified into distinct camps with clear lines of demarcation
between them. By then the phenomenon of "religious pluralism and
moral orthodoxy"[1] had become fully entrenched. The imperial ruler
as arbiter and articulator of moral orthodoxy was unrivalled. Likewise, the heterodox tradition had coagulated around a definable set
of doctrines that espoused an alternative moral universe. In this
chapter we discuss the nature and development of this tradition.[2]

The most characteristic feature of this tradition is the worship
of a central supreme female deity named Wusheng laomu (Eternal
Venerable Mother). Her appearance, most noticeably around the
turn of the sixteenth century, signalled a new and more mature version of unorthodox beliefs. She herself symbolized all the ideas and
practices that could be considered "heterodox." Superseding, but by
no means totally displacing, the Maitreya Buddha as the ultimate
source of eschatological salvation, Eternal Mother inspired numerous
rebellious movements throughout the Ming-Qing period. For this
the government chose to call her believers White Lotus sectarians, as
the White Lotus was the most feared and notorious of all sectarian
organizations since the Yuan dynasty (A.D. 1279–1368).[3] In actuality, however, few if any of her followers used the name White Lotus.
Instead, they adopted a plethora of names and showed much diversity in their practices.[4] For a more truthful description, therefore, we
have decided to refer to them here as Eternal Mother sects and the
religion they subscribed to as the Eternal Mother religion.

The central vision of these sects was salvation through Eternal
Mother and her emissaries. But how did the figure of the Eternal
Mother originate? In what manner did the myth surrounding this

deity evolve? What messages did she have for her believers, and what implications did these messages have for orthodoxy?

The Origin of the Eternal Mother

While most historians of Chinese sectarianism speculate that the Eternal Mother myth may be traced to Luo Qing, (also named Luo Menghong),[5] a Shandong man who lived between 1443 and 1527 in the Ming dynasty, there are arguments advanced that point to a much earlier appearance of the deity, perhaps going back to the beginning of the thirteenth century.[6] The Chinese scholar Ma Xisha located a sacred scroll in the Shaanxi Museum that he has determined first appeared in 1212 and was reprinted in 1290.[7] Entitled *Foshuo Yangshi gui xiu hongluo Huaxiange baojuan* [Precious scroll on the Buddha telling the story of the ghost of Lady Yang embroidering red brocades and her son Huaxiange], this text contains interesting references to the Wusheng laomu and the need for all believers to return to the native place *(jiaxiang).*[8] Yet these references have no organic relationship to the rest of the text, and even Ma himself now suspects that they may be later interpolations.[9] In the absence of further and irrefutable evidence that puts the appearance of the Wusheng laomu belief at a time before Luo Qing, therefore, we are compelled to regard Luo as the precursor in articulating the notion of the Eternal Mother.[10]

A soldier-turned-religious teacher, Luo was the grand patriarch who gave both direction and content to much of Chinese folk sectarianism from the sixteenth century on.[11] His complete writings, known as *Wubu liuce* (Five books in six volumes), were published as a set for the first time in 1509.[12] They served as model for many later sectarian texts and inspired a whole new brand of beliefs, namely, the Eternal Mother religion. To be sure, he never mentioned the Eternal Mother as a saving deity, nor did his writings provide any concrete details of her personality. Yet an examination of his *Wubu liuce* will reveal that most of the basic ideas of the Eternal Mother myth were adumbrated by him. It took only a little imagination on the part of his followers to translate them into full-scale, vivid images. In what follows, we show how these ideas were originally presented and later transformed.

Luo Qing's writings include the following titles: (1) *Kugong wudao juan* [The text of attaining enlightenment through rigorous discipline], referred to herafter as *Kugong juan;* (2) *Tanshi wuwei juan* [The text of lamentation for the world and uncontrived action], hereafter *Tanshi juan;* (3) *Poxie xianzheng yaoshi juan* [The text on the key to refuting heresy and revealing the truth], in two volumes, hereafter *Poxie juan;* (4) *Zhengxin chuyi wuxiuzheng zizai baojuan* [The self-evident precious scroll, needing no cultivation, that rectifies belief and dispels doubts], hereafter *Zhengxin juan;* and (5) *Weiwei budong Taishan shen'gen jieguo baojuan* [The precious scroll, imposing and unperturbed as Mount Tai, which has deep roots and bears fruits], hereafter *Taishan juan.* The *Kugong juan* was the first completed and is thematically the most coherent, with the remaining four providing sometimes rambling expositions of the ideas mentioned in it. Moreover, the *Kugong juan* documents some of the biographical details of Luo Qing, as well as descriptions of his religious odyssey and the arduous path by which he arrived at his spiritual awakening.

Born in 1443 in the Shandong province in North China, Luo Qing was orphaned when he was a young child and was raised to adulthood by his uncle and aunt. As his family had served in the military for many generations, he was a soldier stationed at the Miyun Garrison some 130 Chinese miles northwest of Peking on the Great Wall. Intellectually sensitive and spiritually restless, Luo Qing set out in 1470, at the age of twenty-eight, in search of masters to instruct him on the perennial issues in life and on the human predicament.

The driving forces behind Luo Qing's spiritual quest were his realization of the impermanence of life and his feeling of anxiety caused by the awareness of his own ephemeral self. Subscribing to the conventional Buddhist notion of samsara (incessant transmigration of the soul), Luo was troubled by the gnawing thought of endless and meaningless existences of births and deaths, rebirths and redeaths: "Where can this soul of mine attach itself? Since eons ago it has gone through innumerable births and deaths, in various shapes and forms. Though assuming human form this time, its life span of at most a hundred years is nothing more than a dream, while its next incarnation as another suffering creature is yet to be decided . . . This incessant samsaric transmigration is truly frightening!"[13] From this disturbing observation he concluded that all beings are cut adrift and have gone astray from their native place.[14]

What followed was a thirteen-year spiritual journey during which he studied with different masters and underwent lengthy periods of asceticism and deep meditation. He experimented with the

Pure Land Buddhist practice of *nianfo* (recitation of the name of the Amitabha Buddha), and undertook the Chan (Zen) exercise of inner journeying into his own mind. Then, in 1482, he attained enlightenment at age forty when he saw a stream of white light while he was absorbed in meditation, facing the southwest.[15] This brought about an immediate opening of his mind and the complete illumination of all things. He experienced a total sense of unity with all the myriad phenomena around him, which he described as the sensation of "absolute freedom and ease" *(zongheng zizai)*.

In recounting his spiritual odyssey, Luo Qing revealed a wide spectrum of religious influences to which he had been exposed, as well as a rich array of texts and scriptural sources with which he had become familiar. His *Wubu liuce* thus provide the reader with an encyclopedic appreciation of the religious landscape of late-fifteenth- and early-sixteenth-century China. Of particular interest to us is the way Luo Qing gleaned from his various intellectual and religious sources ideas and concepts with which he later fashioned his own faith.

One such idea is his identification of the Amitabha Buddha as the Eternal Venerable Parent (Wusheng fumu) and the Buddhist believer as infant *(ying'er)*.[16] This represents the earliest recorded usage of "Wusheng fumu," a term that would come to assume great significance in sectarian belief, and one that later would be changed to Wusheng laomu by Luo's followers. From the context in which it occurs, however, it is obvious that Luo Qing did not invent this term but merely repeated what must have been a common or popular reference to the Amitabha Buddha among certain Pure Land groups in the second half of the fifteenth century. These Pure Land believers have apparently employed this parent-child motif to characterize the intimate relationship between the Amitabha Buddha and the human race, as well as the maternal nature of the Amitabha's compassion. In any event, Luo Qing apparently followed the instruction of some of his masters faithfully and devoted himself wholeheartedly to the chanting of the Amitabha Buddha's name with vigor. Thus the text reads:

> With utmost effort, I utter the single cry of Wusheng fumu, lest the Amitabha Buddha will not hear me! I single-mindedly recite the name of the Amitabha Buddha, thinking that if I say it too slowly, my Wusheng fumu in heaven will not hear me![17]

For Luo, and perhaps for some Pure Land practitioners of his time as well, Amitabha Buddha was the Eternal Parent who resided in heaven and who would, with the appropriate demonstration of faith and devotion on the part of the believers, deliver them from endless suffering and allow them to rejoin him in the Pure Land.

Another notion of critical importance for our purposes is "emptiness." As Luo Qing deepened his quest, he came to the conclusion that before the creation of heaven and earth, there existed only the unchanging vacuous emptiness *(xukong)*, or true emptiness *(zhenkong)*.[18] This emptiness antedated the universe and would last longer than it. Limitless and inexhaustible, it is the source of all beings. True emptiness is ultimately omnipresent and pervasive. It already exists in all things, therefore there is no need to seek attachment or entry to it. It is, moreover, all things—from the time of their very creation! This realization is best illustrated by Luo's euphoric proclamation:

> All of a sudden, during my meditation, I experience great joy in my heart. Not belonging to Being, and not belonging to Non-Being, I am True Emptiness. The Mother *(niang)* is me, and I am her—there is originally no distinction. With Emptiness within and without, I am True Emptiness![19]

The reference to "the Mother" here is most intriguing. In Luo's usage, "the Mother" is another name for "True Emptiness," which, as the source of all things, has a motherlike quality. "The names of all the buddhas, the scriptures, the human race, and the myriad things originate from a single word. This word is 'Mother.' The Mother is the Patriarch (Matriarch?), and the Patriarch (Matriarch?) is the Mother *(mu ji shi zu, zu ji shi mu)*."[20] For Luo Qing, however, this "Mother" has no personality and is certainly no deity. "She" is the generative and transformative force in the universe, very much like the Daoist usage of the term in the *Daodejing,* the Daoist classic reportedly authored by Laozi. It can thus be seen that Luo's religious quest was not confined to Buddhist motifs but was instead quite eclectic, involving native Daoist notions as well. Once this highly emotive image was used, however, its personification was only one step away, as we shall see.

This awakening brought Luo Qing's spiritual odyssey to an

end. Having thus thought through the nature of the human predicament and its resolution, Luo was able to draw the conclusion that all the teachings and practices of the other schools were superfluous, if not inimical, to salvation. From then on he felt so sure and confident of his religious understanding that he became a teacher himself and propagated his newfound faith among the people. His teaching, which he called the *wuwei fa* (teaching of actionless action), dispensed with all outward forms of religious piety and theoretical discourse, but insisted only on self-reflection and intuitive understanding.[21] The most interesting part of his teaching, for our purposes at least, remains his discussion of the ontological source and the creative progenitor of the myriad things and how human salvation could be effected with the full understanding and knowledge of it.

Once this ultimate ground of being is identified, Luo Qing can declare with perfect conviction that "before creation I already existed; before heaven and earth came into being I was already there!"[22] Thus salvation involves nothing more than the removal of all previous ignorance and the recognition of one's identity with this ontological source before creation—one's equality with the buddhas, and one's unity with all things. Salvation and final liberation become a matter of reuniting with this ultimate source of being. For Luo Qing, then, salvation is the return to one's "native place." It is the homecoming to this native place of true emptiness that signals the ultimate release from samsara and all human suffering. In this view, Luo Qing's description in the *Wubu liuce* of his spiritual quest and his enlightenment provided all the groundwork for the later evolution of the Eternal Mother belief.

Luo Qing's religious views can thus be summarized as follows: All creatures and beings originate from, and partake of, the same source. This source has various names, including *zhenkong* (true emptiness) and *jiaxiang* (native place). Moreover, it is understood to be eternal and unbegotten *(wusheng)*, and is the parent or mother *(fumu* or *mu)* of the universe and the myriad things. Separation from and ignorance of this origin constitute human suffering, while a return to and unity with it result in salvation. It is thus apparent that Luo's religious writings supplied all the key terms for the later sectarian chant of *zhenkong jiaxiang, wusheng fumu* (native land of true emptiness, eternal venerable parent). To this chant the Ming-Qing sectarians added a whole new mythology of the Eternal Mother and her salvational message for her prodigal children. Yet in an amazing way Luo Qing had already drawn the broad outline of this mythology in his *Poxie juan:*

> Wuji gives birth to heaven and earth, regulates them and provides for the human race. The people of the earth are the poor children: you have been admonished to return home; yet you lack faith. Wuji is our original forebear, Wuji the elder is thinking of her/his descendants. The people of the earth are the poor children; they have experienced numerous kalpas and are lost, failing to recognize their parents. . . . With faith, the poor children can return home, and occupy an exalted position in this vast universe. There will be boundless joy; yet you are not returning. Instead you go through endless samsara in the sea of suffering. With faith, the poor children can return home and fulfill the vow of the elder. The people of the earth are the poor children, while the elder is the Buddha. The Buddha on Mt. Ling is originally me; when I realize this *wusheng,* I can avoid hell. Wusheng is True Thusness *(zhenru),* I myself am originally the Amitabha Buddha.[23]

This depiction of the human predicament and the nature of salvation anticipates much of the Eternal Mother myth which came to be developed later. The human race is alienated from its creator, ignorant of its divine origin, and mired in samsaric suffering. On the other hand, the creator cares for the well-being of her/his children, and is distressed to see them suffer. She/he seeks to enlighten them and beckons them to return. Their reunion with this unceasing, unbegotten, and eternal ground of being marks a genuine salvation. It can thus be seen that while the later sectarian myth has a much stronger eschatological theme and contains more pronounced personality traits for the Eternal Mother, Luo Qing has essentially formulated the main story line.

The Eternal Mother

Indeed, the emotive image of a divine mother who tearfully awaits the return of her estranged and suffering children is so appealing that it did not take long for some sectarians inspired by Luo Qing to propose it.[24] This took place even before Luo's death, in 1527, as evidenced by a sectarian text "reprinted" in 1523.[25] The text is *Huangji jindan jiulian zhengxin guizhen huanxiang baojuan* [Precious scroll of the golden elixir and nine lotuses of the imperial ultimate, which leads to the rectification of beliefs, the taking of refuge in truth, and the return to the native place], hereafter the *Jiulian baojuan*.[26]

A text allegedly composed during the lifetime of Luo Qing, the *Jiulian baojuan* represents both a continuation of his main themes and the addition of new ones. Written probably by a follower of Luo Qing's daughter,[27] it makes frequent references to his teaching. The progenitor of all things, for example, is referred to at one point as "venerable true emptiness," even though she is more commonly addressed as the Eternal Mother. Moreover, the method of cultivation to prepare oneself for the return to the native place is described as *wuwei fa,* a direct echo of Luo's teaching. In deference to him, the principal expositor of the Eternal Mother's salvational message is referred to in this text as "the patriarch of *wuwei,*" who is in turn the incarnation of the Amitabha Buddha. This clearly indicates that Luo Qing was regarded with high esteem by the author of the text. The identification of Luo Qing with the Amitabha Buddha is interesting, as Luo himself has repeatedly insisted that when one is truly enlightened, one is the equal of all the buddhas, especially Amitabha, because one embodies the same buddha nature.[28]

Yet the *Jiulian baojuan* is more than a text that simply repeats or parrots Luo Qing's teaching. It takes Luo's characterization of the ontological ground of being for all things as "parent or mother" as a point of departure and ingeniously creates a vivid, emotive, and homey picture of a mother who tearfully awaits the reunion with her estranged children. In a remarkably well-developed form, the Eternal Mother myth, which was later the shared belief of so many Ming/Qing sectarian groups, unfolds mesmerizingly before the reader and the listener. She is portrayed as the matriarch of all the gods, buddhas, and immortals; the progenitor of the cosmos and the myriad things, and the compassionate savior of the faithful. In addition, the text introduces a distinct eschatological scheme not present in Luo Qing's writings.[29] Finally, the text revealed a much more complex sectarian organizational structure, as well as a far more pronounced sectarian mentality. All these are discussed in this chapter.

The *Jiulian baojuan* opens with the assembly of all the buddhas and immortals called by the Eternal Mother.[30] The gathering notices a distinct fragrance, which is called "the trefoil nine lotus fragrance of the three phases" *(sanyuan ruyi jiulian xiang).* The presence of this fragrance signals an impending change in the kalpa, as it did on two previous occasions, when *wuji* (nonultimate) and *taiji* (supreme ultimate) took charge of the world.[31] Whereupon, the Amitabha Buddha is summoned before the Eternal Mother, who explains to him that he shall descend to earth to save the divine beings created originally by the Eternal Mother to populate the world. Ninety-six myriads in number, they are mired in worldly passions and are totally forgetful of their sacred origin. Four myriads of them have reunited with the Mother when two previous kalpic changes occurred. Now it is Amitabha's turn to locate the rest of the lost souls and to bring them back to her. When they do return, they will escape the Three Disasters of flood, fire, and wind, which will scourge the world.

Unable to disobey this command given by the Mother, the Amitabha Buddha reluctantly leaves this blissful heaven and prepares for his descent. To better enable him to identify the divine beings and facilitate their return, the Eternal Mother entrusts the Amitabha Buddha with numerous "tools," including: *hunyuan ce* (roster of undifferentiated origin), *guijia biaowen* (document for returning home), *jiulian tu* (nine lotus diagram), *sanji xianghuo* (incense of the three ultimates), *shibu xiuxing* (ten-step method of cultivation), *touci shizhuang* (oaths of allegiance and submission), and *ming'an chahao* (overt and covert checking of signs).[32]

The rest of the text describes how the incarnated Amitabha Buddha, now appearing as the patriarch of *wuji*, explains and elaborates on the Eternal Mother's message of salvation to the faithful. With much verbiage and repetition, this message is delivered. The following is typical:

> From the beginningless Beginning until now, the Eternal Mother has undergone numerous transformations. She secures *qian* and *kun* (male and female), administers the cosmos, and creates humanity. The divine beings are *qian* and *kun*. They come to inhabit the world. Entrapped by passions, they obscure their original nature and no longer think of returning ... The Eternal Mother on Mt. Ling longs for her children, with tears welling up in her eyes whenever she thinks of them. She is waiting for the day when, after I have descended to this Eastern Land and delivered this message for her, you will return home to your origin and to your matriarch.[33]

The Amitabha Buddha ends his explanation with the admonition for everyone to "head for Mt. Ling, return home, meet with the Mother, have a reunion between mother and child, and smile broadly."[34]

In the course of acting as the Eternal Mother's messenger, the Amitabha Buddha gives expression to several noteworthy themes. First and foremost is the three-stage salvational scheme. Historical time, according to this scheme, is marked by three great kalpas, each with its respective buddhas in charge. The past age, the age of *wuji*, is ruled by the Dipamkara Buddha (Lamp-lighting Buddha), who sits on a three-petaled lotus flower and hosts the Yellow Sun Assembly (Huangyang hui). The present age, the age of *taiji*, is under the control of the Sakyamuni Buddha, who sits on a five-petaled lotus flower and convenes the Azure Sun Assembly (Qingyang hui). The future age, the age of Imperial Ultimate (Huangji), will be dominated by the Maitreya Buddha, who is seated on a nine-petaled lotus flower and summons the Red Sun Assembly (Hongyang hui).[35] This scheme establishes the basic eschatology of Eternal Mother sectarianism and promises that the salvation of the believers will take place in the near future.

Secondly, Amitabha's teaching reveals a highly "sectarian" character, warning that only the predestined faithful will be saved, while the unbelieving are doomed. Repeatedly such terms as "fated ones" *(youyuan ren)*, "primordial beings" *(yuanren)*, "remnant sentient beings" *(canling)*, "worthies" *(xianliang)*, and "offspring of the imperial womb" *(huangtai)* are used to refer to the religious elect who alone will heed the message of the Mother and return to her. The rest of humanity is expected to perish at the time of kalpic change.[36]

Thirdly, the later sectarian organizational pattern and initiation practices are already mentioned in this text. The terms *"sanzong wupai"* (three schools and five factions), as well as *"jiugan shibazhi"* (nine poles and eighteen branches), characteristic of the organizational structure of later sectarian groups such as the Yuandun (Complete and Instantaneous Enlightenment) sect in the seventeenth century,[37] occur numerous times in this text.[38] Moreover, the practices of registering one's name *(guahao)* and verifying the contracts *(dui hetong)*,[39] both performed at the time of initiation by numerous sectarian groups in the Qing dynasty to ritualize and guarantee the salvation of their members, are also mentioned frequently throughout the text.

The *Jiulian baojuan* thus reveals unmistakably that as the Eternal Mother myth was formulated, the attendant cosmology and eschatology so characteristic of this belief were also developed. At the same time, the sectarian nature of this religion, together with much of its organizational framework and many of its initiation practices, also made their appearance.

Other successors to the Luo Qing tradition also composed texts that further developed the Wusheng laomu belief. A fifth-generation patriarch of Luo Qing's Wuwei sect by the name of Sun Zhenkong reportedly compiled the *Xiaoshi zhenkong saoxin baojuan* (Precious scroll on true emptiness and the sweeping of the mind). In it the entire Eternal Mother myth contained in the *Jiulian baojuan* is repeated. She is referred to either as Wusheng fumu, or Wusheng mu. She is responsible for the creation and the stabilization of the cosmos, as well as the population of the "Eastern world" with her children. Once there, however, her children become mired in desires, lust, and gluttony, and lose sight of their original nature. Out of compassion for the suffering of her children, the Eternal Mother dispatches Patriarch Sun to undertake a universal salvation by calling upon her children to return to their native place, where their Mother awaits them at the Dragon Flower Assembly.[40]

Yet another later patriarch of the Wuwei sect further contributed to the Eternal Mother belief through a concrete portrayal of her as an elderly woman who incarnates in the human world in order to save her children. Mingkong, the eighth-generation patriarch of Luo Qing's tradition, was the author of several texts that describe in detail this Mother in human form. One such text is entitled *Foshuo Dazang xianxing liaoyi baojuan* (Precious scroll relating what the Buddha expounds in the Tripitaka on the meaning of manifesting one's nature). In this the Eternal Mother assumes the persona of a blind elderly woman. With a gesture reminiscent of Princess Miaoshan (the avatar of the bodhisattva Guanyin), Mingkong licks the blind eyes to restore vision to the Mother. Whereupon he is further queried by the Mother before he is designated as the saving patriarch. Thus begins his mission to save the world with the teaching of the Eternal Mother.[41]

Further Development of the Eternal Mother Myth

These texts were followed by a long tradition of sectarian writings that repeated and expanded on the Eternal Mother motif, although in both doctrine and style there was much diversity. A datable text is the *Yaoshi benyuan gongde baojuan* (Precious scroll on meritorious deeds based on the original vow of the buddha of medicine), published in 1543. It echoes much of the language found in the *Jiulian* text, with the same promise of returning home and salvation by the Eternal Mother. Much emphasized is the joy of reunion with the Mother.[42] In 1558, the *Puming rulai wuwei liaoyi baojuan* (Tathagata Puming's precious scroll of complete revelation through nonaction) was completed by the founder of a Yellow Heaven sect (Huangtian dao), whose background and religious awakening bore a strong resemblance to those of Luo Qing.[43] The text also preaches the now familiar theme of salvation by and reunion with the Eternal Mother. It contains vivid descriptions of the encounter between Mother and child, and the following passage is representative:

> When I finally come before the Eternal Mother, I rush into her embrace. Together we weep for joy at our reunion. Ever since our separation on Mt. Ling, I have been left adrift in samsara because of my attachment to the mundane world. Now that I have received the letter from home, from my Venerable Mother, I have in my possession a priceless treasure. Mother, listen to me! Please deliver the multitudes from the sea of suffering![44]

In 1562 a text entitled *Erlang baojuan* (Precious scroll on Erlang) appeared, providing further information on the emerging Eternal Mother myth. Based on the story of Erlang's valiant fight with the Monkey King, a famous and entertaining episode from the classic novel *Journey to the West* (which, incidentally, was given the finishing touches around the same time), the *Erlang baojuan* describes the final subjugation of the Monkey King by the semidivine Erlang, thanks in large measure to the assistance provided by the Eternal Mother.[45] This text also seems to presage the legend surrounding the building of the Baoming Si, Temple Protecting the Ming dynasty, as described hereafter. In it the story of the bodhisattva Guanyin incarnating as a nun by the name of Lü is first being told. According to this text, the nun had tried unsuccessfully to dissuade Emperor Yingzong from fighting the Oirat Mongols prior to his debacle at Fort Tumu in 1449. When Yingzong was restored to the throne in 1457 after his long captivity, he rewarded the nun for her loyalty and courage and built a temple for her, naming it the Baoming Si.[46] The temple had been reportedly in existence since 1462. By the late years of the Jiajing reign (1522–1567), however, it came under the sway of believers of the Eternal Mother religion.

In the 1570s, a sectarian group composed primarily of nuns and affiliated with the Baoming Si in the western suburb of Peking created a sizeable corpus of texts to dramatize its intimate relationship with the Eternal Mother. One of the nuns was a young girl by the name of Guiyuan (Returning to perfection), who produced a set of texts around 1571–1573, when she was said to be only twelve years old. On the model of Luo Qing's collected works, she also named them *Five books in six volumes*. The following passage from the *Xiaoshi dacheng baojuan* (Explanatory precious scroll on the Mahayana teaching), one of her five books, is revealing:

> To illuminate the mind and look into our nature, let us discuss a wondrous teaching. When we return home, there will no longer be any worry. We will be free and totally unimpeded, for we have probed the most mysterious teaching.
>
> Let us deliver all the infants and children and return them home. When we return home, the way will be fully understood and immortality will be secured. We sit upon the lotus flower, enwrapped in a golden light. We are ushered to our former posts; and the children, upon seeing the Mother, smile broadly.
>
> The Venerable Mother is heartened to see you, for today is the time of reunion. We walk the path of enlightenment to attend the Dragon Flower Assembly. The children will rush into the Mother's embrace. They will sit on the nine lotus seat, being free and joyful, with bright illumination all around them. This trip leads us to extreme bliss; the children, upon seeing Mother, burst out laughing![47]

Other texts written by this group of Eternal Mother believers at Baoming Temple include the *Pudu xinsheng jiuku baojuan* (Precious scroll of the new messages of universal salvation from suffering) and the *Qingyuan miaodao xiansheng zhenjun Erlang baojuan* (Precious scroll of the perfect lord Erlang, who is of pure origin, teaches the wondrous way, and manifests his sagely presence).[48] Both of them link the nun Lü, founding abbess of Baoming Temple and now respectfully referred to as Bodhisattva Lü, with the Eternal Mother. In fact, she is asserted to be the incarnation of the Eternal Mother. This group continued to produce texts well into the seventeenth century,[49] when it was known as the West Mahayana sect (Xi dacheng jiao).

Yet another sectarian group active in propagating the Eternal Mother faith was the Red Sun sect (Hongyang jiao), founded by

Han Piaogao, probably in the 1580s.[50] Central to this group's teaching is the doctrine of *linfan shouyuan* (descending to earth to retrieve the primordial beings). Elaborating on the basic Eternal Mother motif, this group asserted that its founder was the youngest son of the Eternal Mother, who had been sent into the world to help with the salvation of the original beings before the world was to be devastated by kalpic disasters. It contributed to the Eternal Mother tradition by standardizing the three-stage scheme, making it a progression from azure sun *(qingyang)*, to red sun *(hongyang)*, and finally to white sun *(baiyang)*.[51] This was the scheme accepted and shared by all Eternal Mother sectarians in the Qing dynasty.[52]

Perhaps by far the most successful and influential sectarian group around the turn of the seventeenth century was the East Mahayana sect (Dong dacheng jiao) founded by Wang Sen of Northern Zhili.[53] Also known as the Incense-smelling sect (Wenxiang jiao), Wang Sen's organization at one point boasted a following of over two million. It was the most systematically organized sect at the time, with a clear division of labor and specific titles for different levels of sect leadership.[54] It is interesting to note that this sect subscribed to the *Jiulian baojuan*,[55] as its leaders were found to have in their possession numerous copies of the text each time the sect was investigated.[56] Wang Sen himself was arrested in 1595, was released through the payment of bribes, and arrested again in 1614. He died in prison, in 1619. His teaching, however, lived on. The apocalyptic message he taught generated a full-scale rebellion in 1622, headed by his follower Xu Hongru and Wang's own son Haoxian.[57] The rebellion lasted three months but was ruthlessly suppressed by the Ming government after heavy fighting. Even then Wang Sen's teaching survived this setback, for his descendants continued to be sectarian practitioners and leaders for the next two hundred years.[58]

It was through one of the offshoots of Wang Sen's organization that the Eternal Mother cult was brought to a fully mature form. This was the Yuandun sect mentioned earlier. Founded by one Gongchang (split-character version of Zhang) in the aftermath of the 1622 rebellion, this sect was responsible for the compilation of the *Gufo tianzhen kaozheng longhua baojing* (The heavenly perfect venerable Buddha's authenticated dragon-flower precious sutra), the most doctrinally developed text on the Eternal Mother religion in Ming-Qing China.[59] Published in the 1650s, this text contains the most mature form of the Eternal Mother myth. It describes the familiar three-stage salvational scheme, the Dragon Flower Assembly, the procreation of humanity by the Eternal Mother, the trapping of her children in the samsaric world, and the joyful return she prepares for them. It also mentions the organizational structure of *sanzong wupai* and *jiugan shibazhi*, which made their first appearance in the *Jiulian baojuan*, as observed earlier. It stresses the importance of the rituals of "registration" *(guahao)* and "verifying the contracts" *(dui hetong)*, as does the *Jiulian baojuan*. But what is most characteristic about the *Longhua jing* is its preoccupation with kalpic disasters, which are asserted to be imminent. Three disasters will take the forms of famines and floods, avalanches and earthquakes, pests and epidemics. There is a palpable sense of urgency in preparing oneself for this cataclysmic devastation not present in other texts.

The Eternal Mother cult thus reached its mature form by early Qing. Thereafter, partly because of governmental vigilance and partly because of the loss of creative momentum, few new sectarian texts were composed. Sometime in the eighteenth century, however, the Eternal Mother belief came to be encapsulated in the eight-character chant of *"zhenkong jiaxiang, wusheng laomu"* (native land of true emptiness, the eternal venerable mother). Thus the vague and hazy ideas that began with Luo Qing finally reached their culminated form as a creedlike chant, binding all the believers of the Eternal Mother into one nebulous but potentially powerful community.

When sectarian writing was resumed in fits and starts in the late nineteenth century, particularly through the *bailuan* (worshiping the phoenix) techniques, it seldom surpassed the grandeur and sophistication of the earlier texts. The scriptures of the Yiguan dao (Unity sect) and the Longhua zhaihui (Dragon Flower Vegetarian Assembly) invariably portray a teary-eyed Eternal Mother, wringing her hands and anxiously waiting for her estranged children to come home. The following passage from the *Jiaxiang shuxin* (Letters from home) of the Yiguan dao is representative:

> In her heavenly abode the Venerable Mother lets out a cry of sadness, with tears running continuously from her eyes and drenching her clothes. This is all because the children of buddhas are attached to the samsaric world. The ninety-six myriads of the imperial womb's offspring know not how to return home. . . . The people of the world are all my children. When they meet with disaster, the Mother is distressed. She dispatches immortals and buddhas to the human world

below to set up the great way in order to convert people from all corners. The Venerable Mother cries in a heart-wrenching way. Is there any way to call her children back?[60]

In the preceding pages, the genesis and development of the Eternal Mother myth have been traced in some detail. What impact did this myth have upon state and society? What kind of challenge, however potential and theoretical, to orthodoxy did it pose? What were the implications of the Eternal Mother belief in ethics and in rituals?[61] These are the questions explored in the remainder of this essay. Three aspects of the Eternal Mother religion are examined: its challenge to state authority, its challenge to patriarchal-familial authority, and its eschatological salvationism.

Challenge to State and Political Authority

By its very nature, folk sectarianism presented a "competing hierarchy of authority" to the government.[62] On this point Max Weber's observation is instructive: "The Confucian subject was expected to practise virtue privately in the five classical social relations. He did not require a sect for this and the very existence of a sect violated the patriarchal principle on which the state rested."[63] Sectarian membership was regarded as dangerous and subversive precisely because "the value and worth of the 'personality' were guaranteed and legitimated not by blood ties, status group, or publicly authorized degree, but by being a member of and by proving oneself in a circle of specifically qualified associates."[64] In other words, the sect had usurped the prerogatives of the state and family to provide meaning and value for the life of the sect member, a decidedly intolerable situation for the authorities. Even more worrisome was the crowd-gathering propensity of the sects. As shall be explained more fully later, folk religious sects performed numerous social functions for their members, including mutual aid and mutual protection. This was particularly popular among the dispossessed and deprived segments of society, which needed these services the most to counter exploitation and other economic hardship. As such these sectarian groups offered themselves as "alternatives" to the state and local communities.[65]

Furthermore, the sectarian nature of the organization of these groups created a far stronger sense of identity and solidarity among the members than existed among ordinary temple-and-shrine goers. This "congregational" power of the sects was potentially trouble some for the government. The statement made by Huang Yubian, the Qing magistrate who zealously hunted down sectarian groups and confiscated their scriptures in the nineteenth century, bears eloquent witness to this official concern. In his celebrated *Poxie xiangbian* (Detailed refutation of heterodoxy), Huang unequivocally declared: "The texts of the heterodox sects make no overt references to sedition and rebellion, yet why is it that members of these sects invariably end up becoming rebels? The cause of rebellion lies in the frequent assembly of large numbers of people."[66] Seen from this standpoint, any popular sect was potentially threatening to the stability that orthodoxy strove to maintain, regardless of its beliefs.

The subversive nature of the sects should not, however, be determined by their inherent power to attract crowds. Their challenge to the state was evidenced by some outright cases of disregard for the government's penal sanctions.[67] It was, of course, the monarch's prerogative to inflict punishment on transgressors of the law. Usually the ruler's threat of punishment was enough to deter most people from breaching the law, given the severity of the penal code. But when applied to some Eternal Mother believers, this threat became empty and ineffectual. In the late years of the Wanli period (1573–1620), officials of the Ministry of Rites complained in one of their memorials: "The sects avoid using the name White Lotus, yet in practice they espouse White Lotus teaching. For every sect there is a different patriarch, and ignorant men and women delude themselves and spread the sects' doctrines. . . . They would rather be executed [by the government] than dare to disobey the order of the sect master."[68] This is a strong indication that some sectarians had turned to another locus of authority—their sect master—and that the emperor had lost his sway over them. Huang Yubian, the nineteenth-century magistrate who made a career of searching out sectarians and criticizing their beliefs, also made the following observation:

> The sectarians blatantly claim that all men who become believers are incarnated buddhas and that all women who become believers are incarnated buddha mothers. . . . Ignorant men and women, who have swallowed the charm water [of the sects], become convinced that they are indeed buddha incarnates. They are therefore eager to return to

heaven. Thus they earnestly practise their religion. Even after they
have been apprehended by the authorities and sentenced to decapitation and slow-slicing, they show no regret.[69]

In other words, some of the sectarians did not fear death, because
they were convinced that they could benefit from it. For them, death
would hasten the recovery of their original divinity. Indeed, it would
enable them to return to their paradise once lost. There was also a
sectarian claim that the heavier the punishment one receives at
death, the more glorious one's ascent to heaven will become. Huang
Yubian describes one such claim he has uncovered: "Non-capital
punishment will enable one to avoid hell, but not enough to reach
heaven. Death by strangulation will enable one to ascend to heaven;
there will be, however, no red capes [to wear in celebration]. Death
by decapitation will enable one to ascend to heaven wearing a red
cape. Death by slow-slicing will enable one to enter heaven wearing
a red gown."[70] Huang Yubian thus acknowledged in despair: "Ignorant men and women are not fearful of violating the law or commit-
ting seditious acts. As they are eager to return to heaven, they are
happy to face capital punishment. Thus penal sanction is useless in
deterring them."[71] This sectarian denial of government authority in
enforcing the law, admittedly commented upon with some exagger-
ation by Huang, was nevertheless a principal factor in earning for the
sects the label of heterodoxy. Their supposed zealous commitment to
their religious beliefs had made them unaccommodating to the rules
and regulations of the state. Yet their unregulated congregation and
their disregard for state authority, serious as they were, paled in comparison to their central beliefs and practices in terms of the potential
challenge they posed to orthodoxy.

Challenge to Patriarchal and Familial Authority

It has been observed earlier that the sects, by virtue of their organization, conferred upon their members a new identity and a sense of
separateness from the rest of society. This new identity as one of the
religious elect, moreover, set the sect member apart even from his
parents, spouse, children, relatives, and friends unless, of course,
they joined him in sect membership. His loyalty was now transferred
to the family of the religious elect, together with whom he awaited

the arrival of the millennium. This disruption to familial and lineage cohesion and the transferring of obligation to a surrogate kinship group was cited, for example, in a memorial to the throne in 1584:

> Nowadays heterodox sects are proliferating. Their assembly places and chanting halls increase in number rapidly. These sectarians would rather be remiss in paying taxes to the government, but dare not be parsimonious in making financial contributions to their sects. They would rather be negligent in keeping appointments with the officials, but dare not be absent from sect meetings. Through incurring debts and selling their valued belongings, they try to meet the demands of their sects.[72]

An official investigating sectarian activities in 1615 charged that the sectarians regarded their fellow believers as more important than their kin: "Though unwilling to contribute to the public coffer, the sectarians support their own organizations with enthusiasm. They treat their own kin with indifference, but embrace their fellow believers with devotion."[73]

What these reports indicate is a new ethics that belittled obligations to the state and kin but instead stressed solidarity with the community of fellow religionists. The bond forged by one's religious affiliation now took precedence over the ties to lineage as well as loyalty to the state. The charge that such severance of traditional ties had resulted in tax resistance is most intriguing, as it certainly brought home to the government how potentially destabilizing and subversive such sectarians could become.

Yet even more serious was the charge of unfiliality leveled against the sectarian followers. The late-Ming scholar Fan Lian reported in his *Yunjian jumu chao* (Eyewitness accounts from Yunjian) that followers of the Wuwei sect refused to perform the prescribed funeral rites for their deceased parents and ancestors.[74] A local gazetteer of Wuxi (in present-day Jiangsu), compiled in 1574, contains the following description of another Wuwei sect:

> The people of Kaiyuan and Yangming are fairly affluent. Since the Jiajing period [1522–1566], they have come to embrace the Wuwei belief. . . and refuse to worship their ancestors. Men and women mingle together to burn incense and take vegetarian meals.[75]

Zhu Guozhen, an observant late-Ming essayist, noted in his *Yongchuang xiaopin* (Short essays from the Yongchuang studio) that Wuwei sectarians in the Wenzhou area in Zhejiang did not worship their ancestors or any other deity.[76]

Though admittedly fragmentary, these accounts appear to be compatible with the basic belief of the Ming-Qing sectarians regarding the relative importance of the Eternal Mother as compared with their own ancestors. Their basic eight-character chant of *zhenkong jiaxiang, wusheng laomu* is indicative of this ethical heterodoxy. One's ultimate native place is not the village or county where one was born and reared but is the realm of true emptiness where one originated and eventually will return. Thus the attachment to the locality and submission to the village power structure is weakened. Moreover, one's ultimate parents are not the biological father and mother, but it is actually the Eternal Mother who makes life possible in the first place. One's obligation to the earthly family and ancestry is therefore undermined and made relative.

This subversive attitude toward family and lineage is further illustrated by the precious scrolls of some sects. The *Xiaoshi zhenkong saoxin baojuan,* mentioned earlier in connection with our discussion of the Eternal Mother belief, relates that its patriarch attained enlightenment despite his total ignorance of and disregard for human relations *(renlun)* and ethical proprieties *(liyi)*.[77] Another scroll, the *Hongyang tanshi jing* (Red sun text of lamentation for the world), contains a picture of Piaogao the patriarch receiving kowtow from his eighty-one-year-old grandfather. This led Huang Yubian to complain vehemently that Piaogao was totally devoid of human feelings, that he knew of no hierarchical distinctions in the family, and therefore in the state as well, and that he deserved the severest punishment in hell.[78]

Such an iconoclastic attitude toward patriarchal authority and the traditional practice of ancestor worship had serious religious and political implications. In religious terms, it was heterodox to deny the validity of the most exalted and lasting aspect of Chinese religious behavior. Politically, it was seditious to dissent from the patriarchal form of authority on which Chinese polity was based. As Weber has so pointedly observed:

> To reject the ancestor cult meant to threaten the cardinal virtue of politics, i.e., piety, and on this depended discipline in the hierarchy

of offices and obedience of subjects. A religiosity which emancipated [the subjects] from believing in the all-decisive power of imperial charisma and the eternal order of pious relations was unbearable in principle.[79]

This countercultural iconoclasm was reflected in another feature of Ming-Qing sectarianism—the disproportionately heavy participation of women and the relative equality they enjoyed with their male counterparts.[80] Though most of the sects had male leaders, it remains true that they were the only large voluntary organization in traditional China that had a sizeable female membership. Indeed, some sects such as the Red Sun sect (Hongyang jiao) were comprised predominantly of women believers.[81] This substantial female participation in sectarianism is also evidenced by the often-cited official charge against the sects: "gathering at night and dispersing at dawn, with men and women mingling together" (yeju xiaosan, nannü hunza). The fact that women could intermingle freely with men in sectarian worship was decidedly objectionable to the guardians of orthodoxy. In their opinion, such unsegregated assembly at night was an open invitation to all kinds of immoral and illicit sexual contacts. Indeed, government sources do contain allegations of lustful behavior and even sex orgies performed by the sectarians.[82]

While some of the allegations may not have been groundless for some groups, for the majority of the female followers of the Eternal Mother faith, deeper and more fundamental reasons for joining the sects can be identified. The female, motherly character of the supreme deity of the believers was a factor that must be reckoned with. In her mature form, the Eternal Mother was no mere goddess who answered people's dire calls for help, as in the case of the bodhisattva Guanyin or the folk goddess Mazu. Instead, she was matriarch of the pantheon of buddhas, gods, and immortals, as well as supreme savior of the human race. In the mature Eternal Mother cult, her position was even more exalted than that of the Jade Emperor, an assertion against which Huang Yubian railed with particular harshness.[83] At her command, awe-inspiring deities such as the Maitreya Buddha would descend to earth to scourge it of all evil elements. Yet her power was tempered by her matronly compassion. In sectarian literature she was portrayed as the concerned mother who tearfully awaited the return of her wayward offspring. Her superiority over all deities, combined with her motherly character, must have formed an

extremely appealing image to those women who were by and large
dissatisfied with their lot in life or unfulfilled in their aspirations.
More importantly, the Eternal Mother motif must have provided a
sense of equality, worth, and power for the female followers, a feeling that was denied them by society at large.

Numerous precious scrolls make reference to this equality
between women and men. The *Longhua jing,* for example, declared:
"Let it be announced to all men and women in the assembly: 'there
should be no distinction between you.'"[84] Similarly, the *Jiuku zhongxiao yaowang baojuan* (Precious scroll on the god of medicine who is
loyal, filially pious, and who delivers people from suffering) proclaims
emphatically that "Men and women are originally not different. Both
receive the pure breath of Prior Heaven *(xiantian yiqi)* from the Venerable Mother."[85] Finally, the *Pujing rulai yaoshi tongtian baojuan*
(Precious scroll by the Pujing Buddha on the key to reaching heaven)
voices a similar theme: "In the realm of Prior Heaven, there are five
spirits of *yin* and five pneuma of *yang.* When men gather the five spirits of *yin,* they become bodhisattvas. When women collect the five
pneuma of *yang,* they become buddhas."[86]

To each of these passages, in particular to the last one, Huang
Yubian reacted with moral outrage. He vehemently accused the sectarians of making a mockery of the proper differentiation between the
sexes. He further charged that these statements were open invitation
to lustful behavior and sexual promiscuity among the sect members.[87] Whether or not these statements encouraged licentiousness
is beside the point. What is noteworthy is their insistence that men
and women are no different and are equally worthy of salvation. To
be sure, such equality may be only theoretical and may exist only in
the the future world. Yet this admission alone is a stark contrast to
the orthodox maxim of "distinctions must exist among the sexes"
(nannü youbie).

In actuality, some sects did implement, up to a point, this egalitarian notion. The Huangtian sect in the seventeenth century, commented on by the famous neo-Confucian scholar Yan Yuan (1635–
1704), referred to its female members as the "alternative way"
(erdao).[88] In view of the orthodox claim of "under heaven there is
no alternative way" *(tianxia wu erdao),* this play on words was clearly
not accidental but was meant to tease the orthodox authority. Yan
Yuan was adamant in his criticism of this blurring of sexual distinctions. He accused the sectarians of "destroying the way of humanity

and disrupting established customs." This, he declared, "was utterly shameless."[89] Prosper Leboucq, a French Catholic missionary who traveled extensively in North China in the 1860s and reported on the activities of the sects in his letters, noted that women were very active in most of the sects. His explanation was that women were given a status equal to men. He further observed that if a wife joined a sect earlier than her husband, then in sectarian matters she would have superiority over him, as seniority within the sects was determined by length of membership.[90]

Sectarian Apocalyptic Eschatology and Salvationism

The one truly distinguishing feature of the belief in the Eternal Mother is its apocalyptic eschatology. By that we mean an acute, burning vision of the imminent and complete dissolution of the corrupt, existing world, and its replacement by a utopian, alternative order. Furthermore, this esoteric knowledge is shared only by a religious electi whose faith and action will guarantee their exclusive survival of this cosmic event.[91] Basic to the Eternal Mother belief is the idea of the kalpa *(jie)*, a drastic and cataclysmic turning point in human history. Originally a Buddhist notion that marks the cyclical passage of time on a cosmic scale, kalpa for the Eternal Mother believers assumed an immediacy and urgency that it originally did not possess.[92] The belief in an eventual occurrence of kalpic crisis was commonly shared by the Ming and Qing Eternal Mother followers. Virtually all the sectarian texts from the sixteenth century on subscribed to a three-stage salvational scheme in which heavenly emissaries would descend to earth at predestined times and at the command of the Eternal Mother to deliver the faithful. While the first two stages, representing past and present, excited little interest, it was the third stage, the stage to come, that created apprehension and fired the imagination of the believers. After all, it was their anticipation that the arrival of this third stage would signal their return to and reunion with the Mother. The third stage, it was widely believed, would be ushered in by a messianic figure (usually the Maitreya Buddha, but in some cases the founding patriarchs of the various sects) whose coming would be accompanied by an unprecedented wave of natural and social upheavals so catastrophic that the heavenly bodies as well as human society would be literally torn asunder and then reconstituted. The following description of the horrors and devasta-

tion of the kalpic turmoil, related with apparent relish by the compilers of the *Longhua jing,* is illustrative:

> In the *xinsi* year [1641?] there will be floods and famines in North
> China, with people in Shandong being the hardest hit. They will prac-
> tise cannibalism upon one another, while millions will starve to death.
> Husbands and wives will be forced to leave one another, and parents
> and children will be separated. Even those who manage to flee to
> northern Zhili will be afflicted by another famine and will perish by
> the roadside. In the *renwu* year [1642?] disasters will strike again with
> redoubled force. There will be avalanches and earthquakes. The Yel-
> low River will overflow its banks and multitudes will be drowned.
> Then the locusts will come and blanket the earth, devouring what
> little crop remains. Rain will come down incessantly and houses will
> crumble. . . . In the *guiwei* year [1643?] widespread epidemics will
> occur.[93]

Keeping in mind that the *Longhua jing* was compiled during the
Ming-Qing transition, and assuming that the specific years mentioned in the text refer to that critical period as the Ming dynasty was
about to fall, the devastation and misery described above may indeed
be offering an uncannily authentic picture of the real situation itself.
Thus the kalpic change, for some of the sectarians at least, was not
an event that might happen in some distant future eons from the
present but was in fact taking place right before their very eyes and
confirmed by their own experience! Their overriding concern was to
"respond" to this kalpic disaster *(yingjie)* and to survive it. The
urgency for action was understandable.

Equally noteworthy in this apocalyptic vision of the sectarians
is the notion of their own "election." Not only was the apocalyptic
conflagration impending, it would at the same time separate the electi
from the doomed. The Eternal Mother believers were convinced that
they belonged to a minority of "saints" destined to survive the cataclysm, which would terminate the existing order. Indeed, they and
they alone would inherit the new age that was soon to dawn, when
they would enjoy the fruits of reunion with the Eternal Mother. All
their religious practices were designed to confirm their election, to
ensure their survival in the final moments of this doomed order, and
to prepare themselves for the eventual admission into the new one.
A corollary of this view was the expected annihilation of the nonbe-

lievers (the wicked and evil ones) prior to the arrival of the millennium. Since the onset of the new age would confirm the salvation of the elect, it was not surprising that some sectarians would look forward to its early arrival when the saved and the doomed would be separated and the latter would be destroyed and cast away without mercy.

The notion of election figures prominently in sectarian texts. The electi are variously referred to as *youyuan ren* (predestined ones), *huangtai zi* (offspring of the imperial womb), and a host of other names.[94] The *Longhua jing,* in particular, contains a pronounced theme of election for the Yuandun sect members. Describing the Dragon Flower Assembly after the kalpa, the text mentions a "city in the clouds" *(yuncheng)* where it will be held. The survivors of the apocalypse will proceed to enter the city gate, where their identity will be individually checked before admission. Those who fail to produce a valid registration or contract will be turned away and cast into oblivion.[95]

While this portrayal reveals glimpses of the bureaucratic tendency in Chinese folk mentality—salvation is seen here as "certified" by registration slips and "confirmed" by admission through the city gate—it nevertheless highlights the sense of solemnity and pride felt by the elect. For this reason, the initiation rituals of *guahao, biaoming* (submitting names), and *dui hetong*[96] performed by the novices at the time of their admission into the sect assumed great significance. These rites not only ritualistically conferred upon the members a new identity, they also dramatized their election as the destined remnant of humanity after the kalpa. Assured of their salvation, many Eternal Mother followers thus concerned themselves with "the age to come" *(laishi),* which meant both "the life one might expect after death and the millennium one might experience in this world."[97] When captured and interrogated, these people repeatedly insisted that the principal motivation for their conversion to sectarianism was to "pray for protection in the life to come." They were confident that they would get it too.

This sense of election was evident in many Eternal Mother sects. An untitled precious scroll in Huang Yubian's *Poxie xiangbian* declared that "all non-believers are destined for hell. Only devout sect members will have direct access to the Celestial Palace, not be condemned to descend into hell."[98] At the time of the Eight Trigrams uprising in 1813, one of the faithful claimed, "In the future, those who are not in our assembly will meet with disasters accompanying the arrival of the kalpa." Another put it more bluntly, "If you join the sect, you live; if you don't, you die."[99] Members of a Yuan Jiao (Perfect Completion) sect in the early part of the nineteenth century held the belief that "when the Maitreya comes to rule the world, there will be chaos for forty-nine days. The sun and moon will alter their course, the weather will change and only those who adhere to the Yuan Jiao will be saved from the cataclysm."[100] It was precisely this exclusionist view of election, which made the sectarians stand apart from their local communities and even kin, that made their commitment to the existing order suspect.

When, and if, they did survive the catastrophic disasters of the kalpa, some sectarians expected to find a radically changed cosmos with a totally different time scale and alternative calendar. The *Puming baojuan* of the Yellow Heaven sect, the first edition of which probably appeared in 1558, has a vivid description of this new world:

> The land is re-arranged; the stars and constellations re-established. Heaven and earth are put in order again. Oceans and mountains are relocated. After nine cycles, the elixir [of life] is refined. Together humans reach the other shore. The compass stops and the two unbroken lines [of a trigram] meet. The eighteen kalpic disasters have run their full course, and the form of all things is about to change. Eighteen months will make one year, and thirty-six hours constitute a day. There will be forty-five days in a month. One day will have one hundred and forty-four quarter-hours, and eight hundred and ten days form one year.[101]

This vision of a reconstituted cosmos with an altered timescale appears to have been shared by other sectarians as well. During the early years of the Daoguang reign (1821–1851), a White Sun sect espoused a similar belief in a thirty-six-hour day for the new age. Moreover, its members claimed that "The *hongyang* [red sun] age is about to have run its full course. It is time to prepare for the arrival of *baiyang* [white sun]. In the present age, the moon remains full until the eighteenth day of each month. When it stays full until the twenty-third day, the kalpa is upon us."[102] It is thus obvious that some sectarians were not content with the thought of a new cosmos but were actively observing phenomena in the night sky, ever ready to detect the first signs of the arrival of the new age.

There was yet another sect that displayed keen interest in astronomical matters. It was the Imperial Heaven (Huangtian dao) sect
of the seventeenth century.[103] Yan Yuan has left a brief account of
this group:

> In my native province of Zhili, the people's mores were uncontami-
> nated prior to the Longqing (1567–1572) and Wanli (1573–1620)
> periods [of the Ming dynasty]. Since the last years of Wanli, however,
> there appeared a Huangtian Sect which has become very popular.
> From the capital to the neighboring prefectures and counties, and
> even down to the distant villages and mountain retreats, members
> of this sect can be found. . . . They rename the stars Can and Shu
> "Cold Mother" and the two constellations Fang and Xin "Warm
> Mother."[104]

The entire eschatology of the Eternal Mother sectarians, represented by the concepts of kalpa, election, and cosmic reconstitu-
tion, was most threatening to orthodox thinking. The notion of kalpa,
to begin with, was predicated on the assumption that the existing
order, with its ethical norms and sociopolitical institutions, was finite,
mutable, and destined to be replaced. Moreover, the new age promised to be a far better substitute. This kind of thinking might create
a frame of mind that expected, even welcomed, the demise of the
present age. It would at least render untenable the orthodox claim
that "Heaven is immutable, so also is the Way" (tian bubian, dao yi
bubian). The notion of kalpic upheaval ran directly counter to this
claim of immutability, for it called for total, cosmic, cataclysmic
change. The validity of the present age, including the existing moral
authority, was at least theoretically undermined, since moral norms
must rest on certain assumptions of stability and continuity.

The threat of the kalpa was further aggravated by its urgency.
It was expected to take place at least in the foreseeable future, if not
here and now. It was to be accompanied by a series of disasters so
severe that the entire realm would become one big chaos (tianxia
daluan). To survive it one could no longer rely on one's own efforts
alone but must entrust oneself to a savior or deliverer, follow his
injunctions, and completely suspend all personal values and judgment. This abandonment and surrender ran counter to the orthodox
teaching that prevailed at the time, made popular by morality books
and religious instructions, which was that one could shape one's

own destiny and receive karmic rewards through moral behavior. For some sectarians, this salvational path of conformity to the moral norm was no longer acceptable. They believed instead in redemption through a messianic figure whose deliverance they eagerly awaited. For the guardians of orthodoxy, this sectarian view of messianic salvation meant total contempt for their teaching and authority.

The idea of election was equally unacceptable to orthodox belief, which subscribed to a universalist approach to salvation. The infinite compassion of the Amitabha Buddha or of the bodhisattva Guanyin was believed to be available to all. Similarly, the saving power of Laozi and the other Daoist deities was all-embracing. The sectarian view that sect membership alone could guarantee salvation was thus assailed with vehemence by the orthodox minded. Huang Yubian thus asked teasingly in his *Poxie xiangbian:* "If those who are practising heterodox religion are the children of the Eternal Mother, then whose children are those who do not follow such deviant ways?"[105] A few paragraphs later, Huang again attacked this sectarian view: "If indeed there is a compassionate Eternal Mother up in Heaven, she should certainly not be discriminating in extending her saving grace, and should treat everyone equally. Why should she be so partial toward the heterodox sectarians?"[106]

The sectarian attention to astronomical matters was found most troubling by the state. The changes in timescale, the alteration in calendrical calculations, the predicted deviation in the movement of the heavenly bodies, and the renaming of the stars all infringed upon the prerogatives of the emperor as the supreme astronomer and diviner. In a culture in which the Son of Heaven claimed a monopoly of interpretation of all astronomical phenomena and of all calendrical calculations, and in an agrarian economy in which such powers conferred enormous control over the timing of planting and harvesting, such sectarian concerns carried serious ethical and political implications. The monarchs of China had traditionally warned that "those who recklessly talk about astronomical phenomena are to be executed" *(wang tan tianxiang zhe zhan)*. It is small wonder that orthodoxy would find this sectarian interest in celestial matters most disturbing.

All in all, the sectarian espousal of an eschatology and the attendant millenarianism posed a direct, frontal challenge to orthodoxy. With little to lose and all the fruits of the coming millennium to gain, some sectarians might be psychologically disposed to take drastic, even violent, action to usher in the new era. Seen in this light, Huang Yubian's bitter attack on the sectarian millennial yearning becomes understandable:

> For those who do not practise heterodox religion, men till the land and women weave their cloth. Food will be plentiful and clothing will be abundant. Is it not delightful? . . . The joy of this world is concrete and tangible, while the bliss of heaven is illusory and unreal. The heterodox sects focus their attention on heavenly bliss, but in the end they lose even the joy of the human world. . . . When they say that they are going to enjoy their blissful paradise, who can prove it? Their claim is not to be believed.[107]

Conclusion

In this chapter we have tried to identify the Eternal Mother belief as the mature and coherent version of heterodoxy in late imperial or early modern China. We have examined the genesis and development of the Eternal Mother belief. We have demonstrated how certain originally abstract and disparate ideas were transformed into vivid imagery and even concrete objects of worship. The argument is advanced that Luo Qing played an important role in the final emergence of the Eternal Mother motif, although he was by no means the first person to have used a similar term. Furthermore, it is asserted that once formed, this Eternal Mother cult began to inform the religious content of most Ming-Qing sectarian groups. The last part of this chapter is concerned with the implications and the heterodox nature of this myth. A number of the sects at different times implicitly or explicitly challenged the power of the monarch through casual discussion of astronomical matters, deliberate defiance of law and punishment, evasion of taxes, and arrogating the power to bestow titles and princely honors on the faithful. Some sectarians also undermined patriarchal and kinship authority with their creation of a new sense of community based not on blood relationship but on religious commitment, as well as their advocacy of the theoretical equality of the sexes. Their otherworldly salvational goals, in the last analysis, were not compatible with the existing social and cultural order. Through their religious affiliations, they subverted the control of society through familial and monarchical authority, replacing the orthodox moral norm with their alternative socioethics.

The most heinous crime in the Chinese tradition was "disloyalty and unfiliality, having no regard for monarch and father" *(buzhong buxiao, wufu wujun)*. The sectarians discussed in this study fit this description of heterodoxy rather well, even though the vast majority of them never raised the banner of rebellion. When describing the Wuwei sect in the Wenzhou area in Zhejiang, Zhu Guozhen noted that "some of the curses these sectarians heaped upon monarch and father are unbearable when heard by loyal subjects and filial sons." [108] Commenting on the Huangtian and several other sects, the philosopher Yan Yuan remarked, "When their houses are temples or nunneries which observe no monastic rules, when they themselves are untonsured monks and nuns, it is rare that they do not worship evil spirits who show contempt for ruler and father; it is also rare that they do not chant heterodox slogans which show contempt for ruler and father." [109] Likewise, Huang Yubian noted repeatedly that sectarian beliefs would result in disloyalty and unfiliality. [110] Seen from the perspective of orthodoxy, these sects would have to be regarded as heterodox. If one may borrow the title of Christopher Hill's famous work on the English sectarians, one can indeed say that many of the Ming-Qing Eternal Mother followers had conceptualized a world "turned upside-down." Commenting on the precious scrolls, Huang Yubian made the following observation:

> The sectarians consider those who lead a tranquil, stable life as "having gone astray from home" . . . They make other people abandon their parents, spouse, and children to join them, and call this "return home." They regard prosperous, law-abiding, and peaceful life as "suffering in samsara," but refer to punishments received after their arrest, including decapitation, slow-slicing, and slaughter of family and lineage members, as "returning to Pure Land and Mt. Ling." What is heterodox they maintain as orthodox, evil as moral, transgression as merit, misfortune as blessing, harm as benefit, and disaster as fortune. [111]

Although only a small number of sectarians ever took up arms to overthrow the existing government, the reversal of values inherent in their belief was what made the sects so threatening to the guardians of orthodoxy. The current value system simply lost its validity and immutability when these sectarians subscribed to an alternative system. Their radically countercultural values, combined with an intense eschatological vision, had made them suspect in the eyes of orthodoxy.

To be sure, most of the sects did not translate this alternative value and practice system into radical political action. In fact, it would be safe to say that the vast majority of the sects remained docile and pacific throughout their history, while their organization remained quite hierarchical and authoritarian. Nevertheless, the existence of this potentially subversive tradition in direct opposition to the orthodox mode of thinking must be recognized, and some sectarians did use this radical tradition to realize their political goals. The resilience and tenacity of this tradition must not be underestimated. Indeed, in studying the historical origins of revolutionary movements such as the Taipings in the nineteenth century and perhaps even the Chinese communists in the twentieth, the Eternal Mother tradition needs to be carefully examined for comparison.

Notes

An earlier version of this chapter was published by Richard Shek in *Journal of Early Modern History* 3, no. 4 (1999).

1. For the detailed discussion of this important concept, see Kwang-Ching Liu, ed., *Orthodoxy in Late Imperial China* (Berkeley: University of California Press, 1990), esp. 15–16.

2. In labelling this tradition "heterodox," we are quite aware that we take an opposite position to that held by Professor Daniel Overmyer, the preeminent authority on the Eternal Mother sects and their scriptures. Professor Overmyer has, over the years, consistently regarded the beliefs and values of these sectarians as supportive of orthodox morality. See his "Attitudes Toward the Ruler and State in Chinese Popular Religious Literature: Sixteenth and Seventeenth Century *Pao-chuan*," *Harvard Journal of Asiatic Studies* 44.2 (1984): 347–379; "Values in Chinese Sectarian Literature: Ming and Ch'ing *Pao-chuan*," in David Johnson, Andrew Nathan, and Evelyn Rawski, eds., *Popular Culture in Late Imperial China* (Berkeley: University of California Press, 1985), 219–254; and his *Precious Volumes: An Introduction to Chinese Sectarian Scriptures from the Sixteenth and Seventeenth Centuries* (Cambridge, Mass.: Harvard University Press, 1999), especially 206–215. Yet ultimately the difference between our interpretation of Eternal Mother sectarian values and Professor Overmyer's is one of emphasis. He acknowledges that there are explicit and implicit values in sectarian beliefs. We will concede that the explicit values are indeed conventional in character, but insist that the implicit ones are radically heterodox. It is interesting to note

that Professor Overmyer also acknowledges the social egalitarianism and eschatological concerns of the sectarians, values that we regard to be heterodox in the Chinese context. See his *Precious Volumes*, 210, 263–266.

3. Susan Naquin has followed this designation and refers to all the Eternal Mother cults since 1500 as White Lotus religion. See her article, "The Transmission of White Lotus Sectarianism in Late Imperial China," in David Johnson et al., eds., *Popular Culture in Late Imperial China*, 255–291. However, Barend J. ter Haar has recently argued in his monograph, *The White Lotus Teachings in Chinese Religious History* (Leiden: E. J. Brill, 1992), that this designation is extremely problematic. We concur with ter Haar's concerns.

4. The *Longhua jing* [Dragon flower sutra], one of the most important sectarian texts belonging to the Eternal Mother tradition and discussed in this chapter in some detail, lists eighteen sects in the mid-nineteenth century, none of which used the name White Lotus. A printed copy of the text is in Richard Shek's possession; see also Sawada Mizuho, *Kōchū haja shoben* [Annotated edition of the *Poxie xiangbian*] (Tokyo: Dokyo kankokai, 1972), hereafter referred to as *Kōchū*. Susan Naquin distinguishes two major types of Eternal Mother sects, which she calls respectively "sutra-recitation sects" and "meditational sects." See her "Transmission of White Lotus Sectarianism," 260–288.

5. Ma Xisha insists that Luo's real name was Luo Menghong. See Ma Xisha and Han Bingfang, *Zhongguo minjian zongjiao shi* [History of Chinese folk religion] (Shanghai: Shanghai renmin chubanshe, 1992), 166. As all studies on Luo published in English use the name of Qing, we will follow suit here.

6. See the article by Ma Xisha, "Zuizao yibu baojuan de yanjiu" [A study of one of the earliest precious scrolls], in *Shijie zongjiao yanjiu* [Study of world religions] (Jan. 1986), 56–72.

7. See ibid., 59.

8. Ibid., 70–71.

9. In a 14 March 1993 conversation with Mr. Ma in Davis, California, he raised this suspicion. Overmyer also doubts the early dating of this text. See his *Precious Volumes*, appendix A, 287–289.

10. In his most recent work, Overmyer discusses a sectarian text with the title of *Foshuo huangji jieguo baojuan* [The precious volume, expounded by the buddha, on the karmic results of the teaching of the imperial ultimate period] in which there are numerous references made to mother-goddesses, some even with the title of "venerable mother" *(laomu)*. But none has the central importance of the Venerable Eternal Mother (Wusheng laomu) of the sixteenth century. Overmyer believes that this text was compiled in the first half of the fifteenth century, because of the listing of a printing date of 24 January 1430 at the end of volume 1. This would place the text almost

eight decades ahead of Luo Qing in the adumbration of the Mother motif. See Overmyer's *Precious Volumes,* 51–52. But the self-professed date of printing of sectarian scriptures is often suspect because of the compilers' eagerness to give the impression of antiquity and therefore authority. This is precisely why Overmyer doubts the dating of the aforementioned *Foshuo Yangshi gui xiu hongluo Huaxiange baojuan,* which has a self-proclaimed first printing date of 1212 and a reprint date of 1290. See note 9. We are yet to be convinced that this *Huangji baojuan* is indeed a fifteenth-century text, as some of the ideas mentioned in it, such as the notion of "retrieving the primordial elements" *(shouyuan),* a euphemistic reference to the salvation of the elect, suggest a sixteenth-century context.

    11. For an earlier bibliography of studies on Luo Qing in Japanese, see Sawada Mizuho, *Zōhō hokan no kenkyū* [An expanded and annotated study of precious scrolls] (Tokyo: Kokusho kankokai, 1975), 458–459; hereafter, *Zōhō.* For more recent works in Japanese, see Asai Motoi, *Min-Shin jidai minkan shūkyō kessha no kenkyū* [Study of folk religious associations in the Ming-Qing period] (Tokyo: Kenbun shuppan, 1990), esp. 23–113. For works on Luo in English, see Daniel L. Overmyer, *Folk Buddhist Religion* (Cambridge, Mass.: Harvard University Press, 1976), 113–129; also his "Boatmen and Buddhas: The Lo Chiao in Ming Dynasty China," *History of Religions* 17.3–4 (Feb.–May 1978): 284–302; also see Richard Shek, "Elite and Popular Reformism in Late Ming: The Traditions of Wang Yang-ming and Lo Ch'ing," in *Rekishi ni okeru minshū to bunka* [The common masses and culture in history] (Tokyo: Kokusho kankōkai, 1982), 1–21; also David E. Kelley, "Temples and Tribute Fleets: The Luo Sect and Boatmen's Associations in the Eighteenth Century," *Modern China* 8.3 (1982): 361–391. The most detailed study of Luo Qing in Chinese is Zheng Zhiming's *Wusheng laomu xinyang suyuan* [Exploring the origins of the Eternal Mother belief] (Taibei: Wenshizhe chubanshe, 1985). See also Song Guangyu's article, "Shi lun 'Wusheng laomu' zongjiao xinyang de yixie tezhi" [On some characteristics of the religious belief in the 'Eternal Venerable Mother'], *Bulletin of the Institute of History and Philosophy,* Academia Sinica 52.3 (Sept. 1981): 559–590. See also Yu Songqing *Ming-Qing bailian jiao yanjiu* [Study of White Lotus sects in Ming and Qing] (Chengdu: Sichuan renmin chubanshe, 1987), and the compendium by Ma Xisha and Han Bingfang, *Zhongguo minjian zongjiao shi* [History of Chinese folk religion] (Shanghai: Shanghai renmin chubanshe, 1992), esp. 165–339. The fullest monographic treatment in English of Luo Qing and his texts is Randall L. Nadeau, "Popular Sectarianism in the Ming: Lo Ch'ing and His 'Religion of Non-Action.'" Ph.D. diss., University of British Columbia, 1990).

    12. Overmyer has, on numerous occasions, discussed at length the content of Luo Qing's writings; see especially his *Precious Volumes,* 92–135. On his part, Richard Shek has provided a full exposition of Luo Qing's ideas

in his "Alternative Moral Universe of Religious Dissenters in Ming-Qing China," in the forthcoming symposium volume entitled *State Religion and Folk Belief in the Early Modern World* (Cambridge: Cambridge University Press, n.d.).

13. *Kugong juan* 1:12b. The edition used in this study is the 1596 reprint, with commentaries.

14. Ibid., 1:14b, 16a; see also *Taishan juan,* section 23.

15. This episode is assigned much significance by most scholars studying Luo Qing's thought. See in particular Kaji Toshiyuki, "Rasō no shinkō no seisei katei to 'hikari' ni tsuite" [On the 'light' and the process of formulation of the cult of Luo Qing], in *Chūtetsu bungaku kaihō* no. 10, (1985); also his "Sen yonhyaku hachijyuni nen no 'hikari'—futatabi goburo-kusatsu o yomu" [The "light" of 1482—again on reading the *Five books in six volumes*], in *Yamane Yukio kyojyu taikyū kinen Mindaishi ronsō* [Essays on Ming history in honor of Professor Yamane Yukio's retirement] (Tokyo: Suiko shoin, 1990) 2:1151–1170.

16. *Kugong juan* 1:18a.

17. Ibid., 1:19a, 20b.

18. Ibid., 1:34a–36a.

19. Ibid., 2:44b.

20. *Taishan juan,* section 4.

21. For a discussion of Luo's religious iconoclasm and his Chan affinity, see Shek, "Elite and Popular Reformism in Late Ming," esp. 7–11; see note 11. See also Zheng Zhiming, *Wusheng laomu xinyang suoyuan,* esp. chaps. 3–5 (pp. 43–188).

22. *Poxie juan,* sections 2, 7.

23. *Poxie juan,* section 24.

24. The motif of the reunion between mother and child may have received inspiration from the Manichaean cosmogonic story. See chapter 2 in this volume.

25. It is more likely that it was the first printing of the text, which had previously existed in manuscript form. On the *Jiulian baojuan,* see also Over-myer, *Precious Volumes,* 136–177.

26. This is one of the most important sectarian texts of the Ming-Qing period. Its influence rivalled that of the *Longhua jing,* to be discussed later in this chapter. Apparently the text has another name, *Wudangshan xuantian shangdi jing* [Sutra of the august lord of mysterious heaven from Mount Wudang]. Mount Wudang has been a major Daoist center since the early Ming. It was associated with the Daoist adept Zhang Sanfeng and the Ming court's fascination with him. See Anna Seidel, "A Taoist Immortal of the Ming Dynasty: Chang San-feng," in *Self and Society in Ming Thought,* Wm. Theodore de Bary, ed. (New York: Columbia University Press, 1970), 483–516. See also Mano Senryū, "Minchō to Taiwazan ni tsuite" [The

Ming Dynasty and Mount Taihe (Wudang)], *Otani gakuho* 38.3 (1959): 59–73; also his "Mindai no Butozan to kangan no shinshutsu" [Mount Wudang in the Ming and the ascendancy of the eunuchs], *Tōhō shūkyō* 22 (Nov. 1963): 28–44. For access to the sutra, Richard Shek would like to thank Susan Naquin, who kindly allowed him to photocopy her copy of it. She had herself acquired it from Mr. Wu Xiaoling in Bejing in 1981.

27. Her religious name is Foguang. In addition to her brother Fozheng, she apparently carried on her father's vocation as well, and became a sect master herself. Ma Xisha speculates that Foguang was instrumental in enabling the Luo Qing tradition to branch off into other major sectarian groups. Ma maintains that Foguang was the mother-in-law of Wang Sen, founder of the Wenxiang jiao (Incense-smelling sect) or Dong dacheng jiao (East Mahayana sect) later. Ma even asserts that Wang might have been the author of this text. See note 53. See Ma's *Zhongguo minjian zongjiao shi*, 552–556; see note 5. Wang Sen's group was found to have given great veneration to the *Jiulian baojuan*, even down to the Qing dynasty. Again, see ibid., 585.

28. See *Poxie juan*, section 6, and *Zhengxin juan*, section 12.

29. It is in this connection that perhaps the *Huangji baojuan* studied by Overmyer makes sense. If the date of printing of this text was actually the fifth year of the reign of Emperor Zhengde (1510) rather than the fifth year of the reign of Emperor Xuande (1430) (the difference attributable to a misprint, as both emperors have the word "de" as the second half of their reign name), then the *Huangji baojuan* can be seen as an intermediary text between Luo Qing's *Wubu liuce* and the *Jiulian baojuan*. The three-stage historical scheme in the *Huangji* text can therefore be incorporated by the *Jiulian* text.

30. *Jiulian baojuan*, section 1. The possible Manichaean influence on the Eternal Mother myth can be speculated about. As Richard Shek has shown in chapter 2 in this volume, Mani's original teaching contains the story of the "Mother of Life" who, having given birth to the Primeval Man, sent him into battle to fight the forces of Darkness. Primeval Man was defeated, his armor of light stripped away, and he lay in a stupor. Later he was rescued by the Living Spirit and was reunited with his mother in a moving scene. The rest of the Manichaean story involves complicated efforts undertaken to retrieve all the light particles left behind by Primeval Man, leading up to the climactic conclusion of the second epoch in cosmic history. Although the main thrust of the two myths differs, the Manichaean motifs of the rescue of Primeval Man, the union with the Mother, and the retrieval of the rest of the light particles lost in Darkness bear a striking resemblance to the later Eternal Mother story of the return of the primordial beings, their union with the Mother, and the deliverance of other primordial beings still mired in ignorance and suffering. It should be noted

that there are scholars who reject any connection between Manichaeism and Chinese sectarianism. See Lian Lichang, "Bailianjiao xingcheng wuguan Mingjiao kao" [The formation of White Lotus religion is unrelated to Manichaeism], *Minjian zongjiao* [Folk religion] 1 (Dec. 1995), 117–126. In his *Cong Monijiao dao Mingjiao* [From Manichaeism to the religion of light] (Taibei: Xinwenfeng chubanshe, 1992), the Taiwanese scholar Wang Jianchuan also discounts any influence the Manichaean religion might have had on Chinese sects. See p. 359.

31. The three-stage scheme of time, namely from *wuji*, through *taiji*, and finally to *huangji*, is outlined in the *Huangji baojuan*, discussed by Overmyer in his *Precious Volumes*, 51–91.

32. Ibid., section 2.

33. Ibid., section 4.

34. Ibid., section 12.

35. Ibid., sections 4, 10, 12. It should be pointed out that in the earlier sections of the text, the Amitabha Buddha is referred to as the Future Buddha (sections 1, 2, and 3). It is only later that the more standard version treating the Maitreya Buddha as the future buddha is presented. It is equally interesting that Amitabha Buddha is at one point called the Sanyang jiaozhu (Patriarch of the Three Suns). See section 2.

36. *Jiulian baojuan*, prologue, sections 6 and 15.

37. See Richard Shek, "Religion and Society in Late Ming: Sectarianism and Popular Thought in Sixteenth and Seventeenth Century China," (Ph.D. diss., University of California, Berkeley, 1980), 287–301.

38. *Jiulian baojuan*, sections 9, 20.

39. Both practices are designed to give the impression of official and bureaucratic recognition of the believers' confirmed status as the saved elect.

40. See Ma Xisha and Han Bingfang, *Zhongguo minjian zongjiao shi*, 230–231.

41. Ibid., 232–234.

42. See Shek, "Religion and society in Late Ming," 226. See also Zheng Zhenduo, *Zhongguo suwenxue shi* [History of Chinese folk literature] (Beijing: Zuojia chuban she, 1954), 2:312–317.

43. For a detailed study of the Yellow Heaven sect, see Richard Shek, "Millenarianism without rebellion: The Huangtian Dao in North China," *Modern China* 8.3 (July 1982): 305–336. See also Sawada Mizuho, "Shoki no Kōtendō" [The early yellow heaven sect], in his *Zōhō*, 343–365. For a reproduced and annotated version of the *Puming baojuan*, see E. S. Stulova, *Baotszuian o Pu-mine* [The precious scroll of Puming] (Moscow: Nauka, 1979). See also Ma Xisha and Han Bingfang, *Zhongguo minjian zongjiao shi*, 406–488. A more recent study of this sect is Wang Jianchuan's "Huangtian dao zaoqishi xintan—jian lun qi zhipai" [New inquiry into the early history of the Huangtian dao—also a discussion of its offshoots], in Wang Jianchuan

and Jiang Zhushan, eds., *Ming-Qing yilai minjian zongjiao de tansuo: Jinian Dai Xuanzhi jiaoshou lunwenji* [An inquiry into folk religion from the Ming-Qing period onward: symposium volume commemorating Professor Dai Xuanzhi] (Taibei: Shangding wenhua, 1996), 50–80. Yu Songqing has also studied two major Huangtian dao texts, including the *Puming rulai wuwei liaoyi baojuan*, in her *Minjian mimi zongjiao jingjuan yanjiu* [A study of the texts and scrolls of secret folk sectarian groups] (Taibei: Lianjing, 1994), 135–186, 205–212.

44. See Stulova, *Baotszuian o Pu-mine*, 80.

45. The content of this precious scroll is given brief description by Wu Zhicheng in his "Bailianjiao de chongbaishen 'Wushengmu'" [The Eternal Mother—a deity worshiped by the "White Lotus"], *Beijing shiyuan xuebao* 2 [Journal of the Beijing Normal College] (1986), 46.

46. For a history of the Baoming Temple, see Thomas Shi-yu Li and Susan Naquin, "The Pao-ming Temple: Religion and the Throne in Ming and Qing China," *Harvard Journal of Asiatic Studies*, 48.1: 131–188.

47. Quoted in Sawada, *Zōhō*, 47–48.

48. Whether this latter text is identical to the one bearing a similar title but appearing earlier is uncertain. See note 45.

49. Sawada, *Zōhō*, 278–279.

50. See Richard Shek, "Religion and Society in Late Ming," 276–287. See also Sawada Mizuho, *"Kōyōkyō shitan"* [A preliminary study of the red sun sect], in his *Zōhō*, 366–408. Ma Xisha has also written extensively on this group. See his *Zhongguo minjian zongjiao shi*, 489–548.

51. See this quote from *Hunyuan jiao hongyang zhonghua baojing* in Sawada's *Zōhō*, 397.

52. Actually, as early as 1579, a certain Wang Duo was known to have organized an Assembly of Three Suns between Heaven and Earth (Tiandi sanyang hui) and had a following of six thousand. He was later captured and executed. See *Ming shilu* [Veritable records of the Ming dynasty], 83:5a, Wanli 7/1/23 (twenty-third day of the first month in the seventh year of Emperor Wanli's reign).

53. Wang Sen (1542–1619) was originally named Shi Ziran, a tanner by trade. He might have been initiated into the entire sectarian movement through his marriage to the granddaughter of Luo Qing. His mother-in-law might have been Foguang, Luo Qing's daughter. See note 27.

54. The most thorough study of Wang Sen's sect has been undertaken by Asai Motoi. See his previously cited monograph, the culmination of over a decade of research and writing, *Min-Shin jidai minkan shūkyō kessha no kenkyū*, esp. 133–310, see note 11. Yu Songqing is also an ardent student of this tradition. See her *Ming-Qing bailian jiao yanjiu*, referred to earlier, in note 11. Ma Xisha also has substantial chapters on this group and its offshoots in his *Zhongguo minjian zongjiao shi*, 549–652, 859–907; see note 5.

Finally, Susan Naquin also studies the later transmission of the Wang Sen tradition in her "Transmission of White Lotus Sectarianism in Late Imperial China," mentioned earlier (see note 3), as well as in her "Connections Between Rebellions: Sect Family Networks in Qing China," *Modern China* 8.3 (July 1982): 337–360.

55. In fact, Ma Xisha actually argues that Wang Sen might have been its author. See Ma Xisha and Han Bingfang, *Zhongguo minjian zongjiao shi,* 610–613.

56. Ibid.; see also Susan Naquin, "Connections Between Rebellions," 340.

57. For a detailed description of this rebellion, see Richard Shek, "Religion and Society in Late Ming," 352–367. See also Xu Hongru's biography by Richard Chu in *Dictionary of Ming Biography* (New York: Columbia University Press, 1976), 1:587–589. Noguchi Tetsurō also has a substantial chapter on this rebellion in his *Mindai byakurenkyōshi no kenkyū,* (Tokyo: Yūzhukaku, 1987), 255–268.

58. See Yu Songqing, *Ming-Qing bailian jiao yanjiu,* 37–56, 131–162; Ma Xisha, *Qingdai bagua jiao* [The eight-trigrams sect of the the Qing dynasty] (Beijing: Renmin daxue chubanshe, 1989), esp. 36–44.

59. For an analysis of the Dragon Flower Sutra, see Richard Shek, "Religion and Society in Late Ming," 176–192. Another treatment is given by Daniel Overmyer, in his "Values in Chinese Sectarian Literature," 238–243; see note 2. Overmyer's *Precious Volumes* also has a chapter devoted to the discussion of the text; see 248–271. See also Sawada Mizuho, "Ryugekyō no kenkyu," [A study of the dragon-flower sutra] in his *Kōchū,* 165–220; see note 4.

60. See Song Guangyu, "Shilun 'Wusheng laomu' zongjiao xinyang de yixie tezhi," 575; see note 11.

61. It should be pointed out that there is no consensus among students of the Eternal Mother tradition over the issue of the political and ethical nature of its doctrine. We have already pointed out that Daniel Overmyer prefers to focus on the "orthodox" and accommodating nature of sectarian thought. He also downplays the "subversive" potential of the sects. What we are offering here is an alternative assessment of the same tradition.

62. See David Kelly's characterization in his "Temples and Tribute Fleets," 370.

63. Max Weber, *The Religion of China: Confucianism and Taoism,* trans. Hans Gerth (New York: Free Press, 1951) 215, 216.

64. Ibid., 218.

65. On this point even Overmyer agrees. See his "Alternatives: Popular Religious Sects in Chinese Society," *Modern China* 7.2 (April 1981): 153–190. As also noted earlier, Overmyer acknowledges the social egalitar-

ianism, the sense of election, and the eschatological vision of the sects. See his *Precious Volumes*, 210–213, 219–222, 229, 263–266.

66. Sawada, *Kōchū*, 67, 113.

67. It should be noted that most of the records of the activities, behavior, and beliefs of the sectarians come from hostile sources written by government officials and unsympathetic literati. There is a decided bias there. Nevertheless, whether real or perceived, these descriptions do reinforce the charge of the sects' subversive or heterodox nature made by such allegations.

68. *Ming shilu* [Veritable records of the Ming dynasty], Wanli 43/5/*gengzi* (*gengzi* day of the fifth month during the forty-third year of Emperor Wanli's reign).

69. Sawada, *Kōchū*, 130.

70. Ibid., 113, 152.

71. Ibid., 152.

72. *Ming shilu*, Wanli 12/12/*xinyu* (*xinyu* day of the twelfth month during the twelfth year of Emperor Wanli's reign).

73. Ibid., Wanli 43/6/*gengzi* (*gengzi* day of the sixth month during the forty-third year of Emperor Wanli's reign).

74. Sawada, *Zōhō*, 61.

75. Quoted in Kawakatsu Mamoru, "Minmatsu Nankyō heishi no hanran" [The Nanking army mutiny in late Ming], in *Hoshi hakase taikan kinen chūgokushi ronshū* [Essays on Chinese history in commemoration of the retirement of Dr. Hoshi Ayao] (Yamagata: Kōbundō shoten, 1978), 198.

76. Zhu Guozhen, *Yongchuang xiaopin* (reprint, Shanghai, 1959), 777.

77. Sawada, *Kōchū*, 161.

78. Ibid., 133–134.

79. Max Weber, *Religion of China*, 216.

80. For a discussion of this interesting subject, see Kobayashi Kazumi, "Kōzōteki fusei no hanran" [The rebellion of the structurally antithetical elements], *Rekishigaku no saiken ni mukete* [Toward a review of historiography], no. 4 (1979), and his "Chūgoku byakurenkyō hanran ni okeru teio to seibo" [Sacred mothers and imperial monarchs in White Lotus rebellions in China], *Rekishigaku no saiken ni mukete*, no. 5 (1980). See also Yu Songqing, *Ming-Qing bailian jiao yanjiu*, 295–311.

81. Sawada, *Zōhō*, 402–403. Suzuki Chūsei, *Chūgokushi ni okeru kakumei to shūkyō* [Revolution and religion in Chinese history] (Tokyo: Todai shuppankai, 1974), 212.

82. Suzuki, ibid., 193; also Sawada, *Kōchū*, 30, 57, 64.

83. Sawada, *Kōchū*, 38.

84. Ibid., 30.

85. Ibid., 97.

86. Ibid., 57.

87. Ibid., 30, 57.

88. Yan Yuan, *Sicun pian* [Four preservations] (Yiwen, 1966; reprint Hong Kong, 1978), 152–153.

89. Ibid.

90. Prosper Leboucq, *Association de la Chine* (Paris: F. Wattelier, 1880), 11–12, 19.

91. For a comparative framework, consult Christopher Rowland, *The Open Heaven: A Study of Apocalyptic in Judaism and Early Christianity* (London: SPCK, 1982) and D. S. Russell, *The Divine Disclosure: An Introduction to Jewish Apocalyptic* (Minneapolis: Fortress Press, 1992).

92. For the early history of eschatological notions among Buddho-Daoist groups, see chapters 1 and 2 in this volume.

93. *Longhua jing*, 3:21. Richard Shek would like to thank Professor Overmyer for supplying him with a photocopy of an early-twentieth-century edition of this text. For the apocalyptic beliefs of some later sects, see Susan Naquin, *Millenarian Rebellion in China: The Eight Trigrams Uprising of 1813* (New Haven: Yale University Press, 1976), 12.

94. See *Longhua jing*, 2:19; 3:21a–b, 22a–b, 23a–b, 24a–b. See also the *Puming baojuan*, in Stulova, *Baotszuian o Pu-mine*, 10, 63, 130, 207.

95. *Longhua jing*, 2:15; 3:16b; 4:5b, 8b.

96. *Longhua jing*, 1:24b; 2:6, 12b, 13b, 14b, 18b; 4:21, 25. See also Sawada *Kōchū*, 63.

97. Susan Naquin, "Transmission of White Lotus Sectarianism," 279.

98. Sawada, *Kōchū*, 116, 152.

99. Quoted in Susan Naquin, *Millenarian Rebellion in China*, 13.

100. Adopted with emendation from Daniel Overmyer, *Folk Buddhist Religion*, 160.

101. See Stulova, *Baotszuian o Pu-mine*, 223–225.

102. Sawada, *Kōchū*, 67. See also his "Dōkō Byakuyōkyō shimatsu," [The full story of the White Sun Sect of the Daoguang period], in his *Zōhō*, 434–435.

103. It is highly probable that this is merely another name for the Yellow Heaven sect, as "imperial" and "yellow" are homophones in Chinese.

104. Yan Yuan, *Sicun pian*, 152–153.

105. Sawada, *Kōchū*, 61.

106. Ibid., 63.

107. Ibid., 37.

108. Zhu Guozhen, *Yongchuang xiaopin*, 77.

109. Yan Yuan, *Sicun pian*, 152–153.

110. Sawada, *Kōchū*, 33, 65.

111. Ibid., 160.

CHAPTER 8

Religion and Politics in the White Lotus Rebellion of 1796 in Hubei

Kwang-Ching Liu

The great White Lotus rebellion of 1796 has been studied in the past from the standpoint of the economic and administrative problems of the time, of the role played by migrant settlers in the mountainous Hubei-Shaanxi-Sichuan border area where the rebellion had spread, and of the strategies and tactics of the Qing government forces, and of the rebels. I know of only a handful of studies in Chinese published in the last fifty years that touch upon the role of religion in this great uprising.[1] The most recent survey of Chinese folk sectarians that has come out of China is comprehensive and valuable,[2] but it has not attempted to relate the great rebellion of 1796 to the characteristics of the religious beliefs that, at least in part, inspired it. A recent study from Taiwan offers a comprehensive documentation of the background of the 1796 Rebellion,[3] yet the work does not do justice to the religious aspects of the movement.

A recent and excellent article in the journal *Late Imperial China* has analyzed in depth the inter-sect rivalry within White Lotus prior to 1796.[4] However, the article does not attempt to cover the events in 1796 themselves.

Based on extensive documentation, especially archival sources that have been published in multivolume sets,[5] this chapter explores the religious factors—beliefs and ethics, as well as sectarian organization and politics—that affected the mid-Qing White Lotus rebellion in its initial phase, centered in Hubei. Analysis here is derived especially from the depositions of the captured rebels, which, although they do not reflect the full reality, nonetheless contain facts that are credible. Susan Naquin has written that "it is difficult to tell if the generally unsophisticated explanations of religious activities given by believers reflect a shallow understanding of the philosophical under-

pinnings of the religion or the hostile atmosphere in which depositions were recorded."[6] Despite their shortcomings, the documents
are indispensable to the study of sectarian history. When judiciously
examined along with other sources, I believe, the information in the
available depositions is enough to make possible the formulation of
certain historical themes.

These sources are of value to social history. Very few of the captured rebels whose depositions are preserved were from the families
of landlords and of other upper-class persons. The bulk of the depositions were given by rebels who were peasants (including many hired
laborers) and by people of various occupations in rural market towns
—water carriers, woodcutters, charcoal burners, pig sellers, carpenters, stonemasons, blacksmiths, yamen runners.[7] The social and historical significance of the uprising of 1796 will be considered afresh
at the end of this chapter, which, it is hoped, will provide some basic
facts regarding the rebellion itself—especially the religious and ethical beliefs and the politics of competition and cooperation among
the sectarian groups in Hubei and eventually in Sichuan as well, in
the closing years of the eighteenth century.

Sectarian Traditions

The White Lotus belief in Hubei in the 1790s may be traced to several sectarian traditions that converged on the province during the
preceding decades.[8] Sect leaders were sometimes landlords and merchants but included farmers and people of marginal occupations.[9] A
great many of the rank and file were engaged in agriculture. Sect
organization among the largely rural people with urban contacts was
chiefly vertical, depending a great deal on the teacher-disciple relationship. Naquin has found two analytically distinct modes of sectarian organization and activities in late imperial China—one characterized by congregational structure and by regular meetings for
recitation of scriptures, the other by a looser structure and by the
practice of meditation and martial arts.[10] The sect heritage in the
background of the 1796 rebellion in Hubei included the characteristics of both modes but was distinguished by an especially pronounced
prophecy of the impending cosmic cataclysm. Reading of scripture in
the form of sutra was sometimes required, but greater emphasis was
put on the daily chanting by each convert of mantralike short verses
that embodied the essential eschatology and soteriology of the Eter-

nal Mother religion. It is not entirely clear what the routine group activities were, except for "incense-burning" worship at the teacher's home at regular though infrequent intervals (say, four times a year). There was, in any case, a continuous effort at recruitment of converts—namely, disciples of existing disciples as well as teachers. Even when the sects were under intense government investigation in Hubei and adjacent provinces in and after 1774, secret initiation ceremonies at the homes of teachers were frequently held. Secret meetings with prestigious senior sectarian figures were sometimes arranged.[11]

Among sectarians that became rebels in 1796 in northern Hubei, a major group centered in the Xiangyang prefecture and were at one time or another identified through religious teachers with the Hunyuan (Undifferentiated Origin) sect. More than two decades earlier, this sect, the early history of which could be traced to at least the late Ming,[12] was headed by Fan Mingde of Luyi county in Guide prefecture, Henan province. Fan was a farmer who also practiced healing. There is evidence that his sect also taught martial arts, as well as rituals that presumably would confer invulnerability. Members were required to recite the sect's sutra at home every evening; they were also to meet at least four times a year to read scripture in assembly. This scripture was *Hunyuan dianhua jing* (Sutra of the undifferentiated origin for enlightenment). Fan Mingde owned a version, and his disciples made handwritten copies. The sutra has an eschatological theme. There is a description of the Dragon Flower Assembly (Longhua hui), at the end of the kalpic disaster, when the Eternal Mother was to be united with her children. Meanwhile, the children were expected to "respond" to the kalpa—that is, by taking some violent action. The sect's mantralike song reads in part:

> Change the universe,
> Change the world;
> The year of rebellion,
> The year at the end of the kalpa.[13]

In the aftermath of the suppression of Wang Lun's rebellion of 1774 in Shandong, the increasingly vigilant Qing government became aware of Fan Mingde's sectarian network. Fan was arrested and executed in 1775, and only a few of his disciples escaped death or banishment to frontier lands. There were, however, followers who continued to teach the doctrine, and they managed to build up a

network in several provinces in central China. One who inherited this
tradition was Liu Zhixie (ca. 1740–1800), a sect teacher from Taihe
county, Anhui, who regularly traveled to Henan and Hubei to pros-
elytize and to hold discussions with local leaders on strategy. Liu was
described by a disciple in Hubei who saw him in the early 1790s as
a tall person "with a broad forehead and sharp chin, with a little
beard."[14] Liu honored as his teacher Liu Song (ca. 1715–1794),
who was described as the patriarch (*jiaozhu*) of the Hunyuan sect. A
disciple of one of Fan Mingde's disciples, Liu Song, also a native of
Luyi county, Henan, was arrested and banished to Longde county,
in Gansu, in 1775 and was still living there in the early 1790s. That
Liu Song's charisma was real is indicated by the fact that even in
exile in remote Gansu, he continued to receive from Liu Zhixie and
from sect leaders in Hubei substantial funds that came from the sect's
initiation fees, a sum of two thousand taels of silver, as of 1794, that
he buried under his bed, presumably to be spent when the sect's
activities had developed further.[15]

The Hunyuan tradition was not the only one in the background of the Hubei sectarians. In 1785, government investigations
in Zaoyang county, Xiangyang prefecture, identified "sutras and

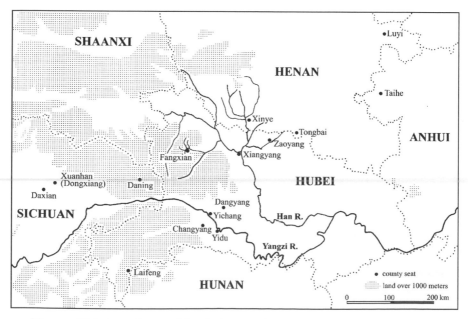

MAP I. Hubei province and bordering provinces

incantations" *(jingzhou)* that seem to have been used by a stone-mason named Sun Guiyuan, who was collecting fees and conducting initiation ceremonies and building a sect network.[16] Sun had been the once-removed pupil of a sect teacher in Ruyang, Henan, named Xu Guotai, who was arrested and executed in 1768 and identified by the officials as "having founded" a Shouyuan (Primordial Retrieving) sect. Xu's teaching was not, however, identical with that of the more famous Shouyuan sect maintained by the Liu family in Shan county, in Shandong. Xu taught vegetarianism, and the officials found him to be in possession of five sutras, including one entitled *Jingxuan* (Careful selection) and another *Shengyi* (Divine will). The mantras Xu taught included the short incantation expressing trust in the Amida Buddha as the "grand guardian of heaven's origin" *(tianyuan taibao)* and the famous creed: "Eternal parent in our home of true emptiness" *(zhenkong jiaxiang, wusheng fumu)*. In 1767, at the time the Qing court sent additional troops to Yunan for the Burmese campaign, Xu had predicted empire-wide rebellion, implying a cosmic crisis.[17]

The millenarian theme continued in the Hubei religious traditions, but the Sun Guiyuan case in 1785 astonished the officials. Sun taught "eating vegetarian food and reciting sutras," yet he and some twenty disciples (including his pupils' disciples) apparently did not use sutras. Instead they taught incantations *(zhouyu)*, which included an enigmatic verse composed of four surnames, suggesting some mysterious seditious movement. In addition, Sun used a chant that began with the line "Herewith a petition to the Religious Teacher in the homeland" that was to be of such importance to Hubei sectarianism.[18] According to the deposition of Sun Guiyuan, he inherited, without understanding their contents, three sutras from Xu Guotai. A disciple's brother was to hand copy the sutras but "did not finish because of illness." All the disciples learned were short incantations that capsulized the White Lotus message.[19]

By the early 1790s, the oral transmission of brief religious texts, often accompanied by prophetic warnings of an untoward event, distinguished White Lotus sectarianism in Hubei—characteristics that seem to have been shared by some sectarian communities in southern Henan and northern Anhui. Yao Yingcai, a disciple of Sun Guiyuan who survived Sun's downfall—the latter was executed by slicing—transmitted the short chants that Sun had taught, even though Yao adopted the new sect name of Sanyi (Three Increases).[20]

From the evidence for the 1790s in Hubei, it is not clear whether
uniform scriptures were used and whether sutra recitation was a regular practice in each sectarian community.[21] What the depositions of
the captured rebels reveal is that they were taught and had learned
the brief sacred chants (*lingwen*, literally, "divine texts")—sometimes
described as "sutra incantations" *(jingzhou)*—that encapsulated the
principal teachings of the Eternal Mother religion. In northern
Hubei, the practice was that the sacred chants were orally transmitted by the teacher, and they were supposed to be recited by the pupil
every morning and evening *(zaowan niansong)*. It was also often said
that incense was burned while the short texts were chanted.[22]

There is no clear evidence as to whether the Hubei sectarians
practiced meditation or breathing exercise along with the recitation
of the chants.[23] Members who joined the sect demonstrated commitment by paying a fee *(genji yin,* literally "foundation silver") and
went through a liminal experience in the initiation ceremony. This
ritual, at which a piece of yellow paper bearing the new member's
name was burned, was known as "submitting the immortality formula" *(shengdan)* or "preparing the immortality formula" *(dadan)*.
The burned document was meant to be a "memorial" to inform
the Eternal Mother of the initiate's commitment as certified by the
teacher. A tally *(hetong)* was given to the disciple by the latter. A
description dated 1794 of this ceremony reads as follows, after
describing a pledge by the new members to keep secrets:

> All who join the sect are first asked to show compliance *(guoyuan)*,
> then taught the secret chants *(lingwen)*, followed by the submission of
> the immortality formula *(shengdan)*. The so-called showing of compli-
> ance is to swear that in following the sect's teaching, one will not
> divulge the identity of the teacher, of the pupils, nor of one's own
> [religion]. What is called submitting the immortality formula is to
> write one's name and native place on a piece of yellow paper and burn
> it against the open sky; this is also called preparing the immortality
> formula *(dadan)*.[24]

It is not clear whether the routine activities of the Hubei sectarians (as opposed to their rituals) fell into any one pattern. Some
sectarians studied martial arts to pass military examinations.[25] A few
leaders in southwestern Hubei practiced spirit possession.[26] However, until the outbreak of rebellion in 1796, there is no evidence that

the sects in Hubei regularly taught either martial arts or the invulnerability cult.[27] The sectarians in Xiangyang are known to have been organized into three "assemblies" *(hui)*, but it is not clear how frequently the assemblies met. Records of sectarian activities in Hubei are few, undoubtedly because after the execution and banishment of a large number of the White Lotus leaders in 1775, sectarians were active only in the underground. Proselytizing went on, however. Sometime in the late 1780s, Liu Zhixie and the leaders in several areas of Hubei sought to introduce greater urgency into their message—undoubtedly in response to the increasing corruption and tyranny of the late Qianlong government, as well as growing despair among the poor. In such harsh times, the religious need for protection against disasters would increase.[28] In the spring of 1788, Liu Zhixie, on a trip to Gansu, obtained Liu Song's approval for changing the Hunyuan sect's name to the Sanyang jiao (Three Suns) sect, thus accentuating the anticipated kalpic change from the era of the Red Sun to that of the White Sun. The sutra of the sect was retained but given a new title, *Sanyang liaodao jing* (Sutra of three suns for understanding the way).[29]

Liu Zhixie's influence in Hubei seems to have been on the rise. Sect leaders in Xiangyang and elsewhere in Hubei found Liu's teaching to be compatible with their own. The charisma of Liu Song, the banished Hunyuan patriarch, continued to be important to the work of proselytizing. Song Zhiqing, a principal sect teacher in Xiangyang, had since the early 1780s followed the teaching of Song Wengao, of Xinye, Henan, who was a disciple once removed of the patriarch of the Primordial Retrieving (Shouyuan) sect. (See figures 1 and 2). As previously mentioned, between 1789 and 1791 Song Zhiqing, along with several other Hubei sectarians, had delivered to Liu Song in Gansu silver amounting to two thousand taels, from the initiation fees they received.[30] The Hunyuan cause and the great prestige of Liu Song had apparently helped in Song Zhiqing's organizational work, but in 1792 Song broke with Liu Zhixie over a matter of great consequence in the preparation for a sectarian rebellion. Song opposed the latter's choice of Liu Song's son as the Maitreya incarnate, and a young man designated by Liu Zhixie himself as heir of the Ming dynasty—a Niuba, a phrase that represents the Ming dynastic name of Zhu (see figure 1), the latter being an ideograph that combines the two ideographs *niu* and *ba*. Song had his own candidates for the role of Maitreya incarnate and that of the Ming heir. Song now founded his own sect—Xitian dacheng jiao (Western-Heaven Great Vehicle).

Song used as scripture *Taiyang jing* (The sun sutra), a sacred book from Henan that apparently was not characteristically sectarian, but he asked his disciples to concentrate on the short divine chants *(lingwen)* that he taught. A disciple later testified that Song had told him: "The *Sun sutra* can be freely given to people. The sacred chant and the tally must be regarded with great care and secrecy when they are taught to others."[31]

FIGURE 1. Examples of two separate characters combined to make a name. (Zhu was the family name of the Ming Dynasty)

Fan Mingde

Wang Huaiyu   Wang Faseng
                                     (son of Wang Huaiyu)
Liu Song

Liu Zhixie

Song Zhiqing

FIGURE 2. Master-disciple relationships of the Undifferentiated Origin (Hunyuan) tradition in Henan and Hubei, in descending order

Song Zhiqing's message was as urgent as Liu Zhixie's. Focusing on the imminent arrival of the ultimate kalpa, he predicted in his divine texts that in the foreseeable future "five demons will descend and there will be calamities of flood and fire; it is necessary to honor the Maitreya Buddha in order to avoid such disaster." Song's candidate for the Maitreya incarnate was a blind man whose face was as if "veiled by yellow sand." Song said that the blind man would open his eyes when the time came. The blind man's son was to be the Ming prince ruling under Maitreya.[32] Song's disciples expanded proselytizing in the Xiangyang area and into Shaanxi and Sichuan.

West and southwest of Xiangyang, in mountainous western Hubei, there was yet another subtradition at work. Wang Yinghu, a sectarian teacher in Fangxian (see map 1) was also a once-removed disciple of Sun Guiyuan. Wang was said to have inherited, in addition to the *Taiyang jing,* some esoteric scripture *(jiejing)* that laid claim to its having originated at least as far back as 1509. This scripture was said to have been "kept in a treasure vault," while the divine chant being taught, as of 1794, was a dire warning of forthcoming disaster: "For seven days and seven nights, there will be dark winds and dark rain" and many will lose their lives. As transmitted to Daning, in Sichuan, by Wang's disciples in 1794, the prediction was that the calamity would take place within a decade (by the next *jiazi* year, i.e., 1804). The Maitreya was, however, already incarnate in a Zhang family in the area of the Shadowless Mountain (Wuying shan), in Henan: he was to assist a Zhu Hongtao (Zhu the Red Peach), who was a Ming heir. This set of crucial charismatic figures was different from that of Liu Zhixie or that of Song Zhiqing.[33]

	Sun Guiyuan	
Yao Yingcai		Ai Xiu
Song Wengao		Wang Yinghu
Song Zhiqing		

FIGURE 3. Master-disciple relationships of the Primordial Retrieving (Shouyuan) tradition in Henan and Hubei, in descending order

Beliefs and Ethics

Several of the Hubei White Lotus sects in the decade before 1796, as suggested in the preceding text, tended to rely on short chants rather than formal scripture for the transmission of religious messages. Such messages were centered, however, on the very core of the Eternal Mother religion—the salvation of the electi who were the Eternal Mother's own children. There is also strong evidence that the sacred chants taught an ethic that was, from the standpoint of Confucianism, blatantly rebellious.

Sectarians of the Hunyuan tradition did not disown deities of the popular religion. The "sutra incantation" (jingzhou) of about a thousand words written on yellow silk, which Liu Zhixie gave out to his followers, was a virtual catalogue of popular deities, from the stove god and city god to the divinities of mountains and stars, and to Sakyamuni himself. There were a score of deities enumerated, but all were servants of the Eternal Mother, waiting on her as she prepared for the salvation of her children. Meanwhile, in anticipation of the forthcoming earthly calamities (dijie), the Eternal Mother wanted the Maitreya Buddha to be especially honored. This text written on silk, found on the person of a captured rebel, was meant, according to his deposition, to be "carried on one's person so as to ward off calamities."[34]

In the early 1790s, Liu Zhixie, Song Zhiqing, and other sect leaders in Xiangyang taught at least three versions of short chants. Four lines of one of the versions are as follows. (Except for the third line, the verse is virtually untranslatable and is offered here in a freely interpreted form.)

> How desolate are talents fit for statesmanship,
> Turn three, four, and five times, and it is the wu year,
> All come to the Dragon Flower Assembly,
> To await Buddha's dharma for the complete preservation.[35]

The "wu year" undoubtedly refers to a future year of the sexagenary cycle. The Dragon Flower Assembly refers to the eventual meeting between the Eternal Mother and her "original children" that is central to White Lotus soteriology.[36] In a short chant that Liu Zhixie was said to have taught, identified by a captured rebel as a "sutra," the term "white lotus" was used:

> Spring wind is warm,
> Summer wind is hot,
> The white lotus blossom
> Is white as snow.[37]

The sacred chant that sectarian teachers in Hubei most commonly taught, according to the depositions of several captured rebels, was one that spells out the central belief of the Eternal Mother religion—and one that is longingly pious in tone. It evokes an acute sense of this-worldly suffering and, in the name of the Eternal Mother, calls on her children to come home:

> Having left the magical mountain and lost our way home,
> We live in this world of suffering and bitterness,
> The Eternal Mother will send a message
> Especially to invite you to return home.[38]

In several versions taught in northern Hubei (from Xiangyang to Fangxian and Yunyang and Yunxi), the sacred chant that was orally transmitted was actually a response to the message from the Eternal Mother. There were at least seven captured rebels from northern Hubei that deposed that the chant they learned began with the following plea to the Eternal Mother:

> Herewith a petition to the Religious Teacher in the homeland—
> My great and merciful old Mother, my Buddha.[39]

Names of popular deities—Amida, the Eight Diamond heroes, and others—were then cited, as if to affirm faith in the protection one would receive in one's journey to the Eternal Mother's embrace. It is especially noteworthy that in at least seven cases the sacred chants as recorded in depositions by the Hubei rebels included the invocation of Nezha,[40] the figure in the novel *Fengshen yanyi* (The investiture of the gods) who, after cutting up his flesh and bones and returning them to his parents, would claim that he no longer owed them anything. In one of the seven cases, the joint deposition of two disciples of Yao Zhifu, the Hunyuan sect leader in Xiangyang, who was close to Liu Zhixie, goes on to give the remainder of the text:

> The disasters of my forebears lay in Five Relations [*wu lun*]—
> In *ren* [benevolence] and *yi* [duty], *li* [ritual] and *zhi* [wisdom];
>   in Heaven, earth, and man,

Cut up bones and return them to father and mother,
Cut up flesh and return it to parents,
One who breaks open the mountain to save the Mother
Is the truly loyal and filial person.[41]

The implication here is, from the Confucian standpoint, outrageous and unacceptable. The chant strongly suggests that only one
who was devoted to the Eternal Mother more than to any other person was "truly" filial (and loyal). The reference to saving the Mother
is reminiscent of the famous Buddhist story of Mulian saving his
mother's soul in Hades, but is perhaps closer to the myth of Chenxiang, the woman who employed an axe to split open the Huashan
mountain, under which her mother was imprisoned.[42] In the White
Lotus context the Eternal Mother looms larger. The sentiment of
putting salvation of one's self above devotion to one's earthly parents
is compatible with a famous passage from a sectarian sutra:

I return home today,
There is nothing I can recompense;
I leave behind the precious scroll,
Recompensing Kindness,
To repay my parents.[43]

Earthly Injustice and "Response to Kalpa"

The distinctive religious ethics taught by the sectarians in Hubei were
accompanied, at least in the early 1790s, by a detailed eschatology—
the impending cosmic calamity and the wonders to be worked by
Maitreya, the messiah who was the Eternal Mother's agent. As indicated above, as early as 1792 Song Zhiqing and Wang Yinghu were
predicting forthcoming calamities.[44] The prophecy took a dramatic
turn within two years, in the spring and summer of 1794, when
imminent apocalypse was predicted:

Dark wind rises in a day and a night
And countless people will be killed,
Bones will heap up in a mountain,
And the flowing blood will form a sea.[45]

As taught by Bai Peixiang, a sect teacher in Fangxian, these lines
were supposed to be from a new "divine text" revealed in Shaanxi.

Bai is said to have taught his disciples in southwestern Hubei that a "true sovereign" *(zhenzhu)* had appeared in Shaanxi, named Li Quan'er (Li the Dog). He was born in 1778 with the two characters *ri* (sun) and *yue* (moon) on his palms—together composing the ideograph Ming (see figure 1). He was said to be the son of Liu Zhixie's sister, and Liu and the mysterious secret-society-like character Zhu Jiutao (Zhu the Nine Peaches) served as Li's principal military and civil advisers, respectively.[46] In the summer of 1794, disciples of Wang Yinghu in Daning, Sichuan, disseminated yet another version of events preparing the way for the apocalypse. Sectarians in Daning not only knew the sacred chants that included invocation of Nezha and other deities, but also announced that the Maitreya was already on earth, born into a Zhang family at Wuying (Shadowless) Mountain in Henan.[47]

Grave earthly disaster now descended upon Hubei from a human source, beginning in the summer of 1794. Reports of sectarian plans for expansion of proselytism and for rebellion were traced by the Qing authorities to Song Zhiqing and other leaders in Hubei and to Liu Song in Gansu. More than twenty leaders, including the two just mentioned, were arrested and executed, and more than a hundred and fifty people believed to be sect members were captured and banished to the frontiers. Pressed by the throne especially to find Liu Zhixie, who had escaped apprehension (itself a dramatic story), an urgent campaign was relentlessly pursued in several provinces—one of Qianlong's last campaigns and the most ruthless.[48] Investigation and persecution continued through 1795; door-to-door searches for lesser leaders were conducted even in villages. The malaise of local government was at its worst. Only "good people," those cleared of suspicion, were given placards to put on their doors. The search for sectarians was sometimes entrusted to gangsterlike figures who, in collusion with yamen underlings and some *baojia* personnel, demanded bribes from anyone who wished to avoid arrest.[49] Some White Lotus members resisted with force, out of outrage, anger, and the desire for revenge. Widespread persecution confirmed the notion that the end of the kalpa was at hand. Behind the revolt of spring 1796 were expectations that gave deeper meaning to the words emblazoned on the sectarian banners: "The officials have forced the people to rebel" *(guan po min fan)*. As two rebels from northwestern Hubei explained, referring to their leaders Lin Zhihua and Zhang Xunlong:

Because local officials, while investigating and apprehending [leaders of] the heterodox religion *(xiejiao)*, have allowed the clerks and runners to engage in extortion and to harass us, resentment and hatred fill the people's minds. Thus Lin Zhihua and Zhang Xunlong have told the people that officials have forced the people to rebel.[50]

The Qing interrogator asked the two rebels a shrewd question. If indeed it was the bureaucracy that was at fault, why then did the White Lotus members pillage peaceful villages and kill innocent people—which seems to be the case? The answer given in the deposition is revealing. The two sectarians claimed that the White Lotus always gave people a chance to join their ranks—and their religion—before doing harm to them. "When we arrive at a village, we pillage for food and compel people to join our group *(ruhuo)*. Those who comply, we will not kill or harm."[51] The implication is that those who would not join proved by their very refusal that they had never been the "original people" *(yuanren)* who were the Eternal Mother's children. In this sectarian view, to destroy those who were not the original progeny of the Eternal Mother was merely "responding to kalpa" *(yingjie)*—separating the wheat from the chaff at a time of final reckoning. Yao Zhifu and his son (who was also a sect teacher) announced to their converts: "Those who would not join [the rebellion] are those who ought to die in the cataclysm." Testimony of the Yaos' converts implies that violence was part and parcel of the "response to the kalpa." Hubei rebels as far south as the Yichang area remembered that before the actual uprising, Yao Zhifu had sent the message that "gathering of the elect" *(shouyuan)* was imminent.[52]

In early 1796 the leaders at both Xiangyang and Fangxian had come to an agreement on the tenth day of the third month (when the year, month, and day were all of the *chen* "horary character") as being auspicious for the uprising.[53] Actually, as the captured rebels from several centers all insisted, the uprising was precipitated by official persecution and harassment. The rebellion first broke out in the first lunar month, 1796, in Yidu and Zhijiang counties, in the foothills of Hubei's western mountain range. The outbreak occurred during the second lunar month in Dangyang, to the north, and in Fangxian and the mountainous counties flanking the latter (see map 1). In Yidu, where the rebels had quickly set up ramparts in the mountains, they announced official titles for hierarchical ranks and promised new recruits and donors future official appointments.[54] In Changyang, one of the leaders was an affluent landowner who claimed to be able to "summon wind and rain and read the stars of the firmament." In Laifeng, in the southwest corner of Hubei, as well as in Yidu, there were cases of leaders who practiced spirit possession and claimed the ability, with the aid of a divine talisman, to provide protection for those who joined the sect, so that they would not be hit by spears, arrows, or gunfire *(kebi qiang jian, duobi qiang pao).*[55] There was no trace of magic or of spirit mediums, however, in the records regarding rebellion in the Xiangyang area that broke out in the third lunar month and which provided the two most effective and long-lasting forces of that year's uprising. The sectarian rebellion in most Hubei counties failed in a matter of months, but the rebellion had meanwhile spread to Sichuan, especially, and a number of leaders from the Xiangyang area, including a woman religious teacher, conducted effective mobile warfare into 1797 and 1798 and exerted an influence on the continued rebellion in Sichuan.

Women's Role and the Status of Widow Qi née Wang

The White Lotus rebellion in Hubei demonstrated its religious basis if only by the prominent role played in it by women sect members. In the context of late imperial Chinese society, it seems that only the faith in an Eternal Mother that transcended heaven could invalidate all the socioethical notions that accompanied heaven and its hierarchical forces of yang and yin.[56] The performance of Hubei's White Lotus women made reality of the famous passage in a sectarian sutra:

> Whether man or woman,
> There is no difference;
> All rely on the Eternal Mother—
> The unitary force [that existed] prior to heaven.[57]

Although most of them were widows who succeeded their deceased husbands as religious teachers, sectarian women in Hubei did assume positions of leadership. A former Qing magistrate, caught in the city of Dangyang, which was occupied by the White Lotus forces in the spring of 1796, wrote of what he had witnessed:

> A woman who has been long in the [White Lotus] religion is honored as Mother Teacher *(shimu)*, . . . When she emerges in a home, five or

six young women will hold tobacco bags and towels for her, and she will be seated at the center of the hall. Both men and women make obeisance: the man puts the palm of his right hand on the back of his left hand, and the woman, the palm of her left hand on the back of her right hand. They kotow in reverence.[58]

In the Qing imperial publication of documents on the suppression of the White Lotus rebellion, there are for the years 1796–1798 at least three cases of Hubei women serving as religious leaders and five instances of women directing battles.[59] Among religious leaders, the most prominent woman was the famous Qi née Wang (Qi Wang shi or Qi er guafu), identified by a literati source as Wang Cong'er. Her husband, Qi Lin, a principal White Lotus leader in Xiangyang who was executed in 1794, was identified by a knowledgeable early-nineteenth-century account as the chief yamen runner of Xiangyang county.[60] From the depositions of his disciples and fellow sectarians, it is known that Qi Lin was the disciple of a White Lotus master in Henan; it is also known that he had been affiliated with both Liu Zhixie and Song Zhiqing.[61] Qi Lin had a chain of disciples, and before he was arrested and executed, in the autumn of 1794, he headed one of the three White Lotus "assemblies" of Xiangyang, identified simply as the Middle Assembly (Zhong hui). The other two assemblies were the Eastern Assembly and the Western Assembly, headed respectively by Ma Delong and Song Zhiqing.[62]

Widow Qi née Wang, who somehow escaped arrest, succeeded to Qi Lin's position in the Middle Assembly. Qing literati writers

Song Wenshi	Liu Zhixie
Song Zhiqing	
Qi Lin *and* Qi née Wang	
Yao Zhifu	

FIGURE 4. Master-disciple relationships of the sectarian heritage of Widow Qi née Wang and Yao Zhifu, in descending order

have fantasized about her background as a member of a traveling theatrical troupe and about her "demonic wickedness." The principal Qing commander who eventually defeated her forces described her—as did the Jiaqing emperor himself in the note of his poem on the event of her defeat and death—as the "chief religious master" *(zong jiao shi)*.[63] Judging from the depositions of Widow Qi's followers and allies, she was not, as is sometimes claimed, serving as overall leader of the Hubei White Lotus groups. She was, however, the leader of one principal White Lotus group that took up arms in the uprising of 1796. Widow Qi fought on horseback herself. She headed a battalion separate from but coordinating closely with Yao Zhifu's. In Widow Qi's battalion were "several hundred women cavalry" and some of these women were given independent missions in the mobile warfare that characterized the White Lotus campaigns.[64]

Sectarian Military Organization

Once the uprising started in the Xiangyang area in the third and fourth lunar months in 1796, the sectarians were on the road and the "assemblies" could not meet in any ordinary way. The term *"hui"* was still used, but it reflected merely the loose affiliation of the forces under the command of several independent religious teachers.[65] The Xiangyang White Lotus rebels now identified themselves with either the Southern Assembly (Nan hui) or the Northern Assembly (Bei hui). The southern *hui* was led by Zhang Hanchao, a fortune-teller who had passed the age of seventy but who lent his prestige to forces led by such staunch fighters as Liu Qirong and Li Chao. The northern *hui* was headed by Widow Qi, who "instructed" *(chuanxi)* Yao Zhifu and six other prominent leaders. According to a deposition, for a time these included Gao Chengjie and Gao Junde, who had been disciples of Song Zhiqing—the able leader who was executed in 1794—at the same time that Qi Lin was. Sectarian organization in Hubei had never emphasized horizontal integration, and it was difficult to do so now. The Gaos did occasionally join Widow Qi in military maneuvers, but this was only when the Gaos were defeated by imperial troops and found it expedient to join forces temporarily.[66]

Widow Qi's effective authority was limited to a few close disciples of her husband and herself, including especially Yao Zhifu, who had emerged as a major teacher in his own right. Yao was a hunchback around sixty years old, a former farmer with a "darkish and wrinkled face, his thin whiskers half-white." Yao probably did most of the military and administrative work under Widow Qi, but the latter was recognized as the Buddhist master *(foshi)* whose authority included making military appointments. In the third lunar month in 1797 when an officer who served under Yao Zhifu was captured by the Qing forces, he was found to be carrying a banner on which was written: "Commanding troops by virtue of the authority of the Buddhist Master" *(foshi,* i.e., Widow Qi). Yao himself apparently enjoyed the position of grand marshal of the army and cavalry *(bingma da yuanshuai)* under Widow Qi's authority.[67]

The aforementioned sectarian officer captured by the Qing forces in the third month of 1797, named Zhou Weicheng, deposed that because he was in charge of the flag, he was often called "marshal" *(yuanshuai).* Captured with Zhou in 1797 was a lower officer holding a smaller flag, also a disciple of Yao Zhifu. This lower officer was supposed to have under him four or five hundred troops.[68] In another sectarian army from Hubei, that of Zhang Hanchao, the forces were organized under vanguard commanders *(xianfeng)* and battalion chiefs and deputy chiefs *(yingzong, yingfu)* as of the fifth lunar month of 1797. (The battalion chief was sometimes called *zongbing,* or commander.) Zhang Hanchao himself was the initial religious master of his forces and one of his sons, Zhang Yuemei, was the grand marshal *(dudu da yuanshuai).*[69]

Difficulty of Wider Coordination

Apparently Widow Qi and her ally Yao Zhifu never attempted to designate a Maitreya incarnate or a Ming pretender. The initial report received by the Qing government that Widow Qi and her disciple Fan Renjie had announced a reign title—Wanli (Ten thousand Advantages)—is not substantiated by other available sources.[70] However, Widow Qi did make an attempt at coordination with other sectarian armies, including those in Sichuan. This aim was apparently shared by the other major sectarian group from Xiangyang, under the command of Zhang Hanchao. Referring to the events of 1797, an associate of Zhang Hanchao later deposed:

> At that time those who make a living from religion *(chijiao de ren)* were unified in mind, and all wanted to see success. Hearing that there are

many [potential supporters in Sichuan] and that the terrain was strategically defensible, we went with Widow Qi *née* Wang to Sichuan to see Xu Tiande.[71]

Pressed by Qing forces, several groups of Xiangyang rebels crossed an upper stream of the Han River, moved into Shaanxi and then to Sichuan in the summer of 1797. Widow Qi and several of her commanders and allies, including Wang Tingzhao, a Hunyuan sect master who was with Zhang Hanchao's army, met with their Sichuan coreligionists Wang Sanhuai and Xu Tiande in the seventh lunar month in 1797. Both Sichuanese leaders had been pupils of Sun Cifeng (Sun Laowu), who was of Xiangyang background and a disciple of Song Zhiqing. Their forces had just suffered a severe defeat, however. Chased by the Qing troops, they fled in the same direction as Widow Qi's adherents, but arranged only a brief meeting with the Hubei leaders. It was literally a meeting on horseback, and the only concrete result was the understanding that two of Widow Qi's affiliates, Fan Renjie and Wang Guangzu, were to remain in Sichuan with their forces. They were given the color yellow for their banners, as differentiated from the blue banner for Xu Tiande and white for Wang Sanhuai.[72]

The idea of "joining forces" *(hehuo)* having been rejected by the Sichuan sectarian leaders, Widow Qi and Yao Zhifu—closely pursued by the Qing forces, who singled them out as principal targets—returned swiftly to Hubei, moved into Shaanxi again that autumn, and again entered Sichuan, only to return to Shaanxi and eventually be surrounded by large Qing forces at the Shaanxi-Hubei border in the third lunar month in 1798. The encirclement narrowed down finally to a steep mountain at the northwestern tip of Hubei. As the enemy closed in, Widow Qi jumped off a high cliff, followed by Yao Zhifu.[73]

More successful, however, was the reentry in Sichuan of Gao Junde, who, as we have seen, was originally a disciple of Song Zhiqing. An able commander, Gao commanded a large force and now gained legitimacy by giving honor to the religious leader Wang Tingzhao. The grandson of a Hunyuan sect teacher, Wang Shan, Wang Tingzhao had spent his boyhood years in the countryside of Luyi, Henan, and was engaged in selling sashes and belts in the Henan-Hubei border region. He joined the uprising in Xiangyang in early

1796. Thanks to his carrying with him two scrolls of White Lotus scriptures (which he seems to have been reluctant to identify), along with a portrait of his grandfather, Wang Tingzhao was very much respected by his Hubei coreligionists, including Zhang Hanchao and his son, Zhang Zhenglong. When the three sectarian assemblies in peacetime Xiangyang were reorganized into the militarized northern and southern assemblies in 1796, Wang Tingzhao gained a principal voice in the southern assembly led by Zhang Hanchao. Wang was with the latter in 1797 in Shaanxi, then with Zhang Zhenglong in Sichuan while dodging the pursuing Qing forces. In the summer of 1798, Wang Tingzhao was welcomed as religious leader by Luo Qiqing, a Sichuanese rebel leader. When Luo, in his turn, was defeated by the Qing armies, he was found to carry the portrait of a sectarian leader given to him by Wang. Wang, meanwhile, had joined the forces of Gao Junde, the Xiangyang sectarian who commanded the strongest Hubei force in Sichuan. By this time Wang had acquired the portraits of seven buddhas, including one of Maitreya. He had announced that the portrait of the Maitreya could "ward off spears and gunfire" (bide qiangpao), but it seems from the depositions that neither Gao Junde nor the Sichuan sectarian leaders believed this.[74]

In the same summer of 1798, Gao Junde, whether out of genuine piety or for reasons of religious politics, honored Wang Tingzhao as the venerable master (lao zhanggui), with authority over Gao's own forces, including the announcement of major appointments.[75] It seems that Gao Junde had so honored Wang despite the fact the latter was of the Hunyuan tradition, whereas Gao himself had been a disciple of Song Zhiqing, whose religious position was more complex. As we have seen, Song had quarreled with Liu Zhixie in 1792 and founded his own Western Heaven Great Vehicle sect, aligning it with his earlier belief in the Shouyuan tradition from Henan. Neither Song nor Liu Zhixie, however, had succeeded in establishing the authority of their respective candidates for the Maitreya and for the Ming heir. Sectarians like Gao Junde who had formerly honored Song as their teacher still needed a creditable religious master, and it seems that role was now partially filled by Wang Tingzhao—the scion of a White Lotus master who was knowledgeable about religion and about the military situation as well. Wang Tingzhao, meanwhile, was considering what he could do to enhance the appeal of the White Lotus cause, fostering greater unity among the militarized sectarians.

Sect Patriarch as "True Sovereign"

Back in the fifth lunar month in 1797, when Wang Tingzhao was with Zhang Hanchao's army in southwestern Shaanxi, he undoubtedly had a hand in producing a proclamation issued by Zhang's commanders. This document, preserved in the original in the First Historical Archives in Beijing, refers to a descendant of the Ming imperial house as "our sovereign" *(wu zhu)*—a potential monarch who, as the document says, would achieve "the rise of the Han people and the extinction of the Manchus" and, moreover, "assume his destined role on behalf of heaven" *(wei tian chengyun)*.[76] Zhang Hanchao announced that a son of his who was twenty-seven years old was the grand marshal that would help install this scion of the Ming house. The proclamation obviously appealed to latent anti-Manchu sentiment among the people and, equally important, to the ancient concept of "mandate of heaven," as well. Such appeals masked, however, a deep religious strategy.

As suggested by the historian Xu Zengzhong, the heaven-favored Ming descendant, though unnamed in the proclamation, was meant to be Wang Faseng, the son of the revered old master of the Hunyuan sect, Wang Huaiyu.[77] (See the preceding figure 1.) Wang Faseng was, like his father, a direct disciple of the founder of the Hunyuan sect, Fan Mingde. He was of a higher generation in sect status than Liu Song, to say nothing of Liu Zhixie (who was a disciple of Liu Song). Wang Faseng had been arrested in 1775 and banished to Lungde county, in Gansu. His father, Wang Huaiyu, somehow escaped apprehension and lived in secret hideouts in the Xiangyang area known only to a few confidants like Liu Zhixie. In the sixth lunar month in 1794, however, Wang Huaiyu died of illness, and later in the year, Liu Song was executed, leaving Wang Faseng —who was to be moved by the Qing authorities from Gansu to Kashgar, in Xinjiang—the senior living patriarch of the Hunyuan sect. Wang Faseng had the reputation of being "well versed in sutras" *(jingdian hao)*, and perhaps only he had the authority to reopen the question of a Maitreya incarnate.[78]

It is all but certain that Wang Tingzhao, who was of the Hunyuan sect and had in his youth met Wang Huaiyu, had identified "our sovereign" mentioned in the 1797 proclamation with Wang Faseng. A curious passage in the proclamation states that it was because of the sectarian troops being in mourning for "our sovereign's father"

(wu zhu fu) that they wore white clothes and held white banners—
white being the color of mourning. Wang Huaiyu's death, known to
some Qing officials in early 1794, would also have been known to
some of his coreligionists. The references to the death of "our sovereign's father" can only be construed as a message to other sectarians
that Wang Faseng, now the senior living patriarch, was "our sovereign"—that while catering to the desire for the restoration of rule by
Han Chinese, the purpose of the rebellion was still, as is also stated
in the proclamation, "to save you all from the present great catastrophe *(danan)*" at the turn of the kalpa.[79]

However, Wang Tingzhao eventually found that he had to
change his strategy—from emphasis on an anti-Qing and pro-Ming
stance to the less ambitious but more solid religious identity of the
sectarian armies. In Sichuan in the summer of 1798, he was honored
as the "religious master" of Gao Junde's forces, despite the fact that
Gao was once an affiliate of Song Zhiqing (who had subscribed to the
Shouyuan teaching from Henan, as well as the Hunyuan teachings of
Liu Zhixie—see figures 2 and 3—and was therefore not simply of the
Hunyuan tradition). Wang Tingzhao still hoped that Wang Faseng,
who he thought was still in Gansu and with whom he tried to establish communication, could help strengthen the common sectarian
cause.[80] But earlier in the same year, Gao's ally, Long Shaozhou,
the leader of a Sichuan White Lotus army who worked closely with
Widow Qi's disciple Fan Renjie, brought yet another White Lotus
master to Sichuan. This was Liu Leng, very likely also of the Hunyuan sect, although this affiliation is as yet undocumented. Remarkably enough, he was from the same native place in Anhui as Liu Zhixie, although the two do not seem to have been relatives. Gao Junde
described Liu Zhixie as a tall man, and Liu Leng as short. Still in his
forties (and therefore younger than Liu Zhixie, who was in his fifties),
Liu Leng was nonetheless believed to be of a higher generation in
sect status in terms of the teacher-pupil relationship. Wang Tingzhao
now enthusiastically supported Liu Leng as the sect patriarch, presumably for all the sects represented in the White Lotus armies in
Sichuan.[81]

Gao Junde was more a man of action than of doctrine. He
seems to have been primarily interested in having a "true sovereign"
to whom he could devote his loyalty and efforts; the precise affiliation of the sect master may have seemed to him to be of less consequence. In his deposition made in Beijing after he was captured and

sent there in late 1799, Gao described his conversations with Wang Tingzhao after the latter joined him as his army's religious master.

> I asked: "In our uprising, whom are we really helping to be the sovereign *(zhu)?*" Wang Tingzhao said: "One called Zhu Tianquan is our sovereign. . . ." I asked: "Where is Zhu Tianquan's native place? Where is he at present? I want to meet him." Wang Tingzhao said: "You cannot see him yet; he has not come out at present." Later Liu Leng arrived and Wang Tingzhao said: "Liu Leng is the sovereign," and Wang did not mention Zhu Tianquan again. I heard that Zhu Tianquan is none other than Liu Leng.[82]

Wang Tingzhao did hint to Gao the true identity of Zhu Tianquan by citing a White Lotus ballad, to the effect that though one is brought up in the Liu family, "only when one gets to the Wang house does one rise [in the world]."[83] Zhu Tianquan was but a fictitious entity, with the Ming imperial surname, Zhu, that could serve Gao Junde's purpose for the moment. But once Liu Leng was ensconced as Long Shaozhou's religious master and had the prospect of winning the allegiance of a large number of sectarian leaders of both Sichuan and Hubei origin, Wang Tingzhao decided to identify him as the sect patriarch and yielded to the authority of Liu Leng, even his own prerogatives as venerable master in Gao Junde's army. When Gao asked him in the summer of 1798 to authorize the appointment of a marshal, Wang replied: "Let us wait till Liu Leng gets here before making the investiture *(feng)*."[84] In late 1799, according to Gao's deposition, there were eleven White Lotus leaders in Sichuan, either of Sichuan or of Hubei origin, who had accepted Liu Leng as the sect patriarch. Liu Leng, with Wang Tingzhao's help, apparently fostered a certain degree of solidarity among Hubei and Sichuan sectarians in a way that Widow Qi had not succeeded in doing. This was undoubtedly a factor in the White Lotus rebellion's lasting beyond 1798.

The First Phase of the Mid-Qing
White Lotus Rebellion: An Interpretation

Despite his solid and basic work on many aspects of the mid-Qing White Lotus rebellion, the late Professor Suzuki Chūsei nonetheless had little substantive to say on the role that religion played in it.[85] Later in his distinguished career, Professor Suzuki advanced his famed hypothesis on the influence of millenarian religion on Asian revolutions, including that of China, of the recent centuries. With the publication in recent decades of archival sources of the mid-Qing period and the appearance of preliminary studies based on these sources, it is now possible to reach a closer view of the bearing of the White Lotus religion itself on the great rebellion from 1796 to 1804.

Evidence presented in this chapter seems to leave little doubt that the Eternal Mother was the principal deity of this religion, as taught by Liu Zhixie, Song Zhiqing, and many other White Lotus teachers in Xiangyang and other centers in Hubei. The elements of this faith that were most pronounced in Hubei in these tumultuous years concerned the immediacy of the eschatological crisis—the imminence of kalpic calamity made more convincing by the worsened abuses of the Qing state. In Hubei in the decade that began in the mid-1780s, prophecy of calamities persisted and was upheld by sect leaders not only in the western mountainous regions but also in the prosperous market-town communities of the northern and southern plains. (See maps 1 and 2.)

That the sectarian leaders in several parts of the province should have presented such dire messages so insistently reflects their reading of the popular mentality—the widespread anxiety to avoid disaster in a precarious life, the willingness to join some collectivity through the teacher-disciple relationship, the investment of hope in a distant and charismatic sect patriarch.

In order to explain this mentality fully, it is necessary to probe into the socio-economic history of the several geographical areas that were so disparate in conditions. In the present chapter, I hope to have demonstrated the assumption that religious phenomena were to a certain degree autonomous. The prophecy of dire calamity as well as the articulation of a blasphemous ethics were to spread from Hubei to Shaanxi and to Sichuan, in the mountainous regions that link the three provinces.

Beginning as early as 1791, several Hubei White Lotus teachers, including especially Sun Cifeng and Chen Jinyu, were active in Sichuan. The message concentrated, as in Hubei, on the Eternal Mother's compassion for her children and on the impending kalpic catastrophe, during which one could save oneself only by reposing faith in collective action of a violent nature. It was probably under Gao Minggui, whose sectarian lineage could be traced to Qi Lin

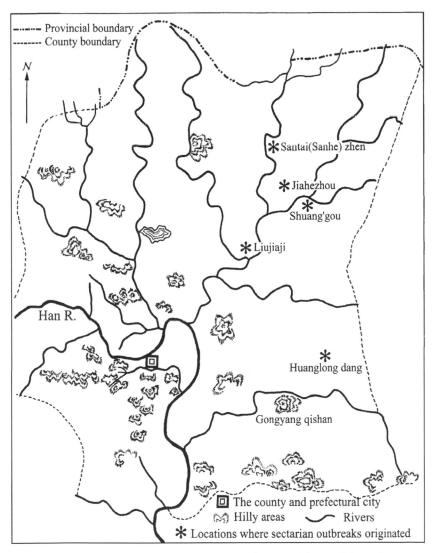

MAP 2. Xiangyang County, showing places where uprisings originated, spring 1796

(Widow Qi's husband), that the White Lotus in Sichuan disseminated an unusual doctrine of Three Refuges, that is, substituting reliance on "the Buddha, the dharma, and the teacher *(shi)*" for that on "the Buddha, the dharma, and the sangha."[86]

The ethical revolt that went with the White Lotus faith was dramatically shown in the sacred chants taught in Hubei, as discussed earlier. Nezha, the "incredible character" of the novel *Fengshen yanyi,* was reverenced as a protective deity.[87] The implication was that being on the verge of reunion with the Eternal Mother, one owed only a secondary obligation to one's own family. The heterodox implications of such teachings are found in the sectarian sayings reported by Peng Yanqing, the retired Qing official caught in Dangyang, Hubei, when it was occupied by the White Lotus forces in 1796: "In Heaven, the Jade Emperor will be changed, and below the earth, the King of Hell will be changed." Moreover, Confucius himself was to be brought to task: "Master Kung will also be criticized. Do not read the Four Books and Five Classics, nor the Nine Books and Thirteen Classics."[88] Such explicit anti-Confucian sayings have not yet been found in the documents regarding the Sichuan sectarians. But the local gazetteers of some eastern Sichuan counties, in recounting the history of the White Lotus rebellion, have preserved garbled passages from the *lingwen* chants taught by Sun Cifeng including: "Pick one's bones and return them to father, one's flesh to mother," and "Break open the mountain and save the [Eternal] Mother; only by being loyal and filial [to her] is one a person."[89]

Whatever dissidence as to social ethics had moved the militant Sichuan sectarians, women are known to have played a large role in sect leadership and in battle in that province, too. In Sichuan, there was no exalted woman Buddhist master comparable to Widow Qi née Wang, but a Widow Chen née Guo wrote on her banner "Revenge for my husband," and she personally directed forces in battle.[90] What is difficult for a contemporary mind to accept is the restriction of the men and women to be saved during the kalpic crisis to the Eternal Mother's original children (in reincarnated form, of course).[91] Rejecting the universalism of mainstream Buddhism, the White Lotus religion believed in the salvation of only the elect—perhaps not unlike some forms of European Christianity. As one White Lotus teacher in Hubei put it: "Those who would not join are those who ought to die during the calamity."[92] Mahayana compassion would not apply to them.

It has been suggested in this chapter that in the Hubei rebellion of 1796, the sectarian belief in cosmic calamity was reinforced by earthly injustice. The rebel slogan, "The officials have forced the people to rebel" *(guan po min fan)* merely confirmed the prophecy that the kalpic crisis was at hand. Slogans used by the sectarian rebels in Sichuan include these lines: "To use weighted scales and differential measurements is unjust! From heaven the star of the Fire Element will descend."[93] Injustice, such as the use of arbitrary weights and measurements in collecting taxes from the common people, was so aggravating that it could justify rebellion.

Joseph Esherick has proposed that, in Chinese millenarianism, the emphasis was more on surviving an impending disaster than on rejoicing in the prospective paradise.[94] This may well be the case, but it may be further suggested that even while surviving a disaster, there is still the question of the legitimacy of government. In the perspective of the Hubei rebellion of 1796, there is little question that as a consequence of cosmic change, if not also as reaction to the Qing dynasty's misrule, the Manchu regime was to be supplanted. It was only natural that for the temporary earthly authority, the sectarians would tend to support restoration of the Ming, the last indigenous dynasty. Yet they did not merely want a Ming heir presiding over a dynastic restoration. Their vision of the future was that the Maitreya Buddha, once he had shepherded the elect through the apocalypse, would preside over the last and longest kalpa of the White Sun. It was unfortunate for the White Lotus rebellion of 1796 that the masters

Qi Lin *and* Qi née Wang		Song Zhiqing
	Sun Cifeng (Sun Laowu)	
	Leng Tianlu	
Xu Tiande		Wang Sanhuai

FIGURE 5. Some sectarian origins of the White Lotus rebellion in Sichuan

of the several sects could not agree on a Maitreya incarnate. Since the sectarians were integrated through teacher-disciple relationships, the task of centralization among the many sets of teacher-disciples was by no means easy. The alliances that were formed at the beginning of the Xiangyang rebellion—the northern and southern assemblies—and the various colors of banners assigned to sectarian commands provided some coordination but hardly unity. In 1798–1799 there were some eleven sectarian commands in Sichuan alone of different provincial backgrounds.

The search for a unified and credible White Lotus authority continued, however. Wang Tingzhao remained hopeful that he could appeal to the most senior Hunyuan sect master living—Wang Faseng. But since the latter had been banished to the frontier, he, too, could not be of immediate use. Greater cooperation between Hubei and Sichuan sectarian armies in Sichuan was promised in the summer of 1798, when Wang Tingzhao supported Liu Leng as the sect patriarch.[95] Wang was attempting what was perhaps a unique ecumenical approach to the problem of White Lotus leadership. It was hoped that the patriarch could bring solidarity to what were actually independent subsects, connected only by religious beliefs and master-disciple relationships. But it appears that Liu Leng was also to fail in charismatic leadership, if only because he was handicapped by a situation in which none of the sectarian armies that honored him as a religious leader could demonstrate military ascendancy. It seems that the rebellion that spread to five provinces never did settle the question of a Maitreya incarnate or that of the "true sovereign" before it was overcome by the combination of an overwhelming number of troops and strategic innovation on the Qing side.

That the rebellion was not more unified in command and that it did not prevail in the end should not, however, blind us to sectarian dedication. Yao Zhifu, the old hunchback who assisted Widow Qi, inspired many subordinates to selfless service. Widow Qi herself risked her life in battle until she jumped off a cliff to her death. Wang Tingzhao seems to have done his best as a religious statesman. He supported Liu Leng while remaining loyal to Wang Faseng—the scion of the most senior Hunyuan master as of 1797. Having been wrongly informed that Wang Faseng was banished to Longde county, Gansu, Wang Tingzhao made two trips to that area, one as late as 1800, in a vain attempt to find him.[96]

There is considerable evidence of the piety of the men and women who participated in the 1796 White Lotus uprising. In the Henan-Hubei-Shaanxi border area, Qing commanders reported that villagers joined the sectarian forces in large groups. "They sometimes mistakenly came to the government camp, saying that they were looking for a certain religious master. Appearing publicly, they recited chants, put their two palms together, and kotowed. In the hilly and out-of-the-way villages of Shanyang county, . . . some inhabitants set fire to their houses themselves and departed with the sectarians." Officers of forces led by Widow Qi and Yao Zhifu, when captured, would not divulge the whereabouts of their superiors even under torture. They merely "closed their eyes and would not utter a word."[97] In Sichuan, in 1799, the Qing strategist Gong Jinghan complained that those who had been exposed for a long period to the White Lotus faith would show "neither fear nor regret, regarding death as if it were a return to their home." In early 1800 a Qing commander in Sichuan reported that in battle, even when gunfire and a rain of arrows were directed at them, sectarian soldiers would "bend their heads low and rush forward without hesitation."[98]

Although this chapter has concentrated on the religious factor in the rebellion of 1796, it does not imply by any means that religion was the only major factor in this great rebellion. The sectarians in Hubei and in parts of Sichuan were well indoctrinated by the mid-1790s with their eschatological expectations. Yet they faced the exigency of survival and the grim prospect of physical persecution, in a society beset with deepening administrative ills and economic hardship. The slogan "The officials have forced the people to rebel," emblazoned on the White Lotus banners, attracted people of all kinds to the rebellion—those who had suffered at the hands of officials and their agents or of rapacious landlords, migrants who had difficulty eking out a living on the hilly lands, feuding lineages or native-place associations among migrants from South China, smugglers and bandits who had long taken advantage of the weakness of law enforcement.[99] As the insurrection expanded, the sectarians were faced with serious problems of discipline, organization, and tactics, and the best of the Qing armies and strategists eventually bore down upon them. Although this essay has emphasized only one major strand of the story, it is hoped that more all-around synthesis will emerge from the work of other scholars.

Notes

The Chinese version of this paper was published in *Ming-Qing dang'an yu lishi yanjiu* [Ming-Qing archives and historical research], ed. First Historical Archives (Beijing: Zhonghua, 1988), 2:776–815. The present essay has incorporated more published materials and a more refined analysis than was possible when the Chinese version, a conference paper, was prepared. In view of the large number of articles in Chinese cited here, references are made only to the journals and books in which the articles appear; the titles of articles themselves are given in English translation, with "in Chinese" noted in each case.

The following abbreviations are used for publications based on archives:

GZD   *Gongzhong dang Qianlong chao zhouzhe* [Palace memorial archive, Qianlong period]. 75 vols. Taibei: National Palace Museum, 1982–1988.

KYQ   *Kang-Yong-Qian shiqi chengxiang renmin fankang douzheng ziliao* [Source materials on the resistance struggles of urban and rural people during the Kangxi, Yongzheng, and Qianlong periods]. 2 vols. Beijing: Zhonghua, 1979.

QDD   *Qingdai dang'an shiliao congbian* [Collection of archival historical sources of the Qing dynasty]. Compiled by China's First Historical Archives. 9th collection. Beijing: Zhonghua, 1983.

QDN   *Qingdai nongmin zhanzheng shi ziliao xuanbian* [Selected materials on the history of peasant wars in the Qing period]. Compiled by History Department of the Chinese People's University and China's First Historical Archives. Vols. 5 and 6. Beijing: Chinese People's University Press, 1983 and 1990.

QZQ   *Qing zhongqi wusheng Bailian jiao qiyi yanjiu ziliao* [Research materials on the five-province White Lotus uprising of the mid-Qing period]. Compiled by Qing history section, Institute of History, Chinese Academy of Social Sciences. 5 vols. Jiangsu: Renmin, 1981.

The following abbreviations are used for archives and reign titles:

JJD   Junji dang (Grand Council copy archive). National Palace Museum, Taiwan.

GZD   Gongzhong dang (Palace memorial archive). National Palace Museum, Taiwan.

QL   Qianlong reign (1736–1795)

JQ   Jiaqing reign (1796–1820)

1. See especially Xu Zengzhong and Lin Yi, "An inquiry into Liu Zhixie's influence in the great Sichuan-Hubei-Shaanxi peasant rebellion" [in Chinese], *Qingshi luncong* 2 (1980), 158–174; Xu Zengzhong, "On two proclamations of the armies of the Sichuan-Hubei-Shaanxi peasant uprising" [in Chinese], in *Zhongguo nongmin zhanzheng shi luncong* [Studies in the history of the Chinese peasant wars] (Henan: Renmin, 1983), 4:191–238; Li Bangzheng, "The White Lotus sect and the peasant uprising in Sichuan" [in Chinese], in *Ming Qing shi guoji xueshu taolun hui lunwen ji* [Proceedings of the International Conference on Ming Qing history] (Tianjin: Renmin, 1982), 1072–1086; Hu Zhaoxi, Huo Datong, and Yang Guang, "A few questions on the Sichuan theater of the White Turban [*sic*] rebellion in the mid-Qing: A preliminary discussion" [in Chinese], in *Zhongguo nongmin zhanzheng shi yanjiu jikan* [Journal of the history of Chinese peasant wars] (Shanghai, 1982), 2:140–159.

2. Ma Xisha and Han Bingfang, *Zhongguo minjian zongjiao shi* [A history of Chinese popular religion] (Shanghai: Renmin, 1993). See also Dai Yi, *Jianming Qing shi* [Concise history of the Qing period] (Beijing: Renmin, 1984), 2:48–61, 382–477.

3. Li Jianmin, "An investigation into the cause of the White Lotus outbreak in Sichuan and Hubei in the first year of the Jiaqing reign of the Qing" [in Chinese], *Bulletin of the Institute of Modern History,* Academia Sinica, 22A (June 1993), 359–396.

4. Blaine Gaustad, "Prophets and Pretenders: Inter-sect Competition in Qianlong China," *Late Imperial China* (June 2000), 1–40. For fuller coverage, see Gaustad, "Religious Sectarianism and the State in Mid Qing China: Background of the White Lotus Uprising of 1796–1804" (Ph.D. diss., University of California, Berkeley, 1994).

5. See the titles in the list of abbreviations for this chapter.

6. Susan Naquin, "The Transmission of White Lotus Sectarianism in Late Imperial China," in David Johnson, Andrew J. Nathan, and Evelyn S. Rawski, eds., *Popular Culture in Late Imperial China* (Berkeley: University of California Press, 1985), 263 n. 17.

7. There were few men of the literati or gentry status among the leaders of the Hubei White Lotus rebellion of 1796. One of the two principal leaders of the uprising in Yidu, in southwestern Hubei, had taught tutorial school *(jiao mengguan);* he does not seem to have had a degree. In Xiangyang prefecture, Zhang Hanchao, in his early seventies, was known to be versed in letters and had practiced divination *(zhanke).* He became the head or figurehead of one of the principal rebel forces arising from the prefecture. See *QZQ,* 5:6, 76–77, 79–80, 116; *QDN,* 5:71–72, 75, 78–81; 6:68–73.

Especially in the hills of southwestern Hubei, leaders and principal supporters of the uprising in early 1796 included landlords. Nie Jieren of Yidu, who provided the hillside headquarters for rebels, acknowledged in his deposition that he had "fairly abundant family wealth and a spacious house." Zhang Xunlong of Changyang owned land tilled by hired laborers. Chen Qiming and Wang Mingfeng, leaders of the uprising in Laifeng, both employed hired laborers. Both were said to be "most respectable" and to have in their families "quite a lot of rice to eat" *(hen yu fan chi); see QZQ,* 5:14–15; *QDN,* 5:208. A few yamen runners had joined the sect. Qi Lin, husband of Widow Qi née Wang, who was executed in 1794 as a sect leader, was said to be the head yamen runner of Xiangyang county. In the Laifeng uprising, two yamen runners from Longshan county (across the border, in Hunan) participated; one of them deposed that he was converted by a sect teacher who was a yamen clerk! In Dangyang, yamen runners played a crucial part in bringing about the city's fall to the sectarians; see *QZQ,* 4:125, 242; 5:28, 30, 34.

The record of rebel depositions often fails to include the occupation of the person who deposed. There is, however, enough such information to suggest the importance of an intermediate group between rural and urban society that provided energy for uprising as well as proselytizing—water carriers, bean-curd sellers, woodcutters, charcoal sellers, pig sellers, carpenters, masons. Blacksmiths, especially, were recruited to make weapons during the preparations for uprising. See *QZQ,* 5:27, 30, 42, 48, 53, 64; *QDN,* 5:147, 216, 281, 291, 324, 411, 681.

Sectarians who composed the rank and file of the uprising included many simply identified as "tilling the land" *(zhongdi)* or "engaged in agriculture" *(wunong).* Some were described as "hired laborers" or "labor helpers" *(yonggong, gugong, or banggong);* in some cases they worked for a landowner who was a convert and were converted by him. See *QZQ,* 5:15, 23, 50, 57, 61, 114, 127, 120, 129; *QDN,* 5:216, 543. Once rebellion broke out and pillaging started, more peasants who were hired laborers, as well as vagrants in town and country would join. Available data suggest that many participants in the sect and in the uprising were from families of recent settlers who had migrated from such provinces as Guangdong, Guangxi, Hunan, and Guizhou. See *QZQ,* 5:13, 18, 23; *QDN,* 5:208, 216, 224, 229, 278, 696. An astonishing number of participants in the uprising were not only poor but also without immediate family—unmarried and without parents or siblings. Among captured rebels at Donghu, near Yichang, there were at least eight such cases, and in Laifeng, thirteen. *QDN,* 5:178–179, 241–248.

8. Cf. Gaustad, "Prophets and Pretenders."

9. Liu Zhixie, the respected itinerant teacher, was supposed to have engaged in trade in cotton and cotton fabric in northern Anhui and in

Henan. Song Zhiqing, the influential Xiangyang sect leader, was also said to have been engaged in commerce. Wang Tingzhao, the Henan sectarian who became a religious master with a Xiangyang rebel force, had been a "hired laborer" in youth but advanced to "selling sashes and belts" *(mai dai zi)*. Yao Zhifu, who played a crucial part in organizing uprisings in Xiangyang, had "borrowed land for farming" in 1793. He was a hunchback, then in his late fifties; it is not certain from the sources whether he himself worked in the fields. *QZQ*, 5:96, 120–121; *QDN*, 5:324; *QDD*, 190.

It must be noted that proselytizing was itself a source of income. Initiation fees paid by the disciples were given at the depositions at various rates (ranging from 200 to 500 cash or, in silver, from 1 to 50 taels for each individual). Wang Lan, a sect leader in Gucheng county, up the Han River from Xiangyang, deposed in 1796 that he had "in four seasons in one year" turned over to Yao Zhifu, his teacher, fees totaling more than 10,000 taels, an incredible amount that may be an error in recording. Wang himself "used six or seven hundred taels [from the initiation fees] to buy farmland property." *QZQ*, 5:10–11, 21 (10,000 taels), 23 and 25 (50 taels), 50–51; *QDN*, 5:102 (300 taels).

10. Naquin, "Transmission of White Lotus Sectarianism," esp. 259–260.

11. See, for example, *QDD*, 161–162; *QZQ*, 5:27, 32, 64, 127.

12. A Japanese authority, Sawada Mizuho, has traced the origins of the Hunyuan sect to 1594, in the late Ming, in the Zhili-Shanxi area. In 1633 a Wang Lunyi of Shandong declared himself the patriarch of the Hunyuan sect and led an uprising. Among the ideas expressed during this rebellion was the belief in the kalpic eras of the Three Suns *(sanyang)*. See Sawada Mizuho, "Preliminary study of the Hunyuan sect" [in Japanese], in his *Zōhō hokan no kenkyū* [An expanded and annotated study of the precious scrolls] (Tokyo: Kokusho kankokai, 1975), 366–408. The recent work of Ma Xisha and Han Bingfang has traced the Hunyuan tradition to influences from Shanxi and Zhili that bore upon the sect teacher Zhang Ren, in Henan, who was arrested and executed in 1756. Like his Shanxi teachers, Zhang Ren taught Daoist-like internal alchemy as well as a millennial vision:

New heaven, new earth, new cosmos,
New person, new books, new constellation,
New person, new world, new immortality *(chang ren)*.

See Ma and Han, *Zhongguo minjian*, chap. 21; the verse translated here is cited on p. 1279. On Zhang Ren and the Shanxi influence, see the extensive discussion in Gaustad, "Religious Sectarianism."

13. *QDD*, 164–171; see also *KYQ*, 2:694–695; *QDN*, 5:7–17. On martial arts and invulnerability, see ibid., 16.

14. Liu Zhixie was a native of Taihe county, Anhui. Having escaped

arrest in 1794, he lived as a fugitive in Xinye and Zheng zhou in Henan, but often visited Hubei secretly. He was described by the captured Hubei rebels as the "old teacher" *(lao shifu)*. More than ten captured rebels acknowledged affiliation with him. *QZQ*, 5:25, 27–28, 38–39, 54, 63, 96, 101–105, 127–128.

15. *KYQ*, 2:820–825; *QDN*, 5:20–24.

16. *QDD*, 173–175.

17. Ibid., 158–164, 173–175. Cf. Naquin, "Transmission of White Lotus Sectarianism," 271–272, 280. See also *GZD-QL*, 60:656.

18. This first line was mentioned in the 1785 memorial from De-zhengo and Wu Yuan regarding the Sun Guiyuan case *(QDD, 174)*. I have been unable to determine whether the entire "sacred chant" as used in 1794–1796 was as it was taught by Sun Guiyuan.

19. *QDD*, 174–175. The three sutras Sun Guiyuan had owned included not only *Wu nü chuandao* [Five women transmitting the Way], honored by the Liu family in Shandong, but also *Jiulian* [Nine lotuses], the sutra reverenced by the long-lasting sectarian family in Zhili, the Wangs. Officials in Hubei found these to be different from the sutras found in the Xu Guo-tai case in 1768; they also remarked that among the sutras found in the Sun Guiyuan case, only *Wu nü chuandao* was found in the Liu Shengguo case in Shandong. Ibid., 174–175.

20. Memorial from GZD-QL, cited in Susan Naquin, "Connections Between Rebellions: Sect Family Networks in Qing China," *Modern China* 8.3 (July 1982): 353–354. On Yao Yingcai, see also *QDD*, 174, 206, 210; Xu Zengzhong and Lin Yi, "An inquiry," 184. Yao owned a pharmacy manufacturing medicated dressings and taught disciples in Zaoyang, Hubei, and Xinye, Henan. He was executed in 1789. See JJD-QL, 40254, 41084, 41214.

21. Captured Hubei rebels would use such phrases to describe their practice as "eat vegetarian food and recite sutra" *(chi cai nian jing)*, or alternatively "eat vegetarian food and recite incantations" *(chi chai nian zhou)*. Liu Zhixie deposed that his own group of sectarians did not observe vegetarianism, although Liu Song deposed that he did. Just as it is impossible to say how widespread vegetarianism was, it is also difficult to tell whether sectarians in Hubei actually read sutra of the *baojuan* (precious scrolls) variety. See following notes 31–40; also *QZQ*, 5:98, 127–128; *QDN*, 5:3–4, 163, 212, 359–360, 715.

22. Phrases such as "burning incense and reciting sacred chants" *(shaoxiang nianzhou* or *nianzhou shaoxiang)* occur in the depositions; see *QZQ*, 5:11, 95. For reciting morning and evening, see ibid., 88. On the oral transmission of *lingwen* chants, see especially ibid., 11, 24–25; *QDN*, 5:279, 291.

23. Liu Zhixie seems to have used a "sutra" that contains an ambig-

uous message regarding self-cultivation common to the syncretic Three Teachings *(san jiao):* "Heaven represents the larger heaven; man represents the smaller heaven. . . . Heaven is born of human nature; man's mind-and-heart does not altogether fit with Heaven. . . . Those who pursue the gentleman's learning can know the Way preceding one's life and the destined place after death." *QZQ,* 5:106. Such ideas had become common in Chinese popular culture and were not exclusive to practitioners of meditation.

24. *QDD,* 179; *QDN,* 5:290–291, 304, 411–412, 680, 689, 693, 696; *QZQ,* 1:3.

25. *QZQ,* 5:22, 59; *QDN,* 5:162, 233–234.

26. *QZQ,* 5:32–33; *QDN,* 5:63, 72, 77, 208. In his deposition, Hu Zhengzhong explicitly identified himself as a spirit medium *(wushi),* with the capacity to be possessed by the deity *(jiang shen).* Ibid., 237.

27. See note 59. Zhang Xiaoyuan, a sectarian of Fuyang, Anhui, later deposed that in 1796 his group in Fuyang had used the "secret signal" *(neihao)* of a verse to identify members in an attempted revolt:

> Buddha in the sky,
> Buddha on earth,
> Buddha in all directions,
> One who has learned the magic to protect one's person *(hushen fa),*
> Will avoid water, fire, and other calamities.

Perhaps this verse implies the practice of an invulnerability cult, but a similar incantation has not been found for Hubei. See *QZQ,* 5:111. On the likelihood of Wang Tingzhao, the Henan sectarian proselytizing in Xiangyang, teaching boxing to his pupils, see note 74.

28. Numerous captured rebels testified to their motivation for joining the sect as being "to avoid calamity" *(mianzai)* or "to ward off calamity" *(xiaozai).* For examples, see *QDN,* 5:162, 275, 280, 290, 292, 411, 680, 715.

29. *KYQ,* 2:819–825; *QDN,* 5:18–24.

30. *QDN,* 5:22, 24; *QDD,* 174, 181–182, 190–192.

31. *QDD,* 194–195; *QDN,* 5:29–30; *QZQ,* 1:4, 9–10, 14–15.

32. *QDD,* 190–191, 201, 203, 206–208; *QDN,* 5:26–27; *QZQ,* 5:103.

33. See Xu Zengzhong and Lin Yi, "An inquiry," 184–187, for an interpretation of the several versions of Maitreya and the Ming heir at this juncture.

34. A copy of the original silk document is preserved in the First Historical Archives in Beijing, and a photocopy is printed in *QDN,* 5:3–4; see also Liu Qirong's deposition, in *QDN,* 5, esp. 359–360. Also see *QZQ,* 5:54.

35. *QZQ,* 5:99; *QDN,* 6:429. This chant may be traced to the Shouyuan tradition of sectarianism in Henan in the mid-1780s. See *GZD,* (1987), 60:656–657.

36. Huang Yubian, *Poxie xiangbian* [Detailed refutation of heterodoxy] (1834 and 1883); see the convenient reprint of the 1834 edition in *Qingshi ziliao*, 3 (Beijing: Zhonghua, 1982), 7.

37. *QZQ*, 5:128.

38. *QZQ*, 5:98–99; *QDN*, 6:428. See also Naquin, "Transmission of White Lotus Sectarianism," 279. The translation is hers.

39. *QZQ*, 5:9–12; *QDN*, 5:290–292, 681. Some lines from a similar response appeared in an official report on the Sun Guiyuan case of 1785. They also appeared in the report on the Xie Tianxiu case from Daning, Sichuan, in 1794. See *QDD*, 174, 178.

40. The invocation of the deity Nacha is documented not only by the depositions cited in note 39 but also by a proclamation issued by the governor-general of Shaanxi and Gansu jointly with the governor of Shaanxi, in the fifth lunar month of 1796, in which the sectarian belief in Nezha is mentioned. See *QZQ*, 5:299; *QDN*, 5:680. On Nezha, see *Fengshen yanyi*, ed. Xu Zhonglin (Hong Kong: Zhonghua, 1970), chaps. 12–14. See Liu Ts'un-yan (Liu Cun'ren), *Buddhist and Taoist Influences on Chinese Novels*, vol. 1: *The Authorship of the Feng Shen Yen I* (Wiesbaden: Otto Harrassowitz, 1962), chap. 11. See also Henri Doré, *Researches into Chinese Superstitions*, trans., D. J. Finn (Shanghai: Tusewei Printing Press, 1914–1933; reprint, Taibei: Chengwen, 1967), 9:111–122.

41. *QZQ*, 5:10–12, and esp. 25; *QDN*, 5:290–292, and esp. 279. See also *QDD*, 178. There is a slight difference between the two versions of the Hubei text published from presumably the same archival source. The last words of the version in *QZQ*, 5:25, are *zhen xiao ren* (truly filial person), but those of the version in *QDN*, 5:179, are *zhong xiao ren* (loyal and filial person).

42. On Mulian, see Stephen F. Teiser, *The Ghost Festival of Medieval China* (Princeton: Princeton University Press, 1988). The best approach to the original Mulian story is in the Tang dynasty *bianwen* (transformation text) translated in Victor H. Mair, *Tun-huang Popular Narrative* (Cambridge: Cambridge University Press, 1983). On Chenxiang, see Yuan Ke, *Zhongguo shenhua shi* [History of Chinese myths] (Shanghai: Xinhua, 1988), 325–326.

43. Cited in Huang Yubian, *Poxie xiangbian*, 3:29.

44. For fuller documentation see *QDN*, 5:28–33; *QDD*, *182*, 188, 190, 192–197.

45. *QZQ*, 5:35; *QDN*, 5:100.

46. *QZQ*, 5:35–37; *QDN*, 5:101–120.

47. *QDD*, 177–180, 187; also see note 32.

48. See Xu Zengzhong and Lin Yi, "An inquiry," 178–179.

49. For the Xiangyang area, the deposition of Li Chao gives the name of a local gentry member who had just bought office and the names of the

baojia personnel and gangsters involved in the extortion of bribes from the sectarians; *QZQ*, 5:79 80; see also 101–102, 105.

50. *QZQ*, 5:61–63; *QDN*, 5:163–165.

51. *QZQ*, 5:63, 68; *QDN*, 5:201, 279.

52. One of Yao Zhifu's disciples (a native of Gucheng county) captured in 1796 deposed that "We, the White Lotus sect, have forty-eight chains (*xian*, literally "lines"). Yao Zhifu is the leader of the nineteenth chain." *QZQ*, 5:21. Presumably the "forty-eight chains" were for the entire province. For three variant characters for *yuan*, see the glossary in this volume. One means "principal," another, "connected by destiny," and the third, "original" children of the Eternal Mother. See Huang Yubian, *Poxie xiangbian*, 2:16, 69, 78–79, 119.

53. *QZQ*, 5:1, 28, 35, 105; *QDN*, 5:76, 101; 6:433.

54. *QZQ*, 5:109, 35–40; *QDN*, 5:76–81, 99–104.

55. *QDN*, 5:63, 72, 161, 208, 233, 237–238.

56. This is not to say that there never was in late imperial China criticism of gender inequality. There was. See, for example, Paul S. Ropp, *Dissent in Early Modern China: Ju-lin wai-shih and Ch'ing Social Criticism* (Ann Arbor: University of Michigan Press, 1981). The issue is whether such criticism rose to the level of worldview.

57. Huang Yubian *Poxie xiangbian*, 2:15, 75.

58. Peng Yanqing, "Dangyang xian bilan ji" [Record of a refugee in Dangyang county], in *QZQ*, 4:279; see also 264–276.

59. See the *Qinding jiaoping sansheng xiefei fanglueh* [Imperially approved military record on the suppression of heterodox bandits in three provinces] (1810; reprint, Taibei: Chengwen, 1970), 12:10, 13:18, 28:25–26, 35b, 32:34, 47:30b–31. Sources cited here include two cases of women in battle supposedly possessed by the Eternal Mother. One of the cases is confirmed by the deposition of Woman Zhou née Deng in *QDN*, 5:233.

60. "Shixiangcun jushi," in *Kanjing jiaofei subian* [Narrative on the suppression of religious rebels], preface dated 1826, reprinted in *QZQ*, 4:126. See also the more colorful notes of Zhou Kai, published in 1840, reprinted in *QZQ*, 5:311–325. My analysis here is compatible with that found in Xu Zengzhong, "An essay on some problems regarding the appraisal of Wang Cong'er" [in Chinese], *Qing shi lun cong* (Beijing: Zhonghua, 1982), 3:164–183.

61. Qi Lin was said to be a disciple of Song Wenshi of Xinye, Henan. See *QZQ*, 5:146. But he also acknowledged Liu Zhixie as master, and offered funds to the exiled patriarch Liu Song. Ibid., 102–103; *QDN*, 5:29, 207.

62. *QZQ*, 5:58; also see 64, cf. 76–77, 103, 118–119, 146; *QDN*, 5:411–412; cf. 6:68–69, 72, 432; *Qinding jiaoping*, 20.41b, 25.38b, 29.18,

32.56, 23b, 34.12b, 36.13, 48.11. See also Deng Zhicheng, *Gudong so ji* [Miscellaneous antiquarian notes] (Beiping, 1926), 6.23.

63. *QZQ*, 5:57–58, 311–312. *QDN*, 5:411–412; *Qinding jiaoping, juan shou* [introduction], 17. See also Zhiang Weiming, ed., *Chuan-Chu-Shaan bailian jiao qiyi ziliao ji* [Collection of materials on the White Lotus Rebellion in Sichuan, Hubei, and Shaanxi]. (Chengdu: Renmin, 1980), 67, 69, 70; Xu Zengzhong, "An essay on some problems," 172. An account by the Qing literatus Zhou Kai refers to Qi as a "licentious, wicked and weak woman," who was yet able to "precipitate the calamitous spirit [of the rebellion]." *KYQ*, 2:830.

64. *QZQ*, 5:57–58, 64, 76–77, 118–119; *QDN*, 5:411–412; 6:68–69, 71–72, 414. *Qinding jiaoping*, 21.41b, 25.38b, 29.18, 32.33b, 34.12b, 49.11, 61.1.

65. *QZQ*, 5:76–77; *QDN*, 6:68–69.

66. *QZQ*, 5:76–77, 82–83, 87; *QDN*, 6:68–69, 192–193, 196–197.

67. *QZQ*, 2:240; 5:118–119. *Qinding jiaoping*, 32.5–6; cf. *QDN*, 5:324, 369. Yao Zhifu was identified by the Qing commanders as early as January 1797 (JQ 1/12/8) as a principal rebel leader. See *GZD*-JQ, 01644. Xu Zengzhong has shown that it was not until April of that year (JQ 2/3/28) that Widow Qi née Wang appeared in a Qing official record. See Xu's "An essay on some problems," 166–169.

68. *Qinding jiaoping*, 32.5–6; *QDN*, 5:369.

69. Xu Zengzhong, "On two proclamations," 200. Xu is of the opinion that Zhang Hanchao was of the Hunyuan persuasion, in contrast to Song Zhiqing's reversion to the Shouyuan tradition in 1792–1793. See also Xu Zengzhong and Lin Yi, "An inquiry," 186.

70. For the single report see *QZQ*, 1:325; cf. 5:249.

71. *QZQ*, 5:154.

72. See ibid., 66, 81, 137–138, 158; *QDN*, 6:286, 292. Wang Sanhuai deposed after he was captured that in 1796 when he met Widow Qi and other sectarians from Hubei, he did not want to join forces with them because "our place in Sichuan does not have to be laid waste by people from Hubei." *QZQ*, 5:70; *QDN*, 6:289–290.

73. *QZQ*, 1:323, 325–326; 5:119–126, 307; *Qinding jiaoping*, 54.28, 60.9, 28–32, 61.1, 3, 64.23, 65.22. *QDN*, 6:68–69.

74. Zhang Xiaoyuan, a sectarian from Fuyang, Anhui, claimed in his deposition made in 1800 that Wang Tingzhao was a relative and that Wang was a "teacher of boxing and cudgeling" *(quan gun jiaoshi)*. Wang denied this in his deposition in 1801. He testified: "In my spare time, I like boxing for fun; this is true. But I have not learned boxing, nor have I taught it." *QZQ*, 5:124; *QDN*, 6:204. Wang's deposition is remarkable for its dryness and stoicism. He insisted that he was illiterate and had played little part among

the sectarian armies! He told little or nothing, even when he was repeatedly tortured.

75. *QZQ*, 5:88, 118; *QDN*, 6:196, 199.

76. Xu Zengzhong, "On two proclamations," 199–200. The original of this proclamation, preserved in the Qing archives, is reproduced in plates in *QZQ*, vol. 1 pl. 1, and in *QDN*, vol. 5, unnumbered illustration.

77. See *QZQ*, 5:16–17; *QDD*, 171–172; Xu Zengzhong, "On two proclamations," esp. 224–225.

78. *QDN*, 5:16–17; 6:210–211. Xu Zengzhong and Lin Yi, "An inquiry," 179–180; *QZQ*, 5:115–116.

79. Ibid., 119, 124–125; *QDN*, 6:72–73, 204–205. Xu Zengzhong and Lin Yi, "An inquiry," 180–181 n. 7. The argument for a reinterpretation of the proclamation is set forth in my article in *Ming-Qing dang'an yu lishi yanjiu* [Ming-Qing archives and historical research], ed. First Historical Archives (Bejing: Zhonghua, 1988), 2:776–815. Xu Zengzhong has emphasized the anti-Manchu political intent of the document; see his "On two proclamations."

80. *QZQ*, 5:88–89, 115; *QDN*, 6:196, 210. On sectarian attempts to contact Wang Faseng in Kashgar as late as 1800, see *QDN*, 5:54–57.

81. *QZQ*, 5:85–89; *QDN*, 6:192–196. For the identification of Liu Leng as sect patriarch *(jiaozhu)*, see *QZQ*, 5:86–87; *QDN*, 6:195.

82. *QZQ*, 5:89; *QDN*, 6:196.

83. This ballad is enigmatic. The surnames "Liu" and "Wang" originally must have referred to the two major sectarian families in North China: see Naquin, "Connections Between Rebellions," 337–357. There is, however, a double meaning here, in that Wang Tingzhao very likely used the verse to refer to the importance of Wang Faseng.

84. *QZQ*, 5:88; *QDN*, 6:196.

85. Suzuki Chūsei, *Shinchō chūkishi kenkyū* [Studies in mid-Qing history] (Toyohashi: Aichi University, 1952); *Chūgokushi ni okeru kakumei to shūkyō* [Revolution and religion in Chinese history] (Tokyo: Tokyo University Press, 1974), chap. 10. For more recent Japanese work that develops Professor Suzuki's themes, see especially Yamada Masaru's article on immigrant society in the Qing period, focused on the 1796 White Lotus Rebellion, in *Shirin* 69.6 (Nov. 1986): 50–89.

86. Hu Zhaoxi, Huo Datong, and Yang Guang, "A few questions on the Sichuan theater," 140–159; Xu Zengzhong, "On two proclamations," 191–199, 226–228, 237. See note 1 for these references.

87. The reference to Nezha as an "incredible character" is from Henri Doré, *Researches into Chinese Superstitions,* trans. M. Kennelly et al. (Shanghai, 1911–), 9:111.

88. Peng Yanqing, "Dangyang," reprinted in *QZQ*, 4:279.

89. See especially *Xuanhan xianzhi* [County gazetteer of Xuanhan, Sichuan] (preface dated 1815; reprint, Taibei: Chengwen, 1976), 10b, 8b (p. 1374). Cf. the discussion in Hu Zhaoxi, Huo Datong, and Yang Guang, "A few questions on the Sichuan theater," 147, citing gazetteers of Sichuan localities. See note 1.

90. Shixiangcun jushi, *Kanjing jiaofei* [Pacification of the religious bandits], in *QZQ*, 4:81, 85; *QDN*, 6:406.

91. It seems that the Eternal Mother's original children would have included those who since that time had taken different forms of life through transmigration. A sectarian sutra declares: "In one net all remnants of souls are gathered; animals in four life-forms are among those returned to the origins." Huang Yubian, *Poxie xiangbian*, 3:85, 89, 128.

92. See notes 50–51, testimony of two disciples of Yao Zhifu and Yao Wenxue.

93. This citation is from *Kai xianzhi* [Gazetteer of Kai county, Sichuan] (1853; reprint, Taibei: Chengwen, 1976), 23.4:463. See also *QZQ*, 4:391.

94. Joseph W. Esherick, *The Origins of the Boxer Uprising* (Berkeley: University of California Press, 1987), 322.

95. See notes 79–83.

96. See note 80 and esp. *QZQ*, 5:115; *QDN*, 6:210.

97. *Qinding jiaoping*, 32.5–6, 36.13; *QDN*, 5:369.

98. Gong Jinghan, "On pacification" [in Chinese], reprinted in *QZQ*, 5:185–187; memorial of 1800 from Eletengpo, cited in Li Bangzheng, "White Lotus," 184. See note 1.

99. See note 1 and the discussion in Wang Yuxin, "Class analysis of the armies of the mid-Qing White Lotus uprising" [in Chinese], in *Zhongguo nongmin zhanzheng shi luncong* (Renmin, 1979), 1:457–498; Feng Zuozhe, "The great White Lotus uprising of five provinces during the Jiaqing period" [in Chinese], in *Qingshi luncong*, (1980), 2:158–174. Note the relevance of Cai Shaoqing, "On the Origins of the Gelaohui," *Modern China* 10.4 (1984): 481–508 and Cheng-yun Liu (Liu Zhengyun), on the Guolu movement in Sichuan: "Kuo-lu: a sworn-brotherhood organization in Szechwan," *Late Imperial China* 6.1 (June 1985): 56–82.

PART IV

Late Qing Perspectives

CHAPTER 9

The Triads and Their Ideology Up to the Early Nineteenth Century:
A Brief History

Wen-hsiung Hsu

In recent years, both Chinese and Western scholars have produced prolific and sophisticated studies on Chinese secret societies that go considerably beyond what Jean Chesneaux and Fei-Ling Davis have done. Some exceptions notwithstanding, these studies wisely eschew the simplistic and rather generalized perception of secret societies as part of a larger tradition of popular revolts that ideologically had been consistent in opposing Confucianism and the imperial government, and which provided a steady source of "popular radicals" and "primitive revolutionaries" who toppled moribund or decadent dynasties throughout Chinese history.

Of particular interest to this volume is an article written by Barend J. ter Haar.[1] Observing that "Triad ritual and mythology derived from a messianic tradition," ter Haar argues that secret societies such as the Heaven and Earth Society (Tiandi hui) had a great deal in common with the religious sectarians.[2] By implication, therefore, they can be understood as posing a cosmological challenge to imperial authority in the same way that some sectarians did, as Richard Shek and Noguchi Tetsurō maintain in chapter 7 in this volume.

This argument, however, is rejected by David Ownby. In his introduction to the same volume in which ter Haar's article appears, Ownby sees secret societies as brotherhood and voluntary associations more akin to Chinese guilds than to "explicitly dissident or revolutionary organizations that consciously challenged accepted norms."[3] Indeed, in his own monographic study on brotherhoods and secret societies, Ownby is even more adamant in drawing a distinction between the Triads and the religious sectarians. Thus he observed: "In stark contrast to the materials generated by the White

Lotus tradition, we find no discussion of salvation, of the elect, of a future world vastly different from that of the present. There is little reason to believe that the apocalyptic images in Tiandi hui manuals and depositions were linked to a full-fledged regimentation of time, space, and social relations. This in turn poses questions about the nature of Tiandi hui 'messianism.'"[4]

To be sure, Triad rituals and symbols are fraught with religious nuances and origins, yet it can be argued, as Ownby does, that they were incorporated "to add a layer of supernatural protection to the more secular protection sought in joining a brotherhood association."[5] Ownby appears to have said the final word when he states, "the point is not whether brotherhood associations were Confucian or anti-Confucian. The point is that the brotherhood associations . . . achieved their fullest capacity in contexts where the Confucian state and Confucian local elite were either weak or absent. In these contexts, brotherhoods provided a form of social organization and a language of social identity that facilitated the cooperation of unrelated individuals in achieving mutual goals."[6]

Fraternal organizations have long provided Chinese with an important means of social affiliation apart from traditional kinship groupings. The secret societies that flourished during the Qing dynasty (1644–1911) may be considered the most active and most important of all fraternal organizations. Qing archives record at least 111 different names of secret societies, some of which were the Triads.[7] The excellent study by Dian H. Murray in collaboration with Qin Baoqi has documented the origins, "founding myths," and development of the Heaven and Earth Society.[8] Written from an alternative perspective (including that of the immigrant society of Taiwan), this chapter offers a concise history of the early Triads up to the early nineteenth century, based on an independent examination of the sources. In the early history of the Triads in Fujian and Taiwan, one sees evidence of the phenomenon of mass psychology, as described by Elizabeth Perry, as well as the dynamics of communal feuding, as explored by Harry Lamley.[9] It is ironic that the rise of the Triads should have received a powerful impetus from the Lin Shuangwen Rebellion in Taiwan in 1787–1788—an outbreak caused by communal strife as well as a sworn brotherhood's compelling duty of mutual aid. Yet the long-term growth of the Triads was to be accompanied by habitual violence that went beyond mutual aid, involving a great deal of outlawry that in today's terms is associated with the underworld of the modern big cities. The setting of the early Triads may have been urban, but not always, and even so was in communities of less density and often in the interstices between communities. Originating on the margins of society, the Triads found in their mobile, autocephalous organization a way to take a share of the wealth and pleasures of the legitimately commercializing society. There were exceptions to this social pattern, however, as with many things regarding the Triads, as discussed in this chapter.

From Sworn Brotherhoods to Triads

The origins of sworn brotherhoods and the Triad groupings they fostered may be best understood in the context of the social dislocation that accompanied demographic movement. First active in Guangdong and Fujian, the Triads were stimulated by the relative mobility of the population together with a constant food-supply shortage. In 1726 the governor of Fujian, Gao Qizhuo, observed that the rice produced in Tingzhou prefecture could feed its residents only for nine months, in Fuzhou for seven or eight months, and in Quanzhou and Zhangzhou for six months, even in a year of good harvest.[10] A bumper rice crop in Guangdong was barely enough to feed half the province's population adequately. In Fujian and Guangdong, grain supply was limited in part by the attention of cultivators to more lucrative crops such as sugar cane, cotton, tobacco, and tea.[11] Along with population growth, average acreage was reduced from 4 *mou* per person in 1753 to 3.75 *mou* per person in 1766 nationwide, but Fujianese peasants could till only an average of 1.7 *mou* of land.[12] And in search of a better life, Fujianese people, especially those in Quanzhou and Zhangzhou prefectures, migrated overseas or inland. A number of Fujianese and Cantonese peasants moved to the mountainous areas abutting Jiangxi to lease land for the cultivation of rice and tea or trekked to Guangxi to farm, dig mines, and engage in other types of manual labor.[13] Many took up other trades that kept them on the move, becoming actors, peddlers, itinerant doctors, fortune-tellers, and porters. The dispossessed became vagrants. Since the local government and lineage organization forbade the appropriation of any funds for aid to them, they were apt to seek social affiliation for mutual help.[14] Those who stayed could find themselves embroiled in lineage feuds, which prompted them to look for protection beyond that offered by kinship ties.

The formation of non-kinship organizations was inspired in large part by the ideas of brotherhood, fidelity, and reciprocity expounded in the two popular novels, *Romance of the Three Kingdoms* and *Water Margin*. The novel *Romance of the Three Kingdoms* introduces the "peach garden sworn brotherhood" *(taoyuan jieyi)*, formed by Liu Bei (161–223), Guan Yu (160–219), and Zhang Fei (d. 221). Although the historical authenticity of this episode is questionable, its theme has been popularized by the novel since the fourteenth century.[15] The founders of the Qing dynasty, Nurhaci (1559–1626) (Taizu [1616–1626]), and Abahai (1592–1643) (Taizong [1627–1643]), were both said to be fond of this novel. Abahai's knowledge of the book reportedly helped him map out his strategy to conquer China.[16] The Qing government generally encouraged the novel's circulation after the publication of the Manchu edition in 1650.[17] The other novel, *Water Margin*, chronicles the adventures of the 108 outlaws pledged in brotherhood toward the end of the Northern Song dynasty (960–1126). It elucidates the main idea of brotherhood, that regardless of social and educational background, "people from the eight directions share the same land, and people of different surnames form one family," bound by "loyalty, sincerity, faithfulness and righteousness in their hearts."[18] Unlike the *Romance of the Three Kingdoms, Water Margin* was repeatedly prohibited from circulating after the seventeenth century. In 1642 the declining Ming court recognized the *Water Margin*'s inspirational contribution to popular uprisings and attempted to ferret out and burn as many copies as possible. During the Qing dynasty, the imperial court banned it at least fifteen times.[19] The interdictive measures, however, did not succeed in thwarting its spread. In Taiwan, for example, both novels remained the favorite books of storytellers, and the plays based on them were openly performed in festivals as late as 1894.[20] The popularity of these two novels helped disseminate the feasible idea of mutual aid and the outlaw ethos of brotherhood.

The practice of brotherhood was further encouraged by the official promotion of the cult of Guan Yu, who was eulogized as having embodied civic virtues and martial spirit in the novel *Romance of the Three Kingdoms*. The Qing imperial court made the worship of Guan Yu a sort of popular cult under its aegis, hoping that the Manchus would emulate his martial spirit and the Han Chinese would internalize his loyalty. Beginning in 1644 the imperial court held an annual ceremony in honor of Guan Yu's birthday and after 1693 issued an official hagiography.[21] So hallowed was his image, blasphemy against it was punishable by death.[22] With this newly created legitimacy, local officials and people from across the country erected temples in homage to him. The circulation of fantastic stories associated with the worship of Guan Yu further assisted in this popularization. According to one account, for example, in the summer of 1787, during the Lin Shuangwen Rebellion, many soldiers recovered from illness after worshiping in Guan Yu temples.[23] They reverently referred to him as Master of Blessings (Enzhugong) or God and Father Guan (Guandi laoye) in some areas.[24] Sworn brothers across the country worshiped him as their patron deity.

Imperial promotion of the Guan Yu cult notwithstanding, the Qing government was the first in Chinese history to ban sworn brotherhoods. It differentiated between two types of brotherhoods—those that used the blood-oath ritual for membership induction and those that formed brotherhoods using a verbal covenant without a blood oath. Since the initiation procedures for the first type implied a deeper commitment to the covenant, authorities dealt with it more harshly. Even before their conquest of China, the Manchus had stipulated that people of different surnames who swore oaths of brotherhood were to be punished by one hundred lashes. In 1661 the penalty was increased to execution. In 1671 a new statute denounced such clandestine groups as seditious, treating sworn brothers as rebels.[25] The governor-general of Fujian, Yao Qisheng (1624–1684), reported in 1680 that soldiers who had deserted, government clerks, pettifoggers, vagrants, and local residents formed sworn brotherhood organizations to commit robberies in Fujian, especially the Zhangzhou area.[26] During the subsequent century, sworn brotherhood associations increased in number and involved themselves in revolts such as the uprising led by Zhu Yigui in southern Taiwan in 1721. In 1729, for example, it was discovered that sworn brothers had formed Peach Garden Society (Taoyuanhui) in Fujian, and Dragon Society (Zilonghui) in Taiwan.[27] The Qing penal code in 1764 specified that the leaders of blood-oath covenants and the leaders of non-blood-oath covenants of more than thirty members were to be sentenced to death by strangulation.[28] Far from inhibiting the growth of brotherhoods, such statutes served only to exacerbate the situation. Villagers in Guangdong's Xiangshan county, for example, formed brotherhoods so openly that they held oath ceremonies in the daytime and placed cannons at street intersections to stave off arrest.[29] To help each other in times of need, people would enter into brotherhoods at any cost.

The early brotherhoods were linked to various voluntary associations for mutual aid. One such group was the benefit association for bereavement, known as the Association for Parents (Fumuhui). The early Association for Parents could be traced to 1728 when twenty-three men formed it in Taiwan's Tainan county. In the oath required by the association, members agreed to contribute a certain amount of cash or grain to defray the expenses of funerals for the deceased parents of fellow members. Although such groups were not actually guilty of any wrongdoing, local authorities sometimes penalized the participants in accordance with the laws against brotherhoods.[30] To protect themselves against persecution, members in some areas carried daggers, calling their groups Small Sword Societies (Xiaodaohui), such as the one organized in Fujian's Zhangpu county in 1742.[31] Other mutual-aid associations bound by covenant adopted different names, the most common being the Heaven and Earth Society.

The origin of the Triads in general and the Heaven and Earth Society in particular is shrouded in mystery.[32] When, where, and by whom the Heaven and Earth Society was founded is still a matter of controversy, although the writings of Cai Shaoqing, Qin Baoqi, and others are persuasive in pointing to a late origin during the Qianlong reign.[33] According to legend, the society was founded in Fujian in 1674, but this is extremely doubtful. The actual founding of the Heaven and Earth Society (that is, when the name was definitely used) does not seem to have been earlier than 1761. Evidence in the Qing archives indicates that in that year, a Fujianese monk by the name of Zheng Kai (Monk Hong Er or Monk Wan, alias Tixi, or Tu Xi, 1722?–1779) formed a Heaven and Earth Society in a place called Guanyinting in Gaoxi(xiang), Zhangpu county, Zhangzhou prefecture of southern Fujian. Sometime before that year, he had become sworn brothers with two Fujianese, Li Shaomin and Tao Yuan, reportedly in Sichuan, where Ma Jiulong and forty-eight other monks later joined.[34] The following year, Zheng Kai succeeded in persuading Chen Biao (d. 1789, an itinerant doctor) and Lu Mao (d. 1789, a local stalwart) to join the society. In 1767 Lu Mao inducted nine villagers and one city dweller, who further recruited mostly from among their own lineages, swelling the size of the organization to 332 members. He gave each member a calico turban for identification and prepared to rise in arms to "manage society in accordance with Heaven's will" *(shuntian dangshi)* on May 1, 1768. But his plan to lead the first revolt of the Heaven and Earth Society in Zhangpu was thwarted by his brother by birth, who captured him with the assistance of the head of their own lineage.[35] Other members of the society, however, continued to expand the organization, attempting to revolt again.

Also in Fujian's Zhangzhou area, after 1768, both Li Shaomin and Chen Biao actively recruited people to join the Heaven and Earth Society. Li Shaomin inducted more members and offered to reward them with one silver dollar for each person they recruited. He showed them a piece of red silk cloth on which was written "Great Ming" (Da Ming) and promised to rob wealthy people before staging a revolt. In 1769 the revolt aborted, however, and Li Shaomin fled the area after eighteen members were apprehended by local officials. The eighteen members ranged in age from twenty-nine to fifty-six, with an average age of forty-four. Their occupations included the following: shopkeepers, fish peddlers, butchers, farmers, and hired hands. In another development, Chen Biao, in 1782, inducted into the society Chen Qu, a clansman of his, and Yan Yan (1762–1788), a cloth merchant. The following year, Yan Yan moved to Taiwan and recruited new members, including Lin Shuangwen.[36] Organized primarily for socioeconomic mutual aid, the Heaven and Earth Society gradually represented a source of public disturbance in South China and Taiwan.

The Heaven and Earth Society came to the close attention of the imperial court during the Lin Shuangwen Rebellion, in 1787–1788, the largest uprising in Taiwan during the Qing period. With his parents Lin Shuangwen had migrated to Taiwan from Fujian's Zhangzhou prefecture in 1773. He once served as a county constable and farmed in Zhanghua, in central Taiwan, an area torn by communal strife between the settlers from Fujian's Zhangzhou and Quanzhou prefectures. Lin became a leader of the Heaven and Earth Society in Taiwan soon after he was inducted into the organization by Yan Yan, on April 4, 1784. Though foreshadowed by communal strife in the Zhanghua area during 1782–1783, the 1787 rebellion itself was triggered by efforts of local officials to prosecute society members. Soon after the rebellion started at Dadun (Taizhong) on January 16, 1787, Lin was made "master of the covenant" *(mengzhu)*, a typical appellation for the leader of a sworn brotherhood. He in turn announced the reign title *shuntian* ("obeying heaven" or "in accordance with heaven's will"), stemming from a common catchword of the society. Lin also followed the traditional rebel practice of conferring official titles upon his associates. The rebellion spread in Chinese-settled areas on the west plains of Taiwan and lasted more than a year, until February 10, 1788, when Lin Shuangwen was captured. The magnitude of the rebellion compelled the imperial court to send nine thousand soldiers from seven mainland provinces to Taiwan and reportedly expend one third of its treasury reserves. The eventual triumph of the government was considered one of Emperor Qianlong's "ten great military achievements."[37] Four years after the rebellion, an article was added to the penal code, outlawing the Heaven and Earth Society by name for the first time.[38] The Qing government was increasingly wary of the activities of the Triads.

In spite of the government's ban, the Triads continued to be active in Taiwan. From 1784 to 1805 the Triads there were formed mostly under the names of the Heaven and Earth Society and the Small Sword Society. The Small Sword Society organized by Zheng Guangcai in Fengshan county in 1794 claimed to have fifty-four members, who had emigrated from southern Fujian. The formation of such a society heightened the tensions between the southern Fujianese and Hakka settlers in Taiwan; and the involvement of the Triads in communal strife prompted an increase in the frequency and scale of social disturbances. In 1795 the Heaven and Earth Society revolted again in Taiwan, under the leadership of Chen Zhouquan.[39] As a matter of fact, Triads were responsible for at least a total of nine uprisings on the island during the nineteenth century. In 1853, when the Small Sword Society planned revolts in both Fujian and Taiwan, twenty-nine of its members were discovered by the authorities in Taiwan, and thirty members were captured on board ships between Taiwan and the mainland.[40]

On the mainland, the Triads were active in Fujian, thriving under the names of Heaven and Earth Society and Adding Brothers Society (Tiandihui), among others. The Adding Brothers Society, which was founded in Pinghe county, Zhangzhou prefecture, in 1775, had a name homonymous with the Heaven and Earth Society, reflecting the nature of its social affiliation—more and more young members were recruited. In 1787 the Heaven and Earth Society led by Zhang Maqiu looted a salt dealer's residence and burned down the barracks south of Zhangpu in Zhangzhou prefecture. The Triads gradually spread to other areas of Fujian. In 1812 their members collected money and plundered villages in Tingzhou prefecture, where Fujian borders on Jiangxi and Guangdong.[41] The Triads remained active in Fujian at least until the mid-nineteenth century.

In Guangdong, the Triads were formed in Tapu and Raoping, of Chaozhou prefecture, before 1790.[42] As Cantonese emigrated to Southeast Asia, they also organized Triads in their adopted lands. A Triad society was formed in Penang, Malaya, as early as 1799.[43] In Guangdong itself, the Triads caused serious social unrest during the first half of the nineteenth century. In 1801 a large Heaven and Earth Society was organized by Chen Lanjisi (literally, Chen "number four with battered shoes") (1776–1802), son of the commissary of the seal at the office of the provincial judge, in Boluo county, Huizhou prefecture. The association claimed to have as many as ten thousand members, including monks and lay vegetarians. With the slogan "carry out the Way in accordance with Heaven's will" *(shuntian xingdao)* displayed on their red flags, they vowed to "pull together [among ourselves in order] to take back the country." Their revolt

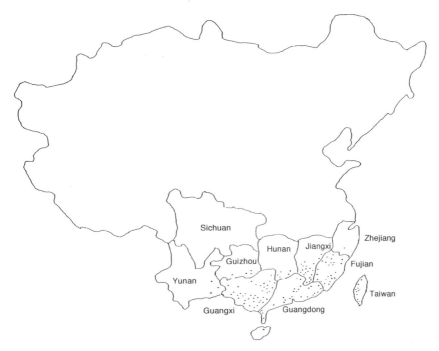

MAP 3. Triad activity areas in South China, 1760s–1830s

the following year lasted over one month and was quelled only after
eight thousand government soldiers and thirteen hundred militia
were sent to seize their strongholds stockpiled with firearms and cannons.[44] After 1811 the Triads adopted the name of Three-in-One
Society (Sanhe hui) and extended their influence to Guangzhou, Jiaying, Qiongzhou, and other prefectures. In Guangzhou's Xiangshan
county, the Triads even formalized their exactions by handing out
receipts to the villagers paying protection fees and trampled on or cut
the crops of those who refused to give them money. During the 1830s
they were known to have held people for ransom, robbed travelers,
broken into stores, pawnshops, and residences, and to have engaged
in salt smuggling and opium trafficking before launching a series of
uprisings and moving elsewhere.[45] The Triads further expanded in
Guangdong after the Opium War of 1841–1842.

In Guangxi, ninety-five people from northern Guangxi, Guangdong, Hunan, and Fujian formed a Heaven and Earth Society in
Pingle county in 1806.[46] As the influx of migrants doubled Guangxi's population from 3.7 million in 1749 to 7.8 million in 1851
(according to an informed estimate), the Triads also proliferated.[47]
It was reported that almost every village in Yulin prefecture had its
Triad "elder brother" (dage).[48] Even the aboriginal Yao people joined
the Han Chinese settlers in organizing the Adding Brothers Society,
in 1821.[49] In any case, after 1828, the Triads were so widespread in
Guangxi that the Qing government sought to control vagrants by
including them in the baojia policing system.[50] Village headmen
admonished residents not to join sworn brotherhoods and risk
becoming "criminals in the view of the imperial court." Well-to-do
families in some areas signed pacts of collective security in order to
take concerted action against the Triads.[51] All these measures not
only failed but also intensified antagonism and politicized the Triads.
In the years 1845–1850, seventy-seven Triad uprisings were reported
in Guangxi alone.[52] When Taiping insurgents rose in arms in Jintian
in May 1850, the Heaven and Earth Society formed by Luo Dagang
three years earlier also joined the rebellion.[53] The Heaven and Earth
Society was to play a role in the Taiping Rebellion.

The Triads also spread to Jiangxi, Hunan, Yunnan, and Guizhou provinces along with the migrants in the early nineteenth century. In Jiangxi they were especially active in Ganzhou and Nanlan
prefectures and the regions adjoining Fujian and Guangdong after
1803.[54] In Jiangxi's Ji'an prefecture, salt-smugglers joined Adding

Brothers Society, Adding Daggers Society, or One Thousand Daggers Society to facilitate their illicit activities.[55] Two Heaven and Earth Societies were separately introduced into Guizhou and Yunnan by people from Guangdong, in 1812.[56] The following year, thirty-four men from Hunan, Guangxi, Guangdong, Fujian, and Jiangxi formed an Adding Brothers Society in Jianghua county in southern Hunan.[57] As more people moved into Hunan from Guangdong to reclaim hilly land, more Adding Brothers Societies were also organized. Some of them formed maurauding hordes, ravaging villages, waylaying travelers, and ransacking houses.[58] The Three-in-One Society had spread to Guizhou and Hunan by 1831, when it claimed to have four other regional groups in Fujian, Guangdong, Yunnan, and Zhejiang, each of which could be identified by the color of its flag.[59] By the 1830s the Triads had become a major social organization outside lineages, native-place associations, and commercial and occupational guilds in southern and southwestern China and Taiwan.

The Triads were organized mostly in the rural areas and rarely in the cities and in the provincial capitals. There is no evidence of Triad involvement in resisting tax payment or of strikes among workers in the agriculturally rich region of Songjiang and Suzhou, in Jiangsu, where handicraft workshops existed. Neither was there any indication of Triad activity at the center of the porcelain industry in Jingdezhen, in Jiangxi.[60] Triads were more likely to be active in marginal regions where government control was not firm, or in areas with ethnically or subethnically mixed population, in places bordering different provinces, and in river ports. Taiwan during the eighteenth century and Guangxi in the early nineteenth century were typical marginal regions characterized by weak political control, providing more latitude for the Triads to develop. The areas with mixed population tended to have a high incidence of intergroup conflict, prompting people to turn to sworn brotherhood and the Triads for organized protection. In Guangdong's Bole county, where the Heaven and Earth Society mustered ten thousand members to revolt in 1801, people from Jiaying and Chaozhou prefectures and from Fujian province often were in contention with local residents over the use of irrigation water.[61] The Triad groups in Taiwan were mostly active in the counties where the settlers from Fujian and Guangdong lived in close proximity and were armed to fight both against the aborigines and against each other. People from Jiangxi also entered the neighboring Jianning, Shaowu, and Tingzhou prefectures of Fujian to join

the Fujianese Triads in the early nineteenth century.[62] In Hunan the
Triads were organized mostly in Chenzhou, Guiyang, and Yongzhou
prefectures bordering Jiangxi, Guangdong, and Guangxi provinces.[63]
Southern Hunan's Jianghua county, for example, is situated roughly
between eastern Guangdong and northwestern Jiangxi, and became
an ideal locale for people from both provinces to establish affiliations
through Triads.[64] Furthermore, people from various places met in
river ports and entered into Triads and other brotherhoods. Wan'an
on the Gan River in Jiangxi was a necessary stop for travelers between
Guangdong and Jiangxi, and the Adding Brothers Society was especially active there. Triad members charged fees and issued passes to
the boats shipping rice on the West River between Zhaoqing, in
Guangdong, and Wuzhou, in Guangxi.[65] In the more established and
densely populated areas, the Triads could also be organized for the
purpose of intergroup fighting.

The Triads were connected with communal strife in Fujian,
Taiwan, Jiangxi, Guangdong, and Guangxi. In Fujian, people practicing pugilism formed associations to engage in fighting with out-
groups before the mid-eighteenth century; the organization of the
Triads intensified this conflict.[66] The Heaven and Earth Society in
Taiwan was first involved in communal strife after it revolted under
the leadership of Lin Shuangwen in 1787–1788. In October 1790,
an immigrant, from Fujian's Zhangzhou prefecture, and a Hakka
settler led forty-seven men to form another Heaven and Earth Society in Taiwan's Nantou area to oppose the immigrants from Fujian's
Quanzhou prefecture. But their plans were discovered by local officials before fighting actually took place.[67] Some Triads were organized specifically for engagement in feuds. In 1797 about one hundred immigrants from southern Fujian joined a Small Sword Society
in northern Taiwan's Danshui area and raised a banner that read
"People from Zhangzhou and Quanzhou prefectures destroy people
from Guangdong," clamoring for fighting.[68] Triad organization
tended to flourish in the regions rife with feuds. In southern Jiangxi's Nanlan and Ganzhou prefectures, an area adjacent to Hunan,
Guangdong, and Fujian provinces, group strife was common and
the Triads were formed. Internecine strife between old and new settlers was rampant in Guangxi's southeastern region, and the Triads
were also more numerous there in the first half of the nineteenth
century.[69] The proliferation of Triads in Guangdong's Huizhou prefecture intensified enmity between old villagers and new settlers,

contributing to the high incidence of communal strife there. Furthermore, the spread of Triads tended to prod villagers to form other voluntary associations to counteract their influence, thus aggravating intergroup strife. In Guangdong's Shunde county, for example, a Sleeping Dragon Society was organized to engage in armed fights with the Three-in-One Society—and the strife lasted until the mid-nineteenth century.[70] With antagonistic organizations involved, intergroup strife could be escalated into popular uprisings. In Yonglan county of Huizhou prefecture, villagers organized an Ox Head Society to protect their cows from being rustled by the Adding Brothers Society. In 1802 the villagers apprehended an Adding Brothers Society member. After discovering that one of their brothers had died in prison, the latter Society mustered between two and three thousand people to loot the member villages of the Ox Head Society members. When local officials intervened, they hoisted a red flag on which was written "Officials compell the people to rebel" in their mountain strongholds equipped with firearms. Their revolt lasted about four months.[71] As the activities of the Triads precipitated more feuds and revolts, their organization became a major concern of provincial and local officials.

The Organization of the Triads

The Triads did not have any centralized organization to oversee regional groups; the lodges or chapters were not actually linked with one another. Each Triad was a localized voluntary organization, independent and self-governing in its own area. A man could organize or join more than one Triad in different places at different times. Chen Silao and Su Ye joined the Heaven and Earth Society in Taiwan in 1786 and both returned to their native Tong'an county in Fujian to recruit two hundred members into their own society in 1792.[72] An organizer could induct people to form a small Triad, but he might also initiate some members who, in turn, would recruit their acquaintances into a separate and bigger society. An enlarged society could consist of several subgroups. A Heaven and Earth Society formed in Guangxi's Shanglin county in 1807, for example, was divided into Heaven and Earth subgroups, with fifteen members each.[73] A small society comprising fewer than thirty members elected an "elder brother," normally the organizer himself, as its leader. A large one, such as the Heaven and Earth Society formed in Guangdong's Haikang county in 1801, was headed by a "general leader" *(zong huishou* or *zong dage)* who supervised several subgroups.[74] Regardless of an individual group's size, its leaders were always recognized as elder brothers.

The organizers or leaders of the Triads came from diverse social backgrounds. Though of modest means, sometimes barely sub-sisting, most of them did have legitimate occupations as scholars, shopkeepers, handicraftsmen, farmers, peddlers, monks, and por-ters. Of the 123 leading members of the Triads recorded in the Qing archives before 1840, roughly half of the total were peddlers, porters, hired hands, soldiers, and "paupers" (see table). Such people tended to have a high degree of geographical mobility, and the Triad asso-ciations facilitated mutual assistance outside their own villages. It appears that after the Opium War, in 1841–1842, more people with a dissident purpose (cf. chapter 10, by David Faure, this volume) served as Triad leaders.[75] Few of these leaders, however, can be iden-

TABLE

Social Backgrounds of 123 Leading Members of the Triads Before 1840

Occupation of the Leading Member	Number
Peddler	26
Porter and hired hand	23
Impoverished scholar	13
Pauper	11
Shopkeeper	11
Peasant	10
Handicraftsman	8
Peasant/small retailer	7
Monk	6
Soldier	5
Watchman	1
Horse peddler	1
Wealthy resident	1
Total	123

Source: Qin Baoqi and Liu Meizhen, "Shilun Tiandihui" [A preliminary treatise on the Heaven and Earth Society], in *Qingshi yanjiuji* [Studies on the history of the Qing dynasty] (Beijing: Zhongguo renmin daxue, 1980), 1:167–168.

tified simply as peasants. As more soldiers, bandits, gamblers, actors, and impoverished degree-holders became leaders, more marginal people were attracted to the Triads.

The Triads drew members from most walks of life, but most likely to join were the less affluent. This was because they had the greatest need for mutual assistance, the organization's main function. Owing to their attachment to land and lineage organization, the relatively settled landlords and peasant tenants normally shunned the Triads. There were exceptions, however. The spread of the Triads in Guangdong in the early nineteenth century was related to the landowners' resistance to taxation and the peasants' refusal to pay rent; they joined separate Triads for different purposes.[76] Residents who took up nonfarming trades and marginal people who were vulnerable to harassment seemed more likely to become Triad members for purposes of protection. Socially marginal people like Hakkas from Guangdong and Fujian joined the Triads in Guangxi, Hunan, Guizhou, and Yunnan in the early nineteenth century. Occupationally marginal people such as vagrants, salt smugglers, bandits, and pirates used the Triads to support their illicit activities.[77] Many vagrants joined the Triads in Taiwan during the eighteenth century and in Guangxi in the early nineteenth century; they even forthrightly acknowledged their vagabondage in the initiation oaths.[78] Pirates not only were members themselves but also involved the Triads in the depredations led by Cai Qian at the beginning of the nineteenth century.[79] In 1807 when the Guangdong government took actions to suppress sea piracy, river bandits scuttled off into Guangxi, forming Triads with migrants from other areas.[80] Itinerant merchants, peddlers, actors, fortune-tellers, and laborers, who were often away from home, entered the Triads to solidify their social relations. In Guangxi's Guanyang county, migrants from Hunan, Guangdong, elsewhere in Guangxi, and local residents, including an actor, a butcher, a barber, some hired hands, and a number of soldiers, joined a Heaven and Earth Society in 1819.[81] In Guangxi's Xunzhou prefecture, where silver mines were opened in the 1820s, the ranks of the Triads were filled primarily by native minority Zhuang and Hakka migrant miners.[82] Though porters and beggars might become individual members, they had their own organization and normally did not form a Triad themselves.[83] The garrison soldiers and local braves were less settled in the communities and they joined the Triads to seek more extra-familial connections.[84] The large number of soldiers, braves, and yamen clerks in the organization further complicated the government's problem of how to deal with the Triads in Taiwan and South China.

In South China, the Triads also drew members from lineages, especially in Fujian and Guangdong. The Heaven and Earth Society organized by Lu Mao in 1767 consisted of 332 members recruited mostly from seven lineages in Fujian's Zhangpu county.[85] Sometimes members' brothers, sons, fathers, and uncles joined the same organization. Zhan Qingzhen, a private tutor from Guangdong's Raoping teaching in southern Fujian's Zhaolan, was inducted into the Heaven and Earth Society by Lü He in 1783. Four years later, Lü recruited more from among his lineage, and Zhan introduced not only his younger brother by birth but also two other men from his own lineage to become members of the Society. In the same year, Zhang Maqiu joined the Heaven and Earth Society together with his father and uncle in Zhangpu.[86] Men from Zheng and Xiao lineages in Guangdong's Chaoyang county joined another Heaven and Earth Society, organized by a pirate, in 1803.[87] The existence of strong lineages also impelled the weak ones to form Triads for self-protection. New settlers who were often also peasant tenants in Guangdong turned to the Adding Brothers Society to counterbalance the influence of powerful lineages in the early nineteenth century.[88] The Triads thus not only became a convenient association to facilitate inter-lineage coordination and cooperation, but they also served as a mode of organization for people without lineage ties to establish social affiliations.

Though the Triads were considered to be a voluntary organization, not all members joined them of their own accord. Initiates were required to pay fees ranging from three hundred cash to two silver dollars, but some members were unable or reluctant to fulfill this obligation. Even if initiation fees were reduced in the course of time, the organization sometimes imposed other financial charges on its members. In Guangxi's Yulin prefecture villagers were forced to pay fees to "turn red" as Triad members, for otherwise they would run the risk of being harassed as "white households."[89] Indeed, some people became Triad members under duress. In some areas Triad leaders compelled wealthy residents to join the organization or be harassed. A Heaven and Earth Society committed several robberies after it was organized in Guangxi's Baise in 1807; when local authorities launched a manhunt, some 508 members conceded that they had been coerced into joining it. The increase in the number of involuntary participants prompted the Qing government in 1819 to grant clemency to those who turned themselves in as rioters forced to have taken part in the disturbances.[90] Some of these pardoned participants might have concealed their Triad membership, for tattling on their organization would disavow their own oaths.

People formally became members after taking an oath in the initiation ceremony. An elaborate ceremony might include the staging of a play, but its most important part was always the blood ritual.[91] The oath stressed the moral paradigm of mutual assistance and spelled out injunctions against any possible breach. An oath text discovered in Jiangxi's Huichang county in 1806 states: "We dare not presumptuously harbor any evil or perfidy in our hearts. We wish to act in concert. In dealing with the outside world, we dare not betray the Grace of God or disavow covenant. After taking the oath, members will be attached to each other like blood brothers. In weal or woe, we support each other. Eminent or humble, we share joys and sorrows. Right or wrong, we receive the gods' blessings. We dare not divulge any secrets. The longer we are members, the more prosperous we become. The old dare not oppress the young, nor the strong bully the weak. We dare not defraud brothers of belongings or seduce brothers' wives. We dare not balk at difficulties or engage in corruption. Various gods will put us to death if we forswear our oath."[92] The oath was sanctified by ritual. As indicated in a nineteenth-century source, the initiates were required to walk under a sword reciting: "I pass under the sword with loyalty and righteousness and will die without loyalty and righteousness."[93] This part of the initiation ceremony later became known conventionally as the rite of "crossing the bridge" *(guoqiao);* and to join a Triad was considered "to be reborn" to "adore the upright" *(baizheng).*[94] After the oath rite, new members formally entered the Triad world of uprightness.

Though adopting the rituals of folk religion, the Triads should not be regarded as religious confraternities. When Qing officials first learned of the existence of the Heaven and Earth Society during the Lin Shuangwen Rebellion in 1787, they called it a "heretical sect" *(xiejiao,* "heterodox teaching" in a broad sense), and some of its own members referred to it as a "sect" *(jiao);* but later neither government officials nor Triad members themselves regarded the association as a sectarian organization.[95] The Triad registers *(huibu)* never contained any sacred scriptures, writings based on divine revelation, or sermons. As Triad initiation ceremonies gradually became ritualized, however, the lives of the members were also more deeply rooted in religious symbols and practices. Starting in the late eighteenth century, the Triads worshiped not only Guan Yu, Monk Hong Er, and the Five Patriarchs (Wuzhu, the five legendary founders of the Heaven and Earth Society), but also the Goddess of Mercy and the God of Earth. The Jade Emperor, Buddha, and other deities were added to the Triad pantheon in the early nineteenth century.[96] The inclusion of commonly worshiped deities suggests that the Triads followed the practices of Chinese folk religion, with no deviation.

The Triads had their own argot, signals, and cryptograms for communications among members. When Monk Hong Er founded the Heaven and Earth Society in 1761, he adopted the phrase "five dots and twenty-one," which made up the Chinese character Hong, as its password and used three fingers as the signal.[97] In the ensuing century this remained the most common means of member recognition with some modifications. In the 1780s, the members identified themselves by pressing three fingers on their chests and using three fingers to serve tea, smoke, and carry things. When looting, they stuck out their little fingers, and the potential victim was to raise a thumb to avoid being robbed.[98] Other methods of identification were also used in the early nineteenth century. For example, they would leave certain buttons of their shirts open, hold umbrellas upside down, and coil up their queues. A formal way to prove membership, of course, was to possess a document, a card, a piece of cloth, or a sheet of paper with such Triad phrases as "Follow Heaven's will."[99] The Triads also adopted elliptical language in their communications. They used the words and phrases "lotus flower" for teacup, "sand" for rice, "storm" for government troops, "single leg" for umbrella, "cruising" for plundering a village, "hitting a partridge" for robbing people, "eating a duck" for attacking a ship, and "attaching oneself to the truth" for believing in popular Daoism or Buddhism.[100] Indeed, to the Qing government, these passwords, signals, and cryptic language made any Triad a "secret society."

There is evidence that the Triads and the White Lotus (the Eternal Mother religion) influenced each other in both religious beliefs and organizational structure in the first half of the nineteenth century. Both emphasized the mutual assistance of brotherhood and worshiped Guan Yu.[101] Futhermore, mutual borrowing of cant phrases and personal names was possible. Both used Mingzhu or

Mingwang but with different connotations: to the White Lotus it sometimes meant Maitreya, while to the Triads, the term signified the Ming ruler. During their uprising in southern Hubei's Changyang county in 1796, the White Lotus rebels used a common catchword of the Heaven and Earth Society, *"tianyun"* (heavenly revolution of destiny), as their reign title, and one of their leaders adopted the name of Zhu Hongtao, a legendary leader of the early Heaven and Earth Society.[102] (See chapter 8, this volume.) Mutual influence was also apparent in their worship of idols and use of organizational names. In 1813, the Triads in Jiangxi's Chongyi county worshiped Ma Chaozhu, a White Lotus leader who led an uprising in Hubei in 1752.[103] On the other hand, a White Lotus sect in Hunan worshiped Wan Yunlong, a legendary founder of the Heaven and Earth Society, in the 1830s.[104] In the 1840s the Blue Lotus (Qinglian) sect in Hunan often called its organization Society of Loyalty and Righteousness (Zhongyitang), a name commonly adopted by the Triads.[105] Around 1847 Dong Yantai, a native of Jiangxi, became an adherent of the Jindan sect of the White Lotus persuasion, worshiping the Eternal Mother (Wusheng laomu), the patron goddess of the White Lotus, and later formed a Triad under the name of Guan Yu Society in Hunan.[106] The relation between the Triads and White Lotus actually was more than sharing idols and organizational names.

The Triads and the White Lotus also collaborated in their revolt against the Qing government. Li Lingkui, a Fujianese who ran a store selling paper in Jiangxi's provincial capital Nanchang, became a proselytizer of the Great Vehicle (Dacheng) sect of the White Lotus persuasion, in 1782. After joining the Heaven and Earth Society in 1801, he formed two associations, Yangpan and Yinpan, which stood for Heaven and Earth respectively. The former was related to the Heaven and Earth Society, and the latter consisted of White Lotus believers. Li's organizations soon spread to other areas in Jiangxi. After he was arrested and executed in August 1803, fifteen hundred of his followers gathered in Shicheng county and rose in arms that November. The uprising, however, was crushed in less than a week.[107] In 1813, when Li Wencheng led his Tianli sect of the White Lotus to revolt in Henan, he sought the collaboration of his sworn brother Huang Jinneng, who had purchased a *jiansheng* degree and was a leader of the Heaven and Earth Society in Guangdong. But this plan did not materialize and Li Wencheng's uprising lasted only three months.[108] Since the interaction between the two organizations persisted, the government in Jiangxi from 1819 to 1831 prosecuted the Heaven and Earth Society in accordance with the law prohibiting the White Lotus—leaders were to face death by strangulation, while followers were to be tattooed and made slaves in the northwestern frontier areas.[109] In spite of government persecution, the alliance of the Triads and the White Lotus persevered in Hunan and Jiangxi in the 1840s.[110] The imperial authorities continued to suppress the Triads primarily because of their insurgent tendencies and subversive ideas.

Triad Ideology Up to the Early Nineteenth Century

The ideology of the Triads was a mixture of inherent and derived ideas. The inherent element, as George Rude suggests, was "based on direct experience, oral tradition or folk-memory and not learned by listening to sermons or speeches or reading books."[111] Among the organizational principles of the Triads were socially accepted norms and notions derived from their involvement in uprisings, from folk literature and theatre, from popular ethnic consciousness, and from the dissenting political idea of opposing the Manchus.

The ideological orientation of the Triads conformed to the traditional cosmological order. The Heaven and Earth Society adopted as its natural symbol the mountain *(shan)* on which heaven and earth were said to join together. Its members considered heaven their father and earth their mother, evincing their appreciation for the harmony of heaven, earth, and humanity; some of them even assumed that they formed a brotherhood with heaven and earth.[112] Actually, the organization itself was so designated because "human life is based on heaven and earth and the name Heaven and Earth Society implies reverence of heaven and earth."[113] The members believed, therefore, that "following Heaven's will" was the natural way of life. They stressed the idea to such a degree that they not only adopted it as their catchphrase but also altered the phrase "implement the way on behalf of heaven" *(titian xingdao)* in *Water Margin* to "implement the way in obedience to heaven's will" *(shuntian xingdao)*.[114] It seems that the Triads never did elaborate on the connotations of "the way," but they evidently took it to mean "principle of the way" *(daoli)*, which had its manifestations in loyalty and correct duty.[115] In orthodox belief, it was the monarch who oversaw the carrying out of the heavenly way, but the Triads vowed to implement it themselves, theoretically in accordance with heaven's will and stressing the concept of "righteousness" in their initiation oaths.

The organizational principle of the Triads incorporated the norms of popular orthodoxy. The quintessence of the Triad norm was "righteousness" *(yi)*, which was more fully expressed by the phrase "spirit of fidelity and uprightness" *(zhongxin yiqi).* [116] In theory, the idea of righteousness enjoined the Triad members to act in conformity with what was right; in practice, it obligated them to abide by their sworn brothers at all costs and forbade all forms of exploitation among themselves. The members, in effect, agreed with the philosopher Mozi (fl. fifth century B.C.) that nothing was more valuable and honorable than righteousness, and interacting righteously would bring them mutual benefit. [117] To join a Triad brotherhood, therefore, was to "form righteousness" *(jieyi)* under oath, which made members "closer to each other than those born from the same womb, and be of the same flesh and bone." [118] To Triad brothers, their moral code outweighed the state's legal code; if a member perpetrated a crime, his sworn brother was duty bound to help him evade the law. [119] It was, therefore, only through righteousness in Triad terms that a member could become a man of integrity, embodying the harmony between heaven and earth. A Triad poem describes the benefits of being an upright member as follows:

> Take it easy and be happy as a fairy;
> Propriety and righteousness are the equal of Heaven.
> Be humane and amiable, you will receive Heaven's blessings;
> Be moral and display equanimity, your descendants will acquire
> virtue. [120]

In exemplifying moral principles pragmatically, the Triad organization not only helped its members understand its norms but also enhanced its appeal to the local populace.

While emphasizing fidelity and uprightness as the basis of fraternal reciprocity among members, the Triads also exalted the cardinal virtue of filial piety and promoted harmony within each member's own family and ties between members' families. The Triads underscored filial piety to one's own parents by including it, as well as fidelity to fellow members' families, in the very first of the thirty-six oaths; unfilial conduct was regarded as the most heinous crime. Such filial piety was even extended to fellow members' parents. [121]

Although the Triad participants were supposed to keep their membership secret from their own parents and wives, they in practice showed great concern for one another's blood families. A document of the Heaven and Earth Society discovered in 1808 stressed that the members "were born and nurtured by the same parents," and should treat other members' parents as their own.[122] Any offense against other members' parents was punished physically—forty strokes with a bamboo stick in the early nineteenth century and 108 heavy blows in later times.[123] The Triads also promoted ancestor worship as an integral part of filial piety. Since proper burial was considered to be the first step to ancestor worship, fellow members provided funds for the burial of other members' deceased parents. One of the main reasons for people to join the Triads, as an organizer of the Heaven and Earth Society revealed in 1788, was for the members to share the cost of funerals.[124] In fact, as previously mentioned, Triad groups in the late eighteenth century were sometimes formed under the name of Association for Parents, in view of their function as benefit associations regarding bereavement.

The Triad brotherhood, in effect, served as a surrogate for actual kinship. The members not only used kinship terms to refer to a sworn brother's family but actually treated that family as kin. They took in their sworn brother, feasted him, and gave him gifts on the occasions of marriage and childbirth. It was also imperative for them to help a sworn brother's family enmeshed in difficulties. If a member was away from home on business or in prison, a brother who neglected the responsibility of looking after that member's family would be subject to having an ear cut off. Indeed, punishment was severe for any breach of trust concerning kinship relationships. A member who had illicit sexual relations with a brother's wife, concubine, or daughter could be put to death "beneath ten thousand knives" or by drowning. A member's obligations to a brother's family continued even after the brother's death, for he was expected to protect the deceased member's family from being oppressed.[125] The Triads also considered it incestuous to marry a brother's widow and would impose the death penalty on any member who did so.[126] The Triads thus not only adopted traditional Chinese kinship norms but also set up sanctions to uphold the quasi-kinship system.

In spite of the Triads' rigid regulations governing members' relationships, their moral paradigm was sometimes flouted and even violated outright. In 1787–1788 during the Lin Shuangwen Rebellion, Zhuang Datian, a rebel leader of the Heaven and Earth Society in southern Taiwan, attempted to extort money from a wealthy member; when he refused, Zhuang killed the fellow member's parents.[127] Another incident took place in Hunan's Lanshan county, where a Three-in-One Society member reportedly committed adultery with his fellow member's wife in 1831.[128] Incidents like these voided the principle that membership was an amulet providing mutual protection and impelled the Triads to formulate more elaborate oaths and stringent rules to specify punishments, some of which were more severe than those enacted in the Qing penal code. The Triads' own compliance structure and regulations in effect rejected the validity of the state judicial system.[129] Yet in theory, filial piety and fidelity to the families of fellow members remained the first of their thirty-six oaths.

In theory, too, the political ideology of the Triads, as they emerged in the last quarter of the eighteenth century, was to challenge the Qing government. According to legend, the Heaven and Earth Society was founded for anti-Qing purposes, but this allegation has not been substantiated by historical evidence. Though their documents showed a trace of Ming restorationism before the nineteenth century, the Triads normally revolted only in response to local officials' efforts to curb their activities. The oath of the Heaven and Earth Society that Lin Shuangwen joined in Taiwan in 1784 included the phrase *"mingzhu chuanzong"* (the Ming ruler will continue the family line), and the initiates were informed of a shibboleth, *mulidoushi* (literally "wood," "establishment," "bushel," and "generation"), which implied the prognostication that the Qing dynasty would fall.[130] It is doubtful, however, that the Society's members took these two phrases seriously, for some of them joined the opponents of the revolt and even led villagers to attack their rebel brothers during the Lin Shuangwen Rebellion in 1787–1788.[131] Throughout this uprising, the rebels never brought up any political slogan with racial overtones. The Triads nonetheless continued their use of politicized phrases. A member of a Heaven and Earth Society in Guangdong captured in 1790 acknowledged that he had been instructed to "follow heaven's will, submit to the Ming, cooperate and be in harmony with each other" *(shuntian fuming he hetong)*.[132] A document of the Heaven and Earth Society that could be traced to Zhejiang in 1793 included the phrase, "oppose the Qing and restore the Ming," but the member in possession of the document, who had bought a *jiansheng* degree, was engaged in such activities as robbery and the abduction of women in Guangxi.[133] The anti-Qing and pro-Ming ideology of the Triads, if only a rationale for their violation of Qing laws, became more pronounced in the course of time. In 1795, when the Heaven and Earth Society under the leadership of Chen Zhou-quan revolted in Taiwan, it clearly indicated a determination "to struggle for the heavenly way and strive for the control of the state" *(zhengtian duoguo)*.[134] Nonetheless, in their revolts until the end of the eighteenth century, Triad persons were not known to have been identified as explicitly declaring support for the slogan of "oppose the Qing and restore the Ming."

As popular uprisings intensified with the White Lotus rebellion in Hubei, Sichuan, and Shanxi in 1786–1804, the Triads in South China also became more politically oriented and began in the early nineteenth century to add clearly ethnic overtones to their slogans. In 1800 the Triads led by Chou Daqin in Guangdong's Yangjiang county spread the pithy catchphrase "restore the Ming throne" *(huifu mingzuo)*, which he copied from a covenant text owned by a southern Fujian man from Zhangzhou. His main purpose in inducting eighty-six people into his organization, however, was to assist in his effort to avenge a brother Triad who had been beaten up by a fellow member belonging to the local gentry.[135] The following year, a Triad organized by a private tutor named Lin Tianshen in Guangdong used these words as part of its initiation vow:

> Restore the Ming, ten thousand surnames have the same origin.
> Together return to the same Hong;
> Mutually rule the country and share the worship of the gods of
>   the soil and grain;
> We gather here in morning and will spread our names in history.[136]

Many followers were at first not aware of such a political cause and expressed their reservations about being initiated, after hearing these words. Lin shrewdly reassured some of his ninety-nine followers that the "old vow" was merely to the effect that "people worked together all of one mind." The vow was actually used to justify their plan to plunder villages.[137] The leaders of the 1802 uprising in Guangdong's Bole county, however, continued to appeal for Ming restoration, writing on their flags the slogan: "The catch phrase *mulidoushi* has been known to the world; following Heaven's will to revive the Ming is our covenant."[138] Yet in Dongwan county in the same province the following year, Cai Tingshi's avowed purpose in organizing a Heaven and Earth Society was to muster some 120 people to loot the house of a merchant of his own lineage who had refused to sell him rice at a lower price.[139] In spite of such activities advancing personal interests, the Triads continued to make statements with racial overtones, as revealed in an oath in Jiangxi in 1806: "Ming princes and officials Li, Zhu, and Hong [three surnames commonly used by the Triads] will transform the state and return it to the house of Han."[140] The beginning of the oath of a Heaven and Earth Society in Guangxi in 1808 disclosed its politicized goal succinctly: "Restore the Ming by removing the Qing" and "make concerted efforts to regain the empire of the authentic ruler."[141] The message tinged with Han ethnocentrism was to become a ready-made catchphrase of the Triads during the nineteenth century.

As the politicized anti-Qing and pro-Ming catchphrase became a convenient slogan to rally disgruntled people for various purposes, the Triads gradually elaborated on its contents. The origin myth of the Heaven and Earth Society developed during the first decade of the nineteenth century further provided it with a historical apologia. A Triad register discovered in Guangxi in 1811 includes a passage tracing the legendary founding of the Heaven and Earth Society by the heroic monks of Shaolin Monastery in the Kangxi period (1662–1722); it also incorporated several poems advocating restoration of the Ming house: "Someday the Yellow River naturally will be utterly pure [*jueqing,* a pun for exterminating the Qing dynasty]. May we not have a chance to restore the Ming?" "People in the world know that the Qing should be eliminated. The covenant [accepted by people as far away as] ten thousand *li* [approximately 3,300 miles] is for the restoration of the Ming." "If the Ming emperor ascends the throne, the unified empire will be perfect." The catechism used by the Triad initiates was also to include such unequivocally political pronouncements as "You cannot smoke until you exterminate the Qing and restore the Ming."[142] Such politically sensitive phrases as "restore the Ming" and "support the Ming" were to appear repeatedly in Triad registers in later times.[143]

Regardless of whether the politicized slogans actually reflected an anti-Manchu sentiment, they did serve to cover the Triads' "strategic" secrets, if not also successfully providing a rationale for their predatory activities. Of the ninety-six Triads whose organizational aims could be traced to the period between the 1790s and 1830s, thirty-nine existed primarily for the purposes of looting other people's houses; twenty-six for mutual protection in emergencies; fifteen for collecting initiation fees; eleven for plundering in villages, towns, and cities; and five for resistance to arrest and participation in communal strife.[144] To this list may be added the wreaking of vengeance, that of a hired laborer in Guangxi's Shanglin county in 1804, when he assembled thirty-one members of an Adding Brothers Society in his attempt to attack a licensed monopolist who had not only refused to sell him saltpeter but had turned him over to local authorities.[145] None of these Triads were organized for the seizure of political power. As the anti-Qing and pro-Ming catchword became stale in the 1840s, the Triads in Guangxi used another slogan, "Rob the rich to relieve the poor," to attract the local populace.[146] For all its appeal, the new slogan was evidently merely intended to justify the Triads' illicit activities.

Although primarily secular organizations, the Triads graced their social ideas with a vague utopian vision. Their dreamland was called the City of Poplars (Muyangcheng), a Buddhist name for paradise, which was also the place where, according to legend, the Heaven and Earth Society was founded. It was a Triad normative *communitas* of comradely harmony, in which righteous people lived.[147] It was supposedly a walled city of affluence where "granaries are filled to the brim with rice." In the initiation ceremony, the city was symbolized by a wooden dipper stuffed with rice and decorated with flags and other paraphernalia.[148] The "truly imposing City" was located in "the Heaven-and-Earth circle" *(qiankun)* and was "as high as one's eyes can reach" and "as broad as the two Capitals and thirteen provinces." Triad members believed it was originally founded by Emperor Taizong (r. 627–649) of the Tang dynasty (618–906) and reestablished by Wan Yunlong of the Heaven and Earth Society. The city was said to be surrounded by 3 moats and 3 layers of wall, and guarded at 4 main gates, 8 side gates, and 21 watchtowers, all of which were erected with the bricks of the Ming dynasty. Inside the city, there were 3 temples, named after the goddess of mercy, Guan Yu, and Gaoxi (a village in southern Fujian where Monk Hong Er proselytized in the years 1762–1779). There were also 3 pagodas, 5 wells, 5 orchards with 108 plum or peach trees, 108 houses, and 108 shops selling a great variety of merchandise. Stationed in the city were a million soldiers who would "exterminate the Qing and restore the great Ming." The city, then, would be "the seat of great peace."[149]

The confraternity was thus transformed into a dreamland of plenty, greatness, and glory. The image of the City of Poplars not only was supposed to enhance the members' anti-Manchu stance, but also served to romanticize their social idea of universal brotherhood.

In summary, then, the secret societies collectively known as Triads in South China and Taiwan had originated in sworn brotherhood for the purpose of facilitating mutual assistance. The members used the association not only to protect themselves but also to participate in communal strife and other illicit activities. Their flouting of the law notwithstanding, the Triads integrated cosmological beliefs with ethical principles and appealed to members with traditional norms anchored in popular orthodoxy. They never directly challenged the Chinese kinship system; in fact, people who lacked family ties found a home in the Triads. Even as the Triads shifted members' loyalty from family to the organization, they recognized the indispensability of kinship relationships and sought to counterbalance the possible debilitating effect of their activities on family ties. The Triads thus should not be regarded as heterodox in the sense of the Chinese term *"xie."* Even in revolt, they never suggested changing the entire system of institutions that supported the state. They launched their first large-scale revolt against government persecution in Taiwan in 1787–1788, but it was not until after 1800 that they regularly used the slogan of "oppose the Qing and restore the Ming." The Ming was, after all, an imperial dynasty. For the ideologically backward-looking Triads, their catchphrase of reestablishing the Ming empire served well as a "myth" that united members for nonpolitical activities in the early nineteenth century.[150] The Triads used the orthodox idea of implementing the Way in accordance with Heaven's will to justify their cause, and insofar as they stimulated Chinese anti-Manchu consciousness, they served as an organizational model for other rebel groups during the nineteenth century.

Notes

The following abbreviation is used in the notes to this chapter:

TDH   Zhongguo renmin daxue Qingshi yanjiusuo (Qing History Research Institute, Chinese People's University) and Zhongguo diyi lishi dang'anguan (Chinese First Historical Archives), eds., *Tiandihui* [The Heaven and Earth Society], 7 vols. (Beijing: Zhongguo renmin daxue, 1980–1988).

1. See Barend J. ter Haar, "Messianism and the Heaven and Earth Society: Approaches to Heaven and Earth Society Texts," in David Ownby and Mary S. Heidhues, eds., *"Secret Societies" Reconsidered* (Armonk, N.Y.: M. E. Sharpe, 1993), 153–176. Also cf. his *Ritual and Mythology of the Chinese Triads* (Leiden: E. J. Brill, 1998).

2. Ibid., 154.

3. Ibid., 15.

4. David Ownby, *Brotherhoods and Secret Societies in Early and Mid-Qing China* (Stanford: Stanford University Press, 1996), 142.

5. Ibid., 4.

6. In Ownby and Heidhues, eds., *"Secret Societies" Reconsidered*, 16.

7. For the variant names of the Triads, see Liu Ziyang, "Qingdai mimi huidang dang'an shiliao gaishu" [A brief survey of the archives of secret societies during the Qing dynasty], in Zhongguo huidangshi Yanjiuhui (Association for the study of the history of Chinese secret societies), ed., *Huidang shi yanjiu* [Studies on the history of secret societies] (Shanghai: Xuelin, 1987), 311. These do not include religious sects. In the Qing archives, 107 religious sects have been identified; see Liu Ziyang, "Qingdai mimi zongjiao dang'an shiliao gaishu" [A brief survey of the archives of religious sects during the Qing dynasty], *Lishi dang'an*, 1986, 3:127–132. Cai Shaoqing has counted 215 secret societies and religious sects; for the names of 175 of these associations, see his *Zhongguo mimi shehui* [Chinese secret societies] (Hangzhou: Zhejiang renmin, 1989), 6–7. Cf. Liu Zhengyun's recent survey cited in the introduction to this volume, note 41.

8. Dian H. Murray, *The Origin of the Tiandihui: The Chinese Triads in Legend and History* (Stanford: Stanford University Press, 1994).

9. Elizabeth J. Perry, *Rebels and Revolutionaries in North China* (Stanford: Stanford University Press, 1980); Harry J. Lamley, "Lineage and Surname Feuds in Southern Fujian and Eastern Guangdong Under the Ch'ing," in Kwang-Ching Liu, ed., *Orthodoxy in Late Imperial China* (Berkeley: University of California Press, 1990), 255–278.

10. *Gongzhongdang Yongzhengchao zouzhe* [Memorials of the reign of Yongzheng in the imperial archives] (Taibei: National Palace Museum, 1978), 7:32. For the constant shortage of rice supply in Fujian, cf. Yeh-chien Wang, "Food Supply in Eighteenth-Century Fujian," *Late Imperial China* 7, no. 2 (1986): 80–111; Zhu Weigan, *Fujian shigao* [A draft history of Fujian] (Fuzhou: Fujian jiaoyu, 1986), 2:474–487; Jiang Jianping, *Qingdai qianqi migu maoyi yanjiu* [Study on the rice trade of the Qing dynasty before the mid-nineteenth century] (Beijing: Beijing Daxue, 1992), 113–120.

11. *Gongzhongdang Yongzhengchao zouzhe*, 8:25; Peng Zeyi, ed., *Zhongguo jindai shougong'ye shi ziliao* [Source materials of handicraft industry in modern China] (Beijing: Zhonghua, 1962), 1:430–431; Maeda Katsutaro, "Shincho no Kōtō ni okeru nomin tōsō no kuban" [The base of peas-

ants' struggle in Guangdong during the Qing dynasty], *Tōyōgakuhō* 51, no. 4 (1969): 458–463; Liu Yongcheng, "Qing qianqi Guangdong Fujian nongcun zhuanyehu jianxi" [A preliminary analysis of the households of specialized occupations in Guangdong and Fujian in the Qing dynasty before the mid-nineteenth century], *Pingzhun xuekan* [Journal of Chinese economic history] 5, no. 1 (Beijing: Guangming ribao, 1989): 135–142; Yamamoto Susumu, "Shindai Kōtō no shohin seisan to Kōsei kome ryūtsū" [The production of commercial crops in Guangdong and the circulation of Guangxi rice during the Qing dynasty], *Tōyōgakuhō* 71, no. 3–4 (1990): 140–148.

12. Guo Songyi, "Qingdai de renkou zengjia he renkou liuqian" [Population growth and migration during the Qing dynasty], in *Qingshiluncong* [Studies on the history of the Qing dynasty] (Beijing: Zhonghua, 1984), 5:105–106.

13. Ibid., 112–115, 120–121; Liu Hang, "Lun Qingdai pengmin de huji wenti" [On the problem of domicile of shanty people in the Qing period], *Zhongguo shehui jingji shi yanjiu* 1 (1983): 17–20.

14. He Changling, comp., *Huangchao jingshi wenbian* [Collection of memorials on statecraft during the Qing dynasty] (Taibei: Shijie, 1964), 42:7b; Luo Ergang, "Taiping tianguo geming qian de renkou yapo wenti" [On the problem of population pressure prior to the Taiping revolution], *Zhongguo shehui jingji shijikan* 8, no. 1 (1949): 63; Wang Yaosheng, "Shilun Qingdai youmin" [Vagrant people in the Qing dynasty], *Zhongguoshi yanjiu* 3 (1991): 77.

15. For discussions, see Song Yuwen, *Sanguo zatan* [Studies on the Three Kingdoms] (Taibei: Wenxing, 1966), 1–6; Huang Huajie, *Guan Gong de renge yu shenge* [The personality and deification of Duke Guan] (Taibei: Shangwu, 1967), 20–23.

16. Li Guangtao, "Qing Taizong yu Sanguo yanyi" [Qing Taizong and *Romance of the Three Kingdoms*], *Bulletin of the Institute of History and Philology*, Academia Sinica, 12 (1946): 251–272.

17. Huang, *Guan Gong*, 142–143, 146.

18. *Shuihu zhuan* [Water Margin] (Beijing: Renmin, 1962), 1155–1156. For the social background of *Shuihu* heroes, see He Xin, *Shuihu yanjiu* [A study of *Water Margin*] (Shanghai: Shanghai wenyi lianhe, 1954), 241–262; Jean Chesneaux, "The Modern Relevance of *Shui-hu chuan*: Its Influence in Nineteenth and Twentieth Century China," *Papers on Far Eastern History* (Australian National University, 1971), 3:13–15.

19. *MingQing neige daku shiliao* [Grand Secretariat archives of the Ming and Qing dynasties] (Shenyang: Dongbei tushuguan, 1949), 1:429–430; *Xiamen zhi* [Gazetteer of Amoy] (Taibei: Bank of Taiwan, 1961), 652–653; Wang Liqi, "Shuihuzhuan yu nongmin geming" [*Water Margin* and peasant revolutions], in *Shuihu yanjiu lunwenji* [Collected essays on the

study of *Water Margin*] (Beijing: Zuojia, 1957), 61–75; Wang Xiaochuan, actually Wang Liqi, ed., *Yuan Ming Qing sandai jinhui xiaoshuo xiqu shiliao* [Historical sources concerning the prohibition and destruction of the novels and plays during the Yuan, Ming, and Qing dynasties] (Beijing: Zuojia, 1958), 15, 17, 24–25, 37, 41, 53, 73, 121; Wu Zhefu, *Qingdai jinhui shumu yanjiu* [A study on the books banned and burned in the Qing dynasty] (Taibei: Jiaxin shuini gongsi wenhua jijinhui, 1969), 68–72.

20. *Fujian shengli* [Regulations and precedents of Fujian province] (Taibei: Bank of Taiwan, 1964), 1019–1020; Sakura Magazo, *Taifeng zazhi* [Miscellaneous notes on Taiwanese customs] (Taibei: Bank of Taiwan, 1961), 30–31.

21. Robert Rulmann, "Traditional Heroes in Chinese Popular Fiction," in Arthur Wright, ed., *The Confucian Persuasion* (Stanford: Stanford University Press, 1960), 174. For the development of the cult of Guan Yu, cf. R. F. Johnston, "The Cult of Military Heroes in China," *New China Review* 3, no. 1 (1921): 49–55; Lewis Hodous, *Folkways in China* (London: Arthur Probsthain, 1922), 164–177; Huang Huajie, *Guan Gong*, 88–122; Winston L. Y. Yang, "From History to Fiction—the Popular Image of Kuan Yu," *Rendition* 15 (spring 1981): 67–79; Prasenjit Duara, "Superscribing Symbols: The Myth of Guandi, Chinese God of War," *Journal of Asian Studies* 48, no. 4 (1988): 780–790.

22. *Xing'an huilan* [Conspectus of penal cases] (Shanghai: Tushu jicheng ju, 1886; reprint, Taibei: Chengwen, 1968), 12.21a–b; translated in Derk Bodde and Clarence Morris, *Law in Imperial China* (Cambridge, Mass.: Harvard University Press, 1967), 290–291.

23. *Qinding pingding Taiwan jilue* [Imperially authorized record of the pacification of the Lin Shuangwen Rebellion] (Taibei: Bank of Taiwan, 1961), 514–515.

24. Hong Minlin, "Qingdai Guanshengdimiao dui Taiwan zhengzhi shehui zhi yingxiang" [Political and social impact of Guan Yu temples on Taiwan in the Qing dynasty], *Taiwan wenxian* 16, no. 2 (1965): 53–59; Michael Saso, *Taiwan Feasts and Customs* (Xinzhu: Chabanel Language Institute, 1968), 24–26; Gerald P. Kramer and George Wu, *An Introduction to Taiwanese Folk Religions* (Taibei: published by the authors, 1970), 27

25. The 1732 edition of *Da Qing huidian* [Collected rules of the great Qing dynasty], cited in He Zhiqing, "Lun Tiandihui de qiyuan" [On the origin of the Heaven and Earth Society], in *Qingshi luncong* 5 (1984): 248. Also see Zhuang Jifa, "Cong Qingdai lüli de xiuding kan mimi huidang de qiyuan ji qi fazhan" [Origin and development of secret societies as seen from the revisions of the statutes and substatutes of the Qing dynasty], *Guoli Taiwan shifan daxue lishi xuebao* 19 (1990): 143.

26. Yao Qisheng, *Youweixuan wengao* (Announcements of Yao Qisheng), cited in Deng Kongzhao, "Cong Kangxi qianqi Fujian huidang

huodong de jitiao shiliao tan Tiandihui qiyuan" [The origin of the Heaven and Earth Society as seen from several items of historical sources concerning the activities of secret societies in Fujian in the early Kangxi period], *Qingshi yanjiu,* 1993, 1:96–98.

27. Chinese First Historical Archives, ed., *Yongzhengchao Hanwen zhupi zouzhe huibian* [Collected Chinese-language memorials with imperial comments of the reign of Yongzheng] (Nanjing: Jiangsu guji, 1989), 16: 246–248.

28. *Gongzhongdang Qianlongchao zouzhe* [Memorials of the reign of Qianlong at the Imperial Archives] (Taibei: National Palace Museum, 1982), 22:805. A clause to the Qing penal code introduced in 1774 stipulated that the leaders of blood-oath brotherhoods consisting of more than twenty members and the leaders of non-blood-oath brotherhoods of more than forty members were to face death by strangulation. *Da Qing lichao shilu* [Veritable records of successive reigns of the great Qing dynasty] (reprint, Taibei: Hualian, 1964), *Gaozong,* 951:10b–11b [13875–13876]; *Da Qing lüli huitong xinzuan* [Comprehensive new edition of the statutes and substatutes of the great Qing dynasty] (1874 ed.; reprint, Taibei: Wenhai, 1964), 22:9a–12b; George Thomas Staunton, trans., *Ta Tsing Leu Lee* (London: Cadell and Davies, 1810), 546–548; Guy Boulais, trans., *Manuel du code Chinois* (Shanghai: Imprimerie de la Mission Catholique, 1924), 468–469.

29. "Zeng Wangyan zougao" [Memorials of Zeng Wangyan], in Graduate Institute of Liberal Arts, Beijing University, ed., *Taiping tianguo shiliao* [Source materials concerning the Taiping Heavenly Kingdom] (Beijing: Kaiming, 1950), 524.

30. *Yongzheng zhupi zouzhe xuanji* [Selections from the memorials to Emperor Yongzheng with the emperor's comments] (Taibei: Bank of Taiwan, 1972), 167–169; *Gongzhongdang Yongzhengchao zouzhe,* 11:67–69; *Qing shilu, Renzong,* 304:24a–25a [4538–4539]. Cf. Sasaki Masaya, *Shinmatsu no himitsu kessha zempen, Tenchikai no seiritsu* [Secret societies in the late Qing period, part 1: The formation of the Heaven and Earth Society] (Tokyo: Gannandō shoten, 1970), 245–249; Zhuang Jifa, "Cong Qingdai lüli kan mimi huidang," 143–144. Another Association for Parents was organized in Guangdong's Chaozhou prefecture in 1731; *Yongzheng Hanwen zhupi zouzhe,* 21:362, 388, 436, 673.

31. Chinese First Historical Archives, ed., *Qianlongchaoshangyudang* [The archives of imperial edicts of the reign of Qianlong] (Beijing: Dangan, 1991), 1:817. *Qing shilu, Gaozong,* 171:20b–21a [2524–2525].

32. For different names of the Tiandihui, see Dai Xuanzhi, "Tiandihui mingcheng de yanbian" [The evolution of the different names of the Tiandihui], *Nanyang daxue xuebao* 4 (1970): 149–165; Wang Ermin, "Mimi zongjiao yu mimi huishe zhi shengtai huanjing ji shehui gongneng" [Ecological and social functions of sects and secret societies], *Journal of the Insti-*

tute of Modern History, Academia Sinica, 10 (1980): 43–45; Qin Baoqi, *Qing qianqi Tiandihui yanjiu* [Study of the Heaven and Earth Society in the early period of the Qing dynasty] (Beijing: Zhongguo renmin daxue, 1988), 136–142.

33. For Qing documents concerning the origin of the Heaven and Earth Society, see *TDH,* 1:3–152. For recent discussions concerning the origin of the society, cf. Cai Shaoqing, "Guanyu Tiandihui de qiyuan wenti" [On the problem concerning the origin of the Heaven and Earth Society], *Beijing daxue xuebao,* (1964), 1:53–64; *Zhongguo jindai huidang shi yanjiu* [Studies on the history of secret societies in modern China] (Beijing: Zhonghua, 1987), 45–65; Dai Xuanzhi, "Origin of the Heaven and Earth Society," Ronald Suleski, trans., *Modern Asian Studies* 11, no. 3 (1977): 405–425; *Zhongguo mimi zongjiao yu mimi huishe* [Secret religious sects and secret societies of China] (Taibei: Shangwu, 1990), 707–726; Sasaki Masaya, *Shinmatsu no himitsu kessha zempen,* 54–86; Weng Tongwen, "Taiyang danchenjie de qiyuan yu Tiandihui" [The origin of the sun's birthday festival and the Heaven and Earth Society], *Shixue huikan* (Yangmingshan, Taiwan, 1976), 7:190–196; "Kangxi chuye yi Wan weixing jituan yudang jianli Tiandihui" [The remaining members of the Wan-surnamed group founded the Heaven and Earth Society in the early years of the Kangxi period], *Shixue huiji* [Collected papers in history], in Zhonghua xueshu yu xiandai wenhua congshu [Chinese learning and contemporary culture series], (Taibei, 1977), 3:437–448; "Lun Fudezhengshenci yuanyu Tiandihui zhi Simuxing" [The temple of the God of Earth originated in the Simuxing of the Heaven and Earth Society], *Dongwu wenshi xuebao* 3 (1978): 1–13; Hu Zhusheng, "Tiandihui qiyuan chutan" [A preliminary study of the origin of the Heaven and Earth Society], *Lishixue jikan* (Beijing, December 1979): 4:62–76; "Tiandihui qiyuan yu Qianlong zhongye shuo boyi" [A rebuttal to the hypothesis that the Heaven and Earth Society began in the middle period of Qianlong], in *Huidangshi yanjiu,* 75–94; Qin Baoqi, "Cong dang'an shiliao kan Tiandihui de qiyuan" [The origin of the Heaven and Earth Society as seen from the archival historical sources], *Lishi dangan* (1982) 2:93–100; "Tiandihui qiyuan Qianlong shuo xinzheng" [New evidence concerning the founding of the Heaven and Earth Society in the Qianlong period], *Lishi dang'an* (1986) 1:92–100; "Ping Tiandihui qiyuan Kangxi shuo" [A critique on the hypothesis that the Heaven and Earth Society began in the Kangxi period], in *Huidang shi yanjiu,* 95–111; *Qing qianqi Tiandihui yanjiu,* 61–107; Zhuang Jifa, "Qingdai Tiandihui qiyuan kao" [On the origin of the Heaven and Earth Society in the Qing period], *Shihuo* 9, no. 12 (1980): 483–494; "Cong guoli gugong bowuyuan diancang Qingdai dang'an tan Tiandihui de yuanliu" [The origin of the Heaven and Earth Society as seen from the Qing archives deposited at the National Palace Museum], *Gugong jikan* 14, no. 4 (1980): 63–91; *Qingdai Tiandihui Yuanliukao* [Studies on the origin and develop-

ment of the Heaven and Earth Society during the Qing dynasty] (Taibei: National Palace Museum, 1981), 6–17; Zhang Xingbo, "Tiandihui de qiyuan" [The origin of the Heaven and Earth Society], in *Ming Qing shi guoji xueshu taolunhui lunwenji* [Papers presented at the international symposium on the history of the Ming and Qing dynasties] (Tianjin: Renmin, 1982), 1040–1052; He Zhiqing, "Tiandihui qiyuan Qianlong shuo zhiyi" [Doubts regarding the founding of the Heaven and Earth Society in the Qianlong period], *Zhongguoshi yanjiu* (1983), 3:149–158; He Zhiqing "Lun Tiandihui de qiyuan," 238–272; "Zhongguo diyi lishi dang'anguan cang Tiandihui mengshu shici ji qi shiliao jiazhi" [The historical value of the oath of the Heaven and Earth Society preserved at Chinese First Historical Archives], in Chinese First Historical Archives, ed., *Ming Qing dang'an yu lishi yanjiu* [Ming Qing archives and historical research] (Beijing: Zhonghua, 1988), 2:816–828; "Wulana deng zouzhe yu Tiandihui qiyuan" [The memorials of Wulana and others and the origin of the Heaven and Earth Society], *Qingshi yanjiu tongxun* (1986), 4:15–20; "Luelun Tiandihui de chuangli zongzhi" [On the purposes of the founding of the Heaven and Earth Society], *Lishi dang'an* (1986), 2:89–96.

34. TDH, 1:97, 111–112, 141; 7:523–525; Qin Baoqi and Li Shoujun, eds., "Youguan Tiandihui qiyuan shiliao" [Historical material concerning the founding of the Heaven and Earth Society], *Lishi dang'an* (1986), 1:37–39. For a discussion, see Qin, "Tiandihui qiyuan Qianlong shuo," 95–100. For Zheng Kai's life, see Fang Qunda, "Tiandihui chuangshiren Tixi heshang kao" [Life of Monk Tixi, the founder of the Heaven and Earth Society], in Cai Shaoqing, ed., *Zhongguo mimi shehui gaiguan* [Collected essays on Chinese secret societies] (Nanjing: Jiangsu renmin, 1998), 322–332. Zhang Tan considers Zheng Kai to be Wan Yunlong; see his "Wan Yunlong de muqin Bi Qiuniang" [Wan Yunlong's mother Bi Qiuniang], *Taiwan fengwu* 33, no. 4 (1983): 57–67.

35. *TDH*, 7:528–533; *Gongzhongdang Qianlongchao zouzhe* 32:153–154, 343–344; 60:1–2; He Zhiqing, "Lun Lu Mao qiyi ji qi xiangguan zhu wenti" [On the Lu Mao uprising and its related problems], in *Zhongguo nongmin zhanzhengshi luncong* [Collected essays on the history of Chinese peasant uprisings] (Beijing: Zhongguo shehui kexue, 1987), 5:358–409; Liu Bohan, "Cong Cui Yingjie deng sanjian zouzhe kan Tiandihui de junshi zuzhi secai" [The militarized organization of the Heaven and Earth Society as seen from three memorials presented by Cui Yingjie and others], *Lishi dang'an* (1987), 2:86–88; Murray and Qin, *Tiandihui*, 18–19.

36. *TDH*, 7:522–527, 534–540; Murray and Qin, *Tiandihui*, 19–20.

37. Another rebel leader Zhuang Datian (1738–1788) was not captured until March 12, 1788, on the southern tip of Taiwan. *TDH*, 1:301; 2:228; *Junjidang* [Grand Council archives] (Taibei: National Palace Museum), 38807, 38813; *Gongzhongdang Qianlongchao zouzhe* [Collected memorials

during the reign of Emperor Qianlong as preserved at Imperial Archives]
(Taibei: National Palace Museum, 1982–1988), 66:864. For original
sources regarding the Lin Shuangwen Rebellion, see *Junjidang; Taiwan dang*
[Archives concerning the rebellions of Lin Shuangwen and Chen Zhou-
quan] (Beijing: Chinese First Historical Archives), nos. 1855–1867, vols.
1–12; *Guangzhongdang Qianlongchao zouzhe*, vols. 62–68; Qianlongchao
shangyudang [Archives of the imperial edicts during the reign of Emperor
Qianlong] (Beijing: Dangan, 1991), vols. 13–16; *Pingding Taiwan jishi benmo*
[A complete chronicle of suppression of the Lin Shuangwen Rebellion in
Taiwan] (Taibei: Bank of Taiwan, 1958); *Qinding pingding Taiwan jilue;
Taian huilu gengji* [Collected source materials on the Taiwanese series, no.
7] (Taibei: Bank of Taiwan, 1964); *Kang Yong Qian shiqi chengxiang renmin
fankang douzheng ziliao* [Materials concerning popular uprisings in urban
and rural areas during the Kangxi, Yongzheng, and Qianlong periods] (Bei-
jing: Zhonghua, 1979), 772–819; *Taiwan Lin Shuangwen qiyi ziliao xuanbian*
[Selected materials of the Lin Shuangwen Rebellion in Taiwan] (Fuzhou:
Fujian renmin, 1984); *TDH*, vols. 1–5.

38. *Da Qing lüli huiji beilan* [Collected references on the statutes and
substatutes of the great Qing] (1904 ed.), 23:16a–17a. Cf. Alexander Wylie,
"Secret Societies in China," in his *Chinese Researches* (Shanghai: n.p., 1897),
113.

39. *TDH*, 6:11–69, 73–78, 86–136; *Tai'an huilu jiji* [Collected source
materials on the Taiwanese series, no. 6] (Taibei: Bank of Taiwan, 1964),
115–128, 393–394; *Qing shilu, Gaozong*, 11476:16a–17a [21890–21891],
11478:11a–12a [21914].

40. Xu Zonggan, *Siweixinzhai zalu* [Miscellaneous notes of Xu
Zonggan] (Taibei: Bank of Taiwan, 1960), 89–91. For this uprising, also cf.
George Hughes, *Amoy and Its Surrounding Districts* (Hong Kong: Printed by
De Souza and Co., 1872), 28–44; Sasaki Masaya, ed., *Shinmatsu no himitsu
kessha shiryohen* [Collected materials concerning the secret societies in the
mid-nineteenth century] (Tokyo: Kindai Chūgoku kenkyū i-inkai, 1967),
246–248; Tang Tianyao, "Guanyu yibawusannian Minnan Xiaodaohui qiyi
de jige wenti" [Several issues concerning the uprising of the Small Sword
Society in southern Fujian in 1853], in *Huidang shi yanjiu*, 152–165.

41. *TDH*, 5:363–374, 424–425, 432–433, 435–436; 6:181, 244; *Qing
shilu, Gaozong*, 1297:28a–29b [19120–19121]; Murray, *Origin of the Tiandihui* 45.

42. *TDH*, 5:419.

43. T. J. Newbold and F. W. Wilson, "The Chinese Secret Triad Society of T'ien-ti-hui," *Journal of the Royal Asiatic Society of Great Britain and
Ireland* 6 (1840): 133.

44. *TDH*, 6:7–28, 31–47, 117–118; *Qing shilu, Renzong*, 103:12b–13a
[1438–1439], 104:2b–4b [1447–1448], 105:2a–3b [1459–1460]; *Huizhou
fuzhi* [Gazetteer of Huizhou prefecture] (1881 ed.; reprint, Taibei: Cheng-

wen, 1966), 18:16b–17a [178–179]; Sasaki Masaya, "Juntoku ken kyōshin to Tōkai jurokusa" [The gentry of Shunde county and Donghai district], *Kindai Chūgoku kenkyū* (Tokyo), 3:203.

45. *TDH*, 6:447–453, 496–500, 508–509, 518, 521; *Qingdai qiju-zhuce, Daoguangchao* [Qijuzhu of the Qing dynasty, the reign of Daoguang] (Taibei: Lianjing, 1985), 21:12445–12448. "Zeng Wangyan zougao," 523–525; *Da Qing shichao shengxun* [Imperial instructions of the ten reigns of the great Qing dynasty] (Reprint; Taibei: Wenhai, 1965), *Renzong*, 101:1b [1018]; Sasaki Masaya, "Kampō jyūnen kōto Tenchikai no hanran" [The Triad uprising in Guangdong in 1854], *Kindai Chūgoku kenkyū senta iho* (Tokyo, April 1963), 2:3.

46. *TDH*, 7:181–189; *Qing shilu, Renzong*, 176:30a–31b [1567–1568].

47. Ibid., 248:23b–24a [3664], 249:10b–11b [3673–3674], 284:31b–32b [4226], 364:15a–b [5350], 371:6b–8a [5441–5442]; *Qing shilu, Xuan-zong*, 3:3a–4a [110], 12:16a–17a [242–243], 16:8a–b [312]. For population increase and resultant change in Guangxi, see Li Peiran, Deng Jiezhang, Zhu Zhefang, and Peng Dayong, "Taiping tianguo qiyi qianye de Guangxi shehui" [Society in Guangxi on the eve of the Taiping Rebellion], in *Taiping tianguo shi xintan* [New studies on the history of the Taiping Rebellion] (Nanjing: Jiangsu renmin, 1982), 164–165; "Lun Qing Daoguangchao yiqian Guangxi renkou zengjia yu Taiping tianguo geming de baofa" [Population increase in Guangxi before the Daoguang period and the outbreak of the Taiping Rebellion], *Taiping tianguo xuekan* (Beijing, 1985), 2:314–349.

48. *Yulin zhouzhi* [Gazetteer of Yulin department] (1984 ed.; reprint, Taibei: Chengwen, 1967), 18:2a [236].

49. *TDH*, 7:411–414.

50. *Qing shilu, Xuanzong*, 131:31a–b [2384], 135:23a–24a [2464], 311:16a–17b [5568–5569]; *Qing qijuzhu, Daoguang*, 10:6350–6352.

51. *Taiping tianguo geming shiqi Guangxi nongmin qiyi ziliao* [Source materials on peasant uprisings in Guangxi during the period of the Taiping Rebellion] (Beijing: Zhonghua, 1978), 1:20–21; *Taiping tianguo qiyi diaocha baogao* [A report on the investigation of the Taiping Rebellion] (Beijing: San-lian, 1956), 99–102; "Baishangdihui chengli qian Jintian diqu de jieji dou-zheng" [Class struggle in the Jintian area before the formation of the God Worshippers' Society], in *Taiping tianguo shi yanjiu wenxuan* [Selected essays on the history of the Taiping Rebellion] (Nanning: Guangxi renmin, 1981), 263, 265.

52. For a list of these seventy-seven Triad uprisings, rebel leaders, and areas of disturbances, see Fang Zhiguang and Cui Zhiqing, "Guangxi Tiandihui qiyi yu Taiping tianguo de xingqi" [Triad uprisings in Guangxi and the outbreak of the Taiping Rebellion], *Taiping tianguo xuekan* (1985), 2:380–385.

53. *Taiping tianguo Guangxi nongmin qiyi*, 1:68. See also Elizabeth Perry, "Taipings and Triads: The Role of Religion in Inter-rebel Relations,"

in Janos M. Bak and Gerhard Benecke, eds., *Religion and Rural Revolt* (Dover, N.H.: Manchester University Press, 1984), 342–353.

54. *TDH*, 6:244–416; *Qing qijuzhu, Daoguang*, 15:9427–9428; 29: 11575–11577. For the development of the Triads in Jiangxi, see also Murray, *Origin of the Tiandihui*, 51–61.

55. *Qing qijuzhu, Daoguang*, 13:7669–7671.

56. *TDH*, 7:420–428.

57. *TDH*, 7:438–440.

58. *TDH*, 7:476–477.

59. *TDH*, 6:518–519, 7:483–491, 494, 506–507, 512–514; *Qing qijuzhu, Daoguang*, 22:12916–12917; "Zeng Wangyan zougao," 523; *Qing shilu, Xuanzong*, 196:9a–11a [3527–3528]; *Da Qing shichao shengxun, Xuanzong*, 82:8b [1412]. For Triad activities in Hunan, Yunnan, and Guizhou, also cf. Murray, *Origin of the Tiandihui*, 77–81.

60. Ibid., 101:1b [1818]; Zhuang Jifa, "Taiping tianguo qishi qian de Tiandihui" [The Heaven and Earth Society before the outbreak of the Taiping rebellion], *Shihuo* 8, no. 12 (1979): 569, 571, 573.

61. *TDH*, 7:40.

62. *TDH*, 6:181, 183–184, 229, 231–233, 300ff. Cf. Zhuang Jifa, "Qingdai Min Yue diqu renkou liudong yu mimi huidang de fazhan" [Migration and the development of secret societies in Fujian and Guangdong in the Qing dynasty], in *Jindai Zhongguo chuqi lishi yantaohui lunwenji* [Collected essays of the symposium on early modern Chinese history] (Taibei: Academia Sinica, 1988), 16.

63. *TDH*, 7:476–477; *Qing shilu, Xuanzong*, 358:4b–6b [5254–5255]; Song Yaping and Wang Chengren, "Shilun Taiping tianguo geming chuqi de Hunan huidang" [The Triads in Hunan in the early period of the Taiping revolution], *Taiping tianguo xuekan* (Beijing, 1987), 4:444–445.

64. *TDH*, 7:438–439, 469–472.

65. Sasaki Masaya, "Kampō jyūnen kōtō Tenchikai," 2.

66. *Da Qing shichao shengxun, Shizong*, 26:5b [314]; *Gaozong*, 197:4a [2601]. For communal strife in southeastern China, see Harry J. Lamley, "Hsieh-tou: The Pathology of Violence in Southeastern China," *Qingshi wenti* 3, no. 7 (1977): 1–39; "Subethnic Rivalry in the Ch'ing Period," in Emily Martin Ahern and Hill Gates, eds., *The Anthropology of Taiwanese Society* (Stanford: Stanford University Press, 1981), 282–318; "Lineage and Surname Feuds in Southern Fujian and Eastern Guangdong under the Ch'ing," in Kwang-Ching Liu, ed., *Orthodoxy in Late Imperial China*, 255–278; "Lineage Feuding in Southern Fujian and Eastern Guangdong under Qing Rule," in Jonathan N. Lipman and Stevan Harrel, eds., *Violence in China* (Albany: State University of New York Press, 1990), 27–64.

67. *TDH*, 5:376–385; *Qing shilu, Gaozong*, 1373:14b–15a [20415–20416]; *Taian huilu jiji*, 378–382; *Taian huilu kuiji*, 63, 65–66, 68.

68. *TDH,* 6:73–86.

69. *Da Qing shichao shengxun, Renzong,* 101:1b [1818]; Zhang Yigui, "Shilun Jintian qiyi qian Guangxi de laike douzheng" [Strife between old and new settlers in Guangxi before the outbreak of the Taiping rebellion in Jintian], in *Taiping tiangkuo shi yanjiu wenxuan,* 65–78.

70. Sasaki Masaya, *Himitsu kessha shiryō,* 51, 241–242; "Zeng Wangyan zougao," 523.

71. Nayancheng, *Nawenyigong zouyi* [Collected memorials of Nayancheng] (1834 ed.), *Jindai Zhongguo shiliao congkan* [Modern Chinese historical materials series] (Taibei: Wenhai, 1968), 5:11, 12a, 14b–16b; *TDH,* 7:95–98, 112, 123–124, 139, 144–146.

72. *TDH,* 5:438, 450–452, 458–481.

73. *TDH,* 7:202.

74. *TDH,* 6:424–425.

75. Lu Baoqian, *Lun wan Qing Liang Guang de Tiandihui zhengquan* [On the political regimes of the Heaven and Earth Society in Guangdong and Guangxi in the late Qing period] (Taibei: Institute of Modern History, Academia Sinica, 1975), 136–142; Peng Dayong, "Jindai chuqi Guangxi Tiandihui yu Shangdihui bijiao yanjiu" [A comparative study of the Heaven and Earth Society and God Worshippers' Society in Guangxi in the early modern period], in *Taiping tianguo shi lunwenji xuji* [Collected essays on the Taiping rebellion, second series] (Nanning: Guangxi renmin, 1989), 430–434.

76. Maeda Katsutaro, "Shincho no Kōtō ni okeru nomin tōsō," 458–471, 476, 483–484.

77. *Da Qing shichao shengxun, Renzong,* 98:5b [1776]; *Xuanzong,* 82:4b [1404].

78. Gustave Schlegel, *Thian Ti Hwui, the Hung League or Heavan-Earth-League* (Batavia: Lange and Co., 1866), 138.

79. For documentation of disturbances created by Cai Qian, see *Tai'an huilu xinji* [Collected source materials on the Taiwanese series, no. 8] (Taibei: Bank of Taiwan, 1964), 7–257. For the Triads and sea piracy, see Sasaki Masaya, "Shunde ken kyoshin to Donghai," 203; *Himitsu kessha shiryō,* 53; Dian H. Murray, *Pirates of the South China Coast, 1790–1810* (Stanford: Stanford University Press, 1987), 90.

80. *Qing shilu, Xuanzong,* 12:16a–b [242]; *Taiping tianguo Guangxi nongmin qiyi ziliao,* 1:27.

81. *TDH,* 7:372–392.

82. *Guixian zhi* [Gazetteer of Guixian] (1934 ed.), 705; *Taiping tianguo diaocha,* 107–108; Liang Renbao, "Taiping tianguo he kuanggong" [The Taiping Rebellion and miners], in *Taiping tianguo shi yanjiu wenxuan,* 51–53.

83. The porters who were concentrated in urban areas had their own

groups, sometimes organized in the form of sworn brotherhood; see Sha Zhengjun, "Shilun Ming Qing shiqi de Jiangnan jiaofu" [Porters in South China during the Ming and Qing periods], *Zhongguo shi yanjiu* (1988), 4:104–106. A beggar couple joined an Adding Brothers Society in Guangdong in 1837. After her husband died in 1841, the woman beggar, née Hsiao, organized 140 beggars into an Earthenware Society (Shabaohui). Cf. Zhou Yumin, "Taiping tianguo shiqi mimi huidang yanjiu de jige wenti" [Several problems concerning the study of the secret societies during the Taiping period], *Lishi jiaoyu*, (Tianjin: Oct. 1988) 12.

84. *Qing shilu, Renzong,* 358:4b–6b [5254–5255], 364:15a–b [5350]; *Xuanzong,* 141:21b [2448]; *TDH,* 6:403–404; "Zeng Wangyan zougao," 524; Banwa jushi, "Yuekou jishi" [An account of rebellion in Guangdong], in *Taiping tianguo shiliao congbian* [Collected source materials of the Taiping Rebellion] (Beijing: Zhonghua, 1961), 1:3; Schlegel, *Thian Ti Hwui,* 138; Sasaki Masaya, *Himitsu kessha shiryō,* 109, 119; Lu Baoqian, *Wan Qing Liang Guang de Tiandihui,* 184–188.

85. He Zhiqing, "Lu Mao qiyi," 394–398.

86. *TDH,* 5:371, 416–423.

87. *TDH,* 6:440–445, 7:97.

88. *TDH,* 7:97; Maeda Katsutaro, "Shincho no Kōtō ni okeru nomin tōsō," 472–474.

89. *Yulin zhouzhi,* 18:2a [236]; *Taiping tianguo Guangxinongmin qiyi ziliao,* 1:88–89.

90. *TDH,* 6:391–393, 7:247–262, 475; Li Huan, ed., *Guochao qixian leizheng chubian* [Biographies of eminent men of the Qing dynasty, first compilation] (1884–1890 ed.; reprint, Taibei: Wenhai, 1966), 247:3a–b [8482].

91. Tanaka Issei, "Etsu-tō Tenchikai no soshiki to engeki" [The organization and stageplay of the Heaven and Earth Society in eastern Guangdong], *Tōyō bunka kenkyūjo kiyō* 111 (1990): 75–77, 92–93.

92. *TDH,* 6:304–305.

93. *TDH,* 6:433.

94. Robert Morrison, "Some Account of a Secret Association in China, Entitled the Triad Society," *Chinese Repository* 14, no. 2 (1845): 62; Schlegel, *Thian Ti Hwui,* 233; William Stanton, *The Triad Society of Heaven and Earth Association* (Hong Kong: Kelly and Walsh, 1900), 93.

95. *TDH,* 1:83, 93, 110–111.

96. *TDH,* 1:11, 6:304, 7:214; *Kang Yong Qian chengxiang douzheng,* 728; Weng Tongwen, "Fudezhengshen yu Tiandihui," 1–13. According to Tao Chengzhang, the "Five Patriarchs" were originally members of the White Lotus sect; see his "Jiaohui yuanliu kao" [On the origins of sects and secret societies], in Xiao Yishan, ed., *Jindai mimi shehui shiliao* [Historical sources on modern secret societies] (Beijing, 1935; reprint, Taibei: Wenhai, 1965), 2:6b–7a.

97. *TDH*, 1:139, 148, 151; 7:523–524.

98. *TDH*, 1:70.

99. *TDH*, 1:3; 6:171, 178, 184, 202, 225, 232, 304–305; 7:181–182, 187.

100. Schlegel, *Thian Ti Hwui*, 230–234; Xiao, *Mimi shehui shiliao*, 6:22a–b; *Taiping tianguo qiyi diaocha baogao*, 80; Cai Shaoqing, *Zhongguo jindai huidang shi*, 437–457.

101. Li Bangzheng, "Bailianjiao yu Sichuan de nongmin qiyi—jianlun zongjiao zai nongmin qiyi zhong de zuoyong" [The White Lotus and peasant uprisings in Sichuan—the role of religion in peasant uprisings], in *Ming Qing shi guoji xueshu taolun lunwenji*, 1074–1075; Yu Songqing, *Ming Qing Bailianjiao yanjiu* [Studies on the White Lotus in the Ming and Qing dynasties] (Chengdu: Sichuan renmin, 1987), 273–274.

102. Feng Zuozhe, "Jiaqing nianjian wusheng Bailianjiao da qiyi" [The uprisings of the White Lotus in five provinces during the Jiaqing period], *Qingshi luncong* 2 (1980): 169; Xu Zengzhong and Lin Yi, "Liu Zhixie zai Chuan, Chu, Shan nongmin da qiyi zhong zuoyong de kaocha" [An examination of the role of Liu Zhixie in the peasant uprisings in Szechwan, Hupeh, and Shanxi], ibid., 189. Ter Haar considers Mingzhu in a Triad to be a savior, the Luminous King, an associate of Maitreya; see his *Ritual and Mythology of the Chinese Triads*, 225–226, 264–266, 274–277.

103. *TDH*, 6:353–354; Zhuang Jifa, "Qingdai Jiaqing nianjian de Tiandihui" [The Heaven and Earth Society in the Jiaqing period of the Qing dynasty], *Shihuo* 8, no. 6 (1978): 266–267; Suzuki Chūsei, "Qianlong ichi-shichi-nen Ma Chaozhu no hanShin undo" [Ma Chaozhu's anti-Qing movement in 1752], in *Ronshū kindai Chūgoku kenkyū* [Studies in modern China] (Tokyo: Yamakawa shuppansha, 1981), 177–193. Also cf. ter Haar, *Ritual and Mythology of the Chinese Triads*, 236–250.

104. Li Xingyuan, *Li Wengonggong zouyi* [Memorials of Li Xingyuan], *Jindai Zhongguo shiliao congkan*, 7:17a–b, 8:12a–16a.

105. *Qing shilu*, *Wenzong*, 38:12b–14a [490–491].

106. *Qing shilu*, *Xuanzong*, 447:15a–17a [7782–7783], 454:4b–5a [7912–7913]; *Ganzhou fuzhi* [Gazetteer of Ganzhou prefecture] (1873 ed.), 23:6b–7b. Also cf. Asai Motoi, "Dōkō Seiren kyoan ni tsuite" [On the case of the Qinglian sect during the Daoguang period], *Tokaishigaku*, (1976), 2:80–81.

107. *TDH*, 6:244–299; Lian Lichang, *Fujian mimi shehui* [Secret societies in Fujian] (Fuzhou: Fujian renmin, 1989), 66–69; ter Haar, *Ritual and Mythology of the Chinese Triads*, 290–291, 377–379.

108. *Kang Yong Qian chengxiang douzheng*, 874–878. For an analysis of this historical document, see Dai Xuanzhi, "Tianlijiao lianhe Tiandihui qibing zhi fenxi" [An analysis of the uprising of the Tianli sect in cooperation with the Heaven and Earth Society], *Guoli zhengzhidaxue lishi xuebao* 2

(1984): 123–135. For this White Lotus rebellion, see Susan Naquin, *Millenarian Rebellion in China: The Eight Trigrams Uprising of 1813* (New Haven: Yale University Press, 1976).

109. *TDH,* 5:368–369, 374–375, 381–382, 384–385, 410–411.

110. Wu Wenrong, *Wu Wenjiegong yiji* [Collected writings of Wu Wenrong], *Jindai Zhongguo shiliao congkan,* 14:4b–15a, 15:16b; *Qing shilu, Xuanzong,* 446:18b–19b [7765–7766], 447:15a–17b [7782–7783]; Noguchi Tetsurō, "Saihi to kaihi" [White Lotus rebels and Triad rebels], in *Chūgoku kingendai shi no shomondai—Tanaka Masayoshi sensei taikan kinen ronsō* [Studies in modern China—essays in honor of Professor Tanaka Masayoshi's retirement] (Tokyo: Kokusho kankokai, 1984), 35–56.

111. George Rude, *Ideology and Popular Protest* (New York: Pantheon Books, 1980), 28, 33.

112. *TDH,* 1:3–4; 7:214. For the symbol of mountain in the Triads, cf. Jean Chesneaux, *Secret Societies in China in the Nineteenth and Twentieth Centuries,* trans. Gillian Nettler (Ann Arbor: University of Michigan Press, 1971), 67.

113. *TDH,* 1:111.

114. *Shuihu,* 1145, 1151, 1156.

115. Zhang Yuluan, "Tan 'titian xingdao' ji qita" [On 'implementing the Way on behalf of heaven' and other problems], in *Shuihu yanjiu lunwen ji,* 77–81; Sakai Tadao, "Hō no minshu no ishiki" [Popular consciousness of Chinese secret societies], *Tōyōshi kenkyū* 31, no. 2 (Sept. 1971): 96–97, 109–110.

116. The phrase often appears in Triad documents, see, for example, Schlegel, *Thian Ti Hwui,* 144; Xiao, *Mimi shehui shiliao,* 5:1b, 3b, 6a–b, 7a, 8a.

117. *Mozi jijie* [Collected commentaries on *Mozi*] (Shanghai: Shijie, 1936), 120, 417, 425.

118. Schlegel, *Thian Ti Hwui,* 145. Since the Chinese character "yi" also signifies "unreal," "artificial," and "foster," the phrase *"jieyi"* could also suggest "becoming foster brothers"; see Sun Shuyu, *Shuihuzhuan de laili xintai yu yishu* [Origin, mentality, and art of *Water Margin*] (Taibei: Shibao, 1981), 278–283.

119. Schlegel, *Thian Ti Hwui,* 153, 155.

120. *TDH,* 1:7, 11.

121. For different versions of Triad oaths and regulations, see Newbold and Wilson, "The Chinese Secret Triad Society," 136–142; "Oath Taken by Members of the Triad Society and Notices of Its Origin," *Chinese Repository* 28, no. 6 (June 1849): 282–287; Schlegel, *Thian Ti Hwui,* 135–143; Stanton, *The Triad Society,* 118–124; J. S. M. Ward and W. G. Stirling, *The Hung Society or the Society of Heaven and Earth* (London: Baskerville Press, 1925), 1:64–70; Xiao, *Mimi shehui shiiao,* 3:4b–12b; Zhu Lin, *Hong-*

men zhi [A treatise on Hung-men] (Shanghai: Zhonghua, 1947; reprint, *Mimi shehui congkan* [Secret societies series], Taibei, 1975), 26 35; Fei ling Davis, *Primitive Revolutionaries of China* (Honolulu: University of Hawai'i Press, 1971), appendix C.

122. *TDH*, 7:214.

123. *TDH*, 7:214; Schlegel, *Thian Ti Hwui*, 153, 161.

124. *TDH*, 1:111.

125. *TDH*, 6:305; 7:214; Newbold and Wilson, "The Chinese Secret Triad Society," 138; "Oath Taken by Members of the Triad Society," 285; Schlegel, *Thian Ti Hwui*, 136, 140, 142, 152–154, 160–162, 164; Stanton, *The Triad Society*, 119–121, 123; Ward and Stirling, *The Hung Society*, 1:65, 69; Xiao, *Mimi shehui shiliao*, 3:1b, 3a–b, 9a, 10a; Zhu Lin, *Hongmen zhi*, 28–31.

126. "Oath Taken by Members of the Triad Society," 286; Ward and Stirling, *The Hung Society*, 1:67; 3:66; Xiao, *Mimi shehui shiliao*, 3:3a, 10a. Some Triads might have different regulations; see Schlegel, *Thian Ti Hwui*, 164.

127. *TDH*, 1:98.

128. *TDH*, 7:512–513.

129. For a discussion, cf. Davis, *Primitive Revolutionaries*, 145–152.

130. *TDH*, 1:69–71; *Pingding Taiwan jilue*, 190, 928; Schlegel, *Thian Ti Hwui*, 24–25. Weng Tongwen has suggested that the phrase alludes to the restoration of Ming emperors; see his "Tiandihui yinyu 'muli doushi' xinyi" [A new interpretation of the argot of the Heaven and Earth Society, 'muli doushi'], *Shixue huikan* 7 (1976): 167–189.

131. *Pingding Taiwan jilue*, 928.

132. *TDH*, 5:413.

133. *TDH*, 5:328.

134. *TDH*, 6:11. *"Zhengtian"* can be translated alternatively as "the struggle for the heavenly mandate."

135. *TDH*, 6:416–420.

136. *TDH*, 6:425. The phrase "ten thousand surnames" *(wanxing)* can also be interpreted as "the surname Wan."

137. Ibid.

138. *TDH*, 7:34.

139. *TDH*, 6:446–453.

140. *TDH*, 7:34; Qin Baoqi and Liu Meizhen, "Shilun Tiandihui" [A preliminary treatise on the Heaven and Earth Society], in *Qingshi yanjiuji* [Studies on the history of the Qing dynasty] (Beijing: Zhongguo renmin daxue, 1980), 160.

141. *TDH*, 7:714.

142. *TDH*, 1:5, 6, 8, 17.

143. For more Triad slogans used after the 1820s, see *TDH*, 7:485,

507, 516; Robert Morrison, "A Transcript in Roman Characters, with a Translation of a Manifesto in the Chinese Language, Issued by the Triad Society," *Journal of the Royal Asiatic Society of Great Britain and Ireland* 1 (1834): 93–95; C. Gutzlaff, "On the Secret Triad Society of China, Chiefly from Papers Belonging to the Society Found at Hong Kong," *Journal of the Royal Asiatic Society of Great Britain and Ireland* 8 (1846): 365–367; Boris Novikov, "The Anti-Manchu Propaganda of the Triads, ca. 1800–1860," in Jean Chesneaux, ed., *Popular Movements and Secret Societies in China, 1840–1950* (Stanford: Stanford University Press, 1972), 49–63.

144. Qin Baoqi, "Tiandihui dang'an shiliao gaishu" [A brief introduction to the historical sources of the Heaven and Earth Society], *Lishi danglan* (1981): 1:116.

145. *TDH,* 7:330–331.

146. *Taiping tianguo diaocha baogao,* 83; Fang Zhiguang and Cui Zhiqing, "Guangxi Tiandihui yu Taiping tianguo," 369.

147. *TDH,* 1:18–19; Schlegel, *Thian Ti Hwui,* 45, 233; Ward and Stirling, *The Hung Society,* 2:38–41; Xiao, *Mimi shehui shiliao,* 4:29a, 5:10a. Ter Haar translates *muyangcheng* "the City of Willows"; see his *Ritual and Mythology of the Chinese Triads,* 80–87, 275–278, 445–446. For a brief discussion of *communitas,* see Victor W. Turner, *The Ritual Process* (Harmondsworth, England: Penguin Books, 1974), 119–122.

148. Stanton, *The Triad Society,* 39; Dai Xuanzhi, "Tiandihui yu Daojiao" [The Heaven and Earth Society and Daoism], *Nanyang daxue xuebao* 6 (1972): 158–159.

149. Schlegel, *Thian Ti Hwui,* 41, 92–99, 128, 193; Xiao, *Mimi shehui shiliao,* 4:8b–11b. Daniel Overmyer has suggested that the transition from Qing back to Ming echoes the concern for rebirth and salvation; see his *Folk Buddhist Religion: Dissenting Sects in Late Traditional China* (Cambridge, Mass.: Harvard University Press, 1976), 202, 259.

150. George Sorel uses "myth" to mean an ideology that expresses the determination of a group to act; see his *Reflections on Violence* (New York: Peter Smith, 1941), 22–32. Ideology is also viewed as "justification"; cf. the Frankfurt Institute for Social Research, *Aspects of Sociology,* trans. John Viertel (Boston: Beacon Press, 1972), 189. Ideology has been described as a "perpetual error" that prevents people from assessing a situation veridically; for a brief discussion, see Gary Schwartz, *Sect Ideologies and Social Status* (Chicago: The University of Chicago Press, 1970), 2–7.

CHAPTER 10

The Heaven and Earth Society in the Nineteenth Century
An Interpretation

David Faure

By virtue of the law of 1792, the Heaven and Earth Society (Tiandi hui) was regarded by the Qing dynasty government as a seditious institution.[1] The law did not specify what constituted the society's characteristics, but it became standard practice to identify it by its peculiar rites. These consisted of an initiation ceremony *(baihui)* in which members drew blood and swore to be brothers to one another, the frequent repetition of certain set phrases, and the use of various finger signs.[2] It did not matter that many groups practicing these rites did not refer to themselves as the Tiandi hui, for, the use of this name having been banned, practicing members sought to evade the law by using aliases. Some of these can be quite easily identified as variations of the original. The name Adding Brothers Society (Tiandi hui) was a homonym, the Father and Mother Society (Fumuhui) was a reference to the worship of heaven as father and earth as mother that was part of the initiation ceremony, and the Three Dots Society (Sandian hui) was a reference to the "water" radical of the character "Hong," which was the adopted surname for all members. Other names, such as the Small Sword Society (Xiaodaohui), were not so obviously related, and, even though the secret society by this name that staged an uprising in Shanghai in 1853 made use of the Heaven and Earth Society's identification symbols, other groups that were known by the same name were not necessarily part of the Heaven and Earth Society.[3]

The history of the nebulous institution is necessarily obscure. To reconstruct it, we depend to a large extent on official records. However, because the Heaven and Earth Society was outlawed, these records, like all crime reports, were written with a strong legal bias and tend to exaggerate its criminal connections. They can be supplemented by two other sources of information: documents that purport to be manuals used by groups said to be affiliated with the society and recorded evidence from overseas Chinese communities, especially in Malaya and Singapore. There, from the mid-nineteenth century, the Ghee Hin and the Hai San Societies, which practiced many of the rituals of the Heaven and Earth Society, came to be regarded as a public-order menace by the British colonial government, and a considerable amount of material was gathered on them as a result. Nevertheless, however useful the reports from overseas Chinese communities are as a supplementary source of information, it must be recognized that they were gathered outside China from a later period, and they might not be totally applicable to events on Chinese soil in the eighteenth century and the early half of the nineteenth century, the period when the Heaven and Earth Society came to be prominently noted in Qing official records. The same caution must be taken in reading the manuals. Except for one that was found during a raid on a Heaven and Earth Society in Guangxi in 1811, all those that are extant are post-Taiping, and most were discovered not in rural China but in Hong Kong and Southeast Asia. In any case, they describe the rituals of the society and not the activities of the affiliated groups. None of our source materials is, therefore, without serious shortcomings, and it should be noted at the outset that account must be taken of their problematic nature in our interpretation.[4]

The Autocephalous Structure

It is now becoming quite clear that the groups said to be affiliated with the Heaven and Earth Society were autocephalous, each having its own headmen and an independent command. However, all of them, by the second or third decade of the nineteenth century, subscribed to the belief that they had a common ancestry, which originated from an anti-Manchu tradition. This belief gave members of these groups a sense of historical purpose and bound them to the view that each was a part of a greater whole. The belief in participation in a wider community designated by a common purpose was expressed in the rituals of the society, but it is an open question if it affected the actions of individual members.

The salient features of the rituals, the activities of individual members, and the organization of the group can best be illustrated by case studies. However incomplete they are, the following four cases are among the best examples from official records:

Case 1. In 1801, a certain Lin Tianshen invited a Fujianese fortune-teller to his house to tell his fortune. The fortune-teller told him about the Heaven and Earth Society, and how as a member he could receive help when he was in trouble. He also taught Lin the secret signs and gave him a ritual text. Later, Lin collected his own disciples. He found seven people, each of whom gave him three hundred cash to buy sacrificial meat and wine, and conducted the brotherhood union *(jiebai)* in a quiet place outside the village. Lin showed his disciples the ritual text, on which was written: "All the surnames that help to restore the Ming have their ancestry from the Hong surname. They will together hold power over the land and enjoy the benefits of the soil. The day they gather, their names will be known for thousands of years."[5]

Case 2. In 1814 Ou Lang, a man of Zhangpu county, Fujian, performed an initiation ceremony *(baihui)* with thirty-six people in Xiapu county, also in Fujian. They took the name Father and Mother Society. Ou taught them the code words "three-eight-twenty-one" for the character "hong." To the question "Where do you come from and where are you going?" he taught them to answer, "From the east to the west." When asked where they would cross the river, they were to say, "Under the bridge." To pick things up and to smoke tobacco, they were to use only three fingers. They had some books, with the names Li, Zhu, Hong, and Abbot Wan written in them. They joined the society to learn these secrets.[6]

Case 3. In 1831 a Ma Shaotang of Kaitai county, Guizhou province, visited Huaiyuan county, Guangxi province, and met a Guangdong boatman, Wu Lao'er. Wu told Ma that in Guangdong there used to be an Adding Brothers Society, which later changed its name to the Triad (Sanhe hui). Members of the society had only to say certain code words and would be spared by bandits. For instance, if they were asked their surnames, they would first give their own surnames and then say that they had been changed to "Hong." All these code words were written in a book in Wu's possession. In this book, Ma saw a hexagonal figure with several lines of characters written on four sides. He also saw the characters written with the "tiger" *(hu)* radical: *"san"* (three), *"shou"* (longevity), *"he"* (combine), *"he"* (harmony) and *"tong"* (sameness), which he did not recognize, and certain lines saying that Tao Bida and Wu Tiancheng were in eldest, second, third, fourth, or fifth branch. There was also a poem, which read:

The five branches left a poem,
[This is] the *hongying* on the body [see note 12] that few people
　　know about,
But those who know [our own] brothers,
Will eventually meet in perfect fellowship.

Wu Lao'er told him that Guangdong belonged to the second branch, under the name Hong Taizong, and used the red banner as insignia. However, even Wu did not know about the other branches.

　　Ma paid Wu seven hundred cash and made a copy of the poem and the code words. He then returned to Kaitai and formed a society with thirty-two people. He passed the code words to one of them, held two initiation ceremonies, and recruited thirty-seven disciples.[7]

Case 4. In 1854 Tang Fengji, a farmer from Hua county in Guangdong province, participated in an initiation ceremony with sixty people from his own village. A certain Huang Yi acted as "mother" (*laomu*, i.e., initiator), and Tang Ya'er served as "maternal uncle" (*jiufu*, i.e., introducer of the novices). After that, he joined a rebel group at Foling Monastery, and was placed under the command of Tang Yasi. He fought against government troops several times, and then the group dispersed. After that, he went to Hong Kong and worked as a cook for a Westerner. He worked there for just one year, returned to his village, and gathered his own group.[8]

　　The anti-Manchu tradition is apparent in the rituals in these examples, but, except for case 4, there is no evidence that the participants in the initiation ceremonies were bent on seditious activities. In any case, they did not have a lasting organization that could successfully carry out a rebellion.

To begin at the individual level, we can only conjecture as to why these people took part in the ceremony. Prima facie, it was a precondition for the privilege of knowing the secret code words and sign language that ensured safety from bandits. Moreover, as members they could receive help in times of trouble. The sort of help needed varied. In one case, an Adding Brothers Society was involved in robbery and killing but was protected from prosecution by a yamen runner who was also a member. In another case, a Triad group in Guangzhou prefecture operated a protection racket at harvest time, collecting 10 to 20 percent of the rent from landlords on the threat of destroying the crops. Not everyone joined voluntarily. A merchant who stayed with a group in Sichuan province for eight months claimed that the bandits killed his porters and forced him to take part in the ceremony; thereafter he served as the teacher to the bandit chief's son and looked after the group's membership records. In Jiangxi province, where some societies also collected money at harvest time, landowners sometimes joined in order to be allowed to pay protection fees. There was no suggestion in any of these examples that sedition, in the sense of an intent to overthrow the government, was ever contemplated. Case 4, the exception, occurred when the Taipings had already upset the local political order, and the initiation was consciously used by many groups—bandits as well as rebels—as a method of recruitment.[9]

The ritual claims were very different. The code words, the secret symbols, and the initiation ceremonies, illustrated in cases 1 through 3, were built around three themes: that the groups that referred to themselves as the Heaven and Earth Society or its variants had a common origin, were committed to reestablishing the Ming dynasty, and were involved in a lasting relationship. Hence, members of one group could reasonably expect help from members of other groups.

Thanks to the manuals that have been published, much is known about these ritual claims. Several complete sets of questions and answers used in the initiation ceremony are preserved in them, parts of which are quoted in case 2. The hexagonal figure referred to in case 3 is part of the Heaven and Earth Society's identification leaflet, the *yaoping* (identification worn on the waist), samples of which may be found in the work of Gustave Schlegel and of Xiao Yishan. The poem and the strange characters are written into the figure, and in Xiao's sample, the different branches of the society

and the names associated with each are recorded above it. In all likelihood, Ma Shaotang in case 3 made a copy of this *yaoping*.[10]

The myth of origin, which was the center of the initiation ceremony, had every characteristic of being the result of the merging of
different traditions. The Heaven and Earth Society, it claimed, originated from the monks of the Shaolin Monastery who helped the
Kangxi emperor conquer a country known as Xilu. As the result of
some treachery, the emperor subsequently attacked the temple,
burned it to the ground, and killed all but five of the monks. These
five escaped, came across five other people who were opposed to the
Manchu regime, and together they swore that they would overthrow
the Qing and restore the Ming. The five monks were, therefore,
known as the "Five Early Founders" *(qian wuzhu),* and the five people who came to their aid as the "Five Later Founders" *(hou wuzhu).*
The group of ten, and others whom they subsequently gathered,
then came across Chen Jinnan, who took them to Zhu Hongying, a
descendant of the Ming emperors. This Chen Jinnan, moreover, had
helped Zheng Chenggong (Koxinga) in his resistance against the
Manchus from Taiwan. The loose linkages in these different stories
suggest several rebellious traditions had been merged as the literature
and the ritual that came to be identified as the Heaven and Earth
Society evolved.[11]

According to J. S. M. Ward and W. G. Stirling, who recorded
W. A. Pickering's eyewitness account of the initiation ceremony in
Singapore in the late nineteenth century, the origin myth was retold
at the beginning of the initiation ceremony. The manuals also show
that it was referred to in many places in the ceremonial questioning
of the novices. For instance, the 1811 manual found in Guangxi has
recorded the following:

Q.   Why are your sleeves big or small?

A.   On the left I wear a tunic and on the right armor.

Q.   Where do you go in armor?

A.   To fight the Qing troops.

Q.   What for?

A.   Because of matters of the state.

Q.   Did you win or lose [when you last fought]?

A. In the first three battles, the Qing army retreated, but in the last
    three, we lost contact with the Little Lord [reference to Zhu
    Hongying]. That is why we have come to pay you this visit.[12]

As the questioning goes on, the set answers explain that originally a hundred and eight people were involved in the fighting,
including the Little Lord. That was the number of monks who went
from the Shaolin Monastery to fight Xilu.

The poem quoted in case 3 is also a reference to the myth. The
Five Later Founders parted but were to meet again. Meanwhile, the
members had close to their bodies the *hongying,* a reference to Zhu
Hongying on the one hand and the identification leaflet *(yaoping)* on
the other. This was to be a lasting relationship among the members
until the Manchus were driven out and the Ming dynasty was
restored.[13]

It would seem from the four cases cited that each Heaven and
Earth Society group was set up through contact with an already
established group but that after the initial contact, the "parent" group
ceased to maintain any relationship with its "offspring." No information went back and forth among the members of the different groups,
and there was no coordination to speak of. In this way, the Heaven
and Earth Society was not even a "network," a term that is often
invoked to refer to the independence of individual units and yet to
imply that they were not totally divorced from one another. Unity
among these groups existed only symbolically on the level of the
myths; we do not even have evidence that bandits genuinely left alone
people who knew the code words or the finger signals.[14]

It is quite misleading, therefore, to think of each Heaven and
Earth Society as a "lodge" and that individual societies were uniformly organized, each including the posts of "master," "first
brother," "second brother," "red staff," "key of the strong box,"
"grass sandal," and so on. Although Schlegel noted the prevalence
of the uniform organization in Southeast Asia, and it was also cited
in at least one memorial of the Xianfeng period (1851–1861), the
description probably applied more aptly to groups that were involved
in the very lucrative business of offering protection to migrants who
worked in the mines and the plantations of Southeast Asia and their
offshoots in their South China home villages. Cases 1 through 4 suggest that in China itself many groups were tiny, their numbers ranging from a handful to sixty members.[15] Moreover, the membership

that was granted through the initiation ceremony was only symbolic: novices who "entered" the society did not thereby become members of functional groups, while officiators at the ceremonies were bearers of tradition, rather than functional leaders. In other words, it was not as a unified organization, but as a set of rituals and traditions, that the Heaven and Earth Society spread.[16]

The Written Word in a Semiliterate Environment

Some factors that contributed to the spread of the Heaven and Earth Society's tradition were intrinsic to the organizational structure of the individual groups and their beliefs. The society permitted proselytizing. The belief in a wider organization that could give individual members support in times of trouble was inherently attractive. Moreover, its secret character could contribute to group solidarity. Much has been written about these aspects of the society, but one aspect to which not a great deal of attention has been given is the use of writing as a tool of organization.[17]

Writing helped to spread the Heaven and Earth Society tradition because its central tenets were written on the identification leaflet, the *yaoping,* distributed to novices. The leaflet was not an invention by the society, but a variation of the record given by the *yamen* for each household registered in the *baojia.* Since beggars and transport workers were not located in households, some officials gave them personal registration leaflets known as the *yaopai* (waist certificates).[18] Thus, what to the historian in hindsight appears to be a membership card, to a member of the Heaven and Earth Society was probably more a registration record. Only in this light can we understand the stress on secret symbols for the purpose of membership identification and not the production of the *yaoping.*

The *yaoping,* distributed to those people who participated in the initiation ceremony, embodied the basic tenets of the Heaven and Earth Society. These were stated in the poem and the notes that were standard portions of the document. There was also an esoteric element, for the *yaoping* included a number of Chinese characters that, though written in nonstandard forms, were not difficult to recognize. The *yaoping* could thus serve as a constant point of reference for the oral traditions associated with the society as well as a symbol for participation in the society's secrets.

However, many of the novices who took part in the initiation ceremony must have been illiterate. To them, the written word not only conveyed a message, it exerted authority. The poem on the *yaoping* and many more poems in the questions and answers in the manuals were recorded not to *illustrate* the history of the society but to *prove* the common ancestry of the different groups.[19] Because most of the participants were illiterate, there was room for the literate to dominate the ceremony by acting as interpreters of the texts, both the *yaoping* and the manuals. According to Ward and Stirling, the novices were not required to know the answers to the questions in the initiation ceremony: the questions were asked by the chief officiator (the *laomu*) and answered on their behalf by the introducer (the *jiufu*).[20] There was thus a theatrical element to the ceremony, in which certain individuals who knew the script acted out for the ones who did not the main tenets of the society. The novices were, of course, not only playing the part of an audience, for by being present and willing to accept the rituals, they were participating with the actors in the re-creation of tradition. This kind of joint participation by actors and audience was quite common in village theater in South China.[21]

The combination of texts and oral tradition was used not only by the Heaven and Earth Society but also by the White Lotus sects, the martial arts societies, and in local Daoist worship.[22] (For the use of the term "Daoist," see note 61.) The use of these texts does not sufficiently explain why the Heaven and Earth Society spread in the nineteenth century, but it does explain why, when it did spread, the practices of different localities were so similar. When the Qing government interpreted the similarities as evidence that the different groups were parts of an immense organization, it had simply left out of consideration the unifying effects of a common literature.

The Seditious Tradition

Since the early Qing, many seditious traditions had existed under cover, and many more were imputed. The theatrical companies of the Pearl River delta, for instance, retained Ming dynasty dress styles and presented anti-Manchu themes under the guise of such popular operas as the *Yang Family Generals*.[23] In 1752 a certain Ma Chaozhu staged an uprising in Hubei province, using the restoration of the Ming dynasty as his slogan, and in 1814 a Heaven and Earth Society was found in Jiangxi that sacrificed to him.[24] Legends of rebels lingered on for decades in rural China even after their defeat, and they could become the intercessors between nature and man just as famous generals, virtuous women, and others might.

Nevertheless, was there a seditious tradition in the early Qing that was distinctly the Heaven and Earth Society's? Although the society traced its origin to the Kangxi period, no one has yet identified from contemporary records either the themes or the groups that could have served as the precursors of the particular seditious traditions associated with the society in the nineteenth century. Arguments that claim a Kangxi origin in the society's seditious traditions draw their evidence mainly from the origin myths, and this evidence is at best suggestive. Articles published in the early 1980s by Qin Baoqi and Liu Meizhen, and the earlier work of Cai Shaoqing, argue that the Heaven and Earth Society originated much later, in the mid-Qianlong period. While Zhuang Jifa disagrees, the evidence he produces also points to a late origin for the seditious tradition in the society, even if not for the society itself.[25]

The center of much dispute on the origin of the Heaven and Earth Society is the testimony of Yan Yan, arrested in connection with the Lin Shuangwen Rebellion in Taiwan in 1786. Yan admitted that he had taught the Heaven and Earth Society's rituals to Lin, and that he himself had learned them from Chen Pi, who had learned them, directly or indirectly, from Abbot Wan, a certain Wan Tixi. In the 1811 text the name Wan Tixi appeared as an alias for Wan Yunlong, one of the founders. According to Yan, the society had been started much earlier, by two men in Sichuan province.[26]

The governor general of Sichuan immediately reported that the Heaven and Earth Society was not known in his province, even though officials had had problems with the Guolu bandits. Based on this claim, the argument has been advanced that the Heaven and Earth Society might have originated with the Guolu. However, the Guolu were not known to have harbored any seditious tradition at that point in time and no justification has been found for this supposed connection.[27] Qing officials found Wan Tixi's son, who testified that his father was also known as Hong Er (Hong the second), did know the finger symbols, and had died in 1779. Other testimonies also alleged that Hong Er was the founder of the society.[28]

As Qin Baoqi and Liu Meizhen point out, it is significant that none of the culprits mentioned the myth of origin involving the monks of the Shaolin Monastery and the conquest of Xilu. They further argue that even the 1811 text was only a prototype of the myth, to which much was added later. Much of the myth, they argue, could have developed from the proselytizing by Wan Tixi, the only proved historical character among the founders. We cannot be certain that Lin Shuangwen did not make use of the origin myth: the sacrificial document that he used made reference to some names associated with it.[29] The case seems strong, nonetheless, for the argument that in the early years of the nineteenth century, there was less emphasis on the myths and a less elaborate ritual than that recorded in later manuals. If this argument is correct, the seditious tradition of the Heaven and Earth Society developed primarily in the nineteenth century.

Zhuang Jifa, on the other hand, places greater emphasis on the statement that the society had originated much earlier than Wan Tixi's time. He subscribes to the argument that the Heaven and Earth Society had originated as alliances among multi-surname groups in local armed feuds. The fictitious surnames Zhu, Hong, and Wan were adopted for the sake of these alliances. The alliances began before Kangxi, and could be traced throughout the Kangxi, Yongzheng, and Qianlong reigns.[30] But they carried no anti-dynastic implication. They employed the ceremony of drawing blood and swearing brotherhood oaths, and their rallying cries included "robbing the rich to relieve the poor," but there was no indication that they wanted to "overthrow the Qing and restore the Ming." Despite the different emphasis, therefore, Zhuang's argument does not refute that of both Qin and Liu, but complements it. The many threads of the Heaven and Earth Society tradition started at different times. The multi-surname alliances started before Wan Tixi, but then they were given an anti-dynastic twist at approximately his time. It was only then that the Heaven and Earth Society took the shape that is now recognized by historians.

Evolution in the Nineteenth Century

When Yan Yan was asked by his interrogators what advantages membership in the Heaven and Earth Society entailed, he answered as follows:

> As for the reason for joining the society, originally it was that one
> could receive financial help for marriages and funerals, and support

if one was involved in a fight. Moreover, if one was stopped by a rob-
ber, one would be left alone if one performed the secret signs of sect
[*jiao*]. Also, when one could preach the creed [*chuanjiao*], one could
be rewarded.[31]

In 1802 Nayancheng, as a senior metropolitan official sent to
Guangdong to investigate an uprising in Boluo county, gave the following account of the Adding Brothers Society that was involved in
an uprising there:

> The name "Adding Brothers Society" began in Zhangzhou and Quan-
> zhou in Fujian. As Huizhou and Chaozhou [Guangdong] are adjacent
> to this part of Fujian, people here have had the practice for a long time
> and it has become local custom. The Guangdong people live in clans,
> but the Hakka [*kejia*] are wild unemployed vagabonds who gather in
> gangs. They become brothers in the Adding Brothers Society so that
> they can help one another in trouble. Some local people also join, but
> 80 to 90 percent are Hakka. Because the local people are afraid of
> being disturbed by these Hakka gangs, and because these gangs steal
> their oxen, which are rare in these mountainous areas, they also set
> up their own societies in the villages. They call these the Ox Heads
> Societies, and every household contributes to them annually. The
> societies by these two names have been hostile to each other for many
> years. Trouble then started in Guishan, Boluo and Yong'an, because
> the Guishan Adding Brothers Society, under its headman Chen
> Yaben, gathered several hundred people to rob from the Ox Heads
> Societies' villages. Before they could do it, they were discovered.[32]

There are other cases in the late eighteenth and early nineteenth century that followed these patterns. It seems that in this
period many Heaven and Earth Societies were fundamentally
mutual-aid groups. (See chapter 9, this volume.) There are two
types. Testimonies in connection with Lin Shuangwen's rebellion
show that many of his associates who were arrested were involved in
local marketing networks. Yan Yan sold cloth, another sold wine, yet
another food, and quite a few worked in roving theatrical companies
from Guangdong. The groups in Boluo were a different type. These
were multi-surname groups in farming villages that were engaged in
local feuds.[33]

Qin Baoqi, who has excellent command of the archives in Beijing, reports that of ninety-six cases in the Jiaqing and Daoguang reigns (spanning 1796 to 1850) in which the leaders of the groups made statements on the aim of the Heaven and Earth Society, twenty-six said it was finding support in times of trouble, fifteen said they wanted to collect money, thirty-nine wanted to rob the rich, five wanted to resist arrest or to prepare for armed feuds, and only eleven wanted to attack the cities, raise their own banners, and rebel.[34] Zhuang Jifa discusses at length some seventy-five cases in the Jiaqing and Daoguang reigns, and while some of these groups obviously subscribed to an anti-dynastic ideology, only a few toward the end of the Daoguang era were actively engaged in rebellion.[35]

It is difficult to tell from existing records if the ideology these groups accepted varied greatly from the myth-of-origin outlines in the Xilu tale. We do know that Wan Tixi came to be more commonly associated with these groups. A text discovered in 1806 listed his name as the earth god, and he was appealed to along with other gods and the founders of the society for religious support. In several cases cited by Zhuang, his name was inscribed on spirit tablets and placed on the altar for the initiation ceremony.[36] It is also known that the tradition spread over a wide geographic area. First found primarily in Fujian and those parts of Guangdong that were on its border, by the early years of the Jiaqing period (1796–1820), the society was reported in Guangxi, Hunan, and Jiangxi. In Guangdong, by the end of the Jiaqing reign, it was found throughout the Pearl River delta.[37]

The Heaven and Earth Society became increasingly associated with criminal activities such as robbery and smuggling. The evidence for the association is not always clear. In at least one instance, when a memorial charged that the Small Sword, the Triad, and the Three Dots Societies were engaged in robbery in Guangdong, local officials protested, arguing that these names were not known among Guangdong bandits even though brotherhood (jiebai) was a common institution.[38] It was a frequent practice for Qing officials to relate banned institutions to crime, and the possibility that legislation might have biased them in their perception of the Heaven and Earth Society must not be ruled out.

The evidence that at least some groups involved in the smuggling of opium might have adopted the ways of the Heaven and Earth Society is nonetheless quite strong. The geographic area most prominently mentioned in the memorials of the Daoguang period (1821–1850) in connection with Heaven and Earth Society activities

was the stretch that included the principal inland routes from Guangdong and Fujian into Jiangxi, that is, from Ganzhou and Nan'an in
Jiangxi to Shaowu in Fujian. In 1840 it was reported in detail how
merchants from Quanzhou and Zhangzhou in Fujian sent opium
inland into Jiangxi via Shaowu. A Fujianese gang known as the Taiping and a Guangdong gang known as the Changsheng constituted
together what was known as the Red Society (Hong hui). Their people were seen carrying opium in bamboo baskets on this route. The
Fujianese tied red wool to their buttonholes, and the Guangdong
people, green wool. They said they themselves were headmen, and
that there were twenty to thirty thousand who were their "brothers,"
an expression that was reminiscent of the Heaven and Earth Society.
A Lin Fumou, who was arrested as a headman, was accused of having distributed red flags and red cloth.[39]

Some memorials also reported that the society might be
involved in salt smuggling, but no concrete evidence was given.[40] As
the opium trade was rapidly expanding, the lucrative returns could
make these groups very powerful on an important trade route. Sedition was not a factor in these reports. That the bands that finally
rebelled were not connected with these smugglers is further evidence
that rebellion and common crime were quite separate issues.

As the case of Li Yuanfa would show, rebellions were prompted
by local circumstances and not the overall orientation of any group.
Li staged an uprising in 1849 in Xinning county in Hunan province,
where the Heaven and Earth Society was organized primarily in connection with local feuds. Groups that were known as the Black and
Red Societies had existed there for many years. In 1849, Li was
thirty-three years old, and unmarried, when he formed his Bazi hui
(Brotherhood Society).[41] According to his testimony, the rain that
year had damaged the crops, and consequently, the price of grain
was high. But the rich refused to sell at a lower price and were not
ordered by the magistrate to do so. There was little relief grain from
the granaries, and even for the little that was provided, the gentry
wanted to charge a high interest to be paid at harvest. Li recruited
his members at this time, and they swore to be brothers. So, one
night, Li gathered three hundred people, entered the city, and captured the prison. At this point they had no alternative but to rebel.
So they forced many people into their band and gave each a piece of
red or blue cloth as identification. It was reported that some of the
groups that were with him had banners with the name Wan Yunlong

(an alias for Wan Tixi) written on them. The rebellion came to be considered as having been organized by the Heaven and Earth Society, but the rebels had adopted the rituals of the society only after the rebellion had developed.[42]

The role of the rituals changed somewhat during the Taiping Rebellion. In the near anarchy that resulted in much of Guangdong and Guangxi, many groups similar to Li Yuanfa's openly fought one another and looted nearby villages.[43] Powerful chieftains came to be known as rice masters *(mifan zhu)*, who received their portions of the spoils as a matter of course when their affiliates looted. Not all of these groups adopted the Heaven and Earth Society's traditions. From the little that is known of them, despite the common use of the word *"tang"* (hall) for these groups, it is not clear that many of them had very much organization.[44]

Traditional historiography on the relationship between the Taiping regime and the Heaven and Earth Society has exaggerated the importance of Hong Daquan, supposed head of the society. Being not one but many independent bands, there could not have been a single leader who represented the society. Moreover, the relationship of these bands to the Taiping regime did not follow a consistent pattern. As Jian Yuwen has pointed out, they did not worship the same gods as the Taipings did, and they had different moral standards and political doctrines.[45] Some of the bands adhered to the Taipings, and Hong Daquan's, to say nothing of Luo Dagang's, must have been completely absorbed in the Taiping regime. Nevertheless, many others remained outside, and several went as far as to set up their own Heaven and Earth Society kingdoms. Most, however, never rose beyond their local settings.[46]

Local legends in Guangxi have given reasons a person might join the Taipings in preference to the Heaven and Earth Society. It was said that the Triads were robbers, but the God Worshipers (the Taipings) were fair and did not rob from the local people. It was also said that one had to pay to become a member of the Triad, but not of the God Worshipers' Society. Moreover, the God Worshipers' Society worshiped the Christian god, Shangdi, who was represented as a male figure, while some of the Triads were said to have worshiped "Mother," a woman, and it seemed that Shangdi must be the stronger of the two. This last point evidently misrepresents the Heaven and Earth Society's tradition but is indicative of the attitudes that might be associated with the different beliefs.[47]

These legends imply that there was choice of group membership for many people in these troubled times. Testimonies of secret-society members in Guangdong taken from the archives of the governor general's yamen (now held in London's Public Record Office) show that the initiation ceremony was actually used as a method of recruitment. Case 4, discussed above, is one such testimony, but several others, taken from a Chen Guanglong's band near Guangzhou in 1853, give a clearer idea of the functions of the ceremony.

Chen used to sell pigeons outside Li Village.[48] He led an uprising on the twenty-first day of the sixth month. Lin Qinglian, who became a member of his force, had taken part in an initiation ceremony only on the previous day, not in Chen's presence. The people who were in this ceremony joined Chen on the twenty-first, with the "maternal uncle" for the ceremony becoming a "commander" *(xianfeng)*, and the "mother," a commander in chief *(yuanshuai)*. Lin was put in charge of a company, the size of which he obviously exaggerated, and was given a sum of money each day for its food. Lin Yazhu, a sixty-year-old who was in Chen's own company, in charge of temple worship, took part in an initiation ceremony on the fifteenth day of the seventh month. Both Lin Qinglian's and Lin Yazhu's bands were set up under the banners of the Hongshun *tang.* According to Lin Yazhu, in the intercalary seventh month, nearby villages contributed roast pork and other things to the rebel camp. Almost immediately after the first initiation ceremony, Chen went with some of his men to the home of Gao Changnian, a member of the gentry, and forced Gao to take part in a ceremony in which Chen seems to have been a mere bystander. Gao was forced to pay several thousand taels of silver, which he could only do by handing over his pawnshop to Chen, who was to sell the goods at a discount. Gao admitted to having participated in the initiation ceremony, when he was first questioned by government officials, although he later denied it. His having gone through the ritual clearly incriminated him, and that could have been one of the rebels' objectives.

Chen's band fought against government troops many times, until the twelfth month, when Chen was killed. Members of the band burned incense to him, allowed his family to remove his belongings to one of the nearby villages, and accepted the leadership of a clansman of his. Meanwhile, officials ordered that his ancestral tombs be destroyed, and when nearby villagers were doing this, people of the Lin surname—who apparently were related to Chen—came and fought against them. Lin Yazhu and Lin Qinglian were arrested during the fight.[49] If other rebel bands were organized in the way Chen Guanglong's was, it would seem that they were gatherings of small groups recruited at the Heaven and Earth Society's initiation ceremonies. One must note the strong religious overtones attached to recruitment: comradeship created through the initiation ceremony overrode lineage and village connections.

It was only in the period of the Taiping Rebellion that the Heaven and Earth Society's tradition was widely involved, for the first time, in overt rebellious activities. Most of the groups that rebelled in this period in Guangdong were small and isolated, and it is no longer possible to trace their history individually, except in formalized official accounts. Nonetheless, the legends that persisted in Cantonese theatrical companies long after the mid-nineteenth century show that the influence of some of these groups was lasting. The rebellion of the actor Li Wenmou became an important landmark in Cantonese theatrical history.

Li Wenmou's rebellion implicated the Qionghua hui, the Cantonese theatrical guild that was based in Foshan. Foshan was *the* center for the theatrical companies, for from there they traveled by the "red boats" to perform in villages all over the Pearl River delta.[50] This practice was well established long before the Taiping Rebellion. Li rebelled in 1853, when Chen Kai, a Foshan boatman, had already declared his own rebellion. According to theatrical legends, during their several months' success in Foshan, Li and his followers, many of them actors, dressed in the Ming dynasty clothes that were standard theatrical costumes. Li joined with Chen, but they were soon defeated by government forces and had to escape into Guangxi, where they set up the Dacheng (Great Accomplishment) kingdom. In Guangxi the rebels captured several counties before they were totally routed by government forces, in 1858. Li died, his group dispersed, and some of his followers joined the Taiping.[51]

The Xilu legend associated with the Heaven and Earth Society was recorded in the 1811 manual found in Guangxi, and thus it clearly predates the Li Wenmou rebellion. Similarities between the Cantonese theatrical traditions and the Heaven and Earth Society's must, therefore, be explained either in terms of a common origin or in terms of borrowing by the theatrical tradition. For instance, there were always two red boats, one known as the "heaven boat" *(tianchuan)* and the other, "earth boat" *(dichuan)*, and this similarity to the concept of the Heaven and Earth Society could simply be due to the common practice of using "heaven" and "earth" as the naming system.[52] Closer to a common origin, in the Xilu legend, the monks belonged to the Shaolin Monastery, and in the theatrical tradition, the staged martial arts also developed out of the fighting style of the Shaolin Monastery. Recalling the Kangxi emperor's burning of the Shaolin Monastery, the theatrical tradition considered the destruction of Foshan during the campaign of suppression by the Qing government to be the "burning of the Qionghua hui." Not only did the legends of the Heaven and Earth Society come to be a part of the theatrical tradition, theatrical traditions also crept into the Heaven and Earth Society's tradition. In the initiation ceremony, the novices were asked about a boat on which they had symbolically traveled in order to come to the society's meeting, and they had to identify the gods that were enshrined aboard the boat. Huaguang was in the bow, Tianhou in the stern, and Guandi in the cabin. As is well known, Huaguang was the actors' god, Tianhou the seafarers, and Guandi, among other things, was the god of justice and comradeship associated with the martial arts. This part of the questioning is absent in the 1811 text, and it is just possible that this was a theatrical tradition blended into that of the Heaven and Earth Society.[53]

After the Taiping Rebellion, the influence of the Heaven and Earth Society in the rural areas of Guangdong, Guangxi, and Fujian seems to have returned to what it was in the Jiaqing and Daoguang periods. However, its influence outside the rural areas in these provinces is a mystery. One must take into account the effects of changes in trade routes, the growth of coastal cities, and emigration. The tradition of the Heaven and Earth Society remained a useful tool for organization, but the purposes of the groups that were formed were changing.

According to a memorial by Zhang Zhidong, which is corroborated by other sources, it seems that the locus of Heaven and Earth Society activities in Guangdong and Guangxi in the post-Taiping period was the area from Huizhou prefecture to the Pearl River delta.[54] Sporadic reports on the society were received from other places, notably from the Leizhou peninsula and Hainan Island.[55] The inland routes into Jiangxi and Hunan were no longer important, for with the advent of the steamer, the coastal traffic took the place of these routes, while the centers of trade shifted to the cities of the littoral, including Guangzhou, Hong Kong, Xiamen, and Shanghai.

Some groups continued to be associated with local feuds and robberies, arrests continued to be made on the sole basis of treasonous
association,[56] and a report from Hainan Island explained that the
society's officers were known as "elder brother," "second brother,"
"red stick," "master," "straw sandal," and so on, corroborating
Schlegel's material gathered in Southeast Asia shortly before this
period.[57] With rare exception, such as the case of Hong Quanfu in
1902, outright rebellion was, as before, far from being the objective
of these groups.[58] However, in 1902 the time was drawing near when
"secret societies" abroad began to take an interest in supporting
revolutionary or anarchist bodies.[59]

The predominance of the Heaven and Earth Society's tradition in overseas Chinese communities must have had its effects on
organization at home, but little concrete evidence has so far been
produced. As is well known, Chinese emigration to Southeast Asia,
America, and Australia advanced rapidly in the nineteenth century.
In Malaya and Singapore, in particular, because of the societies' local
influence, membership and organization must have developed to an
extent unknown in China itself. One must not think of the Malayan
and Singapore societies as an entirely post-Taiping development,
nonetheless. When they were first discovered, in 1825, it was reported
that they had already been in existence for twenty years.[60] As for
direct contact, it seems that the Small Sword Society that rebelled in
Xiamen in 1853 was founded by an overseas Chinese who had
returned from Singapore. Local tradition in Hong Kong also claims
that the underworld in the city just before 1900 was headed by a
Chaozhou man who had returned from Southeast Asia. Hong
Quanfu, apparently, was financed in Hong Kong through strong
overseas connections who believed in secret society activities.[61] It is
inconceivable, given the strong affiliation overseas Chinese people
maintained with their homeland, that there were not other points of
contact.

The Heaven and Earth Society also extended to other places
in China. An obvious example of this extension was the Small Sword
Society that rebelled in Shanghai in 1853, composed primarily of
people from Guangdong. While one must agree that the Elder Brothers Society (Gelao hui) was not simply an extension of the Heaven
and Earth Society, its use of the *shantong* (a recruitment ceremony),
identification leaflets, and banners in its organization was more akin
to the Heaven and Earth Society's tradition than to those either of

the Guolu gangs, which were frequently mentioned in pre-Taiping records, or of the White Lotus, both of which have been proposed as its predecessor.[62] One cannot be certain, however, for the Green Gangs (Qingbang) on the Grand Canal had similar organizational devices, and could well have been a greater source of inspiration.[63]

From the late eighteenth century to approximately 1900, there-fore, the Heaven and Earth Society's tradition, characterized by a peculiar origin myth and a set of secret codes, developed from small beginnings possibly in Fujian and neighboring prefectures in Guang-dong to influence a much wider geographic area. In the process, par-ticularly because it was adopted by local groups during the Taiping Rebellion, the rebelliousness of its doctrine deepened. The groups that made use of the doctrine were, nonetheless, not always associ-ated with rebellious activities.

Orthodox-Heterodox Distinctions

As Dai Xuanzhi has pointed out, much of the Heaven and Earth Society's ritual had originated with orthodox Daoism.[64] What counts as Daoism, as always, is problematic, but Dai uses the term loosely to refer to beliefs and practices forming what he sees as the founda-tion of Chinese popular religion. Participants in the rituals of the Heaven and Earth Society, like participants in village rituals, sought a liminal experience and religious sanction for their behavior. In the initiation ceremony, the gods among whom their founders were listed were acceptable to any village Daoist, and the lamp, the sword, the mirror, the scale, the ruler, the pair of scissors, and the abacus, inserted into the centrally placed rice-filled wooden measure, the *dou,* were objects that had particular meanings within some varieties of Daoist purification ceremonies. The questions and answers that formed the main body of the ceremony were special to the society, but the use of charms and mysterious scripts is reminiscent of Daoist practice. The question of why the Heaven and Earth Society's tra-dition was heterodox is thus intimately bound up with the question of the position of Daoism, particularly as it was practiced in the villages, in the state's orthodox ideology.

Although the Qing government was in general quite open-minded about non-Confucian practices that did not affect the polit-ical order, orthodox China was Confucian, and many village religious

practices, along with the Daoist rituals that served them, were heterodox. The crux of the matter lay in the relation of humanity to the
natural order. In the imperial Confucian order of the Qing dynasty,
the emperor and his officialdom held pride of place in interceding
between man and nature, but Daoist priests officiating at their rituals assumed precisely the same role. The difference was not one of
cosmology. The Daoist, by late imperial times, could accept a hierarchy of gods that reflected government officialdom on earth, but he
sent his petition to Heaven by direct sacrifice, while the Confucian
stressed the role of the emperor or his representative presiding over
worship in communal matters. Whatever their private beliefs, Qing
officials were at least in theory opposed to the Daoist communal purification ceremony *(jiaohui)*, for community rituals involving Daoist
practices could easily threaten the symbolic authority of the state.[65]

Popular religion in Qing China was quite distinct from the state
orthodoxy, in so far as popular worship was closer to the Daoist view
of nature and humanity than the Confucian view. In its stress on the
sanction of the gods for every human activity, popular religion bor-
dered on magic. The individual came to terms with nature through
his own prayers, sacrifice, and the use of religious charms. There
were many aspects of popular religion that the Qing government
could not come to terms with but could not pragmatically ignore. It
took the easy way out, by considering as seditious only those creeds
that embodied an overtly rebellious program or were connected with
groups that had at some time staged an uprising. Officials were
spared the task of probing why a creed might or might not instigate
rebellion, for they had only to see if its tenets fit the definitions of the
law.

As this chapter has argued, the object of a seditious creed was
not necessarily rebellion. But given its seditious nature, the Heaven
and Earth Society's tradition could not be integrated into the official
religious system. As Frederic Wakeman has pointed out, it became
an independent source of political legitimation.[66] Moreover, because
it appealed to the Ming emperors, it turned the tables on the ruling
regime: it was the Manchu regime that was illegitimate in the Heaven
and Earth Society's reference system, while the society, by being the
supporter of the legitimate political order, could claim sanction from
the socioethics as well as the gods of orthodoxy. This belief system
must have been attractive to people who were conscious of them-

selves as criminals, for by becoming rebels loyal to the Ming, they could remove themselves from the religious monopoly of the Qing state and make their own arrangements for protection by the gods.

The self-image of the Heaven and Earth Society as a legitimized body should explain why far from being opposed to most legitimate social practices, it insisted on their enforcement. The regulations of the society were not opposed to filial piety, respect for elders, and larger fidelity—witness loyalty to the Ming. On the contrary, the regulations provided for the observance of these norms in adjusted form.[67] One might even argue that the stress placed on brotherhood among members was not a violation, but a variation, of the Three Bonds; for a member served Heaven and Earth as father and mother, and his relationship to other members must then be equated to that among brothers. Indeed, the group was supposed to take precedence over the family, but through the initiation ceremony, the group became a replica of the family. In the case of the Heaven and Earth Society, even a heterodox doctrine could not escape the symbolic structure of the wider society. Immediate goals and concerns differed, but at the level of the need for justification, the basic concepts —the "categories"—employed by orthodox and heterodox alike were common to Chinese culture.

Notes

Since this chapter was last revised, two monographs have appeared in English on the Heaven and Earth Society. They are David Ownby, *Brotherhoods and Secret Societies in Early and Mid-Qing China* (Stanford: Stanford University Press, 1996), and Barend J. ter Haar, *Ritual and Mythology of the Chinese Triads* (Leiden: E. J. Brill, 1998).

1. The law may be found in Xue Yunsheng, *Duli cunyi congkanben* [Reservations about doubtful matters while perusing the substatues of the Qing code, second edition] (Beijing, 1905; new version punctuated and edited by Huang Qingjia, Taibei: Chengwen, 1970), 365. The law of 1792 referred specifically to Taiwan. In 1811 this was modified to include Guangdong and Fujian. See *Da Qing huidian shili* [Collected statutes on the institutions of the Qing dynasty, with precedents] (1899, reprint, 779:18b–19a). For a historical review of these legal changes, see Robert J. Antony, "Brotherhoods, secret societies, and the law in Qing-dynasty China," in David Ownby and Mary Somers Heidhues, eds., *"Secret Societies" Reconsidered* (Armonk, N.Y.: M.E. Sharpe, 1993), 190–211. A comprehensive discussion

of the historiography on the Heaven and Earth Society may be found in Dian H. Murray (in collaboration with Qin Baoqi), *The Origin of the Tiandihui, the Chinese Triads in Legend and History* (Stanford: Stanford University Press, 1994).

2. See, among the numerous accounts of these rituals, especially Gustave Schlegel, *Thian Ti Hwui, the Hung League, Secret Society in China and India* (Batavia: Lange and Co., 1866; reprint, Singapore: Government Printer, n.d.); J. S. M. Ward and W. G. Stirling, *The Hung Society* or *The Society of Heaven and Earth* (London: Baskerville Press, 1925–1926); and Xiao Yishan, ed., *Jindai mimi shehui shiliao* [Historical sources on modern secret societies] (Beijing, 1935; reprint, Taibei: Wenhai, 1965).

3. On the Shanghai Small Sword Society, see Lu Yaohua, "Shanghai xiaodao hui di yuanliu" [Origins and development of the Small Sword Society in Shanghai], *Shihuo* 3.5 (1973): 207–218, and Shanghai Academy of Social Sciences, Institute of History, *Shanghai xiaodao hui qiyi shiliao huibian* [Collection of historical sources on the Small Sword Society in Shanghai] (Shanghai: Renmin, 1964).

4. The 1811 manual may be found in Chinese People's University, Institute of Qing History, and the Number One Historical Archive of China, eds., *Tiandi hui* [Heaven and Earth Society, hereafter *Tiandi hui*], 1 (1980–1988), 1:3–32. For other manuals, besides those in Schlegel, *Thian Ti Hwui;* Ward and Stirling, *The Hung Society;* and Xiao Yishan, *Jindai mimi,* the most important ones are in Luo Ergang, *Tiandi hui wenxian lu* [Documents of the Heaven and Earth Society] (n.d., n.p., preface dated 1942; reprint, Hong Kong: Shiyong shuju, n.d.). For accounts on activities in Malaya and Singapore, see M. L. Wynne, *Triad and Tabut: A Survey of the Origin and Diffusion of Chinese and Mohammedan Secret Societies in the Malay Peninsula A.D. 1800–1935* (Singapore: Government Printing Office, 1941); Leon Comber, *Chinese Secret Societies in Malaya: A Survey of the Triad Society from 1800–1900* (Locust Valley, N.Y.: J. J. Augustin, 1959); and W. Blythe, *The Impact of Chinese Secret Societies in Malaya, a Historical Study* (London: Oxford University Press, 1969).

5. Zhuang Jifa, *Qingdai Tiandi hui yuanliu kao* [The origins and development of the Heaven and Earth Society of the Qing period] (Taibei: Palace Museum, 1981), 79. The memorial cited in Zhuang may be found in *Tiandi hui,* 6:424–427.

6. *Da Qing lichao shilu* [Veritable records of successive reigns of the Qing dynasty], *Renzong shilu* [Veritable records of the Jiaqing emperor] (Mukden: Manzhouguo guowu yuan, 1937; hereafter *SLJQ,* 304:24a–25b; Zhuang Jifa, *Qingdai Tiandi hui,* 92–93.

7. *Da Qing lichao shilu* [Veritable records of successive reigns of the Qing dynasty], *Xuanzong shilu* [Veritable records of the Daoguang emperor]; hereafter *SLDG,* 196:9a–11b. I have translated this document in full in

David Faure, "Secret Societies, Heretic Sects, and Peasant Rebellions in Nineteenth Century China," *Journal of the Chinese University of Hong Kong* 5:1 (1979): 196.

8. Sasaki Masaya, *Shinmatsu no himitsu kessha* [Late Qing secret societies] (Tokyo: Kindai Chūgoku kenkyū iinkai, 1967), 31–32. For full translation, see David Faure, "Secret Societies," 198–199.

9. *SLJQ*, 296:21a–23a; *SLDG*, 158:18a–b, 168:24a–26a, 280:17b–19a. Compare also *SLJQ*, 176:30a–31b; *SLDG*, 69:10b–11b, 72:26b–28a.

10. Gustave Schlegel, *Thian Ti Hwui*, 27–31, discusses the content of the *yaoping*. For other examples, see Xiao, *Jindai mimi*, 1:25a–26a, and a reproduction of the Shanghai Xiaodao hui's in Shanghai Academy of Social Sciences, Institute of History, comp., *Shanghai Xiaodao hui*, on the fifth page of the plates. In case 3, cf. discussion on Xiao, *Jindai mimi*, 1:26a, in Faure, "Secret Societies," 11.

11. This is the version given in the "Xilu xu," and may be found in Xiao, *Jindai mimi*, 2:3b–7b. For different versions of the legend, see Murray, *The Origins of the Tiandihui*, 197–228.

12. *Tiandi hui*, 1:15.

13. The term *"hongying"* was also used to refer to members of the society, and Schlegel, *Thian Ti Hwui*, 29, gives reasons for translating it as "Hong heroes." It is obviously a pun, referring to the leaflet itself, to Zhu Hongying, and to the member's own person.

14. Frederic Wakeman Jr., "The secret societies of Guangdong, 1800–1856," in Jean Chesneaux, ed., *Popular Movements and Secret Societies in China 1840–1950* (Stanford: Stanford University Press, 1972), 29–47, argues that the groups said to be affiliated with the society were autocephalous, but concedes that they enjoyed "an exchange of information and favors" (30). We have no evidence even of such exchanges.

15. For a very good description of these societies in the Southeast Asian context, see Mary Somers Heidhues, "Chinese organizations in West Borneo and Bangka: *kongsis* and *hui*," in Ownby and Heidhues, eds. *"Secret Societies" Reconsidered*, 68–88.

16. Fei-ling Davis, *Primitive Revolutionaries of China, A Study of Secret Societies in the Late Nineteenth Century* (Honolulu: University of Hawai'i Press, 1971), 101–125, and Jean Chesneaux, *Secret Societies in China in the Nineteenth and Twentieth Centuries*, Gillian Nettle, trans. (Ann Arbor: University of Michigan Press, 1971), 31, confuse the officiating members in the initiation ceremony with offices in the groups that novices supposedly entered. The two works also presuppose a greater degree of uniformity in these offices than the source materials justify. The Xianfeng reference is Zeng Wangyan's memorial in the early 1850s, included in Beijing University Graduate Institute of Letters, comp., *Taiping tianguo shiliao* [Historical materials on the Taiping Heavenly Kingdom] (Beijing: Kaiming shudian, 1950), 523–527.

17. See Jean Chesneaux, "Secret societies in China's historical evolution," in Jean Chesneaux, ed., *Popular Movements*, 1 21, and Lee Poh ping, *Chinese Society in Nineteenth Century Singapore* (Kuala Lumpur: Oxford University Press, 1978), 48–58.

18. Xu Dong, *Baojia shu jiyao* [Essential documents collected from the *Handbook for Baojia Registration*] (ca. 1837, abridged 1871; reprint, Taibei: Chengwen, 1968), 2:16b–36a. The *yaopai* for beggars and transport workers is discussed on 2:34a–35b. There is also a reference to the *yaopai* for workers on the grain transport in *SLDG*, 284:20a–21a.

19. See Xiao, *Jindai mimi*, chap. 4. Poems are usually introduced by the question "What do you have for proof?" In response, the *jiufu* replies, "We have this poem . . ."

20. Ward and Stirling, *The Hung Society*, 53–107.

21. Barbara E. Ward, "Not merely players: drama, art and ritual in traditional China," *Man* (new series) 14 (1979): 18–39.

22. Evidence for this can be found in Chan Hok-lam, "The White Lotus-Maitreya Doctrine and Popular Uprisings in Ming and Qing China," *Sinologica* 10 (1969): 212–233; Shandong University, Department of History, Center for the Teaching and Research of Modern Chinese History, eds., *Shandong Yihe tuan diaocha ziliao xuanbian* [Selected data from field investigation on the Boxers in Shandong] (Jinan: Shandong University, 1980), esp. 113–244; and Michael Saso, *Daoism and the Rite of Cosmic Renewal* (Pullman: Washington State University, 1972).

23. Mai Xiaoxia, "Guangdong xiju shilue," [Brief history of drama in Guangdong], *Guangdong wenwu zhanlan hui, Guangdong wenwu* [Cultural relics of Guangdong] (Hong Kong: Zhongguo wenhua xiejin hui, 1941], chap. 8; Fredrikke Skinsnes Scollard, "Shiwan Pottery Explored," *Journal of the Hong Kong Branch of the Royal Asiatic Society* 18 (1978): 101–112.

24. Lingmu Zhongzheng (Suzuki Chūsei), "Qianlong shiqi nian Ma Chaozhu di fan Qing yundong" [Ma Chaozhu's anti-Qing movement of 1752], *Zhonghua wenshi luncong* 2 (1981): 125–139; Zhuang Jifa, *Qingdai Tiandi hui*, 83.

25. Zhuang Jifa, *Qingdai Tiandi hui*, 161–162; cf. Xiao Yishan, *Jindai mimi*, 3:13a–14a.

26. *Tiandi hui*, 1:110–112, 116–117. David Ownby has recently argued that testimonials, such as Yan Yan's "reveal little evidence of restorationist or anti-Manchu intent at any point before, during, or after the Lin Shuangwen uprising." See David Ownby, "Chinese *Hui* and the Early Modern Social Order: Evidence from Eighteenth-Century Southeast China," in Ownby and Heidhues, eds., *"Secret Societies" Reconsidered*, 34–67; quotation from p. 54.

27. *Tiandi hui*, 1:126–127; Hu Zhusheng, "Tiandi hui qiyuan chutan" [A preliminary investigation of the origins of the Heaven and Earth Society], *Lishi yanjiu* 4 (1979): 62–76; and Cai Shaoqing, "On the Origin

of the Gelaohui," *Modern China* 10.4 (1984): 481–508. See also Cheng-yun Liu, "Kuo-lu: A Sworn-Brotherhood Organization in Sichuan," *Late Imperial China* 6.1 (June 1985): 56–82.

28. *Tiandi hui,* 1:64–65, 137–138.

29. Ibid., 161–162; cf. Xiao Yishan, *Jindai mimi,* 3:13a–14a.

30. See Zhuang Jifa, *Qingdai Tiandi hui,* 12 ff. The argument was first advanced in Weng Tongwen, *Kangxi chuye "yi Wan wei xing" jituan yudang jianli Tiandi hui* [The remnant members of the Wan surname group founded the Heaven and Earth Society in the early years of the Kangxi period], Institute of Humanities and Social Sciences, Nanyang University, Occasional Papers Series, no. 3 (Singapore, 1975).

31. *Tiandi hui,* 1:111.

32. Nayancheng, *Nawenyi gong zouyi* (n.d., n.p., reprint, Taibei: Wenhai, 1966), 5:10b–11b.

33. Cf. *Tiandi hui,* 1: 70–72, 162–166, and Qin Baoqi and Liu Meizhen, "Shilun Tiandihui," 167–168.

34. Qin Baoqi, *Qing qianqi tiandihui yanjiu* [A study of the early Qing Heaven and Earth Society] (Beijing: People's University Press, 1988), 116.

35. Zhuang Jifa, *Qingdai Tiandi hui,* 78–113.

36. Ibid., 88, 98; Chinese People's University Qing History Institute and Department of Archives Unit on the History of Chinese Political Institutions, eds., *Kang-Yong-Qian shiqi chengxiang renmin fankang douzheng ziliao* [Sources on urban and rural people's struggle for resistance and protest in the era of Kangxi, Yongzheng and Qianlong] (Beijing: Zhonghua, 1979), 2:727–729.

37. *SLJQ,* 284:31b–32a, 358:4b–6b, 364:15a–15b; *SLDG,* 12:16a–17a, 26:45a, 101:40a–41b, 158:37b–38a, 176:7a–9a, 214:43b–44b, 233: 11a–12a, 299:5a–6a, 301:34a–35a.

38. *SLDG,* 186:8a–9b.

39. *SLDG,* 335:20b–21b, 337:20b–22b, 338:5a–6a, 339:33a–35a, 340:13b–14a, 346:23a–24b.

40. *SLDG,* 158:37b–38b, 176:7a–9a, 269:4b–6a.

41. The meaning of the term *"bazi"* is obscure in the context. I translate it as it might be used in the phrase *"bai bazi"* or *"bai xiongdi,"* as given in Tian Zongyao, *Zhongguo gudian xiaoshuo yongyu zidian* [Dictionary of terms used in classical Chinese novels] (Taibei: Lianjing, 1985), 458, 650. On Li Yuanfa, Lei Caihao, and the Bangbang hui, translated as "Cudgel Society," see Philip A. Kuhn, *Rebellion and Its Enemies in Late Imperial China: Militarization and Social Change* (Cambridge, Mass.: Harvard University Press, 1970), 107–112.

42. Palace Museum Department of Ming-Qing Archives, comp., *Qingdai Dang'an shiliao congbian* [Collected historical sources from Qing archives] 2 (1978): 13:138–141.

43. In view of the possible effects of the Opium War on local order in Guangdong, it is not clear if the change came in the 1840s or during the Taiping Rebellion. See Wakeman, "The Secret Societies," for an excellent description of Guangdong from 1840 to 1856.

44. See Su Fengwen, comp., *Dangfei zonglu* [Comprehensive record on secret-society bandits] (n.p., 1889, reprinted in Guting shuwu, *Mimi shehui congkan*, series 4, vol. 4, Taibei: Xiangsheng, 1975), 9:4b for the meaning of "rice master." For examples of these groups in Guangxi, see ibid. and Su Fengwen, comp., *Gufei zonglu* [Comprehensive record on bandit gangs] (n.p., 1889, reprinted in Guting shuwu, *Mimi shehui*, series 3, vol. 1).

45. Jian Yuwen, *Taiping tianguo quan shi* [Complete history of the Taiping Heavenly Kingdom] (Hong Kong: Mengjin shuwu, 1962), 1:240–242.

46. There is a vast literature on Hong Daquan. For a summary, see C. A. Curwen, "Taiping Relations with Secret Societies and with Other Rebels," in Jean Chesneaux, ed., *Popular Movements*, 65–84. For more recent arguments, see Cai Shaoqing, "Lun Taiping tianguo yu Tiandi hui di guanxi" [On the relations between the Taiping Heavenly Kingdom and the Heaven and Earth Society], *Lishi yanjiu* (1978): 6:46–61, and Zhuang Jifa, *Qingdai Tiandi hui*, 114–143. See especially Elizabeth J. Perry, "Taipings and Triads: the Role of Religion in Interrebel Relations," in Janos M. Bak and Gerhard Benecke, eds., *Religion and Rural Revolt* (Dover, N.H.: Manchester University Press, 1984), 342–353.

47. Jian Yuwen, *Taiping tianguo quan shi*, 245.

48. The term used here is *"mai baige"* (selling pigeons). Ernest John Eitel, *A Chinese Dictionary in the Cantonese Dialect* (London and Hong Kong: Trüber and Lane, Crawford, 1877) 282, defines *"fang baige"* (releasing pigeons) as "marry a husband under false pretences, cheat," and this can give a totally different twist to Chen's occupation.

49. Sasaki Masaya, *Shinmatsu*, 39–47.

50. Barbara E. Ward, "The Red Boats of the Canton Delta: An Historical Chapter in the Sociology of Chinese Regional Drama," in *Zhongyang yanjiu yuan guoji Hanxue huiyi lunwen ji minzu minhua zu* [Collected essays from the Academia Sinica International Sinological Conference: section on ethnography and culture] (Taibei: Academia Sinica, 1980), 233–257.

51. Lu Baoqian, *Lun wan Qing Liang Guang di Tiandihui zhengquan* [On the political regimes of the Heaven and Earth Society in Guangdong and Guangxi in the late Qing period] (Taibei: Academia Sinica, Institute of Modern History, 1975), 8–22; Taiping tianguo geming shiqi Guangxi nongmin qiyi ziliao bianzhi zu, comp., *Taiping tianguo geming shiqi Guangxi nongmin qiyi ziliao* [Sources on peasant uprisings in Guangxi in the period of the Taiping rebellion] (Beijing: Zhonghua, 1978), 505–722.

52. Barbara E. Ward, "The Red Boats," 4.

53. Mai Xiaoxia, "Guangdong"; Xiao Yishan, *Jindai mimi,* 4:5b–6a.

54. Zhu Shoupeng, *Shi'er chao Donghua lu: Guangxu chao* [Donghua records of twelve reigns: Guangxu reign] (n.d., n.p.; reprint, Taibei: Wenhai, 1963), 2046–2047.

55. Ibid., 2946–2947, 3461–3464, 3661–3664.

56. Ibid., 307, 309.

57. Ibid., 2946–2947.

58. Palace Museum, Department of Ming-Qing Archives, *Qingdai dang'an,* 1:142–151.

59. John Lust, "Secret Societies, Popular Movements, and the 1911 Revolution," in Jean Chesneaux, ed., *Popular Movements,* 165–200.

60. Wynne, *Triad and Tabut,* 74.

61. Ibid., 61–64; Zhang Sheng, *Xianggang heishehui huodong zhenxiang* [The reality of underworld activities in Hong Kong] (Hong Kong: Tiandi tushu, 1980), 38–43; "Bashi nian qian heishehui yuanliu" [Origins and trends of the underworld eighty years ago], *Xinzhi zhoukan* (Hong Kong: 16 June 1980), 15; Zhonghua minguo kaiguo wushi nian wenxian editorial committee, ed., *Zhonghua minguo kaiguo wushi nian wenxian,* series 1, vol. 4 (Taibei: Zhengzhong, 1964), 647–684.

62. Charlton M. Lewis, "Some notes on the Ko-lao hui in late Qing China," in Jean Chesneaux, ed., *Popular Movements,* 97–112; Zhu Jinfu, "Qingdai dang'an zhong youguan Gelao hui yuanliu di shiliao" [Historical sources regarding the origins and development of the Elder Brothers Society in Qing archives], *Gugong bowuyuan yuankan* 2 (1979): 65–71; Zhuang Jifa, *Qingdai Tiandi hui,* 134–139. See also note 27.

63. On the Green Gang, see Faure, "Secret Societies," Chen Guoping, *Qingmen kaoyuan* [Inquiry into the origins of the Green Gang] (Shanghai, 1946; reprint, Hong Kong, 1965), and Hu Zhusheng, "Qingbang shi chutan" [Preliminary inquiry into the history of the Green Gang], *Lishi xue* 3 (1979): 102–120.

64. Dai Xuanzhi, "Tiandi hui yu Daojiao" [The Heaven and Earth Society and Daoism], *Nanyang Daxue xuebao* 6 (1972): 156–161.

65. Cf. Stephan D. R. Feuchtwang, "School Temple and City God," in G. William Skinner, ed., *The City in Late Imperial China* (Stanford: Stanford University Press, 1977).

66. Wakeman, "The Secret Societies," 34–35.

67. These regulations may be found as part of the thirty-six oaths in Xiao Yishan, *Jindai mimi,* 3:1a–12a. For an analysis, see Lu Baoqian, *Lun wan Qing Liang Guang,* esp. 50.

CHAPTER 11

The Taipings in Chinese
Sectarian Perspective

P. Richard Bohr

As the most heterodox of late imperial China's sectarian uprisings, the chiliastic Taiping Rebellion (1851–1864) was the gravest challenge to imperial Confucianism between the time China assimilated Buddhism and the country's twentieth-century revolutions. The Taipings were driven by a syncretistic religion formulated by Hong Xiuquan (1814–1864), a failed examination candidate from a Hakka village in Hua county (near Canton), who sought to transform China into a Heavenly Kingdom of Great Peace and Equality. Intersecting with Hakka ethnicity, domestic decline, and foreign encroachment, Hong's religion incorporated a monotheistic faith, millenarian blueprint, messianic leadership, motivational ritual, puritanical morality, apocalyptic timetable, and theocratic organization. These insurrectionary building blocks enabled the Taipings to control the lower Yangzi valley from 1853 to 1864 and, in the process, to nearly topple the old order.[1]

Natural disaster, population pressure, economic injustice, ethnic tension, lawlessness, and government repression were by no means unique to the Taipings. These conditions stirred antigovernment fervor and eschatological fantasies among many other groups in late Qing China, including the "folk religious sects" (*jiao*) of the Eternal Mother tradition as well as sworn-brotherhood associations (*hui*), which, although not religious sectarians per se, nevertheless wrapped their ideals in pious ritual.[2] Lay religious leaders from the margins of orthodox society often employed vernacular preaching and scriptural exegesis to articulate the helplessness, anxieties, and aspirations of alienated people and expose them to apocalyptic notions that triggered expectations of supernatural liberation from an orthodox order now condemned as evil. In the revivalistic atmosphere of visions, faith healing, preaching, confession, initiation, purification rituals, penitential rites, prayers, incense and food offerings, vegetarian meals, hymn singing, asceticism, calendar reform, an enhanced status for women, gender equality, property sharing, and iconoclastic destruction, they recruited a broad spectrum of followers along ethnic, kinship, and occupational lines into close-knit congregational counter-communities devoted to preparing for the new millennium. Traditionally, the throne endeavored to keep congregational groups from openly challenging what Kwang-Ching Liu identifies as the three pillars of Chinese orthodoxy: adherence to Confucian socioethics, support of kinship institutions, and loyalty to the throne.[3] When the state attacked sectarians for crossing the line, these groups often raised the banner of revolt.[4]

The Taipings were inheritors of this rich, syncretistic tradition and selectively tapped its abundant store of heterodox themes and practices. At the same time, the Taipings were the first Chinese rebels to be inspired by evangelical Protestantism, then being clandestinely introduced into China. Christianity provided Hong with a source of ideas potentially far more explosive than the Daoist utopianism, Maitreyan messianism, and Manichean dualism that had long motivated Chinese sectarians. Ultimately, Hong's interpretation of the Bible became the standard by which he evaluated, reinterpreted, and selectively repudiated China's traditions, both orthodox and heterodox. The resultant synthesis, in which the biblical aspects energized the indigenous elements, became a potent political mix.[5]

This chapter identifies both Chinese and evangelical Christian sources of Taiping heterodoxy, analyzes their role in the rise of the rebellion, and evaluates the Taiping heterodoxy within Chinese and Christian perspectives.

The Only True Heavenly Father

Chinese sectarian movements often began with awe-inspiring creator-deities longing to provide spiritual and material salvation to their earthly followers. The Eternal Mother (Wusheng laomu), for example, was revered as a compassionate creator and matriarch of all deities, who longed to grant salvation to her earthly children at the end of the kalpa. By dispatching such messianic agents as the Maitreya Buddha (the Buddha of the Future), she made her presence felt on earth from time to time.[6] Although this lofty ideal inspired several White Lotus uprisings in the late eighteenth and early nineteenth centuries, polytheistic Eternal Mother faith focused primarily on the reunion of the elect with her, following the destruction of the earthly order and the creation of a new millennial epoch, which was merely alluded to.

The Taipings' monotheistic Heavenly Father (Tianfu), by contrast, was the loving, compassionate God who had burst forth from Europe's and America's evangelical churches during the Great Awakening to declare all people worthy and capable of spiritual salvation, intervening in history to redeem them from sin and physical suffering. He was introduced to Hong Xiuquan by Liang Fa (1789–1855), China's first pastor, who was baptized and ordained by Protestantism's earliest missionaries to the Chinese: Robert Morrison (1782–1834) and William Milne (1789–1822). Because of the emperor's 1724 ban against Christianity, the missionaries could only present the scriptures and evangelical doctrines in books written in a complex language far removed from the Judeo-Christian context for covert dissemination in China. Exposed to evangelical ideals while working as a woodblock carver for Morrison in Canton and for Milne in Malacca, Liang turned to Christianity after concluding that pious Pure Land ritual lacked the transcendent source of morality required for the "virtuous act" needed to "obtain forgiveness" for his youthful "drunkenness," "gambling," "lust," "cheating," and "lying" in Canton, where poverty had forced him to seek employment after a few years of village schooling.[7]

The missionaries' "only true," "sovereign" God as creator, parent, law giver, judge, and redeemer on whom all people depend dominates Liang's *Good Words to Admonish the Age* (*Quanshi liangyan;* hereafter cited as *Good Words*), published in 1832. Through scriptural excerpts, biblical commentary, and homiletical essays, Liang's book pleads for China to reject the polytheistic idol worship and immorality caused by its rebellion against God (whom Liang calls "Heavenly Father"). Liang echoes Milne's admiration of Confucianism's stress on such biblical virtues as filial piety as well as the missionary's rebuke of China as "a land full of idols; a land of darkness and spiritual death!"[8] Like the evangelicals, Liang claims that every human being possesses a God-given "soul," which, connected to the Holy Spirit, reveals God's "secret" spiritual knowledge essential to individual conversion and requires sustained moral action. As the Last Judgment looms, Liang warns, the Heavenly Father gives the Chinese a choice: Those who persist in the sin of rejecting their dependence on the Heavenly Father by attributing his creative powers to man-made images, seek to manipulate his will through "magical arts," and pursue such "materialistic-driven" social evils as gambling, cheating, lying, and tobacco, alcohol, and opium addiction, he will punish with hell; those who repent and are "born again" by trusting in the free gift of the Heavenly Father's grace, believing in the "merit" of Jesus' "atoning death," and obeying the Ten Commandments and the mercy, purity of heart, and peacemaking injunctions of the beatitudes, he will reward with heaven. China's Christian conversion would, in turn, trigger the millennial ingathering of the Heavenly Father's global kingdom.

Liang's portrayal of the evangelicals' universal God seeking personal redemption and society's moral resurgence profoundly affected Hong, who, in 1836, received a copy of *Good Words* at the Canton examination site (where, for a second time, he failed the prefectural test). While Liang found God revealed in the Bible and the mission chapel, Hong, the examination scholar, discovered him illuminated also in his own prophetic visions and China's pre-Confucian texts.[9] Amid Hong's guilt over "failing to repay my obligations to my father and older brothers,"[10] following his third unsuccessful examination attempt in 1837, the Heavenly Father appeared to him in a series of dreams as an imposing sage in a long black robe and blond beard. The frustrated patriarch complained to Hong that although the world's people were "produced and sustained by me . . . they take of my gifts, and therewith worship demons; they purposely rebel against me, and arouse my anger."[11] Hong later concluded that the Heavenly Father had intervened three times in human history—in the flood, the exodus, and Jesus' ministry—to win his ungrateful "children" back to monotheism. In the West, the third intervention through Jesus had been successful. But in China, Confucius had already failed to "expound" the Heavenly Father's "true doctrine" when the philosopher edited the classics before Jesus' birth. In addition, the "old serpent-Devil" (Hong's composite of Buddhism's Yanluo and Satan described in *Good Words*) seduced China's emperors into "rebelling" against the divine "grace and favor" and employing such false "demons" as the "five gods," the "Kitchen God," the "Great Monad," "Empress Earth," and the "Jade Emperor" to sever the people's filial tie to the Heavenly Father and to achieve such "selfish" ends as the first emperor's quest for immortality.[12]

In 1843, after his bitter fourth, and final, examination failure, Hong famously dramatized his obedience to the messianic commission to "behead the heterodox [*xie*]" (in which he was coached in the dream by his "Heavenly Elder Brother" Jesus), "preserve the orthodox [*zheng*]" and "relieve the people's distress."[13] Claiming to be the "true son of heaven" *(tianzi)*, he told his biological father, "I am not your son."[14] Then, with the prophet's anger and missionary activism described in *Good Words*, he deposed his family's door, ox, pig, and dragon gods and the Confucian tablet in the village schoolroom where he taught; offered food, prayers of thanksgiving, and petitions for safety before the carved words for "Heavenly Father"; baptized himself and his cousins Feng Yunshan (1822–1852) and Hong Ren'-gan (1822–1864); made a three-foot "demon slaying" sword with which to "capture all the demons" and unite the world into "harmonious union";[15] denounced idol worship and immoral neighbors; and refused to honor the village gods during the Lantern Festival. He also claimed the Heavenly Father had been China's ancient emperor, whose beneficent, egalitarian rule was usurped by the apostate emperors. Hung was convinced that China now needed to restore God's ancient rule in a new millennium.

A Millennial Blueprint

The geography of Hong's millennial thinking was the frontier region of Xunzhou, in southeastern Guangxi, where he and Feng Yunshan preached among Hong's Hakka relatives in 1844.[16] Hong blamed the region's social, economic, and ethnic polarization on the new domestic crises and international pressures created by the first Opium War (1839–1842) as well as Confucius' hierarchical "partial love," which, having emerged since the loss of the universal love that had prevailed during the Heavenly Father's reign, caused people to become "small," "intolerant," and "shallow," their "loves and hates derived from selfishness." Tragically, people now "love those of their own village, hamlet, or clan, and dislike those of other villages, other hamlets, and other clans."[17] Hence the current licentiousness, family breakdown, killing, robbery, "superstition," shamanism, gambling, and opium smuggling throughout Xunzhou.

The kind of moral anarchy plaguing Xunzhou nurtured a great

deal of Chinese millennial activism. The *Liezi* and *Classic of Great Equilibrium (Taiping jing)*, for instance, depict the emergence of a Daoist paradise of simplicity, personal integrity, communal ownership, and peace in which a virtuous government is responsive to people's spiritual and material needs and achieves harmony among heaven, earth, and society.[18] The Triads, too, had a misty utopian vision in their concept of the "City of Poplars," depicted as an ideal, plentiful state located within the Triad lodges, or "seats of great peace" *(taiping zuo)*. The concept harked back to Ming dynasty norms that reaffirmed orthodox social and political institutions.[19]

Hong's own millennial thinking harked back to pre-imperial days. He was especially inspired by Mozi's (fl. 479–438 B.C.E.) depiction of China's pre-imperial sage-kings believing that, in Hong's words, "the earth, when spoken of in its parts, comprised ten thousand kingdoms, but when spoken of collectively constituted one family."[20] This universalism was, Hong wrote, based on "liberal mindedness" *(liang)*, which also characterized the era of "great community" *(datong)* described in the "Evolution of Rites" chapter of the *Book of Rites*. Hong was the first Chinese of the later imperial era to draw attention to this text, in which he discovered a pre-Confucian commonwealth of "great peace and equality"—both concepts are summed up in the term *taiping*[21]—when all the Chinese people, not just the sages, worshiped and depended upon "the universal Father . . . for every article of clothing and every morsel of food."[22]

Hong's anticipation of a future *taiping* millennium is reminiscent of He Xiu's (128–192) theory of historical evolution from a world of disorder to one of "small tranquility" and finally to the utopia of great community, when the world becomes united as a single family.[23] This millennial hope was reinforced in Hong's time by scholars of the *Gongyang Commentary* on the *Spring and Autumn Annals*, who speculated about the possibility of redemptive history amid China's current age of decadence. For Hong, this utopian inevitability resonated with Liang Fa's hope that "the blessing of eternal great peace [*taiping*]"[24] would be achieved in the biblical promise of the Kingdom of Heaven (Tianguo). For Liang, the Kingdom would come "in power" (1 Corinthians 4:20) at an undetermined time to "remit our sin and save our country" by reaffirming the "Three Bonds" and dynastic rule, by easing the exploitation of the poor by the rich, and by reversing moral decline so that Chinese fathers would once again "become merciful and sons filial, officials incorrupt, and the people happy."[25] This millennial age would also see a self-centered China integrated into "a new heaven and a new earth (2 Peter 3:10)."[26]

Liang's millennial aspirations were contained within the imperial Confucian world. In contrast, Hong's restored millennium (outlined in an 1845 essay entitled "Exhortation on the Origin of Virtue for Awakening the Age") will be ruled directly by the Heavenly Father and managed by civil servants with "talent," "virtue," and "sincerity" who will "cultivate harmony" and extend universal love regardless of biological family relationships. These officials will "be selected" to exercise (in Hong's paraphrase of Confucius) "a public and common spirit"[27] in governing an egalitarian commonwealth of virtuous rule (as Yao and Shun treated their districts evenhandedly), social harmony (as Confucius and Mencius taught people "without distinction," and Tang and Wu eliminated the violent and cruel throughout China), and evenly distributed goods and services (as Yu and Ji cared for the calamity-stricken regardless of their location).

In addition, Hong envisioned, social welfare will be secured by nurturing the young into adulthood, by employing the able-bodied, and by treating orphans, childless men, the sick, widows, and the aged with kindness and compassion. In particular, ethical government will insure justice in business dealings, and the rules of decorum in education. Driven by love, not materialism, the haves and have-nots will care for each other, and there will be no social distinctions, crime, or rebellion against the Heavenly Father. In 1846, Hong expressed his confidence that the millennial role reversal would soon be realized:

> Presently we shall see the world united as one family, enjoying great peace and equality [*taiping*]. How can it be that this perverse and unfeeling world cannot in a day be transformed into an honest and upright world? How can it be that this insulting and encroaching, fighting and killing age cannot in a day be changed into a world where the strong no more oppress the weak, the many overwhelm the few, the wise delude the simple, or the bold annoy the fearful?[28]

Messianic Leadership

Chinese millenarian movements were typically centered around a messianic hero, whose visions and prognostications articulated the grievances of their followers and revealed the utopian society they sought to establish in collaboration with the divine intervention. As Heavenly King (Tianwang), Hong's mission (through which, Hong said, the Heavenly Father was now making his fourth descent into history) was to articulate his millenarian prophecy, help his followers break with the old order, and become God's agent on earth. In this way, Hong thought, he could redeem himself and China. After all, his Confucian education had engendered in him not only the ideal of filial devotion but a sense of the responsibility of the individual who, drawing upon larger cosmic powers, was supposed to rescue a world in precipitous decline. The Cheng-Zhu Confucianism of his examination study imposed the burden of achieving sagehood, and by the nineteenth century, neo-Confucianism oscillated between hope for bringing order to the world through public service on the one hand and introspective self-cultivation on the other. A balance was supposed to be achieved by linking the sage with heaven.[29] But Hong had been unable to connect with immanent heaven. For him, as for Liang, the moral perfection that Confucianism promised could not, in the end, be delivered. Instead, Hong discovered personal and collective salvation at a literal, this-worldly level with the transcendent Heavenly Father, and he endeavored to rescue a world he perceived to be steeped in evil. As Heavenly King, an earthly sovereign, Hong would thereby supersede the Confucian sage as the agent of salvation.

The alienation generated by Xunzhou's deepening polarization was hard on the Hakka immigrants. Living in widely scattered hillside villages, these newcomers from western Guangdong were soon pushed off lands they had only just brought under cultivation because of escalating rents, increasing surtaxes, and intensifying attacks by landlords as well as other tenants and aboriginal groups. Mustering their traditional self-reliance, ethnic solidarity, and dialect uniformity, the Hakka organized self-defense teams, their guerrilla tactics honed in countless feuds during centuries of southward migration from their central China homeland.[30]

Among the dispirited Hakka, Hong and Feng pursued the fervent style of missionary evangelism pioneered by Milne in colonial Malacca and emulated by Liang in his home village near Guangzhou in 1819. (For violating the ban on Christianity, yamen underlings beat the soles of his feet with bamboo.) Claiming that individual salvation would lead to Xunzhou's moral revival, Hong and Feng exhorted their fellow Hakka to turn away from "false spirits" and "perverse things"; to repent by worshiping the "true God," believing in Jesus, and adhering to the Ten Commandments; and to thereby avoid disasters and sickness. In this way, they promised, the people's "souls would ascend to heaven."[31] But those who clung to worldly customs and believed in devils would descend to the "eighteenth level of hell."[32] Hailing Hong and Feng as messengers who "had come down from heaven to preach the true doctrine," over one hundred Hakka requested baptism.[33]

Back in Hua during 1844–1847, Hong continued to preach and set down his social critique and millennial prophecies in handwritten, missionary-style pamphlets intended to persuade "the people to right behavior."[34] (He sent these writings to Xunzhou to be the basis of Feng's evangelism there.) Li Zhenggao (1823–1885), a Hakka disciple in Hua, noted that the Hakka warmed to Hong's teachings because "we lamented the moral and political decline of our country. According to our sentiment, Heaven had decreed that we should curb injustice and promote justice."[35] Hence, Li said, "When we heard his daydreams, our hearts flew to him, and we thought: certainly Heaven had heard our sighs and had chosen this man to bring better times."[36]

In Chinese messianic tradition, saviors often descended as ideal kings to rescue a disadvantaged group and reign over a new dispensation throughout China as secular rulers.[37] In 1846 Hong dreamed that a red sun was placed into his hand. And in a poem of that year, he refers to the traditional notion that a sage appears in China every five hundred years.[38] The sun is an orthodox symbol of the Chinese monarch, a heterodox image of the millennial reign of the Manichean Prince of Radiance (Mingwang), and a Triad restorationist symbol.[39] For Hong, the most recent sage would have been Zhu Yuanzhang (1328–1398), leader of the White Lotus rebels who overthrew the Mongols and founded the Ming dynasty five centuries earlier. Hong, however, did not advocate the Ming's return but instead went beyond the missionaries and Liang Fa in denouncing the imperial system altogether. Nor did he ever claim the emperor's role for himself. Instead, he consistently denied the divinity of both himself and his Heavenly Elder Brother Jesus, insisting that only the Heavenly Father was divine; as vice regent, Hong was merely king, subordinate to the imperial father.

During the spring of 1847, Hong's messianic self-identity

broadened when he studied with Issachar Jacox Roberts (1802–1871), a Baptist from Tennessee who had defiantly built his chapel outside the Canton treaty-port's perimeter. A disciple of Karl Gützlaff (1803–1851), initiator of *blitzconversion* by Chinese evangelists themselves, Roberts offered to give Christian catechism to Hong in the hope of expanding Hong's evangelism so as to spark "the commencement of the outpouring of the Holy Spirit upon this benighted [Chinese] people."[40] To this end, Roberts had Hong memorize the Bible (this was his first exposure to the full scriptures), study congregational organization, broaden his revivalistic preaching style, and visit Canton's other dozen missionaries and their churches (serving a hundred Chinese converts), schools, clinics, libraries, and printing presses, which the Treaty of Nanjing (1842) permitted within the five treaty ports. Hong now sought baptism and ordination to become Roberts' assistant pastor. Roberts, however, refused to baptize Hong, thereby thwarting his church career. Undeterred, Hong returned to Xunzhou, in June 1847, convinced that his millennial dream would still be realized through his messianic commission, the guidance of his newly acquired Bible, and his building of the Heavenly Kingdom.

God Worshiper Ritual and Ethics

Traditionally, Chinese sectarian leaders were regarded as having moral authority derived from spiritual power manifested in visions, heavenly transports, and divine mandates.[41] In Xunzhou's rugged Thistle Mountain frontier area, where Feng Yunshan had been organizing congregations around his cousin's teachings, long-held beliefs in Yao-originated faith healing and mediumship through spirit possession and in trance-induced spirit journeys to supernatural realms made people receptive to a prophet-messiah like Hong Xiuquan.[42]

Structured according to sectarian traditions of lay leadership, egalitarian ethics, and property sharing, the God Worshipers Society (a term taken from *Good Words*) was a multi-village network of a dozen congregations of some two thousand tenants, unemployed miners, charcoal burners, boat people, porters, carpenters, rice pounders, secret-society members, and bandits, along with a few wealthy Hakka landholders, pawnshop owners, merchants, and members of the Zhuang and Yao ethnic minorities recruited by family, lineage, and occupation. By means of the liturgical and moral precepts laid out in his *Book of Heavenly Commandments* (1848), a worship manual, Hong molded the God Worshipers into the vanguard of the coming Kingdom.

Chinese sectarians anticipated the new dispensation by acting out its new values and communal life, beginning with ritual initiation to symbolize rebirth and purification. For example, initiates into the Eternal Mother–oriented Residing in Principles (Zaili) cult crawled through a straw image of the Eternal Mother as a metaphor for rebirth into eternity. Other cults had initiates make written confessions that they ceremonially burned, along with initiation lists, and drink three cups of tea before undergoing ritual purification by washing in a basin. Sectarians regarded penitential rites as essential to both spiritual and physical well-being and practiced ritual repentance through group confession and recitation of prayers for forgiveness. The Triad associations (made up of peddlers, smugglers, dockhands, clerks, runners, and lower-degree holders as well as criminals) also ritualized their sworn brotherhoods before the image of the imperially sanctioned god of war along with those of other patron deities.[43]

The sect members' unity as a new family, celebrated in the White Lotus "precious scrolls" and in the Triads' sworn kinship groups, certainly challenged Confucian precepts.[44] Hong, too, questioned the Confucian family ethic by claiming that the only legitimate basis for kinship was not biological but moral, because, he insisted, only those who worshiped the Heavenly Father and followed his moral principles could be considered his relatives. ("If my own parents, my wife and children, do not believe," he reasoned, "I cannot feel united with them, how much less with other friends. Only the heavenly friendship is true, all other is false.")[45] This idea grew into Hong's conviction that all the world's people were equal as siblings under the same Heavenly Father.

The God Worshipers' initiation into this world family was patterned after the Baptist rite of adult baptism through bodily immersion at Roberts' chapel. After their names were read aloud, initiates bowed before two burning lamps and three cups of tea (which they drank), "confessed" their sins (according to Roberts' practice), and, as water was poured over their heads, vowed "not to worship evil spirits, not to practice evil things, but to keep the heavenly commandments." They then washed in a stream (another Baptist custom) while promising "to purify [myself] from all former sins, put off the old, and regenerate [myself]."[46] The initiates' names and confession texts were then burned, the smoke sent heavenward to the Heavenly Father.

Hong affirmed the God Worshipers' filial dependence on the Heavenly Father. To this end, he cited Liang's quotation from Jesus in Matthew 7:7: "Ask and it shall be given you; seek, and you shall find; knock and it shall be opened to you."[47] To request blessings on the occasion of a birthday, marriage, celebrating a child's first month of life, building a house, and planting crops, the God Worshipers were to offer "animals [including horses and oxen on special occasions], delicacies, tea, and rice." Hong wrote and printed the morning and evening intercessions and thanksgivings for food, clothing, and protection against sickness and calamity, grace before meals, and petitions for peace, stability, prosperity, and freedom from demons and fear. Hong's prayers asked the Holy Spirit "never [to] allow the devilish demons to deceive me" and to "change my [wicked] heart" for help in "repentance" (gaiguo) and "self-renewal" (zixin) so that "my soul may ascend to heaven." Each prayer referred to Jesus' atonement and ended with a line from the Lord's Prayer pledging cooperation with the Heavenly Father so that his "will be done on earth as it is in heaven." After reciting or (if they were illiterate) burning prayer texts, the God Worshipers were to seek purification by washing in a basin or a river.[48] Insisting that the righteous go directly to heaven, Hong banned Buddhist funeral rites.

The liturgy Hong designed welded the God Worshipers into a cohesive fellowship with an exuberant sense of moral purpose. Given Hong's anticlerical bias and his experience with Baptist lay elders in Canton, the Taipings never did develop an ordained clergy. During worship services, the God Worshipers faced the sun to honor Hong, while men and women sat on opposite sides of the room. They called each other "brother" and "sister" according to both Baptist and Hakka customs. An elder prayed for divine mercy and protection, praised the merits of Jesus' atonement, enjoined sincerity of heart, and proscribed image worship. The congregants sang Baptist hymns to the accompaniment of gongs and firecrackers, and concluded with a doxology in praise of Father, Son, and Holy Spirit. (The God Worshipers did not, however, celebrate the Lord's Supper as Roberts did.)

Hong thought that social reform could be accomplished only after individual moral transformation. White Lotus congregations achieved salvation by chanting mantras pronouncing the Eternal Mother's name. And some White Lotus groups adhered to an austere puritanism that stressed dietary and sexual abstinence to repudiate what sectarians saw as the orthodox order's moral bankruptcy. Triads, too, exalted a lofty morality, paramount within which was the ethic of doing the heroically righteous *(i)*, an idea celebrated in China's popular novels. They also espoused such virtues as filial devotion, loyalty, faithfulness, sincerity, reciprocity, and benevolence among sworn siblings.[49]

Like Morrison, Milne, and Liang, Hong initially applauded Confucian ethics, his earliest moral pronouncements seemingly consonant with China's popular "morality books" based on Zheng-Zhu Confucianism. Later, Hong asked his lineage elders to beat adulterers, seducers, the disobedient to parents, thieves, robbers, gamblers, and "all vagabonds plotting evil,"[50] and then advocated fortifying Confucian ethics with such New Testament virtues as forgiveness, charity, modesty, integrity, justice, and faith.[51] Eventually, though, his assessment of the severity of China's decline convinced him that the moral rigor of the Ten Commandments must supersede Confucianism in order to repudiate old values and define the new ones needed to support the coming millennium. Convinced that sin originated in ignorance of the Ten Commandments, Hong wrote commentaries to apply each commandment to conditions in Thistle Mountain, admonishing followers to obey God and parents; to renounce China's "false gods" and apostate emperors; to reject the sins of "materialism" (stealing, killing, and other violence), of "selfishness" (fornication, adultery, lewdness, perversity, seducing others' wives and daughters, and addiction to opium and the "family-destroying juice" of alcohol), and of "efforts to manipulate God's will" (stealing, gambling, witchcraft, and trickery).

Hong's conviction that moral activism in a world partitioned between good and evil must be dramatized by iconoclastic destruction of the old order had historical precedent, both orthodox and heterodox. Richard Shek points out, for example, that the Luojiao sectarians belittled the efficacy of temples, images, clergy, ritual, and ancestor worship.[52] Hong admired the efforts of such Confucian "prophetic heroes" as Han Yü (768–824) to denounce Daoist and Buddhist "heresies," demolish "licentious temples," and condemn "idolatrous rites," but he regretted their failure to reverse China's deepening idolatry. Throughout Thistle Mountain, the God Worshipers destroyed temples, shrines, and religious images, be they dedicated to state Confucianism or to local cults glorifying illicit love, matricide, or Zhuang dog worship. They posted copies of the Ten Commandments amid the debris to demonstrate the limitless power of the Heavenly Father over localized false deities guilty of such sins as "deceiving" the Heavenly Father, "violating the Ten Commandments," "transgressing the law of the state," or "deluding and enslaving men and women."[53]

Apocalyptic Signs and Wonders

C. K. Yang notes that Chinese sectarians have a long tradition of eschatological speculation, which, since the Han period, merged piety with politics during troubled times when divinely appointed messiahs employed scriptural revelation, prophetic preaching, and faith healing to convince their followers that the symptoms of cosmic decay and dynastic decline portended an imminent, cataclysmic end to the prevailing age. The coming apocalypse would, they promised, yield to a utopian era of individual and social salvation.[54] To bring history to this climax, some sect leaders mobilized their followers against governments that they felt oppressed them and that were, in any event, already seeking the sectarians' destruction. One eschatological myth was that of the Maitreya Buddha descending to earth to usher in the third and final kalpa. Later, elements of Manichaeism were introduced. Persian in origin, this dualistic perspective envisioned a heroic struggle between the forces of dark (the orthodox order) and light (the sectarian elite). After the victory of light, the Maitreya Buddha would announce the incarnation of the Prince of Radiance to rule over the new millennium. The Song rebel Fang La (d. 1121), for instance, rose in 1120 to proclaim a new dispensation of equality and plenty following the victory of light.

By the middle of the fourteenth century, the Maitreyan and Manichaean traditions had joined with the salvationist White Lotus cult of Pure Land Buddhism to form a potent millenarian amalgam. During the Yuan dynasty, Han ethnocentrism became a compelling element in this synthesis as White Lotus leaders proclaimed themselves or others to be the reincarnation of a former ideal emperor who would overthrow alien rule and restore conscientious Han government. He would also prepare for the coming of a messiah to preside over the final utopian epoch under the symbol of a white lotus.

One such White Lotus leader was Han Shantong (d. 1351), who claimed to be the reincarnation of both the Maitreya Buddha and the Song emperor Huizong (r. 1101–1125). He preached that the reign of the foreign Mongols presaged the collapse of the present era and advocated apocalyptic combat against the Yuan, so that Han Chinese rule could be restored with the inauguration of a millennium of "great equality" (taiping) to be overseen by the Prince of Radiance (who would, in fact, be Han Shantong's own son).[55]

These sectarian ideals were transmitted from teacher to disciple, often with the help of "precious scrolls," among the White Lotus congregations spreading into central and southern China. After 1775 Eternal Mother millennialism joined with escalating crop failure, social strains, ethnic conflict, and anti-Manchu rhetoric among recent settlers, weak in lineage ties, along the mountainsides of Hubei to unleash the White Lotus rebellion of 1796–1804.[56]

For the God Worshipers, too, trances, visions, dream interpretation, speaking in tongues, faith healing, prognostication, and other ecstatic behavior created a highly charged apocalyptic atmosphere in which the Heavenly Father himself took charge of delivering them from disaster. Xunzhou's doomsday omens of intensifying drought-induced famine and typhus, merchant greed, government malfeasance, ethnic friction, and militarization energized God Worshiper ritual and ethics and unleashed eschatological theories as to the arrival of the promised Kingdom.[57] Moreover, Hong assisted the needy from his sacred treasury, a Hakka-inspired egalitarian community chest, which Hong rationalized through Liang's references to the blessedness of the poor in the beatitudes and to the difficulty the rich would have in entering the "kingdom of heaven" (Matthew 19:23). Initiates contributed their possessions to this fund, from which they were to receive equal shares of the divine bounty. In fact, many Hakka joined the God Worshipers because, as the Taipings' future "Loyal King" Li Xiucheng (1824–1864) later recalled in his confession, "[we] were poor and had nothing to eat."[58]

Scholars note that Chinese messiahs practiced both prophetic condemnation and healing arts. By the end of the Han dynasty, for example, such Daoist-inspired groups as the Yellow Turbans and the Five Pecks of Rice devotees blamed sickness on moral laxity and government malfeasance.[59] Hong, too, denounced Xunzhou merchants for mercilessly raising food prices, and chided local officials for hoarding food aid as famine spread. In addition, Hong used prognostication to "regularly forecast rain or clear weather" and "drew magic charms [in God's name] to cure disease" on the basis of New Testament healing miracles.[60] But it was traditional Hakka shamanism (including some aspects Hong had earlier condemned as "superstition") tied to the Trinity (which Hong had not emphasized beyond giving it symbolic significance in the singing of the doxology) that brought the Heavenly Father and Jesus directly into the God Worshipers' midst to promise an end to suffering, accelerate the millennial timetable, and transform the God Worshipers' religious campaign into political insurrection.

Yang Xiuqing (d. 1856), illiterate boss of the local charcoal workers, used Hakka faith healing and Yao spirit possession techniques to take upon himself—in the name of the "omnipotent" Heavenly Father, the "compassionate" Christ, and the "omniscient" Holy Spirit—the illnesses that resulted from malnutrition and typhus. Yang also served as the medium for the Heavenly Father in prophesying events and publicly reprimanding backsliders identified by the spy network that Yang modeled on Roberts' congregational surveillance system in Canton. Moreover, Hong's cousin-in-law, Xiao Chaogui (d. 1852), invoked Jesus' name and Yao spirit journeys to help the God Worshipers reenact Hong's 1837 vision. He also spoke for Jesus.[61]

Within this ecstatic environment, the divine descents (in the God Worshipers' own words) "display[ed] innumerable [healing] miracles and [prophetic] powers."[62] This attracted increasing numbers of desperate Hakka and instilled a martial zeal in the struggle against the local elite who—offended by Hong's iconoclastic destruction of the very temples that also facilitated market activities, lineage and village alliances, and social services—began sending their militia against the God Worshipers in January 1851. Through Yang and Xiao, the divine oracles affirmed Hong as Heavenly King and counseled obedience to the Ten Commandments as well as Hong's injunctions to obey military orders, endure suffering, fight courageously, respect civilians, and expect execution for disobedience and cowardice. In the struggle against their persecutors, the God Worshipers were to subordinate personal and family interests to the wider millennial cause and reject selfishness and materialism by contributing all their possessions to the sacred treasury.

The fact that Hong's authority as religious founder, prophet, and messiah was now becoming integrated with Yang's and Xiao's folk religious charisma—both sources of authority seemingly anchored within both Christian and Chinese doctrines—has led Joseph W. Esherick to hypothesize that "without some means of making . . . [Taiping] religion comprehensible to a peasantry utterly unfamiliar with Christian eschatology, the rebellion could never have gotten off the ground. I would argue that for the Taiping, this dilemma was resolved by the fact that much of their religious behavior could be understood in terms of ordinary Chinese folk religion."[63]

Hong's congregational structure facilitated the mobilization of thousands of Hakka (who were weak in lineage structure) throughout southeastern Guangxi and adjacent northwestern Guangdong. In the spring of 1851 the Qing government, alarmed by the God Worshipers' loyalty to a transcendent God claiming a status far above that of the Manchu Son of Heaven, assumed they were a traditional rebel threat to the dynasty and attacked them.

A Theocratic Kingdom

Hong's millennial goal of *taiping* was to be realized through a biblically based theocratic Heavenly Kingdom. For Liang, the Heavenly Kingdom meant both a place of heavenly reward for the spiritually saved as well as a purified Confucian order. But for Hong it was the ideal vehicle for reconstituting the ancient commonwealth for the equal distribution of the Heavenly Father's creation. This idea turned Confucianism on its head and offered the reconstruction of state and society in a far more concrete, far-reaching way than what other Chinese rebels proposed. Daoist-inspired responses to moral collapse and administrative decline included the short-lived theocracies of the Five Pecks of Rice sectarians, the Ba ethnic community in southwest China, the Yellow Turbans, and the Northern Wei court in which their messiahs, like the Taipings, combined religious and secular authority.[64] Later, White Lotus rebels appealed to Maitreyan messianism in their quest to overthrow the Mongol emperors and the gentry landlords loyal to the alien dynasty. Yet they soon discovered that Buddhist eschatology, passively awaiting the millennium at the kalpa's end, offered neither an alternative to the existing order nor a concrete plan for reorganizing secular power. Other rebels, too, hailed the coming of a new age and encouraged some sectarian groups to create their own state or "safe area" in the name of Maitreya and approved of necessary military force. But these autonomous devotional groups lacked a comprehensive plan for unifying themselves and centralizing the new millennium.[65]

Hong's Heavenly Father, on the other hand, was to resume his rule of China as emperor, a claim no other religious rebels made for their patron deities. The Taipings' theocratically inspired organizational power, energized with troop discipline, was unparalleled among contemporary rebels and would bring the movement much early success. Following his declaration of the inauguration of the Heavenly Kingdom of Great Peace and Equality (Taiping tianguo) on 11 January 1851 (his birthday), Hong decreed that the Heavenly Kingdom would be implemented by a theocratic hierarchy, which merged religious, military, and civil authority into a single administrative pyramid through Hong and his "brother" kings, with Yang in charge of Feng and Xiao (the latter two were killed in 1852), as well as two other kings, to extend God's sovereignty directly to twenty thousand individual Taipings. In order to reject traditional fatalism, internalize dependence on the Heavenly Father, and enter the new millennium, Feng Yunshan created a hybrid lunar-solar calendar that eliminated the lucky and unlucky days of the old lunar calendar.

Hong promised that compliance with the Ten Commandments (read weekly in public) would bring heavenly rewards. In his *Taiping Rules and Regulations* (1851),[66] Hong spelled out a puritanical code mandating segregation of the sexes (including spouses) into separate camps, strict obedience to officers, self-sacrifice, benevolence to civilians, and the commitment to "uphold and faithfully serve the country to the end."[67] Officers and conscripts were to call each other "brother" and "sister." Battlefield anxiety was generated by the filial bond to the morally demanding Heavenly Father, warrior god, and judge. The threat of summary execution for battlefield cowardice, failure to memorize the Ten Commandments within three weeks of enlistment, and other clearly stated infractions fostered disciplined troops. These included one hundred thousand intrepid Hakka women fighters under the command of Hong's sister, their unbound feet, capacity for physical stamina, and years of self-defense experience helping the Taipings win early victories against disorganized Qing forces.

In a series of evangelistic tracts written in 1852, Hong sought to indoctrinate the growing number of Taiping recruits by calling on all Chinese—including former adversaries among Hakka, original settlers, and aboriginal groups—to unify as a "chosen people" whom the Heavenly Father would deliver from Manchu oppression in a latter-day Exodus. In fact, Hong put the Taiping crusade into the pages of the Old Testament itself by identifying the "demon" Manchus as latter-day Egyptians now enslaving not Jews but Chinese, defiling their women, debasing their culture, and destroying their families.[68] Hong also defined the new Taiping person as one who forges correct relationships with the Heavenly Father and Jesus, inserts liberality, indulgence, and love into the obligations of monarch, civil servants, spouses, and family members and who promotes individual responsibility as the basis of the Taiping state through the regulation of mind, heart, and senses in the practice of honesty, humility, and selfless devotion.[69]

The Guangxi "Old Sisters" and "Old Brothers" fortified the burgeoning ranks of "Heavenly Soldiers" with such assurances as this: "The Heavenly Father and Heavenly Elder Brother rescue mankind. They gave birth to the Heavenly King to guide you forward. Brothers and sisters, this is our great good fortune. Endless blessings await you in the life to come."[70] In camp, the Taipings sang Baptist hymns and concluded their grace with the phrase "Kill the demons!" On the march, they razed religious places and libraries, including some that were architectural wonders. They also killed Buddhist and Daoist clergy, whom Liang and Hong had condemned as venal hypocrites preying on the people's superstitions, as well as Manchus and unrepentant Chinese civil servants. Before battle, the Taipings exulted: "Our Heavenly Father helps us, and no one can fight with him."[71] During battle, Hong encouraged the faithful to:

> Let the demons scheme in a thousand and ten thousand ways;
> They will hardly escape the sure hand of the Heavenly Father.
> Even the rivers and mountains were, in six days, created;
> Each of you who believes in the Spiritual Father shall be a hero.
> High Heaven has commissioned you to exterminate the demons;
> The Heavenly Father and Heavenly Elder Brother constantly
>   look after you.
> Let men and women officers all grasp the sword.[72]

Nanjing as New Jerusalem

In March 1853 one million Taipings captured Nanjing, the former Ming capital. Hong renamed it "New Jerusalem," which, he asserted

in annotating Revelation 3:12, was predestined to be "sent down
from heaven by God" to become His "Heavenly Capital."[73] The
Heavenly Father, depicted with a beard, cap, and wife (called "Heavenly Mother") and as grandfather of Jesus' and Hong's children
(through Hong's heavenly wife, called "First Chief Moon"), was now
forming a new covenant with the Chinese and would soon vanquish
the false emperor in Beijing.

Although Hong styled himself as "Son of Heaven" and borrowed "Heavenly King" from the *Rites of Zhou* and the *Spring and
Autumn Annals,* his self-identity as monarch has no parallel in Chinese history. Although he had earlier intimated a personal connection
to Zhu Yuanzhang, he now claimed to be the reincarnated biblical
priest-king Melchizedek, messianic founder of the first Jerusalem
who prefigured both King David in the Old Testament and Jesus in
the New. As Melchizedek, Hong pointed out in his annotations, he
was "priest of the God Most High" (Genesis 14:18) and "king of
peace" (Hebrews 7:2). He would therefore be the Heavenly Father's
vice-regent in "rebuild[ing] . . . [his] tabernacle."[74]

Hong put himself at the apex of Taiping worship, which was
intended to maintain popular compliance with theocratic rule. On
the "Heavenly Terrace" near his palace, he venerated the Heavenly
Father. He also ordered the "best room" in every building to be
transformed into a "Heavenly Father hall," where Taiping officials
(who also merged religious, civil, and military authority) led worship
services, explained the scriptures, and officiated at Protestant-style
baptisms, weddings, and funerals. Work was banned and military
action discouraged on the Taiping Sabbath. In front of incense-filled
altars of three bowls each of tea, meat, rice, and vegetables, worship
included a recitation of the Ten Commandments (along with Hong's
commentary on them) and the Lord's Prayer; singing hymns and the
doxology; Bible readings; prayers; a sermon praising the Heavenly
Father's omnipotence, Hong's messianic leadership, and the importance of loyalty over filial piety—"A man should only regard his
country, / And not consider his own parents,"[75] Hong wrote—stead-
fastness in patriotic duty, courage, faithfulness, and self-sacrifice in
the struggle against the Manchu "demons"; incense; and gongs and
firecrackers. Before meals at home, the Taipings laid out the twelve
bowls referred to above, lit candles, and, according to one Western
observer, intoned such petitions as this: "Heavenly Father, the Great
God, bless us thy little ones. Give us day by day food to eat and

clothes to wear. Deliver us from evil and calamity, and receive our souls into heaven."[76]

In the Taipings' Heavenly Kingdom, Confucianism was supplanted by a whole new ideological foundation based on (1) the Taiping Bible, which consisted of the first six books of the Old Testament, a complete New Testament, and a third, "True Testament" recording the divine pronouncements made during the descents in 1848–1852; (2) Hong's numerous theological writings; and (3) the Taipings' evangelical tracts. These publications were widely distributed for free and became the basis of the Taipings' universal education and civil service examination.[77]

Theocracy provided the authoritarian state power needed to conscript the populace for public works and military service, implement Hong's millennial plan, assume responsibility for the people's welfare, and mount a cultural revolution against the old order, the scope and depth of which surpassed the missionaries' treaty-port "good works" and even the Christian reformism in the West. Hong ordered all property turned over to the sacred treasury, and trade and commerce were to become a state monopoly. Within separate men's and women's camps (which existed through 1855), units of twenty-five people pursued their occupational specialties to supply the heavenly capital and the far-flung military campaigns. In accordance with the *Rites of Zhou,* all of this was supervised by six central ministries (one for each "king") and fifty administrative units. To repudiate Manchu domination, Hong banned the queue, restored Ming clothing, and created a new system of court nobility and etiquette. He broke the scholars' monopoly of learning by ordering use of a simplified, punctuated vernacular. He also eliminated ancestor worship and similar "idolatrous" notions from some traditional texts, ordered the burning of other books, and he prohibited bribery and torture in judicial proceedings.[78]

Hong's most revolutionary innovations were on behalf of gender equality, an idea shared by White Lotus devotees who believed that because the elect were created by the Eternal Mother and were destined to receive her impartial salvation, they were equal as "brothers" and "sisters." (Within the White Lotus sect called the Great Way Prior to Heaven, women became cult leaders.)[79] The Taipings went much further than this, however, in banning foot-binding, arranged marriage, polygamy, wife purchase, widow suicide, and prostitution —traditions already shunned by the Hakka. And they decreed women's equal access to schools, landholding, work outside the home, government examinations, bureaucratic appointment, military service, and court nobility. Wherever the Taipings conquered territory, the troops were to build refuges for vulnerable women and summarily execute anyone caught violating them. Even though the Taiping kings maintained harems (a Chinese institution with Old Testament parallels) and employed the traditional Confucian rhetoric of women's "Three Obediences," to father, husband, and sons (which nevertheless resonated with the evangelicals' Pauline views of women's inferiority), they imposed monogamy on the rank and file, banned dowries, and encouraged women to marry (and even remarry) of their own free will.

The Heavenly Kingdom's centerpiece was the "Land System," promulgated in 1854, which Jonathan Spence characterizes as "perhaps the most utopian, comprehensive, and authoritarian scheme for human organization ever seen in China up to that time."[80] As the fullest expression of Hong's millennial idealism (laid out in the 1845 essay discussed above), it not only implied the destruction of China's Confucian institutions but went far beyond the social and economic leveling described in the utopian *Rites of Zhou,* by making the state the vehicle of God's love. The *Rites of Zhou* claimed that the king owned all the land. And Sui and Tang officials proposed an idealistic "equal field" system, abandoned in 780 in favor of the "two tax" method of equalizing taxes. By contrast, the Taipings insisted that all land belonged to the Heavenly Father. Hence, Hong wrote, "if there is land, it should be farmed by all; if there is food, it should be eaten by all; if there are clothes and money, they should be worn and used by all. There should be no inequality. Everyone should be equally well fed and clothed."[81] Because equal shares of similar-quality land were to be assigned to all the Heavenly Father's earthly children, the Land System therefore extended to women equal access to landholding.[82]

Conscientious theocratic leadership was needed to manage this utopian plan. The devil, Hong noted, had created idols to assist him in promoting evil in the world. So God, who rules over a just "government of all men and things" and saves people from selfish monarchs and unjust magistrates, has therefore appointed "assistants who aid [him] in protecting mankind, just as a sovereign in ruling a country has officials to aid him in the government."[83] Officials with talent, virtue, and sincerity would therefore be selected by the biblically based examination system to cultivate harmony and extend government to an administrative level based on the "congregation" of twenty-five families. There a sergeant appointed by Hong would insure that men and women received equal amounts of similarly productive land, that rents were abolished and taxes reduced, and that each family kept as much of its produce as it needed, the surplus to be stored in public granaries for the support of local residents and for transfer to hard-hit areas during hard times. The sergeant was also to administer justice; teach both boys and girls in a form of "charity school" envisaged by Milne and implemented briefly by Liang; assist the elderly, sick, disabled, widows, and orphans; defray the costs of marriage feasts, ceremonies for the newborn, and other rituals; and conduct worship services in the local church.

The Taipings proclaimed all people who worshiped God were siblings, to be included in an imminent worldwide millennium under Hong's universal reign. Hong had already prophesied a post–Opium War China taking its rightful place in the new global order:

> China, which is near to us, is governed and regulated by God; so it is in foreign nations, which are far away.... In the world there are many men, all brothers; in the world there are many women, all sisters. Why, then retain partiality for this country against that boundary? How can we think of your swallowing me or of me swallowing you?[84]

By hailing "foreign brothers" who visited Nanjing as their siblings under the same creator—their lord's prayer concluding with the phrase "bless the brothers and sisters of all nations"[85]—the Taipings rejected the claim that the "middle kingdom" was unique.

The Fall of the Heavenly Kingdom

Amid the ebb and flow of military fortune, the Taipings maintained their Heavenly Kingdom for more than a decade. But for all its strengths, the Taipings' theocratic paradigm was fatally flawed. After 1853 Hong, the prophet, priest, and king, confined himself to "heavenly matters," through visions, ritual, Bible study, and an obsession with a missionary translation of *Pilgrim's Progress* (with its evangelical themes of iconoclastic break with the past, apocalyptic combat against demons, obedience to the Ten Commandments, and spiritual odyssey from the City of Destruction to the Celestial City). At the same time, Yang Xiuqing, the shamanic medium, wielded bureaucratic and military authority by issuing the Heavenly Father's frequent commands directly through his "golden mouth." He also portrayed himself as the Christ-like "Comforter," delivering the Taipings from "misery and bitterness," and claimed to be the Holy Spirit monopolizing spiritual secrets (gleaned through his Nanjing-wide spy network). Proclaiming himself "holy" and Hong merely "eminent," Yang implied that his oracles were a superior revelation to Hong's dreams and theological writings. Humiliated in this sibling rivalry, Hong mortally wounded theocratic power by ordering Yang's assassination on 2 September 1856, which also took the lives of twenty thousand members of Yang's court.

Yang wanted to make the Taipings more traditionally sectarian. Yet Hong Ren'gan sought to make them more Christian. Baptized, confirmed in the Lutheran catechism, and having served as an evangelist in Hong Kong for Morrison's and Milne's London Missionary Society during the mid-1850s, Ren'gan witnessed the second generation of evangelical missionaries in China fusing the Bible and Western culture into a concept of Christian ecumene. In 1859 the Heavenly King appointed his cousin "Shield King." Hong Ren'gan immediately became concerned that the Heavenly Kingdom relied too heavily on the Old Testament's "compulsion of human force" and encouraged the Heavenly King to balance vengeance with Christ's "merciful forgiveness" and the loving "influence of the Holy Spirit."[86] To this end, the Shield King installed a stone pillar inscribed with the beatitudes in front of his palace and wrote prayers and exhortations emphasizing such New Testament concepts as conscience, forgiveness, and mercy.

Hong Ren'gan was also convinced that the Kingdom of Heaven should become a vehicle for China's global economic integration and secular progress, because "both heaven and earth have been altogether renovated." Moreover, he thought, only Christian nations could compete in the nineteenth-century world. Hence, the Chinese must now become "new citizens" of a "new civilization."[87] He proposed that China and the Christian West not only forge spiritual bonds but also cooperate in promoting China's institutional and economic development. This would include the banning of infanticide and capital punishment and the creation of missionary-inspired schools, hospitals, adoption agencies, and social welfare institutions. These charitable organizations would be funded by taxes derived from new national wealth created by a Sino-Western, public-private partnership in transportation, commerce, technology, mining, industry, international trade and finance, and establishment of Chinese Christian churches to promote spiritual and material progress. China's new order would be undergirded by the rule of law; safeguarded by a Western-style court system, limited bill of rights, and separation of executive and judicial powers; and modernized by a postal system, patent office, and an educated citizenry informed through universal education, an open press, and political access to Taiping leaders.[88]

The Heavenly King ignored his cousin's reforms, but they probably could not have saved the Heavenly Kingdom. By 1860 the Taiping rank and file were still able to recite the doxology, Hong's prayers, and the Ten Commandments. But centralized military coordination—the very means of extending theocratic control—collapsed. After Yang's death the Heavenly Father's voice no longer rang through the Heavenly Kingdom, and Taiping commanders focused on their own regional enclaves at the expense of an overall, coordinated military strategy. Some virtuous officers did indeed enforce the Ten Commandments, communal ownership, and tax relief. But most jettisoned Land System ideals for traditional land ownership and tax collection to finance their military campaigns. Moreover, by the late 1850s, moral zeal and martial discipline had begun to plummet, even among the Guangxi core believers.

As the loyalist cordon around Nanjing choked off New Jerusalem's food supply during the first half of 1864, Hong told the faithful to eat weeds, which he dubbed "manna," rather than evacuate the city. He himself would ascend to heaven one final time to implore the Heavenly Father's deliverance. But on June 1 of that year, Hong died, his millennial campaign soon to be eradicated by "regional" armies and their gentry patrons loyal to Confucianism and the Manchu throne. Ironically, the loyalists were assisted by Christian mercenaries from Europe and America, whose governments feared that a Taiping victory would impose Hong's concept of global equality and thereby negate the West's commercial privileges in the treaty system with the Qing.

Conclusion

At a terrible cost of between twenty and forty million lives on both sides, no civil war in world history rivals the destructiveness of Hong's religiously inspired millenarian campaign. Some observers marvel at how much Hong actually understood the biblical elements of his religious synthesis.[89] For him, the ultimate theological reality was the filial relationship with God, and monotheism was key to the movement's cataclysmic force. Clearly, Hong emphasized the Old Testament over the New. Adherence to the Ten Commandments fostered a stricter discipline and courage than other rebels were able to muster. Susan Naquin points out that many sectarians wavered between orthodox spheres (when they were led by clergy, worshiped state-approved deities, stressed Chinese familism even within their religious communities, and recited sutras and meditated for health and longevity) and heterodox dimensions (when they abandoned Confucian socioethics, worshiped deities lacking imperial sanction, and allowed women independent action).[90] The Taipings, on the other hand, offered no such ambiguity. Neither the Chinese populace nor the elite ultimately embraced Hong's blatantly heterodox faith.

Nor, in the end, did his foreign brothers and sisters in the West. Hong's monotheistic logic led him to reject Trinitarian Christianity, which he considered polytheistic. Hong denied the divinity of himself and Jesus—if Christ were divine, he wrote in his gloss to Mark 12:28–34, "there would be two Gods"[91]—and identified the Holy Spirit (which Liang had never fully explained) with Yang. Not only did Hong proclaim himself God's second son (crossing out "only" from the phrase "only begotten son" in John 1:18)[92] but made himself, rather than the risen Christ, the center of the forthcoming worldwide Kingdom.

Hong may have been encouraged to de-emphasize Jesus' redemptive role because the missionaries themselves made human beings an important partner with God in salvation. For Hong this idea defused the Christian insistence on original sin and instead reinforced Confucianism's optimistic view of human nature as well as the Chinese religious notion that sin originates in ignorance, wrong "habit," and corrupt "custom" (Hong's terms). And although Hong admired the evangelicals' stress on moral striving, Taiping salvation was achieved not by grace or character change but works, such as public bathing, reciting prayers, and ceasing evil deeds. The number of heads on display throughout Nanjing dramatized the severity with which Hong punished major infractions like opium smoking. Even occasional absence from religious services, spiritual backsliding, and tobacco smoking merited severe beatings. This clearly demonstrates Hong's preference for Old Testament vengeance over New Testament love.

Without a proper understanding of Christ's divinity, resurrection, and atonement, Hong ignored the cross, Easter, Christmas, and the Christian church as a manifestation of Jesus' incarnation. Foreign Christians deplored Hong's self-promotion as sole interpreter of biblical revelation, condemning his rewriting portions of the Bible (editing out Noah's intoxication, for example) to accord with Taiping orthodoxy. After serving as the Taipings' director of foreign affairs in 1860–1862, Issachar Roberts condemned Taiping faith, demanding that it "should be exterminated by the foreigners . . . in the interest of commerce and the Gospel."[93] Apparently, Roberts failed to recall the Christians' own heterodox undercurrents, which had erupted into such millennial cataclysms as the Anabaptists' "New Jerusalem" at Münster three centuries earlier.[94]

Liang Fa, on the other hand, prayed "each hour of the day to the Almighty for His blessings on the Taiping leaders."[95] But as they learned more about Hong's religion after Liang's death in 1855, many other Chinese Protestants scorned Taiping doctrines, including a number of Hakka survivors who sought Christian baptism after the rebellion's suppression.[96] This included Li Zhenggao, who condemned Hong as "a fanatic" with "materialistic . . . ideas about God."[97]

No trace of Taiping religion survived the Heavenly Kingdom's collapse. Yet the Taipings remain the unique instance in which the Bible and Chinese religion were joined to create a powerful insurrectionary surge that claimed to have brought the Kingdom of Heaven to earth. In later years Liang Fa's evangelical Protestantism not only affirmed ongoing missionary Christianity in China but also inspired the rise of indigenous Chinese Christian sects.[98] And the Social Gospel theology anticipated by Hong Ren'gan's modernization proposals had a major impact on China's subsequent national development.[99] However, no other dissident movement was to arise with comparable all-embracing ideological pretensions or with such extreme programs until the twentieth century.

In three respects, the Taipings went beyond traditional sectarian rebellion to presage China's twentieth-century revolutions. First, the Taipings remained faithful to their fundamental principles. In this regard the White Lotus rebels helped to overthrow the Mongols, but Zhu Yuanzhang abandoned White Lotus messianism for Confucian restoration, which he carried out in alliance with the same landowning gentry he had earlier repudiated. After proclaiming himself Ming Taizu (r. 1368–1398), Zhu issued edicts in 1370 banning religious heterodoxy. Ironically, he also mandated that Cheng-Zhu orthodoxy become the basis of the civil service examinations. And the anti-heterodoxy provisions of the Ming-Qing law code added a rationale to the Qing dynasty's suppression of the White Lotus–inspired rebellions of 1774, 1796–1804, and 1813, which sought to restore virtuous Han Chinese rule.

The Taipings refused to compromise theologically, even when this meant sacrificing cooperation with other rebels, such as the Triads and the Nian, when the Manchus were stretched thin fighting various insurrections around the empire. Indeed, the Taipings were convinced they could implement their millennium because they had the ability, through theocratic organization, high troop discipline, and an aggressive preach-and-print evangelism, to maintain power and support indefinitely.

Second, Hong's monotheism prompted the remarkable egalitarianism that established a sibling unity far more cohesive than other sectarians' artificial sibs and stimulated the reconstruction of state and society in a far more explicit way than other rebels proposed. Monotheism also created the puritanical rigor and martial zeal that made the Taipings such formidable fighters, especially in the early years. Before his execution in 1864, Li Xiucheng observed: "After I worshipped God I never dared to transgress in the slightest, but was a sincere believer, always fearing harm from [in a paraphrase from Liang] serpents and tigers."[100] One contemporary Western missionary, astonished by the Taipings' extraordinary discipline, wrote: "There may be defective teaching among [the Taipings]...but it ...is confessedly a moral revolution...[and] is the wonder of the age."[101] And Zeng Guofan (1811–1872), leader of the anti-Taiping forces, observed after capturing New Jerusalem in July 1864: "Not one of the hundred thousand rebels in Nanjing surrendered.... Never before in history has there been so formidable a rebel force."[102]

Third, the Taipings' radicalism surpassed all other sectarians in anticipating the programs championed by Chinese revolutionaries—especially the communists—from the 1920s on.[103] The Taipings were the first rebels to be inspired by a Western ideology and initiate an attempt to reintegrate China within the modern international world. Hong responded to the discovery of a larger community beyond China in terms of redemptive history. He hoped to achieve China's redemption by making it the site of the latest revelation of God, whom the foreigners had continued to worship long after the Chinese had abandoned him at the dawn of imperial government. To this end, Hong was convinced that the Chinese imperial institution must be destroyed by divine means, of which he was the designated instrument. And he never wavered from his conviction that as emperor the transcendent Heavenly Father alone towered high above immanent Confucian heaven.[104] Although the Taipings' religiously inspired ideology and organization fell short of perpetuating the Heavenly Kingdom, their efforts to change China anticipated future endeavors that, while also inspired by millenarian and messianic ideals, relied on strictly secular methods.

Notes

1. Recent English-language scholarship on the Taiping ideology includes Eugene Powers Boardman, *Christian Influence Upon the Ideology of the Taiping Rebellion, 1851–1864* (Madison: University of Wisconsin Press, 1952); P. Richard Bohr, "The Heavenly Kingdom in China: Religion and the Taiping Revolution, 1837–1853," *Fides et Historia*, 17.2 (spring–summer 1985), 38–52; Jen Yu-wen, *The Taiping Revolutionary Movement* (New Haven: Yale University Press, 1973); Jonathan D. Spence, *God's Chinese Son: The Taiping Heavenly Kingdom of Hong Xiuquan* (New York: W. W. Norton, 1996); Philip A. Kuhn, "The Taiping Rebellion," in John K. Fairbank, ed., *The Cambridge History of China*, vol. 10: *Late Ch'ing*, part I (Cambridge: Cambridge University Press, 1978), 264–316; Vincent C. Y. Shih, *The Taiping Ideology* (Seattle: University of Washington Press, 1967); and Rudolph G. Wagner, *Reenacting the Heavenly Vision: The Role of Religion in the Taiping Rebellion* (Berkeley: University of California, Institute of East Asian Studies, 1982). For a PRC perspective, see Xia Chuntao, *Taiping Tianguo zongjiao* [Religion of the Taiping Heavenly Kingdom] (Nanjing: Nanjing University Press, 1992). For further titles, see G. W. Tiedemann, comp., *Bibliography*

of Western Language Materials Concerning the Taiping Tianguo, forthcoming, and Jiang Pingcheng, *Yanjiu Taiping Tianguo shi jushu zongmu* [A comprehensive bibliography of studies on the history of the Taiping Rebellion] (Beijing: Shumu wenxian, 1983).

2. Daniel H. Bays, "Popular Religious Movements in China and the United States in the Nineteenth Century," *Fides et Historia* 15.1 (fall–winter, 1982), 24–38, and Guillame Dunstheimer, "Some Religious Aspects of Secret Societies," in Jean Chesneaux, ed., *Popular Movements and Secret Societies in China, 1840–1950* (Stanford: Stanford University Press, 1972), 23–47.

3. Kwang-Ching Liu, "Introduction: Orthodoxy in Chinese Society," in idem, ed., *Orthodoxy in Late Imperial China* (Berkeley: University of California Press, 1990), 1–24.

4. For an overview of Chinese sectarianism, see chapters 7 and 8, this volume. See also J. J. M. de Groot, *Sectarianism and Religious Persecution in China*, 2 vols. (Amsterdam: Johannes Müller, 1903); Daniel L. Overmyer, *Folk Buddhist Religion: Dissenting Sects in Late Traditional China* (Cambridge, Mass.: Harvard University Press, 1976); idem, "Alternatives: Popular Religious Sects in Chinese Society," *Modern History* 7.2 (1981): 153–190; Richard Shek, "Religion and Society in Late Ming: Sectarianism and Popular Thought in Sixteenth and Seventeenth Century China" (Ph.D. diss., University of California, Berkeley, 1980); C. Stevan Harrell and Elizabeth J. Perry, "Syncretic Sects in Chinese Society: An Introduction," *Modern China* 8.3 (July 1982), 283–303; Robert Weller, "Ideology, Organization and Rebellion in Chinese Sectarian Religion," in Janos M. Bak and Gerhard Benecke, eds., *Religion and Rural Revolt* (Dover, N.H.: Manchester University Press, 1984), 390–406; and T. H. Barrett, "Chinese Sectarian Religion," *Modern Asian Studies* 12 (1978): 333–352.

5. For the nature and role of evangelical Protestantism, see Murray Rubenstein, *The Origins of the Anglo-American Missionary Enterprise in China, 1807–1840* (Lanham, Md.: The Scarecrow Press, 1996); P. Richard Bohr, "The Legacy of William Milne," *International Bulletin of Missionary Research* 25.5 (Oct. 2001): 173–178; and idem, "Christianity and Rebellion in China: The Evangelical Roots of the Taiping Heavenly Kingdom," in Roman Malek, ed., *The Chinese Face of Jesus Christ*, 2 vols. (Sankt Augustin: Monumenta Serica Monograph Series, forthcoming).

6. For Eternal Mother belief, see chapter 7, this volume. See also Erik Zürcher, "Eschatology and Messianism in Early Chinese Buddhism," in W. L. Idema, ed., *Leyden Studies in Sinology* (Leiden: E. J. Brill, 1982); Daniel L. Overmyer, "Folk-Buddhist Religion: Creation and Eschatology in Medieval China," *History of Religions* 12 (1972), 42–70; Chan Hok-lam, "The White Lotus-Maitreya Doctrine in Popular Uprisings in Ming and Ch'ing China," *Sinologica* 10.4 (1969): 212–213; Susan Naquin, *Shantung*

Rebellion: The Wang Lun Uprising of 1774 (New Haven: Yale University Press, 1981); idem, *Millenarian Rebellion in China: The Eight Trigrams Uprising of 1813* (New Haven: Yale University Press, 1976); and Barend J. ter Haar, *The White Lotus Teachings in Chinese Religious History* (Leiden: E. J. Brill, 1992).

7. Quoted in George Hunter McNeur, *China's First Preacher: Liang A-fa* (Shanghai: Guangxue Publishing House, [1934?]), 23, 25. For my theological analysis of Liang's *Good Words,* see P. Richard Bohr, "Liang Fa's Quest for Moral Power," in Suzanne Wilson Barnett and John King Fairbank, eds., *Christianity in China: Early Protestant Missionary Writings* (Cambridge, Mass.: Harvard University Press, 1985), 35–46. For an analysis of the book's political implications, see Philip A. Kuhn, "Origins of the Taiping Vision: Cross-Cultural Dimensions of a Chinese Rebellion," *Comparative Studies in Society and History* 29.3 (July 1977): 350–366.

8. Quoted in Robert Philip, *The Life and Opinions of the Rev. William Milne, D.D.* (London: John Snow, 1840), 110.

9. For my analysis of Hong's theological development see P. Richard Bohr, "The Theologian as Revolutionary: Hung Hsiu-ch'üan's Religious Vision of the Taiping Heavenly Kingdom," in Yen-p'ing Hao and Hsiu-mei Wei, eds., *Tradition and Metamorphosis in Modern Chinese History* (Taibei: Institute of Modern History, Academia Sinica, 1998), 2:907–953. See also Wang Qingcheng, "Hung Hsiu-ch'üan's Early Thought and the Taiping Revolution," C. A. Curwen, trans., *Renditions* 15 (spring 1981): 103–138; and Mao Jiaqi, "Jidujiao, Rujia sixiang he Hong Xiuquan" [Christianity, Confucianism, and Hong Xiuquan], *Nanjing daxue xuebao* [Nanjing University Journal] 2 (1979): 43–53.

10. Quoted in *Taiping tianri* [Taiping heavenly chronicle], in Xiang Da, et al., comps., *Taiping Tianguo* [The Taiping Heavenly Kingdom], in *Zhongguo jindaishi ziliao congkan* [A collection of materials on modern China], 8 vols. (Shanghai: Commercial Press, 1952), 2:632.

11. Quoted in Theodore Hamberg, *The Visions of Hung-Siu-Tshuen, and Origin of the Kwang-si Insurrection* (Hong Kong: The China Mail, 1854), 10. For a scenario of the entire dream sequence, see ibid., 9–13, and Issachar Jacox Roberts, "Taiping Wang," *Putnam's Magazine* 8 (Oct. 1856): 382. For an analysis of Hong's dreams, see Rudolph G. Wagner, "Imperial Dreams in China," in Carolyn T. Brown, ed., *Psycho-Sinology: The Universe of Dreams in Chinese Culture* (Washington, D.C.: Woodrow Wilson International Center for Scholars, 1988), 11–24.

12. Quoted in Jen Yu-wen, *Taiping Tianguo dianzhi tongkao* [Studies on the institutions of the Taiping Heavenly Kingdom], 3 vols. (Hong Kong: Mengjin shuwu, 1958), 3:1727.

13. Quoted in Hamberg, *Visions*, 12.

14. Quoted in *Taiping tianri*, 2:639.

15. Quoted in Hamberg, *Visions*, 25.

16. For a historical analysis of conditions in China during this period, see Kwang-Ching Liu, "Nineteenth-Century China: The Disintegration of the Old Order and the Impact of the West," in Ping-ti Ho and Tang Tsou, eds., *China in Crisis*, 2 vols. (Chicago: University of Chicago Press, 1968), 1:93–178; Frederic Wakeman Jr., *Strangers at the Gate: Social Disorder in South China, 1839–1861* (Berkeley: University of California Press, 1966); and Susan Mann Jones and Philip A. Kuhn, "Dynastic Decline and the Roots of Rebellion," in Fairbank, ed., *Cambridge History of China* 10.1, 108–132.

17. Quoted in Jen, *Tongkao*, 3:1725.

18. Max Kaltenmark, "The Ideology of the *T'ai-p'ing ching*," in Holmes Welch and Anna K. Seidel, eds., *Facets of Taoism* (New Haven and London: Yale University Press, 1979), 19–52; Anna K. Seidel, "The Image of the Perfect Ruler in Early Taoist Messianism: Lao-Tzu and Li-Hung," *History of Religions* 9 (1969–1970): 216–247; and Rolf Stein, "Remarques dur les mouvements Taoisme politico-religieux au 11e siècle après J.C.," *Toung Pao* 40 (1963): 1–78.

19. See Wen-hsiung Hsu's reconstruction in chapter 9, this volume.

20. Quoted in Jen, *Tongkao*, 3:1726.

21. Wolfgang Bauer, *China and the Search for Happiness*, trans. Michael Shaw (New York: The Seabury Press, 1976), 117.

22. Quoted in Jen, *Tongkao*, 3:1728–1729. The missionaries' insistence that all Chinese—not merely the sages—had the right to worship God became a signal theme in *Good Words*. See Bohr, "Legacy of William Milne."

23. Bauer, *Search for Happiness*, 80–85.

24. Liang Fa, *Quanshi liangyan* [Good words to admonish the age], in Mai Jansu, *Liang Fa zhuan* [Life of Liang Fa], 2d ed. (Hong Kong: The Council on Christian Literature for the Overseas Chinese, 1968, appendix), 105.

25. Ibid.

26. Ibid., 121.

27. Quoted in Jen, *Tongkao*, 3:1726.

28. Quoted in ibid.

29. Thomas A. Metzger, *Escape from Predicament: Neo-Confucianism and China's Evolving Political Culture* (New York: Columbia University Press, 1977); and Julia Ching, *Mysticism and Kingship in China: The Heart of Chinese Wisdom* (Cambridge: Cambridge University Press, 1997).

30. For an analysis of the turbulent conditions under which the Hakka lived in Guangxi and Guangdong, see Laai Yi-faai, "The Part Played by the Pirates of Kwangtung and Kwangsi Provinces in the Taiping Insurrection" (Ph.D. diss., University of California, Berkeley, 1949) and J. A. G. Roberts, "The Hakka-Punti War" (Ph.D. diss., Oxford University, 1968). For the

problems of rising militarization, see Philip A. Kuhn, *Rebellion and Its Enemies in Late Imperial China: Militarization and Social Structure, 1796–1864* (Cambridge, Mass.: Harvard University Press, 1970).

31. Quoted in Hamberg, *Visions,* 43.

32. Quoted in Jen, *Tongkao,* 3:1732.

33. Quoted in Hamberg, *Visions,* 28. A number of contemporary observers noted that the Hakka were open to new ideas and were the largest group of Chinese to become Christian. See Nicole Constable, *Christian Souls and Chinese Spirits* (Berkeley: University of California Press, 1994), 23, 139–140. For Hakka influence on the formation of Taiping ideology, see P. Richard Bohr, "The Hakka and the Heavenly Kingdom: Ethnicity and Religion in the Rise of the Taiping Revolution," *China Notes* 18.4 (fall 1980): 133–136.

34. Quoted in Jen, *Taiping tianri,* 2:634. See note 12.

35. Quoted in Jessie G. Lutz and Rolland Ray Lutz, *Hakka Chinese Confront Protestant Christianity, 1850–1900* (Armonk, N.Y.: M. E. Sharpe, 1998), 123.

36. Quoted in Constable, *Christian Souls and Chinese Spirits,* 166.

37. Barend J. ter Haar, "Messianism and the Heaven and Earth Society: Approaches to Heaven and Earth Society Texts," in David Ownby and Mary Somers Heidhues, eds., *"Secret Societies" Reconsidered: Perspective on the Social History of Modern South China and Southeast Asia* (Armonk, N.Y.: M. E. Sharpe, 1993), 153–176.

38. See Hong's poem in Hamberg, *Visions,* 30.

39. Some Eternal Mother sects during the Qing period required daily bowing to the sun during mantra recitations. See Susan Naquin, "The Transmission of White Lotus Sectarianism in Late Imperial China," in David Johnson, Andrew J. Nathan, and Evelyn S. Rawski, eds., *Popular Culture in Late Imperial China* (Berkeley: University of California Press, 1985), 284; William Stanton, *The Triad Society or Heaven and Earth Association* (Hong Kong: Kelly and Walsh, 1900), 46; and Dian H. Murray, in collaboration with Qin Baoqi, *The Origins of the Tiandihui* (Stanford: Stanford University Press, 1994).

40. Quoted in Margaret Morgan Coughlin, "Strangers in the House: J. Lewis Schuck and Issachar Jacox Roberts, First American Baptist Missionaries to China" (Ph.D. diss., University of Virginia, 1972), 316. For Roberts' influence on Hong, see William R. Doezema, "Western Seeds of Eastern Heterodoxy: The Impact of Protestant Revivalism on the Christianity of Taiping Rebel Leader Hung Hsiu-ch'üan, 1836–1864," *Fides et Historia* 25.1 (winter–spring 1993), 73–98; and Teng Yuan Chung, "Reverend Issachar Jacox Roberts and the Taiping Rebellion," *Journal of Asian Studies* 23.1 (1963): 55–67.

41. Frederic Wakeman Jr., "Rebellion and Revolution: The Study of

Popular Movements in Chinese History," *Journal of Asian Studies* 36.2 (Feb. 1977), 205–212.

42. For an exploration of the religious environment of Xunzhou, including its orthodox and heterodox dimensions, see Robert P. Weller, *Resistance, Chaos and Control in China: Taiping Rebels, Taiwanese Ghosts and Tiananmen* (Seattle: University of Washington Press, 1994), chap. 4; and idem, "Matricidal Magistrates and Gambling Gods: Weak States and Strong Spirits in China," in Meir Shahar and Robert P. Weller, eds., *Unruly Gods: Divinity and Society in China* (Honolulu: University of Hawai'i Press, 1996), 250–268. For a close analysis of the God Worshipers' congregational recruitment and membership composition, see Ichisada Miyazaki, "The Nature of the Taiping Rebellion," trans. Charles A. Peterson, *Acta Asiatica* 8 (Mar. 1965): 2–3.

43. See chaps. 9 and 10, this volume. See also C. A. Curwen, "Taiping Relations with Secret Societies and with Other Rebels," in Chesneaux, *Popular Movements*, 65–84 and Elizabeth J. Perry, "Taipings and Triads: The Role of Religion in Interrebel Relations," in Bak and Benecke, eds., *Religion and Rural Revolt*, 342–353.

44. Daniel L. Overmyer, "Values in Chinese Sectarian Literature: Ming and Ch'ing *Pao-chüan*," in Johnson, Nathan, and Rawski, eds., *Popular Culture*, 219–254; and idem, *Precious Volumes: An Introduction to Chinese Sectarian Scriptures from the Sixteenth and Seventeenth Centuries* (Cambridge, Mass.: Harvard University Press, 1999).

45. Quoted in Hamberg, *Visions*, 42.

46. Quoted in ibid., 35.

47. Quoted in Jen, *Tongkao*, 3:1730.

48. Quoted in Franz Michael, in collaboration with Chung-li Chang, *The Taiping Rebellion*, 3 vols. (Seattle and London: University of Washington Press, 1966–1971), 2:115. Hong clearly borrowed from Chinese sectarian ritual traditions, but he did oppose the sectarian insistence on vegetarianism. See Constable, *Christian Souls and Chinese Spirits*, 167.

49. Frederic Wakeman Jr., "The Secret Societies of Kwangtung, 1800–1856," in Chesneaux, *Popular Movements*, 29–47; and Lu Baoqian (Lu Pao-ch'ien), *Lun wan Qing Liangguang di Tiandihui zhengquan* [On the Triad regimes of Guangdong and Guangxi during the late Qing] (Taibei: Institute of Modern History, Academic Sinica, 1975).

50. Quoted in Hamberg, *Visions*, 41–42.

51. Quoted in Jen, *Tongkao*, 3:1725.

52. Richard Shek, "The Ethics of Ming-Qing Folk Religious Sects: The Luojiao Tradition" (paper presented at the thirty-third annual meeting of the Association for Asian Studies, Toronto, 14 March 1981). See also chapter 7, this volume.

53. Quoted in Hamberg, *Visions*, 37.

54. C. K. Yang, *Religion in Chinese Society* (Berkeley: University of California Press, 1967), 218.

55. See chapter 2, this volume. See also Jan Nattier, *Once Upon a Future Time: Studies in a Buddhist Prophecy of Decline* (Berkeley: Asian Humanities Press, 1991); Alan Sponberg and Helen Hardacre, eds., *Maitreya, The Future Buddha* (Cambridge: Cambridge University Press, 1988); E[rik] Zürcher, "'Prince Moonlight': Messianic Eschatology in Early Medieval Chinese Buddhism," *T'oung Pao* 68 (1982): 1–59; and Yuji Muramatsu, "Some Themes in Chinese Rebel Ideologies," in Arthur F. Wright, ed., *The Confucian Persuasion* (Stanford: Stanford University Press, 1960), 241–267.

56. See chapter 8, this volume and Naquin, *Millenarian Rebellion.*

57. For an assessment of the apocalyptic motif in the Taipings' rise, see Michael Barkun, *Disaster and the Millennium* (New Haven: Yale University Press, 1974). Regarding the Taiping Rebellion as an example of "cataclysmic millennium" typology, see Scott Lowe, "The Taiping Revolution and Mao's Great Leap Forward," in Catherine Wessinger, *Millennialism, Persecution, and Violence* (Syracuse: Syracuse University Press, 2000), 220–240.

58. Quoted in C. A. Curwen, trans. and ed., *Taiping Rebel: The Deposition of Li Hsiu-ch'eng* (Cambridge: Cambridge University Press, 1976), 83.

59. Howard S. Levy, "Yellow Turban Religion and Rebellion at the End of the Han," *Journal of the American Oriental Society* 76 (1956): 214–227; Rolf A. Stein, "Religious Taoism and Popular Religion from the Second to Seventh Centuries," in Holmes and Seidel, eds., *Facets of Taoism,* 53–82; and Michael R. Saso, *The Teachings of Taoist Master Chuang* (New Haven: Yale University Press, 1978). During times of calamity, sectarians emphasized ritual purification, corporate exorcism, the communal reading of prayers and sacred vernacular texts, and fasting. See Paul De Witt Twinem, "Modern Syncretic Religious Societies in China," *The Journal of Religion* 5.5 (Sept. 1925): 463–482, and 5.6 (Nov. 1925): 595–606.

60. Quoted in Weller, *Resistance,* 66.

61. See ibid., 56–85. For further material on the Guangxi descents, see Wang Qingcheng, *Tianfu Tianxiong shengzhi* [The sacred declarations of the Heavenly Father and Heavenly Elder Brother] (Liaoning, n.p., 1986).

62. Quoted in Xiang, et al., *Taiping Tianguo,* 1:71.

63. Joseph W. Esherick, *The Origins of the Boxer Uprising* (Berkeley: University of California Press, 1987), 325. This view is supported by the fact that Guanyin herself (whom Hong as Jesus addressed as "younger sister") was thought to have also descended into Thistle Mountain during this time to possess female God Worshipers. Weller, *Resistance,* 82–83.

64. See chapter 1, this volume; Terry F. Kleeman, *Great Perfection: Religion and Ethnicity in a Chinese Millennial Kingdom* (Honolulu: University of Hawai'i Press, 1998); and Richard B. Mather, "K'ou Ch'ien-chih and

the Taoist Theocracy at the Northern Wei Court, 425–451," in Welch and Seidel, eds., *Facets of Taoism*, 103–122.

65. See chapter 2, this volume. Cf. John W. Dardess, "The Transformations of Messianic Revolt and the Founding of the Ming Dynasty," *Journal of Asian Studies* 24.3 (May 1970): 539–558.

66. For Taiping military rules, see *Taiping tiaogui* [Taiping rules and regulations], in Xiang, et al., *Taiping Tianguo*, 1:153–156.

67. Quoted in Michael, *Taiping Rebellion*, 2:107.

68. See *Banxing zhaoshu* [Proclamations by imperial sanction], in Xiang, et al., *Taiping Tianguo*, 1:157–167.

69. See *Yuxue shi* [Ode for youth], in ibid., 1:229–235.

70. Quoted in Jen, *Tongkao*, 3:1862.

71. Quoted in Joseph Callery and Melchior Yvan, *History of the Insurrection in China*, 3d ed., John Oxenford, trans. (New York: Harper and Brothers, 1853), 268.

72. Quoted in Michael, *Taiping Rebellion*, 2:109.

73. Quoted in ibid., 2:235.

74. Quoted in ibid., 2:228.

75. Quoted in ibid., 2:249

76. Quoted in Augustus F. Lindley, *Ti-Ping Tien-Kwoh: The History of the Ti-Ping Revolution*, 2 vols. (London: Day and Son, 1866), 1:361.

77. Rudolph G. Wagner, "Operating in the Chinese Public Sphere: Theology and Technique of Taiping Propaganda," in Chun-chieh Huang and Erik Zürcher, eds., *Norms and the State in China* (Leiden: E. J. Brill, 1993), 104–138.

78. For an overview of Taiping reforms in Nanjing, see Erik Zürcher, "Purity in the Taiping Rebellion," in Walter E. A. van Beek, ed., *The Quest for Purity* (Berlin, New York, and Amsterdam: Mouton de Gruyter, 1988), 203–215; John Lovelle Withers II, "The Heavenly Capital: Nanjing Under the Taiping, 1853–1864" (Ph.D. diss., Yale University, 1983); and Lindley, *Ti-Ping Tien-Kwoh*, 2:691.

79. Marjorie Topley, "The Great Way of Former Heaven: A Group of Chinese Secret Religious Sects," *Bulletin of the School of Oriental and African Studies* 26 (1963): 326–392.

80. Jonathan D. Spence, *The Search for Modern China* (New York: W. W. Norton, 1990), 175. For the text of the Land System, see Xiang, et al., *Taiping Tianguo*, 319–326.

81. Quoted in Lo Yong and Shen Zuji, comps., *Taiping Tianguo shiwenchao* [Poetry and prose of the Taiping Heavenly Kingdom], 2 vols., rev. ed. (Shanghai: Commercial Press, 1934), 136a–136b.

82. Yuji Muramatsu, "Rebel Ideologies," 257–258. Robert A. Scalapino and George T. Yu express their belief that the "combination of puritanism and egalitarianism with respect to male-female relations was quite

possibly the most novel element in the Taipings movement," in *Modern China and Its Revolutionary Process* (Berkeley: University of California Press, 1985), 19.

83. See *Tianli yaolun* [Important observations regarding heavenly principles] in Xiang, *Taiping Tianguo*, 1:327–352.

84. Quoted in ibid., 3:1726. For the Taipings' international relations, see Rudolph G. Wagner, "God's Country in the Family of Nations: The Logic of Modernism in the Taiping Doctrine of International Relations," in Bak and Benecke, eds., *Religion and Rural Revolt*, 354–372.

85. Quoted in Jen, *Tongkao*, 3:1726.

86. Quoted in Michael, *Taiping Rebellion*, 3:756.

87. Quoted in Jen Yu-wen, "New Sidelights on the Taiping Rebellion," *T'ien-hsia Monthly* 1 (1935): 372.

88. For an introduction to Hong Ren'gan's reform ideas, see Teng Ssu-yü, "Hung Jen-kan, Prime Minister of the Taiping Kingdom and His Modernization Plans," *United College Journal* 8 (1970–1971): 87–96. See also Carl T. Smith, *Chinese Christians: Élites, Middlemen, and the Church in Hong Kong* (Hong Kong: Oxford University Press, 1985), chap. 4.

89. See, for example, Doezema, "Western Seeds of Eastern Heterodoxy," 98.

90. Naquin, "Transmission of White Lotus Sectarianism," 288–291.

91. Quoted in Michael, *Taiping Rebellion*, 2:229. Milne himself was uneasy about the potential for downplaying Christ's divinity in Liang's portrayal of Jesus as a boddhisattva figure whose sacrificial death earned Buddhist-style "merit" and whose resurrection seemed more like reincarnation. See Philip, *Life and Opinions*, 229.

92. Spence, *God's Chinese Son*, 289.

93. Issachar Jacox Roberts, "Letter to the Editor," *North-China Herald*, 17 Nov. 1860, 182. For an analysis of contemporary missionary perspectives on Taiping religion, see J. S. Gregory, "British Missionary Reaction to the Taiping Movement in China," *Journal of Religious History* 2 (1963): 204–228; John B. Littell, "Missionaries and Politics in China: The Taiping Rebellion," *Social Science Quarterly* 43 (1928): 566–599; and Rudolph G. Wagner, "Understanding Taiping Christian China: Analogy, Interest and Policy," in Klaus Koschorke, ed., *Christen und Gerwürze: Konfrontation und Interaktion kolonialer und indigener Christentumsvarianten* (Göttingen: 1998), 132–157. For a recent theological assessment of Taiping borrowing from Christianity, see C. S. Song, *The Compassionate God* (Maryknoll: Orbis Books, 1982), chap. 10.

94. See Norman Cohn, *Pursuit of the Millennium*, revised and expanded (New York: Oxford University Press, 1970), esp. chap. 13.

95. Quoted in Wagner, *Reenacting*, 15.

96. Constable, *Christian Souls and Chinese Spirits*, 165–169.

97. Quoted in Lutz and Lutz, *Hakka Chinese,* 128.

98. Adrian A. Bennett and Kwang-Ching Liu, "Christianity in the Chinese Idiom: Young J. Allen and the Early *Chiao-hui hsin-pao,* 1868–1870," in John K. Fairbank, ed., *The Missionary Enterprise in China and America* (Cambridge, Mass.: Harvard University Press, 1974), 159–196; Daniel H. Bays, "The Growth of Independent Christianity in China," in idem, ed., *Christianity in China* (Stanford: Stanford University Press, 1996), 307–316; idem, "Christianity and the Chinese Sectarian Tradition," *Ch'ing-shih wen-t'i* 4.7 (June 1982): 33–52; and idem, "Chinese Popular Religion and Christianity Before and After the 1949 Revolution: A Retrospective View," *Fides et Historia* 23.1 (winter–spring 1991), 69–71. See also Frank K. Flinn, "Prophetic Christianity and the Future of China," in Jeffrey K. Hadden and Anson Shupe, eds., *Prophetic Religions and Politics* (New York: Paragon House, 1986), 307–328.

99. For a discussion of Christianity's impact on Chinese reform, see Paul A. Cohen, "Littoral and Hinterland in Nineteenth Century China: The 'Christian' Reformers," in Fairbank, ed., *Missionary Enterprise,* 197–225. For a perspective on Social Gospel developments in China, see P. Richard Bohr, *Famine in China and the Missionary: Timothy Richard as Relief Administrator and Advocate of National Reform, 1876–1884* (Cambridge, Mass.: Harvard University Press, 1972), chap. 6.

100. Quoted in Curwen, *Taiping Rebel,* 83. Cf. Liang, *Good Words,* 16. For contemporary observations of rank-and-file allegiance to Taiping belief, see Yung Wing, *My Life in China and America* (New York: Arno Press, 1978), 101–103.

101. W. H. Medhurst, "Letter to the Editor," *North-China Herald,* 26 Nov. 1853, 66.

102. Quoted in Withers, "The Heavenly Capital," 231.

103. Lucian Bianco, for example, has written: "The Taipings were in a sense the precursors of the communists." *Origins of the Chinese Revolution, 1915–1949,* trans. Muriel Bell (Stanford: Stanford University Press, 1971), 5.

104. Joseph R. Levenson, "Confucian and Taiping 'Heaven': Political Implications of Clashing Religious Concepts," *Comparative Studies in Society and History* 4.4 (July 1962): 436–453.

CHAPTER 12

Popular and Elite Heterodoxy Toward the End of the Qing

Don C. Price

I n the twilight years of the Qing dynasty, a structure of orthodox principles and institutions crumbled so rapidly that one hesitates to invoke the orthodox/heterodox dichotomy that for centuries was such a robust feature of late imperial China. First, legal protection had been extended to Christians, and then imperial patronage to the Boxers. The examination system was abolished, and constitutionalism endorsed, but not fast enough to satisfy a new constituency composed largely of examination licentiates, stewards of the Confucian tradition. Who was to say any longer where orthodoxy lay? It is therefore only with reservations and partly by analogy that we can venture to discuss elite and popular heterodoxy at the end of the Qing, but there is some justification in doing so.

Orthodoxy crumbled, but the Boxers and secret societies remained heirs to longstanding forms of heterodoxy. It is possible to argue that regard for the institutions of family and monarchy was not entirely negated by secret societies of the Triad variety.[1] The case of the Boxers is complex. Contemporary accounts written during or after the events of 1899–1901 often describe the Boxers as heterodox (*xiejiao, xieshu,* or *xieshuo*), although very few actually identified the Boxers with the White Lotus.[2] The facts yield no easy generalization. Those inspired practitioners of the martial arts were seldom critical of the orthodox socioethical values, and in the end they supported the dynasty, while venting their hatred of Chinese Christians and foreigners.[3] The ballads known to have been sung by the Boxers vaguely suggest impending disaster other than the flood that had occurred—not as vividly, however, as the dire calamity often predicted by the White Lotus sects, the destruction and transformation of the physical and social world, following severe flood, fire, and windstorms.

The Boxers' rituals were nonetheless extraordinary. Their shamanism gave every Boxer a chance to be a medium and to transmit the
pronouncements of Piggy, Sandy, or other figures from the *Journey to
the West* and other novels, familiar to him from folk opera. The Boxers practiced a kind of shamanistic individualism, but to adapt a
phrase from Donald Sutton, the Boxers as mediums did not articulate any clear message.[4]

As for elite heterodoxy, the term is useful primarily to the
extent that it suggests a challenge to the traditional order which was
both political and ideological, and rooted, as was that of popular heterodoxy, in an alternative cosmology. It was with exotic eschatolo-
gies, apocalyptic visions, a mother goddess, extraordinary powers,
and histories of ancient racial enmity that popular heterodoxy had
challenged the underpinnings of Confucian state and society.[5] The
modernized intellectuals of the late Qing, for their part, believed in
progress, equality as the basis of the social and political order, the
power of technology, and a cosmic order characterized by ceaseless
struggle or tending toward a Great Harmony (or both). In either
case, the challenges were inspired and supported by worldviews that
differed from the orthodox amalgam of Han cosmology and neo-
Confucian metaphysics. Radical reformers and revolutionaries in the
late Qing, whatever their similarity to the late Ming Donglin scholars, were not bent on revitalizing a traditional Confucian order.[6] For
them, orthodoxy was not crumbling fast enough, and they were still
struggling to sweep it away.

Where elite and popular heterodoxy gave rise to armed revolt,
forces could be joined, and these alliances have been dealt with in
one way or another in a large and growing body of research, focusing
mainly on relations between secret societies and the revolutionary
movement. On that subject, the existing literature has already provided a wealth of useful observations and generalizations.[7] It is the
purpose of this chapter to address in a more general way the attitudes of the "heterodox elite," revolutionaries and radical reformers,
toward the sects and secret societies. (There is a regrettable asym-
metry in this approach, for it would be no less instructive, although a
good deal more difficult, to analyze the secret societies' reactions to
elite heterodoxy.)[8]

The central questions that arise in a review of the activities and
writings of the reformers and revolutionaries are the following. To
what extent did their new worldviews permit a positive role for pop-

ular heterodox elements in China, beyond that of providing military support for a modern political movement? In particular, to what extent did the elite, for all their iconoclasm, inherit a conviction of their own exclusive qualifications for leadership? And to what extent did their iconoclasm undermine that self-confidence with a recognition that it was not their forebears, but the tradition of popular heterodoxy, which for centuries had held out against the orthodox order?

One approach to these questions might be to look for a recognition of affinities between the cosmologies of the elite and popular heterodoxies. The search is, in fact, almost fruitless. To be sure, popular heterodox ideas at times included a serious devaluation of the kinship, gender, and age hierarchies that were so important to orthodoxy. In their millenarian versions, they looked to the establishment of a qualitatively new and better world order, rather than the restoration of a Confucian golden age. Occasionally they called for some redistribution of wealth.[9] On all these points, a number of reformers and revolutionaries could have acknowledged a debt of influence or a kindred spirit, but no such acknowledgement is to be found, even in writings that otherwise found things to praise in them.

This silence is certainly not the result of ignorance, as we shall see from some of the commentary considered herein, especially that of Tan Sitong and Tao Chengzhang. Rather, it seems that reformers and revolutionaries were simply too confident of the superiority of their modern knowledge to think of intellectual affinities with a backward tradition. And yet, it was not simply the fact that popular heterodoxy was old that disqualified it, for Kang Youwei and Yan Fu found ways to link modern ideas with ancient Chinese ones. It was rather that the modern intellectuals were heirs to a rationalist (albeit parochial) tradition, while popular heterodoxy reflected the beliefs and superstitions of the uneducated. Elite heterodoxy understood modern world history, geography, and science, and on that basis rejected Sinocentrism and the cosmic functions of the son of heaven. It admired the technological power and institutional changes that had brought progress to the West and Japan, and deplored China's stagnation. Thus, elite heterodoxy appealed to men who knew enough of the world beyond China to respect its achievements, to understand the nature of the threat it posed, and to appreciate what might be learned from it (in stark contrast to the Boxers, for example).

To be sure, it has occasionally been suggested that popular heterodoxy provided some inspiration for the elite. S. L. Tikhivinskii

has counted the Taiping land program and Taiping ideology among
the influences on Kang Youwei's utopian thought, but this suggestion
has, I think, been convincingly refuted by Kung-chuan Hsiao.[10] Elements of popular utopianism have also been attributed to the revolutionary Tao Chengzhang, but it seems clear from his own accounts
of the sects and secret societies that Tao was striving to inspire popular heterodoxy with egalitarian utopianism rather than the other way
around.[11] Sun Yat-sen, in some ways a marginal member of the heterodox elite, is reported to have admired the Taipings since childhood, but there is little in his revolutionary program that might be
traced to their influence. Even his abiding concern for the land question seems to have owed more to historical government policy than
to heterodox traditions,[12] and the Gongjin hui (Mutual Advancement Society), an offshoot of his revolutionary party that focused
particularly on secret-society support, found it expedient to abandon
Sun's equalization of land rights.[13] In short, there is little or no evidence that popular heterodox doctrines had any distinctive influence
on elite heterodoxy's vision and programs, with the sole exception of
anti-Manchuism, to which we return later. Kang Youwei's earliest
critique of the traditional Confucian hierarchies and his earliest analysis of China's ills stressed the importance of an expanded view of the
world.[14] This was a theme that ran through the propaganda of the
reform movement, and that remains implicit in much of the revolutionary propaganda. There was thus little inclination on the part of
this elite to acknowledge affinities with the beliefs and aspirations of
untutored and parochial sectarians and secret societies. The latter's
horizons were simply too narrow.

Elite contempt for heterodox beliefs and doctrines is clearly
reflected in the writings of Kang Youwei and Tan Sitong. In fact, on
one of the few occasions when reformers invoked the *zheng/xie*
(orthodox/heterodox) distinction, Kang urged the popularization of
the state cult of Confucius, in the place of illicit *(yin)* local cults and
sacrifices. Abounding in fantastic demons and monsters, such cults,
he charged, merely preyed on the fears and gullibility of the common
man and provided a humiliating object of derision for curious foreigners. Elsewhere, Kang recommended that their wealth be confiscated to support modern schools.[15] Tan, in a somewhat milder tone,
criticized the Zaili jiao, a rapidly growing new sect in Zhili province
that he joined to gain access to their secret canon. Their public literature he had found to be a shallow jumble of Confucian, Buddhist,

Christian, and Islamic doctrines, but their secret book turned out to contain nothing more impressive than a discussion of the mantric uses of *"om mani padme hum."* Tan was sympathetic to the spiritual impulses of the common man and conceded that this sect saved its adherents some money by forbidding opium and alcohol, but he lamented the disappearance of a truly devout cult of Confucius, and regarded heterodox faiths, with their multitude of idols and nature cults, as a distinctly inferior alternative, although better than nothing.[16] As for Tao Chengzhang, discussing the defects of the sects, he asserted that their strength lay in their superstition, but "superstition prevented the further development of their thought and often led them into meaningless actions, sending them blindly to their death."[17]

Hints of a less disdainful attitude toward secret societies also appear in the reform movement's propaganda, which only rarely referred to any form of popular heterodoxy. When one influential book on nineteenth-century history referred to Western revolutionaries as *huidang* (literally, "partisans in association"), this suggested a possibly progressive role for China's secret societies, although before 1898 the reformers did not generally view even Western revolutionaries favorably.[18] But one of Kang Youwei's disciples, the *juren* degree holder Mai Menghua, ventured to compare China's *huidang* (or *huifei*: secret society bandits) with the xenophobic supporters of the Meiji restoration and the "parties which transformed the governments of Europe and America." Even so, he sharply distinguished them from elite patriots, and credited the most enlightened of those leaders (presumably Sun Yat-sen) with only "a little knowledge of Western government."[19]

By 1900 the Boxer Uprising prompted more extensive commentary on popular heterodoxy. At the same time, several of Kang Youwei's reform partisans, driven abroad by the Empress Dowager's coup, returned to China to launch their own uprising through Tang Caichang's Independence Army, itself largely composed of secret-society forces.[20] Thus there was now some necessity for the radical elite to clarify their views about popular heterodoxy and their own outlaw status. The *Qingyi bao* (Journal of disinterested criticism), organ of the reformers in exile, quickly defended the reform martyrs and proscribed and exiled patriots against slander as *luanmin* (rebels) and went on to lay the blame for popular disturbances at the feet of the rulers.[21] But its treatment of the Boxers was uniformly hostile.

The least convincing, perhaps least important, and certainly most problematical basis of criticism was in terms of Confucian ideology. Commenting on the Empress Dowager's term for the Boxers, *"yimin"* (righteous people), Mai Menghua noted that *yi* implied *zhong* (loyalty to prince and country). The Guangxu emperor, himself profoundly dedicated to the country's welfare, was thus the proper object of loyalty on both counts, whereas the Boxers were the minions of anti-Han Manchus and treacherous ministers who had usurped the emperor's authority and were ruining the country. To these rebels *(luanmin, luantu)* or Boxer bandits *(tuanfei)* Mai opposed the true *yimin*, exiled gentlemen of outraged loyalty, heroes of high purpose *(caomao zhongfen zhi shi, haojie you zhi zhi tu)*.[22] In view of Mai's reinterpretation of *zhong*, this criticism of the Boxers is clearly pressing a quasi-orthodox standard into service for political purposes, but it is worth noting that some continuity is asserted between traditional Confucian commitments and the cause of the reformers, and that high purposes are denied to the Boxers.

Pure class prejudice shows up more clearly in a letter to the *Qingyi bao* defending Tang Caichang's Independence Army. These people were hardly rebels and bandits, the author asserted. They were *xiucai* and *juren,* or else people who had studied abroad. One was even related by marriage to Zhang Zhidong. Surely such men were not the type to undertake a rebellion *(luan)!* They could only be motivated by earnest love of prince and country.[23] But Mai's condemnation of the Boxers was based on more than politics and prejudice, for he tended to link sectarianism with ignorance and unrestrained violence. Antiforeign resentment was justified, he conceded, but the Boxers' indiscriminate burning, looting, and slaughtering were not only stupid and counterproductive, opening China to universal contempt and greater dangers than before, they were also the acts of savages and barbarians.[24] As the "southern patriots" (the Independence Army) well understood, the days were gone when China could close her doors to foreigners. Civilized competition, international trade, and international law were here to stay, Mai argued, and China could benefit from the foreigners' culture and wisdom. Japan understood the problem and had put her own house in order so as to cope with the new foreign pressures, and so should China; but these Boxers merely followed in the footsteps of the Red Eyebrows and Yellow Turbans.[25] Far more important than any quasi-orthodox invocation of *zhong* is the major new elite heterodox principle operating here: ideas and actions must be based on a rational understanding of the wider civilized world. Susceptibility to atavistic superstition and xenophobia counted heavily against popular heterodoxy.

Aside from this, barbaric antiforeignism *(yeman ren zhi paiwai)* also contained a serious character defect. It lacked constancy and staying power, so that once it was, inevitably, defeated, it reverted to servility. "They [the formerly antiforeign people] view foreigners as some kind of spirits and celestial deities, serve them as servants do their masters and woo them as wives and concubines do their husbands. Those who formerly hated them as enemies are now happy to be their slaves."[26] Instead of the unreliable extremes, what was needed was an elevated, civilized form of antiforeignism *(wenming ren zhi paiwai)*, namely patriotism, which would know how to promote national strength and employ diplomatic skill.[27]

One veteran of the reform movement who had direct experience with popular heterodoxy was Qin Lishan, a student of Liang Qichao at the Current Affairs Academy in Changsha, and later in Japan. In 1900 he returned to China to assist Tang Caichang's uprising, hoping to enlist the aid of the Boxers. After explaining his mission to a Boxer chief in Tianjin, he was cursed as a half foreigner *(ermaozi)* himself and shown the door. He then went to central China and worked to recruit secret societies for the Independence Army, organizing and leading their forces with some success.[28] Nevertheless, his work with these representatives of popular heterodoxy did not alter his basically contemptuous attitude toward them. Upon his return to Japan he wrote of the necessity of modern political parties, with modern organization, ideas, and purposes. In contrast, he spoke of the White Lotus, Gelao hui, Triads, Big Swords, Little Swords, Boxers, and others as "barbarous groups." If the Taipings, with all their power, could not organize a real government, what could be expected from their defeated latter-day counterparts? Not only was their ideology confined to replacing the Qing autocracy with that of the Ming, even that was beyond their capacity.[29]

Not surprisingly, for heirs to an elite tradition in which education was both intellectual and moral, these comments link criticism of popular ignorance and of popular character defects. But by now the legacy of the Confucian tradition was itself under attack, and in the process, a new citizen ideal was emerging. If not in the realm of worldview and tenets, could one detect in the realm of character some traits that might commend these traditional rebels against orthodoxy? On this point, the radical elite began to evince some ambivalence. The "renovation of the people" that Liang Qichao began to call for in 1902 was not entirely new then. The journal that Qin Lishan helped organize in 1901 was entitled *Guomin bao* (The citizen), and it hammered away at the consciousness and character- istics requisite for a modern citizenry. In fact, Qin had begun to develop these themes even earlier, in the *Qingyi bao,* and so had Mai Menghua, in an article that dwelt on two important qualities: patrio- tism—that is, an enlightened conception of one's own national group and commitment to its interests—and spirit, as opposed to the ser- vility that was identified in several articles as a pernicious legacy of the Chinese tradition.

Mai bewailed China's lack of popular spirit *(minqi).* The pres- ence of this spirit distinguished America, Japan, and the Boer Repub- lic from India, which lacked it. Civilized countries saw its value and fostered it, enhancing the nation's strength. Barbaric countries feared it and suppressed it, forcing their people into the role of slaves and beasts of burden, to the point where the nation itself lost its vitality. This was the case with China. Over the past two thousand years, a servile quality had been cultivated in her people, who consequently took no interest in or responsibility for national affairs. But how about the Boxers? Hadn't their *qi* (spirit) merely caused problems for the country? Mai did not deny that the Boxers had plenty of *qi.* "Their harm," he contended, "lay in their failure to consider the outside world and their indiscriminate xenophobia, not in the abun- dance of their *qi.*"[30] This of course left open the possibility that the Boxers' spirit might be seen as deserving encouragement, even if their barbarism must be purged.

Among Kang's students, Mai was one of the more restrained, and it is little wonder that he never came any closer to a kind word for the Boxers. Among Liang's students, Qin was one of the more radical, but his own personal experience soured him on the Boxers too. Neither were they generally praised by later revolutionaries, partly because the revolutionary camp found it expedient to avoid a truculent posture toward the powers,[31] and partly because the Box- ers had accepted the patronage of the hated Empress Dowager, in contrast to other politically active popular associations with anti- Manchu traditions. In one of the most widely distributed and influ- ential revolutionary tracts, Zou Rong's *Revolutionary Army* (1903), the Boxers were referred to as "bandits *(tuanfei),*" and their uprising categorized as the kind of "barbaric revolution *(yeman zhi geming),*" which served only to worsen the lot of the people.[32]

But there remained considerable ambivalence about the Boxers among those who had become committed to the overthrow of the dynasty. After all, the Boxers did represent popular resistance to foreign domination, they were widely thought to have dampened the powers' enthusiasm for partitioning China, and they enjoyed some sympathy as victims of a terror more brutal than their own, visited upon them by the armies of countries that claimed to be more "civilized." The ambivalence and sympathy was often expressed in subtle and indirect ways, especially at first. Thus Sun Yat-sen and the Xingzhong hui denounced the Boxers to the governor of Hong Kong, asking his support to suppress them and overthrow the Manchus at the same time, though their propaganda organs systematically replaced the word *fei* (bandit), in texts referring to them, with *dang* (party). They also published an occasional speech or letter comparing the Boxers to patriots in Europe, or referring to them as "our country's soldiers."[33]

Likewise, Qin Lishan, by mid-1901 a convert to the revolutionary camp, wrote a short commentary deriding "civilized" Japan's hesitant talk about resisting Russia, as perhaps reflecting a lower level of civilization than the Boxers with their direct action. Elsewhere in his *Guomin bao,* the Boxer mentality was described as "xenophobia when repressed" but "a spirit of independence when properly channeled."[34]

Qin Lishan has also been credited, although not convincingly, with another article, defiantly pro-Boxer, dating to the spring of 1901.[35] The authorship of this remarkable piece is not as important as the fact that protégés of both Liang Qichao and Sun Yat-sen published it in their journal, the *Kaizhi lu* (Record of opening minds). Its message brings together various strands of anti-imperialism, patriotism, and desire for popular strength. The author's point of departure was the intolerable foreign incursions in China, and he could sympathize fully with the Boxer reaction to them. The Boxers, he claimed, knew their own weakness, but love of country and a desperate hope that they might at least stir up the idea of resistance in the people prompted them to act. Their uprising could hardly be explained by a few traitors' exploitation of their superstitions. And despite their defeat, they had planted the idea of independence in the minds of countless Chinese. In the idealized interpretation of this writer, they "represented the *minqi* of China, and were the heralds of anti-foreign resistance *(paiwai zhi xiansheng)*." The Europeans, he said, recognized the principle that men who were courageous in private feuds would be courageous in war. The Boxers were certainly deficient in strength and sophistication, but their self-respect, courage, and implacable wrath had astounded the whole world, and forced the powers to change their plans of partitioning China.[36] Not only could they not be dismissed as "bandits" *(fei)*, they had in fact provided an inspiring example for China's citizens.[37]

By 1903 Sun Yat-sen himself was citing the Boxers as evidence of the Chinese people's courage and patriotism, and proof that China could not be partitioned, points that continued to be made occasionally in revolutionary propaganda. But the anonymous *Kaizhi lu* article (also reprinted in a widely distributed anthology of revolutionary propaganda in 1903) remained the most extensive and articulate revolutionary endorsement of the Boxers.[38]

If the original publishers of this tribute to the Boxers were men of uncertain elite credentials,[39] this does not mean that men of more solid scholar-gentry background were incapable of finding something valuable in popular heterodoxy. Prior to the Boxer uprising, there was within Kang Youwei's reform camp a politically radical wing centered primarily in Changsha. These radicals had begun to distribute anti-Manchu literature and to talk about racial revolution and the establishment of an independent Hunan before the hundred days' reform in 1898. We know that Tan Sitong, Tang Caichang, and the *shengyuan* Bi Yongnian had established contacts with the Gelao hui and considered using them if and when armed action should become necessary.[40] After the Empress Dowager's coup and Tan's martyrdom, Bi, Tang, and other colleagues undertook to mobilize secret societies as the main force for the Independence Army.[41]

In view of the evidence for elite suspicion of popular heterodoxy considered here, what are we to make of these elite radical reformers' early contacts with the secret societies? In part, the answer lies in the fact that secret societies were the only force that might be readily recruited for an uprising. Even Sun Yat-sen, inclined to anti-Manchuism since childhood, tried to stimulate reform through the bureaucracy before turning to revolution, but when he made the turn, he naturally sought anti-Manchu manpower among the secret societies, and as far as we know, sought them out for no other reason.[42] But men like Tan Sitong were of much higher social standing, and we are prompted to ask what might have overcome the predictable prejudices and bridged the usual gaps between them and the secret societies? Too little is known of Tang and Bi to help answer this question, but Tan Sitong's case provides some interesting hints. His upbringing, though scholarly, was not exclusively bookish, and as a young man he had shown an interest in his ancestors' military accomplishments and in the martial arts. He studied the latter, in fact, under Single-Sword Wang the Fifth and Masterarm Ape Hu the Seventh, former outlaws who proposed to make him leader of a small brotherhood dedicated to "righteous knight-errantry."[43] Tan's own accounts of hard riding, hunting, and camp life in the harsh weather and wild wastes of Gansu bespeak a fascination with the strenuous life as an alternative to the quiet scholar-bureaucrat's career. In his *Ren xue* (study of benevolence), Tan declared that if the time were not ripe for heroes to pave the way for a sage ruler, the best alternative was "chivalric knight-errantry *(renxia),* which would at least suffice to foster popular spirit *(minqi),* promote an esteem for courage, and counter oppression *(boluan)....* Confucians disdain knights errant *(youxia),* comparing them to bandits, not knowing that under monarchical oppression there is no other way to save oneself."[44] As John Lust has suggested, the knight-errantry or chivalry *(renxia)* esteemed by secret societies could provide some common ground between them and the disaffected elite. And as Tan himself noted, the ranks of secret societies in the nineteenth century were swelled by demobilized and homeless soldiers banding together for support and protection: they were not initially criminals.[45] While we cannot assume that this adds up to a highly romanticized view of the secret societies for Tan much less for the progressive literati at large, it nevertheless suggests that an appreciation of the martial arts and a measure of alienation from the existing order could predispose some of the heterodox elite in their favor.[46] Indeed, they could even be seen to have certain virtues lacking in the elite. Qin Lishan whose overall evaluation was quite negative, nevertheless found the secret societies' solidarity, loyalty to precepts, and staying power superior to those of the conservatives, reformers, and revolutionaries.[47]

Among Kang Youwei's students, Ou Qujia, another of the radical wing, had more or less defected to the revolutionary cause by 1902, and published a tract entitled *The New Guangdong*, advocating independence for the province under a republican regime. This

tract contained the most extensive information on popular heterodoxy in political propaganda down to that time, and it reflected Ou's
own efforts at recruiting secret societies for political action. In one
way or another it addressed all the issues raised in evaluations of popular heterodoxy down to that point, and having apparently enjoyed
rather wide distribution, provided a baseline for further public discussion and for the crystallization of private attitudes.[48]

Ou's tract was clearly, although not explicitly, a response to
the writings of his former fellow-students Mai and Qin, and perhaps
to the anonymous apologist for the Boxers, as well. He dealt with the
problems raised by the Boxers indirectly, by placing them within the
larger context of popular heterodoxy as a whole. He used the term
sihui (literally, "private associations") to cover sects and secret societies *(huidang)*, but not guilds, Landsmannschaften, clan organizations, et cetera. The southern secret societies he traced back to Ming
loyalism in south China, not believing the myth that they originated
at the Shaolin Monastery.[49] In the north, he traced the origins of
the Small and Big Swords as well as Manchurian mounted bandits
to environmental and economic roots. The various sects, northern
(including White Lotus, Zaili, etc.), southern (various vegetarian
groups), and Moslem, he traced to their various religious origins but
noted that they, like the secret societies, shared an anti-Manchu animus, if only in response to suppression or oppression. Ou dealt with
the Taipings only to invoke their barbarity, stupidity, and ignorance
of foreign affairs as illustrative of the fatal weaknesses of popular
heterodoxy. Such weaknesses, he held, explained why Manchus
could use Chinese to suppress Chinese for centuries, and why Chinese rebels had never attracted any foreign support.[50] The strictures
would apply, mutatis mutandis, to the Boxers as well, although Ou's
brief comments on them had yet a different thrust. He explained the
Boxers as a temporary fusion of the Small and Big Swords, the White
Lotus, the Zaili, Bagua, Guangren, and other sects, manipulated by
the Manchu grandees Ronglu and Gangyi. Although Ou did not
explain in any further detail this divergence from the otherwise universal anti-Manchu pattern, he clearly regarded it as an anomaly.[51]
Thus Ou could accept Mai's criticism of the Boxers, and Qin's criticism of popular heterodoxy in general, without quite dismissing all
secret societies and sects as uniformly and irredeemably worthless.
At least they were mostly anti-Manchu.

For Mai, anti-Manchuism was not necessarily a virtue, and for

Qin, if it meant no more than a return to Ming despotism, it was scarcely worth the trouble. But Ou saw anti Manchuism as part of the resistance to slavery and oppression that Mai and Qin recommended. This did not necessarily mean that the resistance was very consistent or effective, but at least those who resisted were not willing slaves.

Ou summed up a hypothetical critic's objections to the secret societies in the following way:

> These *huidang* are made up of all sorts of people, and are a refuge for scum. They join a society merely for protection against robbery on journeys, or for support in their own extortions.... As for their goal of overthrowing the Manchus and restoring the Han their so-called elders do not even know what that is. Not only do they not carry it out, they're not even concerned to talk about it, or if they do, they say, "Quietly wait for heaven's hour..." They are generally scorned as rascals [*wulai,* literally, "those who have nothing they can depend on"]. It is impossible to do anything with them.

To these objections Ou answered:

> The [real] *wulai* lacks an independent spirit. One who by nature depends on others and cannot arouse his own independent spirit is a slave. To escape slavery, one must extirpate its roots, one must eradicate the temperament which relies on others. To [do that]...one must understand that one is a man who can stand on his own two feet, not an animal who must be cared for by men. So a man who does not depend on others is full of inner strength and confidence, his actions are vigorous and free...fearless, untrammelled, free of regrets, taking the lead without regard for life or death, guided only by honor (*yi*)—this is true independence (*duli*). Of the great mass of secret society members there are few who have this independent spirit. But they stand independent of the dynasty, come and go on their own, secretly band together to protect themselves, covertly constituting an organization of an independent character. However many their imperfections and defects, they must not be faulted too severely![52]

Here, then, is something of the *minqi* that Mai Menghua had called for, as well as reference to a theme prominent in turn-of-the-century reform propaganda; the rejection of stifling government con-

trol and paternalism, and the importance of autonomous public
activity and voluntary popular organizations—in effect, civil society.
Early stated by Liang Qichao,[53] some of the implications of these
ideas for secret societies and popular political initiatives had been
quickly noted by Mai Menghua and Ou himself. Like their counterparts in Japan and the West, Mai argued that China's *huifei*, guided
by gentlemen *(junzi)*, and mobilized by the government, could preserve faith, people, and nation *(jiao, min, guo)*.[54] Ou, for his part, had
declared that the chief agency for reform everywhere was the people,
acting through their own associations.[55] Thus, Ou was invoking in
The New Guangdong an important component of the reformers' conception of popular vitality. He distinguished first between *sihui* and
gonghui. The latter were public organizations devoted in one way or
another to the public welfare and including everything from parlia-
ments to astronomical societies. Such *gonghui* mobilized the intelligence and genius of a nation in competition with others (the "civilized competition" that Mai stresses), causing both *minqi* and the
national prestige to flourish. They were the expression of popular initiative.[56] *Sihui,* on the other hand, were conspiratorial organizations
devoted to terrorism and uprisings, and they arose where tyrannical
governments did not allow public organizations for the pursuit of
justice, the representation of the people's will, and the exchange of
ideas. Such were the Russian nihilists and the Italian Carbonari, and
they performed a great service in forcing the transition from autocracy to full constitutional government. Again disregarding various
voluntary associations in China, Ou concluded that China had no
gonghui at all, but was full of *sihui.*[57]

In Ou's view, then, secret societies represented a manifestation
of the people's genius for organization in opposition to tyranny.
China's scholars had no solidarity, her merchants had none, nor did
her farmers and artisans; and for lack of it China, for all her huge
size and population, was trampled underfoot by foreigners. But a
collection of people who seemed to be neither scholars, merchants,
farmers, nor artisans, and yet could be all of them, now formed a
great invisible organization, indeed something of a basis for (civil?)
society in China *(zhongguo zhi shehui).* They might have strayed from
their lofty ancient purposes, but if men of heroic talent and vision
were to remind them of their origins and oaths they would rise up to
restore China for the Han. "Today's secret societies," Ou declared,
"if they can be reformed so as to follow the leadership of heroes, will

be the source of tomorrow's parliament and assemblies, the basis of tomorrow's political parties. Not only will they equal the illegal societies of the foreign countries; they will take their place among the public bodies of the nations."[58]

For Ou the defects of popular heterodoxy, grave enough to have prevented the attainment of its goals for hundreds of years, could nevertheless be remedied. Its most important qualities were among those Mai and Qin Lishan had singled out as essential to China's revival: independence and backbone, organizational talent and solidarity.

Within a year another former teacher at the Current Affairs Academy in Changsha, the Hunanese *juren* Yang Dusheng, produced a tract obviously inspired by Ou's, entitled *The New Hunan*. In this work, Yang took a somewhat less positive view of popular heterodoxy than Ou. He wrote of the calamity the Boxers had caused China, and bitterly criticized the brutality of the Taipings, even praising Zeng Guofan and Hu Linyi for suppressing them. He wrote of the value and necessity of public organizations for the national welfare, but did not mention heterodox groups as a base for them.[59] He noted the Manchus' use of neo-Confucian orthodoxy and *mingjiao* (the doctrine of hierarchical status) to cultivate a servile mentality among the Chinese,[60] but did not praise the secret societies for resisting them. And yet, in this tract, Yang adumbrated a strategy somewhat similar to Ou's, and it was spelled out in another article that is probably attributable to him. He divided Hunan society into the upper, middle, and lower classes. Of these, the upper class were those who ruled, and were not worth dealing with. The middle class were Yang's audience, presumably relatively powerless scholars.[61] The lower class were the commoners, the working poor, and the secret societies, whose ranks had been swelled by demobilized Hunan Army soldiers. The lower classes had been reduced to the kind of desperation in which only those who became bandits prospered, and their ill-considered antiforeign outbursts only tightened the foreign grip on Hunan. Under these circumstances, it was up to the middle class to assist them. In fact, it was up to the middle class to "educate," that is, propagandize, them, for they were the basis for revolution. And under the rubric of this assistance and education, the first item of business was to reform and mobilize the secret societies, which had extensive contacts with the two other major targets of propaganda—the military and workers.[62]

Yang's writings are not remarkable as an exposition of the potential of secret societies, to which he attributed no particular virtues, and which he seemed to regard as rather crude raw material. They are important, however, as an expression of the views of one of the ringleaders of revolutionary organization among the student population in Japan before the establishment of the three major elite revolutionary organizations—the Huaxing hui, the Guangfu hui, and the Tongmeng hui. After the collapse of Tang Caichang's Independence Army, the next major effort of literati to organize secret societies in China for an uprising was undertaken by Huang Xing's Huaxing hui. Huang Xing (a *shengyuan*) had been a close associate of Yang Dusheng's in Japan, and the strategy for his 1904 uprising more or less followed Yang's blueprint. As Huang analyzed it, in China it was out of the question to undertake a revolution on the European model, relying on the urban population of the capital city. This meant that revolution would have to take whole provinces as its base. In Hunan there was a rise in revolutionary sentiment among students in military academies, and there was some ferment among the urban population. The Triads (Hongmen), on the other hand, were widespread, firmly established, and anti-Manchu. Neither the cadets nor the secret societies were ready to launch a revolution alone, but their combined explosive potential was great. It remained only for revolutionaries drawn from the intellectuals to organize them and light the fuse.[63]

In most of the revolutionary uprisings down to 1911, secret societies played a major role. Yang's and Huang's strategy brought together intellectuals, secret societies, and the military, with some thought of attracting urban workers, although they were never a significant source of recruits. Ou Qujia wanted to convert intellectuals, with propaganda, and have heroic leaders mobilize the secret societies. The Guangfu hui's efforts in Zhekiang were directed toward linking intellectual revolutionaries and secret societies.[64] And Sun Yat-sen relied primarily on overseas Chinese, merchants, and professionals for money and staff down to 1905, and then recruited elite students, but his fighting forces until 1910 were generally drawn from secret societies. The common denominator was almost invariably secret societies. Willy-nilly, when the elite opposition came to contemplate the violent overthrow of the government, secret societies were the logical source of armed force.

So far, the representatives of elite heterodoxy discussed here were, with few exceptions, members of the gentry or potential aspirants to that status, and clearly heirs to the traditions of China's scholar elite. The coincidence of two important developments lends the year 1905 a certain symbolic significance: the traditional examination system was abolished, and Sun Yat-sen, for the first time, managed to bring a large number of student radicals, many of them already degree holders, under his leadership. Sun had intellectual credentials of his own, but they were not traditional, and while the elite revolutionaries (unlike Mai Menghua seven years earlier) no longer saw him as a secret-society leader, in supporting him they were abandoning a claim to a gentry monopoly on leadership. Still, the Chinese students in Japan who constituted the core of Sun's Tongmeng hui, whether they were licentiates or not, had generally received a traditional education and laid great store by their modern knowledge as well. Western knowledge seems to have succeeded to the authority of neo-Confucian rationality. Under the circumstances, it is not surprising that their revolutionary propaganda should continue to express the critical attitudes toward popular heterodoxy that this chapter has addressed thus far.

Even Sun faulted the secret societies for their failure to produce any worthy leaders, and is said to have compared dissension among them to the internal feuds that destroyed the Taipings.[65] While the *Min bao* (the Tongmeng hui organ) paid little attention to popular heterodoxy in general, its only extended commentary on the Taipings was bitterly critical. The author (pseudonymous and unidentifiable) blamed them for clinging to a foreign superstition rather than restoring a rational, intelligent system with effective standards of administrative and military conduct, as Liu Bang and Zhu Yuanzhang had done. The result was internecine feuding and abuse of the populace, fatally weakening the movement. "Our people's subjugation to barbarians for another fifty years is the fault of the Taipings," the author declared. "The only hope for the descendants of the Yellow Emperor is for men of principle to arise and vindicate the goals of the Taipings, but by a different kind of action."[66]

Chen Tianhua (a *shengyuan*) had likewise denounced the superstitious and barbarous Boxers for the calamity they had brought down on China, and cautioned revolutionaries against relying on the secret societies for anything more than an auxiliary force. Guangwudi could not use the Bronze Horsemen or Red Eyebrows to restore the Han, he wrote. How much the less could any great undertaking be accomplished through today's secret societies?[67] Zhang Taiyan (1868–1936), a formidable classical scholar who disdained the examinations, wrote in the *Min bao* stressing the unreliability of the secret societies and the Manchus' ability to manipulate them for their own ends.[68]

But when secret societies were criticized as unreliable allies, the sword of criticism proved to be double-edged. If revolutionary intellectuals needed to be warned against relying on secret societies, this was an indication of their own weakness. Zhang Taiyan called the secret societies inferior to simple bandits, but also called "*xiucai* revolutionaries" inferior to secret societies, for the rebels lacked power, spirit, and self-confidence of their own, and were inclined to hope for the support of high officials.[69] Here Zhang echoed the reform radicals' complaints about the Chinese lack of *minqi,* suggesting that scholars were the most deficient of all. The point had been made as early as 1903, when one radical denounced China's pacifism, and in particular, her scholars *(ru),* men who esteemed empty talk, cautious calculation, and traditional ways. The opposite type, rare in China since the eighteenth century, was the "knight-errant" *(xia),* practical, sanguine, and innovative. "A nation," he declared, "will perish on account of its scholars, or rise through its knights-errant." Quoting the popular saying, "*Xiucai* won't manage to launch a rebellion if they try for three years," this writer urged them to infiltrate various groups in society, and especially to gain the support of the secret societies.[70]

Chen Tianhua, on the other hand, saw the intellectuals' central problem as a shallowness of commitment, which led either to frivolous dissipation or to ill-conceived efforts to borrow secret-society strength to achieve dramatic success.[71] But as he pointed out elsewhere, there were many valiant patriots within the secret societies, and he hoped to enlist their aid. In fact, his uncompleted novel, *The Lion's Roar,* contrasted secret societies favorably with more reputable patriots. The hero of the story, a rustic scholar trained in martial arts and endowed with great physical strength, went to Shanghai to contact the famous *zhishi* (gentlemen of purpose) there, with whom he expected to share his patriotic commitment. To his disappointment, he found that they were wasting all their time in parks, foreign restaurants, and schools, whereupon he went on to Hankou and Sichuan organizing secret-society leaders into a potential revolutionary force.[72] Decadence and posturing among China's new radicals was not confined to Shanghai, however. Criticism in the Tokyo press of the "dissolute and contemptible" ways of Chinese students there, together with newly enacted Qing government measures to control them, were taken as a great insult, and thousands of Chinese students boycotted their classes. Distrusting this reaction, Chen committed suicide to awaken the students to the gravity of their responsibilities and the importance of a sober approach to the task of reviving China.[73]

Chen did not criticize the new elite's shortcomings in order to recommend emulation of the secret societies, and some of those who were moved by his suicide reached back into the neo-Confucian tradition for techniques of self-cultivation that might qualify them for their mission of leadership.[74] In retrospect, intellectuals might have been more sensitive to criticisms about their failure to join in secret-society uprisings against the Manchus, if indeed the overthrow of the Manchus was the immediate task on the agenda. It was less so for Chen than for most revolutionaries.

As the split in elite heterodoxy between reformers and revolutionaries took clear shape, much of the debate between them amounted to advocating different means to similar nationalist and democratic ends, but the simplest counter to the constitutionalist blandishments of reformers and Manchus was anti-Manchuism.[75] Under these circumstances, the evils of the Taipings, so frankly conceded in Ou's and Yang's tracts, and stressed by Liang Qichao when he argued against revolution, were rarely mentioned in the subsequent revolutionary propaganda. In the *Min bao* a portrait of Hong Xiuquan took its place alongside those of Ming Taizu and Sun Yat-sen as one of the great nationalist revolutionaries in China *(minzu geming weiren)*. Pictures of secret-society leaders were harder to come by, but scenes of Manchurian mounted bandits (called "mounted heroes") were also displayed.[76]

In some minor revolutionary journals, writers offered fulsome praise for the Taipings, stressed the potential of secret societies, given the proper leadership, and criticized intellectuals for failure to involve themselves in secret-society uprisings.[77] And in a journal published by a coterie of Chinese anarchists in Paris, one writer urged Chinese revolutionaries to "go to the secret societies!" on the model of the Russian populists' slogan "Go to the people!" Regardless of leadership and outcome, all revolutions depended on popular forces, he argued. In addition to the tactical advantages of their widespread mutual support network in the military and the working classes, the secret societies possessed distinct virtues, including a solidarity and courage greater than those of the radical elite.[78] However debatable these virtues, on one particular count, sects and secret societies could claim the revolutionary intellectuals' respect. They gave the appearance of being traditionally anti-Manchu, whereas the elite's very identity was bound up with a system of recruitment for service to the dynasty. Thus, as the implications of anti-Manchuism were explored, the significance of the secret societies was enhanced. Zhang Taiyan for example, finally used the secret societies to argue against Yan Fu's contention that China remained a state partly dominated by patriarchal kinship and that anti-Manchuism was a reversion to clannish, therefore ethnic, principles. To the contrary, Zhang asserted, the secret-societies' bonds in themselves embodied values transcending those of the patriarchal clan, and they did so in the service of ethnic nationalism *(minzu zhuyi)*. "The secret societies," he claimed, "are just nationalists still deficient in organization."[79]

The revolutionary camp after 1905 produced only one account of popular heterodoxy comparable in scope to that in *The New Guangdong,* and this was Tao Chengzhang's "Inquiry into the Origins of the Sects and Secret Societies." Like Zhang Taiyan, Tao located their primary significance precisely in their antiforeignism. In Tao's view, this was true no less of sects than of secret societies, and could be traced back as far as the White Lotus resistance to the Mongols. Sects, like the Taipings (a vehicle of Triad anti-Manchuism, in his account) and Boxers (descendants of the White Lotus according to him), preyed on popular ignorance and superstition but had the advantage of tight organization and powerful motivation. Secret societies were, in his view, more autonomous and stressed honor and equality, but were correspondingly less disciplined and less highly motivated. Tao did not minimize the tendency of both to lapse into outlawry and inaction, but nonetheless looked forward to the day when they would be reunited in pursuit of their anti-Manchu goal.[80]

Whatever their reservations about the secret societies, *xiucai* revolutionaries continued to count on their support right down to the Wuchang uprising. Among those planning for action in the Yangzi valley at that time was Song Jiaoren. A veteran in efforts to borrow the strength of secret societies, Song had played a major role in Huang Xing's abortive Huaxing hui uprising of 1904. His own early anti-Manchuism was shared with his elder brother, a man who cultivated the martial arts, established ties with local "greenwood heroes" *(lülın haojıe),* and "distinguished strictly between Han and barbarian." Thanks to his brother's help, Song is reported to have had a force of some thirty thousand "heroes" ready for action when plans for the uprising had to be cancelled.[81]

Song's early writings suggest a continuing enthusiasm for the revolutionary potential of secret societies and bandits. During his exile in Japan, this enthusiasm may have been temporarily dampened by Chen Tianhua's warning, but he anxiously followed the progress of the massive secret-society uprising in Jiangxi in late 1906–early 1907, and was heartened by reports of its leaders' enlightened policies.[82] His own next attempt to launch an uprising, undertaken in 1907 on his own initiative, centered on Manchuria, where he planned to mobilize mounted bandits *(mazei)* who had carved out an autonomous territory of their own. Although Song was highly critical of their banditry as well as their tendency to ally themselves with either Russian or Japanese forces, he nevertheless evoked sympathy for these "fellow descendants of our Yellow Emperor, members of the four-hundred million strong Han race," by comparing them to the chivalrous and heroic brigands in *The Water Margin.* Unfortunately for Song's plans, the authorities learned of them shortly after his arrival in Manchuria, and once again they were cancelled.[83] Thereafter, Song's wide-ranging interests focused more and more on modern statecraft—diplomacy, international relations, and comparative government. It was in these fields that he began to make his mark as a pundit in the world of Shanghai journalism in 1911. By this time the constitutional movement, reflecting the strength of the new provincial assemblies and their constituents, had reached a high tide, and Song seems to have been as interested in wooing and prodding this less radical elite into the revolutionary camp as he was in recruiting support within either the New Armies or the secret societies. The major thrust, although not the scope, of his journalistic writings is perhaps best summed up by the title of one short column: "It's Time to Wake Up from the Constitutional Dream."[84]

In the same year, called upon to provide a preface for Hirayama Shū's new book on China's secret societies, Song wrote:

> Today's secret societies do not always act nobly, and their faults are widely criticized. But are they not rich in solidarity and discipline, adherence to their word, disregard of self and readiness to die for

their cause ... ? If their numbers can be better organized and their purposes enlarged, if they can be transformed into parties and labor unions on the European and American model, they will surely advance beyond the factions of the Xin-Han, Sui-Tang, Yuan and late Ming.[85]

Somehow, the apology, praise, and conditional hope sound rather more patronizing than Ou Qujia's blunter criticism eight years earlier. Ou had then seen no evidence of broad, organized political opposition in China except in popular heterodoxy, but by 1911 elite parliamentary activism had begun to leave the backward popular organizations behind.

It has been said that secret societies provided a romantic model for late-Qing revolutionaries, helping to enhance their self-image, and this was to some extent true.[86] Song Jiaoren is a good example. Fond of traditional novels of knight-errantry and brigandage, he invoked the images of greenwood heroes like Lu Da and Wu Song to suggest the potential of modern bandits and secret societies. In fact, revolutionaries very often applied the terms *haojie* and *yingxiong* (both words meaning "heroes") to secret-society members, almost as a matter of convention.

But the names of *Water Margin* heroes could also be invoked in derision (as Qin Lishan did),[87] and it is remarkable how rarely the members of secret societies were called heroes in the *Min bao*. In fact, when *xiucai* revolutionaries cast about for a flattering self-image, they were more likely to picture themselves as modern Western revolutionaries, or historically notable patriots, domestic or foreign.[88] Hong Xiuquan was not really a suitable model, even for Song Jiaoren, who devoured books about world heroes, East and West.[89]

But if sects and secret societies meant something more than just a handy source of infantry, what was it? I would argue that they represented a national potential particularly important at a time when heirs to the literati tradition could no longer rest secure in their own traditional vocation. Few radicals failed to accept the point made so strongly by Yan Fu, Liang Qichao, Mai Menghua, and Ou Qujia: a national survival required a more active and energetic citizenry. This was one of the fundamental components of the heterodox elite's worldview. The particular internal articulation of the traditional world kingship, in which the people were passive recipients of guidance from scholars, officials, and the Son of Heaven, could no longer survive. As Mai Menghua pointed out in 1897, there were three ways the government might deal with the *huifei*. It could coopt them, as Meiji Japan had done with her rebels. It could modernize its institutions, education, and economy on the Western model, as Russia had done since Peter the Great, while (unlike the West) suppressing the concomitant modern expressions of the popular will. Or it could simply concentrate on its army, like Turkey, with no attention at all to its other human resources.[90] With Turkey on the verge of ruin, and Russia, despite her national strength, internally unstable, there was only one policy to choose. The need to cultivate and mobilize natural popular capacities and energies as the basis for a strong country was axiomatic for reformers and revolutionaries alike, and sects and secret societies were repeatedly assimilated to this model.[91] While the elite could broaden the horizons, rectify the commitments, and nurture the talents of the people, their respective roles would no longer be divided, à la Mencius, between those who supplied the brains and those who supplied the muscle.

More specifically, the popular submissiveness so esteemed in the elite tradition was now denounced as servility, and was blamed for China's inability to resist modern imperialism. *Minqi* became important, and examples of popular resistance to the state, generally in the form of sectarian or secret-society traditions, took on great significance. The spirit was there. The orthodox elite had long tried to suppress it. In fact, as some writers noted, they themselves might have something to learn about *qi* from the people.[92]

Finally, revolutionaries took the additional step of assimilating Manchu rule to the general case of foreign rule. If national survival required not just elite, but popular patriotism, where but in secret society and sectarian anti-Manchuism was it to be found? The elite had, by and large, accepted the legitimacy of Manchu rule on the basis of the Confucian principles of loyalty to prince and dynasty, but now that those principles were rejected, the domination of the Han by the Manchus could be seen as pure oppression. As Zhang Taiyan put it, it was *minzu zhuyi* (nationalism) that had transcended the particularisms of the patriarchal order, and that was embodied, albeit in poorly organized form, in the secret societies. Thus the elite heterodox worldview assigned a role to popular energy, organizational initiative, resistance, and nationalism that could be filled only (if, to be sure, imperfectly) by the traditions of popular heterodoxy. At the same time, this worldview altered and in some ways diminished the role of the new elite itself, devalued the values of its orthodox fore-bears, and criticized the weaknesses it had inherited.

In the new radicals' view of popular heterodoxy can be seen the closest approach to populism in late Qing thought. There are adumbrations of Li Dazhao's enthusiasm for the Red Spears and Gu Jiegang's search for national identity and vitality outside China's elite traditions.[93] On the whole, however, elite views of popular heterodoxy were not romantic. As those who were more realistic were well aware, the virtues they detected in popular heterodoxy were at best unevenly distributed among and within the various sects and secret societies, while most of them shared a backwardness and parochialism anathema to the partisans of the future. It was still the role of the radical elite to guide and enlighten them. Popular heterodoxy could provide an indispensable basis for optimism about the Chinese people's prospects for survival in the modern world, but it remained, as well, a symbol of the backwardness yet to be overcome.

Notes

1. See chapters 9 and 10, this volume.

2. Zhongguo shixue hui et al., eds., *Yihe tuan* [The Boxers] (Shanghai: Renmin, 1951, 1960) 1:304, 354, 468, 492; 2:5, 180. The principal sources identifying the Boxers with the Eight Trigrams and the White Lotus were in "Lao Naixuan," ibid., 3:431–490.

3. Joseph W. Esherick, *The Origins of the Boxer Uprising* (Berkeley: University of California Press, 1987). Cf. review article on this book by Kwang-Ching Liu, "Imperialism and Chinese Peasants: Background of the Boxer Rising," *Modern China* 15.1 (Jan. 1989): 102–116.

4. Esherick, *The Origins,* esp. chap. 8; cf. the concluding remarks in chapter 6, this volume.

5. See chapters 7 and 8, this volume, and, for example, Susan Naquin, *Millennarian Rebellion in China* (New Haven: Yale University Press, 1976), part 1.

6. Cf. Frederic Wakeman Jr., "The Price of Autonomy: Intellectuals in Ming and Ch'ing Politics," *Daedalus* (spring 1972): 54–64.

7. For example, Mary Backus Rankin, *Early Chinese Revolutionaries* (Cambridge, Mass.: Harvard University Press, 1971); Liliia N. Borokh, *Soiuz vozrozhdeniia Kitaia* [The Xingzhong hui] (Moscow: Nauka, 1971); several articles in Jean Chesneaux, ed., *Popular Movements and Secret Societies in China, 1840–1950* (Stanford: Stanford University Press, 1972); Vladimir

N. Nikiforov, *Pervye Kitaiskie revolutsionery* [The first Chinese revolutionaries] (Moscow: Nauka, 1980); Cai Shaoqing, "Lun Xinhai geming yu huidang di guanxi" [On the relations between the secret societies and the revolution of 1911], and Wei Jianyou, "Xinhai geming shiqi huidang yundong di xin fazhan" [New developments in the secret society movements in the era of the 1911 revolution), and Wei Yingtao and He Yimin, "Lun Tongmeng hui yu Sichuan huidang" [On the Revolutionary league and the Sichuan secret societies], in *Jinian Xinhai geming qishi zhou nian xueshu taolun hui lunwen ji* [Collection of papers from the conference commemorating the seventieth anniversary of the 1911 revolution] (Beijing: Zhonghua shuju, 1983), 509–529, 530–545, and 546–569; Shao Yong, "Lun Huang Xing yu huidang di guanxi" [On Huang Xing's relations with secret societies], in Lin Zengping and Yang Shenzhi, eds., *Huang Xing yanjiu* [Studies on Huang Xing] (Changsha: Hunan Normal University Press, 1990), 74–83.

8. For the reactions of the secret societies in the Americas to the approaches of the elites, see L. Eve Armentrout Ma, *Revolutionaries, Monarchists, and Chinatowns: Chinese Politics in the Americas and the 1911 Revolution* (Honolulu: University of Hawai'i Press, 1990). There is scattered evidence that some secret-society leaders recognized the need for modern elements in the leadership of an anti-Manchu revolution. See Cai Shaoqing, "Lun Xinhai," 515–516, and Wei Jianyou, "Xinhai geming," 533.

9. Yuji Muramatsu, "Some Themes in Chinese Rebel Ideologies," in Arthur F. Wright, ed., *The Confucian Persuasion* (Stanford: Stanford University Press, 1960), 257.

10. S. L. Tikhvinskii, *Dvizhenie za reformy v Kitae v kontse XIX v. i Kan You vei* [The reform movement in China at the end of the nineteenth century and Kang Youwei] (Moscow: Izdatel'stvo vostochnoi literatury, 1959), 332. Kung-chuan Hsiao, *A Modern China and a New World* (Seattle: University of Washington Press, 1975), 500–501.

11. Rankin, *Early Chinese Revolutionaries,* 150–153; John Lust, "Secret Societies, Popular Movements, and the 1911 Revolution" in Chesneaux, ed., *Popular Movements,* 171, 182; Martin Bernal, *Chinese Socialism to 1907* (Ithaca: Cornell University Press, 1976), 62–63. Cf. Tao Chengzhang, *Zhe'an jilue* [Brief account of the Zhekiang case], especially the appendix "Jiao hui yuan-liu kao" [Inquiry into the origins of the sects and secret societies], in Chai Degeng et al., eds., *Xinhai geming* [The revolution of 1911] (Shanghai: Renmin chubanshe, 1957), 1:540; 3:18–20, 99–111; and Tang Zhijun, ed., *Tao Chengzhang ji* [Works of Tao Chengzhang] (Shanghai: Zhonghua shuju, 1986), 413–426.

12. Harold Z. Schiffrin, "Sun Yat-sen's Early Land Policy," *Journal of Asian Studies* 16.4 (Aug. 1957): 550–553. Feng Ziyou's reminiscences about Sun's ideas of social reform around 1900 referred to the mythical ancient "well-field system," Wang Mang's land policies, and Wang Anshi's

reforms as well as the Taipings and Henry George, and Sun's contacts with
the Miyazaki brothers may also have had some influence, but on the question of a practical present-day policy, Henry George seems to have been
decisive. See Kubota Bunji, "Sun Zhongshan di ping jun diquan lun" [Sun
Yat-sen's theory of land rights equalization], in *Jinian Xinhai geming qishi
zhou nian xueshu taolun hui lunwen ji* [Collection of papers from the conference commemorating the seventieth anniversary of the 1911 revolution],
3:2411–2413, and Xia Liangcai [Xia Liangcai], "Lun Sun Zhongshan yu
Hengli Qiaozhi" [On Sun Yat-sen and Henry George], in *Sun Zhongshan he
ta di shidai* [Sun Yat-sen and his era] (Beijing: Zhonghua shuju 1989),
2:1472–1474.

13. Lust, "Secret Societies," 177; Joseph W. Esherick, *Reform and
Revolution in China: The 1911 Revolution in Hunan and Hubei* (Berkeley: University of California Press, 1976), 153–154, 169.

14. "Jueshi pian" [On awareness and understanding], in San-bao Li,
"A Preliminary Analysis of Kang Youwei's Earliest Extant Essay, *Kangzi
neiwai pian*," *The Tsing Hua Journal of Chinese Studies*, n.s., 11.1–2 (Dec.
1975): 228–230.

15. Zhongguo shixuehui, ed., *Wuxu bianfa* [The Reform of 1898]
(Shanghai: Shanghai renmin chuban she, 1957), 2:221, 231–232.

16. Cai Shangsi and Fang Xing, eds., *Tan Sitong quanji* [The complete
works of Tan Sitong] (Beijing: Zhonghua shuju, 1981), 352–354.

17. *Tao Chengzhang ji*, 423.

18. Don C. Price, *Russia and the Roots of the Chinese Revolution* (Cambridge, Mass.: Harvard University Press, 1974), 91–94.

19. "Lun Zhongguo huifei yi she fa anzhi" [A proper place should be
found for China's secret society rebels], *Shiwu bao* no. 40 (26 Sept. 1897)
(reprint, Taibei: Taiwan Huawen shuju, 1966), 5:2696–2698; pagination
follows that of the reprint edition.

20. Huang Zhangjian, *Wuxu bianfa shi yanjiu* [Studies on the reform
of 1898] (Taibei: Institute of History and Philology, Academia Sinica, 1960),
21–26. Nikiforov, *Pervye Kitaiskie revolutsionery*, 110.

21. Wuyaisheng (Ou Qujia), "Yishi luandang bian" [The distinction
between righteous gentlemen and rebels], *Qingyi bao* no. 18 (18 June 1899)
(photographic reprint, Taibei: Chengwen, n.d.), 3:1123–1130; pagination
follows that of the reprint edition.

22. Shangxin ren (Mai Menghua), "Lun yimin yu luanmin zhi yi"
[On the difference between righteous people and the rebels], ibid., no. 52
(17 Aug. 1900), 7:3361–3363.

23. Xingke (pseud.), "Qinwang luanfei bian" [The distinction
between aiding the king and rebellious bandits], ibid., no. 65 (2 Dec. 1900),
8:4205.

24. Shangxin ren, "Xu lun Yihe tuan shi" [More on the Boxers], ibid.,

no. 47 (7 June 1900), 6:3052–3053; "Lun fei huangshang fu zheng ze guo luan bu neng pingding" [The country's rebellion cannot be pacified unless the emperor resumes governing], ibid., no. 49 (27 June 1900), 6:3176; "Lun yimin yu luanmin zhi yi" [On the difference between righteous people and the rebels], ibid., no. 68 (1 Jan. 1901), 9:4355.

25. "Lun Zhongguo minqi zhi ke yong" [On the usefulness of the Chinese people's spirit], ibid., no. 57 (14 Oct. 1900), 7:3677–3678; "Xu lun Yihe tuan shi," 6:3053–3054; "Paiwai pingyi" [Impartial view on anti-foreignism], 9:4355–4356.

26. Ibid., 4356.

27. Ibid., 4359–4360. Mai's views and the later sympathy for the Boxers foreshadow Chen Duxiu's and others' evolving views of them in the May Fourth era. See Paul A. Cohen, "The Contested Past: The Boxers as History and Myth," *Journal of Asian Studies* 51.1 (Feb. 1992): 82–96.

28. Feng Ziyou, *Geming yishi* [An unofficial history of the revolution] (Taibei: Commercial Press, 1953), 1:85–92. It is highly unlikely that Qin proposed an anti-Manchu revolution to the Boxers, as Feng asserts. For his self-image as a loyalist to the emperor for some time after the failure of Tang's uprising, see "Qianyan" [Preface], in *Qin Lishan ji*, 2–3.

29. "Zhongguo miewang lun" [On the fall of China], *Guomin bao huibian* [Anthology of the *Citizen's Daily*] (photographic reprint, Taibei: Kuomintang Party History Commission, 1968), 48–49. For my identification of Qin as author of this article, see Price, *Russia and the Roots*, 245.

30. "Lun Zhongguo minqi zhi ke yong," 7:3673–3677.

31. A. M. Grigor'ev, *Antiimperialisticheskaia programma kitaiskikh bur-zhuaznykh revoliutsionerov (1895–1905)* [The antiimperialist program of the Chinese bourgeois revolutionaries, 1895–1905] (Moscow: Nauka, 1966), 74.

32. Tsou Jung (Zou Rong), *The Revolutionary Army*, trans. John Lust (The Hague: Mouton, 1968); Chinese text pp. 23, 25.

33. *Sun Zhongshan quan ji* [Complete works of Sun Yat-sen] (Beijing: Zhonghua shuju, 1981) 1:191–194; Kubota Bunji, "Giwadan hyōka to kaku-mei undō" [The revolutionary movement and the evaluation of the Boxers], *Shisō* [Shisō: Journal of Historical Studies, published by the Historical Society of Japan Women's University, Tokyo] (Nov. 1976): 17:14–18.

34. *Guomin bao huibian*, 208.

35. See Kubota, "Giwadan hyōka," 26; Kondō Kuniyasu, *Shingai kakumei: shisō no keisei* [The 1911 revolution: formation of ideology] (Tokyo: Kinokuniya, 1972), 65. This attribution is based on the similarities between this article and others clearly by Qin with respect to the focus on national-ism and popular patriotism, but it ignores his otherwise consistent stress on sophistication and commitment in political organization and action.

36. This point had been disputed by Mai Menghua in "Lun yi he"

[On peace negotiations], *Qingyi bao* no. 61 (30 Oct. 1900), 8:3925, but was later echoed by Hu Hanmin, who, however, did not approve of the Boxers, in "Paiwai yu guoji fa" [Antiforeignism and international law], *Min bao* [The people] no. 9 (15 Nov. 1906), 54–55; no. 7 (5 Sept. 1906), 15; no. 8 (8 Oct. 1906), 69–70.

37. "Yihe tuan you gong yu Zhongguo shuo" [On the Boxers' service to China], reprinted in Zhang Nan and Wang Renzhi, eds., *Xinhai geming qian shi nian jian shilun xuanji* [Selected writings on current events from the decade before the 1911 revolution] (Hong Kong: Sanlian, 1962), 1.1:58–62.

38. Kubota, "Giwaden hyōka," 28–29; Sun Yat-sen, *Quanji*, 223; Kondō, *Shingai kakumei*, 33–34. The reprinted version in the collection *Huangdi hun* [Spirit of the Yellow Emperor] carried a revised title: "Yihe tuan yu Zhongguo zhi guanxi" [The relation of the Boxers to China], which is considerably less positive in tone than the original.

39. The editors of the *Kaizhi lu* were Feng Ziyou, of emigre merchant background, and Zheng Guanyi, who was forced to abandon a traditional education at age fifteen and had gone to live with merchant relatives in Japan. See Feng Ziyou, "Zi xu" (Author's preface), *Geming yishi*, 1:1, 82–83.

40. Huang Zhangjian, *Wuxu bianfa*, 21–26. Nikiforov, *Pervye Kitaiskie revolutsionery*, 110.

41. Ibid., 112.

42. Harold Z. Schiffrin, *Sun Yat-sen and the Origins of the Chinese Revolution* (Berkeley: University of California Press, 1968), 33–41. Liila N. Borokh suggests that Sun admired the secret societies, but seems to be contradicted by her own evidence on this point. See her "Notes on the Early Role of Secret Societies in Sun Yat-sen's Republican Movement," Chesneaux, ed., *Popular Movements*, 137, 140.

43. Douglas David Wile, "Tan Sitong, His Life and Major Work, the *Ren xue*" (Ph.D. diss., University of Wisconsin, 1972), 46–48.

44. Ibid., 56–59; *Quanji*, 19–20, 344.

45. Ibid., 347.

46. For other examples and an analysis of this cluster of attitudes, see Don C. Price, "Early Chinese Revolutionaries: Autonomy, Family and Nationalism," in Academia Sinica, Institute of Modern History, ed., *Family Process and Political Process in Modern Chinese History* (Taibei: Academia Sinica, Institute of Modern History, 1992), 1034–1043.

47. "Zhongguo miewang lun," 49–50.

48. Li Shaoling, *Ou Jujia xiansheng zhuan* [Biography of Ou Jujia] (Taibei: Li Shaoling, 1960), 24.

49. "Xin Guangdong" in ibid., 76–77.

50. Ibid., 90.

51. Ibid., 78–79.

52. Ibid., 83–84.

53. Hao Chang, *Liang Ch'i-ch'ao and Intellectual Transition in China* (Cambridge, Mass.: Harvard University Press, 1971), 106–109.

54. "Lun zhongguo huifei," 2695–2698.

55. Ou Jujia, "Lun da di ge guo bianfa jie you min qi" [How reform in every country in the world has arisen from the people], *Shiwu bao* no. 50 (24 Nov. 1897): 6:3375–3379.

56. "Xin Guangdong," 72.

57. Ibid., 73.

58. Ibid., 84, 91. See also Don C. Price, "From Civil Society to Party Government: Models of the Citizen's Role in the Late Qing," in Joshua Fogel and Peter Zarrow, eds., *Imagining the People: Chinese Intellectuals and the Concept of Citizenship, 1890–1920* (Armonk, N.Y.: M. E. Sharpe, 1997).

59. "Xin Hunan," in Zhang Nan and Wang Renzhi, *Xinhai geming,* 1.2:618–619.

60. Ibid., 618, 635.

61. Ibid., 615.

62. Ibid., 622; "Minzuzhuyi zhi jiaoyu" [Education in nationalism], in ibid., 1.1:408–409.

63. Liu Kuiyi, *Huang Xing zhuanji* [Biography of Huang Xing] (Taibei: Wu Jingwen, 1952), 3.

64. Rankin, *Early Chinese Revolutionaries,* chaps. 7–8.

65. Lust, "Secret Societies," 176. Lust does not document Sun's reference to the Taipings.

66. Xinchuan (pseud.), "Ai Taiping tianguo" [Lament for the Taiping Heavenly Kingdom], *Min bao,* no. 18 (25 Dec. 1907): 99–101.

67. "Chen Xingtai xiansheng jueming shu" [Mr. Chen Xingtai's suicide letter], *Min bao* no. 2 (6 May 1906): 4 (separate pagination). See also his "Jingshi zhong" [A Tocsin for the age], in Chai Degeng, *Xinhai geming,* 2:123; and "Meng huitou" [Turn around!], ibid., 146.

68. Zhang Taiyan, "Geming zhi daode" [Revolutionary morality], *Min bao* no. 8 (5 Oct. 1906): 25–26.

69. Minyi (pseud.), "Ji shier yue er ri ben bao jiyuan jie qingzhu da hui shi ji yanshuoci" [Account of this journal's Dec. 2 anniversary celebration and transcript of the addresses], ibid., no. 10 (9 Jan. 1906): 96–98.

70. Zhuangyou (pseud.), "Guomin xin linghun" [The citizen's new soul], in Zhang Nan and Wang Renzhi, 1.2:574–575. Cf. Baihua daoren (Lin Xie), "Guomin yijian shu" [Views on the citizen], ibid., 1, 2:910.

71. "Chen Xingtai," 4.

72. Chen Xingtai, "Shizi hou" [The lion's roar], *Min bao* no. 7 (5 Sept. 1906): 81–100; no. 8 (5 Oct. 1906): 85–114. Cf. his exhortation to the secret societies in "Meng huitou," 141–142.

73. Ernest P. Young, "Ch'en T'ien-hua" in Chün-tu Hsüeh, ed., *Rev-*

olutionary Leaders of Modern China (New York: Oxford University Press, 1971), 242–245.

74. Don C. Price, "Song Jiaoren: Confucianism and Revolution," *Qingshi wenti* (Nov. 1977): 3.7:50–55.

75. See Michael Gasster, *Chinese Intellectuals and the Revolution of 1911* (Seattle: University of Washington Press, 1969), 83–84. This is not to suggest that anti-Manchuism was simply a counter to constitutionalism, for a number of elite rebels, e.g., Lin Gui, Bi Yongnian, and Song Jiaoren, are reported to have displayed strong anti-Manchu sentiments even before the reform movement, and they surface here and there in Tan Sitong's *Renxue* (*Quanji,* pp. 341–342). The nature and extent of anti-Manchuism still awaits serious investigation. For some preliminary speculations, see Don C. Price, "Nation as Family: Revolution for the Ancestors," (paper read at the forty-fifth annual meeting of the Association for Asian Studies, Los Angeles, 25–28 March 1993).

76. Pictures of Taipings and mounted bandits appear in numbers 4, 5, 13, and the special supplement *Tian tao* [Heaven's chastisement] of the *Min bao.* For Liang's criticism of the Taipings, see "Zhongguo lishi shang geming zhi yanjiu" [A study of revolution in China's history], in Zhang Nan and Wang Renzhi, *Xinhai geming,* 1.2:809.

77. Especially two articles by the pseudonymous Tielang, "Ershi shiji zhi Hunan" [Twentieth-century Hunan], *Dongting bo* [The waves of Lake Dongting (1 Sept. 1906): 1–21, and "Lun ge sheng yi su xiangying Xiang Gan gemingjun" [All provinces should quickly rally to the revolutionary armies in Hunan and Jiangxi], *Han zhi* [The Han banner] (Jan. 1907): 1–16; reprinted in *Ershi shiji zhi Zhina, Dongting bo, Han zhi* (photographic reprint, Taibei: Kuomintang Party Historical Commission, 1968).

78. Fan (pseud.), "Qu yi, yu huidang wei wu" [Go, join ranks with the secret societies!], in Zhang Nan and Wang Renzhi, *Xinhai geming,* 3:188–191.

79. [Zhang] Taiyan, "Shehui tong quan shangdui" [A discussion of *A History of Politics*], *Min bao* no. 12 (6 Mar. 1907): 19.

80. See ibid., 3, 99; and Tao Chengzhang, "Jiao hui yuan-liu kao," 3:99–111.

81. "Song xiansheng Shiqing shi lueh" [A brief account of Mr. Song Shiqing] *Minli bao* [The people's stand], 7 Apr. 1913. For the origins of Song Jiaoren's anti-Manchuism, see Don C. Price, "From Civil Society to Party Government: Models of the Citizen's Role in the Late Qing." For book-length biographies of Song, see K. S. Liew, *Struggle for Democracy* (Berkeley: University of California Press, 1971), and Wu Xiangxiang, *Song Jiaoren: Zhongguo minzhu xianzheng di xianqu* [Song Jiaoren: Pioneer of democratic constitutionalism in China] (Taibei: Wenxing, 1964).

82. Song Jiaoren, *Wo zhi lishi* [My history] (Taibei: Wenxing, 1962; photographic reprint of the Taoyuan, 1920, edition), 300.

83. Jie [Song Jiaoren], "Ershi shiji zhi Liangshan bo" [Twentieth-century Liangshan bo], *Ershi shiji zhi Zhina* no. 1 (1 May 1906): 15. Reprinted in *Ershi shiji zhi Zhina, Dongting bo, Han zhi.*

84. Yufu [Song Jiaoren], "Xianzheng meng ke xing yi" [It's time to wake up from the constitutionalist dream], *Min li bao,* 25 Mar. 1911.

85. Taoyuan yishi [Song Jiaoren], "Xuyan er" [second preface], in Hirayama Shū, *Zhongguo mimi shehui shi* [History of China's secret societies] (n.p.: 1911; photographic reprint, Taibei: Guting shuwu, n.d.). "Xin" refers, of course, to Wang Mang's short-lived and illegitimate dynasty, A.D. 8–24.

86. Rankin, *Early Chinese Revolutionaries,* 15.

87. "Zhongguo miewang lun," 50–51.

88. Price, *Russia and the Roots,* chap. 7. Cf. Rankin, *Early Chinese Revolutionaries,* 38–47.

89. Song, *Wo zhi lishi,* 23–101, passim.

90. "Lun Zhongguo hui fei," 2697–2698.

91. For a curious example, see [Hu] Hanmin, "Jinsheng Gelao hui jishi" [Account of the Elder Brothers Society in Shansi], *Min bao* no. 2 (6 May 1906): "Shiping" [Comments on current events], 1–8.

92. Chongyou (Gao Fengqian), "Lun Zhongguo minqi zhi keyong" [On the usefulness of the Chinese people's spirit], in Zhang Nan and Wang Jenzhi, 1.2:938–939.

93. Maurice Meisner, *Li Ta-chao and the Origins of Chinese Marxism* (Cambridge, Mass.: Harvard University Press, 1967), 248–250; Laurence A. Schneider, *Ku Chieh-kang and China's New History* (Berkeley, Los Angeles, London: University of California Press, 1971), 13–17.

Afterword
The Twentieth-Century Perspective

Kwang-Ching Liu and Richard Shek

We began our inquiry with a reference to J. J. M. de Groot's work. The foregoing chapters have, it is hoped, demonstrated that de Groot's definition of the issue of orthodoxy versus heterodoxy was all too biased and simplistic. We argue that there indeed existed in China a dominant and vibrant orthodox tradition, defined by monarchical/patriarchal authority and the normative power of *lijiao*.[1] Originating at least in the Han dynasty, this orthodox tradition went through numerous challenges and accommodations and, by the late imperial period, became the prevailing religio-ethical standard not only among the educated elites but throughout the different strata of society. The final triumph of this tradition of "correctness" *(zheng)* has to be understood in the context of what is considered "incorrect," "deviant," and outright "heterodox." Thus there is a mutually reinforcing procedure, with what is regarded as "incorrect" helping to consolidate the content of what is "correct," while what is "correct" in turn defines what is ethically and religiously unacceptable.

To be sure, it is extremely difficult, if not entirely impossible, to form an independent, culture-free definition of heterodoxy. There is really no effective way to free oneself from relying on the state or the cultural elite in identifying what is heterodox. For, after all, "heterodoxy" has meaning only in contradistinction to "orthodoxy," and "orthodoxy" is ultimately defined by the state and its cultural elite. Yet orthodoxy and state authority were by no means identical entities. Orthodoxy in the Chinese tradition consisted of a broad spectrum of beliefs and institutions, including ancestor worship, social hierarchy, communal religion, and lineage authority. Antigovernment or antidynastic positions were therefore not necessarily heterodox, if they agreed with or subscribed to the same set of orthodox values—witness the change of dynasties often without basic ideological or institutional change. Only movements that espoused a genuinely alternative worldview and envisioned a radically different social order would qualify as heterodox. Politically motivated rebellions that repeated the dynastic cycle and kept intact the prevailing orthodox values would thus not be heterodox at all by our definition. Seen in this light, religious affiliations and identities per se do not indicate orthodoxy or heterodoxy. In this connection, Steven Sangren's study of religion in a Taiwanese community is most instructive. On the whole question of orthodoxy and heterodoxy, Sangren remarks:

> Structures of value that prize order and legitimate existing social institutions and authority define Chinese orthodoxies, both official and local. Conversely, it is the denial of order as an ultimate value that defines heterodoxies.[2]

By definition, heterodoxy thus has to be antiestablishmentarian in its value orientation and is therefore politically confined to groups out of power. On the rare occasion when it does succeed in toppling the existing and establishes itself as the prevailing value system, it ceases to be heterodox. It is always in an unstable state. Its very nature denies it the possibility of being successful in overthrowing the existing orthodoxy, and remaining heterodox at the same time.

Heterodoxy is never an autonym. On the contrary, some of the commonly identified "heterodox" groups even claim some higher or truer form of "orthodoxy" than the established and governmentally sanctioned traditions. In this connection, Barend J. ter Haar's work, *The White Lotus Teachings in Chinese Religious History,* is highly suggestive. Focusing on a revisionist study of the lay Buddhist phenomenon of the White Lotus, ter Haar convincingly argues that by the late imperial period, "White Lotus" was merely a label and a stereotype, having little "objective" content. This label represents everything that the authorities (whether of the state, community, or family) regarded as incorrect, unacceptable, and heretical. How the groups so labelled saw themselves, and whether the content of their beliefs and behavior merits such a label is no longer a relevant issue. Ter Haar maintains that the only genuine White Lotus were the lay Buddhist associations of the Song, Yuan, and possibly early Ming that dedicated themselves to the worship of Amitabha. These "people of the Way" *(daomin)* founded cloisters to rival the monasteries of established Buddhism, undertook charitable works in the community, and never engaged in rebellious activities.

One of ter Haar's major arguments is that, with a substantial literati membership at least until the early Ming, the White Lotus actually proves to be "a highly coherent, socially well-accepted phenomenon."[3] Thus ter Haar maintains that the White Lotus is far from being the heretical and rebellious tradition it was labelled by late Ming elites and later historians. As he puts it, "the notions of deviance and heresy are only present in the minds of the elites, who are responsible for most of our sources."[4] This means that one has to be mindful of such elite biases and be free from them. Yet in the course of examining the very content of the beliefs and structure of these lay religious groups, ter Haar concedes that "the fact that the [White Lotus] movement placed membership of the common religious household above loyalty to one's own family and lineage and above membership of a group based on place of residence in this explicit way must be considered a violation of Confucian morality."[5] This is precisely what is argued in this volume; namely, that while elite and official sources are used inter alia in our examination of the "heterodox" groups, we are not merely applying labels to such groups. Instead, we seek to determine whether such groups truly espoused ideas and beliefs that can be construed as alternatives to the prevailing order and values.

We argue in this volume that a resilient and potent heterodox tradition did exist in China. Characterized by an "alternative moral universe" in which the orthodox values of order and structure were consciously rejected, this heterodoxy is understood primarily in cultural and religious terms as an antinomian, countercultural, and dissident value tradition that ultimately denied the existing order its legitimacy and immutability. With its origins going back to Daoist, Buddhist, and even Persian sources, this tradition was messianic and eschatological in nature, in the sense that it subscribed to the belief in a saviorlike figure who would bring an end to the present age and usher in a new one. While this heterodox tradition at times led or participated in armed rebellions against the state, it did not always have to have political aspirations itself (as seen in establishing a new kingdom or dynasty), nor did it necessarily have to express explicit antigovernment sentiments. The heterodox nature of a group or a movement did not derive from its political activities, but rather from its beliefs and ethics. It is a view of heterodoxy that is quite independent of state or official proclamations.

Elite Radicalism and Utopianism

It is not the task of the present volume to examine the perpetuation of the heterodox tradition in China into the twentieth century. A few brief observations are offered here, however, to stimulate discussion and perhaps to suggest areas for further study. The Chinese heterodox tradition can be perceived positively in numerous respects. It served as an antidote to the excesses of monarchical and patriarchal power. It included a feminine perspective on viewing reality that otherwise might be absent from the Chinese worldview—witness the faith in the Eternal Mother and the role of women leaders. It also proposed an alternative social order that was more egalitarian. Finally, it envisioned a utopian world whose features expose the inadequacy and imperfection of the existing one. As such, it was a source of utopianism that scholars such as Jin Guantao consider to be highly significant in the making of modern China.[6]

Sometime in the first decade of the twentieth century, a profound radicalism gripped a small but increasing number of Chinese intellectuals. Don C. Price, in chapter 12 of this volume, has found a Chinese elite heterodoxy that arose to challenge certain basic premises of the imperial state. Fired by patriotism and armed with information introduced from abroad, the young Chinese intellectuals began to challenge the age-old neo-Confucian social ethics. The new knowledge that the earth is not flat nor square—and that heaven is essentially the blue sky that envelops the earth—led even gentry literati that had had the old-style scholastic training, to be skeptical of the sacrosanct status of the Son of Heaven. The Qing dynasty having been toppled in 1912, the way was open for a more sweeping and more thorough reexamination of the entire traditional ethical premise. Can the radicalism of the May Fourth generation be further understood from the perspective of this elite heterodoxy?

Secret Societies and Gangsterism

What about the Green Gang (Qingbang) that played such an important part in the life of twentieth-century Shanghai? In what way can the secret societies of the twentieth century be understood in terms of heterodoxy? The origins of the Green Gang are still partly shrouded in mystery. Some historical studies have traced the Green Gang's genesis to the worship of Patriarch Luo Qing (whose central role in the formulation of late Ming sectarian belief has been discussed in chapter 7, this volume) among the boatmen of the Grand Canal carrying tribute rice from the Jiangsu-Zhejiang area to North China. David E. Kelly has argued convincingly that the temples built near the Grand Canal in Hangzhou and Suzhou were religious centers for retired boatmen in search of spiritual solace and material care. Many of them were Luo Qing followers.[7] The work of Ma Xisha and Cheng Xiao has suggested that the Green Gang of the twentieth century could be more directly identified with the smugglers' league that came into being after the complete reorganization of the Grand Canal boatmen in 1853, as a result of the difficulties consequent to the government's increasing use of seagoing junks to move the tribute rice to Tianjin. Among the former boatmen, many took advantage of their familiarity with the waterways and terrain to become big-time smugglers of salt produced in northern Jiangsu, to Anhui, Hubei, and beyond. The network of this illicit trade in time reached the cities of the lower Yangzi, including Shanghai. Memorials to the throne beginning in 1862 referred to this smuggling organization as An-Qing daoyou, meaning "Friends on the same path from Andong and Qinghe" (both places being situated near the intersection of the Huai River and the Grand Canal). Ma and Cheng maintain that these An-Qing daoyou were predecessors of the Green Gang.[8]

The Green and Red Gangs, as well as the Elder Brother Society (Gelao hui), are subjects calling for further research. The latter, founded in the 1840s, gained great cohesion when it spread among the Hunan Army under Zeng Guofan and Zuo Zongtang. Veterans of this army became the leaders of the Elder Brother Society in the port cities of the Yangzi valley. The society played a key role in the anti-Christian movement that broke out in several Yangzi ports in 1891, and in the revolutionary agitations prior to the establishment of the Republic. In chapters 9 and 10, the generalization has been offered that the secret societies of the Triad type, although often engaged in violent activities flouting the law and in some cases even sharing their remote historical roots with the religious sects, were nonetheless quasi-orthodox in that the sworn brotherhood did not call for a restructuring of the hierarchical socioethics. The same generalization, it maybe hypothesized, applies to the Green Gang, and to the Elder Brother Society as well.

Eternal Mother Sectarianism

Meanwhile, the Eternal Mother sectarian tradition of late imperial China survived into the twentieth century, showing much resilience and tenacity. Despite government sanctions and occasional severe persecutions, the sects, using different names and incessantly branching off into new locales with new memberships, continued their existence with their underlying beliefs intact. There were, still, the firm belief in the centrality of the Eternal Mother in a well-developed salvational scheme, an intense eschatological expectation in the form of the three-stage historical time frame, and an acute sense of election and chosenness among the believers.[9]

One of the largest and most influential of the Eternal Mother sects in the twentieth century is the Xiantian dao (Way of Former Heaven). Active throughout China and even expanding overseas into Southeast Asia, this tradition exists under various names.[10] In North China, the Xiantian dao is primarily known as Yiguan dao, a sectarian group that has attracted much government attention and hostility, as well as general suspicion and distrust.[11] The label of "Yiguan dao" is, like the label of "White Lotus" in late imperial China, a blanket reference to numerous proscribed religious groups. The Yiguan dao has been driven underground in China since the Communist Revolution but still commands a substantial following in Taiwan today.[12] It can thus be observed that the Eternal Mother tradition has had a long, uninterrupted existence of over four hundred years!

Maoist Radicalism

What role did religion play in Chinese Communism under Mao? Ironically, it is precisely a certain brand of millenarian and messianic sentiment that informed the history of Chinese Communism. Any student of Mao Zedong's role in history cannot fail to notice the religious symbolism of the Long March, the Yan'an era, and the cult of Mao himself. The Long March helped to foster a belief among the

followers of Mao that he was the prophet who, Moses-like, was destined to succeed in delivering the faithful to the promised land. Similarly, the Yan'an experience created an almost numinous character
for the leadership of the Communist Party, whose modest dwellings
during those hard times were still visited and revered by "successors
of the revolution" decades later as "sacred shrines." Since the 1950s,
moreover, Mao was seen by millions of Chinese as the savior and the
"great star of salvation" *(da jiuxing)* who would usher in a perfect
society free from want and worry.

Li Rui, Mao Zedong's former secretary and biographer,
remembers that at a plenary meeting of the Communist Central
Committee in July 1959, Mao distributed to the participants the section in the *History of the Three Kingdoms,* complete with his own commentaries, of the biography of Zhang Lu.[13] It may be recalled that
Zhang Lu was the head of the Celestial Masters sect (Tianshi dao)
in the second century, the first organized religious Daoist tradition
founded by his grandfather Zhang Daoling. (See chapter 1.) Zhang
Lu was said to have provided his followers with free lodging and
meals and to have replaced civil officials with priests *(jijiu)* who were
also given command over fighting men. Li Rui has found Mao's
interest in people's communes to have complex roots, being influenced by European utopianism, Japanese experiments with the "new
village," and the concepts of equalization *(pingjun zhuyi)* derived
from the programs of a number of peasant rebellions in Chinese history.[14] Maurice Meisner, who has studied European as well as Chinese Marxism, has written that at that historical juncture: "The Great
Leap Forward compaign was a profoundly utopian historical episode,
utopian in the chiliastic fervors and expectations which characterized
the early stages of the movement—and perhaps even more 'utopian'
in the pejorative Marxist sense of the term."[15]

But it was the Great Proletarian Cultural Revolution of 1966–
1976 that brought the chiliasm of Mao to its culmination. Mao
exhorted his young admirers to dare to rebel against not only the
"four olds" of China's past but also the established authority of the
Party and its organizations. Meisner summarizes the fervent messianic sentiments succinctly:

> In an uneasy fusion of traditional Chinese and modern revolutionary
> symbolism, the "Mao-sun" was hailed as the "reddest of all suns"

whose radiance dwelt in the hearts of all true revolutionaries. Drawing on the imagery of Taoist mysticism, the "thoughts of Mao" was
said to be a "magic weapon" that would vanquish his foes, while the
foes themselves were condemned in demonic Buddhist terminology
as hellish "monsters," "demons," "cow-ghosts" and "snake-gods."[16]

At the height of the Cultural Revolution, Mao held himself up as a
messiah who demanded total renunciation of the values of the past
and the present, and an unswerving commitment to the new ethics of
the coming world. This Maoist revolutionism, by our definition, is
thus highly heterodox and inherently unstable. Meisner has shrewdly
noted that during the Cultural Revolution, Mao was revered and
worshiped as a utopian prophet whose vision and instructions were
translated by the masses into new forms of revolutionary action.[17]

To what extent can the Mao cult be described as "chiliastic"?[18]
It is not within the scope of this volume to address the question,
except to say that there was a morphological similarity between the
Cultural Revolution's excesses and the violent response to the kalpa
among the sectarians in late imperial China. As we have argued in the
preceding chapters, the millenarian, anticultural vision was what constituted heterodoxy in China. Recalling Steven Sangren's definition
of "heterodoxy" as the rejection of the existing order, cited earlier,
the irony of Mao's chiliasm becomes apparent. As Meisner has
rightly asserted, "the cult of Mao was wholly antithetical to bureaucratic routinization and the institutionalization of the postrevolu-
tionary state."[19] It was precisely his contempt of and challenge to the
social-political order of China in the 1960s that characterized Mao's
Cultural Revolution. Mao might have thus unwittingly created a new
heterodoxy that rejected the authority of the very political order he
had helped to create! It is thus possible to establish the connected-
ness between Maoism and traditional heterodoxy. Our volume is
therefore not merely an examination of the heterodox cultural pattern of China's past but, it is hoped, will inspire inquiry further into
aspects of China's modern revolution.

Perhaps a final passing comment can be made regarding the
current Falun Gong phenomenon in China. One may wonder if the
Falun Gong can be considered a contemporary expression of the
heterodox impulse. The Chinese government is determined to root
the sect out. A preliminary examination of the teaching of Li Hongzhi (1952–), founder of the movement, reveals the following themes:

1. The current world as we know it is coming to its destined end.
2. We are living in the last stage of time—the "end of the doctrine" *(mofa)* in medieval Buddhist terms.
3. Our age is characterized by moral degeneracy, brought about by spiritual delusion.
4. Established religious organizations and government services are ineffective and irrelevant in dealing with the impending catastrophe.
5. Only the Falun Gong formula for exercise and meditation, and Li Hongzhi's supernatural protective power can provide deliverance from the current mess.
6. We are offspring of higher entities in the cosmos, thus our earthly kinship ties have no ultimacy.

Because of the intense personal cult of its founder-master Li Hongzhi, the Falun Gong is indisputably messianic.[20] Far from being resigned to the prospect of cosmic disaster, Li calls for a sustained human effort. The individual must strive for a rigorous self-cultivation *(xiulian)* to achieve invincibility and spirituality. These goals are to be achieved through *qigong* exercises "at a higher and deeper level." Like Daoists, Li believes in the potential of the body to enhance energy and harness cosmic powers. Like Buddhists, Li prizes compassion and visualizes "salvation of all beings." He pays lip service to science, picturing space travel in a futuristic world. Truth, compassion, forbearance *(zhen shan ren)*, the ultimate values, are to him physical qualities of the universe, not simply moral concepts.[21]

In reality, the Falun Gong is an outgrowth of the daily morning regimen of *qigong* (group calisthenics and breathing exercises) practiced collectively by gatherings at public parks all over China. Participants in *qigong* often engage in meditation as well. From the quasi-mystic belief that rhythmic exercise can enhance human forces and energy, it was perhaps not difficult to go a step further and accept Li Hongzhi's theory that a rigorous, introspective self-training can not only bring health and well-being but also harness the cosmic powers to achieve supernatural feats. A former government clerk turned *qigong* master, Li devoted full time to the propagation of Falun Gong in 1992. By 1998, when for the sake of his personal safety he left China to live in New York, a nationwide network of his cult had been formed: 28,000 Falun Gong training centers all over China, 1,900 regional centers, and 39 national centers. The total number of adherents in the late 1990s is said to have been "tens of millions."[22] Many of the local Falun Gong groups had aroused government suspicion and were often harassed.

On a clear Sunday morning, 25 April 1999, the authorities in Beijing were stunned by the appearance of more than 10,000 Falun Gong adherents staging a quiet demonstration at the leadership compound of Zhongnanhai in central Beijing. Many in the big crowd had traveled day and night from the provinces to be there, most of them reported to be retirees and middle-aged women. They demanded recognition of the Falun Gong as a legitimate organization, so that its adherents could be free from harassment. The demonstration was both quiet and orderly; no slogans urging democracy or self-government were shouted. The government, surprised by the petitioners' obvious capacity for organization, had to accept their demands.[23] Yet only three months later, it banned the Falun Gong as heterodox religion *(xiejiao)*, on the grounds that its teachings flouted science and that, moreover, it had seriously disrupted social order. The whole machinery of the state was to be brought to bear against the movement in the next few months. Falun Gong activists were arrested. Four senior adherents of the sect who were former Party and government officials were tried publicly.

As compared with sectarian heterodoxy in late imperial China, the Falun Gong movement was more open and accessible. Its core adherents, "retirees and provincial policemen, farmers and graduate students,"[24] are more conspicuous and less secretive than the "intermediate group between urban and rural society" that constituted the rank and file of the White Lotus rebellion two hundred years earlier. Beyond the press reports and the treatises written by Li Hongzhi in the early and mid-1990s, there is as yet very little available documentation on the Falun Gong in action. Many Chinese have sympathized with the avowed ideals of the Falun Gong: "Truth, compassion, forbearance *(zhen shan ren)*" succinctly summarized by the simple adage "Be a good person *(zuo haoren)*." Yet there is no reliable way to tell just what this means in terms of socioethical commitment, whether "goodness" entails any reference at all to obligations to family and state. Or is the dominant concern simply individual well-being and salvation? The peaceful and nonpolitical Falun Glong demonstrations in Beijing and in the provincial centers have, to all appearances, turned a page in modern Chinese populism. The Falun Gong movement is very different from the agitations during the Cultural Revolution. Maoism seems to have receded into the background. But it is still unclear whether the Falun Gong, in its turn, carries a new utopian vision and message. Is the Falun Gong heterodoxy in the tradition of the great heterodoxies of the imperial past, or is it something entirely different?

Notes

1. See Kwang-Ching Liu, ed., *Orthodoxy in Late Imperial China* (Berkeley: University of California Press, 1990).

2. P. Steven Sangren, *History and Magical Power in a Chinese Community* (Stanford: Stanford University Press, 1987), 176.

3. Barend J. ter Haar, *White Lotus Teachings in Chinese Religious History* (Leiden: E. J. Brill, 1992), 111.

4. Ibid., 12 n. 28.

5. Ibid., 113.

6. Cf. Jin Guantao's article "Zhongguo wenhua de wutuobang jingshen" [The utopian spirit in Chinese culture], *Ershiyi shiji* [Twenty-first century], no. 2 (Dec. 1990): 16–32.

7. See David E. Kelly, "Temples and Tribute Fleets: The Luo Sect and Boatmen's Associations in the Eighteenth Century," *Modern China* 8.3 (July 1982), 361–391.

8. Ma Xisha and Cheng Xiao, "Cong Luojiao dao Qingbang" [From the Luo sect to the Green Gang], *Nankai shixue* (1984): 1–28. See also Ma Xisha and Han Bingfang, *Zhongguo minjian zongjiao shi* [A history of popular (sectarian) religion in China] (Shanghai: Renmin, 1993), esp. 301–309. Cf. Brian G. Martin, *The Shanghai Green Gang: Politics and Organized Crime, 1919–1937* (Berkeley: University of California Press, 1996), chap. 1.

9. In his classic, *Xianzai huabei mimi zongjiao* [Secret religious sects in contemporary North China] (Beijing, 1948; Taibei reprint: Guting, 1975), Li Shiyu has identified at least fourteen different sects in North China in the 1940s that subscribed to the same broad Eternal Mother belief; see p. 2.

10. For a good discussion of this tradition, see Asai Motoi, "Sentendō no tenkai" [The unfolding of the Xiantian dao], in his *Min-Shin jida minkan shukyō kessha no kenkyū* [A study of the folk religious associations of the Ming-Qing period] (Tokyo: Kenbun shuppan, 1990), 381–438. Some of the names of the sects include Jindan [Golden Elixir], Qinglian [Blue Lotus], and Zhaijiao [Vegetarian Teaching]. For some of the activities of the sect outside China, see Majorie Topley, "The Great Way of Former Heaven: A Group of Chinese Religious Sects," *Bulletin of the School of Oriental and African Studies* 26:2 (1963): 362–392.

11. One of the earliest researchers of the Yiguan dao is Li Shiyu. Li

devoted considerable space to this sectarian group in his *Xianzai huabei mimi zongjiao* (1948; reprint, Taibei: Guting shuwu, 1975), 32–130. The Japanese scholar Kubo Noritada has also written extensively about the sect. See his "Ikkandō ni tsuite" [On the Yiguan dao], *Toyo bunka kenkyūjo kiyō* [Bulletin of the research center on oriental culture, Tokyo University], no. 4 (1953): 173–249. Also his "Ikkando hōkō" [Supplementary study of the Yiguan dao], ibid., no. 11 (1956): 179–212.

12. See Song Guangyu, *Tiandao gouchen* [Retrieving forgotten knowledge about the way of heaven] (Taibei: Yuanyou chubanshe, 1983). See also Lin Wanchuan, *Xiantian dao yanjiu* [A study of the way of former heaven] (Taibei: Qiju shuju, 1985).

13. Li Rui, *Lushan huiyi shilu* [The true record of the Lushan conference] (Hunan jiaoyu chubanshe, preface dated Dec. 1988), 12. We are as yet unable to find Mao's commentaries on the biography of Zhang Lu that were distributed at the conference.

14. Ibid., 10–12.

15. Maurice Meisner, *Marxism, Maoism and Utopianism* (Madison: University of Wisconsin Press, 1982), 193. Meisner writes earlier in the book: "During the rural communization movement, which aroused chiliastic expectations of the more or less immediate advent of a communist utopia, Mao appeared on the new historical stage in the guise of a utopian prophet who promised to lead those who followed his teachings and instructions to a classless and stateless society. Through direct and visionary appeals to the masses, Mao ignored and bypassed regular bureaucratic channels and established state and party procedures—and, for a time, forged a direct bond between himself and the peasant masses, a bond between his own utopian visions and popular aspirations for social change and economic abundance." Ibid., 163.

16. Maurice Meisner, "The Cult of Mao Tze-tung," in his *Marxism, Maoism, and Utopianism*, 168–169.

17. Ibid., 167.

18. The late Maurice Freedman has characterized the Red Guards as "juvenile millenarians." See "Why China?" in G. William Skinner, ed., *The Study of Chinese Society: Essays by Maurice Freedman* (Stanford: Stanford University Press, 1979), 409–412.

19. Meisner, *Marxism, Maoism and Utopianism*, 175.

20. For an authoritative source of Falun Gong beliefs, consult Li Hongzhi's *China Falun Gong* (Hong Kong: Falun Fofa Publishing, 1998); and the much lengthier and fuller Chinese version, *Zhuan Falun* [Turning the Dharma Wheel] (Hong Kong: Falun Fofa Publishing Co., 1998). There are also numerous other books issued by this publisher that present Li's further lectures and record conversations Li had with his followers in different

cities in China as well as abroad, which reveal more of Li's views about his personal role in the future cosmic change.

21. David Ownby, "China's War Against Itself," *New York Times,* 15 Feb. 2001, Op Ed page. The esoteric features of Li's self-cultivation include a wheel with healing power in the lower abdomen, which draws good forces into the body and expels bad ones, and an all-seeing eye in the forehead. Only those predestined to succeed can achieve such wonders, however. Nonetheless, those who have tried and failed can still enjoy good health and fine moral character.

22. In July 1999 the government believed that the Falun Gong had 20 to 60 million members, but the sect itself claimed 100 million members. In November 1999, four months after the sect was banned, Elizabeth Rosenthal reported that the Falun Gong still claimed "tens of millions" of adherents. *New York Times,* 11 and 22 July, and 1 Nov. 1999.

23. In reference to demonstrations in April, the ban in July, and the protests against it, see *New York Times,* 11, 22, 23 July, 25 Aug., and 28, 30, 31 Oct., 1 Nov., and 27 Dec. 1999.

24. *New York Times,* 1 Nov. 1999. Cf. chap. 8 n. 6.

Appendix
A Note on the Usage of the Chinese Terms for Heterodoxy

Kwang-Ching Liu

To buttress the main contents of this volume, it is necessary to offer a discussion of the Chinese terms for heterodoxy. At issue here is the meaning of such phrases as *"yiduan," "xie," "zuodao,"* and *"yao,"* as employed by the state and its officials and by philosophers and clerics. Patterns may be detected in the usage of such terms in imperial China, beyond existing treatment such as is found in J. J. M. de Groot's *Sectarianism and Religious Persecution in China.*[1]

An excellent discussion of some of the Chinese terms for heterodoxy has been offered by Donald Sutton in chapter 6 of this volume. The present disquisition relies especially on the dynastic histories from the Han to the Ming, where the usage varied, emphasizing "evil magic" at first, but eventually moving toward the perverse and heretical by Ming times, indicating a growing intolerance and perhaps reflecting the growing threat of heterodoxy.

The terms *"yiduan"* and *"xie"* originated before the imperial era. It was presumably Confucius (551–479 B.C.) who first used the term *"yiduan"* to denote what to him were strange or alien principles. Confucius is supposed to have said, as in James Legge's translation of the *Analects:* "The study of strange doctrines [*yiduan*] is injurious indeed."[2] The same saying is imaginatively translated by Arthur Waley to read: "He who sets to work upon a different strand [*yiduan*] destroys the whole fabric."[3]

"Xie" is a stronger and more pejorative term than *"yiduan."* As used in the sources of antiquity, including the *Book of Poetry* and the *Analects, "xie"* simply means "evil or depraved."[4] Yet as used in a famous passage in the *Works of Mencius, "xie"* bore the meaning of "perverse or morally misguided." Mencius was speaking of the doc-

trine of Yang Zhu, who advocated a selfish epicureanism, and that of Mo Di, who taught a kind of universal love. Mencius regretted that these two schools of thought were very popular in his time. As compared with Confucianism, Mencius implied, the ethics championed by Yang and Mo were less than human. In Legge's translation, Mencius declares:

> Now, Yang's principle is—"each one for himself," which does not acknowledge *the claims of* the sovereign. Mo's principle is—"to love all equally," which does not acknowledge *the peculiar affection due to* a father. But to acknowledge neither king nor father is to be in the state of a beast. . . . If the principles of Yang and Mo be not stopped, and the principles of Confucius not be set forth, then these perverse speakings [*xieshuo*] will delude the people, and stop up *the path of* benevolence and righteousness. When benevolence and righteousness are stopped up, beasts will be led on to devour men, and men will devour one another.[5]

It was Mencius' view that human nature is good—and good in the sense that benevolence *(ren)* and dutifulness *(yi)*, filial piety and respect for an elder brother are natural feelings. Mencius' words were to be quoted frequently in the imperial times of much later centuries, providing a source for the culturally determined aversion to "heterodoxy."

In the lifetime of Mencius (ca. 372–ca. 289 B.C.), Confucianism was still only one of the "hundred schools" that competed with one another. Even in the Qin state that was destined to unify China (and then lost to the Han in short order), the ideological justification for conducting the intensifying military struggle was still being worked out.[6] The age of orthodoxy had not arrived. It was not until the reign of Emperor Wu (141–87 B.C.) of the former Han dynasty (206 B.C.–A.D. 8) that Confucianism was given preeminence and that the study of the Six Classics, with which Confucians identified themselves, received imperial sponsorship. The Han view of heterodoxy, articulated especially by Dong Zhongshu (ca. 195–ca. 105 B.C.) and Kuang Heng, chancellor under Emperor Cheng (r. 33–7 B.C.), went beyond Mencius's notion of impropriety and perversity.

Dong Zhongshu's cosmos comprised the tripartite division of heaven, earth, and man. He saw nature and human society as linked, following the rhythm of yin and yang and revolving according to the

Five Operating Phases (Wuxing).[7] The imperial sovereign played a crucial role, for it was through his morally transformative influence *(jiaohua)*—as well as the government over which he was supreme—that the equilibrium between the social and the natural cosmos was maintained. Should the throne's moral influence be lacking and should government be so unjust as to cause dire poverty and destitution among the people, the usual rhythm of nature would be disrupted.[8] There would be eclipses of the sun, unexplained fires in the imperial capital, long droughts that would destroy the harvest. Such prodigies and calamities would be portents of further disasters for the dynasty.

It was in the context of such a cosmology that Dong Zhongshu's followers conceived of good and evil—the correct and the deviant. Dong saw rectitude as represented by the proper action of the sovereign. "According to the text of the *Spring and Autumn Annals,* the principle of the Kingly Way *(wangdao)* is found in correctness *(dezhi yü zheng)*. . . . That is, [for the sovereign] to model oneself on the action of heaven in the sphere below, to rectify one's action and model oneself on the Kingly Way." When the monarch's government departs from rectitude and his officials are allowed to tyrannize the people and when punishments are administered unjustly, then evil ether *(xieqi)* will be created in abundance, the harmony between yin and yang will be undermined, and there will be supernatural manifestations of evil *(yaonie)*.[9]

As chancellor to Emperor Cheng, Kuang Heng, who in the main followed Dong Zhongshu's theories, won imperial endorsement for a "religious reform" in 31 B.C. What seemed particularly abhorrent to Kuang were the various forms of unorthodox sacrifice *(yinsi)*—in this context meaning worship that was believed to be contrary to the dominant heaven-earth-man tripartite cosmology.[10] Kuang Heng advocated the proper sacrifices to heaven and earth outside the imperial capital, at sites south and north of the city respectively. These were first performed by Emperor Cheng in 31 B.C. Meanwhile several hundred former shrines for worship dedicated to a host of colorful spirits were abolished in the empire at large and at a center of worship in the vicinity of the capital. Kuang Heng himself is believed to have used the term *"yinsi"* in reference to the shrines abolished. Other learned officials referred to the heterodox spirits as "deviant" *(zuodao)* or "wizardly" *(yao)*, a term that can also be translated as "supernaturally evil."[11]

As peasant rebellions arose in the late Han period, it was inevitable that imperial astronomers would try to link the eruptions in the social realm with prodigies in the natural realm. The *History of the Later Han Dynasty* ascribed a host of socially undesirable phenomena to abnormal and demonic forces—intrigues among noblemen and high officials, bizarre costumes worn by decadent men and women, unfilial acts, magical archers, deformed dragons and horses.[12] A number of peasant rebellions were believed to have been led by "demonic sorcerers" *(yaowu)*, who could collect an armed band with their "wizardly spells" *(yaoyan)*.[13] The major rebellion, that of the Yellow Turbans, arose in present-day Henan in A.D. 184. The Yellow Turbans were believed to practice healing by charms and incantations, as well as spirit possession and sorcery. Not only did their leader, Zhang Jue, have imperial pretensions, identifying himself with the "Yellow Heaven," his scripture, the *Taiping jing* (The classic of the great equilibrium), was believed to have included "heterogeneous messages from spirit possession" *(wuxi zayü)* and was described as "wizardly and outrageously heterodox" *(yaowang bujing)*.[14] The contemporaneous Daoist movement in Sichuan, the Way of Five Pecks of Rice (Wudoumi dao), led by Zhang Lu and persisting in a larger area for some thirty years (sometimes with the uneasy recognition of the government), was dubbed the ghostly way *(guidao)*, its adherents described as wizardly rebels *(yaozei)*, its doctrines as wizardly delusions *(yaowang)*.[15]

There were, of course, other words and phrases used by Chinese historiographers to describe popular rebellions—for example, *"kou"* (robbers), *"zei"* (bandits, rebels), *"ni"* (rebels), *"pan"* (defectors). However, following the usage of the *History of the Later Han Dynasty*, rebels who claimed to perform magical feats or who propagated a religious message were almost always referred to in the standard dynastic histories as *"yaozei"* (which may be translated simply as "heterodox rebels") or by variants of the phrase such as *"yaodang"* (heterodox partisans) or *"yaozhong"* (heterodox bands). The utterances of such rebels would be *yaoyan* (heterodox words or incantations) and their supernatural claims *yaoshu* (heterodox magic).[16] Such was the case, for example, with the Daoist millenarian movement led by Sun En that broke out in 399.[17] In *Old History of the Tang Dynasty*, the Maitreyan revolt of 715, led by Cui Ziyan, was labelled *yaozei*, while the great Huang Chao rebellion of the late Tang, because its leaders were smugglers and bandits with no religious message, was merely referred to as *dao* (robbers) or *zei* (rebels), even after Huang Chao had declared his pretensions as founder of a new dynasty in 880.[18] The early Song peasant rebellion that broke out in 994, led by Wang Xiaopo and Li Shun, was merely described as *zei* and *kou*. However, the leader of the Maitreyan revolt of 1047, Wang Ze, was identified as a *yaoren* (wizard).[19] The Manichaean Fang La rebellion (1120–1122), with its strange practices and disrespectful scriptures (see chapter 2), was described as *yao* and *zuodao,* both meaning heterodox.[20]

The case can be made, however, that these terms should be translated as "heretical" in this context, for what was considered particularly pernicious by the authorities was the report that the Manichaeans did not practice ancestor worship and that they recited strange-sounding scriptures that were outside the Buddhist and Daoist canon. In European religious history, a distinction has been made between heterodoxy and heresy, and it would be appropriate to make a similar distinction here.[21] Yet the Chinese historiographical terminology continued to be stereotyped. Even the colorful rebellions of the late Yuan period, with the White Lotus sectarians in open revolt, received routine treatment. The Red Turbans under Han Lin'er and Liu Futong were described in the *History of the Yuan Dynasty* simply as *yaokou* (heterodox bandits). Liu, a principal leader of the Red Turbans, was identified as *yaoren* (wizard).[22] Indeed, such language continued to be used by the officials of the Ming period to describe the "White Lotus" revolts that broke out from time to time.[23] In the Shandong rebellion of 1420, the woman leader Tang Sai'er was described as a heterodox woman *(yaofu)*. Several cases of revolt in the early and mid-sixteenth century ascribed to the "White Lotus Society (Bailian she)" were depicted as heterodox rebels *(yaoren)* deluding the people with heterodox words *(yaoyan).*[24]

Was there then a gap between language and reality, semantics and the changing facts? Indeed this seems to be the case, for especially during the Ming dynasty, the term for heterodoxy, "*xie,*" began to be used in a malignant context. Partly on the basis of the Yuan dynasty statutes, the Ming adopted in its law code severe penalties for shamans that practiced spirit possession and black magic *(shiwu jiajiang xieshu)* as well as the proscription of a number of religious sects specified by name: Maitreyan (Mile), White Lotus (Bailian), Manichaean (Mingzun), and White Cloud (Baiyun).[25] Although the term "*yaozei*" was still widely used in referring to the sectarian rebels, the phrase *"xiejiao"* (heresy or heretical doctrine) began to be used by officials, along with its variant forms, *"xieshuo"* (heretical discourse) and *"xieshu"* (heretical magic).[26] By the mid-Qing period, *"xiejiao,"* which needs to be translated as "heresy" to suggest the abhorrence in which it was held, became the standard term, used in the scholars' notebooks as well as imperial edicts.

Historically, the deep meaning of such terms as *"xiejiao"* or *"xiefa"* (heretical doctrine) must be traced to the age of religious polemics in medieval China when Buddhism, Daoism, and Confucianism were often in deadly contention at the courts of rulers who chose to honor one or more of the three religions. The well-known persecution of Buddhism in the Northern Wei was inspired by Cui Hao, a Confucian minister who brought to the sovereign's attention the Daoist divine Kou Qianzhi. (See chapter 1, this volume.) The imperial edicts of 444–446 attacked the Buddhists for practicing what was referred to as *yaoxie* (evil heresy), and Buddhism itself as a barbarian-inspired heretical delusion *(xie wei)*.[27] In the early Tang dynasty, Fu Yi (555–639), a Confucian with an interest in Daoism, attacked Buddhism as disloyal and arrogant toward monarchs and parents and for its *yaoshu* (supernaturally evil books) and *xiefa* (heretical doctrine). In a debate at court with a Buddhist, he attacked Buddhism not only as a barbarian faith but also as *xiejiao* (heresy):

> Propriety *(li)* starts with service to the parents and ends in submission to the emperor. If the principles of loyalty and filial piety are manifest, the duty of a servitor and of a son will be fulfilled. The Buddha, however, went out of his city and left his family; he turned his back on his father, and as an individual [subject] he defied the Son of Heaven.[28]

As in the Six Dynasties period, Confucians and Daoists often joined in attacking Buddhism, but the Buddhists were not slow in counterattacking. Despite their continued insistence that the monks need not make obeisance before the ruler, the Buddhist apologetics argued that Buddhism essentially reinforced the throne's moral and cultural influence and stressed filial piety as well. When pressed by Confucian and Daoist criticism, Buddhists also used strong language. Responding to Fu Yi's charge that Buddhism was heresy, Falin, an eminent cleric at a great monastery in Chang'an, lashed back, declaring that Fu's assertion was a *xiejian* (heretical opinion) and Fu himself a *xieren* (heretic). Falin argued that Fu not only maligned Buddhism, but betrayed the dynasty's interest as well.[29] It seems that Buddhists were the first to initiate that distinct genre in Chinese literature—works or anthologies devoted to *poxie* (decisively refuting heresies). The famous Buddhist encyclopedia *Fayuan zhulin* (Forest of gems in the garden of law), compiled by Daoshi in 668, included a two-*juan* work entitled *Poxie bian* (A book to refute heresies). Daoists were scathingly attacked for their role in the late-Han Yellow Turban rebellion and, in more recent history, for the "heretical magic" *(xieshu)* used, for example, by the Daoist priests in the revolt between 366 and 372 in Eastern Jin territory.[30]

In the post-Tang era, as Buddhism—and Daoism—became further domesticated, the phrase *"xiejiao"* seems to have been rarely used against any of the Three Religions, Confucianism, Daoism, and Buddhism. The neo-Confucian philosophers of Song and Ming regarded Buddhism and Daoism as unorthodox *(yiduan)*, but the term in their usage is a moderate one. In fact, a significant number of neo-Confucians were interested in reconciling Confucianism with aspects of those religions.[31] Meanwhile, the term *"xie"* in the forms of *"xieshuo"* (heretical discourse) and *"xiejiao"* (heretical doctrine) began to be applied to sectarian groups that seemed to be especially dangerous to the established order.

The first explicit interdiction of a religious sect (in contrast to the general suppression of Buddhism as decreed in Northern Wei, Northern Zhou, and the late Tang) seems to have taken place only under the Song dynasty in 1132 in regard to the Manichaeans, ten years after the Fang La rebellion had ended. The Chinese Manichaeans, with their strange customs and scriptures, "eating vegetables and serving the devil," were condemned in this edict as a heterodox sect *(yaojiao)*.[32] Meanwhile, in an unrelated development, a lay Buddhist association was founded with which the monk Mao Ziyuan (1086–1166) was identified. This group, which came to be led by married priests, was attacked as practicing heresy *(xiejiao)* in the mid-thirteenth century, by Zhiqing, a Buddhist writer of the Tiantai school.[33] In what was probably still another unrelated development, a popular sect identified as White Lotus assembly (Bailian hui) was discovered in 1281 by officials of the Yuan dynasty to be practicing "heterodox magic" *(zuodao luanzhen zhi shu)*. The "White Lotus teachings" (Bailian jiao) were banned forthwith by imperial edict.[34] As late as 1300, a pious adherent of the White Lotus religion *(jiao)* defended it in a memorial to the throne and urged that a distinction be made between the genuinely devout and those who were "heretical and deluded" *(xiemei).*[35] In 1308, when activities of married White Lotus clerics in the Jiangxi area were reported, a statute reiterated the prohibition against the White Lotus temples and hostels—the new accusation against the sectarians including that they held nocturnal meetings in mixed company.[36] Despite this prohibition, the White Lotus sect continued to develop, absorbing Maitreyan as well as Manichaean beliefs sometime in the ensuing decades, and played a major part in the great rebellion of the Yuan-Ming transition. The Yuan statutes prohibiting the White Lotus, Manichaean, and other sects were later incorporated into the Ming code by authority of Zhu Yuanzhang (Ming Taizu, r. 1368–1398), who had been a Buddhist novice in his youth and for many years served under a White Lotus-Manichaean military regime.[37]

Yet the term for heresy, *"xiejiao,"* was not standardized during the Ming dynasty. As noted above, the White Lotus insurgents of the fifteenth and sixteenth centuries were referred to as *"yaozei"*—the ancient term for heterodox rebels. The Xu Hongru rebellion of 1622 was still ascribed to *yaozei.*[38] For the mid-Ming period, an account in the *History of the Ming Dynasty* does refer to Bailian xiejiao (White Lotus heresy), but then, that history was not compiled until the early Qing period.[39] It was not until the Kangxi reign (1662–1722) that a substatute was added to the Qing code, which was originally a mere copy of the Ming code, to the effect that the sectarians were identified with *xiejiao.* It seems that this new legal rehetoric was the invention of the Manchu court in Manchuria, before the Qing conquest of China.[40] In any case, with the Yongzheng emperor's amplified instructions on the Kangxi sacred edict and with the compilation of a near-definitive edition of the Qing code to be published in the early Qianlong period, in 1740, the branding of the sectarians as heretics was explicitly stated, and local officials were adjured in accordance with the statutes to root out and eliminate this heresy.[41]

But, then, what was the content of this heresy? What did it advocate, and in what way did it originate? If it was heresy, it was heresy as opposed to what? What forms of rebellion either would or would not qualify as heretical, and what forms of dissidence did evolve during the latter part of the Qing dynasty on the eve of and in conjunction with China's response to the West? What were the values—and doctrines—of Chinese heterodoxy as opposed to the venerated socioethical orthodoxy? These are some of the questions addressed in this volume, and it is hoped that it will stimulate discussion.

Notes

1. J. J. M. de Groot, *Sectarianism and Religious Persecution in China: A Page in the History of Religions*, 2 vols. (Amsterdam: Johannes Müller, 1903; reprint, Shannon, Ireland: Irish University Press, 1973).

2. James Legge, trans., *The Chinese Classics*, rev. 2d ed. (Oxford: Oxford University Press, 1893–1895) vol. 1, *Confucian Analects*, 150.

3. Arthur Waley, trans., *The Analects of Confucius* (London, 1938; Vintage paperback, New York, n.d.), 91.

4. In the *Book of Poetry:* "His thoughts are without depravity" *(si wu xie)*; see Legge, *The Chinese Classics*, 4:613. In the *Analects:* "The Master said, '*In the Book of Poetry* are three hundred pieces, but the design of them all may be embraced in one sentence—Having no depraved thoughts *(si wu xie)*,'" ibid., 1:145. *"Xie"* also appears in the *Book of Historical Documents:* "In your employment of men of worth, let none come between you and them. Put away evil without hesitation *(qu xie wu yi)*," ibid., 3:55. Although this section of the *Book of Historical Documents* is believed to be a later redaction, the word *"xie"* was often used in later centuries in this sense, for example by the first emperor of Ming, Zhu Yuanzhang, referring to officials he considered evil or depraved. See, for example, "Dagao sanbian" [Third grand pronouncement, 1386], in *Mingchao kaiguo wenxian* [Documents on the founding of the Ming dynasty] (reprint, Taibei: Xuesheng, 1966), 244, 399, 402.

5. Legge, *The Chinese Classics*, 2:2826. Elsewhere in the *Works of Mencius*, he says: "When words are one-sided, I know how *the mind of the speaker* is clouded over. When words are extravagant [*yin*], I know how *the mind* is fallen and sunk. When words are all-depraved [*xie*], I know how the *mind has departed from principle.*" Ibid., 191; italics appear in the original.

6. See Derk Bodde, "The State and Empire of Ch'in," in Denis Twitchett and Michael Lowe, eds., *The Cambridge History of China*, vol. 1, *The Ch'in and Han Empires, 221 B.C.–A.D. 220* (Cambridge: Cambridge University Press, 1986), esp. 30, 72–81.

7. See the discussion in Kwang-Ching Liu, "Socioethics as Orthodoxy: A Perspective," in Liu, ed., *Orthodoxy in Late Imperial China* (Berkeley: University of Berkeley Press, 1990), esp. 55–64.

8. *Han shu* [History of the Han dynasty] (Beijing: Zhonghua, 1962), 56:2498–2499.

9. Ibid, 56:2500–2502.

10. For Kuang Heng's definition of *"yinsi,"* see note 11. For post-Han usage of this term, see Rolf A. Stein, "Religious Taoism and Popular Religion from the Second to the Seventh Centuries," in Holmes Welch and Anna Seidel, eds., *Facets of Taoism* (New Haven: Yale University Press, 1979), 57.

11. *Han shu,* 4:1253–1263; 81:3334–3344. Michael Lowe, *Crisis and Conflict in the Han Empire* (London: George Allen and Unwin, 1974), chap. 5.

12. *Hou Han shu* [History of the Later Han dynasty] (Beijing: Zhonghua, 1965); *Zhih* [Treatises], 12:3255–3259, 3261; 13:3265, 3270–3276; 14:3297, 3299, 3301; 17:3341–3352.

13. An Zozhang, comp., *Qin-Han nongmin zhanzheng shiliao huibian* [Compendium of historical sources regarding peasant rebellion in the Qin and Han period] (Beijing: Zhonghua, 1982), 240–241.

14. Ibid., 336–344; Paul Michaud, "The Yellow Turbans," *Monumenta Serica: Journal of Oriental Studies* 17 (1958): 47–127.

15. An Zozhang, comp., *Qin-Han nongmin,* 363–367; also see chapter 1, this volume.

16. These terms may be conveniently located in the series of collections of historical sources on peasant rebellions compiled by scholars of the PRC, cited here in notes 13, 17–20, 22–23, 33, 39. Cf. Kao Yu-kung, "A Study of the Fang La Rebellion," *Harvard Journal of Asiatic Studies* 24 (1962–1963): 18 n. 3.

17. Zhang Zexian and Zhu Dawei, comps., *Wei-Jin nanbei chao nongmin zhanzheng shiliao huibian* [Compendium of historical sources regarding peasant rebellion during the Wei-Jin and Southern and Northern dynasties] (Beijing: Zhonghua, 1980), 1:231–273. See also chapter 1, this volume.

18. Zhang Zexian, comp., *Tang wudai nongmin zhanzheng shiliao huibian* [Compendium of historical sources regarding peasant rebellion during the Tang dynasty and the Five Dynasties] (Beijing: Zhonghua, 1979), 1:53–54; 2:325–331 and passim.

19. Su Jinyuan and Li Chunpu, comps., *Songdai san ci nongmin qiyi shiliao huibian* [Compendium of historical sources for three peasant rebellions during the Song dynasty] (Beijing: Zhonghua, 1963), 15–25; and passim; *Song shi* [History of the Song dynasty] (Beijing: Zhonghua,, 1977), 28:9770–9771.

20. Su Jinyuan and Li Chunpu, comps., *Songdai san ci,* 93–105 and passim; Kao Yu-kung, "A Study of the Fang La Rebellion," 57–60; also chapter 2, this volume.

21. Webster's *New International Dictionary of the English Language* (2d edition, 1955) draws the following distinction between the two antonyms of orthodox—heterodox and heretical: "That is heterodox which is at variance

with accepted doctrine (especially religious); that is heretical which is perniciously heterodox or erroneous." For discussion of these terms in the European classical and medieval contexts, see, inter alia, the introduction in Edward Peters, ed., *Heresy and Authority in Medieval Europe* (Philadelphia: University of Pennsylvania Press, 1980), esp. 13–26; Jeffrey Burton Russell, *Dissent and Order in the Middle Ages: The Search for Legitimate Authority* (New York: Twayne Publishers, 1992), 2–5, 101–102. See also Sheila McDonough, "Orthodoxy and Heterodoxy" in Eliade, ed., *The Encyclopedia of Religion*, 11:124–129.

22. Yang No, Chen Gaohua, Zhu Guozhao, and Liu Yan, comps., *Yuandai nongmin zhanzheng shiliao huibian, zhongbian* [Compendium of historical sources regarding peasant wars during the Yuan dynasty, part 2] (Beijing: Zhonghua, 1985), 1:5, 7, and passim.

23. The use and abuse of the term "White Lotus" has been thoroughly examined in Barend J. ter Haar, *The White Lotus Teachings in Chinese Religious History* (Leiden: E. J. Brill, 1992), in this instance, especially chapter 4.

24. See Li Shoukong, "Mingdai bailian jiao kaolue" [A brief study of the Ming dynasty White Lotus sect], in Tao Xisheng et al., *Mingdai Zongjiao* [Religion in the Ming period]. *Mingshi luncong* [Collected studies on the Ming dynasty] (Taibei: Xuesheng, 1968), 10:36–43. See also Xie Guozhen, comp., *Mingdai nongmin qiyi shiliao xuanbian* [Selected historical sources regarding peasant uprisings during the Ming dynasty] (Fuzhou: Fujian renmin, 1981), 3, 8–9, 38–40, 119, 122–126.

25. Huang Zhangjian, ed., *Mingdai lü li huibian* [A compendium of the Ming code and substatutes] (Taibei: Institute of History and Philology, Academia Sinica, 1979), 2:589.

26. See Li Shoukong, "Mingdai bailian jiao," 42–44, for references to *xiejiao* and *xieshuo* in sources for which 1551 and 1597 are given as dates.

27. *Wei shu* [History of the Northern Wei dynasty] (Beijing: Zhonghua, 1974), 1:97; 8:3033–3034.

28. *Jiu Tang shu* [Old history of the Tang dynasty] (Beijing: Zhonghua, 1975), juan 79, 2714–2717. On Fu Yi, see Arthur F. Wright, *Studies in Chinese Buddhism* (New Haven: Yale University Press, 1990), 112–123. Fu Yi's reference to Buddhism as *xiejiao* is also quoted in Falin, *Poxie lun* [A discourse decisively refuting heresies, 622], in *Taishō shinshū daizōkyō* [The Buddhist canon, newly compiled during the Taisho reign] (Tokyo: Taisho shinshu daizokyo kankokai, 1924–1929; hereafter cited as T.), 52:476, top column.

29. T. 52:476–477. On the background of Buddhist apologetics and Chinese anti-Buddhist writings, see Erik Zürcher, *The Buddhist Conquest of China: The Spread and Adaptation of Buddhism in Early Medieval China* (Leiden: E. J. Brill, 1959, 1972), chaps. 5 and 6.

30. Daoshi, *Fayuan zhulin* [Forest of gems in the garden of the law, 668], in T. 53, no. 2122, 704–705. See also Zhang Zexian and Zhu Dawei, eds., *Wei-Jin nanbei chao*, 1:224–231.

31. See, inter alia, Judith Berling, *The Syncretic Religion of Lin Chao-en* (New York: Columbia University Press, 1980); and Cynthia Brokaw, *The Ledgers of Merit and Demerit* (Princeton: Princeton University Press, 1991).

32. Documents from *Song huiyao* [Collected statutes of the Song dynasty], cited in Su Jinyuan and Li Chunpu, *Songdai san ci*, 108–109; see also 128, 134. On the background of this interdiction, see Mou Runsun, "Songdai Moni jiao" [Manichaeism during the Song dynasty] in Songshi yanjiu hui, ed., *Songshi yanjiu* [Studies in Song history] (Taibei: Zhonghua congshu weiyuan hui, 1958), 79–100. A Tang edict issued at the time of the Cui Ziyan Maitreyan revolt in 715 warned the Buddhists against "heretical ways" *(xiedao)* and urged local officials to apprehend those Buddhists "wearing long hair and white clothes and deluding people with the false claim of a Maitreya incarnate." The edict also warned against such sectarians' making "false pronouncements on [public] misfortune or fortune, even producing their own short sutras." Zhang Zexian, comp., *Tang Wudai*, 54. It is not clear whether this injunction amounted to a permanent interdiction of Maitreyanism.

33. Zhiqing (fl. 1260–1270), *Fozu tongji* [A comprehensive record of the Buddha and Buddhist patriarchs, 1269], T. 49:425. See Daniel Overmyer, *Folk Buddhist Religion: Dissenting Sects in Late Traditional China* (Cambridge, Mass., Harvard University Press, 1976), 35, 91–94; ter Haar, *The White Lotus Teachings*, chap. 3.

34. Yang No and Chen Gaohua, comps., *Yuandai nongmin zhanzheng shiliao huibian, shang-bian* [A compendium of historical sources regarding peasant wars in the Yuan dynasty, part I] (Beijing: Zhonghua, 1985), 32.

35. Ibid., 129.

36. Ibid., 145.

37. Huang Zhangjian, *Mingdai lü li*, esp. 2:589–592. On the Yuan origins of this part of the Ming code, see Shen Jiaben, *Ming lü mu jian* [Notes on the section titles of the Ming code], in idem, *Shen Jiyi xiansheng yishu, jiabian* [Writings of the late Mr. Shen Jiaben, first series] (Beijing, ca. 1929; reprint, Taibei: Wenhai, 1964), 2:800–801. For background, see John W. Dardess, "The Transformation of Messianic Revolt and the Founding of the Ming Dynasty," *Journal of Asian Studies* 29.3 (1970): 539–558.

38. Li Shoukong, "Mingdai bailian jiao," 45–47; Xie Guozhen, *Mingdai nongmin*, 149–158.

39. The *Ming shi* was compiled between 1679 and 1735 and printed in 1739. See *Ming shi* [History of the Ming dynasty] (Beijing: Zhonghua, 1974), 1.

40. An edict of the Qing monarch Taizong issued in Mukden in 1642 banned the Society of Good Friends (Shangyou hui) and branded it *xiejiao*. A Ming statute of the Wanli period (1573–1620) merely identified Shangyou as the followers of "heterodoxy which deludes the people" *(zuodao huozhong)*. The 1642 Qing edict was issued after more than 300 such sectarians had been arrested, of whom 16 were executed. *Da Qing shi chao sheng xun* [Sacred instructions from ten reigns of the Great Qing] (reprint, Taibei: Wenhai, 1965), Taizong reign, 93. Cf. Huang Zhangjian, *Mingdai lü li,* 2:591–592. The Society of Good Friends was found to be active in Zhili and Shaanxi in 1643. Reports on the Zhili group described the sectarians (including women) as *zuodao yaoren* and on the Shaanxi group (including a woman leader) as *yaozei* as well as adherents of *xiejiao*. Xie Guozhen, *Qing chu nongmin qiyi ziliao jilu* [Collected source materials regarding peasant uprisings in the early Qing] (Shanghai: Xinzhishi, 1956), 72–73, 250–251; Frederic Wakeman Jr., *The Great Enterprise: The Manchu Restructure of the Imperial Order in Seventeenth-Century China* (Berkeley: University of California Press, 1985), 2:681–682.

41. The substatutes of the Qing code are assigned approximate dates in Xue Yunsheng, *Du li cunyi* [Doubts raised while perusing the substatutes of the Qing code, Peking, 1905] (punctuated edition, Taibei: Chengwen, 1970), esp. 3:421–425. For Kangxi's *Sacred Edict* and Yungzheng's elaborations on heterodoxy and heresy, see *Da Qing huidian shili* [Collected statutes of the Qing dynasty, with cases and precedents] (1899 edition; reprint, Taibei: Chongwen, 1963), 10332–10349, esp. 10339–10340.

Glossary

Ai di 哀帝
Akizuki Kan'ei 秋月觀暎
Andong 安東
An-Qing daoyou 安清道友
anzhen 安鎮

babao chuixun 八寶垂訓
bagua 八卦
bai bazi 拜把子
Bai Peixiang 白培相
bai xiongdi 拜兄弟
baihui 拜會
Bailian 白蓮
Bailian hui 白蓮會
Bailian jiao 白蓮教
Bailian zong 白蓮宗
bailuan 拜鸞
Baise 百色
Baiwu 白烏
baiyang 白陽
baiyi 白衣
Baiyun 白雲
baizheng 拜正
baji 八極
Bang Hu 棒胡
Bao Jing (Bao Xuan) 鮑靚（鮑玄）
Bao Jingyan 鮑敬言
bao 報
bao'en 報恩
baoguo 報國
baojia 保甲

baojuan 寶卷
Baoming Si 保明寺
Baopuzi 抱朴子
Bazi hui 把子會
Beifang taiping zhenjun
　　北方太平真君
benlai mianmu 本來面目
Bi Yongnian 畢永年
bian zhengxie 辨正邪
biaoming 標名
bide qiangpao 避得槍炮
biji 筆記
bili 鄙俚
Bingding fu 丙丁符
Bingling gong 炳靈公
biqiu 比丘
Bohutong 白虎通
boluan 撥亂
Boluo 博羅
buduan 不端
bufa 步法
bufeng zhengdao 不奉正道
bugang 步罡
bujing 不經
buyi 補遺
buzhen 不真
buzheng 不正
buzhong buxiao, wufu wujun
　　不忠不孝，無父無君

Cai Qian 蔡牽

491

Cai Shaoqing 蔡少卿

Cai Tingshi 蔡廷仕

canling 殘靈

Cao Cao 曹操

Cao E 曹娥

caomao zhongfen zhi shi, haojie you
zhi zhi tu
    草茅忠憤之士，豪傑有志之徒

chan 禪

Chang Ahan jing 長阿含經

Changyang 長陽

Chaoyang 潮陽

Chaozhou 潮州

Chen Biao 陳彪

Chen Jinyu 陳金玉

Chen Lanjisi 陳爛屐四

Chen Pi 陳丕

Chen Qu 陳曲

Chen Silao 陳四老

Chen Tianhua 陳天華

Chen Yaben 陳亞本

Chen Yuan 陳垣

Chen Zhouquan 陳周全

chen 辰

chengfu 承負

chenghuang 城皇

chengyi 誠意

Cheng-Zhu 程朱

Chengzong 成宗

Chengzu 成祖

Chenxiang 沉香

Chenzhou 郴州

chenzi zhi dao 臣子之道

Chi wangye 池王爺

chicai shimo 吃菜事魔

Chongyi 崇義

Chou Daqin 仇大欽

Chu 楚

chuanjiao 傳教

Chuci 楚辭

chujia 出家

Chunqiu 春秋

Chunqiu fanlu 春秋繁露

churen 初人

ci 祠

Cui Hao 崔浩

Cui Ziyan 崔子晶

dadaoren 大道人

da jiuxing 大救星

Da Loutan jing 大樓炭經

Da Ming 大明

da nan 大難

da shenren 大神人

dacheng 大乘

Dadao jialingjie 大道家令誡

Dadun 大墩

dage 大哥

dahua 大化

dajie chuizhi 大劫垂至

dajie 大劫

danding 丹鼎

dang 黨

Danglai zhenjun 當來真君

Danshui 淡水

Danyang 丹陽

Dao'an 道安

Daojiao 道教

daoli 道理

Daolu si 道錄司

daomin 道民

Daosheng 道生

daoshi 道士

Daoshi 道世

Daoxuan 道玄

Dapu 大埔

daren 大人

Daren xiansheng zhuan 大人先生傳

datong 大同

Dayun guangming si 大雲光明寺

Dazhou jianding zhongjing mulu
    大周鑒定眾經目錄

Dehu zhangzhe jing 德護長者經

Deng Zhimo 鄧志謨

Deqing 德清
diling 帝靈
diqi 地祇
Diqi yuanshuai 地祇元帥
ditong 地統
diwang 帝王
dixian 地仙
diyi guizi 第一貴子
Dong dacheng jiao 東大乘教
Dong Yantai 董言台
Dong Zhongshu 董仲舒
Donglin 東林
Dongping wang 東平王
Dongwan 東莞
Dongyue dadi 東嶽大帝
dou 斗
du 度
Du Guangting 杜光庭
duan gong 端公
dui hetong 對合同
duli 獨立
Duren jing 度人經

Enzhugong 恩主公
erdao 二道
Erlang baojuan 二郎寶卷
ermaozi 二毛子
lerzong sanji 二宗三際

fa 法
faguan 法官
Faguo 法果
Fajing jing 法鏡經
Falun Gong 法輪功
Famiejin jing 法滅盡經
faming 法名
Fan Lian 范濂
Fan Mingde 范明德
Fan Renjie 樊人傑
Fan Zushu 范祖述
Fang La 方臘
fangshi 方士

fanmin 凡民
Fanwang jing 梵綱經
Faqing 法清
fashi 法師
Fayuan zhulin 法苑珠林
fazhu 法主
fei 匪
fei qi gui 非其鬼
fei zhengdao 非正道
feiseng feisu 非僧非俗
Feixian duren jing 飛仙度人經
Feng Menglong 馮夢龍
Feng Yunshan 馮雲山
Fengshan 鳳山
Fengshen yanyi 封神演義
foshi 佛師
Foshuo Dazang xianxing liaoyi baojuan 佛說大藏顯性了義寶卷
Foshuo Yangshi gui xiu hongluo Huaxiange baojuan 佛說楊氏鬼繡紅羅化仙哥寶卷
Fozu tongji 佛祖統記
Fu Yi 傅奕
fuchi zhengdao 扶持正道
Fude zhengshen 福德正神
fuji 扶乩
fulu 符籙
Fumu enzhongjing 父母恩重經
Fumuhui 父母會
fuzheng quxie 扶正去邪
fuzhi gangchang 扶植綱常

gaiguo 改過
gan 肝
Gan 贛
gangchang lunli 綱常倫理
Gangyi 剛毅
Ganzhou 贛州
Gao Chengjie 高成傑
Gao Junde 高均德
Gao Panlong 高攀龍
Gao Qizhuo 高其倬

Gaoshang yuegong taiyin yuanjun xiaodao xianwang lingbao jingming huangsushu 高上月宮太陰元君孝道仙王靈寶淨明黃素書

Gaoxi 高溪

Ge Chaofu 葛巢父

Ge Hong 葛洪

gejian 革諫

Gelao hui 哥老會

gengshen 庚申

gengsi 庚巳

gong 公

gong 宮

gong'an 公案

Gongchang 弓長

Gongguo ge 功過格

gonghui 公會

Gongjin hui 共進會

Gongyang 公羊

gu 蠱

Gu Jiegang 顧頡剛

guahao 掛號

guan 觀

Guan Mile pusa shangsheng doushuaitian jing 觀彌勒菩薩上生兜率天經

Guan Yu 關羽

Guandi laoye 關帝老爺

guang 光

Guangfu hui 光復會

Guangwu di 光武帝

Guangxu 光緒

Guangzhou 廣州

Guanjing 觀經

Guanjingshu 觀經疏

Guanyang 灌陽

Guanyin 觀音

Guanyin ting 觀音亭

Gufo tianzhen kaozheng longhua baojing 古佛天真考證龍華寶經

guidao 鬼道

guijia biaowen 歸家標文

guijian 貴賤

guishen 鬼神

Guiyang 桂陽

guiyi zhengdao 皈依正道

Guiyuan 歸元

guo 國

Guo Pu 郭樸

Guo Pusa 郭菩薩

Guo Xiang 郭象

Guo Ziyi 郭子儀

Guomin bao 國民報

guoqiao 過橋

Haikang 海康

Han Lin'er 韓林兒

Han Piaogao 韓飄高

Han Shantong 韓山童

Han Shizong 韓世忠

Han Yu 韓愈

haojie 豪傑

he 和

He Chong 何充

He Shouzheng 何守證

He Xinyin 何心隱

He Xiu 何休

He Zhengong 何真公

heshun 和順

heyixiang 合一相

Hirayama Shū 平山周

Hong 洪

Hong Er 洪二

Hong hui 紅會

Hong Mai 洪邁

Hong Ren'gan 洪仁玕

Hong Xiuquan 洪秀全

Hongmen 洪門

hongyang 紅陽

Hongyang hui 紅陽會

Hongyang jiao 弘陽教

Hongyang tanshi jing 弘陽嘆世經

hongying 紅英

Hongzhou 洪州

hou wuzhu 後五主

Housheng daojun 後聖道君
Hu Huichao 胡惠超
Hu Linyi 胡林翼
Hu Qingxu 胡清虛
Hua 花
Huainanzi 淮南子
Huan Xuan 桓玄
Huang Gongjin 黃公瑾
Huang Jinneng 黃錦能
Huang-Lao 黃老
Huang Xing 黃興
Huang Yuanji 黃元吉
Huang Yubian 黃育楩
Huang Zongxi 黃宗羲
Huangchao jingshi dadian
　　皇朝經世大典
huanghu ziran 恍惚自然
Huangji 皇極
Huangji baojuan 皇極寶卷
Huangji jindan jiulian zhengxin
　　guizhen huanxiang baojuan
　　皇極金丹九蓮正信皈真還鄉寶卷
Huanglu dazhai 黃籙大齋
Huanglu zhaiyi 黃籙齋儀
huangtai 皇胎
huangtai zi 皇胎子
Huangtian dao 黃天道
Huangting neijing jing 黃庭內景經
Huangyang hui 黃陽會
huangzhong daoqi 黃中道氣
Huaxing hui 華興會
huazhu 化主
huchi zhengdao 護持正道
hui 會
Hui'an 惠安
huibu 會簿
Huichang 會昌
huidang 會黨
huifei 會匪
huifu mingzuo 恢復明祚
Huiguan 慧觀
Huiyuan 慧遠
Huizhou 惠州

Huizhou 徽州
Huizong 徽宗
hunmin 混冥
hunyuan 混元
hunyuan ce 混元冊
Hunyuan dianhua jing 混元點化經
Hunyuan jiao hongyang zhonghua
　　baojing 混元教弘陽中華寶經
huren 戶人

ji 紀
Ji 稷
Ji'an 吉安
jian 賤
jiang 將
Jiang Cong 姜聰
jianghu fayou 江湖法友
Jianghua 江華
jiangjun 將軍
Jiangyin 江陰
jiansheng 監生
Jianwen di 簡文帝
jiao (teaching) 教
jiao (festival) 醮
jiaozhu 教主
jiaxiang 家鄉
Jiaxiang shuxin 家鄉書信
Jiaying 嘉應
jie (integrity) 節
jie (kalpa) 劫
jiebai 結拜
jiecheng yidao 竭誠醫禱
jieyi 結義
jieyuan 結緣
jijiu 祭酒
Jile pian 雞肋篇
jin 謹
Jin Guantao 金觀濤
Jin Hongzhou Xishan shi'er zhenjun
　　neizhuan
　　晉洪州西山十二真君內傳
Jindan 金丹
jing 淨

jing dian hao 經典好

Jingang keyi 金剛科儀

Jingdezhen 景德鎮

jingming 淨明

Jingming daoshi Jingyang Xu
　Zhenjun zhuan
　淨明道士旌陽許真君傳

Jingming ji gongguobu 淨明記功過簿

Jingming lingbao zhongxiao zhi dao
　淨明靈寶忠孝之道

Jingming zhongxiao dafa
　淨明忠孝大法

Jingming zhongxiao dao 淨明忠孝道

Jingming zhongxiao quanshu
　淨明忠孝全書

Jingshi tongyan 警世通言

jingtu 淨土

Jingtu shengxianlu 淨土聖賢錄

jingxuan 精選

Jingyang 旌陽

Jingyanggong tieshu zhenyao
　旌陽宮鐵樹鎮妖

jinjian gudu 金蠶蠱毒

Jintian 金田

jiufu 舅父

jiugan shibazhi 九干十八支

Jiuku zhongxiao yaowang baojuan
　救苦忠孝藥王寶卷

jiulian tu 九蓮圖

juan 卷

jueqing 絕清

jun (equity) 均

jun (sovereign) 君

junzi 君子

juren 舉人

Kaizhi lu 開智錄

Kang Senghui 康僧會

Kang wang 康王

Kang Youwei 康有為

kaozheng 考證

kejia 客家

Kou Qianzhi 寇謙之

kuan 寬

Kuang Heng 匡衡

kuang 狂

kuanyu 寬裕

Kubo Noritada 窪德忠

Kugong wudao juan 苦功悟道卷

kun 坤

laishi 來世

Langong 蘭公

Langye 琅琊

Lanshan 藍山

lao zhanggui 老掌櫃

lao zhenkong 老真空

Laojun yinsong jiejing 老君音誦誡經

laomu 老母

Laozi 老子

Lei Qiong 雷瓊

Li 李

li (ritual) 禮

li (distance) 里

Li Changling 李昌齡

Li Chao 李潮

Li Dazhao 李大釗

Li Fuyan 李復言

Li Hong 李洪，李弘

Li Hongzhi 李洪志

Li Lingkui 李凌魁

Li Mingzhong 李銘中

Li Puwen 李普文

Li Rui 李銳

Li Shaomin 李少敏

Li Wencheng 李文成

Li Xiucheng 李秀成

Li Zhenggao 李正高

lian 廉

Lian Lichang 連立昌

liang 量

Liang Fa 梁發

Liang Qichao 梁啟超

Lianshe 蓮社

lianshen 廉慎

Lianzong baojian 蓮宗寶鑒

Liao Kang 廖康

Liezi 列子

ligong buguo 立功補過

ligui 厲鬼

Liji 禮記

Lijia Dao 李家道

lijiao 禮教

Lin 林

Lin Lingsu 林靈素

Lin Shuangwen 林爽文

Lin Tianshen 林添申

linfan shouyuan 臨凡收元

Ling 凌

ling 靈

Lingbao 靈寶

Lingbao jing 靈寶經

Lingbao jingming mifa 靈寶淨明密法

Lingbao jingming xinxiu jiulao
    shenying fumo mifa
    靈寶淨明新修九老神應伏魔密法

Lingbao jingmingyuan xingqian shi
    靈寶淨明院行遣式

lingguang 靈光

Lingshu ziwen shangjing
    靈書紫文上經

Lingwen xu 靈文序

Lishi zhenjun tidao tongjian
    歷世真君體道通鑒

Liu An 劉安

Liu Bang 劉邦

Liu Bei 劉備

Liu Deren 劉德仁

Liu Qirong 劉啟榮

Liu Song 劉松

Liu Yan 劉焉

Liu Yimin 劉遺民

Liu Yu (Yuzhen zi) 劉玉（玉真子）

Liu Yuanran 劉淵然

Liu Zhixie 劉之協

liyi 禮義

Long Shaozhou 龍紹周

Longhua hui 龍華會

Longhua jing 龍華經

Longhua zhaihui 龍華齋會

Longshu jingtuwen 龍樹淨土文

Lu Can 陸粲

Lu Da 魯達

Lü He 呂河

Lu Mao 盧茂

Lü Shinang 呂師囊

Lu Xiujing 陸修靜

Lu Xun 盧循

luan 亂

luanmin 亂民

luantu 亂徒

lülin haojie 綠林豪傑

Luo Dagang 羅大綱

Luo Menghong 羅夢鴻

Luo Qing (Luozu) 羅清（羅祖）

Luo Rufang 羅汝芳

Luojiao 羅教

Lushan 盧山

Lushan lianzong baojian
    盧山蓮宗寶鑒

Lutu zhenjing 錄圖真經

Ma Chaozhu 馬朝柱

Ma Delong 馬德隆

Ma Jiulong 馬九龍

Ma Shaotang 馬紹湯

Ma Xisha 馬西沙

mai baige 賣白鴿

Mai Menghua 麥孟華

Mao Ziyuan 茅子元

mazei 馬賊

Mazu 媽祖

Meiji 明治

mengzhu 盟主

miao 廟

Mile xiasheng, mingwang chushi
    彌勒下生，明王出世

min 民

Min bao 民報

Ming jiao 明教

Ming Taizu 明太祖

ming zun 明尊

ming (destiny) 命

ming (radiance) 明

ming'an chahao 明暗查號

mingfen 名分

mingjiao 名教

Mingkong 明空

Mingwang 明王

mingzhu 明主

mingzhu chuanzong 明主傳宗

minqi 民氣

minzu geming weiren 民族革命偉人

minzu zhuyi 民族主義

mixin 迷信

Miyun 密雲

Mo (Moni) 魔（摩尼）

Mo wang 摩王

mofa 末法

Moni guangfo 摩尼光佛

Moni jiao 摩尼教

motou 魔頭

Mouzi lihuoi lun 牟子理惑論

Mozi 墨子

mu ji shi zu, zu ji shi mu
母即是祖，祖即是母

Mulian 目連

mulidoushi 木立斗世

Muramatsu Yuji 村松祐二

Muyangcheng 木楊城

Muyi 母乙

Muzi Gongkou 木子弓口

Nan hui 南會

Nan'an 南安

Nanchang 南昌

nannü heqi zhi shu 男女合氣之術

nannü hunza 男女混雜

nannü youbie 男女有別

Nantou 南投

Nayancheng 那彥成

Nian 捻

nianfo 念佛

niang 娘

Noguchi Tetsurō 野口鐵郎

nubi 奴婢

Ou Lang 歐狼

Ou Qujia 歐榘甲

paiwai zhi xiansheng 排外之先聲

peishen 陪神

Peng Shaosheng (also Jiqing,
Chimu) 彭紹升（際清，尺木）

ping 平

ping qi zhi 平其治

Pinghe 平和

Pingjun 平君

Pingle 平樂

poxie 破邪

Poxie lun 破邪論

Poxie xiangbian 破邪詳辯

Poxie xianzheng yaoshi juan
破邪顯正鑰匙卷

pu 樸

Pu Songling 蒲松齡

Pudu 普度

Pudu xinsheng jiuku baojuan
普度新聲救苦寶卷

Puixian pusa shuo zhengming jing
普賢菩薩說證明經

Pujing rulai yaoshi tongtian baojuan
普靜如來鑰匙通天寶卷

Puming rulai wuwei liaoyi baojuan
普明如來無為了義寶卷

qi 氣

Qi Lin 齊林

Qi Wang shi 齊王氏 (Qi Er guafu
齊二寡婦), see Wang Cong'er

qian wuzhu 前五主

qian 乾

qiankun 乾坤

qianshou 錢收

Qieluo wang 伽羅王

qigong 氣功

Qin Baoqi 秦寶琦

Qin Lishan 秦力山

Qingbang 青幫
Qinghe 清河
Qinglian 青蓮
qingyang 青陽
Qingyang hui 青陽會
Qingyi bao 清議報
*Qingyuan miaodao xiansheng zhenjun
    Erlang baojuan*
    清源妙道顯聖真君二郎寶卷
qionghua 瓊花
Qiongzhou 瓊州
Qiu Daoren 丘道人
qizheng renlun, fenming xingzu
    齊整人倫，分明姓族
Quanshi liangyan 勸世良言
Quanzhen 全真
Quanzhen dao 全真道
Quanzhou 泉州
quxie fuzheng 袪邪輔正

Raoping 饒平
Ren Jiyü 任繼愈
Ren xue 仁學
ren (humanity) 仁
ren (endurance) 忍
renlun 人倫
renxia 任俠
rilu 日錄
rong 容
Ronglu 榮祿
rongren 容忍
ru 儒
Ruan Ji 阮籍
ruzhe 儒者

Sandian hui 三點會
sangang 三綱
sanguan 三官
Sanhehui 三合會
Sanhuang jing 三皇經
sanhun qipo 三魂七魄
sanji xianghuo 三極香火
sanjie 三階

sanshi (three worms) 三尸
sanshi (three eras) 三世
Santan 三壇
sanyuan ruyi jiulian xiang
    三原如意九蓮香
Sanyuan 三原
sanzai 三災
sanzong wupai 三宗五派
Sawada Mizuho 澤田瑞穗
se xianghao 色相好
Seng You 僧佑
sengjia 僧伽（家）
Shabao hui 沙包會
shamen 沙門
Shamen bujing wangzhe lun
    沙門不敬王者論
shan 山
Shandao 善導
shang shangcheng 上上乘
Shanglin 上林
Shangqing 上清
shangsheng 上生
shanhao zhai 善好宅
shanshu 善書
shanyou 善友
Shao Yizheng 邵以正
Shaolin 少林
she 社
shefu 社夫
shen 神
shengong miaoji 神功妙濟
shengren 聖人
shengyi 聖意
shengyuan 生員
Shenri erbenjing 申日兒本經
Shenri jing 申日經
shenwu 神巫
Shenxiao 神霄
Shenzhou jing 神咒經
shenzhu 神主
shibu xiuxing 十步修行
Shicheng 石城
shidafu 士大夫

shi'er zhenjun 十二真君

shijie 尸解

Shimen zhengtong 釋門正統

shimu 師母

shipo 師婆

shishan 十善

shiwei 失位

shiwu 師巫

shiwu jiajiang xieshu 師巫假降邪術

Shiyi 十翼

shizhi youming 始制有名

Shouluo biqiu jing 首羅比丘經

shou ren hunpo 收人魂魄

shouzhuo xiejing 收捉邪精

Shujun 蜀郡

Shun 舜

shun 順

Shunde 順德

shuntian 順天

shuntian dangshi 順天當世

shuntian fuming he hetong
　順天服明合和同

shuntian xingdao 順天行道

sidian 祀典

sihui 私會

Sijiao xinglu 四教行錄

Siming Zhili 四明知禮

sisheng 四聖

Song Jiaoren 宋教仁

Song Lian 宋濂

Song Wenshi 宋文世

Song Zhiqing 宋之清

Song Zixian 宋子賢

Songjiang 松江

Su Ye 蘇葉

suan 算

Sui-Tang 隋唐

Sun Cifeng 孫賜奉 (Lao Wu 老五)

Sun En 孫恩

Sun Guiyuan 孫貴遠

Sun Yat-sen 孫逸仙

Sun Zhenkong 孫真空

Suzuki Chūsei 鈴木中正

taibao 太保

taihe 太和

Taiping 太平

Taiping dao 太平道

Taiping guangji 太平廣記

Taiping jing 太平經

Taiping qi 太平氣

Taiping tianguo 太平天國

taiping zuo 太平坐

Taiqing 太清

Taishang dongxuan lingbao
　baxianwang jiaojie jing
　太上洞玄靈寶八仙王教戒經

Taishang dongyuan shenzhou jing
　太上洞淵神咒經

Taishang ganying pian 太上感應篇

Taishang laojun 太上老君

Taishang lingbao jingming dongshen
　shangpin jing
　太上靈寶淨明洞神上品經

Taishang lingbao jingming feixian
　duren jingfa
　太上靈寶淨明飛仙度人經法

Taishang lingbao jingming rudao pin
　太上靈寶淨明入道品

Taishi 太始

Taisui 太歲

Taiwei xianjun gongguoge
　太微仙君功過格

Taiwu 太武

Taiyi 太一

Taiyin 太陰

Taizong 太宗

Taizu 太祖

Tan Sitong 譚嗣同

tan 壇

tang 堂

Tang Caichang 唐才常

Tang Fengji 湯逢吉

Tang Yasi 湯亞四

Tanshi wuwei juan 嘆世無為卷

Tanyao 曇曜

Tao Bida 桃比達

Tao Chengzhang 陶成章
Tao Yuan 桃元
taoyuan jieyi 桃園結義
Taoyuanhui 桃園會
ti 體
tian bubian, dao yi bubian
 天不變，道亦不變
Tiandi sanyang hui 天地三陽會
tiandi shihua de jun 天地施化得均
Tiandihui (Adding Brothers
 Society) 添弟會
Tiandihui (Heaven and Earth
 Society) 天地會
Tianfu 天父
Tianguo 天國
Tianli 天理
tianli zhi ziran 天理之自然
tianlü 天律
tianming 天命
Tianpeng 天蓬
Tianpeng zhou 天蓬咒
tianshen 天神
Tianshi 天師
Tianshi dao 天師道
Tianshi daotu 天師道徒
Tiantai 天台
Tianwang 天王
tianxia daluan 天下大亂
tianxia wu erdao 天下無二道
tianxian 天仙
Tianyou 天猷
tianyun 天運
tianzhen 天真
tianzi 天子
tianzun 天尊
tiaoshen 跳神
tidian tianxia shenmiao
 提點天下神廟
Tieshu ji 鐵樹記
tiju 提舉
Tingzhou 汀州
titian xingdao 替天行道
Tixi 提喜

tiyong 體用
Tong'an 同安
Tongmeng hui 同盟會
tongji 童乩
touci shizhuang 投詞誓狀
Tu Long 屠龍
Tu Xi 涂喜
tuanfei 團匪
tudishen 土地神

Wan 萬
Wan Tixi 萬提喜
wan xing 萬姓
Wan Yunlong 萬雲龍
Wan'an 萬安
wang 妄
Wang Anshi 王安石
Wang Bi 王弼
Wang Cong'er 王聰兒 (see Qi Wang
 shi)
Wang Faseng 王法僧
Wang Gen 王艮
Wang Haoxian 王好賢
Wang Huaigu 王懷古
Wang Ji 王幾
Wang Jianchuan 王見川
Wang Juzheng 王居正
Wang Rixiu 王日休
Wang Sen 王森
wang tan tianxiang zhe zhan
 妄談天象者斬
Wang Tingzhao 王廷詔
Wang Yangming 王陽明
Wang Yinghu 王應琥
Wang Ze 王澤
Wang Zhe 王喆（哲）
wangdao 王道
wangsheng 往生
Wangshengji 往生記
wangye 王爺
Wanli 萬曆
wanshou 萬壽
wei 位

Wei Huacun 魏華存

Weiling Wen yuanshuai 威靈溫元帥

Weiwei budong Taishan shen'gen jieguo baojuan
巍巍不動泰山深根結果寶卷

wen (plague) 瘟

wen (warmth, name) 溫

Wen Qiong 溫瓊

Wen yuanshuai 溫元帥

wenming ren zhi paiwai
文明人之排外

Wenxiang jiao 聞香教

Wu 吳

wu (shaman) 巫

wu (realizing) 悟

wu (nothing) 無

wu (material) 物

Wu 武

Wu Han 吳

Wu Lao'er 吳老二

Wu Meng 吳猛

Wu Song 武松

Wu Tiancheng 吳天成

Wubu liuce 五部六冊

Wudoumi dao 五斗米道

wuji 無極

Wuji shengzu 無極聖祖

wuju xiaohan 無拘霄漢

wulai 無賴

wuming 無名

wu'ni 五逆

Wuqian wen 五千文

wusheng fumu 無生父母

Wusheng laomu 無生老母

wushi 巫師

wushu 巫術

Wutong 五通

Wutong shen 五通神

wuwei 無為

wuwei fa 無為法

Wuwen shizhe 五瘟使者

wuxi 巫覡

wuxi zayu 巫覡雜語

Wuxian 五顯

wuxing weiqi zhi ren 無形委氣之人

Wuyue 五嶽

wuzhe 巫者

Wuzhou 梧州

Wuzu 五祖

Xi dacheng jiao 西大乘教

Xi Kang 嵇康

xia 俠

xianfeng 先鋒

xian Tian er Tian buwei
先天而天不違

Xiang Haiming 向海明

Xiang'er 想爾

xiangde 相得

Xiangfa jueyi jing 像法決疑經

xiangfa 像法

Xiangshan 香山

xiangtong 相通

xianliang 賢良

xian¹ren (immortal) 仙人

xian²ren (worthy) 賢人

Xiantian dao 先天道

xiantian yiqi 先天一氣

xiao (xiaoshun) 孝（孝順）

Xiao Baozhen 蕭抱真

Xiao Chaogui 蕭朝貴

Xiao mingwang 小明王

Xiao Qiong 蕭瓊

xiao 孝

xiaodao mingwang zhi fa
孝道明王之法

Xiaodao Wu-Xu er zhenjun zhuan
孝道吳許二真君傳

xiaodao 孝道

Xiaodaohui 小刀會

Xiaojing 孝經

Xiaoshi dacheng baojuan
銷釋大乘寶卷

Xiaoshi zhenkong saoxin baojuan
銷釋真空掃心寶卷

xiaoshuo 小說

Xiaodi wang 孝悌王

Xiaoyaoshan wanshougong zhi
逍遙山萬壽宮誌

xiaoyou 孝友

xiapin 下品

xiasheng 下生

xie 邪

xiefa 邪法

xiegui 邪鬼

xiejian 邪見

xiejiao 邪教

xiemei 邪昧

xieqi 邪氣

xieshen 邪神

xieshu 邪術

xieshuo 邪說

Xilu 西魯

xin 信

xing 性

Xingzhong hui 興中會

Xin-Han 新漢

Xishan Xu zhenjun bashiwu hualu
西山許真君八十五化錄

Xishan 西山

Xitian dacheng jiao 西天大乘教

xiucai 秀才

xiulian 修煉

xiuzhen zhi shi 修真之士

Xu Hongru 徐鴻儒

Xu Hui 許翽

Xu Mai 許邁

Xu Mi 許謐

Xu Shoucheng 徐守誠

Xu Su 許肅

Xu Sun 許遜

Xu Sun zhenren zhuan 許遜真人傳

Xu Tiande 徐天德

Xu Yi 徐異

Xu Zengzhong 許曾重

Xuan di 玄帝

Xuantian shangdi 玄天上帝

xuanxue 玄學

xueshi 血食

Xujing 虛靖

xukong 虛空

Xunzhou 潯州

Yan Fu 嚴復

Yan Yan 嚴煙

Yan Yuan 顏元

Yang Dusheng 楊篤生

Yang Xi 楊羲

Yang Xiuqing 楊秀清

Yangjiang 陽江

Yangpan 陽盤

yangqi 陽氣

Yanluo 閻羅

yao (demon) 妖

Yao (tribe) 瑤

Yao (older name of above) 猺

Yao Qisheng 姚啟聖

Yao Zhifu 姚之富

yaodang 妖黨

yaokou 妖寇

yaonie 妖孽

yaopai 腰牌

yaoping 腰憑

yaoren 妖人

Yaoshi benyuan gongde baojuan
藥師本願功德寶卷

yaoshu 妖術

yaowang 妖妄

yaowu 妖巫

yaoxie 妖邪

yaoxie mogui 妖邪魔鬼

yaoyan 妖言

yaozei 妖賊

yaozhong 妖眾

Ye Fashan 葉法善

yecha 夜查，叉

yeju xiaosan, nannu hunza
夜聚曉散，男女混雜

yeman ren zhi paiwai 野蠻人之排外

yeman zhi geming 野蠻之革命

yi 義

yiduan 異端

Yiguan dao 一貫道
Yijian zhi 夷堅志
Yijing 易經
yimin 義民
yin 淫
yinci 淫祠
yinde 陰德
ying'er 嬰兒
yingfu 營副
yingjie 應劫
yingxiong 英雄
yingzong 營總
Yinpan 陰盤
yinsi 淫祀
yinyang 陰陽
Yinzhi wen 陰騭文
Yisheng 翊聖
yitai 以太
yiyi 義邑
yiyuan 一元
yong 用
Yong'an 永安
Yongzhou 永州
youde zhi jun 有德之君
Yousheng 佑聖
Youwei guan 遊帷觀
Youxuanzi 又玄子
youyuan ren 有緣人
Yu Bing 庾冰
Yu Xiangdou 余象斗
yu 裕
Yu 禹
yuan (connection) 緣
yuan (origin) 原
yuan (principal) 元
Yuan Jiao 圓教
Yuandun jiao 圓頓教
yuanqi 元氣
yuanren 原人
*Yuanshi dongzhen cishan xiaozi
    bao'en chengdao jing*
    元始洞真慈善孝子報恩成道經
Yubu 禹步

Yuchang 豫昌
Yue Fei 岳飛
Yue 越
Yueguang tongzi 月光童子
Yulanpen jing 盂蘭盆經
Yulin 鬱林
Yulong 玉隆
Yulong wanshou gong 玉隆萬壽宮
yuncheng 雲城
Yunji qiqian 雲笈七籤
Yunjian jumu chao 雲間據目抄
Yunzhong yinsong xinke zhi jie
    雲中音誦新科之誡
Yuzhang 豫章
Yuzhang huiguan 豫章會館

Zaili 在理
Zaili jiao 在禮教
Zeng Gong 曾鞏
Zeng Guofan 曾國藩
Zeng Shaonan 曾紹南
zhai 齋
Zhan Qingzhen 詹清真
Zhang Fei 張飛
Zhang Gui 張珪
Zhang Hanchao 張漢潮
Zhang Heng 張衡
Zhang Jixian 張繼先
Zhang Jue 張角
Zhang Jun 張俊
Zhang Junfang 張君房
Zhang Ling (Zhang Daoling)
    張陵（張道陵）
Zhang Lu 張魯
Zhang Maqiu 張媽求
Zhang Taiyan 章太炎
Zhang Xiu 張修
Zhang Yuemei 張月梅
Zhang Zehong 張澤洪
Zhang Zhenglong 張正隆
Zhang Zhidong 張之洞
Zhang Zongyan 張宗演
Zhanghua 漳化

Zhangpu 漳浦

Zhangzhou 漳州

Zhanmu (Shenmu) 諶母

Zhao Shiyan 趙世延

Zhao'an 詔安

Zhaoqing 肇慶

Zhen dadao jiao 真大道教

Zhen Dexiu 真德秀

zhen shan ren 真善忍

zhen yuan ben 真元本

zhenfu 真符

zhenfu zhi xin 貞婦之信

Zheng Chenggong 鄭成功

Zheng Guangcai 鄭光彩

Zheng Kai 鄭開

zheng 正

Zheng 鄭

zheng/xie 正邪

zhengdao 正道

zhengdao buzhen 正道不振

zhengfa 正法

Zhengfu xianying weilie zhongjing
   wang 正福顯應威烈忠靖王

zhengjiao 正教

zhengqi 正氣

zhengshen 正神

zhengtian duoguo 爭天奪國

*Zhengxin chuyi wuxiuzheng zizai
   baojuan* 正信除疑無修證自在寶卷

zhengxin (belief) 正信

zhengxin (mind) 正心

Zhengyi 正一

Zhengyi dao 正一道

Zhengyi mengwei zhi dao
   正一盟威之道

zhengzhi 正直

zhenjing 真精

zhenkong 真空

zhenkong jiaxiang 真空家鄉

zhenkong jiaxiang, wusheng fumu
   真空家鄉無生父母

zhenkong jiaxiang, wusheng laomu
   真空家鄉無生老母

zhenren 真人

zhenru 真如

zhenshen 真身

zhenzhu 真主

Zhidao xuanying 至道玄應

Zhipan 志槃

zhiping 執平

Zhiqing 志磬

zhishi 志士

Zhiyi 智顗

zhong 忠

Zhong Shigui 鍾士貴

zhongxiao 忠孝

Zhongxiao dao 忠孝道

zhongguo zhi shehui 中國之社會

zhonghe 中和

Zhongjing wang 忠靖王

Zhongling 鐘陵

zhongmin 種民

zhongshu 忠恕

zhongxiao lianshen zhi dao
   忠孝廉慎之道

zhongxiao zhi dao 忠孝之道

zhongxin yiqi 忠心義氣

Zhongyitang 忠義堂

Zhou Defeng 周德峰

Zhou Weicheng 周惟成

zhou 州

zhouyu 咒語

Zhu Guozhen 朱國楨

Zhu Hongtao 朱洪桃

Zhu Hongying 朱洪英

Zhu Tianquan 朱天全

Zhu Xi 朱熹

Zhu Yigui 朱一貴

Zhu Yuanzhang 朱元璋

zhu 祝

zhuan yi lidu wei shou 專以禮度為首

zhuang 壯

Zhuang 莊

Zhuang Datian 莊大田

Zhuang Jiyu 莊繼裕

Zhuangzi 莊子

zhuanlun shengwang 轉輪聖王

zhufa yiling zhaowu dashi taibao
　助法翊靈昭武大使太保

Zhuhong 株宏

zhui 追

zhujian miexie 誅奸滅邪

zhushen 主神

zhusheng 諸生

Zhuzi yulei 朱子語類

Zilonghui 子龍會

ziran 自然

zixin 自新

Zizhi lu 自知錄

zizhu zhi quan 自主之權

zong jiao shi 總教師

zongheng zizai 縱橫自在

zong huishou 總會首

Zongjian 宗鑒

Zongmi 宗密

zongpai 宗派

zonq dage 總大哥

Zou Rong 鄒容

zumi 租米

zunbei daxiao jie ruyi
　尊卑大小皆如一

zuo haoren 做好人

zuodao 左道

Contributors

P. RICHARD BOHR, Professor of History, College of Saint Benedict and Saint John's University in Minnesota

DAVID FAURE, Lecturer, Institute for Chinese Studies, University of Oxford

WEN-HSIUNG HSU, Professor Emeritus of Asian Studies, Northwestern University

PAUL R. KATZ, Associate Professor, Institute of History, National Central University, Taiwan

WHALEN W. LAI, Professor of Religious Studies, University of California, Davis

KWANG-CHING LIU, Professor of History, Emeritus, University of California, Davis

TETSURŌ NOGUCHI, Professor Emeritus, Tsukuba University, Japan

DON C. PRICE, Professor of History, University of California, Davis

RICHARD SHEK, Professor of Humanities and Religious Studies, California State University, Sacramento

DONALD S. SUTTON, Professor of History and Anthropology, Carnegie Mellon University

Index

Production Notes for
Liu / *Heterodoxy in Late Imperial China*

Cover and interior designed by the production
staff of the University of Hawai'i Press with text
in Adobe Plantin and display type in Beanie

Composition by Josie Herr in QuarkXPress

Printing and binding by The Maple-Vail Book
Manufacturing Group

Printed on 60 lb. Sebago Eggshell